New Perspectives on

Microsoft® Windows Vista™

Comprehensive

What is the Microsoft Business Certification Program?

The Microsoft Business Certification Program enables candidates to show that they have something exceptional to offer – proven expertise in Microsoft Office programs. The two certification tracks allow candidates to choose how they want to exhibit their skills, either through validating skills within a specific Microsoft product or taking their knowledge to the next level and combining Microsoft programs to show that they can apply multiple skill sets to complete more complex office tasks. Recognized by businesses and schools around the world, over 3 million certifications have been obtained in over 100 different countries. The Microsoft Business Certification Program is the only Microsoft-approved certification program of its kind.

What is the Microsoft Certified Application Specialist Certification?

The Microsoft Certified Application Specialist Certification exams focus on validating specific skill sets within each of the Microsoft® Office system programs. The candidate can choose which exam(s) they want to take according to which skills they want to validate. The available Application Specialist exams include:

- Using Windows Vista™
- Using Microsoft® Office Word 2007
- Using Microsoft® Office Excel® 2007
- Using Microsoft® Office PowerPoint® 2007
- Using Microsoft® Office Access 2007
- Using Microsoft® Office Outlook® 2007

What is the Microsoft Certified Application Professional Certification?

The Microsoft Certified Application Professional Certification exams focus on a candidate's ability to use the 2007 Microsoft® Office system to accomplish industry-agnostic functions, for example Budget Analysis and Forecasting, or Content Management and Collaboration. The available Application Professional exams currently include:

- Organizational Support
- Creating and Managing Presentations
- Content Management and Collaboration
- Budget Analysis and Forecasting

What do the Microsoft Business Certification Vendor of Approved Courseware logos represent?

The logos validate that the courseware has been approved by the Microsoft® Business Certification Vendor program and that these courses cover objectives that will be included in the relevant exam. It also means that after utilizing this courseware, you may be prepared to pass the exams required to become a Microsoft Certified Application Specialist or Microsoft Certified Application Professional.

For more information:

To learn more about Microsoft Certified Application Specialist or Professional exams, visit
www.microsoft.com/learning/msbc.
To learn about other Microsoft Certified Application Specialist approved courseware from Course Technology, visit
www.course.com.
*The availability of Microsoft Certified Application exams varies by Microsoft Office program, program version and language. Visit www.microsoft.com/learning for exam availability.
Microsoft, the Office Logo, Outlook, and PowerPoint are either registered trademarks or trademarks of Microsoft Corporation in the United States and/or other countries. The Microsoft Certified Application Specialist and Microsoft Certified Application Professional Logos are used under license from Microsoft Corporation.

New Perspectives on

Microsoft® Windows Vista™

Comprehensive

June Jamrich Parsons
Dan Oja

Joan & Patrick Carey
Carey Associates

Lisa Ruffolo

COURSE TECHNOLOGY
CENGAGE Learning™

Australia • Brazil • Japan • Korea • Mexico • Singapore • Spain • United Kingdom • United States

COURSE TECHNOLOGY
CENGAGE Learning

New Perspectives on Microsoft Windows Vista—Comprehensive is published by Course Technology.

Acquisitions Editor: Kristina Matthews

Senior Product Manager: Kathy Finnegan

Product Manager: Erik Herman

Associate Product Manager: Brandi Henson

Editorial Assistant: Leigh Robbins

Senior Marketing Manager: Joy Stark

Marketing Coordinator: Jennifer Hankin

Developmental Editor: Judy Adamski

Senior Content Project Manager:
    Catherine G. DiMassa

Composition: GEX Publishing Services

Text Designer: Steve Deschene

Cover Designer: Elizabeth Paquin

Cover Art: Bill Brown

For product information and technology assistance, contact us at
Cengage Learning Customer & Sales Support, 1-800-354-9706

For permission to use material from this text or product, submit all requests online at **cengage.com/permissions**
Further permissions questions can be emailed to
permissionrequest@cengage.com

ISBN-13: 978-1-4239-0602-5

ISBN-10: 1-4239-0602-0

Course Technology
25 Thomson Place
Boston, Massachusetts 02210
USA

Cengage Learning is a leading provider of customized learning solutions with office locations around the globe, including Singapore, the United Kingdom, Australia, Mexico, Brazil, and Japan. Locate your local office at:
international.cengage.com/region

Cengage Learning products are represented in Canada by Nelson Education, Ltd.

For your lifelong learning solutions, visit **course.cengage.com**

Purchase any of our products at your local college store or at our preferred online store **www.ichapters.com**

Disclaimer: Any fictional data related to persons or companies or URLs used throughout this book is intended for instructional purposes only. At the time this book was printed, any such data was fictional and not belonging to any real persons or companies.

Microsoft and the Windows Vista logo are either registered trademarks or trademarks of Microsoft Corporation in the United States and/or other countries. Course Technology is an independent entity from the Microsoft Corporation, and not affiliated with Microsoft in any manner.

Printed in the United States of America
2 3 4 5 6 7 8 9 11 10 09 08

Preface

The New Perspectives Series' critical-thinking, problem-solving approach is the ideal way to prepare students to transcend point-and-click skills and take advantage of all that Microsoft Windows Vista has to offer.

In developing the New Perspectives Series for Microsoft Windows Vista, our goal was to create books that give students the software concepts and practical skills they need to succeed beyond the classroom. We've updated our proven case-based pedagogy with more practical content to make learning skills more meaningful to students.

With the New Perspectives Series, students understand *why* they are learning *what* they are learning, and are fully prepared to apply their skills to real-life situations.

"I really love the Margin Tips, which add 'tricks of the trade' to students' skills package. In addition, the Reality Check exercises provide for practical application of students' knowledge."
—Terry Morse Colucci
Institute of Technology, Inc.

About This Book

This book provides comprehensive coverage of the new Microsoft Windows Vista operating system, and includes the following:

- Complete coverage of Microsoft Windows Vista basics so that students can use the operating system with confidence and ease
- Guidance around the Windows Vista desktop, Start menu, and file system, teaching students how to start Windows, run programs, and organize files
- Exploration of the exciting new features in Windows Vista, including Windows Aero, the Navigation pane and updated Address bar in folder windows, new file and folder views, Windows Sidebar, Windows Calendar, and Windows Meeting Space
- Opportunities for personalizing Windows Vista, navigating the Web, exchanging e-mail, and finding files with the updated Search tools
- Presentation of advanced skills, including managing multimedia files, using mobile computers to connect to networks and the Internet, maintaining hardware and software, and enhancing system performance
- Expanded and in-depth coverage of managing computer security with Windows Vista, including Internet Explorer and Windows Mail security features, and working with innovative tools such as Windows Photo Gallery, the Windows Mobility Center, Windows Defender, and the new Control Panel
- New business case scenarios throughout, which provide a rich and realistic context for students to apply the concepts and skills presented
- Certification requirements for the Microsoft Certified Application Specialist exam, "Using Windows Vista™"

System Requirements

This book assumes a typical installation of Microsoft Windows Vista Ultimate with the Aero color scheme turned on. (Note that most tasks in this text can also be completed using the Windows Vista Home Premium or Business editions.) The browser used for any steps that require a browser is Internet Explorer 7.

The New Perspectives Approach

Context

Each tutorial begins with a problem presented in a "real-world" case that is meaningful to students. The case sets the scene to help students understand what they will do in the tutorial.

Hands-on Approach

Each tutorial is divided into manageable sessions that combine reading and hands-on, step-by-step work. Colorful screenshots help guide students through the steps. **Trouble?** tips anticipate common mistakes or problems to help students stay on track and continue with the tutorial.

InSight

InSight Boxes

New for Windows Vista! InSight boxes offer expert advice and best practices to help students better understand how to work with the software. With the information provided in the InSight boxes, students achieve a deeper understanding of the concepts behind the software features and skills.

Tip

Margin Tips

New for Windows Vista! Margin Tips provide helpful hints and shortcuts for more efficient use of the software. The Tips appear in the margin at key points throughout each tutorial, giving students extra information when and where they need it.

Reality Check

Reality Checks

New for Windows Vista! Comprehensive, open-ended Reality Check exercises give students the opportunity to complete practical, real-world tasks, such as managing their files and folders and personalizing the Windows Vista environment.

Review

In New Perspectives, retention is a key component to learning. At the end of each session, a series of Quick Check questions helps students test their understanding of the concepts before moving on. Each tutorial also contains an end-of-tutorial summary and a list of key terms for further reinforcement.

Apply

Assessment

Engaging and challenging Review Assignments and Case Problems have always been a hallmark feature of the New Perspectives Series. Colorful icons and brief descriptions accompany the exercises, making it easy to understand, at a glance, both the goal and level of challenge a particular assignment holds.

Reference Window

Task Reference

Reference

While contextual learning is excellent for retention, there are times when students will want a high-level understanding of how to accomplish a task. Within each tutorial, Reference Windows appear before a set of steps to provide a succinct summary and preview of how to perform a task. In addition, a complete Task Reference at the back of the book provides quick access to information on how to carry out common tasks. Finally, each book includes a combination Glossary/Index to promote easy reference of material.

Our Complete System of Instruction

Coverage To Meet Your Needs

Whether you're looking for just a small amount of coverage or enough to fill a semester-long class, we can provide you with a textbook that meets your needs.

- Brief books typically cover the essential skills in just 2 to 4 tutorials.
- Introductory books build and expand on those skills and contain an average of 5 to 8 tutorials.
- Comprehensive books are great for a full-semester class, and contain 9 to 12+ tutorials.

So if the book you're holding does not provide the right amount of coverage for you, there's probably another offering available. Visit our Web site or contact your Course Technology sales representative to find out what else we offer.

Student Online Companion

This book has an accompanying online companion Web site designed to enhance learning. This Web site, www.course.com/np/office2007, includes the following:

- Student Data Files
- PowerPoint presentations

CourseCasts – Learning on the Go. Always available...always relevant.

Want to keep up with the latest technology trends relevant to you? Visit our site to find a library of podcasts, CourseCasts, featuring a "CourseCast of the Week," and download them to your mp3 player at http://coursecasts.course.com.

Our fast-paced world is driven by technology. You know because you're an active participant—always on the go, always keeping up with technological trends, and always learning new ways to embrace technology to power your life.

Ken Baldauf, host of CourseCasts, is a faculty member of the Florida State University Computer Science Department where he is responsible for teaching technology classes to thousands of FSU students each year. Ken is an expert in the latest technology trends; he gathers and sorts through the most pertinent news and information for CourseCasts so your students can spend their time enjoying technology, rather than trying to figure it out. Open or close your lecture with a discussion based on the latest CourseCast.

Visit us at http://coursecasts.course.com to learn on the go!

Instructor Resources

We offer more than just a book. We have all the tools you need to enhance your lectures, check students' work, and generate exams in a new, easier-to-use and completely revised package. This book's Instructor's Manual, ExamView testbank, PowerPoint presentations, data files, solution files, figure files, and a sample syllabus are all available on a single CD-ROM or for downloading at www.course.com.

Skills Assessment and Training

SAM 2007 helps bridge the gap between the classroom and the real world by allowing students to train and test on important computer skills in an active, hands-on environment.

SAM 2007's easy-to-use system includes powerful interactive exams, training or projects on critical applications such as Word, Excel, Access, PowerPoint, Outlook, Windows, the Internet, and much more. SAM simulates the application environment, allowing students to demonstrate their knowledge and think through the skills by performing real-world tasks.

Designed to be used with the New Perspectives Series, SAM 2007 includes built-in page references so students can print helpful study guides that match the New Perspectives textbooks used in class. Powerful administrative options allow instructors to schedule exams and assignments, secure tests, and run reports with almost limitless flexibility.

Blackboard

Online Content

Blackboard is the leading distance learning solution provider and class-management platform today. Course Technology has partnered with Blackboard to bring you premium online content. Content for use with *New Perspectives on Microsoft Windows Vista, Comprehensive* is available in a Blackboard Course Cartridge and may include topic reviews, case projects, review questions, test banks, practice tests, custom syllabi, and more.

Course Technology also has solutions for several other learning management systems. Please visit http://www.course.com today to see what's available for this title.

Acknowledgments

I would like to thank the following reviewers for their contributions in the development of this text: Anton Bruckner, Sinclair Community College; Ken McDaniel, Santa Barbara Business College; and Deborah Meyer, St. Louis Community College–Forest Park. Their valuable insights and excellent feedback helped to shape this text, ensuring it will meet the needs of instructors and students both in the classroom and beyond.

Many thanks to everyone on the New Perspectives team for their guidance, insight, and encouragement, including Kristina Matthews, Cathie DiMassa, and Brandi Henson. Special thanks to Kathy Finnegan, whose thoughtfulness and good humor make this book more engaging and useful, and to Judy Adamski, who shepherded this text over many hurdles. I also appreciate the careful work of Nicole Ashton, John Freitas, Serge Palladino, Danielle Shaw, Marianne Snow, and Susan Whalen, Manuscript Quality Assurance testers. Additional thanks go to June Parsons, Dan Oja, and Joan and Patrick Carey, on whose previous work this book is based.

–Lisa Ruffolo

Brief Contents

Table of Contents

Windows Vista Level II Tutorials

Tutorial 3 Personalizing Your Windows Environment
Changing Microsoft Windows Vista Desktop Settings . . . .*WIN 97*

Tutorial 4 Working with the Internet and E-Mail
Communicating with Others . . . .*WIN 159*

Windows Vista Level III Tutorials

Tutorial 7 Managing Multimedia Files

Working with Graphics, Photos, Music,
and Movies ....*WIN 321*

Tutorial 8 Connecting to Networks with Mobile Computing

Accessing Network Resources ....*WIN 401*

Objectives

Session 1.1
- Start Windows Vista and tour the desktop
- Explore the Start menu
- Run software programs, switch between them, and close them
- Manipulate windows
- Identify and use the controls in menus, toolbars, and dialog boxes

Session 1.2
- Navigate your computer with Windows Explorer and the Computer window
- Change the view of the items in your computer
- Get help when you need it
- Turn off Windows Vista

Exploring the Basics of Microsoft Windows Vista

Investigating the Windows Vista Operating System

Case | Metro Learning Center

Metro Learning Center is a small but growing training company in Des Moines, Iowa. It offers academic tutoring and supplemental classes to help high school students and others prepare for college and other postsecondary education. In addition to classes that help students prepare for entrance exams, develop study and research skills, and earn high school equivalency diplomas, Metro Learning Center provides general training for using computers productively. Laura Halverson is the director of computer education at Metro, and she coordinates demonstrations and classes on developing computer skills, ranging from basic introductions to computers, Windows, and the Internet, to more advanced topics such as using word-processing programs, designing Web pages, and setting up home networks. Laura recently hired you as a computer trainer, and so far you have taught introductory classes on searching the Internet and exchanging e-mail. Now she asks you to prepare a demonstration on the fundamentals of the Microsoft Windows Vista operating system. She has scheduled demos with a few nonprofit agencies in Des Moines and surrounding communities and offers to help you identify the topics you should cover and the skills you should demonstrate. Overall, she suggests starting with turning on the computer and then explaining how to open and close programs, work with windows and dialog boxes, and navigate the computer. Finally, she wants you to demonstrate ways to turn off Windows Vista.

In this tutorial, you will start Windows Vista and practice some fundamental computer skills. Then, you'll learn how to navigate with the Computer window and Windows Explorer. Finally, you'll use the Windows Vista Help system, and turn off Windows Vista.

Starting Data Files

There are no starting Data Files needed for this tutorial.

Session 1.1

Starting Windows Vista

Laura Halverson begins helping you plan the demonstration by first defining the operating system. She explains that the **operating system** is software that helps the computer perform essential tasks such as displaying information on the computer screen and saving data on disks. (Software refers to the **programs**, or **applications**, that a computer uses to complete tasks.) Your computer uses the **Microsoft Windows Vista** operating system—**Windows Vista** for short. Windows is the name of the operating system, and Vista indicates the version you are using. Microsoft has released many versions of Windows since 1985 and is likely to continue developing new versions.

Much of the software created for the Windows Vista operating system shares the same look and works the same way. This similarity in design means that after you learn how to use one Windows Vista program, such as Microsoft Office Word (a word-processing program), you are well on your way to understanding how to use other Windows Vista programs. Windows Vista allows you to use more than one program at a time, so you can easily switch between your word-processing program and your appointment book program, for example. Windows Vista also makes it easy to access the **Internet**, a worldwide collection of computers connected to one another to enable communication. All in all, Windows Vista makes your computer an effective and easy-to-use productivity tool.

Windows Vista starts automatically when you turn on your computer. After completing some necessary startup tasks, Windows Vista displays a Welcome screen. Depending on the way your computer is set up, the Welcome screen might list only your user name or it might list all the users for the computer. Before you start working with Windows Vista, you must click your user name and perhaps type a password. A **user name** is a unique name that identifies you to Windows Vista, and a **password** is text—often a confidential combination of letters and numbers—that you must enter before you can work with Windows Vista. After selecting your user name, the Windows Vista desktop appears and the Welcome Center window opens, which provides information about your computer and how to set it up according to your preferences.

To begin your demo of Windows Vista, Laura asks you to start Windows Vista.

To start Windows Vista:

1. Turn on your computer. After a moment, Windows Vista starts and the Welcome screen appears.

   Trouble? If you are asked to select an operating system, do not take action. Windows Vista should start automatically after a designated number of seconds. If it does not, ask your instructor or technical support person for help.

   Trouble? If this is the first time you have started your computer with Windows Vista, messages might appear on your screen informing you that Windows is setting up components of your computer.

2. On the Welcome screen, click your user name and enter your password, if necessary. The Welcome Center window opens on the Windows Vista desktop, as shown in Figure 1-1. Your desktop might look different.

   Trouble? If your user name does not appear in the list of users on the Welcome screen, ask your instructor or technical support person which name you should click.

   Trouble? If you need to enter a user name and a password, type your assigned user name, press the Tab key, type your password, and then click the Continue button or press the Enter key to continue.

   Trouble? If the Welcome Center window does not open and only the desktop appears, continue with Step 3.

Welcome Center window open on the Windows Vista desktop

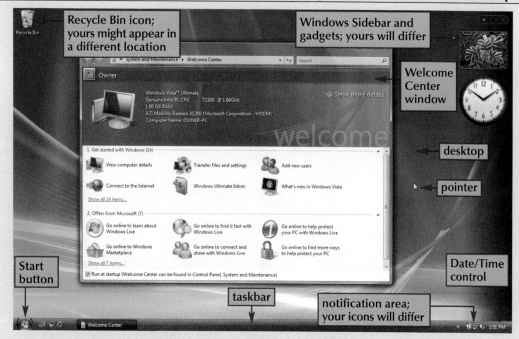

Recycle Bin icon; yours might appear in a different location

Windows Sidebar and gadgets; yours will differ

Welcome Center window

desktop

pointer

Start button

Date/Time control

taskbar

notification area; your icons will differ

3. Look at your desktop and locate the objects labeled in Figure 1-1. The objects on your desktop might differ or appear larger or smaller than those in Figure 1-1, depending on your monitor's settings. Figure 1-2 describes the purpose of each of these objects.

Elements of the Windows Vista desktop   **Figure 1-2**

Element	Description
Icon	A small picture that represents an object available to your computer
Pointer	A small object, such as an arrow, that moves on the screen when you move the mouse
Desktop	Your workplace on the screen
Sidebar and gadgets	A place on the desktop where Windows stows gadgets, which are small, handy programs such as sticky notes and clocks
Date/Time control	An element that shows the current date and time and lets you set the clock
Notification area	An area that displays icons corresponding to services running in the background, such as an Internet connection
Taskbar	A strip that contains buttons to give you quick access to common tools and the programs currently running
Start button	A button that provides access to Windows Vista programs, documents, and information on the Internet
Welcome Center window	A window that lists tasks first-time users can perform to quickly set up their computers

Trouble? If a blank screen or animated design replaces the Windows Vista desktop, your computer might be set to use a **screen saver**, a program that causes a monitor to go blank or to display an animated design after a specified amount of idle time. Press any key or move your mouse to restore the Windows Vista desktop.

The Windows Vista screen uses a **graphical user interface** (**GUI**, pronounced *gooey*), which displays icons that represent items stored on your computer, such as programs and files. A computer **file** is a collection of related information; typical types of files include text documents, spreadsheets, digital pictures, and songs. Your computer represents files with **icons**, which are pictures of familiar objects, such as file folders and documents. Windows Vista gets its name from the rectangular work areas called **windows** that appear on your screen as you work, such as the Welcome Center window shown in Figure 1-3. You will learn more about windows later in this tutorial.

Figure 1-3   **Welcome Center window**

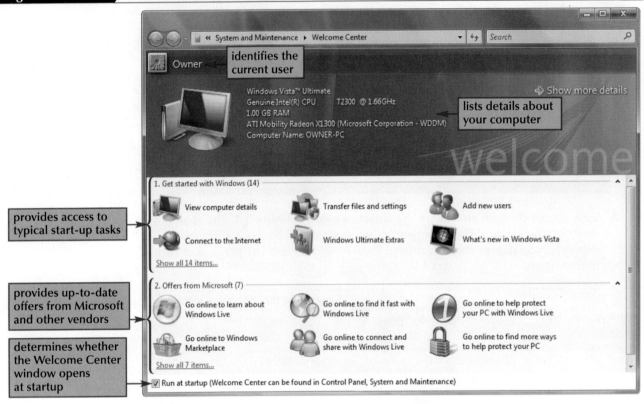

The user interface in Windows Vista is called **Aero**, and is available in two versions. The Aero experience features a semitransparent glass design that lets you see many objects at the same time, such as two or more overlapping windows. (Aero is available only in the following versions of Windows Vista: Business, Enterprise, Home Premium, and Ultimate.) Aero also offers other features for viewing windows that are demonstrated later in this tutorial. To take advantage of the Aero experience, your computer requires hardware with features designed for enhanced graphics. (The Microsoft Web site at *www.microsoft.com* has detailed information about these requirements.) Otherwise, you can use the basic version of Aero, which provides the same elements as the enhanced experience, including windows and icons, but not the same graphic effects. This book assumes that you are using the Aero experience. If you are using the Basic experience, the images on your screen will vary slightly from the figures, and some features will not be available. (These are noted throughout the book.)

Touring the Windows Vista Desktop

In Windows terminology, the background area displayed on your screen when Windows Vista starts represents a **desktop**—a workspace for projects and the tools that you need to manipulate your projects. When you first start a computer, it uses **default settings**, those preset by the operating system. The default desktop you see after you first install Windows Vista, for example, displays an abstract image that shades from blue to green to yellow. However, Microsoft designed Windows Vista so that you can easily change the appearance of the desktop. You can, for example, change images or add patterns and text to the desktop.

Interacting with the Desktop

To interact with the objects on your desktop, you use a **pointing device**. Pointing devices come in many shapes and sizes. The most common one is called a **mouse**, so this book uses that term. If you are using a different pointing device, such as a trackball or touchpad, substitute that device whenever you see the term *mouse*. Some pointing devices are designed to ensure that your hand won't suffer fatigue while using them. Some are attached directly to your computer, whereas others work like a TV remote control and allow you to access your computer without being plugged into it.

You use a pointing device to move the pointer over objects on the desktop, or to **point** to them. The pointer is usually shaped like an arrow ↖, although it changes shape depending on the pointer's location on the screen and the tasks you are performing. As you move the mouse on a surface, such as a mouse pad, the pointer on the screen moves in a corresponding direction.

When you point to certain objects, such as the objects on the taskbar, a ScreenTip appears near the object. A **ScreenTip** tells you the purpose or function of the object to which you are pointing.

During your demo, Laura suggests that you acquaint Metro Learning Center clients with the desktop by viewing ScreenTips for a couple of desktop objects.

To view ScreenTips:

▶ **1.** Use the mouse to point to the **Start** button ⊕ on the taskbar. After a few seconds, you see a ScreenTip identifying the button, as shown in Figure 1-4.

Viewing ScreenTips ◀ **Figure 1-4**

▶ **2.** Point to the time displayed at the right end of the taskbar. A ScreenTip for today's date (or the date to which your computer's calendar is set) appears.

Clicking refers to pressing a mouse button and immediately releasing it. Clicking sends a signal to your computer that you want to perform an action with the object you click. In Windows Vista, you perform most actions with the left mouse button. If you are told to click an object, position the pointer on that object and click the left mouse button, unless instructed otherwise.

When you click the Start button, the Start menu opens. A **menu** is a group or list of commands, and a **menu command** is text that you can click to complete tasks. If a right-pointing arrow follows a menu command, then you can point to the command to open a **submenu**, which is a list of additional choices related to the command.

The **Start menu** provides access to programs, documents, and much more. To explore the Start menu, Laura suggests you click the Start button to open the Start menu.

To open the Start menu:

▶ **1.** Point to the **Start** button ● on the taskbar.

▶ **2.** Click the left mouse button. The Start menu opens. An arrow ▶ points to the All Programs command on the Start menu, indicating that you can view additional choices by navigating to a submenu. See Figure 1-5; your Start menu might show different commands.

Figure 1-5 ▶ Start menu

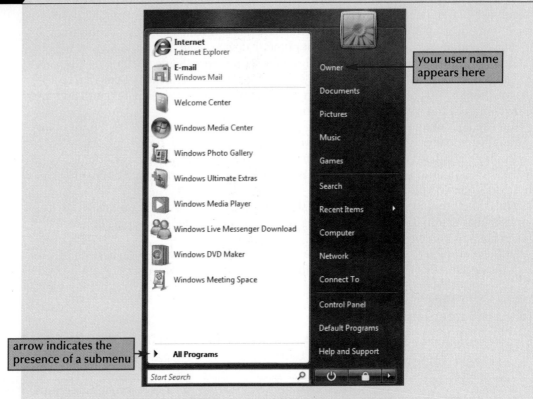

You need to select an object before you can work with it. To **select** an object in Windows Vista, you usually need to point to and then click that object. Windows Vista often shows you that an object is selected by highlighting it, typically by changing the object's color, putting a box around it, or making the object appear to be pushed in.

Depending on your computer's settings, you can select certain objects by pointing to them. To demonstrate selecting a menu command by pointing, Laura suggests that you point to the All Programs command on the Start menu to open the All Programs submenu.

To select a menu command:

▶ **1.** Click the **Start** button ● on the taskbar.

Start button shortcut menu ◀ **Figure 1-8**

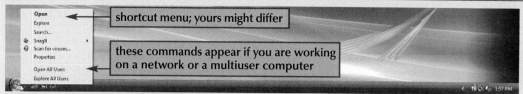

- shortcut menu; yours might differ
- these commands appear if you are working on a network or a multiuser computer

Trouble? If the shortcut menu does not open and you are using a trackball or a mouse with three buttons or a wheel, make sure you click the button on the far right, not the one in the middle.

Trouble? If your menu looks slightly different from the one in Figure 1-8, it is still the correct Start button shortcut menu. Its commands often vary by computer.

▶ 3. Press the **Esc** key to close the shortcut menu. You return to the desktop.

Now that you've opened the Start menu and its shortcut menu, you're ready to explore the contents of the Start menu.

Exploring the Start Menu

Recall that the Start menu is the central point for accessing programs, documents, and other resources on your computer. The Start menu is organized into two **panes**, which are separate areas of a menu or window. Each pane lists items you can point to or click. See Figure 1-9.

Start menu ◀ **Figure 1-9**

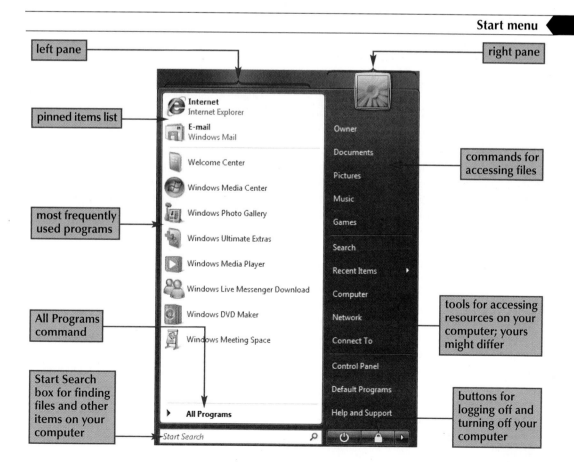

- left pane
- right pane
- pinned items list
- commands for accessing files
- most frequently used programs
- All Programs command
- tools for accessing resources on your computer; yours might differ
- Start Search box for finding files and other items on your computer
- buttons for logging off and turning off your computer

The left pane organizes programs for easy access. The area at the top of the left pane is called the **pinned items list**. Pinned items stay on the Start menu until you remove them. By default, Windows Vista lists the Web browser and e-mail program on your computer in the pinned items list. You can pin other items to this list if you like. When you use a program, Windows Vista adds it to the **most frequently used programs list**, which appears below the pinned items list. Windows Vista can list only a certain number of frequently used programs—after that, the programs you have not opened recently are replaced by the programs you used last.

Near the bottom of the left pane is the All Programs command, which you have already used to display the All Programs submenu. The All Programs submenu provides access to the programs currently installed on your computer. You'll use the All Programs submenu shortly to start a program.

The **Start Search box** helps you quickly find anything stored on your computer, including programs, documents, pictures, music, videos, Web pages, and e-mail messages. When you want to use the Start Search box, you open the Start menu and type one or more words related to what you want to find. For example, if you want to find and play the Happy Birthday song, you could type *birthday* in the Start Search box. Windows Vista searches your computer for that song and displays it and any other search results in the left pane of the Start menu where you can click the song to play it.

From the right pane of the Start menu, you can access common locations and tools on your computer. For example, the **Documents folder** is your personal folder, a convenient place to store documents and other work. **Computer** is a tool that you use to view, organize, and access the programs, files, and drives on your computer.

From the lower section of the right pane, you can open windows that help you work effectively with Windows Vista, including **Control Panel**, which contains specialized tools that help you change the way Windows Vista looks and behaves, and **Help and Support**, which provides articles, demonstrations, and steps for performing tasks in Windows Vista. (You'll explore Windows Help and Support later in this tutorial.) Finally, you also log off and turn off your computer from the Start menu. When you **log off**, you end your session with Windows Vista but leave the computer turned on.

Now that you've explored the Start menu, you're ready to use it to start a program.

Reference Window | Starting a Program

- Click the Start button on the taskbar, and then point to All Programs.
- If necessary, click the folder that contains the program you want to start.
- Click the name of the program you want to start.

or

- Click the name or icon of the program you want to start in the pinned items list or the most frequently used programs list on the Start menu.

Laura mentions that Windows Vista includes an easy-to-use word-processing program called WordPad. Suppose you want to start the WordPad program and use it to write a letter or report. You open Windows Vista programs from the Start menu. Programs are usually located on the All Programs submenu or in one of its folders. As mentioned earlier, a **folder** in Windows Vista is a container that helps to organize the contents of your computer. In the All Programs submenu, a folder contains programs that share a similar purpose. For example, the Accessories folder contains standard useful programs, such as a calculator. WordPad is stored in the Accessories folder because it is a typical accessory you can use for basic word processing.

To start the WordPad program from the Start menu:

▶ **1.** Click the **Start** button ⊕ on the taskbar to open the Start menu.

▶ **2.** Point to **All Programs** to open the All Programs submenu.

▶ **3.** Click **Accessories**. The Accessories folder opens, as shown in Figure 1-10.

Start menu and related submenus ◀ Figure 1-10

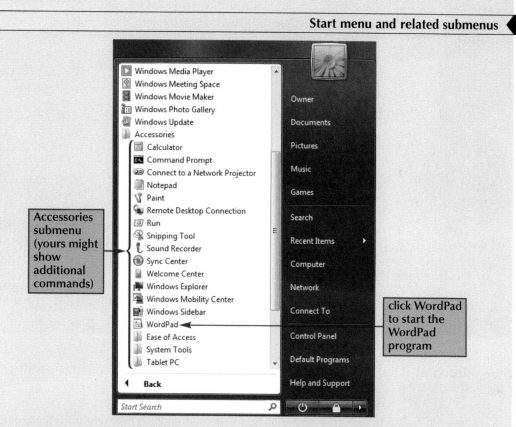

Trouble? If a different menu or folder opens, point to Back to return to the initial Start menu, point to All Programs, and then click Accessories.

▶ **4.** Click **WordPad**. The WordPad program window opens, as shown in Figure 1-11.

Figure 1-11 **WordPad program window**

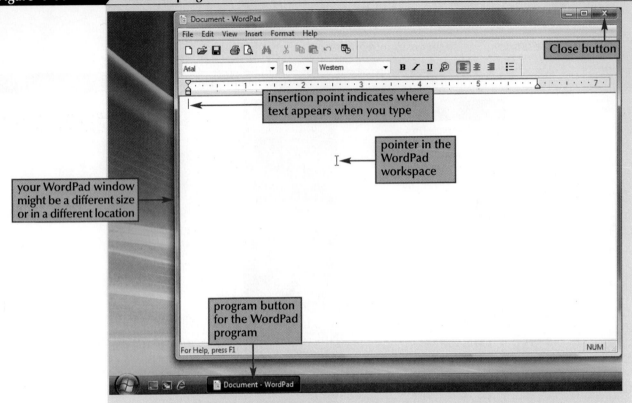

Trouble? If the WordPad program window fills the entire screen, continue with the next step. You will learn how to manipulate windows shortly.

When a program is started, it is said to be open or running. A **program button** appears on the taskbar for each open program. You click a program button to switch between open programs. When you are finished using a program, you can click the Close button located in the upper-right corner of the program window to **exit**, or close, that program.

To exit the WordPad program:

▶ **1.** Click the **Close** button [X] in the upper-right corner of the WordPad window. The WordPad program closes and you return to the Windows Vista desktop.

Now that you have started one program, you can start another program and run two at the same time.

Running Multiple Programs

One of the most useful features of Windows Vista is its ability to run multiple programs at the same time. This feature, known as **multitasking**, allows you to work on more than one task at a time and to switch quickly between projects. To demonstrate multitasking, Laura suggests that you start WordPad and leave it running while you start Paint, which is a program used to draw, color, and edit digital pictures.

To run WordPad and Paint at the same time:

▶ **1.** Start WordPad again.

▶ **2.** Click the **Start** button 🔵 on the taskbar.

▶ **3.** Point to **All Programs**, and then click **Accessories**.

▶ **4.** Click **Paint**. The Paint program window opens, as shown in Figure 1-12. Now two programs are running at the same time.

Two programs open ◀ **Figure 1-12**

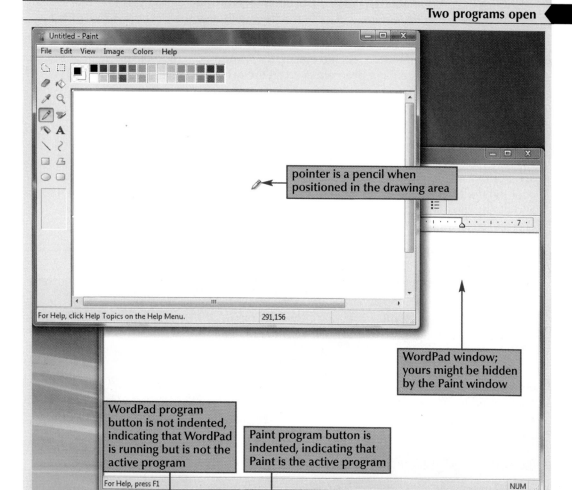

Trouble? If the Paint program window fills the entire screen, continue with the next set of steps. You will learn how to manipulate windows shortly.

The **active program** is the one you are currently using—Windows Vista applies your next keystroke or command to the active program. Paint is the active program because it is the one in which you are currently working. If two or more program windows overlap, the active window appears in front of the other windows. The program button for the active program is indented on the taskbar. The WordPad program button is still on the taskbar, indicating that WordPad is still running even if you can't see its program window. The taskbar organizes all the open windows so you can quickly make a program active by clicking its taskbar button.

Tip

In the Aero experience, when you point to a program button on the taskbar, a small picture appears that shows you a miniature version of the program window, including its contents.

Switching Between Programs

Because only one program is active at a time, you need to switch between programs if you want to work in one or the other. The easiest way to switch between programs is to use the program buttons on the taskbar.

To switch between WordPad and Paint:

▶ **1.** Click the program button labeled **Document - WordPad** on the taskbar. The WordPad program window moves to the front, and now the Document - WordPad button looks pushed in, indicating that WordPad is the active program.

▶ **2.** Click the program button labeled **Untitled - Paint** on the taskbar to switch to the Paint program. The Paint program is again the active program.

You can also use the Switch between windows button on the Quick Launch toolbar to switch from one open window to another. When you click the Switch between windows button, Windows activates **Flip 3D**, which displays all your open windows in a rotated stack so you can see the windows from the side, the way you view the spine of a book. See Figure 1-13. To flip through the stack, you press the Tab key or scroll the wheel on your mouse. Clicking any window in the stack makes that window the active program and closes Flip 3D; you click outside the stack to close Flip 3D without changing the current active window.

| Figure 1-13 | Windows Flip 3D |

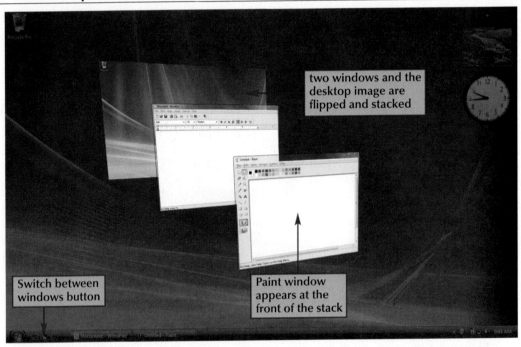

Note that Flip 3D is only available in the Aero experience. If you are using the Basic experience, clicking the Switch between windows button opens a task switcher window that displays a generic icon for each program that is running. See Figure 1-14. You can point to an icon to display information about the program it represents. Clicking an icon makes that program the active program and closes the task switcher window; clicking outside the task switcher window closes it without changing the current active window.

Clicking the Switch between windows button in the Basic experience — **Figure 1-14**

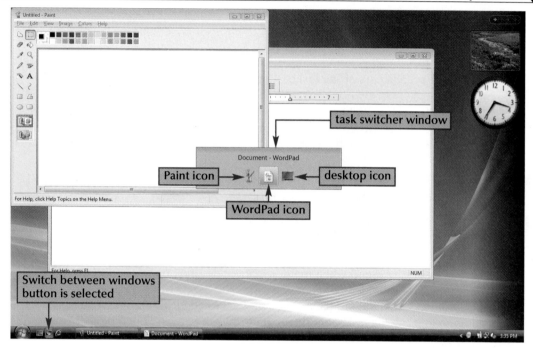

If you like to use keyboard shortcuts and are working in the Aero experience, you can also switch from one window to another using Windows Flip. When you hold down the Alt key and press the Tab key once, Windows Flip displays thumbnails (miniature versions) of your open windows. See Figure 1-15. While continuing to hold down the Alt key, you can press the Tab key to select the thumbnail for the program you want; you release the Alt key to close Windows Flip. (If you are using the Basic experience, the Alt+Tab keyboard shortcut opens the task switcher window shown in Figure 1-14.)

Windows Flip — **Figure 1-15**

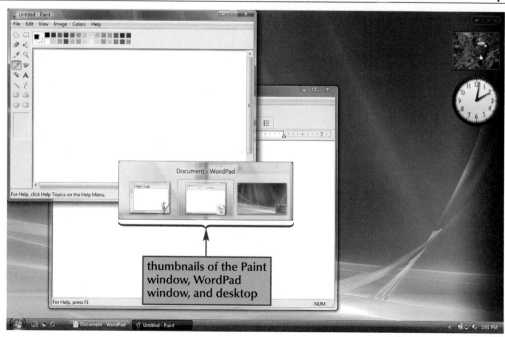

To switch between program windows using Flip 3D:

▶ 1. Click the **Switch between windows** button ▣ on the taskbar. Windows arranges the Paint and WordPad windows and the desktop in a stack, with the Paint window at the top of the stack.

   Trouble? If the Switch between windows button does not appear on your taskbar, right-click a blank part of the taskbar, point to Toolbars, and then click Quick Launch. Then complete Step 1.

   Trouble? If a task switcher window similar to the one shown in Figure 1-14 opens when you click the Switch between windows button, you are not using the Aero experience. Click outside the task switcher window and then read, but do not perform, the remaining steps.

▶ 2. Press the **Tab** key to flip the WordPad window to the front of the stack. The Paint window moves to the back of the stack.

▶ 3. Click the **WordPad** program window to turn off Flip 3D and make WordPad the active program.

Flip 3D is especially useful when many windows are open on the desktop, and the one you want to use is hidden by other windows. Flip 3D provides a handy alternative to switching windows from the taskbar, which can get crowded with program buttons.

In addition to using the taskbar and Flip 3D to switch between open programs, you can also close programs from the taskbar.

Closing Programs from the Taskbar

You should always close a program when you are finished using it. Each program uses computer resources, such as memory, so Windows Vista works more efficiently when only the programs you need are open. Laura reminds you that you've already closed an open program using the Close button in the upper-right corner of the program window. You can also close a program, whether active or inactive, by using the shortcut menu associated with the program button on the taskbar.

To close WordPad and Paint using the program button shortcut menus:

▶ 1. Right-click the **Untitled - Paint** button on the taskbar. The shortcut menu for the Paint program button opens. See Figure 1-16.

Figure 1-16	Program button shortcut menu

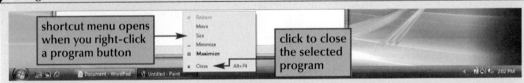

▶ 2. Click **Close** on the shortcut menu. The Paint program closes, and the program button labeled "Untitled - Paint" no longer appears on the taskbar.

   Trouble? If a message appears asking if you want to save changes, click the Don't Save button.

▶ 3. Right-click the **Document - WordPad** button on the taskbar, and then click **Close** on the shortcut menu. The WordPad program closes, and its program button no longer appears on the taskbar.

Now that you've learned the basics of using the Windows Vista desktop, you're ready to explore other Windows Vista features, including windows and dialog boxes.

Using Windows and Dialog Boxes

When you run a program in Windows Vista, the program appears in a window. Recall that a window is a rectangular area of the screen that contains a program, text, graphics, or data. A window also contains **controls**, which are graphical or textual objects used for manipulating the window and for using the program. Figure 1-17 describes the controls you are likely to see in most windows.

Window controls   Figure 1-17

Control	Description
Menu bar	Contains the titles of menus, such as File, Edit, and Help
Sizing button	Lets you enlarge, shrink, or close a window
Status bar	Displays information or messages about the task you are performing
Title bar	Contains the window title and basic window control buttons
Toolbar	Contains buttons that provide you with shortcuts to common menu commands
Window title	Identifies the program and document contained in the window
Workspace	Includes the part of the window where you manipulate your work—enter text, draw pictures, and set up calculations, for example

Laura mentions that the WordPad program is a good example of a typical window. She suggests that you start WordPad and identify its window controls.

To look at the window controls in WordPad:

▶ **1.** Start WordPad.

▶ **2.** On your screen, identify the controls that are labeled in Figure 1-18.

Figure 1-18   **WordPad window controls**

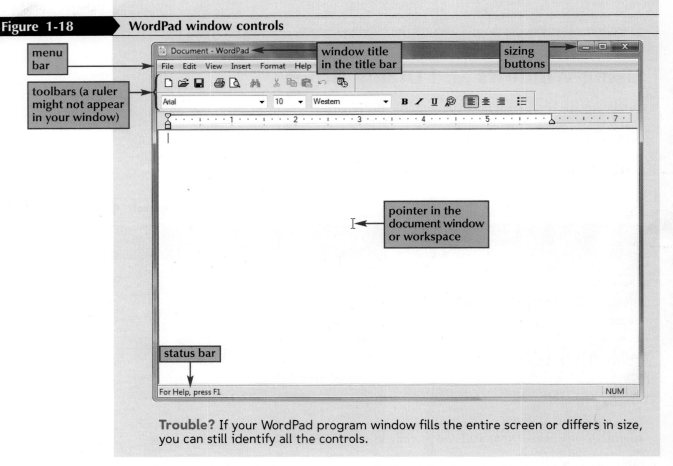

Trouble? If your WordPad program window fills the entire screen or differs in size, you can still identify all the controls.

After you open a window, you can manipulate it by changing its size and position.

Manipulating Windows

In most windows, three buttons appear on the right side of the title bar. The first button is the Minimize button, which hides a window so that only its program button is visible on the taskbar. Depending on the status of the window, the middle button either maximizes the window or restores it to a predefined size. You are already familiar with the last button—the Close button. Figure 1-19 illustrates how these buttons work.

Window buttons   **Figure 1-19**

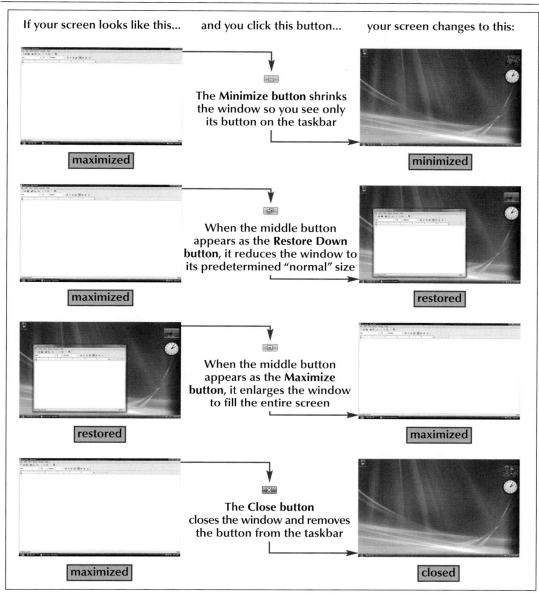

Now that WordPad is open, Laura encourages you to show students how to use its window controls to manipulate the program window. You can use the Minimize button when you want to temporarily hide a window but keep the program running.

To minimize the WordPad window:

▶ 1. Click the **Minimize** button [⬚] on the WordPad title bar. The WordPad window shrinks so that only the Document - WordPad button on the taskbar is visible.

Trouble? If the WordPad program window closed, you accidentally clicked the Close button. Use the Start button to start WordPad again, and then repeat Step 1. If you accidentally clicked the Maximize or Restore Down button, repeat Step 1.

You can redisplay a minimized window by clicking the program's button on the taskbar. When you redisplay a window, it becomes the active window.

To redisplay the WordPad window:

▶ **1.** Click the **Document - WordPad** button on the taskbar. The WordPad window is redisplayed.

The taskbar button provides another way to switch between a window's minimized and active states.

▶ **2.** Click the **Document - WordPad** button on the taskbar again to minimize the window.

▶ **3.** Click the **Document - WordPad** button once more to redisplay the window.

The Maximize button enlarges a window so that it fills the entire screen. Laura recommends that you work with maximized windows when you want to concentrate on the work you are performing in a single program.

To maximize the WordPad window:

▶ **1.** Click the **Maximize** button 🔲 on the WordPad title bar.

Trouble? If the window is already maximized, it fills the entire screen, and the Maximize button doesn't appear. Instead, you see the Restore Down button. Skip this step.

The Restore Down button reduces the window so that it is smaller than the entire screen. This feature is useful if you want to see more than one window at a time. Also, because the window is smaller, you can move the window to another location on the screen or change the dimensions of the window.

To restore a window:

▶ **1.** Click the **Restore Down** button 🗗 on the WordPad title bar. After a window is restored, the Restore Down button 🗗 changes to the Maximize button 🔲 .

You can use the mouse to move a window to a new position on the screen. When you click an object and then press and hold down the mouse button while moving the mouse, you are **dragging** the object. You can move objects on the screen by dragging them to a new location. If you want to move a window, you drag the window by its title bar. You cannot move a maximized window.

To drag the restored WordPad window to a new location:

▶ **1.** Position the mouse pointer on the WordPad title bar.

▶ **2.** Press and hold down the left mouse button, and then move the mouse up or down a little to drag the window. The window moves as you move the mouse.

▶ **3.** Position the window anywhere on the desktop, and then release the left mouse button. The WordPad window stays in the new location.

▶ **4.** Drag the WordPad window to the upper-left corner of the desktop.

You can also use the mouse to change the size of a window. When you point to an edge or corner of a window, the pointer changes to the resize pointer, which is a double-headed arrow, similar to ⬁ . You can use the resize pointer to drag an edge or corner of the window and change the size of the window.

To change the size of the WordPad window:

▶ **1.** Position the pointer over the lower-right corner of the WordPad window. The pointer changes to ⬉. See Figure 1-20.

Preparing to resize a window   **Figure 1-20**

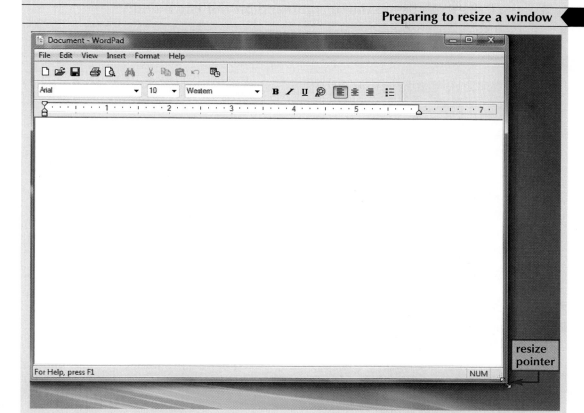

▶ **2.** Press and hold down the mouse button, and then drag the corner down and to the right.

▶ **3.** Release the mouse button. Now the window is larger.

▶ **4.** Practice using the resize pointer to make the WordPad window larger or smaller.

You can also use the resize pointer to drag any of the other three corners of the window to change its size. To change a window's size in any one direction only, drag the left, right, top, or bottom window borders left, right, up, or down.

Selecting Options from a Menu

Many Windows Vista programs use menus to organize the program's features and available functions. The menu bar is typically located at the top of the program window, immediately below the title bar, and shows the names of the menus, such as File, Edit, and Help.

When you click a menu name, the choices for that menu appear below the menu bar. Like choices on the Start menu, these choices are referred to as menu commands. To select a menu command, you click it. For example, the File menu is a standard feature in some Windows Vista programs that contains the commands typically related to working with a file: creating, opening, saving, and printing. Menu commands that are followed by an ellipsis (...) open a dialog box. A **dialog box** is a special kind of window in which you enter or choose settings for how you want to perform a task. For example, you use the Page Setup dialog box to set margins and some printing options.

Tip

If you open a menu, and then decide not to select a command, you can close the menu by clicking its name again or by pressing the Esc key.

Because the Page Setup dialog box contains many typical controls, Laura suggests you use the Page Setup command on the WordPad File menu to open that dialog box.

To select the Page Setup menu command on the File menu:

▶ **1.** Click **File** on the WordPad menu bar to open the File menu. See Figure 1-21.

Figure 1-21	File menu

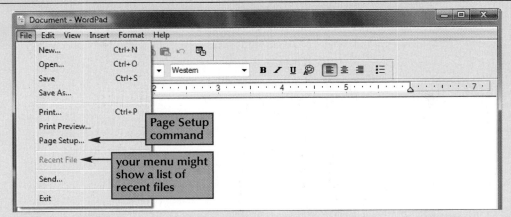

▶ **2.** Click **Page Setup** to open the Page Setup dialog box.

▶ **3.** After examining the dialog box, click the **Cancel** button to close the Page Setup dialog box.

When you select options in the Page Setup dialog box that you want to retain, you click the OK button instead of the Cancel button.

Not all commands immediately carry out an action—some show submenus or ask you for more information about what you want to do. The menu gives you visual hints about what to expect when you select an item. These hints are sometimes referred to as **menu conventions**. Figure 1-22 shows examples of these menu conventions.

Figure 1-22	Examples of menu conventions

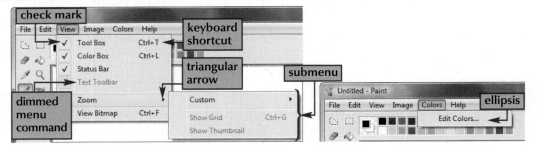

Figure 1-23 describes the Windows Vista menu conventions.

Menu conventions ◀ **Figure 1-23**

Convention	Description
Check mark	Indicates a toggle, or on/off switch (like a light switch), that is either checked (turned on) or not checked (turned off)
Ellipsis	Three dots that indicate you can make additional selections after you select that command. Commands without dots do not require additional choices—they take effect as soon as you click them. If a command is followed by an ellipsis, a dialog box opens so you can enter details about how you want a task carried out.
Triangular arrow	Indicates the presence of a submenu. When you point to a menu option that has a triangular arrow, a submenu appears.
Dimmed command	Command that is not currently available
Keyboard shortcut	Key or combination of keys that you can press to select the menu command without actually opening the menu

Using Toolbars

Many Windows Vista programs include one or more toolbars, which are typically displayed near the top of the program window. A toolbar is a row, column, or block of buttons or icons that gives you one-click access to frequently used menu commands. Just as menu commands are grouped on menus according to task, the buttons on a toolbar are also grouped and organized by task.

Toolbars, Menus, and Ribbons | InSight

Some Windows Vista programs such as Microsoft Office 2007 combine the toolbars and menu bar into a single component called the Ribbon. The Ribbon organizes commands into logical groups that are displayed on a tab. Each tab is designed for a particular activity, such as writing or designing a page. Many buttons on the Ribbon are similar to the buttons on a toolbar—they perform a command with one click. Buttons with arrows work like menus—you click a button to display a menu of related options.

Laura reminds you that Windows Vista programs often display ScreenTips to indicate the name or function of a window component such as a button. She suggests exploring the WordPad toolbar buttons by looking at their ScreenTips.

To determine the names and descriptions of the buttons on the WordPad toolbar:

▶ **1.** Position the pointer over the **Print Preview** button ⬚ on the WordPad toolbar, which is located immediately below the menu bar. After a short pause, the Screen-Tip for the button appears near the button, and a description of the button appears in the status bar at the bottom of the window.

▶ **2.** Move the pointer to each of the remaining buttons on the WordPad toolbar to display its name.

You select a toolbar button by clicking it, which performs the button's command. One of the buttons you pointed to on the WordPad toolbar is called the Undo button. Clicking the Undo button reverses the effects of your last action. Laura says you can see how this works by typing some text, and then clicking the Undo button to remove that text.

To use the Undo button on the WordPad toolbar:

▶ **1.** Type your name in the WordPad window.

▶ **2.** Click the **Undo** button ↰ on the WordPad toolbar. WordPad reverses your last action by removing your name from the WordPad window.

Besides menus and toolbars, windows can contain list boxes and scroll bars, which you'll learn about next.

Using List Boxes and Scroll Bars

As you might guess from the name, a **list box** displays a list of available choices from which you can select one item. In WordPad, the Date and Time dialog box includes a list box that contains formats for displaying the date and time. You can choose a date and time format from the Available formats list box in the Date and Time dialog box. List box controls usually include arrow buttons, a scroll bar, and a scroll box. A scroll bar appears when the list of available options is too long or wide to fit in the list box. You use the arrows and scroll box to move through the complete list.

To practice using a list box and scroll bar, Laura advises you open the Date and Time dialog box in WordPad and select a date format.

To use the list box in the Date and Time dialog box:

▶ **1.** Click the **Date/Time** button 🗐 on the WordPad toolbar to open the Date and Time dialog box, which lists the current date in many formats. See Figure 1-24.

Figure 1-24 ▶ List box

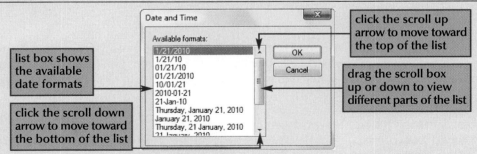

▶ **2.** To scroll down the list, click the **scroll down arrow** button on the scroll bar.

▶ **3.** Drag the **scroll box** to the top of the scroll bar by pointing to the scroll box, pressing and holding down the left mouse button, dragging the scroll box up, and then releasing the left mouse button. The list scrolls back to the beginning.

▶ **4.** Find a date format similar to "January 21, 2010" in the Available formats list box, and then click that date format to select it.

▶ **5.** Click the **OK** button to close the Date and Time dialog box. The current date is inserted into your document in the format you selected.

A list box is helpful because it includes only those options that are appropriate for your current task. For example, you can select only dates and times in the available formats from the list box in the Date and Time dialog box—no matter which format you choose, WordPad recognizes it. Sometimes a list might not include every possible option, so you can type the option you want to select. In this case, the list box includes an arrow on its right side. You can click the list arrow to view options and then either select one of the options or type appropriate text.

Buttons can also have arrows. The arrow indicates that the button has more than one option. Rather than crowding the window with a lot of buttons, one for each possible option, including an arrow on a button organizes its options logically and compactly into a list. Toolbars often include list boxes and buttons with arrows. For example, the Font Size button list box on the WordPad toolbar includes an arrow. To select an option other than the one shown in the list box or on the button, you click the arrow, and then click the option that you want to use.

Laura suggests you select a different font size using the arrow on the Font Size button list box.

To select a new font size from the Font Size button list box:

▶ **1.** Click the **Font Size button arrow** `10 ▾` on the WordPad toolbar.

▶ **2.** Click **18**. The Font Size list closes, and the font size you selected appears in the list box.

▶ **3.** Type a few characters to test the new font size.

▶ **4.** Click the **Font Size button arrow** `10 ▾` on the WordPad toolbar again.

▶ **5.** Click **12**.

▶ **6.** Type a few characters to test this type size. The text appears in 12-point text.

Dialog boxes also contain scroll bars and list boxes. You'll examine a typical dialog box next.

Working with Dialog Boxes

Recall that when you select a menu command or item followed by an ellipsis (...), a dialog box opens that allows you to provide more information about how a program should carry out a task. Some dialog boxes organize different kinds of information into groups. For example, the Print dialog box in Figure 1-25 includes the Select Printer and Page Range groups. Within these groups, you usually find tabs, option buttons, check boxes, and other controls that the program uses to collect information about how you want it to perform a task. Figure 1-25 displays examples of common dialog box controls.

Figure 1-25 Examples of dialog box controls

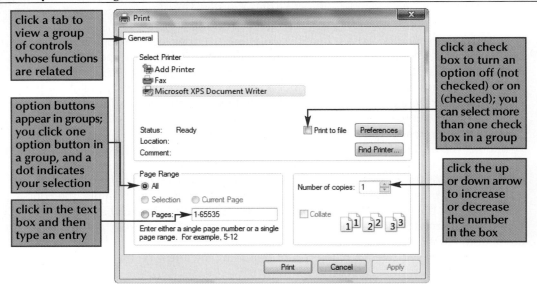

click a tab to view a group of controls whose functions are related

option buttons appear in groups; you click one option button in a group, and a dot indicates your selection

click in the text box and then type an entry

click a check box to turn an option off (not checked) or on (checked); you can select more than one check box in a group

click the up or down arrow to increase or decrease the number in the box

Laura says a good way to learn how dialog box controls work is to open a typical Windows Vista dialog box in WordPad, such as the Options dialog box. You use this dialog box to determine how text fits in the WordPad window and which toolbars appear. You'll remove the check mark from a check box and select an option button, and then see how these settings affect the WordPad window. Note that by default the status bar appears at the bottom of the WordPad window and that the ruler uses inches.

To work with a typical Windows Vista dialog box:

1. Click **View** on the WordPad menu bar, and then click **Options**. The Options dialog box opens, by default, to the Rich Text tab.

   Trouble? If the Options dialog box does not display the Rich Text options, click the Rich Text tab.

2. Click the **Status bar** check box to remove the check mark.

3. Click the **Options** tab to select the measurement units that the WordPad ruler uses.

4. Click the **Centimeters** option button.

5. Click the **OK** button. WordPad accepts your changes and closes the Options dialog box.

Examine the WordPad window and note that the ruler now uses centimeters instead of inches, and the status bar no longer appears at the bottom of the window. You can use the Options dialog box again to restore the WordPad window to its original condition.

To restore the WordPad window:

1. Click **View** on the WordPad menu bar, and then click **Options**. The Options dialog box opens.

2. On the Rich Text tab, click the **Status bar** check box to insert a check mark.

3. Click the **Options** tab, and then click the **Inches** option button.

▶ **4.** Click the **OK** button. The WordPad window now includes a status bar and a ruler that uses inches as its measurement unit.

▶ **5.** Click the **Close** button [X] on the WordPad title bar to close WordPad.

▶ **6.** When you see the message "Do you want to save changes to Document?" click the **Don't Save** button.

Tip

You can also close a program window by clicking File on the menu bar, and then clicking Close or Exit.

In this session, you started Windows Vista and toured the desktop, learning how to interact with the items on the desktop and on the Start menu. You also started two Windows programs, manipulated windows, and learned how to select options from a menu, toolbar, and dialog box.

Session 1.1 Quick Check | Review

1. What does the operating system do for your computer?
2. A(n) _____ is a group or list of commands.
3. Name two ways to change the size of a window.
4. In Windows Vista, right-clicking selects an object and opens its

   _____ .
5. How can you access the programs listed on the All Programs submenu?
6. True or False. When you're not sure what to do with an object in Windows Vista, it's a good idea to right-click the object and examine its shortcut menu.
7. Even if you can't see an open program on your desktop, the program might be running. How can you tell if a program is running?
8. Why should you close a program when you are finished using it?

Session 1.2

Exploring Your Computer

To discover the contents and resources on your computer, you explore, or navigate, it. **Navigating** means moving from one location to another on your computer, such as from one file or folder to another. Windows Vista provides two ways to navigate, view, and work with the contents and resources on your computer—Computer and Windows Explorer.

Navigating with the Computer Window

When you use Computer, a window opens showing your computer, its storage devices, and other objects. The icons for these objects appear in the right pane of the Computer window. The Computer window also has a left pane, called the Navigation pane, which shows icons and links to other resources. As shown in Figure 1-26, this window also contains a toolbar with buttons that let you perform common tasks, and a Details pane at the bottom of the window that displays the characteristics of an object you select in the Computer window.

Figure 1-26   **Relationship between your computer and the Computer window**

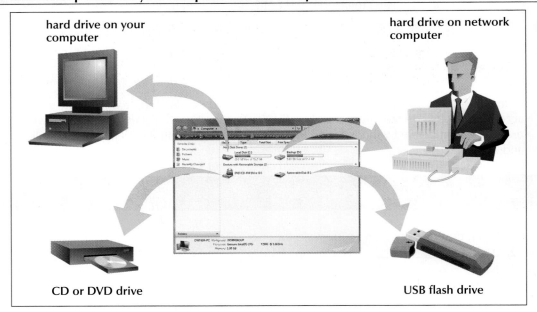

Each storage device you can access on your computer is associated with a letter. If you have an older computer, it might have one or more 3.5-inch disk drives; the first one is drive A and the second is drive B. The first hard drive is usually drive C. (If you add other hard drives, they are usually drives D, E, and so on.) If you have a CD or DVD drive or plug a USB flash drive into a USB port, it usually has the next available letter in the alphabetic sequence. If you can access hard drives located on other computers in a network, those drives sometimes (although not always) have letters associated with them as well. Naming conventions for network drives vary. In the example shown in Figure 1-26, the network drive has the drive letter D.

You can use Computer to keep track of where your files are stored and to organize your files. In this session, you will explore the contents of your hard disk, which is assumed to be drive C. If you use a different drive on your computer, such as drive E, substitute its letter for C throughout this session.

Laura Halverson, the director of Metro Learning Center, is helping you plan a demonstration of the basics of Windows Vista. She wants you to start this session by opening the Computer window and exploring the contents of your computer.

To explore the contents of your computer using Computer:

► **1.** If you took a break after the previous session, make sure that your computer is on and Windows Vista is running.

► **2.** Click the **Start** button 🔘 on the taskbar, and then click **Computer**. The Computer window opens. See Figure 1-27. Your window might look different.

Computer window ◄ Figure 1-27

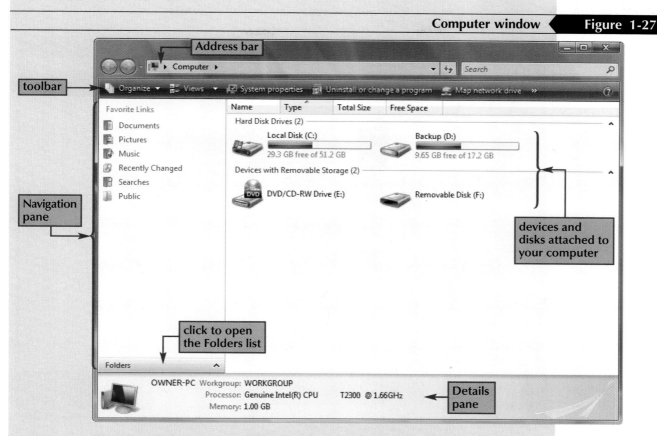

3. In the Navigation pane, click the **Music** folder. A window opens showing the contents of that folder. See Figure 1-28.

Figure 1-28 Contents of the Music folder

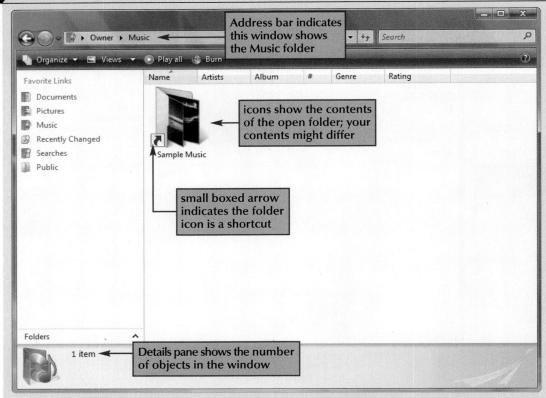

The Music folder is a convenient location for storing your music files. Many digital music players use this location by default when you rip, download, play, and burn music. Note that in Figure 1-28, the Sample Music icon represents a **shortcut**, a special type of file that serves as a direct link to another location that your computer can access, such as a folder, document, program, Windows tool, or Web site.

Trouble? If your window looks different from Figure 1-28, you can still perform the rest of the steps. For example, your window might contain a different number of folders and files.

▶ 4. Double-click the **Sample Music** icon to open the Sample Music folder. The right pane of the window shows the contents of the folder you double-clicked. You can learn more about the contents of a folder by selecting one or more of its files.

▶ 5. Click the first file listed in the Sample Music folder to select it. See Figure 1-29.

Viewing files in a folder ◄ Figure 1-29

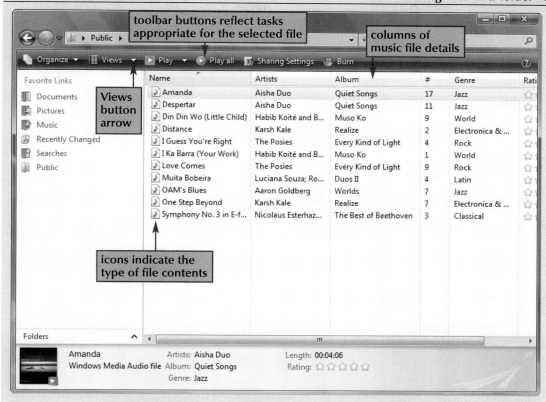

As you open folders and navigate with the Computer window, the contents of the toolbar change so that they are appropriate for your current task—in Figure 1-29, the toolbar lists actions to take with the selected music file, such as Play all and Burn.

Laura mentions that you can change the appearance of most windows to suit your preferences. You'll change the view of the Computer window next so you can see the file icons more clearly.

Changing the View

Windows Vista provides at least six ways to view the contents of a folder—Extra Large Icons, Large Icons, Medium Icons, Small Icons, List, Details, and Tiles. The default view is Details view, which displays a small icon and lists details about each file. The icon provides a visual cue to the type of file. Although only Details view lists all file details, such as the file size and the date it was modified, you can see these details in any other view by pointing to an icon to display a ScreenTip.

Selecting a View | InSight

The view you select depends on your preferences and needs. When you display files in one of the large icon views, the icon displays a preview of the file's content. The preview images are big and easy to see, though the window can show fewer files. When you display files using smaller icons, the window can show more files but the preview images are not as easy to see.

Reference Window | **Changing the Icon View**

- In a folder window, click the Views button arrow on the toolbar, and then click a view.
or
- To cycle through the views listed on the Views menu, click the Views button more than once.
or
- Click the Views button arrow on the toolbar, and then drag the slider.

To practice switching from one view to another, Laura says you can display the contents of the Sample Music folder in Large Icons view. To do so, you'll use the Views button on the toolbar.

To view files in Large Icons view:

1. In the Sample Music folder window, click the **Views button arrow** on the toolbar. See Figure 1-30.

   Trouble? If you click the Views button instead of the arrow, you cycle through the views. Click the Views button arrow, and then continue with Step 2.

Figure 1-30 ▶ **Preparing to change views**

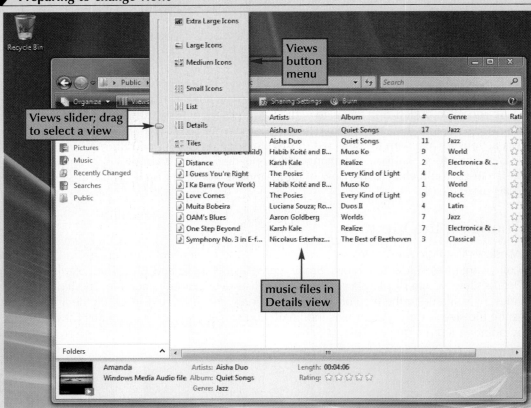

Tip

To change the appearance of the icons using the Views button, you can also drag the Views slider to select an icon size or set a size somewhere between the predefined views.

2. Click **Large Icons**. The window shows the same files, but with larger icons than in Details view.

▶ **3.** Click the **Views button arrow** on the toolbar, and then click **Details** to return to Details view.

No matter which view you use, you can sort the file list by filename or other detail, such as size, type, or date. If you're viewing music files, you can sort by details such as artist or album title, and if you're viewing picture files, you can sort by details such as date taken or size. Sorting helps you find a particular file in a long file listing. For example, suppose you want to listen to a song by a certain artist, but can't remember the song title. You can sort the music file list in alphabetic order by artist to find the song you want.

To sort the music file list by artist:

▶ **1.** Click the **Artists** button at the top of the list of files. The up-pointing arrow on the Artists button indicates that the files are sorted in ascending (A–Z) alphabetic order by artist name.

▶ **2.** Click the **Artists** button again. The down-pointing arrow on the Artists button indicates that the sort order is reversed, with the artists listed in descending (Z–A) alphabetic order.

▶ **3.** Click the **Close** button ❌ to close the Sample Music window.

Now Laura says you can compare Computer to Windows Explorer, another navigation tool.

Navigating with Windows Explorer

Like Computer, Windows Explorer also lets you easily navigate the resources on your computer. Most of the techniques you use with the Computer window apply to Windows Explorer—and vice versa. Both let you display and work with files and folders. By default, however, Windows Explorer also lets you see the hierarchy of all the folders on your computer. Viewing this hierarchy makes it easier to navigate your computer, especially if it contains many files and folders.

Laura suggests that during your Windows Vista demo, you compare navigation tools by using Windows Explorer to open the same folders you opened in the Computer window. As with other Windows Vista programs, you start Windows Explorer using the Start menu.

To start Windows Explorer:

▶ **1.** Click the **Start** button 🟦 on the taskbar, point to **All Programs**, click **Accessories**, and then click **Windows Explorer**. The Windows Explorer window opens, as shown in Figure 1-31. By default, when you start Windows Explorer from the All Programs submenu, the Documents folder opens. The Address bar shows the name of the open folder.

Figure 1-31	Windows Explorer window

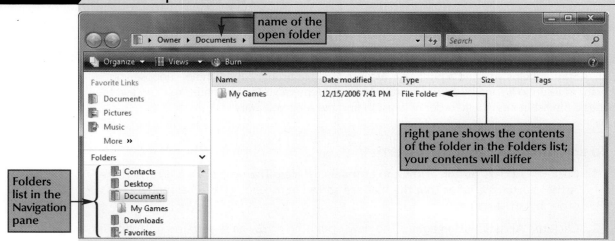

Trouble? If your Windows Explorer window looks slightly different from the one displayed in Figure 1-31, the configuration of your computer probably differs from the computer used to take this picture. Continue with Step 2.

2. If the Windows Explorer window is not maximized, click the **Maximize** button on the Windows Explorer title bar.

Windows Explorer has the same tools and features you used in the Computer window: the Navigation pane, toolbar, Details pane, and file list in the right pane. However, the default Navigation pane in Windows Explorer includes a Folders list, which displays the folders on your computer. In the Folders list, you can click any folder to navigate directly to it.

The Folders list organizes your files and folders based on their location in the hierarchy of objects on your computer. Initially, the Folders list shows the main objects you can access from your desktop, including the Documents folder. If your desktop contains other folders or objects, those are displayed as well. The right pane of the Windows Explorer window displays the contents of the object selected in the Folders list. When you point to the Folders list, triangles appear next to some icons. An open triangle ▷ indicates that a folder contains other folders that are not currently displayed in the Folders list. Click the triangle to open the folder and display its subfolders. A filled triangle ◢ indicates the folder is open, and its subfolders are listed below the folder name. To display the contents of a folder or object in the right pane of Windows Explorer, click the name of the folder or object.

InSight	**Navigating with Windows Explorer and the Computer Window**

Navigating with Windows Explorer usually involves clicking triangles in the Folders list to open objects and find the folder you want, and then clicking that folder to display its contents in the right pane. In contrast, navigating with the Computer window usually involves double-clicking folders in the right pane to open them and find the file you want. In general, it's easier to navigate your computer using the Folder list because it shows the hierarchy of folders on your computer.

To compare Windows Explorer to the Computer window, Laura suggests that you open the same folder you opened before using the Computer window.

To open a folder:

▶ **1.** Click the **Music** folder in the Folders list. The contents of the Music folder appear in the right pane of the Windows Explorer window, and the folder you opened is selected in the left pane.

Trouble? If the Music folder does not appear in the Folders list, click the open triangle icon next to your personal folder (the one with your name).

▶ **2.** In the right pane, double-click **Sample Music**. The same music files you displayed earlier appear in the window.

▶ **3.** Click the **Close** button ⊠ on the title bar to close the window.

Before completing your demonstration, Laura says it is always a good idea to show people how to get help when they need it.

Getting Help

Windows Vista Help and Support provides on-screen information about the program you are using. Help for the Windows Vista operating system is available by clicking the Start button and then clicking Help and Support on the Start menu.

When you start Help for Windows Vista, the Windows Help and Support window opens, which gives you access to Help files stored on your computer as well as Help information stored on the Microsoft Web site. If you are not connected to the Web, you have access to only the Help files stored on your computer.

Laura suggests that you start Windows Vista Help, and then explore the information provided in the Windows Help and Support window.

To start Windows Vista Help:

▶ **1.** Click the **Start** 🗗 button on the taskbar.

▶ **2.** Click **Help and Support**. The home page of Windows Help and Support opens. See Figure 1-32. The contents of the home page differ depending on whether you are connected to the Internet.

Tip

For Help with a program such as WordPad, first start the program, and then click Help on the program's menu bar.

Tip

You can also start Windows Vista Help and Support from the Computer window or Windows Explorer by clicking the Help button (a circled question mark) on the toolbar.

Figure 1-32 **Windows Help and Support window**

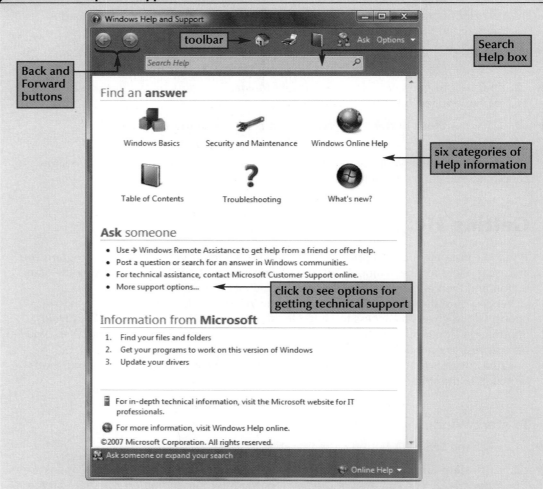

Trouble? If the Help and Support window does not display the page you see in Figure 1-32, click the Home icon on the toolbar at the top of the window to view Help contents.

The home page in Windows Help and Support organizes the vast amount of help and support information into six categories: Windows Basics, Security and Maintenance, Windows Online Help, Table of Contents, Troubleshooting, and What's new? The Windows Basics topics are designed for novice Windows users, and What's new? is for users who are familiar with earlier versions but who are new to Windows Vista. You are more likely to use Windows Online Help and the Table of Contents when you are more experienced and are looking for an answer to a particular question. (You need an Internet connection to use Windows Online Help.) Security and Maintenance provides articles about keeping your computer and Windows Vista in top condition, and Troubleshooting guides you step by step through procedures to help you solve problems.

To view the topics in a category, you click a category icon in the Find an answer section of the Windows Help and Support home page. Click a topic to open an article providing detailed information about that topic or instructions for performing a task. You can also use the toolbar to navigate Windows Help and Support. For example, click the

Home button to return to the Windows Help and Support home page. In addition to buttons providing quick access to pages in Windows Help and Support, the toolbar contains two other navigation buttons—the Back button and the Forward button. You use these buttons to navigate the pages you've already opened. Use the Back button to return to the previous page you viewed. After you do, you activate the Forward button, which you can click to go to the next page of those you've opened.

If you can't find the topic you want listed in any of the Help categories, the word that you are using for a feature or topic might be different from the word that Windows Vista uses. You can use the Search Help box to search for all keywords contained in the Help pages, not just the topic titles. In the Search Help box, you can type any word or phrase, click the Search Help button, and Windows Vista lists all the Help topics that contain that word or phrase.

Viewing Windows Basics Topics

Windows Vista Help and Support includes instructions on using Help itself. You can learn how to find a Help topic by using the Windows Basics category on the Windows Help and Support home page.

To view Windows Basics topics:

▶ 1. Click **Windows Basics**. A list of topics related to using Windows Vista appears in the Windows Help and Support window.

▶ 2. Scroll down to the "Help and support" heading, and then click **Getting help**. An article explaining how to get help appears, with the headings in the article listed in the "In this article" section.

▶ 3. Click **Getting help with dialog boxes and windows**. The Windows Help and Support window scrolls to that heading in the article.

▶ 4. Click the **Back** button on the toolbar. You return to the previous page you visited, which is the Windows Basics: all topics page. The Forward button is now active.

You can access the full complement of Help pages by using the Table of Contents.

Selecting a Topic from the Table of Contents

The Table of Contents logically organizes all of the topics in Windows Help and Support into books and pages. In the Table of Contents, you click a book to display the titles of its pages. Click a page to get help about a particular topic. For example, you can use the Table of Contents to learn more about files and folders.

To find a Help topic using the Table of Contents:

▶ 1. Click the **Help and Support home** button 🔘 on the Windows Help and Support toolbar.

▶ 2. Click **Table of Contents** on the home page. A list of books appears in the Windows Help and Support window.

▶ 3. Click **Files and folders** to display the list of pages included in the Files and folders book.

▶ 4. Click the topic **Working with files and folders**. The page you selected opens in the Windows Help and Support window.

▶ **5.** In the first line below the "What are files and folders" heading, click the word **file**, which is green by default. A tip shows the definition of *file*.

▶ **6.** Click a blank area of the Windows Help and Support window to close the tip.

Another Help tool is the Search Help box, a popular way to find answers to your Windows Vista questions.

Searching the Help Pages

If you can't find the topic you need by using Windows Basics or the Table of Contents, or if you want to quickly find Help pages related to a particular topic, you can use the Search Help box. Laura provides a typical example. Suppose you want to know how to exit Windows Vista, but you don't know if Windows refers to this as exiting, quitting, closing, or shutting down. You can search the Help pages to find just the right topic.

To search the Help pages for information on exiting Windows Vista:

▶ **1.** Click in the Search Help box. A blinking insertion point appears.

▶ **2.** Type **shutdown** and then click the **Search Help** button 🔍. A list of Help pages containing the word *shutdown* appears in the Windows Help and Support window. See Figure 1-33.

Figure 1-33 ▶ Search Help results

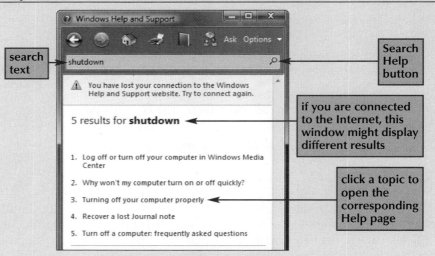

▶ **3.** Click the **Turning off your computer properly** topic. The article appears in the Windows Help and Support window.

If this article did not answer your question, you could click the **Ask someone or expand your search** link at the bottom of the Windows Help and Support window. Doing so opens a page listing other ways to get Help information.

▶ **4.** Click the **Close** button ❌ on the title bar to close the Windows Help and Support window.

If you are connected to the Internet, you can use Windows Online Help to find up-to-date information about Windows Vista on the Microsoft Web site. From the Help and Support home page, you can also contact Microsoft support or get in touch with other users of Windows Vista.

Now that you know how Windows Vista Help works, Laura reminds you to use it when you need to perform a new task or when you forget how to complete a procedure.

Turning Off Windows Vista

When you're finished working in Windows Vista, you should always turn it off properly. Doing so saves energy, preserves your data and settings, and makes sure your computer starts quickly the next time you use it.

You can turn off Windows Vista using a Lock button command or the Power button at the bottom of the Start menu. If your computer provides a Sleep option, you can click the Power button to put your computer to sleep. Windows saves your work, and then turns down the power to your monitor and computer. A light on the outside of your computer case blinks or turns yellow to indicate that the computer is sleeping. Because Windows saves your work, you do not need to close your programs or files before putting your computer to sleep. To wake your desktop computer, you press any key or move the mouse. To wake a notebook computer, you might need to press the hardware power button on your computer case instead. The screen looks exactly as it did when you turned off your computer.

If your computer does not provide a Sleep option or you otherwise need to shut down your computer, you can click the arrow next to the Lock button and then select a turn off command such as Shut Down or Restart. You sometimes need to shut down or restart your computer after installing new programs or hardware. Unlike putting your computer to sleep, shutting down closes all open programs, along with Windows itself, and then turns off your display and computer completely. Because shutting down doesn't save your work, you must save your files first.

Instead of using the Sleep, Shut Down, or Restart command, your school might prefer that you select the Log Off command on the Lock button menu. This command logs you off of Windows Vista but leaves the computer turned on, allowing another user to log on without restarting the computer. Check with your instructor or technical support person for the preferred method at your lab.

Log Off or Turn Off?		InSight

If more than one person uses your computer, you should generally log off Windows rather than turning off the computer. That way, the computer is ready for someone else to use. In either case, it's a good idea to log off (or shut down) when you're finished working to prevent an unauthorized person from accessing and changing your work.

In addition to the Shut Down, Restart, and Log Off commands, your Lock button menu might include the Standby and Cancel commands. You choose Standby when you want to put your computer into an idle state in which it consumes less power, but is still available for immediate use. Choose Cancel if you do not want to end your Windows session, but want to return to your previous task.

Laura suggests that you compare putting your computer to sleep and shutting down Windows Vista.

To turn off Windows Vista:

▶ 1. Click the **Start** button 🏵 on the taskbar and then point to the **Power** button ⏻.

▶ 2. If the Power button is yellow, click the **Power** button ⏻. Windows Vista saves your work, and then puts the computer to sleep. Wait a few moments, and then press any key or move the mouse. (If you are using a notebook computer, you might need to press the hardware power button, usually located on your computer case.)

   Trouble? If your Power button is not yellow or does not look like the Power button in Step 1, skip to Step 3.

▶ 3. Click the **Start** button 🏵 on the taskbar and then point to the arrow next to the Lock button 🔒.

▶ 4. Click **Shut Down**. Windows Vista turns off the computer.

   Trouble? If you are supposed to log off rather than shut down, click Log Off instead and follow your school's logoff procedures.

In this session you learned how to start and close programs and how to use multiple programs at the same time. You learned how to work with windows and the controls they provide. Finally, you learned how to get help when you need it and how to turn off Windows Vista. With Laura's help, you should feel comfortable with the basics of Windows Vista and well prepared to demonstrate the fundamentals of using this operating system.

Review | **Session 1.2 Quick Check**

1. The _____ command on the Start menu provides access to your computer, its storage devices, and other objects.
2. Explain how to open a folder in the Folders list and display its subfolders.
3. When you navigate from the Computer window displaying the drives on your computer to the Sample Music folder, what happens to the toolbar in the Computer window?
4. How can you decide which view to use to display file and folder icons in the Computer window or Windows Explorer?
5. In the Windows Explorer window, what appears in the right pane when you click a folder icon in the left pane?
6. In Windows Help and Support, the _____ page organizes a vast amount of help and support information into six categories.
7. How can you quickly find Help pages related to a particular topic in the Windows Help and Support window?
8. Instead of using the Shut Down command on the Lock button menu, you can end your session with Windows Vista by clicking the _____ _____ at the bottom of the Start menu.

Key Terms

active program
Aero
application
click
Computer
control
Control Panel
default settings
desktop
dialog box
Documents folder
double-click
drag
exit
file
Flip 3D
folder
graphical user
    interface (GUI)

Help and Support
icon
Internet
list box
log off
menu
menu command
menu convention
Microsoft Windows Vista
most frequently used
    programs list
mouse
multitask
navigate
operating system
pane
password
pinned items list

point
pointing device
program
program button
right-click
screen saver
ScreenTip
select
shortcut
shortcut menu
Start menu
Start Search box
submenu
user name
window
Windows Vista

Practice	**Review Assignments**

Practice the skills you learned in the tutorial.

There are no Data Files needed for the Review Assignments.

The day before your first Windows Vista demonstration for Metro Learning Center clients, Laura Halverson offers to observe your tour of the operating system and help you fine-tune your demo. You'll start working on the Windows Vista desktop, with no windows opened or minimized. Complete the following steps, recording your answers to any questions according to your instructor's preferences:

1. Start Windows Vista and log on, if necessary.
2. Use the mouse to point to each object on your desktop. Record the names and descriptions of each object as they appear in the tips.
3. Click the Start button. How many menu items or commands are on the Start menu?
4. Start WordPad. How many program buttons are now on the taskbar? (Don't count toolbar buttons or items in the notification area.)
5. Start Paint and maximize the Paint window. How many programs are running now?
6. Switch to WordPad. What are two visual clues that tell you that WordPad is the active program?
7. Close WordPad, and then restore the Paint window.
8. Open the Recycle Bin window. Record the number of items it contains.
9. Drag the Recycle Bin window so that you can see both it and the Paint window.
10. Close the Paint window from the taskbar.
11. Click the Organize button on the toolbar in the Recycle Bin window. Write down the commands on the menu. Point to Layout, and then click Menu Bar to display the menu bar.
12. Use any menu on the Recycle Bin menu bar to open a dialog box. What steps did you perform? What dialog box did you open? What do you think this dialog box is used for? Click Cancel to close the dialog box.
13. Click the Organize button on the toolbar, point to Layout, and then click Menu Bar to close the menu bar. Close the Recycle Bin window.
14. Open the Computer window, maximize it, and then open the Public folder in the Navigation pane. (*Hint*: If the Folders list is open, click the Folders button to close the list so you can see all of the folders in the Navigation pane.)
15. Open any folder in the Public folder that interests you. List the name and contents of that folder.
16. Close all open windows.
17. Start Windows Explorer. Use the Folders list in the Navigation pane to navigate to the same folder you opened in Step 15. What steps did you perform?
18. Change the view of the icons in the right pane of the Windows Explorer window. What view did you select? Describe the icons in the Windows Explorer window.
19. Close the Windows Explorer window.
20. Open Windows Help and Support.
21. Use the What's new? topics to learn something new about the Windows Vista desktop. What did you learn? How did you find this topic?
22. Use the Table of Contents to find information about the topic of mobile PCs, an enhanced feature in Windows Vista. How many topics are listed? What is their primary subject matter?
23. Use the Search Help box to find information about the topic of mobile PCs. How many topics are listed?
24. Close Help, and then close any other open windows.

25. Turn off Windows Vista by using the Sleep command, shutting down, or logging off.
26. Submit your answers to the preceding questions to your instructor, either in printed or electronic form, as requested.

| Apply | **Case Problem 1** |

Use the skills you learned in the tutorial to explore the contents of a computer for a client of At Your Service.

There are no Data Files needed for this Case Problem.

At Your Service   At Your Service is a small business with three locations in Boulder, Colorado, that provides troubleshooting and repair services for desktop and notebook personal computers. Roy Farwell, the manager of the west side branch, has hired you to do on-site troubleshooting and repair. You are preparing for a visit to a client who is new to Windows Vista and wants to determine the contents of his computer, including sample media files and related programs already provided in folders or menus. Complete the following steps:

1. Start Windows Vista and log on, if necessary.
2. From the Start menu, open the Computer window.
3. List the names of the drives on the computer.
4. Click the Documents link in the Navigation pane. Does the Documents folder contain any subfolders? If so, what are the names of the subfolders? If your Documents folder does not contain subfolders, click the Pictures and Music links in the Navigation pane and identify the contents of one of those folders.
5. Display the Folders list in the Computer window. (*Hint:* Click the Folders button near the bottom of the Navigation pane.) Where is the Documents folder located in the folder structure of your computer?
6. Open the Pictures folder, and then open a folder containing images, if necessary. View the files as Extra Large Icons.
7. Navigate to a folder that contains graphics, music, or other media files, such as videos or recorded TV. Point to a file to open the ScreenTip. What type of file did you select? What details are provided in the ScreenTip?
8. Close the Computer window, and then start Windows Explorer. In the Folders list, navigate to the Public folder.
9. Open the Public Pictures folder in the Public folder. Describe the contents of this folder. (If you cannot access the Public Pictures folder, return to the Pictures folder.) Open a subfolder, and then double-click a file icon. Describe what happens.
10. Close all open windows, and then use the Start menu to open a program that you could use with picture files. What program did you start?
11. Open Windows Help and Support, and then find and read topics that explain how to use a program you started in a previous step.
12. Close all open windows.
13. Submit your answers to the preceding questions to your instructor, either in printed or electronic form, as requested.

| Apply | | **Case Problem 2** |

Use the skills you learned in the tutorial to work with Windows Vista installed on a computer for a garden center.

There are no Data Files needed for this Case Problem.

Dover Landscapes After earning a degree in horticulture and working as a master gardener and landscape designer in Dover, Delaware, Liz Borowski started a garden center specializing in native plants and environmental designs. So that she can concentrate on landscape designs and marketing, she hired you to help her perform office tasks as her business grows. She asks you to start by teaching her the basics of using her computer, which runs Windows Vista. She especially wants to know which programs are installed on her computer and what they do. Complete the following steps:

1. Open the Start menu and write down the programs on the pinned items list.
2. Start one of the programs on the pinned items list and then describe what it does. Close the program.
3. Open the Start menu and write down the programs on the most frequently used programs list.
4. Start one of the programs on the most frequently used programs list and then describe what it does. Close the program.
5. Open the Accessories folder on the All Programs submenu, and examine the list of programs in the Accessories folder and its subfolders.
6. Use Windows Help and Support to research one of the programs you examined in the previous step, such as Calculator or Notepad. Determine the purpose of the program and how to perform a task using that program.
7. Use the Search Help box in Windows Help and Support to list all the Help topics related to the program you researched in the previous step.

⊕ **EXPLORE**   8. Start the program you researched. Click Help on the program's menu bar (or click the Help button) and then click each command on the Help menu to explore the Help topics. Compare these topics to the ones included in the Windows Help and Support window.

⊕ **EXPLORE**   9. Open and read a Help topic in the program. Find a similar topic in Windows Help and Support, and then read that topic. Compare the topics, if they are different, to determine when you would be likely to use Windows Help and Support, and when you'd use the program's Help.

10. Close all open windows.
11. Submit the results of the preceding steps to your instructor, either in printed or electronic form, as requested.

| Challenge | | **Case Problem 3** |

Extend what you've learned to customize the Windows Explorer window for a financial consultant.

There are no Data Files needed for this Case Problem.

Vernon Taylor Moe Vernon and Brett Taylor recently started their own small firm called Vernon Taylor in Bloomington, Indiana, which analyzes the finances of Bloomington businesses and recommends ways to plan for growth and success. Most of these businesses want to provide employee benefits while increasing revenues and profits. Brett Taylor uses his Windows Vista computer to write reports, study and compare data, and communicate with clients. He typically uses the Windows Explorer window to work with his files, but suspects he is not taking full advantage of its features. As his new assistant, he asks you show him around the Windows Explorer window and demonstrate how to customize its appearance. Complete the following steps:

1. Start Windows Explorer. Click the Organize button on the Windows Explorer toolbar, and write down any commands that seem related to changing the appearance of the window.

EXPLORE
2. Select a command that lays out the Windows Explorer window so that it displays a single pane for viewing files. Then restore the window to its original condition.

3. Navigate to a folder containing graphic files, such as the Pictures folder. Double-click the Sample Pictures folder to open it. (If your computer does not contain a Sample Pictures folder, open any folder that displays pictures.) Display the icons using Large Icons view.

4. Change the view to Details view. Describe the differences between Large Icons and Details view.

EXPLORE
5. Click the Slide Show button on the toolbar. Describe what happens, and then press the Esc key.

6. With the Details pane open, click a picture file. Describe the contents of the Details pane.

EXPLORE
7. Repeatedly click the Views button to cycle from one view to another. Describe the changes in the window.

8. Display the window in Details view.

EXPLORE
9. Close the Folders list. (*Hint*: Click the Folders button.) On the Organize button menu, click Folder and Search Options to open the Folder Options dialog box. Select the option that uses Windows classic folders, and then click the OK button. Describe the changes in the Sample Pictures window.

EXPLORE
10. Open the Folder Options dialog box again, click the Restore Defaults button, and then click the OK button.

11. Open the Windows Help and Support window and search for information about folder options. Find a topic explaining how to show or hide file extensions for known file types. Record your findings.

12. Close all open windows.

13. Submit the results of the preceding steps to your instructor, either in printed or electronic form, as requested.

| Research | **Case Problem 4** |

Work with the skills you've learned, and use the Internet, to provide information to an academic tour company.

There are no Data Files needed for this Case Problem.

Go and Learn Tours   Years after spending their college junior year abroad in Salzburg, Austria, Rebecca Springer and Betsy Modine decided to start a travel service for people who wanted to learn about the history, art, literature, and music of Austria. Betsy spends most of the year in Washington, D.C., marketing the business and enrolling travelers on a Go and Learn tour. Rebecca works part-time in the Washington, D.C., office and often travels to Salzburg to organize the local lecturers. Both use laptop computers running Windows Vista to run their business when they are on the move. They have hired you as a consultant to help them use and maintain their computers. For your first task, Betsy asks you to help her research wireless networks. She wants to set up a wireless network in the Go and Learn office so that she and Rebecca can easily connect to the Internet wherever they are working. You suggest starting with Windows Help and Support, and then expanding to the Internet to search for the latest information. Complete the following steps:

1. In Windows Help and Support, find information about the hardware Betsy and Rebecca need to set up a wireless network.

2. On the Windows Help and Support home page, use the Windows Online Help link to visit the Microsoft Web site containing Windows Vista information.

3. Use the Search text box on the Microsoft Web site to search for information about setting up a wireless network.

4. Choose a topic that describes how to set up a wireless network for a home or small office, and then read the topic thoroughly.

5. Write one to two pages for Betsy and Rebecca explaining what they need to set up a wireless network and the steps they should perform.

6. Submit the results of the preceding steps to your instructor, either in printed or electronic form, as requested.

Assess | **SAM Assessment and Training**

If you have a SAM user profile, you may have access to hands-on instruction, practice, and assessment of the skills covered in this tutorial. Log in to your SAM account (**http://sam2007.course.com**) to launch any assigned training activities or exams that relate to the skills covered in this tutorial.

Review | **Quick Check Answers**

Session 1.1

1. The operating system is software that helps the computer perform essential tasks such as displaying information on the computer screen and saving data on disks.
2. menu
3. Drag a border or corner of the window or restore or maximize the window.
4. shortcut menu
5. Click the Start button, and then point to the All Programs command.
6. true
7. Its button appears on the taskbar.
8. to conserve computer resources such as memory

Session 1.2

1. Computer
2. Point to the Folders list, and then click an open triangle next to a folder.
3. Some buttons change to let you perform tasks appropriate for music files, such as Play All and Burn.
4. The view you select depends on your preferences and needs. In large icon views, icons are big and easy to see, though the window can show only a few files. Small icon views display more files, but the icons are not as easy to see.
5. the contents of the folder you clicked
6. home
7. Use the Search Help box.
8. Power button

Ending Data Files

There are no ending Data Files needed for this tutorial.

Objectives

Session 2.1
- Develop file management strategies
- Plan the organization of your files and folders
- Explore files and folders
- Find files quickly

Session 2.2
- Create folders
- Select files and folders
- Name, copy, move, and delete files
- Work with new files

Session 2.3
- Sort, group, and stack files
- Set the appearance of a folder window
- Compress and extract files
- Copy files to removable media

Organizing Your Files

Managing Files and Folders in Windows Vista

Case | Azalea Inn

The Azalea Inn is a hotel in a historic mansion in Mobile, Alabama, owned by Andrew and Marilynne Ambrose. The Azalea Inn hosts travelers visiting Mobile, and it is a popular site for wedding parties and receptions, especially when the azaleas are in bloom. The Azalea Inn holds a ball during Mobile's Azalea Festival, an annual spring event. Andrew, the marketing manager, has worked hard to position the Azalea Inn at the center of the Azalea Festival. Andrew and Marilynne hired you to assist with marketing, particularly in using computer tools to track repeat customers and measure the success of marketing campaigns. Before you begin, Andrew asks you to organize the files on his new computer. Although he has only a few files, he wants to use a logical organization to help him find his work as he stores more files and folders on his new computer.

In this tutorial, you'll work with Andrew to devise a strategy for managing files. You'll learn how Windows Vista organizes files and folders, and you'll examine Windows Vista file management tools. You'll create folders and organize files within them. You'll also use techniques to display the information you need in folder windows, and explore options for working with compressed files.

Starting Data Files

Tutorial.02 →

Tutorial
Azalea Inn.jpg
Brochure.rtf
Flyer.rtf
Logo.bmp
Marketing Budget.txt
Pink Azalea.jpg
Purple Azalea.jpg
Rate List.mht

Review
Alabama.jpg
Business Plan.rtf
Event Form.xls
Letterhead.bmp
Mobile.jpg
Schedule.rtf

Case1
Bing Cherry.jpg
Buffet.jpg
Class Descriptions.rtf
Fruit Bowl.jpg
Image for Ad.bmp

Case1
Ingredients.txt
Menu-Fall.rtf
Menu-Spring.rtf
Menu-Summer.rtf
Menu-Winter.rtf

Case2
Hanson-BreakEven.xls
Hanson-Commissions.xls
Hanson-General Ledger.xls
Hanson-Tax Reminders.txt

Case2
Moore-BreakEven.xls
Moore-Expenses.xls
Moore-General Ledger.xls
Moore-TaxReminders.txt

Case4
Checklist.txt
Contacts.mdb
Customer Satisfaction.mht
Milestones.ppt
Staff Training.ppt

Session 2.1

Getting Prepared to Manage Your Files

Knowing how to save, locate, and organize computer files makes you more productive when you are working with a computer. Recall that a file, often referred to as a **document**, is a collection of data that has a name and is stored on a computer. After you create a file, you can open it, edit its contents, print it, and save it again—usually with the same program you used to create it. You organize files by storing them in folders, which are containers for your files. You need to organize files and folders so that you can find them easily and work efficiently.

A file cabinet is a common metaphor for computer file organization. A computer is like a file cabinet that has two or more drawers—each drawer is a storage device, or **disk**. Each disk contains folders that hold documents, or files. To make it easy to retrieve files, you arrange them logically into folders. For example, one folder might contain financial data, another might contain your creative work, and another could contain information you're collecting for an upcoming vacation.

A computer can store folders and files on different types of disks, ranging from removable media—such as **USB drives** (also called USB flash drives), **compact discs (CDs)**, and **3.5-inch disks**—to **hard disks**, or fixed disks, which are permanently stored on a computer. Hard disks are the most popular type of computer storage because they can contain many gigabytes of data, millions of times more data than a 3.5-inch disk, and are economical.

To have your computer access a removable disk, you must insert the disk into a **drive**, which is a computer device that can retrieve and sometimes record data on a disk. See Figure 2-1. A hard disk is already contained in a drive, so you don't need to insert it each time you use the computer.

| Figure 2-1 | Computer drives and disks |

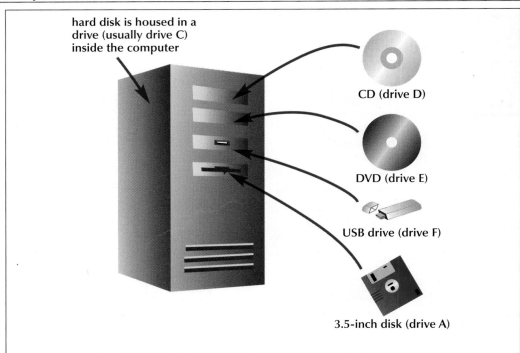

hard disk is housed in a drive (usually drive C) inside the computer

CD (drive D)

DVD (drive E)

USB drive (drive F)

3.5-inch disk (drive A)

A computer distinguishes one drive from another by assigning each a drive letter. Recall from Tutorial 1 that if your computer has a 3.5-inch disk drive, it is drive A. The hard disk is usually assigned to drive C. The remaining drives can have any other letters, but are usually assigned in the order that the drives were installed on the computer—so your USB drive might be drive D or drive F.

Understanding the Need for Organizing Files and Folders

Windows Vista stores thousands of files in many folders on the hard disk of your computer. These are system files that Windows Vista needs to display the desktop, use drives, and perform other operating system tasks. To ensure system stability and to find files quickly, Windows organizes the folders and files in a hierarchy, or **file system**. At the top of the hierarchy, Windows stores folders and important files that it needs when you turn on the computer. This location is called the **root directory** and is usually drive C (the hard disk). The term *root* refers to another popular metaphor for visualizing a file system—an upside-down tree, which reflects the file hierarchy that Windows uses. In Figure 2-2, the tree trunk corresponds to the root directory, the branches to the folders, and the leaves to the files.

Windows file hierarchy | **Figure 2-2**

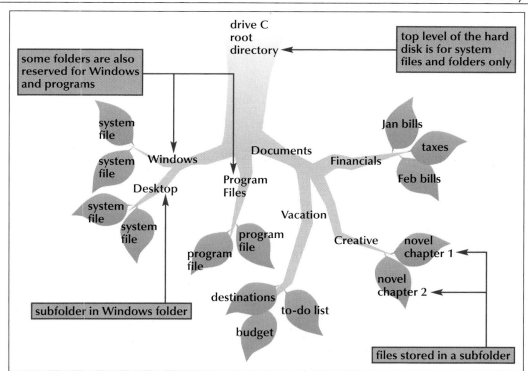

Note that some folders contain other folders. An effectively organized computer contains a few folders in the root directory, and those folders contain other folders, also called **subfolders**.

The root directory, or top level, of the hard disk is for system files and folders only—you should not store your own work here because it could interfere with Windows or a program. (If you are working in a computer lab, you might not be allowed to access the root directory.)

Do not delete or move any files or folders from the root directory of the hard disk; doing so could mean that you can't run or start the computer. In fact, you should not reorganize or change any folder that contains installed software because Windows Vista expects to find the files for specific programs within certain folders; if you reorganize or change these folders, Windows Vista can't locate and start the programs stored in that folder. Likewise, you should not make changes to the folder (usually named Windows) that contains the Windows Vista operating system.

Because the top level of the hard disk is off-limits for your files—the ones that you create, open, and save on the hard disk—you must store your files in subfolders. If you are working on your own computer, you should store your files within the Documents folder. If you are working in a computer lab, you will probably use a different location that your instructor specifies. If you simply store all your files in one folder, however, you will soon have trouble finding the files you want. Instead, you should create folders within a main folder to separate files in a way that makes sense for you.

Even if you store most of your files on removable media, such as USB drives, you still need to organize those files into folders and subfolders. Before you start creating folders, whether on a hard disk or removable disk, you should plan the organization you will use.

Developing Strategies for Organizing Files and Folders

The type of disk you use to store files determines how you organize those files. Figure 2-3 shows how you could organize your files on a hard disk if you were taking a full semester of business classes. To duplicate this organization, you would open the main folder for your documents, create four folders—one each for the Basic Accounting, Computer Concepts, Management Skills II, and Professional Writing courses—and then store the writing assignments you complete in the Professional Writing folder.

If you store your files on removable media, such as a USB drive or rewritable CD, you can use a simpler organization because you do not have to account for system files. In general, the larger the medium, the more levels of folders you should use because large media can store more files and, therefore, need better organization. For example, if you were organizing your files on a 128-MB USB drive, you could create folders in the top level of the USB drive for each general category of documents you store—one each for Courses, Creative, Financials, and Vacation. The Courses folder could then include one folder for each course, and each of those folders could contain the appropriate files.

Organizing folders and files on a hard disk ◄ Figure 2-3

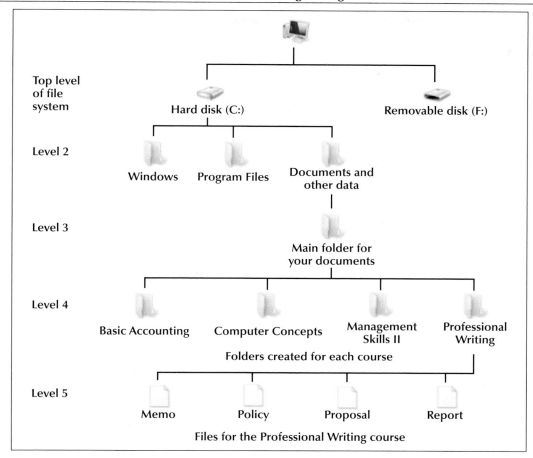

Top level of file system

Hard disk (C:)   Removable disk (F:)

Level 2   Windows   Program Files   Documents and other data

Level 3   Main folder for your documents

Level 4   Basic Accounting   Computer Concepts   Management Skills II   Professional Writing

Folders created for each course

Level 5   Memo   Policy   Proposal   Report

Files for the Professional Writing course

If your computer has a 3.5-inch disk drive, you could also organize these files on 1.44-MB 3.5-inch disks. Because the storage capacity of a 3.5-inch disk is much less than that of a USB drive, you would probably use one 3.5-inch disk for your courses, another for creative work, and so on. If you had to create large documents for your courses, you could use one 3.5-inch disk for each course.

If you work on two computers, such as one computer at an office or school and another computer at home, you can duplicate the folders you use on both computers to simplify transferring files from one computer to another. For example, if you have four folders in your Documents folder on your work computer, you would create these same four folders on your removable medium as well as in the Documents folder of your home computer. If you change a file on the hard disk of your home computer, you can copy the most recent version of the file to the corresponding folder on your removable medium so that it is available when you are at work. You also then have a **backup**, or duplicate copy, of important files that you need.

Planning Your Organization

Now that you've explored the basics of organizing files on a computer, you can plan the organization of your files for this book by recording your answers to the following questions:

1. How do you obtain the files for this book (on a USB drive from your instructor, for example)? _____

2. On what drive do you store your files for this book (drive A, C, D, for example)? _____

3. Do you use a particular folder on this drive? If so, which folder do you use? _____

4. Is this folder contained within another folder? If so, what is the name of that main folder? _____

5. On what type of disk do you save your files for this book (hard disk, USB drive, CD, or network drive, for example)? _____

If you cannot answer all of these questions, ask your instructor for help.

Exploring Files and Folders

As mentioned in Tutorial 1, Windows Vista provides two tools for exploring the files and folders on your computer—Windows Explorer and Computer. Both display the contents of your computer, using icons to represent drives, folders, and files. However, by default, each presents a slightly different view of your computer. Windows Explorer shows the files, folders, and drives on your computer, making it easy to navigate, or move from one location to another within the file hierarchy. Computer shows the drives on your computer and makes it easy to perform system tasks, such as viewing system information. Most of the time, you use one of these tools to open a folder window that displays the files and subfolders in a folder.

InSight	**Using Folder Windows**

The term *folder window* refers to any window that displays the contents of a folder, including the Computer, Windows Explorer, and Recycle Bin windows, and the Save As and Open dialog boxes (which you'll examine later in this tutorial). In all of these windows, you can use the same techniques to display folders and their contents, navigate your computer, and filter, sort, group, and stack files. Instead of distinguishing between Computer and Windows Explorer, think of managing your files in a folder window.

The Windows Explorer and Computer windows are divided into two sections, called panes. The left pane is the Navigation pane, and contains a **Favorite Links list**, which can provide quick access to the folders you use often. (You'll work with the Favorite Links list later in the tutorial.) The right pane lists the contents of your folders and other locations. If you select a folder in the Navigation pane, the contents of that folder appear in the right pane. In addition to the Favorite Links list, the Navigation pane can display a Folders list, which shows the hierarchy of the folders and other locations on your computer.

If the Folders list showed all the folders on your computer at once, it could be a very long list. Instead, you open drives and folders only when you want to see what they contain. If a folder contains undisplayed subfolders, an expand icon ▷ appears to the left of the folder icon. (The same is true for drives.) To view the folders contained in an object, you click the expand icon. A collapse icon ◢ then appears next to the folder icon; click the collapse icon to hide the folder's subfolders. To view the files contained in a folder, you click the folder icon, and the files appear in the right pane. See Figure 2-4.

Tip

To display or hide the Folders list in a folder window, click the Folders bar in the Navigation pane.

Viewing files in Windows Explorer　　　　**Figure 2-4**

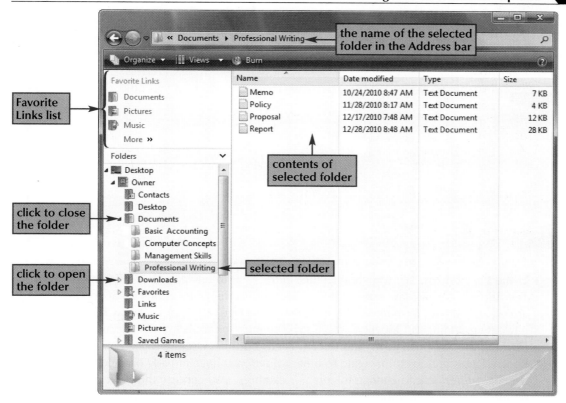

Using the Folders list helps you navigate your computer and orients you to your current location. As you move, copy, delete, and perform other tasks with the files and folders in the right pane of a folder window, you can refer to the Folders list to see how your changes affect the overall organization.

Both Windows Explorer and Computer let you view, organize, and access the drives, folders, and files on your computer. In addition to using the Folders list, you can navigate your computer in other ways:

• **Opening drives and folders in the right pane**: To view the contents of a drive or folder, double-click the drive or folder icon in the right pane of the folder window. For example, to view the contents of the Professional Writing folder shown in Figure 2-5, you can double-click the Professional Writing icon in the right pane.

Figure 2-5 Viewing folders in Windows Explorer

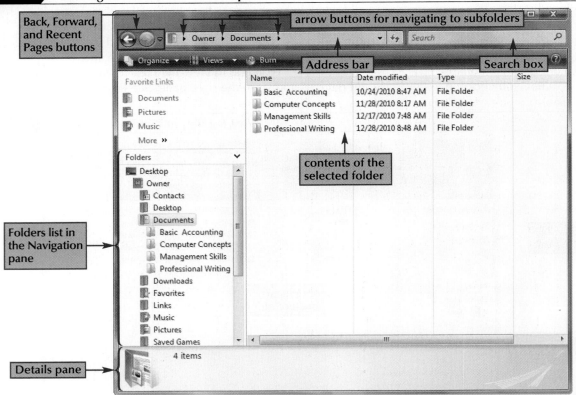

- **Using the Address bar**: You can use the Address bar to navigate to a different folder. The Address bar displays your current folder as a series of locations separated by arrows. Click a folder name, such as "Owner" in Figure 2-5, or an arrow button to navigate to a different location. You'll explore these controls later in the tutorial.
- **Clicking the Back, Forward, and Recent Pages buttons**: Use the Back, Forward, and Recent Pages buttons to navigate to other folders you have already opened. After you use the Address bar to change folders, for example, you can use the Back button to return to the original folder. As with the Address bar arrow button, you can click the Recent Pages button to navigate to a location you've visited recently.
- **Using the Search box**: To find a file or folder stored in the current folder or its subfolders, type a word or phrase in the Search box. The search begins as soon as you start typing. Windows finds files based on text in the filename, text within the file, and other characteristics of the file, such as tags (descriptive words or phrases you add to your files) or the author. For example, if you're looking for a document named September Income, you can type *Sept* in the Search box. Windows searches the current folder and its subfolders, and then displays any file whose filename contains a word starting with *Sept,* including the September Income document.

These navigation controls are available in Windows Explorer, Computer, and other folder windows, including many dialog boxes. In fact, all of these folder windows share common tools. By default, when you first open Computer, it shows all the drives available on your computer, whereas Windows Explorer shows the folders on your computer. However, by changing a single setting, you can make the two windows interchangeable. If you open the Folders list in Computer, you have the same setup as Windows Explorer. Likewise, if you close the Folders list in the Windows Explorer window, you have the same setup as in the Computer window.

Andrew is accustomed to starting Windows Explorer when he wants to manage his files. You'll use Windows Explorer to manage files in the rest of this tutorial.

Using Windows Explorer

Windows Vista provides a personal folder for your subfolders and files. Your personal folder is labeled with the name you use to log on to the computer, such as *Andrew*. Your personal folder contains folders that most users open frequently, such as Pictures, Music, and Favorites. Your personal folder also contains a **Documents folder**, which is designed to store your data files—the memos, reports, spreadsheets, presentations, and other files that you create, edit, and manipulate in a program. Although the Pictures folder is designed to store graphics and the Music folder is designed to store music files, you can store graphics, music, or any other type of file in the Documents folder, especially if doing so makes it easier to find these files when you need them. If you are working in a computer lab, you might not be able to access the Documents folder, or you might be able to store files there only temporarily because that folder is emptied every night. Instead, you might permanently store your Data Files on removable media or in a different folder on your computer or network.

When you start Windows Explorer, it opens to the Documents folder by default. If you can't access the Documents folder, the screens you see as you perform the following steps will differ. However, you can still perform the steps accurately.

To examine the organization of your computer using Windows Explorer:

▶ **1.** Click the **Start** button 🌑 on the taskbar, point to **All Programs**, click **Accessories**, and then click **Windows Explorer**. The Windows Explorer window opens.

▶ **2.** Scroll the Folder list, if necessary, and then click the **expand** icon ▷ next to the Computer icon. The drives on your computer appear under the Computer icon, as shown in Figure 2-6. The contents of your computer will differ.

Figure 2-6 ▶ **Viewing the contents of your computer**

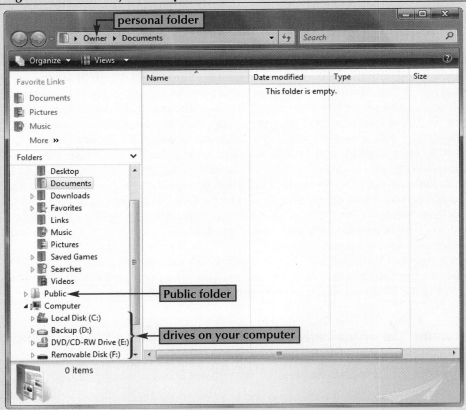

> 3. Click the **expand** icon ▷ next to the Local Disk (C:) icon. The contents of your hard disk appear under the Local Disk (C:) icon.
>
>   **Trouble?** If you do not have permission to access drive C, skip Step 3 and read but do not perform the remaining steps.
>
>   Documents is still the selected folder. To view the contents of an object in the right pane, you can click the object's icon in the Folders list.
>
> 4. Click **Public** in the Folders list. Its contents appear in the right pane. Public is a built-in Windows Vista folder that contains folders any user can access on this computer.

You've already mastered the basics of navigating your computer with Windows Explorer. You click expand icons in the Folders list until you find the folder that you want. Then, you click the folder icon in the Folders list to view the files it contains, which are displayed in the right pane.

Navigating to Your Data Files

To navigate to the files you want, it helps to know the **file path**, a notation that indicates a file's location on your computer. The file path leads you through the folder and file organization to your file. For example, the Logo file is stored in the Tutorial subfolder of the Tutorial.02 folder. If you are working on a USB drive, for example, the path to this file might be as follows:

F:\Tutorial.02\Tutorial\Logo.bmp

This path has four parts, with each part separated by a backslash (\ ):

- **F**: The drive name; for example, drive F might be the name for the USB drive. If this file were stored on the primary hard disk, the drive name would be C.
- **Tutorial.02**: The top-level folder on drive F
- **Tutorial**: A subfolder in the Tutorial.02 folder
- **Logo.bmp**: The full filename with the file extension

If someone tells you to find the file F:\Tutorial.02\Tutorial\Logo.bmp, you know you must navigate to your USB drive, open the Tutorial.02 folder, and then open the Tutorial folder to find the Logo file. Windows Explorer and Computer can display the full file path in their Address bars so you can keep track of your current location as you navigate.

You can use Windows Explorer to navigate to the Data Files you need for the rest of this tutorial. Refer to the information you provided in the "Planning Your Organization" section and note the drive on your system that contains your Data Files. In the following steps, that drive is assumed to be Removable Disk (F:), a USB drive. If necessary, substitute the appropriate drive on your system when you perform the steps.

Tip

To display the file path in a folder window, click to the right of the text in the Address bar.

To navigate to your Data Files:

▶ **1.** Make sure your computer can access your Data Files for this tutorial. For example, if you are using a USB drive, insert the drive into the USB port.

   Trouble? If you don't have the starting Data Files, you need to get them before you can proceed. Your instructor will either give you the Data Files or ask you to obtain them from a specified location (such as a network drive). In either case, make a backup copy of your Data Files before you start using them so you will have the original files available in case you need to start over. If you have any questions about the Data Files, see your instructor or technical support person for assistance.

▶ **2.** In the Windows Explorer window, click the **expand** icon ▷ next to the drive containing your Data Files, such as Removable Disk (F:). A list of the folders on that drive appears.

▶ **3.** If the list of folders does not include the Tutorial.02 folder, continue clicking the **expand** icon ▷ to navigate to the folder that contains the Tutorial.02 folder.

▶ **4.** Click the **expand** icon ▷ next to the Tutorial.02 folder to expand the folder, and then click the **Tutorial.02** folder. Its contents appear in the Folders list and in the right pane of the Windows Explorer window. The Tutorial.02 folder contains the Case1, Case2, Case4, Review, and Tutorial folders, as shown in Figure 2-7. (Because Case Problem 3 does not require any files, the Tutorial.02 folder does not include a Case3 folder.) The other folders on your system might vary.

Figure 2-7 — Navigating to the Tutorial.02 folder

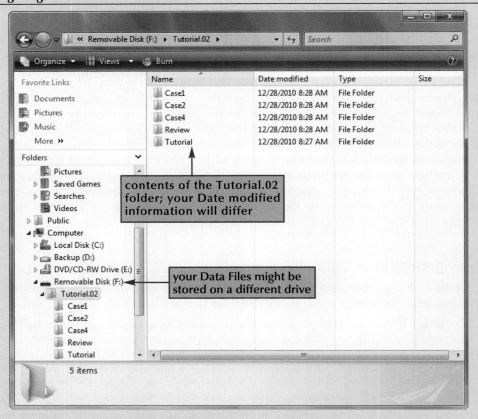

5. In the left pane, click the **Tutorial** folder. The files it contains appear in the right pane. You want to view them as medium icons.

6. Click the **Views button arrow** on the toolbar, and then click **Medium Icons**. The files appear in Medium Icons view in the Windows Explorer window. See Figure 2-8.

Because the icons used to identify types of files depend on the programs installed on your computer, the icons that appear in your window might be different from the ones shown in Figure 2-8.

Although you changed the view of the files in the Tutorial folder to Medium Icons view, other folders continue to display files in the default Details view unless you change the view.

Next, you can navigate with the Address bar to compare using that technique to using the Folders list.

Navigating with the Address Bar

Recall that the Address bar, located at the top of every folder window, displays your current folder as a series of locations separated by arrows. For example, in Figure 2-9, the Address bar shows the Tutorial.02 and Tutorial folders separated by an arrow, indicating that Tutorial is the current folder and it's stored in the Tutorial.02 folder. If a chevron button ⟨⟨ appears, you can click it to list the folders and drives containing the locations displayed in the Address bar. In Figure 2-9, the first item in this list is Removable Disk (F:), which contains the Tutorial.02 folder. The next item in this list is Computer, which contains Removable Disk (F:). This list also includes locations at higher levels in the folder hierarchy of your computer, such as Computer and Recycle Bin.

To change your location, you can click or type a folder name in the Address bar. For example, you can click Tutorial.02 to navigate to that folder. You can also type the path to the folder you want or type the name of a standard, built-in Windows folder, such as Documents, Favorites, Music, or Pictures.

Figure 2-9 ▶ **Navigating with the Address bar**

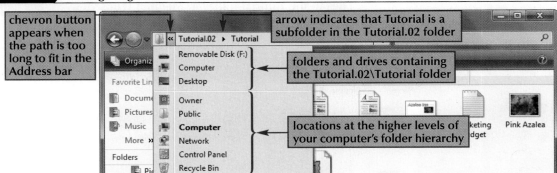

After you've navigated to a location by any method, you can click the Back, Forward, and Recent Pages buttons to revisit folders you've already opened. For example, if you navigate first to drive F:, then to the Tutorial.02 folder, and then to the Tutorial folder, you can click the Back button to open your previous location, the Tutorial.02 folder. When you do, the Forward button becomes active. You can then click the Forward button to again open the next location in your sequence, the Tutorial folder. To navigate to any recent location, click the Recent Pages button, and then click a location in the list.

To navigate using the Address bar and Back button:

▶ **1.** In the folder window displaying the contents of your Tutorial folder, click the **chevron** button `«` on the Address bar, and then click the drive containing your Data Files, such as Removable Disk (F:), in the list. The window displays the contents of the drive containing your Data Files.

   Trouble? If the drive containing your Data Files is not listed in the chevron button menu, click Computer.

▶ **2.** Click the **arrow** button `▶` to the right of Computer, and then click **Local Disk (C:)**.

   Trouble? If Local Disk (C:) does not appear in the list of drives on your computer, click any other drive.

▶ **3.** Click the **Back** button `◀` on the Address bar one or more times to return to the drive containing your Data Files.

▶ **4.** Click the **Recent Pages** button `▾` to display a list of locations you visited, and then click **Tutorial.02**. The subfolders in your Tutorial.02 folder appear in the right pane.

Leave the Windows Explorer window open so that you can work with other file and folder tools.

Using the Search Box to Find Files

After you use a computer awhile, you're likely to have many hundreds of files stored in various folders. If you know where you stored a file, it's easy to find it—you can use any navigation technique you like to navigate to that location and then scan the file list to find the file. Often, however, finding a file is more time consuming than that. You knowthat you stored a file somewhere in a standard folder such as Documents or Music, but finding the file might mean opening dozens of folders and scanning many long file lists. To save time, you can use the Search box to find your file quickly.

The **Search box** appears next to the Address bar in any folder window. To find a file in the current folder or any of its subfolders, you start typing text associated with the file. This search text can be part of the filename, text in the file, tags (keywords you associate with a file), or other file properties. By default, Windows searches for files by examining the filenames and contents of the files displayed in the folder window, including files in any subfolders. If it finds a file whose filename contains a word starting with the search text you specify, it displays that file in the folder window. For example, you can use the search text *inn* to find files named Azalea Inn and Innsbruck Plans. Windows also looks for files that contain a word starting with your search text. If it finds one, it displays that file in the folder window. For example, using *inn* as the search text also finds files containing words such as inning, inner, and innovate.

Andrew asks you to find a digital photo of azaleas. He knows he gave you at least one photo of an azalea along with the other files he wants you to organize. You can find this file by starting to type *azalea* in the Search box.

To use the Search box to find a file:

▶ **1.** In the folder window displaying the contents of your Tutorial.02 folder, click in the Search box.

▶ **2.** Type **a** and then pause. Windows Vista examines the names and the contents of the files in the Tutorial.02 folder and its subfolders, searching for a file whose filename or contents includes a word starting with *a*. Many files in the Tutorial.02 folder meet this criterion. You can continue typing to narrow the selection.

▶ **3.** Type **za** so that the search text is now *aza*. Only eight files have filenames or contents that include a word beginning with *aza*. See Figure 2-10.

Searching for a file — Figure 2-10

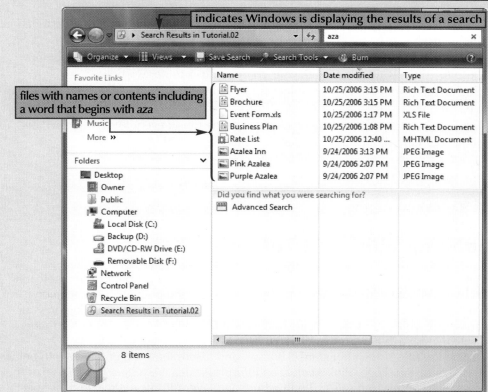

> **Trouble?** If only three files appear in the search results, click the Search in File Contents link in the right pane to search the file contents in addition to filenames.
>
> ▶ **4.** Click each file and view the information in the Details pane, which displays a thumbnail of the file contents and the file properties, such as the filename, file type, and other details.

Three of the files you found using *aza* as the search text have filenames that contain words starting with *aza*: Azalea Inn, Pink Azalea, and Purple Azalea. Five of the files you found contain text that match your criterion. By examining the file contents and properties in the Details pane, you found two photos of azaleas for Andrew—the Pink Azalea file and the Purple Azalea file.

In this session, you examined why you need to organize files and folders and began to plan your organization. You also navigated your computer using Windows Explorer and learned how to navigate to your Data Files using the Folders list and the Address bar. Finally, you used the Search box to find files quickly based on their filenames and contents.

Review | **Session 2.1 Quick Check**

1. What is the term for a collection of data that has a name and is stored on a disk or other storage medium?
2. The letter *C* is typically used for the _____ drive of a computer.
3. What are the two tools that Windows Vista provides for exploring the files and folders on your computer?
4. True or False. One way to find files using the Search box is to type text contained in the file itself.
5. What is the notation you can use to indicate a file's location on your computer?
6. Describe three ways to navigate your computer in a folder window.
7. True or False. Your Documents folder is labeled with the name you use to log on to the computer.
8. The _____ , which is located at the top of every folder window, displays your current location as a series of links separated by arrows.

Session 2.2

Managing Files and Folders

After you devise a plan for storing your files, you are ready to get organized by creating folders that will hold your files. You can do so using Computer or Windows Explorer. For this tutorial, you'll create folders in the Tutorial folder. When you are working on your own computer, you will usually create folders within the Documents folder and other standard folders, such as Music and Pictures.

Examine the files shown in Figure 2-8 again and determine which files seem to belong together. Azalea Inn, Logo, Pink Azalea, and Purple Azalea are all graphics files that the inn uses for marketing and sales. The Brochure and Flyer files were created for a special promotion the inn ran during the spring Azalea Festival. The other files are for general inn management.

One way to organize these files is to create three folders—one for graphics, one for the Azalea Festival, and another for the management files. When you create a folder, you give it a name, preferably one that describes its contents. A folder name can have up to 255 characters. Any character is allowed, except / \ : * ? " < > or |. Considering these conventions, you could create three folders as follows:

- **Marketing Graphics folder**: Azalea Inn, Logo, Pink Azalea, and Purple Azalea files
- **Festival folder**: Brochure and Flyer files
- **Management folder**: Rate List and Marketing Budget files

Before creating the folders, you show your plan to Andrew. You point out that instead of creating a folder for the graphics files, he could store them in the Pictures folder that Windows provides for photos, clip art, drawings, and other graphics. But Andrew wants to keep these marketing graphic files separate from any other files. He also thinks storing them in a subfolder along with the Festival and Management subfolders will make it easier to find his marketing files later.

Guidelines for Creating Folders | InSight

Keep the following guidelines in mind as you create folders:

- **Keep folder names short and familiar**: Long folder names can be more difficult to display in their entirety in folder windows, so use names that are short but clear. Choose names that will be meaningful later, such as project names or course numbers.
- **Develop standards for naming folders**: Use a consistent naming scheme that is clear to you, such as one that uses a project name as the name of the main folder, and includes step numbers in each subfolder name, such as 01Plan, 02Approvals, 03Prelim, and so on.
- **Create subfolders to organize files**: If a file listing in a folder window is so long that you must scroll the window, consider organizing those files into subfolders.

Andrew asks you to create the three new folders. After that, you'll move his files to the appropriate folder.

Creating Folders

You've already seen folder icons in the windows you've examined. Now, you'll create folders within the Tutorial folder using the Windows Explorer toolbar.

Creating a Folder in a Folder Window | Reference Window

- In the Folders list, click the drive or folder in which you want to create a folder.
- Click Organize on the toolbar, and then click New Folder.
- Type a name for the folder, and then press the Enter key.

or

- Right-click a folder in the Folders list or right-click a blank area in the folder window, point to New, and then click Folder.
- Type a name for the folder, and then press the Enter key.

Now you can create three folders in your Tutorial folder as you planned—the Marketing Graphics, Festival, and Management folders.

To create folders using Windows Explorer:

▶ 1. If necessary, start Windows Explorer, and then navigate to the **Tutorial** folder included with your Data Files. Click the **Tutorial** folder in the left pane and change to **Medium Icons** view, if necessary.

▶ 2. Click the **Organize** button on the toolbar, and then click **New Folder**. A folder icon with the label "New Folder" appears in the right pane. See Figure 2-11.

| Figure 2-11 | Creating a folder in the Tutorial folder |

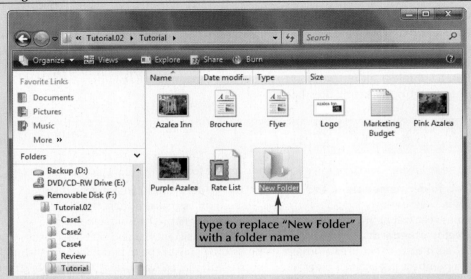

Trouble? If the "New Folder" name is not selected, right-click the new folder, click Rename, and then continue with Step 3.

Windows uses "New Folder" as a placeholder, and selects the text so that you can replace it with the name you want.

▶ 3. Type **Marketing Graphics** as the folder name, and then press the **Enter** key. The new folder is named "Marketing Graphics" and is the selected item in the right pane.

You are ready to create a second folder. This time, you'll use a shortcut menu to create a folder.

▶ 4. Right-click a blank area in the right pane, point to **New** on the shortcut menu, and then click **Folder**. A folder icon with the label "New Folder" appears in the right pane with the "New Folder" text selected.

▶ 5. Type **Festival** as the name of the new folder, and then press the **Enter** key.

▶ 6. Using the toolbar or the shortcut menu, create a folder named **Management**. The Tutorial folder now contains three new subfolders.

Now that you've created three folders, you're ready to organize your files by moving them into the appropriate folders.

Moving and Copying Files and Folders

If you want to place a file into a folder from another location, you can either move the file or copy it. **Moving** a file removes it from its current location and places it in a new location you specify. **Copying** also places the file in a new location you specify, but does not remove it from its current location. Windows Vista provides several techniques for moving and copying files. The same principles apply to folders—you can move and copy folders using a variety of methods.

Moving a File or Folder in a Folder Window | Reference Window

- Right-click and drag the file or folder you want to move to the destination folder.
- Click Move Here on the shortcut menu.

or

- Right-click the file or folder you want to move, and then click Cut on the shortcut menu.
- Navigate to and right-click the destination folder, and then click Paste on the shortcut menu.

Andrew suggests that you move some files from the Tutorial folder to the appropriate subfolders. You'll start by moving the Marketing Budget file to the Management folder.

To move a file using the right mouse button:

▶ **1.** Point to the **Marketing Budget** file in the right pane, and then press and hold the *right* mouse button.

▶ **2.** With the right mouse button still pressed down, drag the **Marketing Budget** file to the **Management** folder. When the "Move to Management" ScreenTip appears, release the button. A shortcut menu opens.

▶ **3.** With the left mouse button, click **Move Here** on the shortcut menu. The Marketing Budget file is removed from the main Tutorial folder and stored in the Management subfolder.

   Trouble? If you release the mouse button before you've dragged the Marketing Budget file all the way to the Management folder and before seeing the "Move to Management" ScreenTip, press the Esc key to close the shortcut menu, and then repeat Steps 1 through 3.

▶ **4.** In the right pane, double-click the **Management** folder. The Marketing Budget file is in the Management folder.

▶ **5.** Click the **Back** button ⊙ on the Address bar to return to the **Tutorial** folder. The Tutorial folder no longer contains the Marketing Budget file.

The advantage of moving a file or folder by dragging with the right mouse button is that you can efficiently complete your work with one action. However, this technique requires polished mouse skills so that you can drag the file comfortably. Another way to move files and folders is to use the **Clipboard**, a temporary storage area for files and information that you have copied or moved from one place and plan to use somewhere else. You can select a file and use the Cut or Copy commands to temporarily store the file on the Clipboard, and then use the Paste command to insert the file elsewhere. Although using the Clipboard takes more steps, some users find it easier than dragging with the right mouse button.

You'll move the Brochure file to the Festival folder next by using the Clipboard.

To move files using the Clipboard:

1. Right-click the **Brochure** file, and then click **Cut** on the shortcut menu. Although the file icon is still displayed in the folder window, Windows Vista removes the Brochure file from the Tutorial folder and stores it on the Clipboard.

2. In the Folders list, right-click the **Festival** folder, and then click **Paste** on the shortcut menu. Windows Vista pastes the Brochure file from the Clipboard to the Festival folder. The Brochure file icon no longer appears in the folder window.

3. In the Folders list, click the **Festival** folder to view its contents in the right pane. The Festival folder now contains the Brochure file. See Figure 2-12.

Figure 2-12 ▶ Moving a file

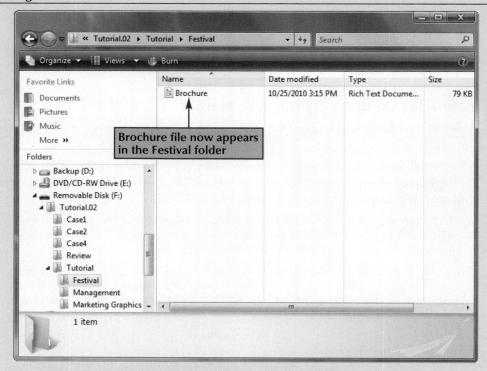

You'll move the Flyer file from the Tutorial folder to the Festival folder.

4. Click the **Back** button on the Address bar to return to the Tutorial folder, right-click the **Flyer** file in the folder window, and then click **Cut** on the shortcut menu.

5. Right-click the **Festival** folder, and then click **Paste** on the shortcut menu.

6. Click the **Forward** button on the Address bar to return to the Festival folder. The Festival folder now contains the Brochure and Flyer files.

Tip

To use keyboard shortcuts to move files, click the file you want to move, press Ctrl+X to cut the file, navigate to a new location, and then press Ctrl+V to paste the file.

One way to save steps when moving or copying multiple files or folders is to select all the files and folders you want to move or copy, and then work them as a group. You'll see how to do that next.

Selecting Files and Folders

You can select multiple files or folders using any of several techniques, so you can use the most convenient method for your current task. First, you open the folder that contains the files or folders you want to select. Then select the files or folders using any one of the following methods:

- To select files or folders that are listed together in a window, click the first item, hold down the Shift key, and then click the last item.
- To select files or folders that are listed together in a window without using the keyboard, drag the pointer to create a selection box around all the items you want to include.
- To select files or folders that are not listed together, hold down the Ctrl key, and then click each item you want to select.
- To select all of the files or folders, click Organize on the toolbar, and then click Select All.
- To clear the selection of an item in a selected group, hold down the Ctrl key, and then click each item you want to remove from the selection.
- To clear the entire selection, click a blank area of the window.

Copying Files and Folders

When you copy a file or folder, you make a duplicate of the original item. You can copy a file or folder using techniques similar to the ones you use when moving.

Copying a File or Folder in a Folder Window | Reference Window

- Right-click and drag the file or folder you want to move to the destination folder.
- Click Copy Here on the shortcut menu.

or

- Right-click the file or folder you want to copy, and then click Copy on the shortcut menu.
- Navigate to and right-click the destination folder, and then click the Paste on the shortcut menu.

You'll copy the four graphics files from the Tutorial folder to the Marketing Graphics folder now.

To copy files using the Clipboard:

▶ **1.** Return to the Tutorial folder window, and then click the **Azalea Inn** file.

▶ **2.** Hold down the **Ctrl** key, click the **Logo** file, click the **Pink Azalea** file, click the **Purple Azalea** file, and then release the **Ctrl** key. Four files are selected in the Tutorial folder window.

▶ **3.** Right-click a selected file, and then click **Copy** on the shortcut menu. Windows Vista copies the files to the Clipboard.

▶ **4.** Right-click the **Marketing Graphics** folder, and then click **Paste** on the shortcut menu. Windows copies the four files to the Marketing Graphics folder.

Now that you have copied files using the Copy and Paste commands, you can use the right-drag technique to copy the Rate List file to the Management folder. As with moving files, to right-drag a file, you point to the file, hold down the right mouse button, and then drag the file to a new location. When you release the mouse button, however, you click Copy Here (instead of Move Here) on the shortcut menu to copy the file.

To copy a file:

▶ **1.** Right-drag the **Rate List** file from the Tutorial folder to the Management folder.

▶ **2.** Release the mouse button, and then click **Copy Here** on the shortcut menu.

When you move or copy a folder, you move or copy all the files contained in the folder. You'll practice moving and copying folders in the Case Problems at the end of this tutorial.

There is a third way to copy or move a file or folder. You can drag the file or folder (using the left mouse button) to another location. Whether the file or folder is copied or moved depends on where you drag it. A ScreenTip appears when you drag a file to a new location—the ScreenTip indicates what happens when you release the mouse button. Figure 2-13 summarizes how to copy and move files and folders by dragging.

Figure 2-13 ▶ **Dragging to move and copy files**

Drag a File or Folder:	To:
Into a folder on the same drive	Move the file or folder to the destination folder
Into a folder on a different drive	Copy the file or folder to the destination folder

Although the copy and move techniques listed in Figure 2-13 are common ways to copy and move files and folders, be sure you can anticipate what happens when you drag a file or folder.

Naming and Renaming Files

As you work with files, pay attention to **filenames**—they provide important information about the file, including its contents and purpose. A filename such as Car Sales.docx has three parts:

- **Main part of the filename**: The name you provide when you create a file, and the name you associate with a file
- **Dot**: The period (.) that separates the main part of the filename from the file extension
- **File extension**: Usually three or four characters that follow the dot in the filename

The main part of a filename can have up to 255 characters—this gives you plenty of room to name your file accurately enough so that you'll know the contents of the file just by looking at the filename. You can use spaces and certain punctuation symbols in your filenames. Like folder names, however, filenames cannot contain the symbols \ / ? : * " < > or | because these characters have special meaning in Windows Vista.

A filename might display an **extension**—three or more characters following a dot—that identifies the file's type and indicates the program in which the file was created. For example, in the filename Car Sales.docx, the extension *docx* identifies the file as one created by Microsoft Office Word 2007, a word-processing program. You might also have a file called Car Sales.xlsx—the *xlsx* extension identifies the file as one created in Microsoft Office Excel 2007, a spreadsheet program. Though the main parts of these filenames are identical, their extensions distinguish them as different files. The filename extension also helps Windows identify what program should open the file. For example, the .txt extension in a file named Agenda.txt indicates that it is a text file and can be opened by programs associated with that extension, such as WordPad, Notepad, and Microsoft Word. You usually do not need to add extensions to your filenames because the program that you use to create the file adds the file extension automatically. Also, although Windows Vista keeps track of extensions, not all computers are set to display them.

Be sure to give your files and folders meaningful names that will help you remember their purpose and contents. You can easily rename a file or folder by using the Rename command on the file's shortcut menu.

Guidelines for Naming Files | InSight

The following are best practices for naming your files:

- **Use common names**: Avoid cryptic names that might make sense now, but could provide confusion later, such as nonstandard abbreviations or imprecise names like Stuff08.
- **Don't change the file extension**: Do not change the file extension when renaming a file. If you do, Windows might not be able to find a program that can open it.
- **Find a comfortable balance between too short and too long**: Use filenames that are long enough to be meaningful, but short enough to be read easily on the screen.

Andrew notes that the Brochure file in the Festival folder could contain the information for any brochure. He recommends that you rename that file to give it a more descriptive filename. The Brochure file was originally created to store text specifically for the Azalea Festival brochure, so you'll rename the file Azalea Festival Brochure. As you do, you can use the Recent Pages button, which appears next to the Forward button on the Address bar. You can click the Recent Pages button to display a list of folders you've opened recently. Click a folder name in the Recent Pages list to select that folder in the Folders list and display its contents in the right pane.

To rename the Brochure file:

▶ 1. Click the **Recent Pages** ⊡ button on the Address bar, and then click **Festival**. The contents of the Festival folder appear in the right pane.

▶ 2. Right-click the **Brochure** file, and then click **Rename** on the shortcut menu. The filename is highlighted and a box appears around it.

▶ 3. Type **Azalea Festival Brochure**, and then press the **Enter** key. The file now appears with the new name.

   Trouble? If you make a mistake while typing and you haven't pressed the Enter key yet, press the Backspace key until you delete the mistake, and then complete Step 3. If you've already pressed the Enter key, repeat Steps 2 and 3 to rename the file again.

   Trouble? If your computer is set to display file extensions, a message might appear asking if you are sure you want to change the file extension. Click the No button, right-click the Brochure file, click Rename on the shortcut menu, type "Azalea Festival Brochure.rtf", and then press the Enter key.

All the files that originally appeared in the Tutorial folder are now stored in appropriate subfolders. You can streamline the organization of the Tutorial folder by deleting the duplicate files you no longer need.

Deleting Files and Folders

You should periodically delete files and folders you no longer need so that your main folders and disks don't get cluttered. In a folder window, you delete a file or folder by deleting its icon. When you delete a file from a hard disk, Windows Vista removes the file from the folder, but stores the file contents in the Recycle Bin. The **Recycle Bin** is an area on your hard disk that holds deleted files until you remove them permanently; an icon on

Tip

To retrieve a deleted file from the hard disk, double-click the Recycle Bin, right-click the file you want to retrieve, and then click Restore.

the desktop allows you easy access to the Recycle Bin. When you delete a folder from the hard disk, the folder and all of its files are stored in the Recycle Bin. If you change your mind and want to retrieve a file deleted from your hard disk, you can use the Recycle Bin to recover it and return it to its original location. However, after you empty the Recycle Bin, you can no longer recover the files it contained.

When you delete a file from removable media, such as a USB drive, it does not go into the Recycle Bin. Instead, it is deleted as soon as its icon disappears, and you cannot recover it.

Andrew reminds you that because you copied the Azalea Inn, Logo, Pink Azalea, Purple Azalea, and Rate List files to the subfolders in the Tutorial folder, you can safely delete the original files. As is true for moving, copying, and renaming files and folders, you can delete a file or folder in many ways, including using a shortcut menu or selecting one or more files and then pressing the Delete key.

To delete files in the Tutorial folder:

▶ **1.** Use any technique you've learned to navigate to and open the **Tutorial** folder.

▶ **2.** Click **Azalea Inn**, hold down the **Shift** key, click **Rate List** (the last file in the file list), and then release the **Shift** key. All the files in the Tutorial folder are now selected. None of the subfolders should be selected.

▶ **3.** Right-click the selected files, and then click **Delete** on the shortcut menu. Windows Vista asks if you're sure you want to delete these files.

▶ **4.** Click the **Yes** button.

So far, you've worked with files using Windows Explorer and Computer, but you haven't viewed any of their contents. To view file contents, you open the file. When you double-click a file in Windows Explorer or Computer, Windows Vista starts the appropriate program and opens the file. You'll have a chance to try these techniques in the next section.

Working with New Files

The most common way to add files to a drive or folder is to create new files when you use a program. For example, you can create a text document in a word-processing program, a drawing in a graphics program, or a movie file in a video-editing program. When you are finished with a file, you must save it if you want to use the file again. To work with the file again, you open the file in an appropriate program; you can usually tell which programs can open a file by examining the filename extension or file icon.

Before you continue working with Andrew's files, you decide to create a to-do list to summarize your remaining tasks. You'll create the to-do list file, save it, close it, and then reopen it to add some items to the list.

Creating a File

You create a file by starting a program and then saving the file in a folder on your computer. Some programs create a file when you open the program. When you open WordPad, for example, it starts with a blank page. This represents an empty (and unsaved) file. You start typing and, when you are finished, you save your work using the Save As dialog box, where you can select a location for the file and enter a filename that identifies the contents. By default, most programs save files in common folders such as Documents, Pictures, and Music, which makes it easy to find the files again later.

The to-do list you want to create is a simple text document, so you can create this file using Notepad, the basic text-editing program that Windows Vista provides.

To create a Notepad file:

▶ **1.** Start Notepad by clicking the **Start** button 🔵 on the taskbar, pointing to **All Programs**, clicking **Accessories**, and then clicking **Notepad**. The Notepad program window opens. See Figure 2-14.

Creating a file ◀ **Figure 2-14**

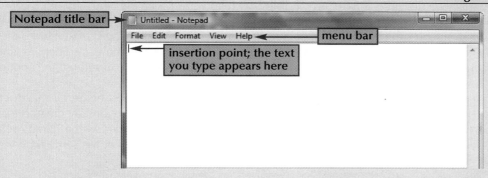

▶ **2.** Type the following text in the Notepad window, pressing the **Enter** key at the end of each line, including the last line:

To Do for Andrew's Files

1. Arrange files in a folder window.

2. Show and hide file extensions.

3. Compress and extract files.

The Notepad title bar indicates that the name of this file is "Untitled." To give it a more descriptive name, preserve the contents, and store the file where you can find it later, you must save the file.

Saving a File

As you are creating a file, you should save it frequently so you don't lose your work. When you save a new file, you use the Save As dialog box to specify a filename and a location for the file. When you open a file you've already created, you can usually click a toolbar button to save the file with the same name and location. If you want to save the file with a different name or in a different location, however, you use the Save As dialog box again to specify the new name or location. You can create a folder for the new file at the same time you save the file.

As a special type of folder window, the Save As dialog box can contain the same elements as all folder windows, such as an Address bar, Search box, Navigation pane, and right pane displaying folders and files. To display all of these navigation tools, you click the Browse Folders button to expand the Save As dialog box. Then you can specify the file location, for example, using the same navigation techniques and tools that are available in all folder windows. In addition, the Save As dialog box always includes a File name text box where you specify a filename, a Save as type list box where you select a file type, and other controls for saving a file. If the expanded Save As dialog box covers too much of your document or desktop, you can click the Hide Folders button to collapse the dialog box so it hides the Navigation pane, right pane, and toolbar. You can still navigate with the Back, Forward, and Recent Pages buttons, the Address bar, and the Search box, and you can still use the controls for saving a file, but you conserve screen space.

Now that you've created a to-do list, you need to save it. The best name for this document is probably "To-Do List." However, none of the folders you've already created for Andrew seems appropriate for this file. It belongs in a separate folder with a name such as "Daily Documents." You can create the Daily Documents folder at the same time you save the to-do list file.

To save the Notepad file:

▶ **1.** In the Notepad window, click **File** on the menu bar, and then click **Save As**. The Save As dialog box opens.

▶ **2.** If the Navigation pane does not appear in the Save As dialog box, click the **Browse Folders** button. If necessary, also click the **Folders** button to display the Folders list. See Figure 2-15.

Figure 2-15 ▶ **Saving a new file**

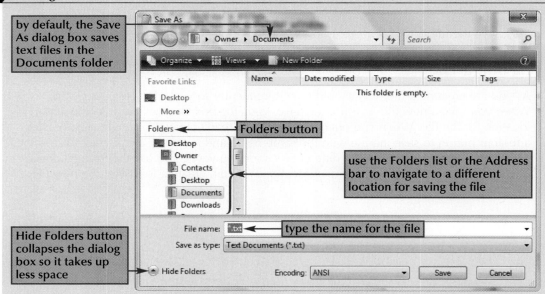

By default, Notepad saves files in the Documents folder. You want to create a folder in the Tutorial folder for this document.

▶ **3.** Use any technique you've learned to navigate to the **Tutorial** folder in the Save As dialog box.

▶ **4.** Click the **New Folder** button on the toolbar. A new folder appears in the Tutorial folder, with the "New Folder" name highlighted and ready for you to replace.

▶ **5.** Type **Daily Documents** as the name of the new folder, and then press the **Enter** key. The Daily Documents folder opens. Now you are ready to specify a filename and save the to-do list file in the Daily Documents folder.

▶ **6.** Click in the **File name** text box, and then type **To-Do List**. Notepad automatically provides a .txt extension to this filename.

▶ **7.** Click the **Save** button. Notepad saves the To-Do List file in the Daily Documents folder. The new filename now appears in the Notepad title bar.

▶ **8.** Click the **Close** button 🗙 to close Notepad.

Next, you can open the file to add another item to the to-do list.

Opening a File

If you want to open a file in a running program, you use the Open dialog box, which is a folder window with additional controls for opening a file, similar to the Save As dialog box. You usually click an Open button on a toolbar or you click File on the menu bar and then click Open to access the Open dialog box, which you use to navigate to the file you want, select the file, and click the Open button. If the program you want to use is not running, you can open a file by double-clicking it in a folder window. The file usually opens in the program that you used to create or edit it. If it's a text file with a .txt extension, for example, it opens in a text editor, such as Notepad. If it's a text file with a .docx extension, it opens in the Microsoft Word 2007 word-processing program.

Not all documents work this way. Double-clicking a digital picture file usually opens a picture viewer program, which displays the picture. To actually edit the picture, you need to use a graphics editor program. When you need to specify a program to open a file, you can right-click the file, point to Open With on the shortcut menu, and then click the name of the program that you want to use.

> **Tip**
>
> To select the default program for opening a particular type of file, right-click the file, point to Open With on the shortcut menu, and then click Choose Default Program. Click a program, and then click the OK button.

To open and edit the To-Do List file:

▶ **1.** In the right pane of the Tutorial folder window, double-click the **Daily Documents** folder.

▶ **2.** Double-click the **To-Do List** file. Notepad starts and opens the To-Do List file.

Trouble? If a program other than Notepad starts, such as WordPad, click the Close button to close the program, right-click the To-Do List file, point to Open With, and then click Notepad.

▶ **3.** Press **Ctrl+End** to move the insertion point to the end of the document, and then type **4. Review how to customize folder windows.**

Because you want to save this file using the same name and location, you can use the Save command on the File menu to save your work this time.

▶ **4.** Click **File** on the menu bar, and then click **Save**. Notepad saves the To-Do List file without opening the Save As dialog box because Notepad uses the same name and location as the last time you saved the file.

As long as Notepad is still open, you can create another simple text file that describes the graphics in the Marketing Graphics folder.

To create and save another file:

▶ **1.** Click **File** on the menu bar, and then click **New** to open a new, blank document.

> **2.** Type the following text in the Notepad window, pressing the **Enter** key at the end of each line:
>
> **Marketing Graphics files:**
>
> **Azalea Inn: Photo of the inn**
>
> **Logo: Copy of the inn's logo for stationery and ads**
>
> **Pink Azalea: Photo of pink azaleas**
>
> **Purple Azalea: Photo of a purple azalea**
>
> **3.** Click **File** on the menu bar, and then click **Save**. The Save As dialog box opens.
>
> **4.** Navigate to the **Marketing Graphics** folder.
>
> **5.** Click in the File name text box, and then type **Graphic Descriptions**.
>
> **6.** Click the **Save** button. Notepad saves the Graphic Descriptions file in the Marketing Graphics folder.
>
> **7.** Click the **Close** button [X] to close Notepad.

Tip

The first time you save a file, selecting Save on the File menu opens the Save As dialog box so you can specify a name and location for the new file.

In this session, you managed files and folders by creating folders and then selecting, moving, and copying files. You also renamed and deleted files according to your organization plan, and then created a file, saved it in a new folder, and opened and edited the file.

Review | **Session 2.2 Quick Check**

1. _____ a file removes it from its current location and places it in a new location you specify.
2. True or False. The advantage of moving a file or folder by dragging with the right mouse button is that you can efficiently complete your work with one action.
3. Describe two ways to select files that are listed together in a window.
4. When you drag a file into a folder on the same hard disk, are you moving or copying the file to the destination folder?
5. What does a filename extension indicate about a file?
6. True or False. You should periodically delete files and folders you no longer need so that your main folders and disks don't get cluttered.
7. The _____ is an area on your hard disk that holds deleted files until you remove them permanently.
8. When you first create a file, what must you do if you want to use the file again?

Session 2.3

Refining Your Organization

Your main tasks when managing files are to formulate a logical plan for organizing your files, create the folders you need to store the files, and then move and copy your existing files into those folders. As you create files using programs, save them in an appropriate folder and use filenames that help you identify the file contents. Performing these basic management tasks helps you keep track of your files so you can easily find information when you need it.

To refine your organization, you can fine-tune the view of your files and folders in a folder window. Changing the view can often help you find files and identify those that share common features, such as two versions of the same file. One way to change the view is to sort your files. **Sorting** files and folders means to list them in a particular order, such as alphabetically by name or type or chronologically by their modification date. You can also **filter** the contents of a folder to display only files and folders with certain characteristics, such as all those you modified yesterday. In short, sorting reorganizes all of the files and folders in a list, while filtering displays only those files and folders that share a characteristic you specify. Both actions change your view of the files and folders, not the items themselves.

Windows Vista provides two other ways to change the view of your files and folders—stacking and grouping. When you **stack** files, you arrange all of the files in the list into piles, called stacks. If you stack by type, for example, Windows displays Microsoft Word documents in one stack and photo files with a .jpg extension in another stack. If you want to view only the Word documents, open the appropriate stack. Unlike a stack, which hides the files it contains behind an icon, a **group** displays a sequential list of all the files in a folder, grouped according to a file detail. When you group your files by type, for example, Windows separates the files into several groups, with each group displaying all the files of the same type.

You want to show Andrew these four ways to change the view of his files so he can choose one that makes the most sense for him or his current task.

Sorting and Filtering Files

To sort or filter the files listed in a folder window, you use the column headings in the right pane of the window. To sort files by type, for example, click the Type column heading. You can sort files in ascending order (A to Z, zero to nine, or earliest to latest date) or descending order (Z to A, nine to zero, or latest to earliest date). To switch the order, click the column heading again. Sorting is often an effective way to find a file or folder in a relatively short file list. By default, Windows Vista sorts the contents of a folder in ascending alphabetic order by filename, so a file named April Budget appears at the top of the list, and a file named Winter Expenses appears at the end. You can change the sort criterion to list files according to any other file characteristic.

If you are working with a longer file list, filtering the list might help you find the file you want. To filter the contents of a folder, you click the arrow to the right of a column heading, and then click a file property such as a filename, date created or modified, author, or file type, and Windows displays only files and folders with those properties. For example, if you want to list only music files by a particular artist, you can filter by that artist's name.

All of the views, including Extra Large Icons and Large Icons, provide column headings corresponding to file details, so you can sort and filter in any view. However, only Details view lists all the file details in these columns—the other views list only some details and provide the others in the Details pane or in the ScreenTip that appears when you point to an icon. This means Details view is usually the most effective one for sorting and filtering.

> **Tip**
>
> To sort by a file detail that does not appear as a column heading, right-click any column heading and then select a file detail; the column heading appears in the folder window so you can sort by that detail.

To sort and filter the files in the Marketing Graphics folder:

▶ 1. Navigate to the **Marketing Graphics** folder in the Tutorial folder.

▶ 2. Click the **Views button arrow** on the toolbar, and then click **Details**.

▶ 3. Click the **Size** column heading to sort the files in descending order according to file size. An indented sort arrow appears at the top of the Size column heading. The sort arrow points down to indicate the column is sorted in descending order.

Trouble? If the Size column does not appear in your folder window, right-click any column heading and then click Size. Then complete Step 3.

▸ 4. Click the **Size** column heading again to reverse the sort order. The sort arrow now points up, indicating the column is sorted in ascending order.

▸ 5. Right-click any **column heading** to display a list of file details. Details with a check mark are displayed in the folder window. If Tags is listed with a check mark, click **Tags** to remove this column from the folder window.

▸ 6. Right-click any **column heading** again, and if Rating is listed with a check mark, click **Rating** to remove this column from the folder window. If Date taken is also listed with a check mark, repeat this step to remove the **Date taken** column.

▸ 7. If the Date modified column heading does not appear in your folder window, right-click any **column heading**, and then click **Date modified** to display this column. Your folder window should now display only the Name, Size, and Date modified columns.

Trouble? If your folder window contains columns other than Name, Size, and Date modified, right-click any column heading, and then click the name of the column you want to remove from the folder window.

▸ 8. Click the **Date modified** column heading to sort the files chronologically by the date they were modified. See Figure 2-16.

Figure 2-16 ▸ **Sorting files by date modified**

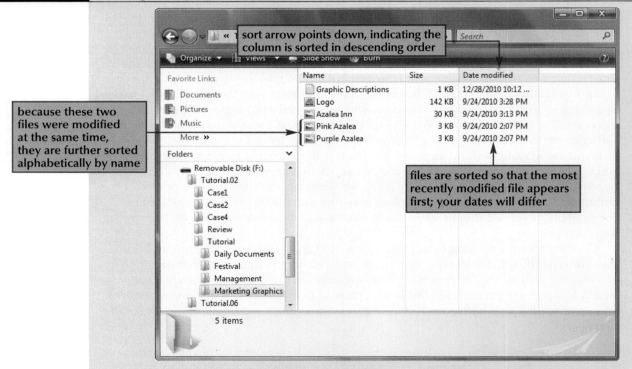

To compare sorting and filtering, you can filter the files by their modified date to display only the files you modified today.

▸ 9. Point to the **Date modified** column heading, and then click its arrow button to display a list of filtering, grouping, and stacking options.

▸ 10. Click the **Today** check box to select today's date. The folder window displays only the Graphic Descriptions file. See Figure 2-17.

Trouble? If you modified the Graphic Descriptions file on a different date, click that date on the calendar.

Trouble? If you clicked Today rather than the check box, repeat Steps 9 and 10 to select today's date.

Filtering to display files modified today ◀ **Figure 2-17**

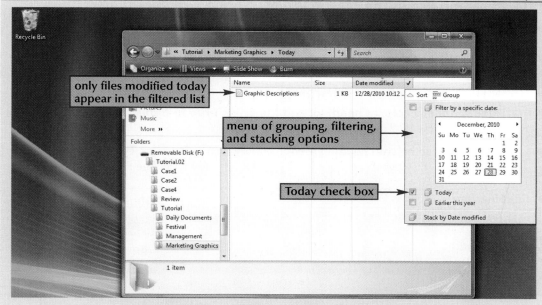

Note that you can filter by two or more properties by selecting the corresponding check boxes.

▶ **11.** Click a blank area of the window to close the list. A check mark appears next to the Date modified column heading to indicate the file list is filtered by a Date modified detail.

Next, you can stack and group the files in the Marketing Graphics folder and compare these views to the ones displayed when you sorted and filtered the files.

Stacking and Grouping Files

Stacking and grouping are similar ways to change your view of files and folders, and are especially effective when working with long file lists. You can stack or group files according to any file detail currently displayed in the folder window. To stack files by author, for example, click the Authors column heading list arrow, and then click Stack by Authors. Windows arranges the contents of the folder into stacks, one for each author, such as one for files you wrote and another for files your colleague wrote. Only stack icons appear for each group of files, not the files themselves. To view the files you wrote, double-click the stack with your name.

To group files, you click a column heading list arrow, and then click Group. When you group files by author, for example, Windows divides the folder window into sections, with one section listing files you wrote and another section for files your colleague wrote. Stacking and grouping files have similar results—the only difference is that stacking hides the files behind a stack icon, while grouping displays the files in different sections in the folder window.

Before stacking or grouping files, you must remove any filters you are using in the folder window. If you don't, you'll rearrange only the files that appear in the filtered list. After removing the filter, you'll stack and then group the files in the Marketing Graphics folder by type.

To stack and group the files in the Marketing Graphics folder:

▶ **1.** In the Marketing Graphics folder window, click the **check mark** on the Date modified column heading, and then click the **Today** check box (or the **Filter by a specific date** check box if you selected a date on the calendar earlier) to clear the check box. Click a blank area of the folder window. The complete list of Marketing Graphics files appears in the window.

▶ **2.** Right-click any **column heading**, and then click **Type** to display that column in the folder window.

▶ **3.** Click the **Type column heading arrow**, and then click **Stack by Type**. Windows hides the files and displays three stack icons, one for each file type. See Figure 2-18.

Figure 2-18	Stacking files

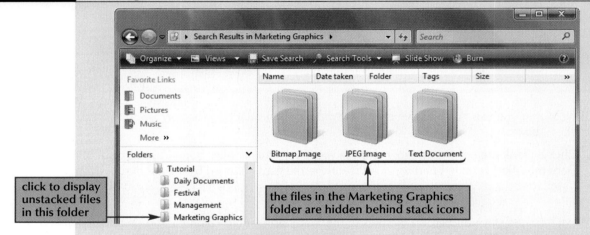

click to display unstacked files in this folder

the files in the Marketing Graphics folder are hidden behind stack icons

▶ **4.** Double-click the **JPEG Image** stack icon. (JPEG is a typical file type for photographs.) Windows displays the three JPEG files in the stack.

▶ **5.** Click **Marketing Graphics** in the Folders list to show the unstacked files in that folder.

▶ **6.** Click the **Type column heading arrow**, and then click **Group**. Windows arranges all five files in the Marketing Graphics folder into three groups, one for each file type. See Figure 2-19.

Grouping files ◀ **Figure 2-19**

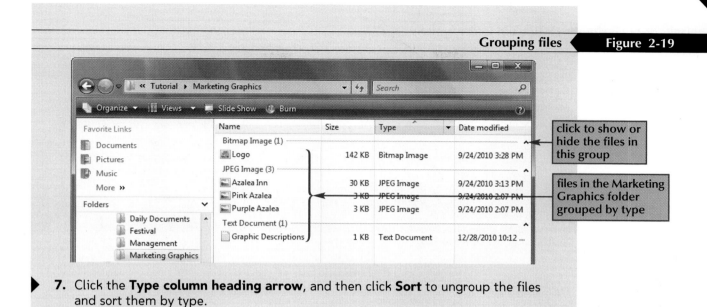

7. Click the **Type column heading arrow**, and then click **Sort** to ungroup the files and sort them by type.

After showing Andrew how to sort, filter, stack, and group files in a folder window, he mentions that he might want to hide or show elements of the folder window itself, such as the Navigation pane or the Details pane. You'll show him how to customize the folder window elements next.

Customizing a Folder Window

You can change the way your folder windows look and work to suit your needs. For example, you can hide the Details pane or the Navigation pane to devote more space to file lists. To do so, you use the Layout command and the Folder and Search Options command on a folder window's Organize button. The Layout command lists the panes you can display in a folder window. When you select the Folder and Search Options command, the Folder Options dialog box opens, where you can select settings that change the behavior and appearance of the folder window. Figure 2-20 summarizes the ways you can customize the appearance of a folder window. Note that the Folder and Search Options command is not available for the Save As and Open dialog boxes.

Figure 2-20   **Layout and folder options**

Layout Options	
Option	**Description**
Menu Bar	Hide or show the menu bar in this window only.
Search Pane	Display buttons for conducting a search (not available in the Save As and Open dialog boxes).
Details Pane or Preview Pane	Hide or show the Details pane when you are viewing folder contents or the Preview pane when you select one or more items.
Navigation Pane	Hide or show the Navigation pane.

Folder Options Dialog Box Setting	
Settings on the General Tab	**Description**
Use Windows classic folders	Turn off the Navigation pane, Preview pane, and toolbar in all folders. (To turn the panes back on, click Show preview and filters.)
Restore Defaults	Restore the original settings for your folders.
Settings on the View Tab	**Description**
Always show icons, never thumbnails	Always show static icons of files and never show thumbnail previews of files. Use this setting if the thumbnail previews are slowing down your computer.
Show hidden files and folders	Display files and folders marked as hidden. Use this setting if you need to work with files that are usually hidden from view, such as user files that have been marked as hidden.
Display simple folder view in Navigation pane	Display folders with lines that connect folders and subfolders.
Hide extensions for known file types	Show or hide extensions as a part of filenames.
Restore Defaults	Restore the original settings on the View tab.

You'll show Andrew how to change the layouts in a folder window, and then how to customize the appearance of the folder contents. Finally, you'll demonstrate how to add items and make other changes to the Navigation pane.

Changing the Layout of a Folder Window

You can change the layout of a folder window by showing or hiding one or more of the following elements: the Navigation pane, Preview pane, Details pane, and menu bar. Recall that the Navigation pane appears on the left side of a folder window and lets you change the view to other folders. You can click an item in the Favorite Links list in the Navigation pane to open a built-in Windows folder, such as the Documents folder. If you often go to the same folder, you can also drag that folder to the Favorite Links list to make it one of your favorite locations. The Details pane appears at the bottom of a folder window and displays details about the folder and its contents. The Preview pane appears at the right side of a folder window and displays the contents of many kinds of files; if you select an e-mail message, text file, or picture, for example, you can see its contents in the Preview pane without opening the file in a program. Figure 2-21 shows a folder window with all the panes open.

Folder window displaying the Navigation, Details, and Preview panes ◀ Figure 2-21

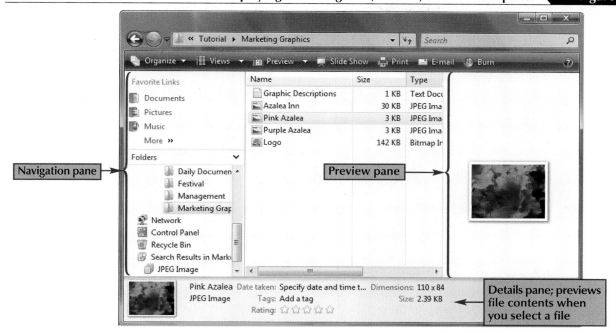

You have also used the toolbar to perform many tasks, particularly to change the appearance of your files and folders. If you used previous versions of Windows, such as Windows XP, you probably performed many of these same tasks using a menu bar. As in programs, Windows Vista folder windows can display a menu bar that shows the names of the menus, such as File, Edit, and Help. The folder window menu bar in Windows Vista is hidden by default because you can use the toolbar or the shortcut menu that opens when you right-click a file or folder to perform the tasks associated with the menu bar commands.

Andrew is accustomed to the folder windows in Windows XP, so he asks you to display the menu bar and hide the Details pane. The Marketing Graphics folder window should currently be open in Details view, with files sorted according to type.

To change the layout of a folder window:

▶ 1. Click **Organize** on the toolbar, point to **Layout**, and then click **Details Pane** to close the Details pane.

▶ 2. Click **Organize** on the toolbar, point to **Layout**, and then click **Menu Bar** to display the menu bar in folder windows. See Figure 2-22.

Figure 2-22 ▶ **Folder window displaying the Navigation pane and menu bar**

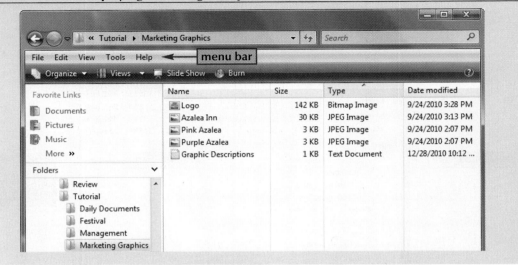

Another way to customize a folder is to change its type. If you store mostly pictures in a folder, for example, right-click the folder, and then click Properties on the shortcut menu. In the folder's Properties dialog box, click the Customize tab, click the Use this folder as a template arrow button, and then click a folder type, such as Pictures and Videos. That folder window then includes features, such as toolbar buttons, designed for working with pictures and videos.

Customizing the File List

Recall that although Windows Vista refers to a file extension to identify a file's type, file extensions are not displayed by default in a folder window. Windows hides the extensions to make filenames easier to read, especially for long filenames. If you prefer to display file extensions, you can show them in all the folder windows.

Another type of file not displayed by default in a folder window is a hidden file. A **hidden file** is not listed in a folder window, though it is actually stored in that folder. Windows hides many types of files, including temporary files it creates before you save a document. It hides these files so that you do not become confused by temporary filenames, which are similar to the names of the files you store on your computer. You can also use a file's Properties dialog box to hide files. Keep in mind that hidden files still take up space on your disk. Windows Vista also hides system files by default, which are those the operating system needs to work properly. You should keep these files hidden unless a reliable expert, such as a technical support professional, instructs you to display them. You use the Folder Options dialog box to show and hide filename extensions, hidden files, and system files.

You can change folder settings in the Marketing Graphics window to show the filename extensions in all windows.

To show filename extensions:

▶ **1.** Click the **Organize** button on the toolbar, and then click **Folder and Search Options** to open the Folder Options dialog box.

▶ **2.** Click the **View** tab. See Figure 2-23. The settings on the View tab of your Folder Options dialog box might differ.

Folder Options dialog box | **Figure 2-23**

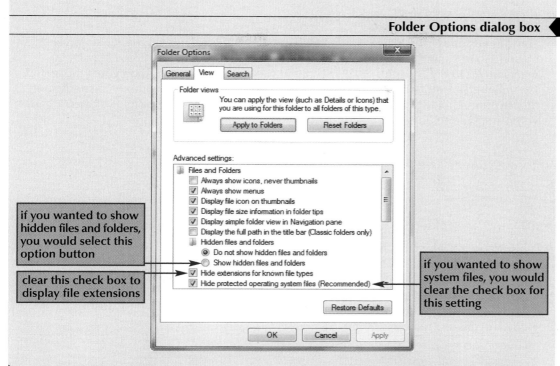

if you wanted to show hidden files and folders, you would select this option button

clear this check box to display file extensions

if you wanted to show system files, you would clear the check box for this setting

▶ **3.** In the Advanced settings section, click the **Hide extensions for known file types** check box to clear the box and display file extensions.

Trouble? If the Hide extensions for known file types check box is already cleared, skip Step 3.

▶ **4.** Click the **OK** button. The Marketing Graphics folder window should look similar to Figure 2-24.

Folder window showing file extensions | **Figure 2-24**

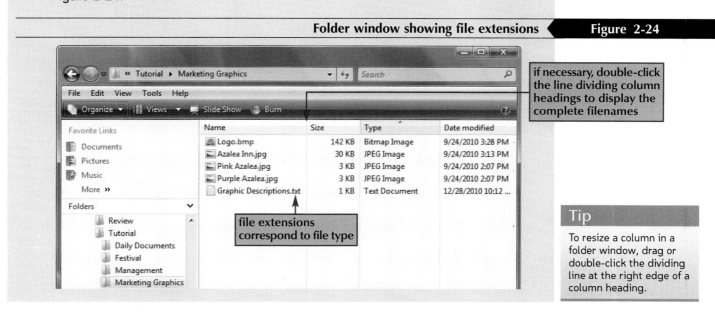

if necessary, double-click the line dividing column headings to display the complete filenames

file extensions correspond to file type

Now the file list in the Marketing Graphics folder window includes file extensions. Next, you can customize the Navigation pane by changing its appearance and adding a folder to the Favorite Links list.

Customizing the Navigation Pane

Tip

When you delete a folder link in the Favorite Links list, you remove only the link, not the folder itself.

You can customize the Navigation pane by moving the links in the Favorite Links list and by adding, renaming, and removing items in the list. First, you'll add the Daily Documents folder to the Favorites Links list so you can access it quickly. Then you'll move and rename this link to distinguish it from the Documents link. When you rename an item in the Favorites Link list, you rename the link only, not the actual file or folder. Later, when you restore the settings on your computer, you'll delete this link.

To customize the Navigation pane:

▶ 1. Use any navigation method you've learned to display the folders in the Tutorial folder.

▶ 2. Click the **Folders** button in the Navigation pane to close the Folders list.

▶ 3. Drag the **Daily Documents** folder from the Tutorial folder to the end of the Favorite Links list in the Navigation pane. When an insertion line appears at the end of the list, release the mouse button to insert a new link named Daily Documents. See Figure 2-25.

Figure 2-25 | Daily Documents folder as a link in the Favorite Links list

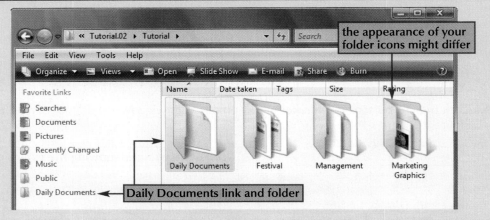

▶ 4. In the Favorite Links list, drag the **Daily Documents** folder to the top of the list.

▶ 5. Right-click the **Daily Documents** link in the Favorite Links list, and then click **Rename** on the shortcut menu. The Rename dialog box opens.

▶ 6. Type **Daily Projects** as the new name of this link, and then click the **OK** button. The link is renamed, but the Daily Documents folder in the Tutorial folder still has its original name. See Figure 2-26.

Daily Documents link moved and renamed to Daily Projects ◄ **Figure 2-26**

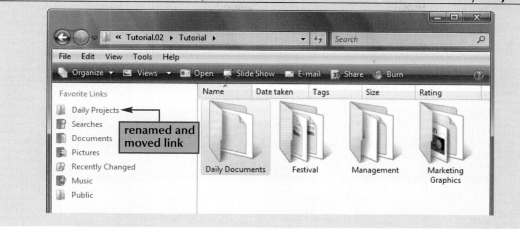

Now that you've refined your file organization and customized the folder window, you are ready to show Andrew two final tasks—compressing and extracting files.

Working with Compressed Files

If you transfer files from one location to another, such as from your hard disk to a removable disk or vice versa, or from one computer to another via e-mail, you can store the files in a **compressed (zipped) folder** so that they take up less disk space. You can then transfer the files more quickly. When you create a compressed folder using Windows Vista's compression tool, a zipper appears on the folder icon.

You compress a folder so that the files it contains use less space on the disk. Compare two folders—a folder named Pictures that contains about 8.6 MB of files and a compressed folder containing the same files, but requiring only 6.5 MB of disk space. In this case, the compressed files use about 25 percent less disk space than the uncompressed files.

You can create a compressed folder using the Send To Compressed (zipped) Folder command on the shortcut menu of one or more selected files or folders. Then, you can compress additional files or folders by dragging them into the compressed folder. You can open files directly from a compressed folder, although you cannot modify the file. To edit and save a compressed file, you must extract it first. When you **extract** a file, you create an uncompressed copy of the file in a folder you specify. The original file remains in the compressed folder.

If a different compression program has been installed on your computer, such as WinZip or PKZIP, the Send To Compressed (zipped) Folder command might not appear on the shortcut menu. Instead, it might be replaced by the name of your compression program. In this case, refer to your compression program's Help system for instructions on working with compressed files.

Andrew suggests you compress the files and folders in the Tutorial folder so that you can more quickly transfer them to another location.

To compress the folders and files in the Tutorial folder:

▶ **1.** In the Navigation pane, click the **Folders** button to open the Folders list again.

▶ **2.** Select all the folders in the Tutorial folder, right-click the selected folders, point to **Send To**, and then click **Compressed (zipped) Folder**. After a few moments, a new compressed folder with a zipper icon appears in the Tutorial window.

Trouble? If the Send To Compressed (zipped) Folder command does not appear on the shortcut menu, a different compression program is probably installed on your computer. Click a blank area of the Tutorial window to close the shortcut menu, and then read but do not perform the remaining steps.

▶ 3. Type **Zipped Files**, and then press the **Enter** key to rename the compressed folder. See Figure 2-27.

| Figure 2-27 | Creating a compressed file |

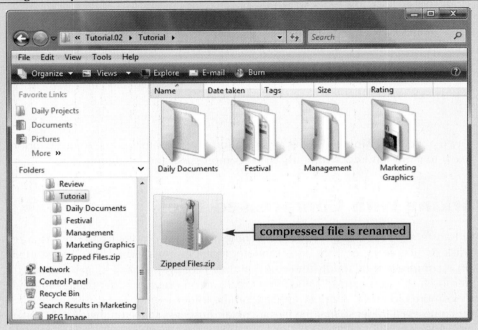

compressed file is renamed

You open a compressed folder by double-clicking it. You can then move and copy files and folders in a compressed folder, although you cannot rename them. When you extract files, Windows Vista uncompresses and copies them to a location that you specify, preserving the files in their folders as appropriate.

| InSight | **Understanding Compressed File Types** |

Some types of files, such as JPEG picture files (those with a .jpg or .jpeg file extension), are already highly compressed. If you compress JPEG pictures into a folder, the total size of the compressed folder is about the same as the collection of pictures uncompressed. However, if you are transferring the files from one computer to another, such as by e-mail, it's still a good idea to store the compressed files in a zip folder to keep them together.

To extract the compressed files:

▶ 1. Right-click the **Zipped Files.zip** compressed folder, and then click **Extract All** on the shortcut menu. The Extract Compressed (zipped) Folders Wizard starts and opens the Select a Destination and Extract Files dialog box.

Trouble? If you are using a different compression program, the Extract All command might not appear on the shortcut menu. Read but do not perform the remaining steps.

2. Press the **End** key to deselect the path in the text box, press the **Backspace** key as many times as necessary to delete "Zipped Files," and then type **Extracted**. The final three parts of the path in the text box should be "\Tutorial. 02\Tutorial\Extracted." See Figure 2-28.

Extracting files from a compressed file ◀ Figure 2-28

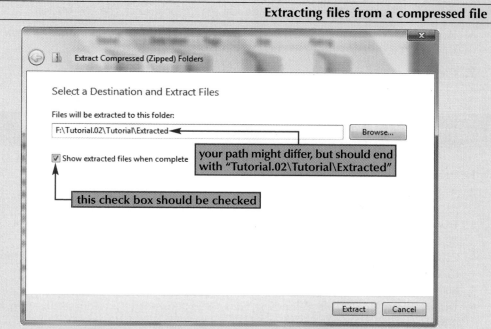

3. Make sure the Show extracted files when complete check box is checked, and then click the **Extract** button. Windows extracts the files, and then opens the Extracted folder, showing the Daily Documents, Festival, Management, and Marketing Graphics folders.

4. Open each folder to make sure it contains the files you worked with in this tutorial.

5. Close the Extracted folder window.

You tell Andrew that you have finished organizing the files on his Windows Vista computer. Before you end your Windows Vista session, however, you should restore your computer to its original settings.

Restoring Your Settings

If you are working in a computer lab or a computer other than your own, complete the steps in this section to restore the original settings on your computer.

To restore your settings:

1. In the Tutorial folder window, click the **Organize** button on the toolbar, point to **Layout**, and then click **Details Pane** to display the Details pane in the folder window.

2. Click the **Organize** button on the toolbar, point to **Layout**, and then click **Menu Bar** to hide the menu bar.

▶ **3.** Click the **Organize** button on the toolbar, and then click **Folder and Search Options** to open the Folder Options dialog box.

▶ **4.** Click the **View** tab.

▶ **5.** In the Advanced settings section, click the **Hide extensions for known file types** check box to check the box and hide file extensions. Click the **OK** button.

▶ **6.** Right-click the **Daily Projects** link in the Navigation pane, click **Remove Link** on the shortcut menu, and then click **Yes** in the Delete File dialog box.

▶ **7.** Close all open windows.

Review | **Session 2.3 Quick Check**

1. Explain the difference between sorting and filtering files.
2. You sort, filter, stack, and group files in a folder window using the _____ _____ , which correspond to file details.
3. True or False. Renaming or deleting a link in the Favorite Links list renames or deletes the corresponding folder in the file list.
4. Explain what happens in a folder window when you click the arrow on the Date Created column and then click today's date.
5. Name two ways that you can change the layout of a folder window.
6. True or False. By default, Windows hides file extensions in a folder window to make the filenames easier to read.
7. Under what circumstances would you store files in a compressed folder?
8. When you _____ a file, you create an uncompressed copy of the file and folder in a folder you specify.

Review | **Tutorial Summary**

In this tutorial, you examined the Windows Vista file organization, noting that you need to organize files and folders to work efficiently. You learned about typical file management strategies, whether you are working on a hard disk or a removable disk. Then, you applied these strategies to organizing files and folders by creating folders, moving and copying files, and renaming and deleting files. You also learned how to copy files to a compressed (zipped) folder and then extract files from a compressed folder.

Key Terms

3.5-inch disk	drive	hidden file
backup	extension	move
Clipboard	extract	Recycle Bin
compact disc (CD)	Favorite Links list	root directory
compressed (zipped) folder	file path	Search box
copy	file system	sort
disk	filename	stack
document	filter	subfolder
Documents folder	group	USB drive
	hard disk	

| Practice | **Review Assignments** |

Practice the skills you learned in the tutorial.

For a list of Data Files in the Review folder, see page 47.

Andrew has saved a few files from his old computer on a removable disk. He gives you these files in a single, unorganized folder, and asks you to organize them logically into subfolders. Before you do, devise a plan for managing the files, and then create the subfolders you need. Also rename, copy, move, and delete files, and perform other management tasks to make it easy for Andrew to work with these files and folders. Complete the following steps, recording your answers to any questions in the spaces provided:

1. Use Computer or Windows Explorer to navigate to and open the Tutorial.02\Review folder provided with your Data Files.
2. Examine the six files in the Review folder included with your Data Files, and then answer the following questions:
   - How will you organize these files? _____
   _____
   - What folders will you create? _____
   _____
   - Which files will you store in these folders? _____
   _____
3. In the Review folder, create three folders: Financial, Planning, and Travel.
4. Move the **Business Plan** and **Event Form** files from the Review folder to the Financial folder. Move the **Alabama**, **Letterhead**, and **Mobile** files to the Travel folder. Move the **Schedule** file to the Planning folder.
5. Copy the **Letterhead** file in the Travel folder to the Planning folder.
6. Rename the **Event Form** file in the Financial folder to **Promotional Events**. Rename the **Mobile** file in the Travel folder to **Historic Mobile**.
7. Return to the Review folder and use the Search box to find a file containing the text *Executive Summary*. Rename this file **Business Plan Form**.
8. Create a Notepad file that includes the following text:
   Agenda for Board Meeting
   7 p.m. Welcome and introductions
9. Save the Notepad file as **Agenda** in the Planning folder. Close the Notepad window.
10. Navigate to the Planning folder, open the **Agenda** file, and then add the following agenda item:
    7:15 Review business plan
11. Save the **Agenda** file with the same name and in the same location. Open a new document, and then type the following text:
    Financial Contact List
    Corgan, Richard (Banker) 555-4187
12. Save the file as **Contact List** in the Financial folder. Close Notepad.
13. Navigate to the Financial folder and make sure the Date modified column is displayed in the folder window. (*Hint*: Right-click a column heading, and then click the Date modified if you need to display this column.) Sort the files by Date modified. How many files appear in the folder window? Filter the files by today's date (or the date you created the two text files). How many files appear in the folder window?
14. Remove the filter, and then stack the files by type.
15. Navigate to the Travel folder, and then display file extensions in the folder window. Group the files by size.

16. Change the layout of the folder window by hiding the Details pane.
17. Display the Review folder, and then add the Travel folder to the top of the Favorite Links list in the Navigation pane. Rename the link **Travel Info**.
18. Click the Travel Info link, and then press the Alt+Print Screen keys to capture an image of the folder window. Start Paint, and then press the Ctrl+V keys to paste this image in a file. Save this file as **Review** in the Tutorial.02\Review folder provided with your Data Files. Close Paint.
19. Restore your computer's settings by displaying the Details pane, hiding file extensions in the folder window, and removing the Travel Info link from the Favorite Links list in the Navigation pane.
20. Create a compressed (zipped) folder in the Review folder named **Zipped Review Files** that contains all the files and folders in the Review folder.
21. Extract the contents of the Zipped Review Files folder to a new folder named **Extracted** in the Review folder. (*Hint*: The file path will end with "\Tutorial. 02\Review\Extracted.")
22. Close all open windows.
23. Submit the results of the preceding steps to your instructor, either in printed or electronic form, as requested.

Apply	**Case Problem 1**

Use the skills you learned in the tutorial to manage files and folders for a catering service.

For a list of Data Files in the Case1 folder, see page 47.

Rossini Catering Sharon Rossini owns Rossini Catering in Providence, Rhode Island, and provides catering services to businesses and others for conferences, weddings, and other events. Specializing in authentic regional Italian dishes, Sharon's clientele has expanded as word of her innovative menus has spread throughout Providence. She recently started offering cooking classes and was surprised to discover that her class on fruit plates was among the most popular. Knowing you are multitalented, Sharon hired you to help her design new classes and manage other parts of her growing business, including maintaining electronic business files and communications. Your first task is to organize the files on her new Windows Vista computer. Complete the following steps:

1. In the Tutorial.02\Case1 folder provided with your Data Files, create three folders: **Classes**, **Fruit Pictures**, and **Menus**.
2. Move the **Menu-Fall**, **Menu-Spring**, **Menu-Summer**, and **Menu-Winter** files from the Case1 folder to the Menus folder.
3. Rename the four files in the Menus folder to remove "Menu-" from each name.
4. Move the three JPEG files from the Case1 folder to the Fruit Pictures folder.
5. Copy the remaining three files to the Classes folder. Also copy the **Ingredients** and **Class Descriptions** files to the Menus folder.
6. Delete the **Class Descriptions**, **Ingredients**, and **Image for Ad** files from the Case1 folder.
7. Open the Recycle Bin folder by double-clicking the Recycle Bin icon on the desktop, and then complete the following steps:
   a. Sort the contents of the Recycle Bin by filename in descending order.
   b. Filter the files by their deletion date to display only the files you deleted today. (*Hint*: If you deleted files from the Case1 folder on a different date, click that date on the calendar.)
   c. Do the Class Descriptions, Ingredients, and Image for Ad files appear in the Recycle Bin folder? Explain why or why not.
   d. Remove the filter, and then close the Recycle Bin window.

8. Make a copy of the Fruit Pictures folder in the Case1 folder. The name of the duplicate folder appears as "Fruit Pictures - Copy". Rename the Fruit Pictures - Copy folder as **Ad Photos**.

9. Locate and move the **Image for Ad** file to the Ad Photos folder. Rename this file **Green Grapes**.

10. Find a file in the Case1 subfolders that contains the text **Fruit plate**. Copy this file to the Classes folder and rename it **Sample Menu**.

11. Send one copy of each graphic file from the Ad Photos folder to a new compressed folder named **Illustrations** in the Case1 folder.

12. Close all open windows.

13. Submit the results of the preceding steps to your instructor, either in printed or electronic form, as requested.

| Challenge | **Case Problem 2** |

Use the skills you learned in the tutorial to manage files and folders for an accounting firm.

For a list of Data Files in the Case2 folder, see page 47.

Lincoln Small Business Accountants   Jack Takamoto is the vice president of Lincoln Small Business Accountants, a firm in Lincoln, Nebraska, that provides accounting services to local small businesses. You work as Jack's assistant and devote part of your time to organizing client files. Jack recently upgraded to Windows Vista and asks you to examine the folder structure and file system on his computer, and then begin organizing the files for two clients. Complete the following steps:

⊕ EXPLORE

1. Start Windows Explorer and then click each link in the Favorite Links list on the Navigation pane to open each folder. (*Hint*: Click the More button to display links hidden by the Folder list.) Describe the contents of each folder in the Favorite Links list.

2. Open the Pictures folder and open a subfolder, if necessary, to display two or more picture files. Change the view to Extra Large Icons. Stack the files by Name. (*Hint*: Click the arrow button on the Name column, and then click Stack by Name.) Press the Alt+Print Screen keys to capture an image of the folder window. Start Paint, and then press the Ctrl+V keys to paste this image in a file. Save the file as **Case2Step2** in the Tutorial.02\Case2 folder provided with your Data Files. Close Paint, and then close the folder window displaying stacked picture files.

3. Examine the files in the Tutorial.02\Case2 folder provided with your Data Files. Based on the filenames and the descriptions displayed in the Details pane, devise an organization plan for the files.

4. In the Tutorial.02\Case2 folder, create the folders you need according to your plan.

5. Move the files from the Case2 folder to the subfolders you created. When you finish, the Case2 folder should contain at least two subfolders and the Case2Step2 file.

6. Rename the files in each subfolder so that they are shorter but still clearly reflect their contents.

7. Search for a file that contains *refund* in the contents.

8. Open the text document you found, and then add the following note at the end of the file: **Client expects a tax refund this year.** Save and close the file.

9. Open the window for one of the subfolders you created. Display the menu bar in the folder window.

✦ EXPLORE 10. Click View on the menu bar and then click Tiles to change the view of the folder window. Press the Alt+Print Screen keys to capture an image of the folder window, and then save the image as **Case2Step10** in the Tutorial.02\Case2 folder provided with your Data Files. Close Paint.

✦ EXPLORE 11. Send all the spreadsheet files (that is, all but the text documents) in the Case2 sub-folders to a new compressed folder named **Spreadsheets** in the Case2 folder. (*Hint*: After you create the compressed folder, drag spreadsheet files from other subfolders to the new compressed folder.)

12. Restore your computer by hiding the menu bar in the folder window.

13. Close all open windows.

14. Submit the results of the preceding steps to your instructor, either in printed or electronic form, as requested.

| Challenge | **Case Problem 3** |

Extend what you've learned to discover other methods of managing files for a home healthcare organization.

There are no Data Files needed for this Case Problem.

MedFirst Hospital Home Health Services Anders Guillickson is the director of the MedFirst Hospital Home Health services (MHHH) in Nashville, Tennessee. The company's mission is to connect licensed practical nurses with people who need health care at home, usually as part of their recovery from surgery. Anders has a dedicated staff of nurses who are just starting to use Windows Vista notebook computers to record the details of their home visits. Anders hires you as a part-time trainer to teach the nurses how to use their computers efficiently. They report that their major problem is finding files that they have saved on their hard disks. Anders asks you to prepare a lesson on how to find files in Windows Vista. Complete the following:

✦ EXPLORE 1. Windows Vista Help and Support includes topics that explain how to search for files on a disk without looking through all the folders. Click the Start button and then click Help and Support to open Windows Help and Support. Use one of the following methods to locate topics on searching for files.
   - On the Home page, click Table of Contents. On the Contents page, click Files and folders, then Finding and organizing, then Finding files and folders, and then click the Find a file or folder topic.
   - In the Search Help box, type **searching for files**, and then click the Search Help button. Click Find a file or folder.

✦ EXPLORE 2. Click the Show all link to show the complete contents of the Find a file or folder topic. Read the topic and click any See also links that provide information about finding files and folders to provide the following information:
   a. Identify three ways to search for files.
   b. If you do not know the entire name of a file, how can you find the file?
   c. Explain how you can save a search so you can use it again.

✦ EXPLORE 3. Use Windows Vista Help and Support to locate topics about organizing and finding files using properties and tags.

4. Write a short description of one procedure for finding files and folders that was not covered in the tutorial.

5. Submit the results of the preceding steps to your instructor, either in printed or electronic form, as requested.

Research		**Case Problem 4**

Work with the skills you've learned, and use the Internet, to organize the files for an architectural design firm.

For a list of Data Files in the Case4 folder, see page 47.

Green Building Arts   Green Building Arts is an architectural design firm in St. Paul, Minnesota, known for designing environmentally responsible buildings. They have been at the forefront of creating healthier and more resource-efficient models of construction, renovation, and maintenance. Maggie O'Donnell is the operations manager for Green Building Arts, and you assist her in setting up systems so that the architects can work effectively. Maggie has recently installed Windows Vista on the firm's desktop and note-book computers. She has a collection of files she can't open with any program installed on her Windows Vista computer. You offer to help her identify the file types and organize the files. Complete the following:

1. Examine the files in the Tutorial.02\Case4 folder provided with your Data Files. Use the Folder Options dialog box to display the file extensions for these files. List the file extensions not already discussed in this tutorial.

⊕ EXPLORE

2. Use your favorite search engine to find information about each file type you listed in Step 1. For example, search for MDB files to learn what type of program can open files with an .mdb extension.

3. Based on what you learned about the file types, sketch an organization for these files. Then create the subfolders you need in the Case4 folder.

4. Move the files from the Case4 folder to the subfolders you created.

5. Open the **Checklist** file in Notepad, read the contents, and then close Notepad. Based on the contents of the Checklist file, move it to a different folder, if necessary.

⊕ EXPLORE

6. Right-click the **Checklist** file, and then click Open With. Select a program other than Notepad to use to open the file. Type your name at the beginning of the file, click File on the menu bar, and then click Save As. Use the Save As dialog box to save the file as a different type, such as .rtf or .doc, but using the same location. (*Hint:* Click the Save as type arrow and then click a file type.) Close the program window.

7. Double-click any other file in a Case4 subfolder and describe what happens.

⊕ EXPLORE

8. If a program did not start when you double-clicked the file in Step 6, right-click the file, and then click Open With. Select a program that Windows Vista suggests. Describe what happens.

9. Double-click another file in a Case4 subfolder and describe what happens. Be sure to choose a file other than the one you chose for Step 7.

10. Close all open windows.

11. Submit the results of the preceding steps to your instructor, either in printed or electronic form, as requested.

Review | **Quick Check Answers**

Session 2.1

1. file
2. hard; hard disk
3. Windows Explorer and Computer
4. True
5. file path
6. Folders list; Address bar; Back, Forward, and Recent Pages buttons; Search box; opening folders in the right pane of a folder window
7. False
8. Address bar

Session 2.2

1. Moving
2. True
3. Click the first item, hold down the Shift key, and then click the last item. Click an item, hold down the Ctrl key, and then click the rest of the items. You can also drag the pointer to create a selection box around all the items you want to include.
4. moving
5. The extension identifies the file's type and indicates the program in which the file was created.
6. True
7. Recycle Bin
8. save the file

Session 2.3

1. Sorting reorganizes all of the files and folders in a list, whereas filtering displays only those files and folders that share a characteristic you specify. Both actions change your view of the files and folders, not the items themselves.
2. column headings
3. False
4. Only the files and folders created today appear in the filtered list.
5. by showing or hiding the Navigation pane, Details pane, Preview pane, or menu bar
6. True
7. If you transfer files from a hard disk to a removable disk or from one computer to another via e-mail, you can compress the files so that they take up less disk space and transfer more quickly.
8. extract

Ending Data Files

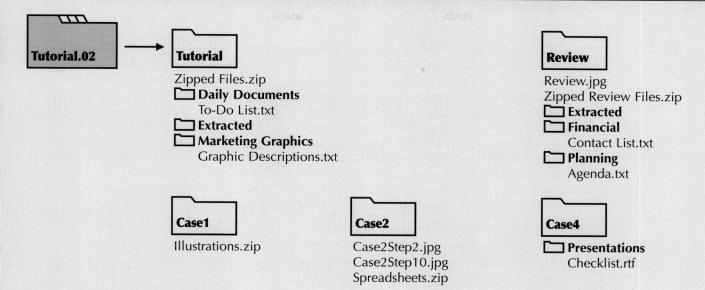

Tutorial.02 →

Tutorial
Zipped Files.zip
📁 **Daily Documents**
    To-Do List.txt
📁 **Extracted**
📁 **Marketing Graphics**
    Graphic Descriptions.txt

Review
Review.jpg
Zipped Review Files.zip
📁 **Extracted**
📁 **Financial**
    Contact List.txt
📁 **Planning**
    Agenda.txt

Case1
Illustrations.zip

Case2
Case2Step2.jpg
Case2Step10.jpg
Spreadsheets.zip

Case4
📁 **Presentations**
    Checklist.rtf

Reality Check

Even if you are familiar with some features of Windows Vista or regularly use your computer for certain tasks, such as accessing Web sites or exchanging e-mail, take some time to explore the basics of Windows Vista on your computer. Then organize the files and folders you use for course work or for other projects on your own computer. Be sure to follow the guidelines you learned for developing an organization strategy, creating folders, naming files, and moving, copying, deleting, and compressing files. As you work through this Reality Check exercise, you will first record settings on your computer. To do so, you can capture and save images of the desktop and windows you open by pressing Alt+Print Screen to capture an image of the screen, and then saving the image in a WordPad or Paint file. You can print these images for references if you experience problems with your computer later or want to restore these settings. Complete the following tasks:

1. Start Windows Vista and log on, if necessary.
2. In case you ever need to restore your computer, you should now capture and save images of your current desktop, the Start menu, the Computer window showing the drives on your computer, and your Documents folder.
3. Start Windows Explorer and open a folder in the Documents folder that you are likely to use often. Make sure the Folders list in the Navigation pane shows the location of this folder on your computer. Capture and save an image of this window.
4. To get acquainted with programs that are included with Windows Vista, start at least two accessory programs that are new to you. Open the File menu in each program, and then capture and save the image of each window.
5. Using the toolbar or menu bar in the new programs, find a dialog box in each program that you are likely to use. Capture and save images of the dialog boxes.
6. Use Windows Help and Support to find information about a feature or technique covered in this tutorial. Choose a topic that you want to know more about. Capture and save an image of the Windows Help and Support window displaying information about this topic.
7. Use a program such as Word or Notepad to create a plan for organizing your files. List the types of files you work with, and then determine whether you want to store them on your hard disk or on removable media. Describe the folders and subfolders you will use to manage these files. If you choose a hard disk as your storage medium, make sure you plan to store your work files and folders in a subfolder of the Documents folder.
8. Use both Windows Explorer and Computer to navigate to your files. Determine which tool you prefer for managing files, if you have a preference.
9. Create the main folders you want to use for your files. Then create the subfolders you will use.
10. Move and copy files to the appropriate folders according to your plan, and rename and delete files as necessary.
11. Create a backup copy of your work files by creating a compressed file and then copying the compressed file to a removable medium, such as a USB flash drive.
12. Submit your finished plan to your instructor, either in printed or electronic form, as requested.

Objectives

Session 3.1
- Access common tools on the desktop
- Customize Windows Sidebar
- Create and use short-cuts on the desktop

Session 3.2
- Use Control Panel
- Customize the desktop
- Activate a screen saver
- Change display settings

Session 3.3
- Modify the taskbar
- Customize taskbar toolbars
- Change Start menu settings
- Pin items on the Start menu

Personalizing Your Windows Environment

Changing Microsoft Windows Vista Desktop Settings

Case | Ptolemy Cartography

Ptolemy Cartography is a small business in Charlottesville, Virginia, that specializes in creating historical maps of American locations. Holly Devore started Ptolemy Cartography with Sarah Liner about two years ago. Since then, the business has continued to grow, with Sarah traveling often to meet with potential clients and conduct on-site research and Holly running operations in Charlottesville.

You have been working for Ptolemy Cartography as the office manager for a few months, providing general assistance to Holly, Sarah, and the staff, including the cartographers, project managers, and interns. The company uses computers to research historical documents online, create and illustrate maps, manage company finances, and communicate with clients and each other. Holly recently upgraded the office computers to Windows Vista. She's heard that Windows Vista makes it easy to change settings to suit the needs of her business. She asks you to customize the company's computers so that everyone can access important files and computer resources. She also wants the desktop to reflect the Ptolemy Cartography corporate image. Holly suggests that you start by personalizing her Windows Vista computer, and then apply the changes to the other office computers.

In this tutorial you add and change Windows Vista tools and icons on the desktop, including shortcuts to folders and devices. You'll also work with Control Panel to change settings and personalize the desktop. Finally, you'll modify the taskbar and customize the Start menu.

Starting Data Files

Tutorial.03 →	Tutorial	Review	Case1	Case2	Case3	Case4
	Haleakala.jpg	Charleston.jpg	DaVinci	Beaux Arts.jpg	Bald Island.jpg	(none)
	Hawaii District 1.gif	Explorers.jpg	Tank.jpg	Colonial.jpg	Bar Island.jpg	
	Hawaii District 2.gif	James River.jpg	Last Supper.jpg	For Sale.jpg	Birch Grass.jpg	
	Hawaii Facts.txt	NF Facts.txt	Mona Lisa.jpg	Schoolhouse.jpg	Bridge.jpg	
	Hawaiian Islands.gif	NF Map.gif	Polyhedra.bmp	Syracuse Facts.txt	Cad Summit.jpg	
	Maui.jpg	NF Outline.gif	Vasari.txt	Victorian.jpg	Driving Directions.txt	
	Navigation.bmp	North America.gif	Vitruvian Man.jpg		Peregrine.jpg	
	Volcano.jpg	US 1800.jpg				

Session 3.1

Accessing Common Tools on the Desktop

As you know, when you start Windows Vista, the large area you see on your screen is called the desktop. When you first install Windows Vista, the desktop displays at least a background image, Recycle Bin icon, taskbar, Windows Sidebar, and the Welcome Center window by default. See Figure 3-1. Your desktop might include different icons or windows.

Figure 3-1 ▶ Default Windows Vista desktop

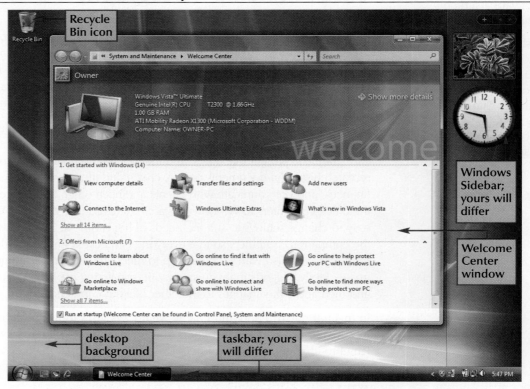

Because the desktop provides your first view of the computer and its contents, it should contain the items you want to access when you start your computer. Depending on how you work, these items might include tools such as Windows Explorer or Computer, programs and devices you use often, and the Documents folder. **Desktop icons** are the most visual and easiest way to access these resources. Figure 3-2 shows the types of icons you can include on the desktop and the objects they represent.

Types of desktop icons ◀ Figure 3-2

Icon	Description
	User's folder desktop icon
	Network desktop icon
	Computer desktop icon
	Control Panel desktop icon
	Recycle Bin desktop icon (full and empty)
	Printer shortcut icon
	Drive shortcut icon
	Folder shortcut icon
	Document shortcut icon

You are already familiar with some icons on your desktop that represent useful Windows tools, such as the Recycle Bin. As Figure 3-2 shows, you can place additional icons on the desktop that represent objects you want to access quickly and frequently, such as other Windows tools, printers, drives, programs, and documents. Windows provides desktop icons for frequently used tools, such as the Recycle Bin, Computer, and your Documents folder. You can add or remove these icons according to your work preferences. Besides these built-in desktop icons, you can use **shortcuts**, which are icons that provide quick ways to start a program or open a file, folder, or other object without having to find its permanent location on your computer. Shortcut icons include a small arrow in the lower-left corner, a reminder that the icon points to an item that is stored elsewhere on the computer. If you double-click a shortcut, its associated file, folder, device, or program opens. When you delete a shortcut icon, you delete only the shortcut—the file or resource it represents remains in its original location. You typically create shortcuts on the desktop (or elsewhere, such as in a folder or on the taskbar) to locations, files, and devices that you use often.

Shortcut icons can simplify tasks you perform regularly. For example, you can create a shortcut icon to a USB flash drive, and then drag files to the shortcut icon to copy them to the flash drive. If you create a shortcut icon for your printer, you can print a file by dragging it to the printer's shortcut icon. You also can create a shortcut icon for a program you use often, and then double-click the icon to start the program. Many programs provide a shortcut icon on the desktop when you install the program.

Sarah Linder is in Hawaii this week meeting with the tourism board and gathering data to create historic maps of the islands. This gives Holly time to work with you to customize her computer so she can work more efficiently. She wants you to start by adding icons to the desktop for system tools she uses often. You'll also explore Windows Sidebar and show her how to change it to suit her preferences and work style. Then you'll show her how to create shortcut icons on the desktop, including those for a USB flash drive, folder, and printer.

Adding Icons to the Desktop

Windows provides five standard desktop icons that can be displayed on the desktop. Besides the Recycle Bin, you can include the Computer icon on the desktop to provide easy access to the Computer window, which you can use to navigate the drives and folders on your computer. If you display the desktop icon for your personal folder (that is, the folder containing the current user's files), you can quickly find and open the folders containing your documents. Display the Network icon to access a window that lists the connections, shared computers, and other resources on your network. You can also add the Control Panel icon to the desktop. Control Panel contains specialized tools you use to change the way Windows looks and behaves. You'll work with Control Panel later in this tutorial.

Reference Window | **Displaying Standard Desktop Icons**

- Right-click an empty area of the desktop, and then click Personalize on the shortcut menu.
- In the left pane of the Personalization window, click Change desktop icons.
- In the Desktop Icon Settings dialog box, click to select a check box for each icon you want to add to the desktop.
- Click the OK button.

Holly mentions that the Windows tools she uses most frequently are her personal folder, Computer, and Control Panel. You'll add these icons to Holly's desktop. Make sure your computer is turned on and displaying the Windows desktop before you perform the following steps.

To display standard desktop icons:

▶ **1.** Close the Welcome Center window, if necessary.

▶ **2.** Right-click the **desktop**, and then click **Personalize** on the shortcut menu. The Personalization window opens, listing tasks you can perform to personalize Windows Vista.

▶ **3.** In the left pane, click **Change desktop icons**. The Desktop Icon Settings dialog box opens. See Figure 3-3.

Figure 3-3 ▶ **Desktop Icon Settings dialog box**

standard Windows icons you can display on the desktop →

preview of the icons →

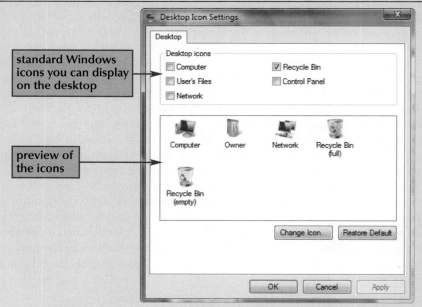

Trouble? If the settings in your Desktop Icon Settings dialog box differ from those in Figure 3-3, note the current options, and change them so they match those in Figure 3-3.

▶ **4.** Click the **Computer**, **User's Files**, and **Control Panel** check boxes.

The Recycle Bin check box is already selected, indicating that Windows is display-ing the Recycle Bin icon on the desktop. Note that the Recycle Bin icon has two appearances, one when it is empty, and another when it contains deleted items.

5. Click the **OK** button. The icons for your personal folder and for Computer and Control Panel appear on the desktop.

6. Click the **Close** button ▨ to close the Personalization window.

Now that you've added desktop icons for Holly, you can customize their appearance to suit her preferences.

Changing the Appearance of Desktop Icons

You can change the size and appearance of desktop icons depending on how you like to work. For example, Windows displays desktop icons at a medium size by default. If you have only a few icons on your desktop or prefer working with large icons, you can resize the desktop icons so they are larger. On the other hand, if you are familiar with previous versions of Windows or use many icons on your desktop, you might prefer Classic icons, which are smaller than the default size.

If you like a clean, uncluttered desktop, you can hide all of your desktop icons and show them only when you need to use one. Hiding the icons doesn't delete them—it only hides them until you show them again. You can also change the standard arrangement of the icons on the desktop. By default, Windows lists the icons in columns along the left side of your desktop, and aligns the icons to an invisible grid so that they are evenly spaced on the desktop. You can change this arrangement to match your preferences, such as arranging the icons on the right or along the top of the desktop.

Besides personalizing the size and arrangement of the desktop icons, you can change the icon images. For example, the Computer icon shows an image of a desktop computer. If you work on a notebook or tablet computer, you might want to change this image.

Holly asks you to show her the desktop with large and Classic icons to see if she wants to use those sizes. She also wants to know how to move the icons on the desktop and then hide them for privacy when interns use her computer. You can perform all of these tasks using the View command on the desktop shortcut menu.

To change the size and location of desktop icons:

1. Right-click the **desktop**, point to **View** on the shortcut menu, and then click **Large Icons**. The icons on the desktop now appear in a larger size.

2. Right-click the **desktop**, point to **View** on the shortcut menu, and then click **Classic Icons**. The icons appear in their smallest size.

Next, you'll show Holly how to move the desktop icons so they no longer are aligned along the left side of the desktop.

3. Right-click the **desktop**, point to **View** on the shortcut menu, and then click **Auto Arrange** to remove the check mark. When the Auto Arrange command is unchecked, you can move the icons anywhere on the desktop.

Trouble? If the Auto Arrange command is not checked, skip Step 3.

4. Drag the **Computer** icon to the right of the Recycle Bin icon. Note that Windows aligns the Computer icon to a grid, maintaining a standard amount of space between the two icons. See Figure 3-4.

Figure 3-4 Arranging icons on the desktop

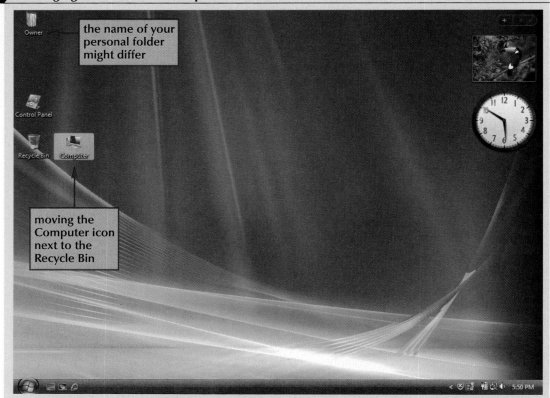

> **5.** Right-click the **desktop**, point to **View** on the shortcut menu, and then click **Align to Grid** to clear the check mark. When the Align to Grid command is unchecked, you can change the icons so they are no longer aligned to each other.
>
>   **Trouble?** If the Align to Grid command is not checked, skip Step 5.

> **6.** Drag the **Computer** icon closer to the Recycle Bin icon.
>
>   Finally, you can use the View command on the desktop shortcut menu to hide and then show the desktop icons.

> **7.** Right-click the **desktop**, point to **View** on the shortcut menu, and then click **Show Desktop Icons** to remove the check mark. When Show Desktop Icons is unchecked, Windows hides the icons so only the desktop appears on your screen.

> **8.** Right-click the **desktop**, point to **View** on the shortcut menu, and then click **Show Desktop Icons**. A check mark appears next to the command, indicating that Windows is displaying the icons on the desktop.

Because she works on a notebook computer, Holly likes the idea of changing the image for the Computer icon on the desktop. To do so, you use the Personalization window, which you opened earlier to select the Windows icons to display on the desktop.

To change the image of the Computer icon:

▶ **1.** Right-click the **desktop**, and then click **Personalize** on the shortcut menu. The Personalization window opens.

▶ **2.** In the left pane, click **Change desktop icons**. The Desktop Icon Settings dialog box opens.

▶ **3.** In the list of desktop icons, click the **Computer** icon, and then click the **Change Icon** button. The Change Icon dialog box opens and highlights the current image. See Figure 3-5. Note the icon currently used for Computer so you can restore it later.

Change Icon dialog box ◀ Figure 3-5

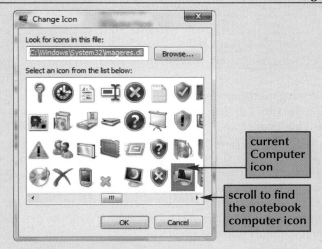

current Computer icon

scroll to find the notebook computer icon

▶ **4.** Scroll the list of images to the right, and then click the **notebook computer** image, which is in the top row and three columns to the right of the current image.

Trouble? If the notebook computer image does not appear in your Change Icon dialog box, click any other suitable image.

▶ **5.** Click the **OK** button to close the Change Icon dialog box, and then click the **OK** button to close the Desktop Icon Settings dialog box. The Computer icon on the desktop now appears as a notebook computer.

▶ **6.** Close the Personalization window.

The standard Windows desktop icons provide quick access to common Windows tools. You can also personalize another feature to save time when you're performing common tasks—the Windows Sidebar.

Using the Windows Sidebar

Windows Sidebar is a long vertical bar displayed by default on the right side of your desktop. It contains miniprograms called **gadgets**, which offer information at a glance and are similar to tools you might keep on your physical desk, such as a pad of sticky notes, an address book, or a calendar. Windows provides a collection of built-in gadgets, which are described in Figure 3-6.

Figure 3-6 ▶ **Windows Sidebar gadgets**

Gadget	Use to:
Calendar	Display the current date and browse a monthly calendar.
Clock	Display the time in your time zone or any other around the world.
Contacts	Keep track of contact information, including e-mail addresses and phone numbers.
CPU Meter	Gauge system performance.
Currency	Convert from one currency to another.
Feed Headlines	Track news headlines, sports scores, and entertainment information.
Notes	Jot down notes and reminders.
Picture Puzzle	Move the pieces of the puzzle to create an image.
Slide Show	Show a continuous slide show of pictures on your computer.
Stocks	Track your favorite stocks.
Weather	Check the weather in cities around the world.

At least two of these gadgets appear on the Sidebar by default: the Clock and the Slide Show. Besides using the Clock gadget to show the current time for your time zone, you can show one or more additional clocks to display the current time for other time zones around the world. In the Slide Show gadget, you can display any pictures stored on your computer, set the speed for playing the show, and change the transition effect between pictures. The Calendar and the Feed Headlines gadgets are two other popular gadgets. The Calendar shows the current date by default and a monthly view when you click it. The Feed Headlines gadget lists frequently updated headlines so you can keep up with the news from your desktop. The headlines are supplied by a Web site that publishes a **feed**, which is online content that is updated often.

InSight	**Understanding Feeds**

A feed, or Really Simple Syndication (RSS) feed, is Web site content that is frequently updated, such as news or Web logs (more commonly called *blogs*). A feed often has the same content as the information provided on a Web site, but it can be delivered directly to your desktop, where you can use the Feed Headlines Sidebar gadget to display the changing content. If you want to keep with news, sports scores, or other frequently updated information, use Internet Explorer to subscribe to a feed on a Web site. Then keep the Feed Headlines gadget open on your desktop so you can view the changing information at a glance.

Holly wants to display a second Clock gadget in the Sidebar and set it to Hawaii time so she can call Sarah at appropriate times while she's visiting the islands. When Sarah returns from Hawaii, Holly can change the second clock to a different time zone or remove it. **Note:** The following steps are designed for the default Windows Vista Sidebar. If you are using a customized Sidebar, read but do not perform the steps in this section.

To add a second Clock gadget to the Sidebar:

▶ 1. Click the **Add Gadgets** button ➕ at the top of the Sidebar. The gadget gallery opens, showing the gadgets that are currently installed on your computer. Any of these gadgets can be added to the Sidebar. See Figure 3-7.

Gadget gallery ◄ **Figure 3-7**

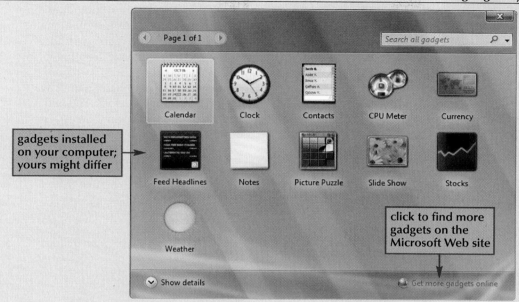

gadgets installed on your computer; yours might differ →

click to find more gadgets on the Microsoft Web site

Trouble? If the Sidebar is not open, click the Start button on the taskbar, point to All Programs, click Accessories, and then click Windows Sidebar.

2. Double-click the **Clock** gadget. A second clock opens in the Sidebar. See Figure 3-8.

Buttons on the Clock gadget ◄ **Figure 3-8**

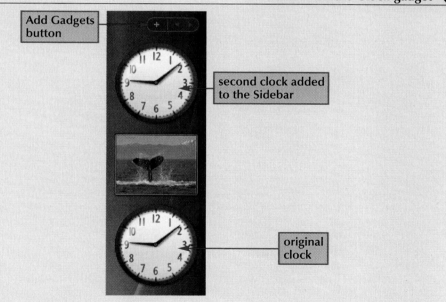

Add Gadgets button

second clock added to the Sidebar

original clock

3. Close the gadget gallery.

Next, you'll show Holly how to customize the second Clock gadget to display Hawaiian time.

Customizing the Windows Sidebar

You can customize many of the Sidebar gadgets to suit your preferences, including the Clock, the Slide Show, Notes, Picture Puzzle, Stocks, and Weather. For example, you can select the pictures you want to display in the Slide Show and choose a color for the Notes pad. In addition, you can customize the Sidebar itself by hiding it, keeping it on top of other windows, and adding, removing, and detaching gadgets.

First, you will customize the second Clock gadget to display the current time in Hawaii and then change its appearance to distinguish it easily from the original clock. You will also name the second clock so you can tell at a glance that it displays Hawaiian time.

To customize the second Clock gadget:

▶ **1.** Point to the new **Clock** gadget at the top of the Sidebar, and then click the **Options** button 🔍 . The Clock dialog box opens. See Figure 3-9.

Figure 3-9 ▶ **Clock dialog box**

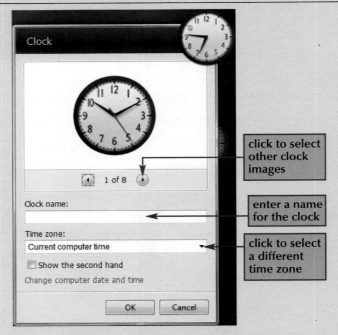

click to select other clock images

enter a name for the clock

click to select a different time zone

Trouble? If your computer uses a Sidebar other than the default Windows Vista Sidebar, your dialog box might differ. Read but do not perform steps 2–5.

▶ **2.** Click the **Next** button ⊙ until you select clock image 6 of 8.

▶ **3.** Click in the **Clock name** text box, and then type **Hawaii** as the name of the clock.

▶ **4.** Click the **Time zone** arrow, and then click **(GMT–10:00) Hawaii**.

▶ **5.** Click the **OK** button. The new Clock gadget now has a new appearance, name, and time.

Because the Windows Sidebar is designed to keep handy tools at your fingertips, you can customize it in many ways to fit your work style. One way to personalize the Sidebar is to keep it on top of other windows, so it always appears on the desktop. In that case, when you maximize a window, it widens only as far as the left edge of the Sidebar, and the maximized window and the Sidebar appear side by side.

Holly expects to use the Sidebar regularly. Because she has a wide monitor on her notebook computer, she plans to keep the Sidebar on top of other windows when she finds herself using gadgets often.

To keep the Sidebar on top of other windows:

▶ **1.** Right-click a blank spot on the Sidebar, and then click **Properties** on the shortcut menu. The Windows Sidebar Properties dialog box opens.

▶ **2.** Click the **Sidebar is always on top of other windows** check box.

▶ **3.** Click the **OK** button. Windows will show the Sidebar even if you maximize other windows or open them so that they overlap the Sidebar.

▶ **4.** Double-click the **Computer** icon on your desktop, and then click the **Maximize** button 🔲 to maximize the window. The Computer window expands only as far as the Sidebar. See Figure 3-10.

Maximized window with Sidebar set to stay on top of other windows ◀ **Figure 3-10**

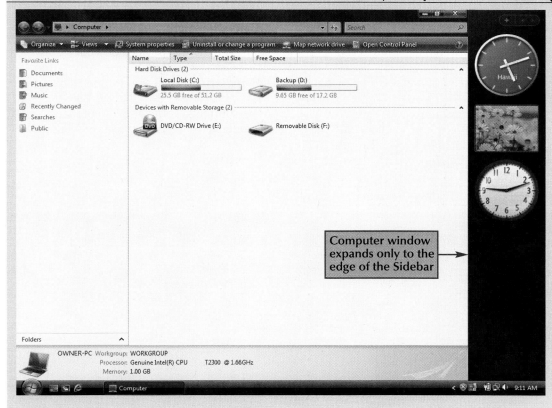

Computer window expands only to the edge of the Sidebar

▶ **5.** Close the Computer window.

Finally, Holly asks you to remove the Slide Show gadget from the Sidebar because she does not plan to use it right now. If your Sidebar does not display the Slide Show gadget, read but do not perform the following step.

...get, right-
...Detach from
...he shortcut
...then drag the
...a different spot
...n the desktop.

To remove a gadget from the Sidebar:

1. Point to the **Slide Show** gadget, and then click the **Close** button ✕ .

Trouble? If a dialog box opens asking if you want to close this gadget, click the Close Gadget button.

So far, you've explored how to personalize your desktop by displaying Windows desktop icons and gadgets you use often. These are standard tools that Windows provides to simplify or enhance your computer work. However, other items you access often include documents, folders, and drives, and are different from the items other users access often. In addition, the folders you use frequently one week might differ from those you'll use frequently next week. To personalize your desktop to provide quick access to these items, you can create and use shortcuts.

Using Shortcuts

You can create shortcuts to access drives, documents, files, Web pages, programs, or other computer resources such as a printer. For example, you can easily open a document from the desktop by creating a shortcut icon for the document. A shortcut icon for a document works much the same way as a document icon does in a folder window—you can double-click the shortcut icon to open the document in the appropriate program. However, a shortcut icon is only a link to the actual document. If you move the icon, for example, you move only the shortcut, not the document itself. One advantage of using shortcut icons is that if your desktop becomes cluttered, you can delete the shortcut icons without affecting the original documents.

You can also create shortcut icons for the folders, drives, and devices on your computer. This way, you can access your local hard disk, for example, directly from the desktop, instead of having to open Windows Explorer or Computer and then navigate to the hard disk.

Windows Vista provides several ways of creating shortcuts. For example, you can right-click an object and choose Create Shortcut on the shortcut menu. Figure 3-11 summarizes the techniques you can use to create shortcuts. The one you choose is a matter of personal preference.

Figure 3-11 ▶ **Methods for creating shortcuts**

Method	Description
Drag (for drives and devices only)	To create a drive shortcut on the desktop, use Computer or Windows Explorer to locate the drive icon, and then drag the icon to the desktop. For locations other than the desktop, hold down the Alt key as you drag.
Right-drag	Use Computer or Windows Explorer to locate and select an icon, hold down the right mouse button, and drag to a new location. Release the mouse button and click Create Shortcuts Here on the shortcut menu.
Right-click, Create Shortcut	Use Computer or Windows Explorer to locate an icon, right-click the icon, click Create Shortcut on the shortcut menu, and then drag the shortcut icon to a new location.
Right-click, Send To	To create a shortcut on the desktop, use Computer or Windows Explorer to locate an icon, right-click the icon, point to Send To, and then click Desktop (create shortcut).

Next, you'll create a shortcut to a USB flash drive. You could use any technique listed in Figure 3-11, but you'll use the drag method because it involves the fewest steps.

Creating a Shortcut to a Drive

To create a shortcut to a drive, you can open the Computer or Windows Explorer window, and then drag the drive icon from the window to the desktop. Windows Vista creates a shortcut icon that looks like a drive icon with a shortcut arrow, and includes an appropriate label, such as "Removable Disk (F) – Shortcut." Note that if you drag a document icon from a folder window to the desktop, you move the actual document from its original location to the desktop. However, you cannot move a drive, program, or other computer resource—its location is fixed during installation—so when you drag a drive icon to the desktop, you automatically create a shortcut.

When you create a shortcut to a USB flash drive, you can insert the drive in a USB port, and then double-click the shortcut to view your Data Files, or you can move or copy documents to the drive without having to start Windows Explorer or open the Computer window.

Holly regularly copies image files from her computer to a USB flash drive, and wants to use a shortcut to simplify the task. You'll show her how to create a shortcut on her desktop to a USB flash drive.

The Steps in this tutorial assume that your Data Files are stored on Removable Disk (F:), a USB drive. If necessary substitute the appropriate drive on your system when you perform the steps.

To create a shortcut to a USB flash drive:

▶ **1.** If necessary, insert the USB flash drive containing your Data Files into a USB port on your computer.

   Trouble? If you don't have the starting Data Files, you need to get them before you can proceed. Your instructor will either give you the Data Files or ask you to obtain them from a specified location (such as network drive). In either case, make a backup copy of your Data Files before you start using them so you will have the orginal files available in case you need to start over. If you have any questions about the Data Files, see your instructor or technical support person for assistance.

   Trouble? If you do not have a USB flash drive, insert a different type of removable disk, such as a Zip disk, but not a CD, into the appropriate drive.

▶ **2.** Double-click the **Computer** icon on the desktop. Resize the Computer window so you can see the icons along the left side of the desktop. You need to see both the desktop icons and the Computer window to drag effectively.

▶ **3.** Point to the **Removable Disk (F:)** icon, press and hold the left mouse button and then drag the **Removable Disk (F:)** icon from the Computer window into an empty area of the desktop. (Your flash drive might have a different name or be associated with a different drive letter—substitute that name or drive letter for the remaining steps.)

▶ **4.** Release the mouse button. A shortcut labeled "Removable Disk (F) – Shortcut" now appears on the desktop. (Yours might be in a different location.) See Figure 3-12.

Figure 3-12 ▸ **Shortcut to a removable disk**

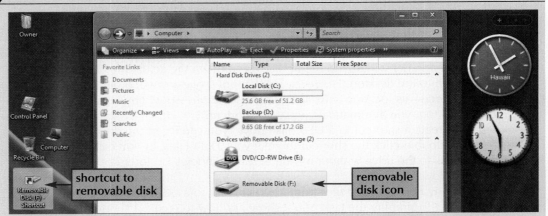

Trouble? If you dragged with the right mouse button instead of the left, a short-cut menu appears when you release the mouse button. Click Create Shortcuts Here to add the Removable Disk (F) – Shortcut to the desktop.

▸ **5.** Point to the **Removable Disk (F) – Shortcut** icon to view its ScreenTip, which indicates the permanent location of the drive on your computer.

Holly received a few files from Sarah containing map images. She can use the shortcut on the desktop to copy the files from the USB flash drive to a new folder for Hawaiian maps.

To use the removable disk shortcut:

▸ **1.** In the Navigation pane of the Computer window, click **Pictures** to open the Pictures folder.

▸ **2.** Click the **Organize** button on the toolbar, and then click **New Folder** to create a new folder in the Pictures folder.

▸ **3.** Type **Hawaii Maps** as the name of the new folder, and then press the **Enter** key.

▸ **4.** Double-click the **Hawaii Maps** folder to open it.

▸ **5.** Double-click the **Removable Disk (F) – Shortcut** icon on the desktop. A new window opens showing the contents of the USB flash drive.

▸ **6.** Open the **Tutorial.03** folder and then the **Tutorial** folder.

▸ **7.** Select all of the files in the Tutorial folder, and then drag them to the right pane of the **Hawaii Maps** folder window. All eight files appear in the Hawaii Maps folder.

▸ **8.** Close the Hawaii Maps folder window.

Using a shortcut to a drive saves a few steps when you transfer files from one computer to another. If you regularly use certain folders and documents, you can save even more time by creating shortcuts to those items. In fact, Holly expects to receive more documents from Sarah while she's working in Hawaii, and she plans to store those in the Hawaii Maps folder. In addition, Holly plans to use the Hawaii Facts file as a template for creating basic maps of the islands. You'll show her how to create a shortcut to the Hawaii Maps folder and the Hawaii Facts file to save her time.

Creating Shortcuts to Folders and Documents

Creating shortcuts to folders and documents is similar to creating shortcuts to drives—with one crucial difference. Instead of dragging a drive icon from a window to the desktop, you right-drag the folder or document icon to the desktop. (That is, you press and hold the right mouse button as you drag.) Recall that you cannot move a drive by dragging its icon from a window to another location; because the drive's location is fixed during installation, dragging a drive icon to the desktop automatically creates a shortcut. However, if you drag a folder or document icon from Computer to the desktop, you move the folder or document from its original location to the desktop.

| **Keeping a Clean Desktop** | | InSight |

Storing actual files and folders on the desktop instead of shortcuts can slow your computer's performance and make it difficult to find documents when you need them. Instead, follow good file management principles and store your documents and other files in your personal folder and its subfolders. Create desktop shortcuts only to the few documents and folders you use often.

You'll show Holly how to create a shortcut to the Hawaii Maps folder using the right-drag method. Then you'll create a shortcut to the Hawaii Facts document using a different method—the Send To menu. When you right-click a file or folder and point to Send To on the shortcut menu, Windows displays a list of the drives and other locations on your computer, including the desktop. If you send an item to the desktop in this way, you create a shortcut to that file or folder.

To create a shortcut to a folder:

▶ 1. In the Tutorial folder window, click **Pictures** in the Navigation pane to display the contents of the Pictures folder, including the Hawaii Maps folder. Resize the window as necessary to see both the Hawaii Maps folder icon in the window and the icons on the left side of the desktop.

▶ 2. Point to the **Hawaii Maps** folder, press and hold the right mouse button, and then drag the **Hawaii Maps** folder icon from the Pictures window onto the desktop, and then release the mouse button. A shortcut menu appears listing the tasks you can perform with this document. Recall that you can use the shortcut menu to copy or move a document as well as create a shortcut to it.

▶ 3. Click **Create Shortcuts Here**. An icon labeled "Hawaii Maps – Shortcut" appears on the desktop.

▶ 4. Point to the **Hawaii Maps - Shortcut** icon to display the ScreenTip, which indicates the location of the original folder. See Figure 3-13.

> **Tip**
>
> To create a shortcut to a program, open the Start menu, right-drag the program to the desktop, and then click Create Shortcuts Here on the shortcut menu.

| Figure 3-13 | Creating a shortcut to the Hawaii Maps folder |

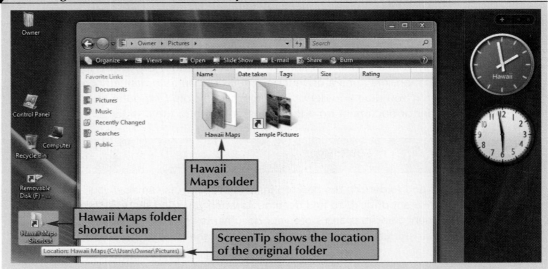

> **5.** Close the Pictures window.

Now you can test the folder shortcut and create another shortcut on the desktop, this time to the Hawaii Facts document.

To test the folder shortcut and create a shortcut to a document:

> **1.** Double-click the **Hawaii Maps-Shortcut** icon on the desktop. A window opens displaying the contents of the Hawaii Maps folder. Resize the window as necessary to see the contents of the Hawaii Maps folder and a blank area on the left side of the desktop.

> **2.** Right-click the **Hawaii Facts** document in the Hawaii Maps window, and then point to **Send To**. The Send To menu opens. See Figure 3-14.

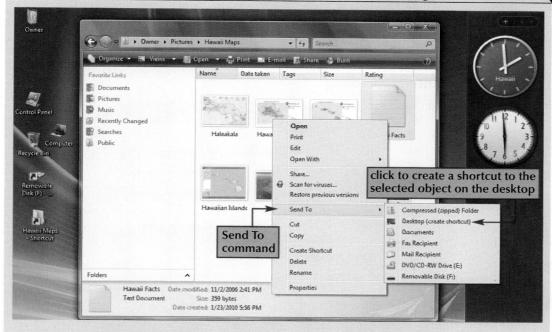

Creating a shortcut using the Send To menu | Figure 3-14

3. Click **Desktop (create shortcut)**. An icon labeled "Hawaii Facts - Shortcut" appears on the desktop.

4. Double-click the **Hawaii Facts - Shortcut** icon on the desktop to open this document in Notepad.

5. Close all open windows.

You now have three shortcuts on the desktop that provide efficient ways to open the Hawaii Maps folder, the Hawaii Facts document, and a USB flash drive. Next, you want to add a printer shortcut to the desktop so that Holly can easily print documents without starting a program.

Creating a Shortcut to a Printer

You can create a printer shortcut in much the same way you created a shortcut for the USB flash drive: by locating the printer device icon in the Printers window, and then dragging the icon onto your desktop. You also can use the other techniques listed in Figure 3-11 to create a shortcut to a printer on the desktop. To open the Printers window, you can use the Start Search text box on the Start menu. (Recall that you can find programs and files on your system by using this text box.) After you create a printer shortcut icon, you can print a document by dragging its icon to the printer shortcut icon on the desktop.

Holly often prints documents to use as a reference when she's working on a map. Instead of starting WordPad or another program, opening the Print dialog box, selecting print settings, and then clicking OK, she can print by dragging a document to a printer shortcut icon. You'll show her how to create a printer shortcut using the Create Shortcut command.

To create a printer shortcut:

1. Click the **Start** button on the taskbar, and then type **Printers** in the Start Search text box. When the Printers icon appears in the left pane of the Start menu, click **Printers**. The Printers window opens. If necessary, resize the window so you can see both the window and the desktop.

2. Right-click the icon for the default printer (the one with the default icon ✓) to select it.

3. Click **Create Shortcut** on the shortcut menu. Windows creates a shortcut to the default printer on the desktop. Because printer names are often long, you can rename the shortcut icon so it's easier to read.

4. Right-click the **printer shortcut icon** you just created on the desktop, and then click **Rename** on the shortcut menu.

5. Type **Office Printer** as the name of the printer shortcut icon, and then press the **Enter** key. See Figure 3-15.

Figure 3-15 ▶ **Creating a shortcut to a printer**

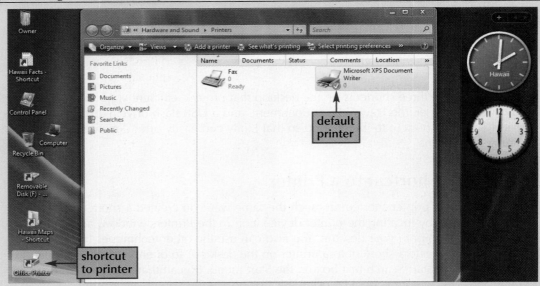

6. Close the Printers window.

Now you can show Holly how to print the Hawaii Facts document using the Office Printer and Hawaii Facts – Shortcut icons. Make sure your default printer is installed, attached to your computer, and turned on before you perform the following steps.

To print the Hawaii Facts document using the printer shortcut icon:

▶ **1.** Using the left mouse button, drag the **Hawaii Facts - Shortcut** icon to the **Office Printer** icon on the desktop.

When you release the mouse button, Windows Vista opens the Hawaii Facts document in Notepad or another text-editing program, prints the document, and then closes Notepad.

Now that your desktop contains a variety of icons, including standard desktop icons and shortcuts, you can arrange the icons so they are easy to access.

Organizing Icons on the Desktop

By default, Windows displays the Recycle Bin icon in the upper-left corner of the desktop. When you add other desktop icons to the desktop, Windows lists them above the Recycle Bin. When you add custom shortcut icons, such as the Hawaii Facts - Shortcut icon, Windows lists them below the Recycle Bin in the order that you add them to the desktop. You can change this order by selecting a sort option to list the shortcut icons by name, size, type, or date modified. These sort options are similar to the ones you use when sorting files and folders in a folder window. Sorting by name organizes the icons in alphabetical order by the icon name. Sorting by size organizes them according to the size of their source files (unless the icon is a shortcut to a program—then Windows uses the size of the shortcut itself). Sort by type when you want to keep shortcuts to files of the same type, such as text documents, next to each other on the desktop. Sort by date modified to arrange the icons according to the date you modified the shortcuts.

Before you organize the icons on the desktop, restore the original Auto Arrange and Align to Grid settings. Then you can sort the shortcut icons by name to make them easy to find.

To restore the desktop settings and sort the icons:

▶ **1.** Right-click the **desktop**, point to **View** on the shortcut menu, and then click **Auto Arrange** to select that option.

▶ **2.** Right-click the **desktop**, point to **View** on the shortcut menu, and then click **Align to Grid** to select that option.

▶ **3.** Right-click the **desktop**, point to **Sort By** on the shortcut menu, and then click **Name** to select that option. The shortcut icons are organized on the desktop in alphabetical order. See Figure 3-16.

Figure 3-16	Desktop icons sorted by name

shortcut icons grouped together, and then listed alphabetically

Finally, you can delete a shortcut icon to verify that doing so does not affect its associated device, drive, folder, or document.

Deleting Shortcut Icons

If you delete a document icon in a folder window, you also delete the document. If you delete a shortcut icon, however, you don't delete the document itself, because it is stored elsewhere. You delete only the shortcut that links to the document. The same is true for other types of shortcuts, including those to folders, drives, and devices. You can verify this by deleting the Hawaii Facts – Shortcut icon on the desktop when the Hawaii Maps folder is open.

To delete a shortcut:

▶ 1. Double-click the **Hawaii Maps – Shortcut** icon on your desktop. Arrange the Hawaii Maps window so that it doesn't overlap the Hawaii Facts - Shortcut icon on the desktop.

▶ 2. Click the **Hawaii Facts – Shortcut** icon on the desktop, and then press the **Delete** key.

▶ 3. Click the **Yes** button if you are asked if you are sure you want to send these items to the Recycle Bin.

▶ 4. Verify that the Hawaii Facts document is still stored in the Hawaii Maps folder, and then close the folder window.

Because you selected Auto Arrange and Align to Grid using the View command on the desktop shortcut menu, Windows rearranges the icons so they remain in a single column and are aligned to one another on the desktop.

So far, you have learned how to access the tools you need from the desktop by displaying system icons and customizing the Windows Sidebar and gadgets. You have also learned how to create desktop shortcuts to a drive, folder, document, and printer, and then organize all the icons on your desktop. Next, you'll learn how to work with Control Panel to continue to customize the desktop and personalize your Windows experience.

Session 3.1 Quick Check | Review

1. To change the size of the icons on the desktop, you can use the _____ command on the desktop shortcut menu.
2. When you delete a shortcut icon, what happens to the file or resource it represents?
3. Describe the two appearances the Recycle Bin icon can have on your desktop.
4. Name three gadgets you can display in the Sidebar.
5. True or False. Although you can customize the Sidebar gadgets, you cannot customize the Sidebar itself.
6. Name three ways you can create a shortcut to the USB flash drive on your desktop.

Session 3.2

Using Control Panel

You've worked with the Windows Sidebar and with standard desktop and shortcut icons to personalize your desktop. You can also personalize other parts of Windows Vista using Control Panel. **Control Panel** is a window that contains specialized tools you use to change the way Windows Vista looks and behaves. Some of these tools help you adjust settings that make your computer more fun to use. For example, use the Personalize tool to select a desktop background image or the sounds Windows plays to signal events such as Windows shutting down or the Recycle Bin emptying. You can also use the Personalize tool to change the **theme**, which is a background plus a set of sounds, icons, and other elements. Other Control Panel tools help you set up Windows so that your computer is easier to use. For example, you can change display settings so that the desktop, icons, and windows are sharp and clear, and you can change mouse settings to switch the default buttons if you are left-handed.

All of the Control Panel tools provide access to dialog boxes that let you select or change the **properties**, or characteristics, of an object. Recall that you already used the Windows Sidebar Properties dialog box to change one of the Sidebar's properties (to keep the Sidebar on top of other windows).

If you added the Control Panel icon to the desktop, you can open Control Panel by double-clicking that icon. Otherwise, you open Control Panel from the Start menu.

To open Control Panel:

▶ **1.** Double-click the **Control Panel** icon on your desktop. The Control Panel window opens. See Figure 3-17. Your Control Panel window might differ.

Figure 3-17 ▶ **Control Panel**

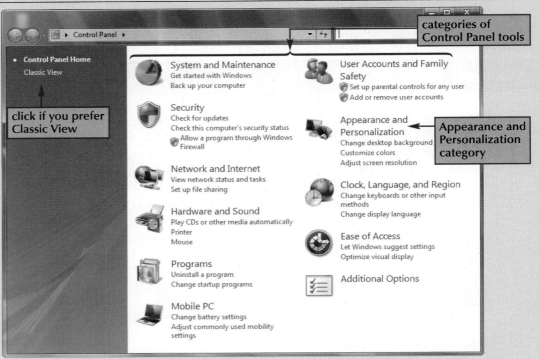

Trouble? If your desktop does not display a Control Panel icon, click the Start button on the taskbar, and then click Control Panel.

Trouble? If a message appears indicating that the Control Panel is not available, you might be in a computer lab with limited customization access. Ask your instructor or technical support person for options.

Tip

When you are more comfortable with Control Panel, you can click the Classic View link in the left pane of Control Panel to switch to Classic View, which displays each tool separately.

By default, the Control Panel window shows tasks in the right pane and related links in the left pane. This default view is called Category View, which groups similar tools into categories. See Figure 3-18.

Control Panel Category	Description
System and Maintenance	Schedule maintenance checks, increase the space on your hard disk, or configure energy-saving settings.
Security	Maintain Windows security settings and keep Windows up to date.
Network and Internet	Set Internet options, view network status, and set up file sharing and perform other network tasks.
Hardware and Sound	Change the sound scheme or individual sounds on your computer, configure the settings for your sound devices, and change the settings for your printer, keyboard, mouse, camera, and other hardware.
Programs	Install and uninstall programs and Windows features, set options for default settings and programs, and work with Windows programs, such as Sidebar.
Mobile PC	Change battery settings and adjust other common mobility settings for a laptop computer.
User Accounts and Family Safety	Change user account settings, passwords, and associated pictures.
Appearance and Personalization	Change the appearance of desktop items, apply a theme or screen saver, or customize the Start menu and taskbar.
Clock, Language, and Region	Change the date, time, and time zone, the language you use on your computer, and the format for numbers, currencies, dates, and times.
Ease of Access	Change computer settings for vision, hearing, and mobility.
Additional Options	Optional category that covers software other than built-in Windows software.

To open a category and see its related tools, you click the appropriate link. For example, you can open the Appearance and Personalization window to change the desktop background or to set a theme.

To open the Appearance and Personalization category:

▶ **1.** In the right pane of Control Panel, click **Appearance and Personalization**. The Appearance and Personalization window opens, showing the tasks and tools related to personalizing your computer's appearance. See Figure 3-19.

| **Appearance and personalization options in Control Panel**

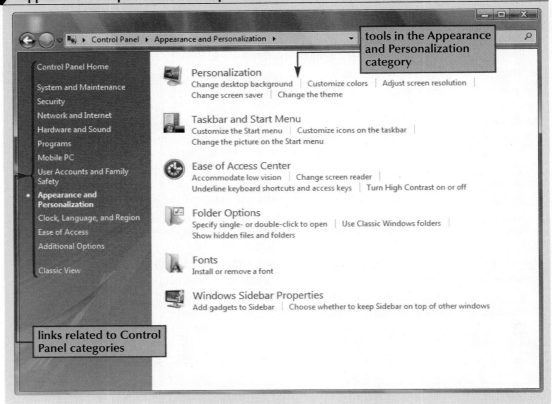

The Appearance and Personalization window, like the other Control Panel category windows, lists tasks and tools in the right pane and links to other Control Panel tools in the left pane. To change the desktop background, for example, you click the appropriate task in the right pane. The Desktop Background window opens so you can select a new desktop background and set other background options.

Holly wants her office computers to reflect the company image of Ptolemy Cartography. She'd like the desktop itself to be more appealing to her and her employees. You will work with the desktop properties to change the desktop background and other elements.

Changing the Desktop

In Windows Vista, you can think of all the parts of your computer—the operating system, the programs, and the documents—as individual objects. For example, the desktop, taskbar, drives, programs, and documents are all objects. Each object has properties that you can examine and usually change to suit your needs and preferences. The desktop has many properties, including the image it displays and its font. You can change the properties of an object using the Properties command on its shortcut menu or by using Control Panel. In this session, you will use Control Panel to change desktop properties.

Changing the Desktop Background

- Open the Control Panel window and switch to Category View, if necessary.
- Click Change desktop background in the Appearance and Personalization category.
- Select an image in the Desktop Background window or click the Picture Location arrow or the Browse button to select images stored in a different location.
- Select a positioning option, if necessary.
- Click the OK button.

Changing Your Desktop's Background

You can change the desktop background, or its **wallpaper**, to display one of the images that Windows Vista provides, or you can select your own graphic to use as wallpaper. When you change the background, you are not placing a new object on the desktop; you are only changing its appearance. You can also determine how you want to position the picture—resized to fit the screen, tiled (repeated across the screen), or centered on the screen. If you center the wallpaper on the screen, you can select a color to frame the background image.

Holly wants the staff computers in the Ptolemy Cartography offices to share a company look. You and Holly decide to examine the desktop backgrounds that Windows Vista provides to see if one is suitable.

To change the desktop background:

▶ 1. In the Appearance and Personalization window, click **Change desktop background** in the Personalization category. The Desktop Background window opens. See Figure 3-20. Your Desktop Background window might differ.

Desktop Background window ◄ **Figure 3-20**

2. Scroll the wallpapers as necessary, and then click the **palm tree branch** image in the Vistas category. (The ScreenTip indicates this image is named img19.) Windows displays the image you selected on the desktop.

3. Click the **OK** button.

Tip

You can make any picture on your computer your desktop background by right-clicking the picture, and then clicking Set as Desktop Background.

After examining the desktop, Holly doesn't think the palm tree image is right for her company after all—Ptolemy Cartography specializes in historical maps of the United States, and the desktop should illustrate that somehow. She mentions that she has an image file of historical maps that she has used in marketing materials. That image might be right for the desktop background.

You'll show Holly how to display her graphic as the desktop background. First, however, you'll close the Windows Sidebar so you can continue to experiment with desktop wallpapers.

To use a graphic image as a desktop background:

Tip

You can open the Sidebar again by clicking its icon in the notification area of the taskbar.

1. Right-click the **Sidebar**, and then click **Close Sidebar**.

2. In the Appearance and Personalization window, click **Change desktop background** to open the Desktop Background window again.

3. Click the **Browse** button to open the Browse dialog box.

4. Navigate to the **Hawaii Maps** folder in the Pictures folder, and then double-click the **Navigation** image file. The Navigation image appears in the Desktop Background window and on the desktop.

5. Minimize the Desktop Background window. See Figure 3-21.

Figure 3-21 | **Navigation image as the desktop background**

Holly's image used as a desktop background

Holly thinks the Navigation image is perfect for the standard wallpaper for Ptolemy Cartography, though the image is too large. You suggest centering the wallpaper image and selecting a coordinating color to frame the image.

To reposition the wallpaper and select a desktop color:

▶ **1.** Restore the Desktop Background window.

▶ **2.** In the How should this picture be positioned? section, click the **Center** option button (point to the positioning images to display their names).

▶ **3.** Minimize the Desktop Background window to verify that Windows centered the Navigation wallpaper on the desktop, and then restore the Desktop Background window.

▶ **4.** Click **Change background color**. The Color dialog box opens.

▶ **5.** In the Basic colors, click the **brown square** in the fifth row, second column. Then click the **OK** button.

▶ **6.** Minimize the Desktop Background window. Windows displays the Navigation image in the center of the desktop with a brown frame. See Figure 3-22.

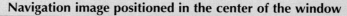 **Navigation image positioned in the center of the window** Figure 3-22

brown background

Navigation desktop image

Holly likes the Navigation wallpaper but comments that the colors of the taskbar and desktop icons are not coordinated with that wallpaper. She also wants to change the font of the desktop icon labels to match the font Ptolemy Cartography uses in its marketing materials, which is Palatino. You'll show her how to change the window colors and the font of the desktop elements.

Changing the Appearance of Desktop Elements

Besides changing the desktop background, you can use the Window Color and Appearance tool in Control Panel to set the color of windows, the Start menu, and the taskbar. To set the color of a broader range of Windows elements, such as buttons, ScreenTips, and the background of program windows, you can specify a **color scheme**, which is a set of colors you apply to Windows elements. Windows Vista includes a collection of color schemes. The default color scheme for most Windows editions is Windows Aero (light blue with glassy effects); for other editions, the color scheme is Windows Basic (also light blue, but without the glassy effects). If you select a color for the windows, Start menu, and taskbar using the Window Color and Appearance tool, Windows integrates this color into the color scheme. For example, if you select graphite as the color and are using the Windows Aero color scheme, title bars shade from black to transparent.

You can also use the Window Color and Appearance tool to change the properties of the text for Windows elements, including icons, window title bars, and buttons. For example, you can increase the size or change the font of the text for desktop icons.

To change the window colors and icon font:

▶ 1. Click the **Desktop Background** button on the taskbar to restore the Desktop Background window, and then click the **Back** button ⊙ to return to the Appearance and Personalization window.

▶ 2. Click **Personalization** to open the Personalization window. You can perform the rest of your changes in this session from this window.

▶ 3. Click **Window Color and Appearance**. The Window Color and Appearance window opens. See Figure 3-23.

| **Figure 3-23** | **Window Color and Appearance window** |

Tip

You can select a custom default color for windows by clicking the Show color mixer button on the Window Color and Appearance window, and then dragging the Hue, Saturation, and Brightness sliders.

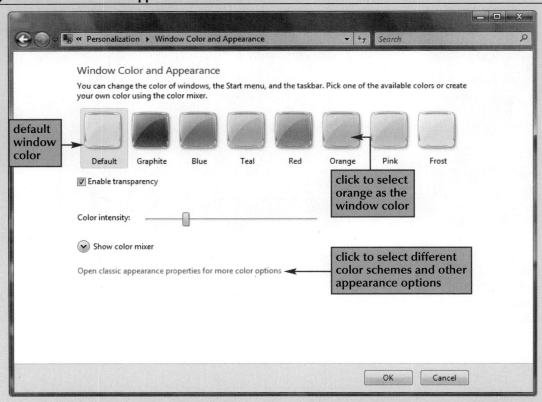

Trouble? If you are not using the Aero experience, the Appearance Settings dialog box opens instead of the Windows Colors and Appearance window. Skip Steps 4 and 5. The color of your window elements will differ from those shown in the figures.

▶ **4.** Click **Orange**. The title bar and border change to orange, which coordinates with Holly's Navigation wallpaper.

Now you want to change the font for the desktop icon labels.

▶ **5.** Click **Open classic appearance properties for more color options**. The Appearance Settings dialog box opens. This dialog box lists the color schemes you can use on your computer.

▶ **6.** Click the **Advanced** button. The Advanced Appearance dialog box opens. See Figure 3-24.

Advanced Appearance dialog box ◀ Figure 3-24

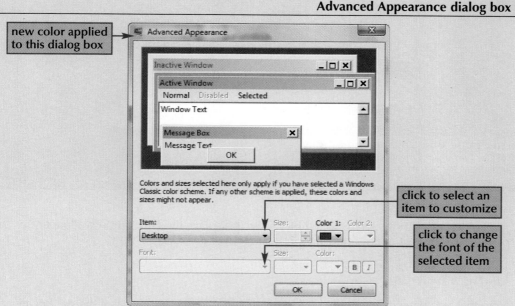

▶ **7.** Click the **Item** arrow, and then click **Icon**. The controls for selecting font properties become active.

▶ **8.** Click the **Font** arrow, and then click **Palatino Linotype**.

▶ **9.** Click the **OK** button to close the Advanced Appearance dialog box.

▶ **10.** Click the **OK** button to close the Appearance Settings dialog box and apply your changes to the desktop, and then minimize the Personalization window. See Figure 3-25.

Figure 3-25 Personalized desktop

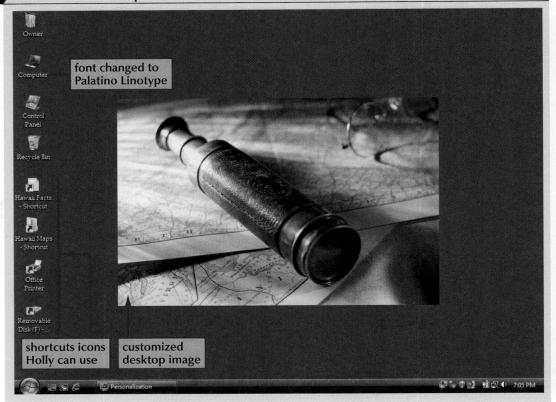

The desktop is now personalized for Holly. It displays the Navigation wallpaper, orange window elements, and Palatino icon labels.

Using Themes

Now that you have changed the desktop, you can save the settings as a theme. Recall that a theme is a collection of customized elements, such as colors and graphics, that you apply to your desktop. If you save your current settings as a theme, you can apply all the changes—the Navigation wallpaper, orange window elements, and Palatino icon labels—at the same time, without selecting the individual settings again. You can save the desktop settings you created for Holly as a theme called Ptolemy.

To save the desktop settings as a theme:

▶ 1. Restore the Personalization window, and then click **Theme**. The Theme Settings dialog box opens. See Figure 3-26.

Theme Settings dialog box | **Figure 3-26**

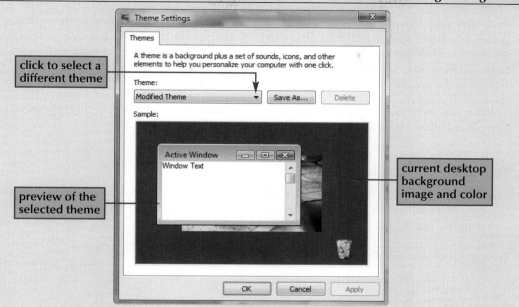

click to select a
different theme

preview of the
selected theme

current desktop
background
image and color

▶ **2.** Click the **Theme** arrow to view the themes you can use on your computer. By default, the themes include at least a Windows Vista and a Windows Classic theme. Your computer might also have themes that correspond to some wallpaper backgrounds in the Desktop Background window.

▶ **3.** Click **My Current Theme**. The My Current Theme option includes all the appearance and personalization properties currently set for Windows.

▶ **4.** Click the **Save As** button.

▶ **5.** In the Save As dialog box, click the **Browse Folders** button, and then navigate to the **Hawaii Maps** folder in your Pictures folder. In the File name text box, type **Ptolemy** as the name of this theme.

▶ **6.** Click the **Save** button. The Ptolemy theme now appears in the Theme list.

▶ **7.** Click the **OK** button to close the Theme Settings dialog box.

Now that you've saved the Ptolemy theme, you can personalize another element of the Windows environment—the screen saver.

Activating a Screen Saver

A **screen saver** blanks the screen or displays a moving design whenever you haven't worked with the computer for a specified period of time. Screen savers are entertaining and handy for hiding your data from the eyes of others if you step away from your computer. When a screen saver is on, you restore your desktop by moving your mouse or pressing a key. Windows Vista comes with several screen savers. Some show an animated design and others play a slide show of the pictures stored on your computer.

You can select how long you want the computer to sit idle before the screen saver starts. Most users find settings between 3 and 10 minutes to be the most convenient. You can change this using the options on the Screen Saver Settings dialog box.

InSight | **Using a Screen Saver for Security**

To enhance the security of your computer and prevent unauthorized people from accessing your files, take advantage of a security setting available in the Screen Saver Settings dialog box. If you select the On resume, require logon screen check box in this dialog box, you can dismiss a screen saver and return to your desktop only after you enter the password you use to log on to Windows Vista.

Holly wants to examine the screen savers that Windows provides and then choose the most appropriate one for her company.

To activate a screen saver:

▶ **1.** In the Personalization window, click **Screen Saver**. The Screen Saver Settings dialog box opens. See Figure 3-27. Note the name of the current screen saver so you can restore it later.

Figure 3-27 Screen Saver Settings dialog box

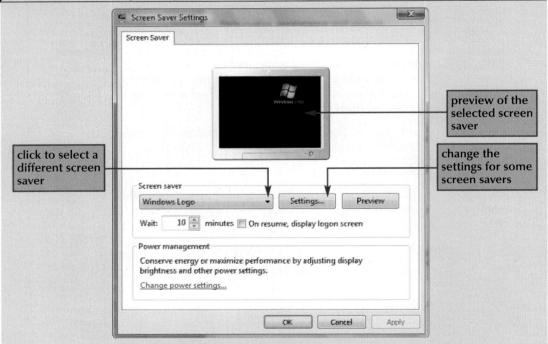

preview of the selected screen saver

click to select a different screen saver

change the settings for some screen savers

▶ **2.** Click the **Screen saver** arrow to display the screen savers installed on your computer.

▶ **3.** Click **Windows Energy**. The animated screen saver plays in the Preview window.

Holly likes that screen saver, but it's not appropriate for her desktop theme. You suggest the Photos screen saver, which plays a slide show of the pictures and videos stored in the Pictures folder, by default. You can change this to any location on the computer, including the Hawaii Maps folder.

▶ **4.** Click the **Screen saver** arrow, and then click **Photos**. The preview window plays a slide show of the graphic files stored in the Pictures folder.

▶ **5.** Click the **Settings** button to open the Photos Screen Saver Settings dialog box. You use this dialog box to specify which files to include in the slide show and other settings, such as the slide show speed.

▶ **6.** Click the **Browse** button. The Browse For Folder dialog box opens.

▶ **7.** Click the **Hawaii Maps** folder in the Pictures folder, and then click the **OK** button.

▶ **8.** Click the **Save** button to close the Photos Screen Saver Settings dialog box. The pictures in the Hawaii Maps folder appear in the Preview window.

▶ **9.** Click the **OK** button to close the Screen Saver Settings dialog box.

After your computer is idle for a few minutes, the screen saver will start, playing a slide show of the maps.

Now that you have worked with the properties for the desktop background, theme, and screen saver, you're ready to explore the display properties that affect the computer monitor itself. The Display Settings dialog box lets you change the sharpness of the images on the desktop and the number of colors your monitor displays.

Changing Display Settings

Use the Display Settings dialog box to control the display settings for your monitor, such as the size of the desktop and whether to use more than one monitor. Windows chooses the best display settings, including screen resolution, refresh rate (also called monitor flicker), and color, based on your particular monitor. The settings you can change depend on your monitor type, so some options in your Display Settings dialog box might be dimmed, indicating they do not apply. Generally, however, you can set the screen resolution and color quality. **Screen resolution** refers to the clarity of the text and images on your screen. At higher resolutions, items appear sharper and smaller, so more items fit on the screen. At lower resolutions, fewer items fit on the screen, but they are larger and easier to see. At very low resolutions, however, images might have jagged edges. The color quality is determined by the number of colors the monitor can assign to a single **pixel**, short for *picture element*, the smallest part of an image on a computer monitor. Computer monitors display images by drawing thousands of pixels in columns and rows, and the more colors each pixel can display, the higher the color quality and the richer the image. Setting your monitor to its highest color quality enhances your Windows experience, though it might slow the performance of your computer.

Selecting the Best Display Settings for Your Monitor	InSight

Display settings vary depending on whether you have an LCD or CRT monitor. (Notebooks and other devices with flat screens often use LCD monitors, while desktop computers sometimes have CRT monitors, which use tubes similar to those in a television.) LCD monitors display vivid color, so use at least a 32-bit color setting. The recommended resolution for a CRT monitor depends on its size. For a 15-inch monitor, use 1024 x 768; for a 17-inch to 19-inch monitor, use 1280 x 1024; and for a 20-inch or larger monitor, use 1600 x 1200.

Changing the Size of the Desktop Area

The Display Settings dialog box has a Resolution slider bar that lets you change the size of the desktop area. You can drag the slider bar to increase or decrease the resolution, or sharpness, of the image. The resolution is measured horizontally and vertically in pixels. If you select a low resolution, such as 800 x 600, the desktop can display fewer objects, but the objects look bigger. If you select a high resolution, such as 1280 x 800 or 1600 x 1200, the desktop can display more objects, though they look smaller.

To change the screen resolution:

▶ **1.** In the Personalization window, click **Display Settings** to open the Display Settings dialog box. Close the Personalization window, and then note the original setting in the Screen resolution area so you can restore it later. See Figure 3-28.

Figure 3-28 | **Display Settings dialog box**

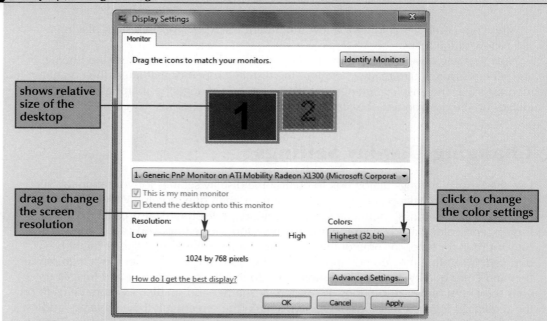

shows relative size of the desktop

drag to change the screen resolution

click to change the color settings

▶ **2.** To select the 1280 by 800 resolution, if it is not already selected, drag the **Resolution** slider to that setting. The preview area shows the relative size of the new resolution.

   Trouble? If your monitor does not display a 1280 by 800 resolution, choose a different resolution, such as 1280 by 720 or 1280 by 768.

▶ **3.** To select the 1024 by 768 resolution, if possible, drag the **Resolution** slider to that setting.

▶ **4.** Return the slider to its original setting. Leave the Display Settings dialog box open.

While changing the screen resolution increases or decreases the sharpness of the images, the number of colors your monitor displays determines how realistic the images look. However, the higher the resolution and color setting, the more resources your monitor needs; the best settings for your computer balance sharpness and color quality with computer resources.

Changing the Colors Setting

You can also use the Display Settings dialog box to change the Colors setting, which specifies the number of colors available to your computer to create shading and other realistic effects. Holly's computers use Highest (32 bit) color, which includes millions of colors.

To view the color settings:

▶ **1.** Click the **Colors** arrow to display the list of color settings available to your monitor. Most contemporary monitors allow at least a Medium (16 bit) setting, which displays up to 835,000 colors.

▶ **2.** Click **Highest (32 bit)**. Depending on your monitor, your screen can now display up to 16 million colors, which allows realistic shading and gradation.

Trouble? If Highest (32 bit) doesn't appear in your Colors list, skip Step 2.

▶ **3.** Click the **Cancel** button to close the Display Settings dialog box without accepting any changes.

You used Control Panel and its tools to change the properties of Holly's desktop, including the background and the appearance of desktop elements, such as windows and icons. You also changed the window colors, saved Holly's color scheme as a theme, activated a screen saver, and experimented with the display settings. You and Holly can now change the desktops of other computers in her office so they all reflect the corporate image of Ptolemy Cartography.

Session 3.2 Quick Check | Review

1. True or False. A theme is a background image plus a set of sounds, icons, and other elements.
2. What is the purpose of Control Panel?
3. Windows Vista includes a collection of _____ , which are sets of colors you apply to Windows elements.
4. Why might you use a screen saver?
5. What does it mean to say that a monitor's resolution is 1024 x 768?
6. At _____ screen resolutions, items appear sharper and smaller, so more items fit on the screen.
   a. low
   b. high
   c. 32-bit
   d. 16-bit

Session 3.3

Modifying the Taskbar

As you know from previous tutorials, the bar that contains the Start button and appears by default at the bottom of the desktop is the **taskbar**. The taskbar is divided into four sections. You are already familiar with the Start button, which you click to open the Start menu. By default, the taskbar also displays the **Quick Launch toolbar**, which contains buttons you can click to start programs you use often. The middle section of the taskbar displays program buttons, which you click to manipulate windows. The far-right section of the taskbar is the **notification area**, which shows the current time, program icons, and system status information. Figure 3-29 shows the taskbar with these default sections.

Figure 3-29 | Default taskbar sections

Tip

To close all the windows in a taskbar group, right-click the group's taskbar button, and then click Close Group.

Figure 3-29 shows the taskbar buttons organized into groups. As you open additional windows, taskbar buttons shrink to accommodate new buttons. When the taskbar becomes crowded, Windows groups the buttons for the same program into a single button. In Figure 3-29, for example, five folder windows are grouped on the Windows Explorer button, which shows the name of the group (Windows Explorer) and the number of items in the group (5). To display a menu of the windows in the group, you click the taskbar button. To activate a window, you click its name in the menu.

Recall that if you are using Windows Aero and you point to a taskbar button, Windows displays a preview of the corresponding window. The preview is designed to help you identify a window by more than the title alone. If a window is playing a video or animation, it also plays in the preview. When you point to a grouped taskbar button, a stack of previews appears, with only the top preview visible.

You can personalize the taskbar to suit your preferences. For example, you can change its size and position or hide it altogether. In addition, you can display toolbars on the taskbar. These toolbars can contain buttons for the icons on your desktop, for programs you use often, and for Web pages to which you want quick access. Including toolbars on the taskbar makes it easy to navigate your computer and open programs, documents, and Web pages without minimizing windows or closing dialog boxes that might be open on the desktop.

InSight | Monitoring the Notication Area

The icons in the notification area of the taskbar let you access some computer settings, such as the system time, and communicate the status of programs running in the background. Background programs are those programs that Windows runs to provide a service, such as an Internet connection. If you suspect trouble with a program running in the background, click the Show hidden icons button on the taskbar to display all the icons in the notification area. Then point to an icon to display its status or name. For example, point to the network icon to determine whether your computer is connected to a network. Sometimes an icon displays a notification, or small pop-up window, to notify you about a change in status, such as when you add a new hardware device to your computer. Read the notification to find out whether you need to respond or correct a problem.

So far you've shown Holly how to work with many properties of the Windows Vista desktop. Now you can personalize two other parts of the Windows Vista desktop: the taskbar and the Start menu. You'll start by showing her how to work with the taskbar.

Moving and Resizing the Taskbar

When you first install Windows Vista, the taskbar is locked in its position at the bottom of the desktop. That way, as you learn your way around Windows, you always have access to the Start menu so you can start programs and shut down Windows. Before you can move or resize the taskbar, however, you must unlock it. You can do so by right-clicking the taskbar to open its shortcut menu, and then clicking the Lock the Taskbar command. This command is listed with a check mark by default to indicate that it is selected, so clicking it again removes the check mark, indicating the taskbar is no longer locked.

When Holly is working with graphics programs, she occasionally drags objects onto the taskbar by accident. You'll show her how to move the taskbar to the top of the desktop, where it's out of her way. First, however, you need to unlock the taskbar.

Moving and Resizing the Taskbar | Reference Window

- Make sure the taskbar is unlocked. To do so, right-click any blank spot on the taskbar, and then click Lock the Taskbar on the shortcut menu to remove the check mark.
- To move the taskbar, click a blank spot on the taskbar, hold down the left mouse button, and drag the taskbar to a new location (the top, bottom, left, or right edge of the desktop).
- To resize the taskbar, point to a taskbar border until a resize pointer appears, and then drag the border to a different height or width.

To move the taskbar:

▶ 1. Right-click a blank spot on the taskbar, and then, if necessary, click **Lock the Taskbar** on the shortcut menu to uncheck this command.

   Trouble? If the Lock the Taskbar command is already unchecked, skip Step 1.

▶ 2. Drag the taskbar to the top of the desktop. See Figure 3-30. Notice that the icons on the desktop moved down slightly to make room for the newly positioned taskbar.

> **Tip**
>
> You can also select commands on the taskbar shortcut menu that let you cascade windows, stack them, or show them side by side.

Moving the taskbar to the top of the desktop ◀ **Figure 3-30**

▶ 3. Drag the taskbar back down to the bottom of the desktop.

Holly has also noticed that when she has several programs running simultaneously, the icons for those programs fill up the notification area. She often refers to these icons, and wants to display them without sacrificing space for her taskbar buttons. You'll show her how to solve that problem by increasing the size of the taskbar.

To increase the size of the taskbar:

▶ **1.** Point to the upper edge of the taskbar until the pointer changes to ↕.

▶ **2.** Drag up to increase the height of the taskbar. See Figure 3-31.

| Figure 3-31 | Resizing the taskbar |

taskbar is twice as high

▶ **3.** Drag the upper border of the taskbar to return it to its original height.

Resizing the taskbar is one way to change its appearance. You also can change other taskbar properties, such as those that determine when the taskbar appears.

Setting Taskbar Appearance Properties

In addition to resizing and relocating the taskbar, you can set taskbar appearance properties using the Taskbar and Start Menu Properties dialog box, which you open from a shortcut menu or Control Panel. Using this dialog box, you can increase the amount of screen space available for your program windows by hiding the taskbar. In this case, the taskbar is not closed, removed, or minimized, but hidden either under the border of the desktop or under the program windows open on the desktop. It still remains active and accessible—you can point to the area of your screen where the taskbar would be located to redisplay the taskbar.

By default, the taskbar appears on top of windows on the desktop, but you can change this setting in the Taskbar and Start Menu Properties dialog box so that program windows and dialog boxes cover the taskbar when necessary. You can also use the Taskbar and Start Menu Properties dialog box to determine whether to show the Quick Launch toolbar on the taskbar, group similar taskbar buttons, and show window previews in the Aero experience.

You'll show Holly how to increase the amount of screen space by hiding the taskbar and by letting windows cover the taskbar.

To set taskbar appearance properties:

▶ **1.** Right-click a blank area on the taskbar, and then click **Properties** on the shortcut menu. The Taskbar and Start Menu Properties dialog box opens. See Figure 3-32.

Taskbar and Start Menu Properties dialog box Figure 3-32

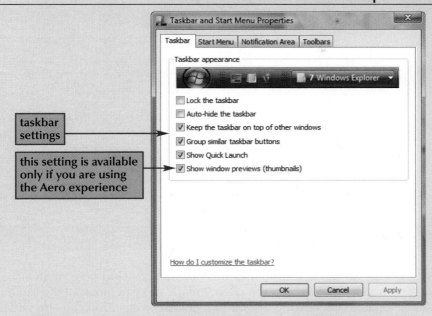

taskbar settings

this setting is available only if you are using the Aero experience

Note the options currently selected in this dialog box so you can restore them later.

2. Click to select the **Auto-hide the taskbar** check box, and then click the **Apply** button. Windows hides the taskbar.

   Trouble? If the Auto-hide the taskbar check box is already selected, skip Step 2.

3. Point to the bottom of the desktop to redisplay the taskbar.

4. In the Taskbar and Start Menu Properties dialog box, click the **Auto-hide the taskbar** check box to remove the check mark, and then click the **Apply** button. The taskbar appears in its default position at the bottom of the desktop.

5. Click the **Keep the taskbar on top of other windows** check box to remove the check mark, and then click the **Apply** button.

   Trouble? If the Keep the taskbar on top of other windows check box does not contain a check mark, skip Step 5.

6. Drag the Taskbar and Start Menu Properties dialog box to your taskbar. When you release the mouse button, the dialog box overlaps the taskbar.

7. Restore the options in this dialog box to their original state, and then click the **OK** button to close the dialog box.

The taskbar shortcut menu also includes options relating to toolbars, which you'll work with next.

Working with Taskbar Toolbars

One way to customize the taskbar is to use it to display toolbars. By default, it displays the Quick Launch toolbar, which contains icons for starting Internet Explorer, switching windows, and showing the desktop. Figure 3-33 describes the toolbars you can include on the taskbar. Your taskbar might be able to display additional toolbars.

Taskbar Toolbar	Description
Address	Use to open any Web page you specify. Open the Address bar by double-clicking it.
Windows Media Player	Use to display controls for playing music and other media, including Play, Stop, and Pause buttons.
Links	Use to access links to product information on the Web and add Web links by dragging them to the toolbar. Open the Links toolbar by clicking the double chevron (>>).
Desktop	Use to access items on your desktop, such as the Recycle Bin and Computer, from the taskbar. Open the Desktop toolbar by clicking the double chevron (>>).
Quick Launch	Use to access icons you can click to quickly open programs, show the desktop, or perform other tasks.
New	Create a custom taskbar toolbar to store shortcuts to folders, documents, or other objects you use often.

The New taskbar toolbar is a custom toolbar you can create to store shortcuts to folders, documents or other objects you use often. In fact, you can move all the shortcut icons you created from the desktop to a custom taskbar toolbar. You can also add program icons to the Quick Launch toolbar, such as those for your e-mail or other programs you use often.

Customizing the Quick Launch Toolbar

You can customize the Quick Launch toolbar by adding program icons to it. To do so, you locate the program you want on the Start menu or on the desktop, and then drag its icon to the Quick Launch toolbar, where you create a shortcut to the program. By default, the Quick Launch toolbar can display only three icons so it doesn't take up too much of the taskbar. If the toolbar contains more than three icons, Windows hides the additional icons. However, you can resize the Quick Launch toolbar to show all of its icons or easily display the hidden icons even if you don't resize the toolbar. You customize the Quick Launch toolbar by working directly with it on the taskbar.

Holly often uses the Windows Photo Gallery program to view pictures of maps and other images. You'll show her how to add that program to the Quick Launch toolbar.

To customize the Quick Launch toolbar:

1. Click the **Start** button ⊕ on the taskbar, and then point to **All Programs**. The Windows Photo Gallery program appears in the All Programs menu.

   Trouble? If the Windows Photo Gallery program does not appear in the All Programs menu, point to Back or click the Accessories folder to find the program.

2. Drag **Windows Photo Gallery** from the Start menu to a blank area on the Quick Launch toolbar until an insertion line appears. See Figure 3-34.

Adding a program to the Quick Launch toolbar | **Figure 3-34**

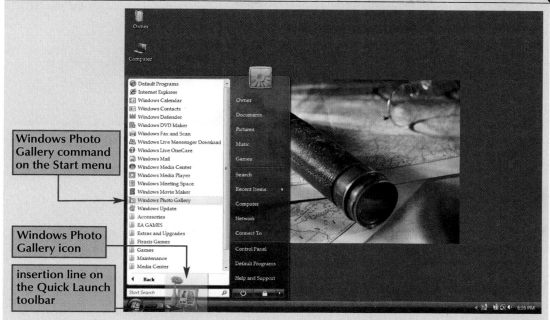

Windows Photo Gallery command on the Start menu

Windows Photo Gallery icon

insertion line on the Quick Launch toolbar

   3. Release the mouse button to add a shortcut icon to the Quick Launch toolbar. Depending on where you dragged the program icon, the shortcut to the Windows Photo Gallery program might be hidden.

   4. Click the **expand** button ❯ on the Quick Launch toolbar to display the hidden icons.

   5. Click a blank area of the desktop, and then point to the **toolbar-sizing handle** ▮ **on the Quick Launch toolbar.**

   6. When the pointer changes to ⇔, drag the handle to the right to widen the Quick Launch toolbar so it shows all of its icons.

Quick Launch might be the only taskbar toolbar you need. However, you can add other toolbars to the taskbar to facilitate your work.

Adding Toolbars to the Taskbar

You can include several toolbars on the taskbar in addition to the Quick Launch toolbar. You can add these toolbars using the Toolbars tab on the Taskbar and Start Menu Properties dialog box or by using the taskbar's shortcut menu.

Holly often has several programs running at once, filling up the screen and hiding the desktop. She understands the benefit of placing icons on the desktop, but wants to access those desktop icons without having to minimize all of her open windows. You suggest that she place a Desktop toolbar on her taskbar, which contains all the icons on the desktop, though it displays only its name, Desktop, by default. Like the Quick Launch toolbar, the Desktop toolbar includes an expand button that you can click to display all of the icons that appear on the desktop. You can also resize the Desktop toolbar, though it typically takes up a lot of room on the taskbar. You'll show Holly how to add the Desktop toolbar to the taskbar, and then use it to open her personal folder, which is one of the icons on her desktop.

To display the Desktop toolbar:

▶ **1.** Right-click a blank area of the taskbar, point to **Toolbars** on the shortcut menu, and then click **Desktop**. The Desktop toolbar appears on the taskbar. See Figure 3-35.

Figure 3-35	Displaying the Desktop toolbar

modified Quick Launch toolbar

click to display all the icons on the Desktop toolbar

▶ **2.** Click the **expand** button ⟩⟩ on the Desktop toolbar to display a menu of its icons.

▶ **3.** Click a blank area on the desktop to close the menu, point to the left border of the Desktop toolbar until the pointer changes to ⟷, and then drag left until you see your user folder, such as Owner.

▶ **4.** Click **your user folder** icon on the Desktop toolbar menu to open this folder, and then close the folder window.

Holly likes having the icon for her personal folder on the Desktop toolbar, but wants to see more icons on it. She wants the toolbar to look more like the Quick Launch toolbar, with no names next to the icon and no title displayed for the toolbar. You can modify the toolbar's appearance by changing its properties.

Modifying the Appearance of a Taskbar Toolbar

You can modify the appearance of a taskbar toolbar by showing or hiding its title and by showing or hiding the text labels for each icon. On the taskbar shortcut menu, these commands are checked by default. To hide the title and text labels, you uncheck both commands. You'll modify the Desktop toolbar by hiding its title and text labels.

To modify the appearance of the Desktop toolbar:

▶ **1.** Right-click a blank area in the Desktop toolbar, and then click **Show Text** on the shortcut menu to uncheck this command.

Trouble? If the Show Text command does not appear on the shortcut menu, you probably right-clicked one of the buttons on the Desktop toolbar. Be sure to click a blank area on the toolbar.

Trouble? If the Show Text command does not appear with a check mark on the shortcut menu, skip Step 1.

▶ **2.** Right-click a blank area in the Desktop toolbar again and click **Show Title** on the shortcut menu to uncheck this command.

Trouble? If the Show Title command does not appear with a check mark on the shortcut menu, skip Step 2.

Figure 3-36 displays the final appearance of the toolbar. Note that each item on the desktop is matched by an item in the toolbar and that the icons are small, like those on the Quick Launch toolbar.

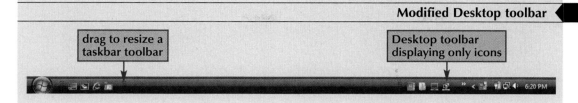

Modified Desktop toolbar — Figure 3-36

drag to resize a taskbar toolbar

Desktop toolbar displaying only icons

Now Holly can access all the items on her desktop without minimizing open windows.

Creating a Custom Toolbar

If the standard taskbar toolbars that Windows Vista provides do not meet your needs, you can create your own taskbar toolbar. For example, if you often work with documents contained in folders in the Documents folder, you could add each folder to a custom toolbar so you can access those documents quickly. To create a custom toolbar, you use the New Toolbar command on the taskbar shortcut menu.

Creating a Custom Taskbar Toolbar | Reference Window

- To create a custom toolbar, right-click a blank area of the taskbar, point to Toolbars, and then click New Toolbar.
- In the New Toolbar – Choose a folder window, click the folder or object you want to turn into a toolbar, and then click the Select Folder button.

Holly experiments with the Desktop toolbar, and notices that when she clicks the Computer icon on the Desktop toolbar it opens the Computer window. Holly asks you to create a taskbar toolbar displaying the icons in the Computer window so she can access her computer's drives easily.

To create a toolbar for Computer window icons:

▶ 1. Right-click a blank area on the taskbar, point to **Toolbars**, and then click **New Toolbar** on the shortcut menu. The New Toolbar – Choose a folder window opens, showing the hierarchy of objects on your computer, which is familiar to you from your work with Computer and Windows Explorer.

▶ 2. Click **Computer** in the Navigation pane of the New Toolbar – Choose a folder window, and then click the **Select Folder** button. The Computer toolbar appears on the taskbar.

▶ 3. To modify the appearance of the Computer toolbar, right-click a blank spot on the Computer toolbar and click **Show Text** on the shortcut menu to remove the check mark.

▶ 4. Right-click a blank spot on the Computer toolbar again and click **Show Title** on the shortcut menu. See Figure 3-37.

Figure 3-37 ▸ **Toolbars on the taskbar**

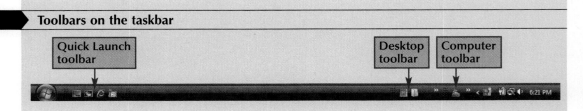

Having seen how to create and modify toolbars on the taskbar, now you can turn to the other major element you can open from the taskbar—the Start menu.

Customizing the Start Menu

Most of the items on the Start menu are created for you by Windows Vista or by the various programs you install. However, you also can determine the content and appearance of your Start menu, removing items you don't use and adding those you do. In addition, Windows Vista personalizes the left pane of the Start menu as you work to show the programs you use most frequently. You can organize the Start menu and control its appearance to use it most effectively.

Controlling the Appearance of the Start Menu

Recall that the picture associated with the current user appears at the top of the Start menu. When you point to commands in the right pane of the Start menu, this picture changes. For example, when you point to the Documents command, the picture shows an image of a folder containing documents. Although you can't change the images associated with commands, you can change the user picture to personalize the Start menu.

You'll select a user picture for Holly that fits the appearance of her desktop.

To change the user picture on the Start menu:

▸ 1. Click the **Start** button 🔵 on the taskbar, and then click the **user picture** at the top of the right pane. The User Accounts window opens. See Figure 3-38.

User Accounts window   **Figure 3-38**

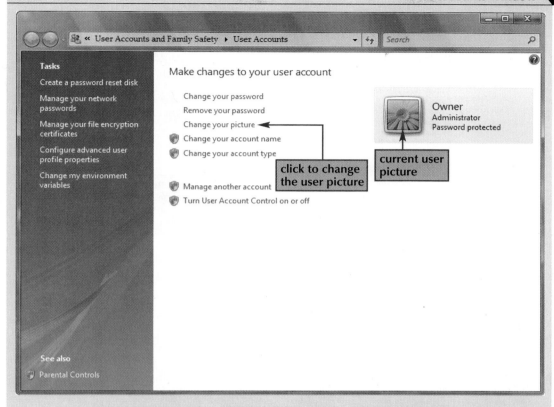

> **2.** Click **Change your picture**. The Change Your Picture window opens, displaying a collection of pictures you can use on the Welcome screen and Start menu.

> **3.** Click the image of the **bass clef**, which is the first picture in the collection.

> **4.** Click the **Change Picture** button.

> **5.** Click the **Start** button 🪟 again to verify the new user picture, and then point to the commands in the right pane to see the picture change to reflect the current command.

> **6.** Click the **Start** button 🪟 to close the Start menu.

> **7.** Close the User Accounts window.

Another feature of the Start menu you can control is whether the menu displays small or large icons. The default is to use large icons, but you can fit more commands on the Start menu by changing this to the smaller icon style. Because the Start button is considered part of the taskbar, you change settings for the Start menu using the same dialog box you used earlier to control the appearance of the taskbar.

To change the size of the icons on the Start menu:

> **1.** Right-click the **Start** button 🪟 on the taskbar, and then click **Properties** on the shortcut menu. The Taskbar and Start Menu Properties dialog box opens to the Start Menu tab.

> **2.** Click the **Customize** button. The Customize Start Menu dialog box opens. See Figure 3-39.

Figure 3-39 **Customize Start Menu dialog box**

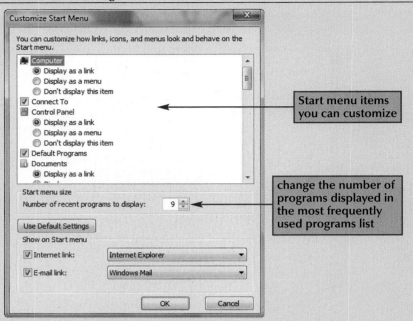

3. Scroll the list of items you can customize. At the bottom of the list, click the **Use large icons** check box to remove the check mark.

4. Click the **OK** button and then click the **Apply** button. The Taskbar and Start Menu Properties dialog box stays open. Before you open the Start menu to view the small icons, you can drag this dialog box out of the way.

5. Drag the Taskbar and Start Menu Properties dialog box to the right side of the desktop.

6. Click the **Start** button 🟦, view your changes, and then click the **Start** button 🟦 again to close the menu.

Now that you have plenty of room on the Start menu, you can learn how to add items to it.

Pinning an Item to the Start Menu

Recall that the upper-left area of the Start menu is the pinned items list, which contains shortcuts to programs you use often. By default, the Internet Explorer and Windows Mail shortcuts appear in the pinned items list. Below the pinned items is the most frequently used programs list. As you open programs, Windows Vista adds their shortcuts to this area. For example, if you use Paint often, Windows Vista adds a Paint shortcut to the most frequently used programs list on the Start menu. The items on the right of the Start menu open dialog boxes or submenus. See Figure 3-40.

Typical Start menu ◀ Figure 3-40

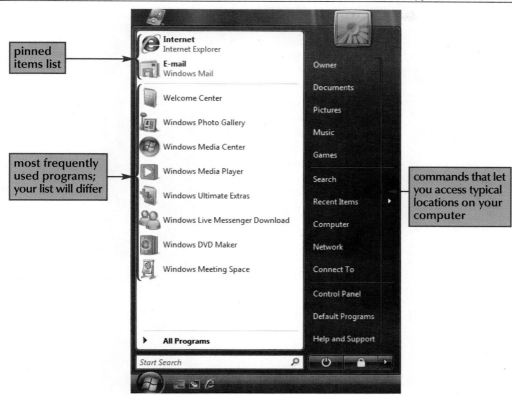

pinned items list

most frequently used programs; your list will differ

commands that let you access typical locations on your computer

A popular way to modify the Start menu is to pin and unpin programs. You can also move the program icons in the pinned items list to change their order. In addition, you can add and remove commands from the right pane of the Start menu. For example, you can remove the Recent Items command to keep your work private.

Holly has become accustomed to using Windows Explorer to navigate her computer. Instead of clicking the Start button on the taskbar, pointing to All Programs, clicking the Accessories folder, and then clicking Windows Explorer, you can pin the Windows Explorer icon to the Start menu for easy access.

To pin Windows Explorer to the Start menu:

▶ **1.** Click the **Start** button 🏵 on the taskbar, point to **All Programs**, and then click the **Accessories** folder.

▶ **2.** Right-click **Windows Explorer**, and then click **Pin to Start Menu** on the short-cut menu.

▶ **3.** Point to **Back** on the Start menu to verify that Windows Explorer is now pinned to the top of the Start menu. See Figure 3-41.

Tip

To add a folder shortcut to the Start menu, drag the folder from a window to the Start button.

Figure 3-41 **Windows Explorer pinned to the Start menu**

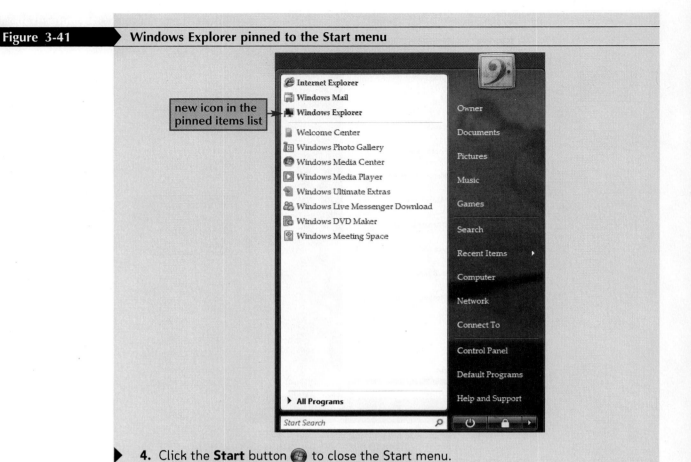

4. Click the **Start** button 🌀 to close the Start menu.

Besides adding programs to the pinned items list, you can add commands to the right pane of the Start menu.

Adding Commands to the Right Pane of the Start Menu

You can add or remove items—such as Computer, Control Panel, and Pictures—that appear on the right side of the Start menu. You can also change some items so that they appear as links or menus.

Holly wants to see how she could use the Start menu to access the Printers folder, which displays all the printers she can use from her computer. Besides the default printer, she also uses a color printer and plotter when creating maps. She asks you to add the Printers command to the Start menu.

To add the Printers command to the Start menu:

▶ 1. With the Taskbar and Start Menu Properties dialog box still open on the desktop, click the **Customize** button. The Customize Start Menu dialog box opens.

   Trouble? If the Taskbar and Start Menu Properties dialog box is not open on your desktop, right-click the Start button on the taskbar, and then click Properties.

▶ 2. Scroll the Start menu items, and then click the **Printers** check box.

▶ 3. Click the **OK** button, and then click the **Apply** button.

▶ 4. Click the **Start** button 🔵 on the taskbar to verify that the Printers command is now displayed in the right pane.

Holly can now open the Printers folder by clicking the Printers command on the Start menu.

Selecting Start Menu Settings

The Customize Start Menu dialog box lists options and settings for your Start menu. For example, you can display a command on the Start menu as a link or as a submenu. If you display a command as a link, you click it to open the appropriate dialog box or window. For example, the Computer command appears on the Start menu as a link by default—you click Computer to open its window. If you display a command as a submenu, you point to the command until a submenu appears, and then you click a command on the submenu. Instead of a link, you can display the Computer command as a submenu. When you point to Computer, a submenu appears listing the contents of the Computer window, including your local hard disk. Figure 3-42 describes the settings you can select for your Start menu.

Start menu settings

Start Menu	Description
Computer	Display this item as a link you click to open the Computer window, as a submenu that lists the contents of Computer, or don't display this item.
Connect To	Display an item that lets you select a network to which you can connect.
Control Panel	Display this item as a link you click to open Control Panel, as a submenu that lists individual tools or categories in Control Panel, or don't display this item.
Default Programs	Display an item that lets you choose the default programs you use for Web browsing, e-mail, playing music, and other activities.
Documents	Display this item as a link you click to open the Documents folder, as a submenu that lists the contents of Documents, or don't display this item.
Enable context menus and dragging and dropping	When you move items on the Start menu, display menus as you drag that indicate the actions you can take.
Favorites menu	Display this item to list your favorite Web sites, files, and folders.
Games	Display this item as a link you click to open the Games folder, as a submenu that lists the contents of the Games folder, or don't display this item.
Help	Display this item to open the Help and Support window.
Highlight newly installed programs	Before you start a newly installed program for the first time, highlight the program name.
Music	Display this item as a link you click to open the Music folder, as a submenu that lists the contents of Music, or don't display this item.
Network	Display this item to open the Network window.
Open submenus when I pause on them with the mouse pointer	Instead of clicking to open a submenu, open the submenu when you point to an item and pause.
Personal folder	Display this item as a link you click to open your personal folder, as a submenu that lists the contents of your personal folder, or don't display this item.
Pictures	Display this item as a link you click to open the Pictures folder window, as a submenu that lists the contents of Pictures, or don't display this item.
Printers	Display this item to open the Printers window.
Run command	Display the Run command to open the Run dialog box.
Search	Display this item to open a Search Results window where you can search the contents of your computer.
Search communications	When searching your computer, have Windows search e-mail and other types of electronic communications.
Search favorites and history	When searching your computer, have Windows search your Web browsing history and the Web sites designated as favorites.
Search files	When searching, have Windows skip searching files, search the index of files on your computer, or search only the current user's files.
Search programs	When searching your computer, search for installed programs.
Sort All Programs menu by name	Display the folders and programs on the All Programs menu in alphabetic order by name.
System administrative tools	Display this item on the All Programs menu, on the All Programs menu and the Start menu, or don't display this item.
Use large icons	Display large program icons on the Start menu.

Holly wants to display the Computer item as a submenu so she has another easy way to access her USB flash drive. The Computer submenu will then contain a shortcut icon that she can click to quickly open her USB flash drive.

To change the Computer command on the Start Menu to display a submenu:

▶ **1.** With the Taskbar and Start Menu Properties dialog box open on the desktop, click the **Customize** button. The Customize Start Menu dialog box opens.

▶ **2.** Click the **Display as a menu** option button under the Computer icon.

▶ **3.** Click the **OK** button, and then click the **Apply** button. Now you can test the Computer submenu on the Start menu.

▶ **4.** Click the **Start** button 🪟 on the taskbar, and then point to **Computer**. The icons in the Computer window appear in the submenu. See Figure 3-43.

New Computer submenu on the Start menu ◀ Figure 3-43

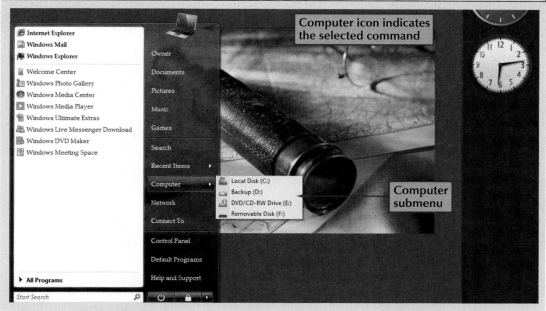

▶ **5.** Click **Removable Disk (F:)** or other item on the Computer submenu. The contents of this drive appear in the Computer window.

▶ **6.** Close all open windows and dialog boxes.

Now that you've finished personalizing the Windows Vista environment on Holly's computer, you should restore the computer to its original settings.

Restoring Your Settings

If you are working in a computer lab or a computer other than your own, complete the steps in this section to restore the original settings on your computer.

To restore your settings:

▶ 1. Right-click the **desktop**, click **Personalize** on the shortcut menu.

▶ 2. Click **Change desktop icons**. Click check boxes to restore the original settings. By default, only the Recycle Bin appears on the desktop.

▶ 3. In the list of desktop icons, click **Computer**, and then click the **Restore Default** button. Click the **OK** button to close the Change Icon dialog box, and then click the **OK** button to close the Desktop Icon Settings dialog box. Minimize the Personalization window.

▶ 4. Right-click the **desktop**, point to **View** on the shortcut menu, and then click **Medium Icons**.

▶ 5. Click a **shortcut icon** on the desktop, hold down the **Ctrl** key, and then click all the other **shortcut icons** you created in this tutorial. Press the **Delete** key to delete the shortcuts, and then click the **Yes** button, if necessary.

▶ 6. Navigate to the **Hawaii Maps** folder in the Pictures folder, and then move it to the **Tutorial.03\Tutorial** folder provided with your Data Files. Delete the original files in the Tutorial.03\Tutorial folder, which should now contain only the Hawaii Maps folder. Close all folder windows.

▶ 7. Open the Sidebar. (Click the **Windows Sidebar** icon 🖼 in the notification area of the taskbar.) Right-click the **Sidebar**, click **Properties** on the shortcut menu, click the **Sidebar is always on top of other windows** check box, and then click the **OK** button. Remove the Hawaii clock from the Sidebar and redisplay the **Slide Show** gadget.

▶ 8. In the Personalization window, click **Theme**. Click the **Theme** arrow, and then click **Windows Vista**. Click the **OK** button to close the Theme Settings dialog box.

▶ 9. In the Personalization window, click **Desktop Background**. Click the **Location** arrow, click **Windows Wallpapers**, scroll to the Vistas category, if necessary, and then click the image that originally appeared on your desktop. By default, this is img24 in the Vistas category. Click the **Fit to Screen** option button, and then click the **OK** button.

   Trouble? If img24 does not appear in the Desktop Background window, click the Browse button, and then double-click img24.

▶ 10. In the Personalization window, click **Window Color and Appearance**, and then click **Default**.

   Trouble? If you are not using the Aero experience, the Appearance Settings dialog box opens when you click Window Color and Appearance. Click Windows Vista Basic in the Color scheme list.

▶ 11. If you are using the Aero experience, click **Open classic appearance properties for more color options**. In the Appearance Settings dialog box, click the **Advanced** button, click the **Item** arrow, and then click **Icon**. Click the **Font** arrow, click **Segoe UI**, click the **OK** button to close the Advanced Appearance dialog box, and then click the **OK** button to close the Appearance Settings dialog box.

▶ 12. In the Personalization window, click **Screen Saver**. Click the **Screen saver** arrow, and then click the original screen saver, which is **Windows Logo** by default. Click the **OK** button to close the Screen Saver Settings dialog box.

▶ **13.** On the Quick Launch toolbar, right-click the **Windows Photo Gallery** icon, click **Delete**, and then click the **Yes** button. Resize the **Quick Launch** toolbar to display only three icons.

▶ **14.** Right-click a blank area of the taskbar, point to **Toolbars**, and then click **Desktop** to remove this toolbar from the taskbar. Do the same to remove the **Computer** toolbar from the taskbar.

▶ **15.** Right-click the taskbar, and then click **Lock the Taskbar** on the shortcut menu.

▶ **16.** Click the **Start** button 🟦 on the taskbar, click the **user picture**, click **Change your picture**, click the original user picture, and then click the **Change Picture** button. Close the User Accounts window.

▶ **17.** Right-click the **Start** button 🟦 , click **Properties**, click the **Customize** button, click the **Use large icons** check box to select it, click the **Printers** check box to remove the check mark, click the **Display as a link** option button under the Computer icon, click the **OK** button to close the Customize Start Menu dialog box, and then click the **OK** button to close the Taskbar and Start Menu Properties dialog box.

▶ **18.** Click the **Start** button 🟦 , right-click **Windows Explorer**, click **Unpin from Start menu**, and then click the **Start** button 🟦 again to close the menu.

▶ **19.** Close all open windows.

Session 3.3 Quick Check | Review

1. Before you can move or resize the taskbar, you must make sure the _____ _____ _____ command on the task bar shortcut menu is not selected.
2. After you hide the taskbar, explain how you can redisplay it.
3. True or False. Only Windows Vista can set the user picture that appears on the Start menu—you cannot change it.
4. On the Start menu, the Internet Explorer and Windows Mail shortcuts appear in the _____ _____ _____ by default.
5. You can display a Start menu command as a link. Identify the other way you can display a command on the Start menu.
6. Identify the four main sections of the taskbar.

Tutorial Summary | Review

In this tutorial, you added icons to the desktop, and then customized and arranged those icons. You also explored the Windows Sidebar and its gadgets by customizing the Sidebar and adding and removing gadgets. You used Control Panel to personalize the desktop by changing the desktop background, setting the appearance of desktop elements, and applying a visual theme. You also selected a different screen saver and changed the display settings. To personalize the taskbar, you moved and resized the taskbar, set its appearance properties, and added toolbars to the taskbar. You also customized the Start menu by changing its appearance, pinning programs to the menu, and adding and changing commands.

Key Terms

color scheme

Control Panel

desktop icon

feed

gadget

notification area

pixel

property

Quick Launch toolbar

screen resolution

screen saver

shortcut

taskbar

theme

wallpaper

Practice	**Review Assignments**

Practice the skills you learned in the tutorial.

For a list of Data Files in the Review folder, see page 97.

You already worked with Holly's notebook computer to personalize its Windows environment. Ptolemy Cartography keeps a computer in its conference area for any employee or intern to use when they need one. Holly asks you to customize that computer so it is appropriate for the company. Holly is also preparing a map of Newfoundland, and wants to store current Newfoundland maps and historical map images on that computer for her employees to use as models. As you perform the following steps, note the original settings of the desktop and other items so you can restore them later. Complete the following steps:

1. Change the desktop icon settings on your computer to display the Computer and Control Panel icons in addition to the default Recycle Bin icon. Change the image for the Computer icon so that it displays any other appropriate image. Close all open windows.
2. Change the size of the desktop icons to display the icons in their smallest size.
3. Customize the Windows Sidebar to display two clocks. One clock should display the time in your time zone. Set the other clock to display the time in the Atlantic Time zone. Select clock 4 of 8, and name it Atlantic.
4. Insert the USB flash drive or other removable media containing your Data Files in the appropriate drive, and then create a shortcut to this drive on the desktop. Name the shortcut Removable Disk Shortcut.
5. Use the Removable Disk Shortcut to move the files from the Tutorial.03\Review folder to a new folder named Historical Maps in your Pictures folder.
6. On the desktop, create a shortcut to the Historical Maps folder. Then create a shortcut to the **NF Facts** text document. Test the shortcut by double-clicking the NF Facts shortcut to start Notepad and open the document.
7. Sort the desktop icons by size so that the Computer icon is the last icon in the list.
8. Change the desktop wallpaper to display any image in the Historical Maps folder.
9. Change the icon font to MS UI Gothic.
10. Save the current desktop settings as a theme named Historical, and store the theme in the Historical Maps folder.
11. Change the screen saver to play a slide show of the images in the Historical Maps folder.
12. Increase the height of the taskbar so it is about twice as high as its current setting.
13. Add the Paint icon to the Quick Launch toolbar. If necessary, modify the Quick Launch toolbar so that it displays all of its icons.
14. Change the appearance of the Start menu so that it displays small icons.
15. Change the user picture on the Start menu so it displays chess pieces.
16. Pin WordPad to the Start menu, and then change the Documents command from a link to a menu. Close all open windows.
17. Open the Start menu, and then press the Print Screen key to capture an image of your desktop with the Start menu open. Open Paint, and then press Ctrl+V to paste the image in a Paint file. Save the file as **ReviewDesktopXY**, where XY are your initials, in the Tutorial.03\Review folder provided with your Data Files.
18. Use the shortcuts on your desktop to move the Historical Maps folder from the Pictures folder on your hard disk to the Tutorial.03\Review folder provided with your Data Files. Close Paint.

19. Restore the settings on your computer. Restore the image of the Computer icon, and then display the original set of icons on the desktop. Change the size of the desktop icons to Medium, and change the font back to Segoe UI. Restore the Windows Sidebar to its original appearance. Delete the shortcut icons on the desktop. Restore the desktop wallpaper and the screen saver to their original images. Resize the taskbar to its original size, and return the Quick Launch toolbar to its default state. Lock the taskbar. Change the user picture to display the original image. Remove WordPad from the pinned items list, change the Documents command from a submenu to a link, and use large icons on the Start menu.

20. Close any open windows.

21. Submit the results of the preceding steps to your instructor, either in printed or electronic form, as requested.

| Apply | **Case Problem 1** |

Use the skills you learned in the tutorial to set up Windows for an engineering firm.

For a list of Data Files in the Case1 folder, see page 97.

Da Vinci Engineering   When Hank Van Hise started his own engineering firm in Columbus, Ohio, he named it after Leonardo da Vinci, one of his engineering heroes. Da Vinci Engineering is an environmental engineering firm that participates in public works projects such as building dams and bridges while minimizing their effect on the environment. When he is not on site, Hank manages 15 employees in an office in downtown Columbus. He has hired you to help him run the office. Because he just installed Windows Vista on the office computers, he asks you to personalize the desktop on his computer. As you perform the following steps, note the original settings of the desktop and other items so you can restore them later. Complete the following steps:

1. Change the desktop icon settings on your computer to display the Computer, User's Files, and Control Panel icons. Change the image for the User's Files icon so that it displays any other appropriate image.

2. Change the size of the desktop icons to display the icons in their largest size.

3. Open the Windows Sidebar, if necessary, and then customize it to display the Notes gadget.

4. Insert the USB flash drive or other removable media containing your Data Files in the appropriate drive, and then create a shortcut to this drive on the desktop. Name the shortcut Removable Disk Shortcut.

5. Use the Removable Disk Shortcut to move the files in the Tutorial.03\Case1 folder to a new folder named Leonardo in your Documents folder.

6. On the desktop, create a shortcut to the Leonardo folder. Then create a shortcut to the **Vasari** text document, an account of the life of Leonardo da Vinci by one of his contemporaries. Test the shortcut by double-clicking the Vasari shortcut to start Notepad and open the document.

7. Create shortcuts to two other files in the Leonardo folder.

8. Sort the desktop icons by type.

9. If you are using Windows Aero, change the color of the window title bars and borders to Graphite.

10. Open the Screen Saver Settings dialog box and select the Ribbons screen saver. Move the dialog box to the middle of the desktop. Minimize any other open windows.

11. Increase the height of the taskbar so it is about twice as high as its current setting.

12. Add the WordPad icon to the Quick Launch toolbar.

13. Change the user picture on the Start menu so it displays a robot.

14. Pin the Windows Photo Gallery program to the Start menu, and then remove the Pictures item from the Start menu.

15. Open the Start menu, and then press the Print Screen key to capture an image of your desktop with the Start menu open. Open Paint, and then press Ctrl+V to paste the image in a Paint file. Save the file as **Case1Desktop*XY***, where XY are your initials, in the Tutorial.03\Case1 folder provided with your Data Files.

16. Move the Leonardo folder to the Tutorial\Case1 folder.

17. Restore the settings on your computer. Restore the image of the User's Files icon, and then display the original set of icons on the desktop. Change the size of the desktop icons to Medium. Sort the icons by name. Delete the shortcut icons on the desktop. Restore the Windows Sidebar to its original appearance. Restore the windows to their default color and the screen saver to its original image. Return the Quick Launch toolbar to its default state, and resize the taskbar to its original size. Lock the taskbar. Change the user picture to display the original image. Remove Windows Photo Gallery from the pinned items list, and then return the Pictures item to the Start menu.

18. Close any open windows.

19. Submit the results of the preceding steps to your instructor, either in printed or electronic form, as requested.

Apply	**Case Problem 2**

Use the skills you learned in the tutorial to personalize the Windows environment for a small real estate office.

For a list of Data Files in the Case2 folder, see page 97.

B&B Realty Ed Bolton and Kevin Bestmuller own B&B Realty in Syracuse, New York, and concentrate on home sales and appraisals. One way they distinguish their business from other realty agencies is by providing computers in their downtown office and inviting people to browse real estate listings, learn about architectural styles, and find local businesses that can help them prepare a house for sale or restore a fixer-upper. Some of this information is stored on the office computers, and some, such as the Multiple Listings Service, is on the Web. You are the office manager and work with the agents and clients to use B&B Realty resources. After installing Windows Vista on all the office computers, Ed asks you to personalize the desktop so it reflects the B&B company image. As you perform the following steps, note the original settings of the desktop and other items so you can restore them later. Complete the following steps:

1. Change the desktop icon settings on your computer to display the Network and Control Panel icons in addition to the default Recycle Bin icon. Change the image for the Network icon so that it displays any other appropriate image.

2. Change the size of the desktop icons to display the icons in their smallest size.

3. Open the Windows Sidebar, if necessary, and then close all gadgets except the Clock. Add the Calendar and Contacts gadgets to the sidebar.

4. Insert the USB flash drive or other removable media containing your Data Files in the appropriate drive, and then create a shortcut to this drive on the desktop. Name the shortcut Removable Disk Shortcut.

5. Use the Removable Disk Shortcut to move the files in the Tutorial.03\Case2 folder to a new folder named Houses in the Documents folder.

6. On the desktop, create a shortcut to the Houses folder. Then create a shortcut to the **Syracuse Facts** text document. Test the shortcut by double-clicking the Syracuse Facts shortcut to start Notepad and open the document.

⊕ EXPLORE

7. Create a shortcut to WordPad on the desktop. (*Hint*: Right-click WordPad on the Start menu, point to Send To, and then click Desktop (create shortcut).

8. Create a shortcut to your printer on the desktop.

9. Arrange all of the desktop icons in a row along the top of the desktop. (*Hint*: Turn off the Auto Arrange option on the desktop shortcut menu before moving the icons.)

10. Change the desktop wallpaper to display any image in the Houses folder. Tile the image on the desktop.

11. Change the color of the window title bars and borders to teal.

12. Save the current desktop settings as a theme named B&B, and store the theme in the Houses folder.

13. Change the screen saver to Windows Energy.

14. Auto-hide the taskbar.

15. Display the Desktop toolbar on the taskbar. Add the Paint icon to the Quick Launch toolbar. Modify the Quick Launch toolbar so that it displays all of its icons.

16. Remove the Connect To item from the Start menu.

17. Close all open windows.

⟠ EXPLORE

18. Open the Start menu, and then press the Print Screen key to capture an image of your desktop with the Start menu open. Open Paint, and then press Ctrl+V to paste the image in a Paint document. Save the document as **Case2DesktopXY**, where XY are your initials, in the Tutorial.03\Case2 folder provided with your Data Files. Click File on the Paint menu bar, click Page Setup, click the Landscape option button, and change the value in the Adjust to text box to 45. Click the OK button, and then close Paint.

19. Use the printer shortcut on the desktop to print the **Case2DesktopXY** document.

20. Use the shortcuts on your desktop to move the Houses folder from the Documents folder on your hard disk to the Tutorial.03\Case2 folder provided with your Data Files.

21. Restore the settings on your computer. Restore the image of the Network icon, and then display the original set of icons on the desktop. Change the size of the desktop icons to Medium, and move them into a column on the left side of the desktop. Auto-arrange the icons. Restore the Windows Sidebar to its original appearance. Delete the shortcut icons on the desktop. Restore the desktop background and screen saver to their original images. Restore the taskbar to its default state. Restore the Start menu to its original condition.

22. Close any open windows.

23. Submit the results of the preceding steps to your instructor, either in printed or electronic form, as requested.

| Challenge | **Case Problem 3** |

Extend what you've learned to discover other ways to customize Windows for a nature conservancy.

For a list of Data Files in the Case3 folder, see page 97.

Acadia Nature Conservancy Ellie Larsen is the director of the Acadia Nature Conservancy in Augusta, Maine. The mission of the organization is to protect the most ecologically important lands and waters in Maine. Ellie organizes projects to study and preserve the natural history and diversity of Maine's plants, animals, and natural habitats. Because of your earlier work for the Acadia Nature Conservancy as a dedicated volunteer, Ellie hired you as a project assistant. Ellie recently upgraded to Windows Vista, and she asks you to customize her computer. As you perform the following steps, note the original settings of the desktop and other items so you can restore them later. Complete the following steps:

1. Change the desktop icon settings on your computer to display all of the built-in desktop icons. Change the image for the Computer icon so that it displays any other appropriate image.

2. Insert the USB flash drive or other removable media containing your Data Files in the appropriate drive, and then create a shortcut to this drive on the desktop. Name the shortcut Removable Disk Shortcut.

3. Use the Removable Disk Shortcut to move the files in the Tutorial.03\Case3 folder to a new folder named Nature in the Pictures folder.

4. On the desktop, create a shortcut to the Nature folder. Then create a shortcut to the **Driving Directions** text document. Test the shortcut by double-clicking the Driving Directions shortcut to start Notepad and open the document. Close all open windows.

✦ EXPLORE
5. On the desktop, create a shortcut to the Windows Photo Gallery program. (*Hint*: Right-drag the Windows Photo Gallery program icon from the Start menu to the desktop, and then click Create Shortcuts Here on the shortcut menu.) Use the Windows Photo Gallery shortcut to start the program and view the photos stored on your computer. Resize the Windows Photo Gallery window to display three columns of images, and then drag the window to the middle of the desktop.

✦ EXPLORE
6. Open the Windows Sidebar, if necessary, and make sure it displays only the Slide Show and Clock gadgets. Right-click the Slide Show gadget, and then click Options to open the Slide Show dialog box. Click the Folder arrow, and then click Pictures to play a slide show of the images in the Pictures folder and its subfolders. (Make sure the Include subfolders check box is selected.) Click the Shuffle pictures check box, and then click the OK button.

✦ EXPLORE
7. Add the Picture Puzzle gadget to the Sidebar. Right-click the Picture Puzzle gadget, and then click Options to open the Picture Puzzle dialog box. Display image 10 of 11 in the Picture Puzzle, and then close the Picture Puzzle dialog box.

8. Change the desktop background image to img21.jpg in the Vistas category.

9. If you are using the Aero experience, change the color of the window title bars and borders to frost.

10. Save the current desktop settings as a theme named Acadia, and store the theme in the Nature folder.

✦ EXPLORE
11. Open the Customize Start Menu dialog box, and then change the Number of recent programs to display setting to 4. Click the OK button on all open windows except for the Windows Photo Gallery window.

12. Open the Start menu, and then press the Print Screen key to capture an image of your desktop with the Start menu open. Open Paint, and then press Ctrl+V to paste the image in a Paint file. Save the file as **Case3DesktopXY**, where XY are your initials, in the Tutorial.03\Case3 folder provided with your Data Files.

13. Use the shortcuts on your desktop to move the Nature folder from the Pictures folder on your hard disk to the Tutorial.03\Case3 folder provided with your Data Files.

14. Restore the settings on your computer, and then close all open windows.

15. Submit the results of the preceding steps to your instructor, either in printed or electronic form, as requested.

Create	**Case Problem 4**

Using Figure 3-44 as a guide, personalize the desktop for a Caribbean marina developer.

There are no Data Files needed for this Case Problem.

Island Marinas   After sailing to the Cayman Islands one winter, John Chang settled in Miami, Florida, and started Island Marinas, a company that consults with the municipal governments on Caribbean islands to help them build and maintain marinas. John hired you to manage the Miami office while he travels, and you recently upgraded to Windows Vista. After working with a client in the Bahamas, John shows you a screenshot of that client's desktop. See Figure 3-44. He thinks this desktop would be appropriate for the Island Marinas computers, and asks you to re-create it on your computers.

Figure 3-44

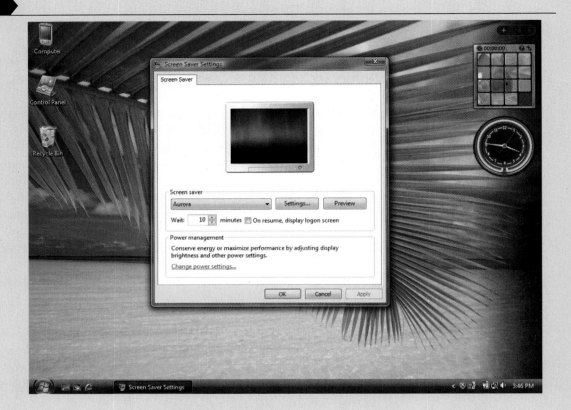

To create this Windows environment, complete the following:

1. Select the following Windows Vista settings:
   - Img19.jpg desktop background
   - Blue window and appearance color
   - Aurora screen saver
   - Sidebar open with a Clock gadget showing image 4 of 8 and the second hand displayed and with the Picture Puzzle gadget displaying image 8 of 11
   - Computer, Control Panel, and Recycle Bin desktop icons, with the Computer icon image showing a handheld computer
2. Open the Screen Saver Settings dialog box.
3. Capture an image of the desktop, and then save the image in a Paint file named **Case4DesktopXY**, where XY are your initials, in the Tutorial.03\Case4 folder provided with your Data Files.
4. Restore the original settings, and then close all open windows.
5. Submit the results of the preceding steps to your instructor, either in printed or electronic form, as requested.

| Assess | SAM Assessment and Training |

If you have a SAM user profile, you may have access to hands-on instruction, practice, and assessment of the skills covered in this tutorial. Log in to your SAM account (**http://sam2007.course.com**) to launch any assigned training activities or exams that relate to the skills covered in this tutorial.

| Review | Quick Check Answers |

Session 3.1

1. View
2. The file or resource it represents remains in its original location.
3. The Recycle Bin icon has two appearances, one when it is empty, and another when it contains deleted items.
4. The Clock, Slide Show, and Feed Headlines are three gadgets that can appear on the Sidebar by default. You can also display gadgets such as sticky notes, a calendar, and an address book.
5. false
6. 1) Drag the USB flash drive icon from the Computer or Windows Explorer window to the desktop; 2) Right-drag the USB flash drive icon from the Computer or Windows Explorer window to the desktop, and then click Create Shortcuts here; 3) Right-click the USB flash drive icon in the Computer or Windows Explorer window, point to Send To, and then click Desktop (create shortcut).

Session 3.2

1. true
2. You can use Control Panel to change the way Windows looks and behaves.
3. color schemes
4. Screen savers are entertaining and offer security by hiding your data from others.
5. The monitor displays 1024 pixels across and 768 pixels down.
6. b

Session 3.3

1. Lock the taskbar
2. Point to the area of your screen where the taskbar is usually located, which is at the bottom of the desktop by default.
3. false
4. pinned items list
5. as a menu
6. Start button, Quick Launch toolbar, middle area for taskbar buttons, and notification area

Ending Data Files

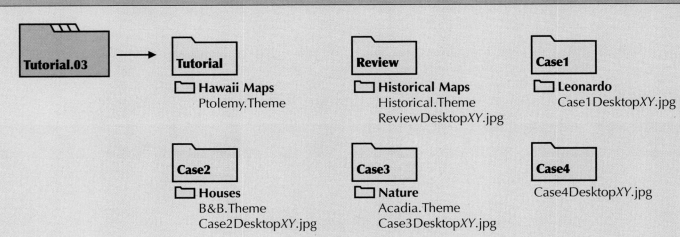

Tutorial.03 →

Tutorial
📁 **Hawaii Maps**
Ptolemy.Theme

Review
📁 **Historical Maps**
Historical.Theme
ReviewDesktop*XY*.jpg

Case1
📁 **Leonardo**
Case1Desktop*XY*.jpg

Case2
📁 **Houses**
B&B.Theme
Case2Desktop*XY*.jpg

Case3
📁 **Nature**
Acadia.Theme
Case3Desktop*XY*.jpg

Case4
Case4Desktop*XY*.jpg

Working with the Internet and E-Mail

Communicating with Others

Case | Entrée Tours

David Sanchez started Entrée Tours in Fort Collins, Colorado, to run bus and van tours in states west of the Mississippi River for low-mobility travelers. David's clients include people who ride in wheelchairs or otherwise need assistance to visit scenic destinations in Colorado and other Rocky Mountain states. The state of Colorado is especially well equipped to provide accessible travel, and David has so far focused on conducting tours to one of the many adaptive skiing and snowboarding programs available at Colorado resorts. He has formed productive partnerships with van operators and businesses that rent scooters and other wheeled forms of personal transportation.

Recently, David hired you as a travel planner to help him expand his business. In addition to Entrée Tours' popular ski and snowboard vacations, David wants to expand to offer sightseeing, birdwatching, and wilderness trips. One of your main tasks is to research western destinations that are suitable for Entrée Tours and find information that states and businesses provide for adaptive travelers. You regularly use Microsoft Internet Explorer to gather this information on the Web. You also use Windows Mail to exchange e-mail with Entrée Tours' contacts and clients. David asks you to get him up to speed in using these programs.

In this tutorial, you'll explore how the Internet and the Web work, and use Internet Explorer to visit and organize Web pages. You'll also examine e-mail technology and use Windows Mail to send, receive, and reply to e-mail messages. You'll use two programs that work with Windows Mail to help you manage your contacts and schedule.

Starting Data Files

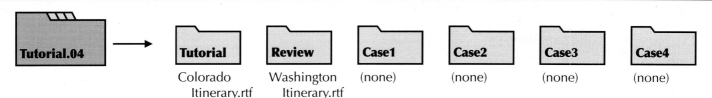

Tutorial.04 →	Tutorial	Review	Case1	Case2	Case3	Case4
	Colorado Itinerary.rtf	Washington Itinerary.rtf	(none)	(none)	(none)	(none)

Session 4.1

Exploring the Internet and the World Wide Web

When you connect two or more computers to exchange information and resources, they form a **network**. You can connect networks to each other to share information across a wide area. The worldwide, publicly accessible collection of networks is called the **Internet**, and it consists of millions of computers linked to networks all over the world. The Internet lets you access and exchange information using services such as electronic mail (e-mail), online newsgroups, file transfer, and the linked documents of the **World Wide Web**, better known as the **Web**. See Figure 4-1.

Figure 4-1	Connecting computers to the Internet

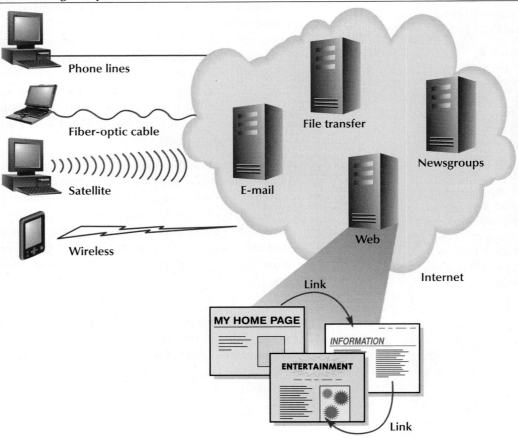

As Figure 4-1 shows, the Web is a service that the Internet provides. Whereas the Internet is a collection of networks connected by communication media such as fiber-optic cables and wireless connections, the Web is a collection of documents connected by hyperlinks. A **hyperlink** (or **link**) is text, a graphic, or combination of both in a Web document that targets another part of the document or a different document altogether. You click the link to display the targeted information. For example, in Figure 4-2, you can click links on the first Library of Congress Web document to display related information.

Web page with links to Web pages containing additional information ◀ Figure 4-2

Each hyperlinked text document—or hypertext document—on the Web is called a **Web page** and is stored on an Internet computer called a **Web server**. A **Web site** is a collection of Web pages that have a common theme or focus, such as all the pages containing information about the Library of Congress, a bookseller and its products, or a local literacy foundation. The Web is appealing because it generally displays up-to-date information in a colorful, lively format that can use sound and animation.

When you want to find information on the Web, you can use a Web directory or a search engine. A **Web directory** is a Web page that organizes links to Web sites in topical categories, such as technology or recreation. Yahoo! is a well-known Web directory. **Search engines** are Web sites that conduct searches to retrieve Web pages. To work with a search engine, you enter a word or expression as the search criterion. The search engine lists links to Web pages that fit your criterion. Popular general search engines include Google and Ask.com.

Using Web Browsers

To access documents on the Web, you need a **browser**—a program that locates, retrieves, and displays Web pages. Your browser allows you to visit Web sites around the world; interact with Web pages by clicking links; view multimedia documents; transfer files, images, and sounds to and from your computer; conduct searches for specific topics; and run programs on other computers. The browser included with Windows Vista is called Internet Explorer.

When you attempt to view a Web page, your browser locates and retrieves the document from the Web server and displays its contents on your computer. The server stores the Web page in one location, and browsers anywhere in the world can view it.

For your browser to access the Web, you must have an Internet connection. In a university setting, your connection might come from your campus network. If you are working on a home computer, you have a few options for connecting to the Internet. You might use your phone line and computer modem to establish a **dial-up connection**. More likely, you are using a **broadband connection**, a high-capacity, high-speed medium for connecting to the Internet. Popular broadband technologies include a **digital subscriber line (DSL)**, which is a high-speed connection through your telephone lines, and **digital cable**, which uses a cable modem attached to cable television lines. A **wireless connection** uses infrared light or radio-frequency signals to communicate with devices that are physically connected to a network or the Internet. Home connections also require an account with an **Internet service provider (ISP)**, a company that sells Internet access. The ISP provides instructions for connecting your computer to one of its servers, which is connected to the Internet. You can then use your browser to visit Web sites and access other Internet services.

Getting Started with Microsoft Internet Explorer

Microsoft Internet Explorer, the Web browser that comes with Windows Vista, lets you communicate, access, and share information on the Web. When you start Internet Explorer, it opens to your **home page**, the Web page a browser is set to open by default. The default home page for Internet Explorer is the MSN Web page, a Microsoft Web site with links to information and services. Your computer manufacturer or school might have set up a different home page.

Your first step in showing David how to research travel destinations is to start Internet Explorer.

To start Internet Explorer:

Tip

You can also start Internet Explorer by clicking its icon on the Quick Launch toolbar.

▶ **1.** Click the **Start** button 🔵 on the taskbar, and then click **Internet Explorer**.

Trouble If a Dial-up Connection dialog box opens, enter your user name and password, and then click the Connect button. If you do not know your user name or password, ask your instructor or technical support person for help; you must have an Internet connection to complete the steps in this tutorial.

▶ **2.** If necessary, click the **Maximize** button 🔲 to maximize the Internet Explorer window. Figure 4-3 shows the MSN main page in the Internet Explorer window. You might have a different home page.

Internet Explorer window | **Figure 4-3**

Figure 4-3 shows the following elements of the Internet Explorer window.

- **Title bar**: Shows the name of the open Web page and includes the resizing buttons
- **Toolbar**: Contains buttons you can click to perform common tasks, such as moving to the next or previous page and printing a Web page
- **Address bar**: Shows the address of the Web page; you can also type an address here.
- **Web page area**: Shows the current Web page
- **Status bar**: Shows information about the browser's actions; for example, indicates that a page is loading or is done loading
- **Live Search box**: Provides a way to search for Web pages
- **Home button**: Click to open the Web page specified as the home page for your browser.
- **Tab**: Each Web page you open can appear on a tab, letting you switch from one Web page to another.
- **URL**: Uniform resource locator; the address of the Web page you want to visit

Now you're ready to use Internet Explorer to open and view a Web page.

Opening a Page on the Web

To find a particular Web page among the billions stored on Web servers, your browser needs to know the **uniform resource locator (URL)** of the Web page. URLs are like addresses—they indicate the location of a Web page. A URL can consist of the following four parts, which are also shown in Figure 4-4:

- Protocol to use when transferring the Web page
- Address of the Web server storing the page
- Pathname of the folder containing the page
- Filename of the Web page

Figure 4-4 | **Parts of a URL**

The URL for most Web pages starts with *http*, which stands for **Hypertext Transfer Protocol**, the most common way to transfer information around the Web. (A **protocol** is a standardized procedure used by computers to exchange information.) When the URL for a Web page starts with *http://*, the Web browser uses Hypertext Transfer Protocol to retrieve the page.

The server address indicates the location of the Web server storing the Web page. In *www.loc.gov*, the *www* indicates that the server is a Web server, *loc* is the name the Library of Congress chose for this Web site, and *.gov* means that a government entity runs the Web server. Other common types of Web servers in the United States are .com (commercial), .net (network server providers or resources), .org (not-for-profit organizations), and .edu (educational institutions). The server address in a URL corresponds to an Internet Protocol (IP) address, which identifies every computer on the Internet. An **IP address** is a unique number that consists of four sets of numbers from 0 to 255 separated by periods, or dots, as in 216.35.148.4. An IP address identifies each server or computer connected to the Internet. Although computers can use IP addresses easily, they are difficult for people to remember, so domain names were created. A **domain name** identifies one or more IP addresses, such as loc.gov in Figure 4-4. URLs use the domain name in the server address part of an address to identify a particular Web site.

In addition, each file stored on Web servers has a unique pathname, just like files stored on a disk. The pathname in a URL includes the names of the folders containing the file, the filename, and its extension. The filename extension for Web pages is usually *html*, or just *htm*. In Figure 4-4, the pathname is library/index.html, which specifies a file named index.html stored in a folder named library.

Not all URLs include a pathname. If you don't specify a pathname or filename in a URL, most Web browsers open a file named index.htm or index.html, which is the default name for a Web site's main page.

Opening a Web Page Using a URL

One way to open a Web page in Internet Explorer is to provide a URL, which you can often find in advertisements, informational materials, and on the Web. When you have the URL for a Web page you want to view, you can enter it in the Address bar of Internet Explorer.

In most cases, URLs are not case sensitive, so you can enter a URL using all lowercase or all uppercase text. However, if the Web server storing a Web page uses the UNIX operating system, the URL might be case sensitive. For mixed case URLs, it's safer to enter them using the mixed case exactly as printed.

Opening a Web Page Using a URL	Reference Window

- Click the Address box on the Address bar.
- Type the URL of the Web page you want to open, and then press the Enter key.

The first Web page you want to open for David is for the Colorado State tourism office. You'll open the page by entering a URL for the New Perspectives Online Companion Web page, and then click a link on that page to go to the Colorado State tourism Web page.

To open a page on the Web using a URL:

▶ **1.** Click the **Address** box on the Address bar. The contents of the Address box, which should be the URL for your home page, are selected. Anything you now type replaces the selected URL.

   Trouble? If the contents of the Address box are not selected, drag to select the entire address.

▶ **2.** Type **www.course.com/np/vista** in the Address box, and then press the **Enter** key. Internet Explorer adds the *http://* protocol for you, and then opens the Web page for the New Perspectives on Windows Vista Online Companion.

   Trouble? If you receive a Not Found error message, you might have typed the URL incorrectly. Repeat Steps 1 and 2, making sure that the URL in the Address box matches the URL in Step 2. If you still receive an error message, ask your instructor or technical support person for help.

▶ **3.** In the list of Online Companion links, click Windows Vista, and then click the **Tutorial 4** link.

▶ **4.** Click the link for **Colorado State Tourism** to open the main page for the Colorado State tourism Web site. See Figure 4-5. This page plays a slide show of images to promote Colorado. The images you see might be different from those in the figures.

Figure 4-5   **Opening the Colorado State tourism Web page**

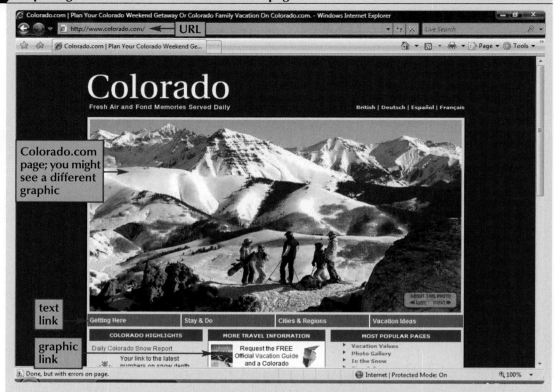

Internet Explorer confirms that you are viewing the Colorado State tourism Web page by displaying the name of the Web page in the title bar and on the page tab.

Because Web content changes frequently, the Web pages you open might differ from the figures in this tutorial.

InSight | **Home Page or Main Page?**

The term *home page* has at least two definitions. The definition already introduced in this tutorial is the Web page a browser is set to open by default. The main page for a Web site is also called a home page, though this tutorial uses *main page* to avoid confusion. On a Web site, pages link to and are organized in relation to the main page.

You can show David how to explore the information the Colorado Web site provides by navigating links on its main page.

Navigating with Links

The main page for a typical Web site includes plenty of links to help you navigate to its Web pages, and those pages also include links you can click to navigate from one page to another. Recall that links can be text, images, or a combination of both. Text links are usually colored and underlined, though the exact style can vary from one Web site to another. To determine whether something on a Web page is a link, point to it. If the pointer changes to 🖑 and a URL appears in the status bar of your Web browser, the text or image is a link you can click to open a Web page. For some graphic links, a ScreenTip also appears next to your pointer.

You'll show David how to navigate the Colorado Web site by clicking links to find information about travel destinations in Colorado that are accessible to low-mobility travelers.

To navigate a Web site using links:

▶ 1. Point to **Vacation Ideas** on the Colorado main page. The pointer changes to 🖑 and the URL for that link appears in the status bar. On this page, pointing to the Vacation Ideas link also displays a menu. See Figure 4-6.

Pointing to a link ◀ | **Figure 4-6**

Vacation Ideas menu

Vacation Ideas link

URL for the Vacation Ideas page

Trouble? If the Colorado main page does not include a Vacation Ideas link, point to any other similar link and substitute that link when you perform Step 2.

▶ 2. Click **Vacation Ideas** to open the Vacation Ideas Web page. See Figure 4-7. The Web page you open might look different.

Figure 4-7 | **Vacation Ideas Web page**

3. Click **Accessible Colorado** to open the Accessible Colorado Web page, which describes activities, transportation, and resources for low-mobility travelers.

   Trouble? If the Accessible Colorado link does not appear on the current Web page, click any other link on the page.

Besides clicking links to navigate from one Web page to another, you can use tools that Internet Explorer provides.

Navigating with Internet Explorer Tools

Recall that when you use Windows Explorer and Computer, you can click the Back and Forward buttons to navigate the devices and folders on your computer. Internet Explorer includes similar buttons. As you navigate from one Web page to another, Internet Explorer keeps track of the pages you visited. To return to the previous page, you can click the Back button. To retrace even earlier pages, continue clicking the Back button. After you click the Back button, you can click the Forward button to continue to the next page in the sequence.

You can also use the Recent Pages menu to revisit a Web page in the sequence. Click the arrow next to the Forward button, and then select a page in the list.

To return to previously viewed Web pages:

1. Click the **Back** button ⬅ to return to the Vacation Ideas Web page.

2. Click the **Forward** button ➡ to return to the Accessible Colorado page.

Trouble? If you opened different Web pages in the previous set of steps, substitute the names of the pages as appropriate in Steps 1 and 2.

▶ **3.** Click the **Recent Pages** button ☑ to open the Recent Pages menu, and then click **Colorado.com | Plan Your Colorado Weekend** to return to the Colorado main page.

▶ **4.** Close Internet Explorer.

One limitation of the Back, Forward, and Recent Pages buttons is that they apply only to your current session in the browser. If you close and then restart Internet Explorer, it starts keeping track of a fresh sequence of pages. To revisit Web pages you opened in previous sessions, you can use the History list.

Using the History List

To open any Web page you've visited in the last 20 days, you can use the History list, which is available in the Internet Explorer Favorites Center. The Favorites Center organizes Web page links and other information, including the History list. (You'll explore the Favorites Center shortly.) The History list includes the Web sites you visited today, last week, two weeks ago, and three weeks ago. You can also change the setup in the History list to view pages by date, by site, by the number of times visited, and in the order visited today. You can also search the pages in the History list to locate a specific Web site you've recently visited.

David wants to open the Web page on the Colorado Web site that provides accessibility information. Because you already closed Internet Explorer, you can't use the Back button to return to that page. You'll use the History list to revisit the Accessible Colorado Web page.

To use the History list:

▶ **1.** Start Internet Explorer.

▶ **2.** Click the **Favorites Center** button ☆ on the toolbar to open the Favorites Center.

▶ **3.** Click the **Pin the Favorites Center** ◀ button on the Favorites Center toolbar to keep the Favorites Center open.

> **Tip**
>
> To display feeds you subscribe to, click the Feeds button on the Favorites Center toolbar.

Trouble? If your Pin the Favorites Center button does not appear on your Favorites Center toolbar, the Favorites Center is already pinned to the Internet Explorer window. Skip Step 3.

▶ **4.** If the History button in the Favorites Center is not currently selected, click the **History** button to display the History list. See Figure 4-8.

Displaying the History list ◀ **Figure 4-8**

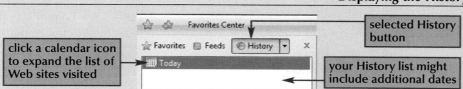

click a calendar icon to expand the list of Web sites visited

selected History button

your History list might include additional dates

Trouble? If your History list is not organized by date as shown in Figure 4-8, click the History button arrow and then click By Date.

▶ **5.** Click **Today** in the History list. The list expands to show the Web sites you visited today.

> 6. Click **colorado (www.colorado.com)** to expand the list to show the pages you visited on that Web site.
>
> 7. Click **Colorado.com | Colorado Vacation Ideas and Travel Tips for Accessible Colorado Vacations**. The corresponding Web page opens in Internet Explorer. See Figure 4-9.

Figure 4-9	**Revisiting a Web page**

Next, you want to show David how to open other Web pages without closing the Accessible Colorado Vacations Web page.

Managing Multiple Web Pages

If you want to open a new Web page without closing the one you're currently viewing, you can use **tabbed browsing**, a feature in Internet Explorer that lets you open more than one Web page in the single browser window. To use tabbed browsing, you open a tab for each new page you want to view. On the new tab, you open a Web page as you usually do. You can also open a new tab by pressing the Ctrl key as you click a link on a Web page or by right-clicking the link and then clicking Open in New Tab on the shortcut menu. You can then switch from one Web page to another by clicking their tabs. If you have two or more tabs open, you can use the Quick Tabs button to display a thumbnail of each Web page so you can see all of your open pages at once. You click a thumbnail to switch to the corresponding page. To close a tab, you click its Close button.

Now that you've explored a few pages on the Colorado tourism site, you want to compare that information to the state of Colorado Web page, which provides instructions for applying for hunting and fishing licenses, buying state park passes, reserving campsites in state parks, and other information David's clients often want to know. You'll show David how to open a new tab in Internet Explorer, and then use it to open the state of Colorado Web page.

To open a second Web page on a new tab:

▶ **1.** Click the **New Tab** button [ ] on the toolbar. (This button changes to [ ] when you point to it.) A blank page opens on the new tab. See Figure 4-10.

Opening a new tab   **Figure 4-10**

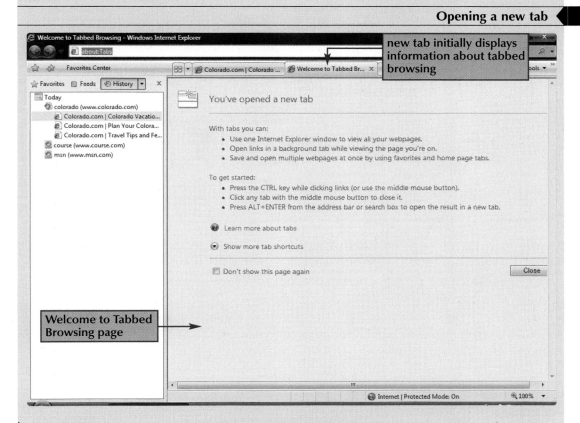

2. In the History list, click the **course (www.course.com)** folder.

3. Click the link to the **New Perspectives on Microsoft Office 2007 and Windows Vista** page. The Microsoft Windows Vista Online Companion Web page opens on the new tab.

4. Click the **Tutorial 4** link.

5. Click the **State of Colorado** link. The main page for the state of Colorado appears on the new tab. See Figure 4-11. Your Web page might differ.

Figure 4-11	State of Colorado Web page on the new tab

6. Right-click the **Visiting – Activities** link, and then click **Open Link in New Tab** on the shortcut menu. The Visiting – Activities Web page opens in a new tab.

   Trouble? If the Visiting – Activities link does not appear on the current Web page, right-click a different link on the page.

7. Click the **Quick Tabs** button 🔲 on the toolbar. Thumbnails appear showing a miniature version of each open Web page. See Figure 4-12.

Tip

You can also switch to a different Web page by clicking the Tab List button and then clicking the name of a Web page.

Thumbnails of the open Web pages | **Figure 4-12**

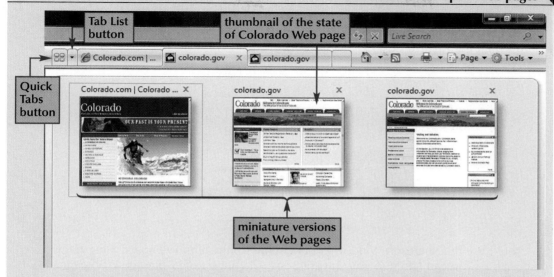

> **8.** Click the first **colorado.gov** thumbnail to display the main state of Colorado Web page.

Although tabbed browsing helps you manage open Web pages, the Favorites Center helps you organize Web pages you open often. You'll show David how to use the Favorites Center next.

Using the Favorites List

As you explore the Web, you'll find pages that are your favorites, those you visit frequently. You can save the location of your favorite Web pages in the **Favorites list**, a collection of links to the Web pages that you visit often. To display the Favorites list, you open the Favorites Center, where you can manage the Favorites list, feeds, and the History list. The Favorites list initially includes a few Web sites that Microsoft provides, such as a link to MSN.com. Your computer manufacturer might also include a few links in the Favorites list. If you find a Web page you want to visit often, you can add it to your Favorites list. When you want to retrieve one of your favorite Web pages, you can click its link in the Favorites list and display the page in your browser. As your list of favorite pages grows, you can organize the links into folders. For example, you could create a Favorites folder for travel Web sites and another for news Web sites.

To display the Favorites list:

▶ **1.** Click the **Favorites** button in the Favorites Center. Internet Explorer displays the Favorites list. See Figure 4-13. Your Favorites list might be different.

| Figure 4-13 | Displaying the Favorites list |

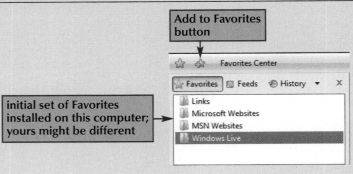

You'll use the Microsoft Windows Vista Online Companion Web page later in this tutorial, so you can add it to your Favorites list. The Accessible Colorado Web page also provides the kind of information you often need when organizing trips for Entrée Tours. You'll also add that page to the Favorites list.

Adding an Item to the Favorites List

To add a Web page to the Favorites list, you access the page in Internet Explorer, and then you use the Add to Favorites command. By default, Windows Vista adds the new page to the end of the Favorites list. If you organize the Web pages into folders, you can add a Web page to one of the folders. You can store the page using the title of the Web page as its name, or you can change the name if you like.

| Reference Window | **Adding a Web Page to the Favorites List** |

- Open the Web page in Internet Explorer.
- Click the Add to Favorites button on the toolbar, and then click Add to Favorites.
- Enter a new name for the Web page and select a folder, if necessary.
- Click the OK button.

If you are working on a network, you might not be able to change the content of the Favorites list. In that case, read through the following steps and examine the figures, but do not perform the steps.

To add Web pages to your Favorites list:

▶ **1.** In the Address box, start typing the address for the Online Companion page for this tutorial: **oc.course.com/np/Office2007/vista.cfm#tut**. After you type the first few characters, Internet Explorer displays the complete address below the Address box. Click the complete address to return to the Online Companion page for Windows Vista Tutorial 4.

▶ **2.** Click the **Add to Favorites** button 🌟 on the Favorites Center toolbar, and then click **Add to Favorites**. The Add a Favorite dialog box opens, displaying the name of the Web page in the Name text box.

▶ **3.** Type **Online Companion** in the Name text box, and then click the **Add** button. A link for the Windows Vista Online Companion appears in the Favorites list.

▶ **4.** Click the **Colorado.com** tab to open that Web page.

▶ **5.** Click the **Add to Favorites button** 🏠 and then click **Add to Favorites**.

▶ **6.** Type **Accessible Colorado** in the Name text box, and then click the **Add** button to add the Web page to the Favorites list.

Next, you can organize your favorite Web pages into folders.

Organizing the Favorites List

As you add more items to the Favorites list, you can organize its links by deleting some and moving others to new folders. Using folders is an excellent way to organize your favorite files and pages.

Organizing the Favorites List	Reference Window

- Click the Add to Favorites button on the Favorites Center toolbar, and then click Organize Favorites to open the Organize Favorites dialog box.
- To create a new folder, click the New Folder button.
- To move a link into a Favorites folder, drag the link to the folder or select the item, click the Move to Folder button, select the new folder for the item, and then click the OK button.
- To remove an item from the Favorites list, select the item, and then click the Delete button.
- Click the Close button to close the Organize Favorites dialog box.

To organize your Favorites list:

▶ **1.** Click the **Add to Favorites** button 🏠 on the Favorites Center toolbar, and then click **Organize Favorites**. The Organize Favorites dialog box opens.

▶ **2.** Click the **New Folder** button, type **Windows Vista** for the new folder name, and then press the **Enter** key.

▶ **3.** Click the **New Folder** button, type **Colorado Travel** for the new folder name, and then press the **Enter** key.

▶ **4.** In the Organize Favorites dialog box, drag the **Online Companion** link to the **Windows Vista** folder.

▶ **5.** Drag the **Accessible Colorado** link to the **Colorado Travel** folder.

▶ **6.** Click the **Close** button to close the Organize Folders dialog box. The two new links you added are now stored in the Windows Vista and Colorado Travel folders in the Favorites list. See Figure 4-14.

Tip

If the number of items in the Favorites list makes it difficult to drag links to folders, you can use the Move to Folder button in the Organize Favorites dialog box instead of dragging.

Figure 4-14   **New folders in the Favorites list**

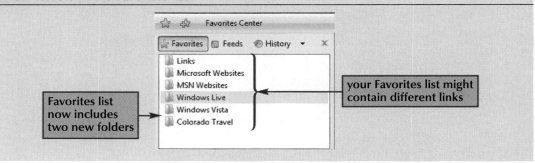

Before you finish showing David how to use Internet Explorer, he asks you to print the Visiting and Activities Web page on the state of Colorado Web site so he can use it for reference when he's away from the computer.

Printing a Web Page

If you want to refer to the information you find on the Web when you don't have computer access, you can print a Web page. Although Web pages can be any size, printers usually use 8.5 × 11-inch sheets of paper. Sometimes, Web pages include a link for printing a Web page, such as "Printer Friendly Format," indicating that the Web site formats the page for a standard size sheet of paper before printing. However, not all Web pages provide such an option. You should therefore preview the page before you print it so see how it will look when printed. In the Print dialog box, you can change the page orientation from portrait (8.5 × 11 inches) to landscape (11 × 8.5 inches) if necessary to print all the information, and specify that you want to print some or all of the document.

Before printing the Visiting and Activities Web page, you'll show David how to preview the page. You can then determine whether to print the information in portrait or landscape orientation and whether to print the entire document or only some pages.

To preview and then print a Web page:

▶   **1.** Click the second **colorado.gov** tab to display the Visiting and Activities Web page in Internet Explorer.

▶   **2.** Click the **Print button arrow** 🖨 ▾ and then click **Print Preview** to open the Print Preview window. See Figure 4-15.

Previewing a Web page before printing Figure 4-15

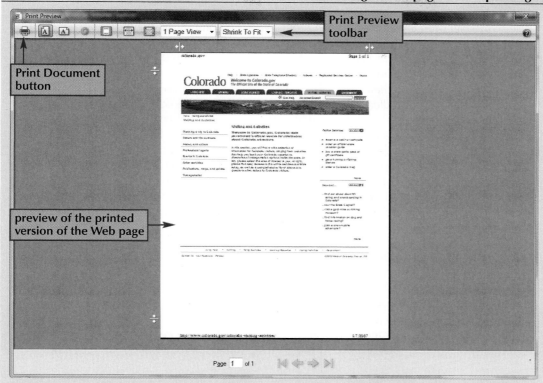

Print Preview toolbar

Print Document button

preview of the printed version of the Web page

▶ **3.** Click the **Print Document** 🖶 button to open the Print dialog box.

▶ **4.** In the Page Range section, click the **Pages** option button, and make sure the Pages text box shows "1".

  Trouble? If a value other than "1" appears in the Pages text box, select the text in the text box, and then type 1.

▶ **5.** Click the **Print** button to print the first page of the Visiting and Activities Web page.

Some printers are set up to print headers and footers in addition to the Web page itself, so when you retrieve the page from your printer, you might find the page's title, its URL, the date, and other similar information at the top and bottom of the page.

Saving Web Pages

Although a Web page appears in your browser window and you can add the page to your Favorites list or find it in your History list, the page itself is still stored on a remote computer (a computer located elsewhere on the Internet). You can save the Web page and store it on your computer by clicking the Page button on the Internet Explorer toolbar, and then clicking Save As. You can also save a graphic image displayed on a Web page. However, doing so is not always legal or ethical. Many of the images displayed on Web pages are the intellectual property of someone else, usually the person who took the photograph, commissioned the logo, or created the drawing. Just as owners have rights to physical property, creators of intellectual property (original works including art and photographs) have rights to their work. You need to be aware of these **intellectual property rights** because Web content such as software, video, music, and images are easy to copy in their digital form. However, if this material is protected by copyright, you usually cannot copy or share it unless you receive permission from the owner. The term **copyright** applies to the originator's exclusive legal right to reproduce, publish, or sell intellectual property. Copyright laws protect intellectual property—if you copy someone else's work without giving that person credit, you are committing plagiarism.

Before you copy or save the graphics, images, sounds, videos, or other information on Web sites that you visit, you need to find out if and how you can use the materials. If you want to use material you find on a Web site, first get permission from the owner of the site. Often, Web sites include their copyright and permission-request information on their main pages. Some Web sites indicate that the material is free, but almost everything on the Internet is copyrighted. Even if you think that information or material you found is not copyrighted, you should always request permission to use it. You might be able to copy a photo to your computer, for example, but you don't have the right to reproduce it in your own work.

As you examine the permission information on Web sites, you might encounter the term **fair use**. This term applies to material that can be used for educational or nonprofit purposes, as opposed to commercial profit. Information that is considered factual or materials that are so old that copyright protection no longer applies fall under the category of fair use. You should still give credit to any Web site that you use in your research.

Because you printed the information David needs, you don't need to save the Visiting and Activities Web page or any of its content. You can also access this page later by using your Favorites list. You're ready to close Internet Explorer. If you only have one tab open, you close Internet Explorer the way you do any other program: click the Close button on the title bar. If more than one tab is open, however, you can choose to close a tab to leave a Web page instead of closing the entire program. To close the tab for the current Web page, you click the Close Tab button. If you have more than one tab open and exit Internet Explorer, it asks if you want to close all tabs before exiting the program.

To close tabs and exit Internet Explorer:

▶ **1.** Point to the tab for the Visiting and Activities Web page, and then click the **Close Tab** button ☒ . The Visiting and Activities Web page closes.

▶ **2.** Click the **Close** button ▭☒▭ on the Internet Explorer title bar. A dialog box opens and asks if you want to close all tabs.

▶ **3.** Click the **Close Tabs** button to close the remaining two tabs and exit Internet Explorer.

So far, you have learned about the structure of the Internet and the Web and how to use Internet Explorer to open, navigate, and organize Web pages. In the next session, you'll use another service the Internet provides—e-mail.

Review | **Session 4.1 Quick Check**

1. Explain the relationship of the Internet and the Web.
2. A _____ _____ is a collection of Web pages that have a common theme or focus.
3. True or False. A browser is a program that lets you create and publish Web pages.
4. When you start Internet Explorer, what does it display by default?
5. The address of a Web page is called a(n) _____ .
6. Name two ways to open a Web page in Internet Explorer.
7. Describe three ways you can open a Web page you visited recently.
8. True or False. The Favorites list includes only those links that Microsoft or your computer manufacturer initially provided.

Session 4.2

Getting Started with Windows Mail

Windows Mail, one of the tools that comes with Windows Vista, allows you to send, receive, and manage **electronic mail** or **e-mail**—electronic messages transferred between users on a network such as the Internet. You can send e-mail to and receive e-mail from anyone in the world who has an e-mail address, regardless of the operating system or type of computer the person is using.

Examining How E-Mail Works

An **e-mail message** is a simple text document that you can compose and send using an **e-mail program**, such as Windows Mail. When you send a message, it travels from your computer, through the network, and arrives at a computer called an **e-mail server**. Typically, the system administrator of your network or ISP manages the e-mail server.

The e-mail server stores the e-mail messages until the recipients request them. Then the server forwards the messages to the appropriate computers. Because e-mail uses this **store-and-forward technology**, you can send messages to anyone on the network, even if they don't have their computers turned on. When it's convenient, your recipients log on to the network and use their e-mail programs to receive and read their messages. Figure 4-16 illustrates sending and receiving e-mail messages.

Sending and receiving e-mail ◀ Figure 4-16

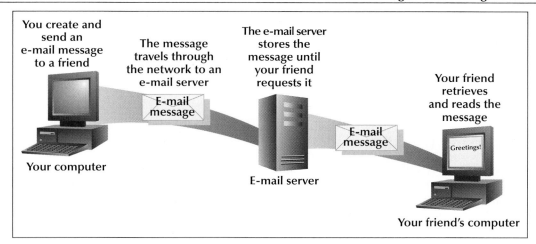

As Figure 4-16 shows, to send and receive e-mail, you must be able to access an e-mail server on the network. If your computer is part of a network at a college or university, for example, you log on to the network to access its services. An e-mail server provides mail services to faculty, staff, and students who have access to the network. When someone sends you a message, it is stored on your e-mail server until you log on to the network and use an e-mail program to check your mail. The e-mail server then transfers new messages to your electronic mailbox. You use an e-mail program to open, read, print, delete, reply to, forward, and save the mail.

If your computer is not part of a network, you can access an e-mail server on the Internet. To do so, you open an **e-mail account** with a service that provides Internet access. For example, e-mail accounts are included as part of the subscription fee for most ISPs. E-mail accounts are also provided free of charge by advertiser-supported Web sites, such as Yahoo! and Google. After you establish an e-mail account, you can connect to the Internet to send and receive your e-mail messages.

Addressing E-Mail

Just as you must address a piece of ordinary mail, you need to supply an address for an e-mail message. The e-mail address you enter directs the message to its destination. Your e-mail address is included in the message as the return address, so your recipients can easily respond to your message. Anyone who has an e-mail address can send and receive electronic mail. If you work for a company or attend a school that provides e-mail, a system administrator probably assigns an e-mail address for you. Other times, you create your own e-mail address, though it must follow a particular format. See Figure 4-17.

| Figure 4-17 | **Typical format of an e-mail address** |

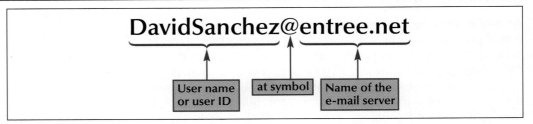

The **user name**, or **user ID**, is the name entered when your e-mail account is set up. The @ symbol signifies that the e-mail server name is provided next. In Figure 4-17, *DavidSanchez* is the user name and *entree.net* is the e-mail server.

The easiest way to learn a person's e-mail address is to ask the person. You can also look up an e-mail address in a network or Internet directory. Most businesses and schools publish a directory listing e-mail addresses of those who have e-mail accounts on their network. Many Web sites also provide e-mail directories for people with e-mail accounts on the Internet, such as *www.worldemail.com* and *www.people.yahoo.com*.

When you sign up for an e-mail account, you can send your new e-mail address to friends, colleagues, and clients. If your e-mail address changes, such as when you change e-mail services, you can subscribe to an e-mail forwarding service so you don't miss any mail sent to your old address.

Observing E-Mail Etiquette

Because e-mail is a widespread form of communication, you should follow standard guidelines when using e-mail. Most of these guidelines are commonsense practices, such as using appropriate language. Others might be new to you. For example, you should understand that e-mail is not private. When you correspond with others using e-mail, the information you send can be read by other users, especially if you work for a corporation or private institution. Your correspondents can easily forward your message to others, deliberately or inadvertently revealing information you consider confidential. It's a good idea to be professional and courteous about what you say to and about others.

Another guideline is to provide meaningful information in the subject line. Most e-mail programs show the subject line, date, and sender address for incoming mail. Let your correspondents know the purpose of your message by including information in the subject line that concisely and accurately describes the message contents. For example, a subject such as "Staff meeting rescheduled" is more informative than "Meeting."

Keep the following guidelines in mind when you are composing e-mail messages so that you use e-mail to communicate effectively, without offending or annoying your correspondents.

- **Reply only as necessary**. When you want to respond to an e-mail message, you can click the Reply button to reply to the original sender or you can click the Reply All button to respond to everyone who received the original message. When you use the Reply All button, make sure that everyone listed as recipients really needs to receive the message so that you are not flooding electronic inboxes with unnecessary e-mails.
- **Include your response first**. When you reply to an e-mail, you can include text from the original message. If you do, make sure that your response is at the top of the message so your recipients can find it easily.
- **State your subject clearly**. As mentioned earlier, include a brief summary of your message in the subject line so your recipients know what it's about.
- **Don't e-mail sensitive or confidential information**. Keep in mind that e-mail is not private, and your recipients can forward your message to others, either intentionally or accidentally.
- **Be concise and direct**. People often read e-mail messages while they are doing something else. As a courtesy to your correspondents and to make sure your message is read, get right to the point and keep your messages short.
- **Avoid abbreviations**. Although you should strive to be brief, don't overcompensate by using nonstandard abbreviations. Stick to the abbreviations that are common in business writing, such as FYI and ASAP.
- **Don't use all capital letters**. Using all capital letters as in "SEND ME THE REPORT TODAY" makes it look like you're shouting and can be difficult to read.
- **Pause and reread before sending**. Be sure to read the e-mails you write before you send them, and consider how they could be received. A message that you intend to be funny could be misinterpreted as rude. If you wrote an e-mail in anger, calm down and revise your message before sending it. After you send an e-mail message, you can't retrieve or stop it.

Setting Up Windows Mail

To use e-mail, you need an Internet connection, an e-mail program such as Windows Mail, and an e-mail address. Make sure you have an Internet connection and e-mail address before performing the steps in this section. Windows Vista provides Windows Mail, so you don't need to install that e-mail program separately.

After you set up an account with an e-mail service provider (usually this is your ISP), you add your account to Windows Mail so you can use it to exchange e-mail. If you are in a university or other institution, this has probably been done for you, but if you are using your own computer, you probably have to add it yourself. At a minimum, Windows Mail needs to know your e-mail address, password, and the names of your incoming and outgoing e-mail servers. The type of server you specify corresponds to the type of account you have with your service provider. Windows Mail supports the following types of e-mail accounts:

- **Post Office Protocol 3 (POP3):** These servers hold incoming e-mail messages until you check your e-mail; then they deliver it to your computer. After delivering messages, e-mail servers usually delete them. POP3 is the most common account type for personal e-mail.

- **Internet Message Access Protocol (IMAP)**: With this type of account, your e-mail is stored on an e-mail server, not on your computer. You can access your e-mail directly on the server, and then preview, delete, and organize messages. IMAP is usually used for business e-mail accounts.
- **Simple Mail Transfer Protocol (SMTP)**: These accounts are for outgoing e-mail. You use them with a POP3 or IMAP account for incoming e-mail.

The first time you start Windows Mail, a series of dialog boxes guides you through the process of setting up an account. The following steps show you how to set up a Windows Mail account. If you already have an e-mail account, read but do not perform the following steps.

David Sanchez has an e-mail account with Entrée Tours, but he hasn't set up Windows Mail to use that account. Because this is the first time you're starting Windows Mail on his Windows Vista computer, you'll show him how to set up Windows Mail to use his Entrée Tours account.

Tip

If Windows Mail is your default e-mail program, you can start it by clicking the Start button and then clicking E-mail.

To set up Windows Mail:

▶ **1.** Click the **Start** button ⊕ on the taskbar, point to **All Programs**, and then click **Windows Mail**. The Windows Mail program starts. If this is the first time you started Windows Mail, the Your Name dialog box opens, requesting your display name.

Trouble? If you have already set up Windows Mail, the main Windows Mail window opens instead of the Your Name dialog box. Read but do not perform the rest of the steps.

Trouble? If the main Windows Mail window opens instead of the Your Name dialog box and you have not set up an e-mail account yet, click Tools on the menu bar, click Accounts, click the Add button, click E-mail Account, and then click the Next button to open the Your Name dialog box.

Trouble? If a dialog box opens asking if you want Windows Mail to be your default mail program, click the Yes button only if you are using your own computer and want to use Windows Mail as your mail program. If you are using a school or institutional computer, click the No button or ask your technical support person for assistance.

▶ **2.** Enter the name you want to appear as the sender of the e-mails you send, such as **David Sanchez**. Click the **Next** button. The Internet E-mail Address dialog box opens.

▶ **3.** Enter your e-mail address, such as **DavidSanchez@entree.net**, and then click the **Next** button. The Set up e-mail servers dialog box opens.

▶ **4.** Click the **Incoming e-mail server type arrow**, if necessary, to select the type of incoming e-mail server you use. (Your ISP typically provides this information.) Enter the name of your incoming e-mail server, such as **pop.entree.net**, and your outgoing e-mail server, such as **smtp.entree.net**. If your server requires a user name and password when sending mail in addition to when receiving it, click the **Outgoing server requires authentication** check box.

▶ **5.** Click the **Next** button. The Internet Mail Logon dialog box opens.

▶ **6.** Enter your e-mail user name and password. (Your ISP might provide this information initially, though you can often change it.) Click the **Next** button.

▶ **7.** The Congratulations dialog box opens. If you do not want to download your e-mail now, click the **Do not download my e-mail at this time** check box. Click the **Finish** button.

Trouble? If a dialog box opens asking if you want to import mail from another e-mail program, do not import the e-mail unless your instructor indicates that you should do so.

Now you can show David how to send and receive e-mail.

Sending and Receiving E-Mail Using Windows Mail

The Windows Mail program installs with Windows Vista so you can compose, send, and receive e-mail messages. After you set up an e-mail account, you're ready to start using Windows Mail to manage your e-mail.

To start Windows Mail:

▶ **1.** Start Windows Mail, if necessary. (Click the **Start** button 🪟 on the taskbar, point to **All Programs**, and then click **Windows Mail**.) The main Windows Mail program window opens. See Figure 4-18. The e-mail account shown in the figures in this tutorial belongs to David Sanchez. Your screens will therefore look different from the figures.

Windows Mail window ◄ **Figure 4-18**

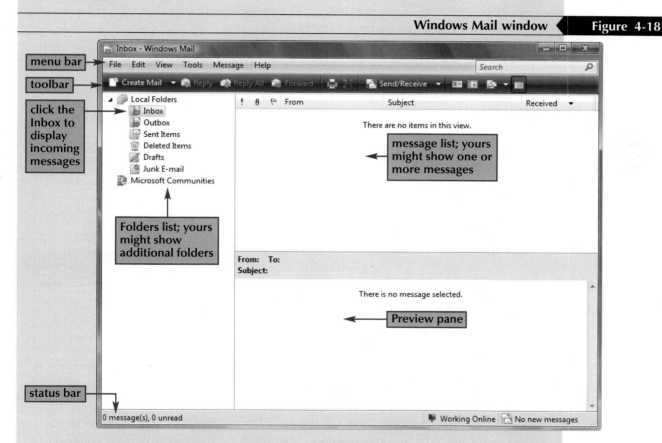

Trouble? If the Folders list does not appear in the Windows Mail window, click View on the menu bar, click Layout, click the Folder List check box, and then click the OK button.

Trouble? If this is the first time you started Windows Mail, your Inbox contains a Welcome message from Microsoft Windows Mail. You do not need to do anything with this message now.

In addition to the standard Windows components, such as the title bar, Close button, and scroll bars, the Windows Mail window includes the following elements:

- **Menu bar**: Provides menus of commands for working with e-mail, accounts, and Windows Mail
- **Search box**: Lets you find e-mail messages by searching for text contained in any part of the message
- **Toolbar**: Provides buttons for frequently performed commands, such as creating, replying to, and forwarding e-mail
- **Folders list**: Displays the default Windows Mail folders, including the Inbox, Outbox, Sent Items, Deleted Items, Drafts, and Junk E-mail folders. Windows Mail organizes your e-mail into these folders automatically. You can create additional folders for the messages you create and receive.
- **Message list:** When you start Windows Mail, it displays a list of the messages in your Inbox by default. These are the messages you've received. If you select a different folder, Windows Mail displays those messages in the list.
- **Preview pane**: Displays the contents of the selected message

Now that you've identified the parts of the Windows Mail window, you're ready to show David how to create and send a message.

Creating and Sending E-Mail Messages

An e-mail message uses a format similar to a standard memo: it typically includes Date, To, and Subject lines, followed by the content of the message. The To line indicates who will receive the message. Windows Mail automatically supplies the date you send the message in the Date line (as set in your computer's clock). If more than one account is set up in Windows Mail, a From line might appear so you can select the account you want to use for sending the message. The Subject line, although optional, alerts the recipient to the topic of the message. Finally, the message area contains the content of your message. You can also include additional information, such as a Cc line, which indicates who will receive a copy of the message, or a Priority setting, which indicates the importance of the message.

InSight | **Using the Cc and Bcc Lines**

In the To line, restrict the e-mail addresses to those of your primary recipients. Use the Cc (courtesy copy) line for secondary recipients who should receive a copy of the message. If you are sending an e-mail message to a large group of people, use the Bcc (blind courtesy copy) line. (Click the Cc button to specify that you want to use an additional Bcc line.) Windows Mail sends an individual message to each person listed in the Bcc line, and the only other e-mail address that appears is the sender's.

To send an e-mail message, you first compose the message and then click the Send button on the message window. Windows Mail sends the message from your computer to your e-mail server, which routes it to the recipient.

Creating and Sending an E-Mail Message

- Click the Create Mail button on the toolbar.
- Enter the e-mail address of the recipient in the To box.
- Click the Subject box and then type the subject of the message.
- Click the message area and then type the content of the message.
- Click the Send button.

To create and send an e-mail message:

▶ **1.** Click the **Create Mail** button on the Windows Mail toolbar. The New Message window opens. See Figure 4-19.

New Message window ◀ **Figure 4-19**

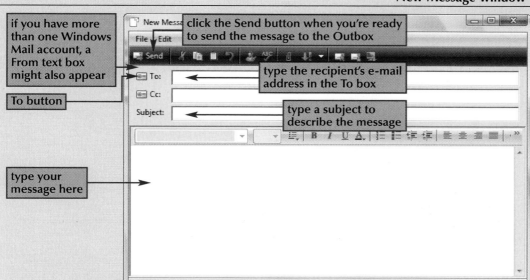

if you have more than one Windows Mail account, a From text box might also appear

To button

click the Send button when you're ready to send the message to the Outbox

type the recipient's e-mail address in the To box

type a subject to describe the message

type your message here

▶ **2.** Type your e-mail address in the To text box.

Trouble? If you're not sure what e-mail address you should enter, check with your instructor or technical support person.

▶ **3.** Click the **Subject** text box, and then type **Test e-mail**.

▶ **4.** Click in the message area, type **This is just a practice test message**, press the **Enter** key, and then type your name.

▶ **5.** Click the **Send** button on the toolbar. Windows Mail places the message in the Outbox. After a few moments, Windows Mail removes the message from the Outbox, sends the message to your e-mail server, and then places a copy of the sent message in the Sent Items folder.

To make sure your message has been sent, you can open the Sent Items folder to see all the messages you have sent.

Trouble? If, after several seconds have passed, Windows Mail still displays "(1)" to the right of the Outbox folder in the Folders list, indicating that there is one unsent message, then Windows Mail is not configured to send messages immediately. In that case, click the Send/Receive button on the toolbar to send your message.

> **6.** Click the **Sent Items** folder in the Folders list. Your message appears in the right pane of the Windows Mail window. See Figure 4-20.

| Figure 4-20 | Sent Items folder |

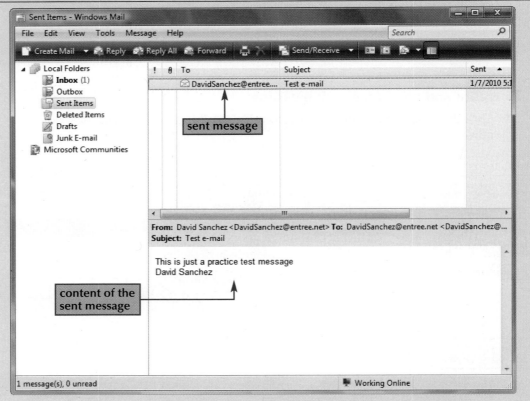

If you had wanted to send this message to many people, you could have typed more than one e-mail address in the To or Cc text boxes. You must separate each address with a comma or semicolon. You can also add the e-mail addresses of people (your contacts) to Windows Contacts, which you'll do shortly.

Receiving and Reading E-Mail Messages

Windows Mail automatically checks to see if you've received e-mail whenever you start the program and periodically after that. (Every 30 minutes is the default.) Windows Mail also checks for received e-mail when you click the Send/Receive button. E-mail you receive appears in your Inbox. By default, the Inbox shows only the name of the sender, the subject, and the date you received the message. Mail you have received but have not read yet appears in bold. To preview a message, you click the message in the list to display its contents in the Preview pane, or you can double-click the message to open it in a separate window. In either case, you can print the messages you receive.

▶ **2.** Click the **Send/Receive** button on the toolbar. Windows Mail retrieves your messages from your e-mail server, routes them to your Inbox, and displays the number of unread messages to the right of the Inbox folder. The content of the selected message appears in the Preview pane. See Figure 4-21. Your Inbox folder might contain additional e-mail messages from other people.

Inbox folder ◀ **Figure 4-21**

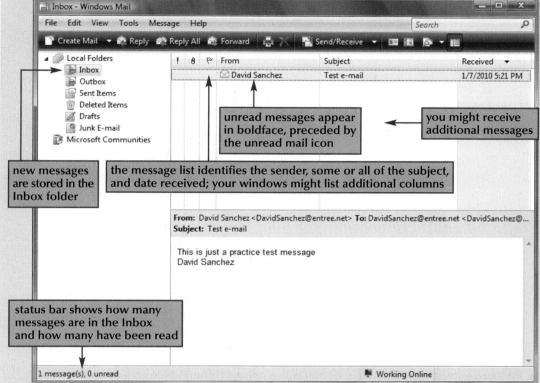

new messages
are stored in the
Inbox folder

unread messages appear
in boldface, preceded by
the unread mail icon

the message list identifies the sender, some or all of the subject,
and date received; your windows might list additional columns

you might receive
additional messages

status bar shows how many
messages are in the Inbox
and how many have been read

Trouble? If a dialog box opens requesting your user name and password, enter the information and continue with Step 3. See your instructor or technical support person if you need help entering the correct user name or password.

Trouble? If the message you sent doesn't appear in the Inbox, wait a few minutes, and then click the Send/Receive button again.

Trouble? If you received more than one message, click Test e-mail in the message list to display the message in the Preview pane.

▶ **3.** Double-click **Test e-mail** in the message list. The Test e-mail message window opens. See Figure 4-22.

Figure 4-22 ▶ **Reading a message**

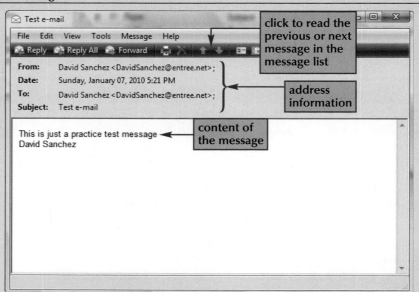

4. Read the message, and then click the **Close** button [X] to close the Test e-mail window.

When you are working with e-mail in your Inbox, you can change the width of the columns in the message list by dragging the dividing line between column headers. You can also click a column button to sort columns. For example, if you click the From column button, Windows Mail sorts messages in the current folder alphabetically by name. The default sort order is by date and time received, with newest messages at the beginning of the list.

Next, you'll show David how to perform another common e-mail task—replying to the messages you receive.

Replying to E-Mail Messages

Some of the e-mail you receive asks you to provide information, answer questions, or confirm decisions. Instead of creating a new e-mail message, you can reply directly to a message that you receive. When you reply to a message, Windows Mail inserts the e-mail address of the sender and the subject into the proper lines in the message window, and includes the text of the original message.

InSight	**Using Reply and Reply All**

You can reply to messages by clicking the Reply or Reply All button. If the original message was sent to more than one person, click the Reply button to respond to only the original sender. Use the Reply All button to respond to all the other recipients as well. Keep in mind the e-mail etiquette guideline about using the Reply All button carefully so that the only messages people receive from you are those they need to read.

You can reply to an open message or to one selected in your message list.

To reply to the Test e-mail message:

▶ **1.** With the Test e-mail message selected in the message list, click the **Reply** button on the toolbar. The Re: Test e-mail window opens. See Figure 4-23.

Replying to a message ◀ **Figure 4-23**

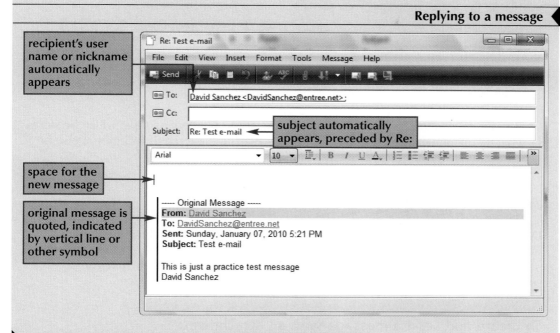

recipient's user name or nickname automatically appears

subject automatically appears, preceded by Re:

space for the new message

original message is quoted, indicated by vertical line or other symbol

▶ **2.** In the message area, type **This test was successful**.

▶ **3.** Click the **Send** button on the toolbar. If necessary, click the **Send/Receive** button on the toolbar to send the message.

Depending on his preferences, David might want to delete the e-mail messages he's read. You'll show him how to delete e-mail messages next.

Deleting E-Mail Messages

After you read and respond to your messages, you can delete any message you no longer need. When you delete a message, it moves to the Deleted Items folder. Messages remain in the Deleted Items folder until you empty, or permanently delete, the folder contents. This folder might be set up to permanently delete its contents when you close Windows Mail. If not, you should do so periodically by right-clicking the Deleted Items folder in the Folders list, clicking Empty 'Deleted Items' Folder on the shortcut menu, and then clicking the Yes button to confirm the deletion.

To delete the Test e-mail message:

▶ **1.** Click **Test e-mail** in the message list, and then click the **Delete** button ✕ on the toolbar. The Inbox message list no longer displays the Test message.

InSight | **Dealing with Junk E-Mail**

Junk e-mail, or spam, is unsolicited e-mail, often containing advertisements, fraudulent schemes, or legitimate offers. Windows Mail includes a junk e-mail filter that analyzes the content of the e-mail messages you receive and moves suspicious messages to the Junk E-mail folder, where you can examine and manage them as necessary. To reduce the amount of junk e-mail you receive, avoid posting your e-mail address on Web sites or other public areas of the Internet. If a Web site requests your e-mail address, read its privacy statement to make sure it doesn't disclose your e-mail address to others. Finally, never respond to junk e-mail—you're likely to receive even more spam.

David mentions that clients often request itineraries of upcoming trips, which he stores in separate documents. You'll show him how to attach a file to an e-mail message so he can reply to clients and provide the documents they request.

Attaching a File to a Message

Besides sending e-mail to others, you can also transfer files by attaching the files to messages. You can send any kind of file, including documents, pictures, music, or videos.

You'll show David how to send and open an e-mail message that includes an attachment. As before, you'll create a test message and send it to yourself.

To create and send a message with an attachment:

▶ 1. Click the **Create Mail** button on the toolbar.

▶ 2. Type your e-mail address in the To box.

▶ 3. Click the **Subject** box, and then type **Itinerary you requested**.

▶ 4. Click the **Attach File To Message** button 📎 on the toolbar. The Open dialog box opens.

▶ 5. Navigate to the **Tutorial.04\Tutorial** folder provided with your Data Files, and then double-click **Colorado Itinerary**. Windows Mail attaches the file to the message. See Figure 4-24.

Attaching a file to a message ◀ **Figure 4-24**

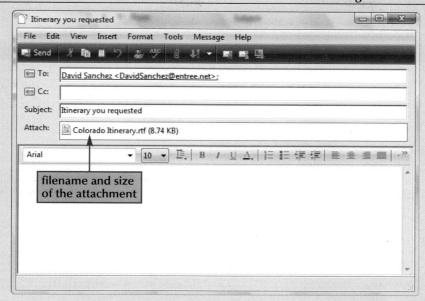

filename and size
of the attachment

▶ **6.** In the message area, type **This is a test e-mail message with a file attachment.**

▶ **7.** Click the **Send** button on the toolbar.

 Trouble? If a Spelling dialog box opens indicating that a word you typed is not in the dictionary, click the Ignore button.

▶ **8.** If necessary, click the **Send/Receive** button on the toolbar to send the message.

When you receive a message that contains an attachment, you can choose to save or open the attached file. You should open files only from people you know and trust—some people spread harmful software, called **viruses**, in e-mail attachments. To open the file, you need to make sure the program used to create the attachment is installed on your computer. If it's not, you can sometimes use a text editor, such as Word-Pad or Notepad, to open and read the attached file.

The Colorado Itinerary document you attached to the test message is a text file, so you can open it on your computer.

To receive and open a message with an attachment:

▶ **1.** When the Itinerary you requested message appears in your Inbox, click the message in the message list so the contents appear in the Preview pane.

 Trouble? If the message you sent doesn't appear in the Inbox, wait a few minutes, and then click the Send/Receive button.

▶ **2.** Click the **paper clip** icon in the Preview pane to display a list of attachments and options, including those for saving or opening the attachment. See Figure 4-25.

Figure 4-25 | Message with a file attachment

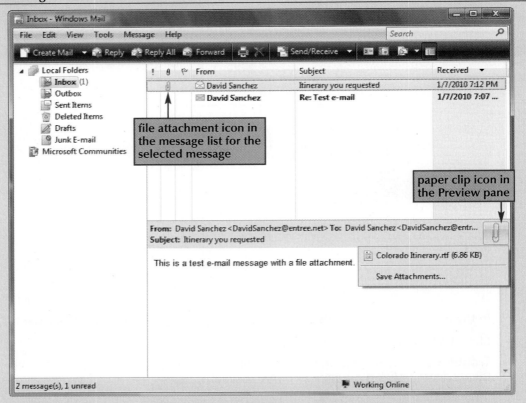

3. Click **Colorado Itinerary.rtf (6.86 KB)**. The file opens in a word-processing pro-gram, such as Word or WordPad. You could save the document now if necessary.

   Trouble? If a message box appears and asks if you want to open the file, click the Open button.

4. Close the word-processing program.

InSight | **Avoiding E-Mail Viruses**

Windows Mail blocks certain types of file attachments that are commonly used to spread e-mail viruses, including files with the following filename extensions: .exe, .pif, and .scr. If Windows Mail blocks an attachment in an e-mail message, an Information bar appears below the toolbar and displays a message letting you know that it has blocked an attachment. If you need to send a file to someone, check to see if it has a blocked filename extension. If it does, compress the file in a zip folder—Windows Mail does not block attach-ments with a .zip extension by default.

Another bit of e-mail etiquette applies to attachments. If you attach a large file to an e-mail message, it might take a long time for your recipient to download your message. Most e-mail servers limit the size of the files you can attach; some allow files no larger than 1 MB. Check with your correspondents before sending large file attachments to find out about size restrictions and set up a convenient time to send the attachment.

Adding Information to Windows Contacts

You can use Windows Contacts to keep track of all your e-mail correspondents—it works like an address book for Windows Mail. You can also use Windows Contacts on its own to save information about people and organizations. In addition to storing e-mail addresses, you can store related information such as street addresses, home phone numbers, and personal information such as anniversaries and birthdays. When you create an e-mail message, you can click the To button to open a dialog box listing your contacts. Click the name you want, and then click the To button to indicate that you want to send a message to this contact.

You can add contact information to Windows Contacts by creating a new contact, and then entering as much information as you want about that contact in the contact's Properties dialog box. When you send an e-mail message to someone, you can add their information to Windows Contacts by right-clicking their e-mail address and then clicking Add Sender to Contacts.

To retrieve a contact's information and address for an e-mail message quickly, you can give the contact a nickname. When you enter the nickname as the recipient of an e-mail message, Windows Mail enters the correct e-mail address. You can also add pictures to contacts, making it easier to identify and remember people.

> **Tip**
>
> To use Windows Contacts on its own, click the Start button, point to All Programs, and then click Windows Contacts.

Adding a Contact in Windows Mail | Reference Window

- Click Tools on the menu bar, and then click Windows Contacts.
- Click the New Contact button on the toolbar.
- Enter contact information in the Properties dialog box for the new contact.
- Click OK.

or

- Click an e-mail message in the message list.
- Click Tools on the menu bar, and then click Add Sender to Contacts.
- Enter contact information in the Properties dialog box for the new contact.
- Click OK.

You'll show David how to use Windows Contacts in Windows Mail to add a new contact.

To add a contact:

▶ 1. Click the **Contacts** button 🖼 on the Windows Mail toolbar. The Contacts window opens, listing your contacts. Because you sent an e-mail to yourself, you are already listed in the Contacts window.

▶ 2. Click the **New Contact** button on the toolbar. The Properties dialog box opens to the Name and E-mail tab. See Figure 4-26.

Figure 4-26 **Entering contact information**

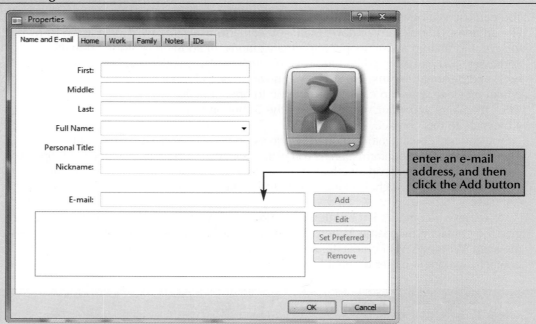

enter an e-mail address, and then click the Add button

3. Type **David** in the First text box, press the **Tab** key twice, and then type **Sanchez** in the Last text box.

4. Click the **Nickname** text box, and then type **David Sanchez**.

5. Click the **E-mail** text box, type **DavidSanchez@entree.net**, click the **Add** button, and then click the **OK** button.

6. Click **David Sanchez** in the list to view his detailed contact information. See Figure 4-27.

Adding a new contact **Figure 4-27**

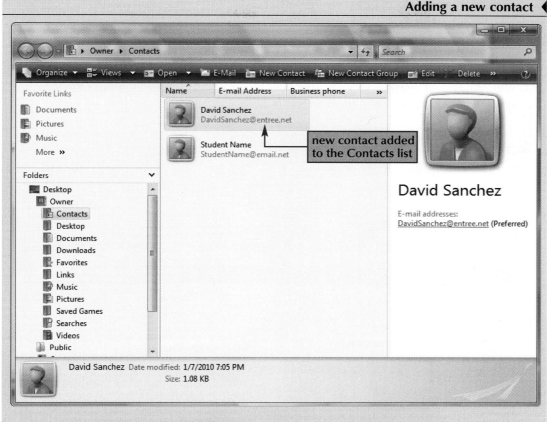

▶ **7.** Click the **Close** button ▗X▖ to close the Contacts window.

You're finished showing David how to use Windows Mail to exchange e-mail. Next, you want to help him manage his schedule with the Windows Calendar.

Managing Your Schedule with Windows Calendar

Windows Calendar is another tool available in Windows Mail and on its own. You use it to schedule appointments, track tasks, and stay on top of deadlines. Windows Calendar also lets you schedule recurring events, such as weekly staff meetings, and set reminders so you don't miss an important appointment. When you schedule an event, Windows Calendar blocks out the time in your schedule, helping you avoid scheduling conflicts.

You can also use Windows Calendar to subscribe to Web calendars, which you can share with others who have Web access. Windows Calendar works with calendars in the iCalendar format (.ics). Many major sports teams, television and radio shows, and academic institutions offer calendars in this format on the Internet that include events such as games, shows, lectures, and other special events. When you subscribe to one of these calendars, you can set how often you want to update your personal calendar with the subscription calendar's event dates.

In Windows Calendar, you can enter either appointments or tasks. Appointments take place at a specified time and place and have a duration, such as one hour or all day. Tasks are activities you want to complete within a particular period of time. Tasks have start and end dates, but don't have to be performed at a certain time.

Because David works so often at his computer, he is ready to use an electronic calendar full time. You'll show him how to start Windows Calendar, schedule an appointment, add a task to his task list, and then personalize the view of his calendar.

Starting Windows Calendar

Tip

To use Windows Calendar on its own, click the Start button, point to All Programs, and then click Windows Calendar.

As with Windows Contacts, you can start Windows Calendar on its own from the Start menu or when you're working in Windows Mail.

To start Windows Calendar:

▶ **1.** Click the **Windows Calendar** button 🔳 on the Windows Mail toolbar. The Windows Calendar window opens, showing your schedule for the day. See Figure 4-28.

Figure 4-28 ▶ **Windows Calendar**

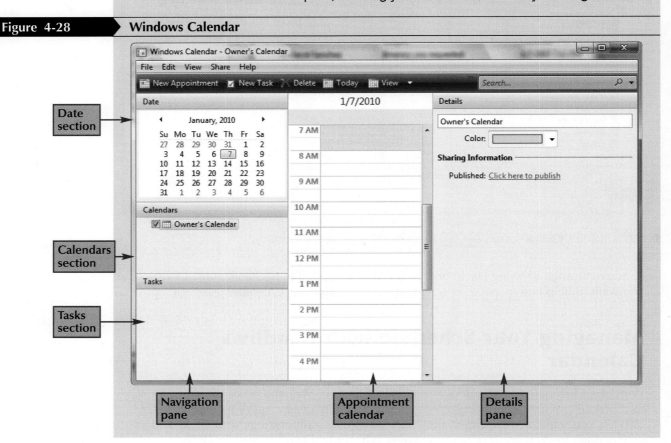

Figure 4-29 describes the parts of the Windows Calendar window.

Parts of the Windows Calendar window ◀ **Figure 4-29**

Calendar section	Description
Navigation pane	The Navigation pane includes a monthly calendar showing today's date, a list of calendars you are using (including Web calendars you subscribe to), and a list of tasks.
Date section	This part of the Navigation pane displays a calendar for the current month, with today's date highlighted. You can select another date in the month by clicking it. You can also use the left or right arrow keys to open calendar pages for other months.
Calendars section	This part of the Navigation pane shows the calendars in use on your computer. You can keep calendars for each user or only for yourself. You can also maintain calendars for different purposes, such as a professional and a social calendar.
Tasks section	This part of the Navigation pane shows your task list, including completed and pending tasks.
Appointment calendar	The middle pane shows a calendar in a daily, weekly, or monthly format. Click the View button arrow on the toolbar to change the view of the appointment calendar.
Details pane	The Details pane shows details about the selected calendar, appointment, or task.

Now that you've started Windows Calendar, you can use it to schedule appointments and track tasks.

Scheduling Appointments and Creating Tasks

When you schedule appointments, you can specify that they are recurring, such as training that takes place once a week, sales meetings scheduled once a month, or birthdays and other annual events. You can also set a reminder message to appear minutes, hours, days, or weeks before the scheduled appointment.

Scheduling an Appointment in Windows Calendar | Reference Window

- Click the New Appointment button on the Windows Calendar toolbar.
- Type a description of the appointment, and then press the Enter key.
- In the Location box, enter the location of the appointment.
- If you have more than one calendar, click the Calendar arrow, and then select the calendar you want to use to schedule the appointment.
- If you are scheduling an all-day appointment, click the All-day appointment check box.
- In the Start and End date boxes, click the arrow, and then click a date on the calendar.
- In the Start and End time boxes, click the arrows to change the times, or click to select the times and then enter the times you want.
- To specify a recurring appointment, click the Recurrence arrow, and then click how often the appointment recurs.
- To set a reminder, click the Reminder arrow, and then click an amount of time.
- To invite someone to the event, click an e-mail address in the Invite box, and then click the Invite button. If the e-mail address does not appear in the list, type an e-mail address in the Attendees box and press the Enter key, or click the Attendees button to select an address from your Contacts list.

The first appointment David wants to schedule is the weekly Wednesday morning staff meeting, which is usually an hour long. He also wants to receive a reminder message 15 minutes before a meeting.

To schedule an appointment:

▶ **1.** Click the **New Appointment** button on the toolbar. An appointment block is highlighted in the appointment calendar, and the Details pane shows the details you can enter for the new appointment. See Figure 4-30.

| Figure 4-30 | Scheduling an appointment |

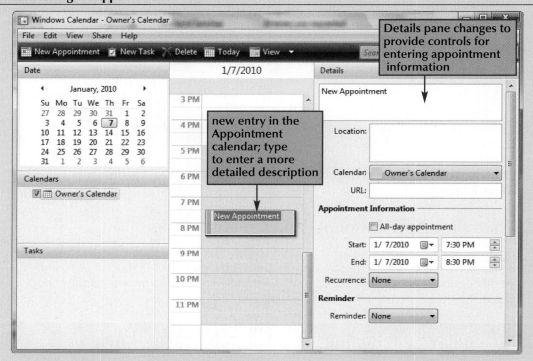

▶ **2.** Type **Weekly staff meeting** as the appointment description, and then press the **Enter** key. The new Weekly staff meeting entry appears in the Appointments calendar.

▶ **3.** In the Details pane, click in the **Location** box, and then type **West conference room**.

▶ **4.** Click the **Start** arrow, and then click the date for this coming Wednesday on the calendar.

▶ **5.** Click the **hour** value in the Start time text box, and then type **9** so the time appears as 9:00 AM.

   Trouble? If the minutes display a value other than 00, click the minutes and type 00. If the time is followed by PM, click PM and then type A to change this to AM.

▶ **6.** Click the **Recurrence** arrow, and then click **Weekly** to specify that this is a recurring appointment.

▶ **7.** Click the **Reminder** arrow, and then click **15 minutes** to set a reminder to appear 15 minutes before each staff meeting. A dialog box opens asking if you want to change the entire series. This means you will receive a reminder before every staff meeting.

▶ **8.** Click the **Change the series** button.

You've created an appointment for David's weekly staff meeting, and specified that Windows Calendar display a reminder message 15 minutes before the meeting. When David receives the reminder, he can dismiss it or have Windows Calendar remind him again in five minutes. (Dismissing a reminder means you won't be reminded again until the next occurrence of the appointment.)

Creating a task is similar to creating an appointment. When you create a task, you can assign it a priority and also set a reminder message to appear on a specified date.

To prepare for the next weekly staff meeting, David wants to present a new slate of tours to the Canadian Rockies. He's running out of time to finish it, so this task has a high priority. He also wants to be reminded about this task on its due date. You'll show him how to add this task to the Tasks list.

To create a task:

▶ **1.** Click the **New Task** button on the toolbar. A new task appears in the Task list and the Details pane shows the details you can enter for the new task. See Figure 4-31.

Creating a task ◄ Figure 4-31

▶ **2.** Type **Prepare list of new Canadian tours**, and then press the **Enter** key. The new task is listed in the Tasks section of the Navigation pane.

▶ **3.** In the Details pane, click the **Priority** arrow, and then click **High** to assign this task a high priority.

▶ **4.** Click the **Due date** button, and then click this coming Wednesday in the calendar.

▶ **5.** Click the **Reminder** arrow, and then click **On date**. Windows Calendar will send you a reminder on Wednesday indicating that the list of Canadian tours is due. See Figure 4-32.

Figure 4-32 | **Completed task**

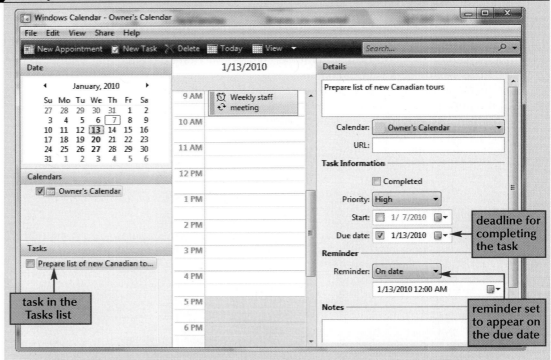

Besides maintaining calendars on your own computer, you can subscribe to Web calendars. If you want to share your appointments with others, you can publish your calendar.

Sharing a Calendar

Recall that many organizations, including sports teams and television shows, offer Web calendars that include special events. You can subscribe to one of these calendars and then update your personal calendar with the subscription calendar's event dates. To see a list of calendars you can subscribe to online, click Share on the Windows Calendar toolbar, click Subscribe, and then click the Windows Calendar Web site link.

You can also publish your own calendar on the Web so that others can see and share it. If you want, you can publish your personal schedule with password protection, so that you can choose who can access and view it. You can also share your calendar by printing it in a daily, weekly, or monthly format.

Reference Window | **Subscribing to a Web Calendar**

- Click the Subscribe button on the Windows Calendar toolbar.
- In the first wizard dialog box, enter the address of the Web calendar you want to use, and then click the Next button.
- The next steps vary depending on the calendar you choose. Follow the instructions in the wizard, and then click the Finish button to subscribe to the calendar.

Publishing a Web Calendar

- Click Share on the Windows Calendar menu bar, and then click Publish.
- In the Calendar name text box, type the name of the calendar you want to share.
- In the Location to publish calendar text box, enter the URL of the Web site or other location where you want to publish the calendar, or click the Browse button to navigate to the location.
- Click the Automatically publish changes made to this calendar check box if you want new appointments and other changes to appear on the published calendar.
- Click the Notes, Reminders, or Tasks check boxes to include those details on the published calendar.
- Click the Publish button.

Another way to share a calendar is to print it. You can print the calendar using one of many formats: Day, Work Week, Week, or Month. The Work Week option prints only Monday through Friday, while the Week option includes weekends. David wants to print his calendar using the Work Week format.

To print a calendar:

▶ 1. Click **File** on the menu bar, and then click **Print**. The Print dialog box opens. See Figure 4-33.

Printing a calendar ◀ Figure 4-33

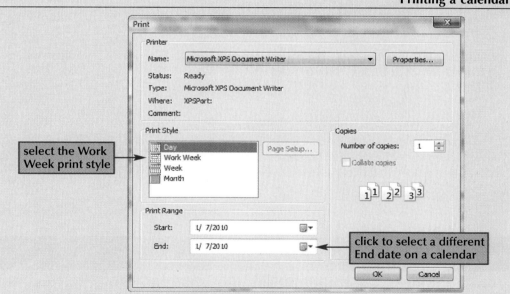

select the Work Week print style

click to select a different End date on a calendar

▶ 2. In the Print Style box, click **Work Week**.

▶ 3. In the Print Range section, click the **End** arrow, and then use the calendar to select the date one week from today.

▶ 4. Click the **OK** button to print the calendar.

▶ 5. Close all open windows.

Now that you've finished exploring the Internet and e-mail on David's computer, you should restore the computer to its original settings.

Restoring Your Settings

If you are working in a computer lab or a computer other than your own, complete the steps in this section to restore the original settings on your computer.

To restore your settings:

▶ 1. Start Internet Explorer, click the **Tools** button, click **Delete Browsing History**, click the **Delete all** button, and then click the **Yes** button.

▶ 2. Click the **Add to Favorites** button ☆ on the Favorites Center toolbar, and then click **Organize Favorites**.

▶ 3. Click the **Windows Vista** folder, click the **Delete** button, and then click the **Yes** button. Click the **Colorado Travel** folder, click the **Delete** button, and then click the **Yes** button. Click the **Close** button to close the Organize Folders dialog box.

▶ 4. Click the **Close** button ✕ to close the Favorites Center.

▶ 5. Close Internet Explorer.

▶ 6. Start Windows Mail, click the **Itinerary you requested** message in the Inbox, and then click the **Delete** button ✕ on the Windows Mail toolbar. Do the same to delete the **Re: Test e-mail** message.

▶ 7. Click the **Sent Items** folder in the Folders list, select the **Test e-mail**, **Re: Test e-mail**, and **Itinerary you requested** messages, and then click the **Delete** button ✕ .

▶ 8. Right-click the **Deleted Items** folder in the Folders list, click **Empty 'Deleted Items' folder**, and then click the **Yes** button.

▶ 9. Click the **Contacts** button ⊞ on the Windows Mail toolbar. Select **your name** and **David Sanchez** in the list of contacts, right-click the selection, click **Delete** on the shortcut menu, and then click the **Yes** button. Close the Windows Contacts window.

▶ 10. Click the **Windows Calendar** button ▦ on the Windows Mail toolbar. Right-click the appointment you added to the calendar, click **Delete** on the shortcut menu, and then click the **Delete the series** button. Right-click the task you added to the Tasks list, and then click **Delete** on the shortcut menu.

▶ 11. Close all open windows.

Review | Session 4.2 Quick Check

1. A(n) _____ is a simple text document that you can compose and send using Windows Mail.
2. Identify the user name and the e-mail server name in the following e-mail address: HalWilson@chambers.net.
3. True or False. You can send messages to anyone on the Internet or network, even if they don't have their computers turned on.
4. Explain the purpose of the Sent Items folder in Windows Mail.
5. Why should you open e-mail file attachments only from people you know and trust?
6. True or False. You can open Windows Contacts when you are working in Windows Mail or you can open it from the Start menu.
7. In Windows Calendar, you can enter appointments or _____ .

Tutorial Summary | Review

In this tutorial, you explored the structure of the Internet and the role of the Web. You learned how to use Internet Explorer to access Web pages and navigate with links and other tools. You used the Internet Explorer Favorites list to maintain a list of Web pages you visit often, and you learned how to print and save Web pages. You also explored e-mail technology to learn how e-mail works. You sent and received e-mail messages, replied to messages, and sent an e-mail message with a file attachment. Finally, you used Windows Contacts and Windows Calendar to manage your contacts, appointments, and tasks.

Key Terms

broadband connection
browser
copyright
dial-up connection
digital cable
digital subscriber
   line (DSL)
domain name
electronic mail (e-mail)
e-mail account
e-mail address
e-mail message
e-mail program
e-mail server
fair use
Favorites list

home page
hyperlink
Hypertext Transfer
   Protocol (HTTP)
intellectual property rights
Internet
Internet Protocol (IP)
   address
Internet service
   provider (ISP)
link
network
protocol
search engine
store-and-forward
   technology

tabbed browsing
uniform resource
   locator (URL)
user ID
user name
virus
Web
Web directory
Web page
Web server
Web site
wireless connection
World Wide Web

Practice	**Review Assignments**

Practice the skills you learned in the tutorial.

Data File needed for the Review Assignments: Washington Itinerary.rtf

You already showed David how to conduct research on tours in Colorado for low-mobility travelers. He also needs information about accessible travel in the state of Washington. Some of his clients want to use wheelchairs or scooters on hiking trails, and then fish on a lake or stream. You'll use Internet Explorer to research this information. Complete the following steps:

1. Start Internet Explorer, and go to the Windows Vista Online Companion Web page (*www.course.com/np/vista*).
2. Click Windows Vista, and then click the Tutorial 4 link.
3. Open the Washington State Accessible Outdoor Recreation Guide Web page on a new tab by pressing the Ctrl key and clicking the Washington State Parks link in the Review section on the Online Companion Web page.
4. Click a link on this page to find more information about accessible hiking trails in coastal Washington. Find at least one location that provides accessible fishing for low-mobility people.
5. Return to the Online Companion Web page, press Ctrl, and then click the Accessible Trails link to open that Web page on a new tab.
6. In the Washington State Accessible Trails section, click a few links to learn about trails in various parts of Washington State that are accessible to wheelchairs and scooters. Do the same in the Other Links on Accessibility section. Find at least two pages that provide information that people in wheelchairs and scooters can use to access wilderness fishing spots.
7. Use the History list or other Internet Explorer tools to navigate to a Web page you think will be especially useful to Entrée Tours, and then add it your Favorites list.
8. Print the first page of a Web page you added to your Favorites list.
9. Start Windows Mail and create an e-mail message. Enter your e-mail address in the To box, your instructor's e-mail address in the Cc box, and the following text in the Subject box: **Best spots for Entrée Tours in Washington State**.
10. In the message area, write a message describing the best places in Washington State for disabled and low-mobility travelers, based on your research.
11. Attach the **Washington Itinerary** file to the message. (This file is stored in the Tutorial.04\Review folder provided with your Data Files.)
12. Send the message, and then add your e-mail address and your instructor's e-mail address to the Contacts list.
13. Add an appointment to Windows Calendar to meet with David at Entrée Tours today for 30 minutes. Set a reminder to appear five minutes before the appointment. Add yourself and your instructor as invitees. Then print the calendar using the Day view.
14. Restore your computer by clearing the History list in Internet Explorer, deleting the Web pages you added to the Favorites list, deleting the e-mails you sent and received, emptying the Deleted Items folder, deleting yourself and your instructor from the Contacts list, and deleting the appointment you created on the Windows Calendar.
15. Close Internet Explorer and Windows Mail.
16. Submit the results of the preceding steps to your instructor, either in printed or electronic form, as requested.

| Apply | | Case Problem 1 |

Use the skills you learned in the tutorial to conduct research for an organization promoting astronomy for kids.

There are no Data Files needed for this Case Problem.

Supernova Center Gordon Bernhardt is the director of the Supernova Center, a non-profit organization in Santa Fe, New Mexico, that promotes astronomy and planetary science for kids from kindergarten through eighth grade. Gordon wants to take advantage of the astronomy information posted on the Web by national science organizations and compile it for science teachers. Recently, Gordon hired you to help provide outreach to educators. To prepare for an upcoming presentation at an educators conference, you want to pull together some innovative ideas for teaching astronomy in the classroom. Complete the following steps:

1. Start Internet Explorer, and go to the Windows Vista Online Companion Web page (*www.course.com/np/vista*).
2. Click Window Vista, and then click Tutorial 4 link. Maximize the Internet Explorer window.
3. On new tabs, open the four astronomy Web pages by clicking the links in the Case 1 section for Astronomy for Kids – 1, Astronomy for Kids – 2, Starchild Learning Center, and
   Windows to the Universe.
4. Click links and use the Internet Explorer tools to find three Web pages that provide ideas for teaching astronomy in the classroom.
5. Save the three Web pages you found in Step 4 in your Favorites list in a folder named Astronomy.
6. Pin the Favorites Center to the Internet Explorer window, if necessary, so that the Favorites list stays open. Open the Astronomy folder in the Favorites list to display the Web pages you found.
7. With the Internet Explorer window displaying the contents of the Astronomy folder and at least four tabs containing Astronomy Web pages suitable for school-age children, press the Alt+Print Screen keys to capture an image of the Internet Explorer window. Start Paint, paste the screen image in a new Paint file, and then save the file as **Astronomy Web pages** in the Tutorial.04\Case1 folder provided with your Data Files.
8. Start Windows Mail and create an e-mail message addressed to you and your instructor. Enter the following text in the Subject box: **Ideas for astronomy lessons**.
9. In the message area, write a message describing one of the ideas you found for teaching astronomy to students in grades kindergarten through eighth grade.
10. Attach the **Astronomy Web pages** file to the message, and then send it.
11. Add an appointment to Windows Calendar to make a presentation to the educators conference one month from today. Set a reminder to appear two days before the conference. Add yourself and your instructor as invitees. Then print the calendar showing the presentation appointment using the Week view.
12. Restore your computer by clearing the History list in Internet Explorer, deleting the folder you added to the Favorites list, deleting the e-mails you sent and received, emptying the Deleted Items folder, and deleting the appointment you created on the Windows Calendar.
13. Close Internet Explorer and Windows Mail.
14. Submit the results of the preceding steps to your instructor, either in printed or electronic form, as requested.

| Apply | Case Problem 2 |

Use the skills you learned in the tutorial to research museum services for an art restoration company.

There are no Data Files needed for this Case Problem.

Leroux Fine Art Restoration Evelyn Leroux is the owner of Leroux Fine Art Restoration, a company in Philadelphia, Pennsylvania, that provides expert restoration services to authenticate, conserve, and scientifically study paintings. Her specialty is early American portrait painting. Evelyn often works with the conservation departments of Philadelphia museums to restore paintings and is interested in expanding her company to work with museums around the United States. As her marketing and sales assistant, you offer to research the restoration services provided by museums outside of Philadelphia. Complete the following steps:

1. Start Internet Explorer, and go to the Windows Vista Companion Web page (*www. course.com/np/vista*).

2. Click WIndows Vista, and then click the Tutorial 4 link. Maximize the Internet Explorer window.

3. On additional tabs, open the three museum Web pages by clicking the links in the Case 2 section for the Metropolitan Museum of Art, the Minneapolis Institute of Arts, and Smithsonian Museums.

4. Click links and use the Internet Explorer tools to find at least one Web page for each museum that describes its restoration or conservation services. For the Metropolitan Museum of Art, you can access the Objects Conservation page from the Features page in the Works of Art category. For the Minneapolis Institute of Arts, restoration is considered a online educational resource. (*Hint*: Look for a "Restoring a Master-work" link.) For the Smithsonian, look for links to the Museum Conservation Institute, which is part of Smithsonian Research.

5. Save the Web pages you found in Step 4 in your Favorites list in a folder named Restoration.

⊕ **EXPLORE** 6. On the Web site for the Metropolitan Museum of Art, find a page that provides the terms and conditions and frequently asked questions (FAQ) about copying images. (*Hint*: Look for an FAQs link at the bottom of the main page, and then click a link describing Web site terms and conditions.) Save this page as a single HTML file named **Met FAQ** in the Tutorial.04\Case2 folder provided with your Data Files. (*Hint*: Click the Page button on the Internet Explorer toolbar, click Save As, click the Save as type arrow, click Webpage, HTML only (*.htm; *.html), enter the filename, and then click the Save button.)

⊕ **EXPLORE** 7. On the Metropolitan Museum of Art Web site, find a portrait of George Washington. (*Hint*: On the main page, click the Permanent Collection link.) Right-click the image, click Save Picture As on the shortcut menu, and then save the image as a file named **Washington** and store it in the Tutorial.04\Case2 folder provided with your Data Files.

8. Start Windows Mail and create an e-mail message addressed to you and your instructor. Enter the following text in the Subject box: **American portraits**.

9. In the message area, write a message listing examples of the types of art objects the Metropolitan Museum, the Minneapolis Institute of Arts, or the Smithsonian restores.

10. Attach the **Met FAQ** and **Washington** files to the message, and then send it.

11. Add two tasks to Windows Calendar to research restoration services at museums and to write a report on your findings. Set the priority for both tasks to Medium. Set the Start and Due date for the research task to today. Set the Start date for the report task to today and the Due date to one week from today. Set a reminder for the report task to the day before the due date.

12. Mark the research task as completed, and then print the calendar showing both tasks using Month view.

13. Restore your computer by clearing the History list in Internet Explorer, deleting the folder you added to the Favorites list, deleting the e-mails you sent and received, emptying the Deleted Items folder, and deleting the tasks you created on the Windows Calendar.

14. Close Internet Explorer and Windows Mail.

15. Submit the results of the preceding steps to your instructor, either in printed or electronic form, as requested.

Challenge | Case Problem 3

Go beyond what you've learned to help a start-up magazine find information about gardening in the upper Midwest.

There are no Data Files needed for this Case Problem.

Northern Gardening Magazine   The Northern Gardening Magazine is a new monthly periodical published in St. Paul, Minnesota, for gardeners in the upper midwestern states of Michigan, Wisconsin, Minnesota, North Dakota, and South Dakota. Michael Nilsson is the publisher and a master gardener. He hired you as his director of communications, and asked you to find Web sites providing basic information for the readers of Northern Gardening Magazine. Complete the following steps:

1. Start Internet Explorer, and go to the Windows Vista Online Companion Web page (*www.course.com/np/vista*).

2. Click Windows Vista, and then click the Tutorial 4 link. Maximize the Internet Explorer window.

3. On additional tabs, open the gardening Web pages by clicking the links in the Case 3 section for the UM Extension, the UW Extension, and the Minnesota Department of Natural Resources.

4. Click links and use the Internet Explorer tools to find at least one Web page for each site that recommends gardening techniques or plants for residents of the upper Midwest. (*Hint*: If the Web site provides a Search tool, type **gardening** in the Search box.)

⊕EXPLORE   5. Save the group of open tabs in your Favorites list as a tab group named Gardening. (*Hint*: Click the Add to Favorites button, click Add Tab Group to Favorites, name the group Gardening, and then click the Add button.)

⊕EXPLORE   6. On the Web site for the Minnesota Department of Natural Resources, find a page explaining how to landscape with native plants. Save this page as a single HTML file named **Native Plants** in the Tutorial.04\Case3 folder provided with your Data Files. (*Hint*: Click the Page button on the Internet Explorer toolbar, click Save As, click the Save as type arrow, click Webpage, HTML only (*.htm; *.html), enter the filename, and then click the Save button.)

⊕EXPLORE   7. On the main Web page for the UW Extension agriculture topics, click the Urban Horticulture link, and then click a link for Wisconsin Garden Facts. On the Wisconsin Garden Facts page, look for files you can download. For example, look for a WORD or PDF link next to the name of an article. (PDFs, or Portable Document Files, are files containing text and images that you can often download from a Web site and read with a program called Adobe Reader. DOC files are Microsoft Word documents, which you can also open in WordPad.) Right-click the link to the file, click Save Target As, and then save the file as **Wisconsin Horticulture** in the Tutorial.04\Case3 folder provided with your Data Files.

8. Start Windows Mail and create an e-mail message addressed to you and your instructor. Enter the following text in the Subject box: **Midwestern gardening**.

9. In the message area, write a message listing a few types of plants that can be grown in the upper Midwest.

10. Attach the **Native Plants** and **Wisconsin Horticulture** files to the message, and then send the message.

11. Add one task to Windows Calendar to research gardening in Michigan tomorrow. Add an appointment to meet with Michael to discuss next month's issue of Northern Gardening Magazine two days from today at 1:00 in the afternoon. Set a reminder to appear the same day as the task. Set another reminder to appear 30 minutes before the meeting. Print the calendar showing the task and appointment using the Work Week view.

12. Restore your computer by clearing the History list in Internet Explorer, deleting the folder you added to the Favorites list, deleting the e-mails you sent and received, emptying the Deleted Items folder, and deleting the appointment and task you created on the Windows Calendar.

13. Close Internet Explorer and Windows Mail.

14. Submit the results of the preceding steps to your instructor, either in printed or electronic form, as requested.

Challenge | Case Problem 4

Go beyond what you've learned to help a booster club promote women's college volleyball.

There are no Data Files needed for this Case Problem.

Volleyball Boosters   Volleyball Boosters is a club in Kalamazoo, Michigan, that supports and promotes women's college volleyball teams at small American colleges. Felicia Andrade, the club president, recently hired you as a part-time assistant. You help Felicia write the club newsletter and organize promotional events. Felicia wants you to visit college Web sites periodically to make sure they are promoting their women's volleyball teams. Complete the following steps:

1. Start Internet Explorer, and go to the Windows Vista Online Companion Web page (*www.course.com/np/vista*).

2. Click Windows Vista, and then click the Tutorial 4 link. Maximize the Internet Explorer window.

3. On additional tabs, open the college Web pages by clicking the links in the Case 4 section for Hiram College, Kalamazoo College, Mount Holyoke College, and Northland College.

4. Click links and use the Internet Explorer tools to find at least one Web page for each college that describes or reports on the women's volleyball team.

⊕EXPLORE

5. Save the group of open tabs in your Favorites list as a tab group named Volleyball. (*Hint*: Click the Add to Favorites button, click Add Tab Group to Favorites, name the group Volleyball, and then click the Add button.)

⊕EXPLORE

6. On the Web site for any of the four colleges, find a schedule for the current or upcoming volleyball season. Click the Print button arrow, click Print Preview, and examine the schedule image. Using the buttons on the Print Preview toolbar, adjust the image of the schedule so that it will print on one page. Then click the Print Document button on the Print Preview toolbar to print the schedule.

⊕ **EXPLORE**

7. Close the Print Preview window, click the Page button on the Internet Explorer tool-bar, and then click Send Page by E-mail. Address the message to you and your instructor. Enter the following text in the Subject box: **Volleyball Schedule**. Then send the e-mail message.

⊕ **EXPLORE**

8. Start Windows Mail and click the Send/Receive button to receive the e-mail. Click the Volleyball Schedule message in the message list, click File on the menu bar, and then click Save As. Save the e-mail message as **Volleyball Schedule** in the Tutorial.04\Case4 folder provided with your Data Files.

⊕ **EXPLORE**

9. Start Windows Calendar, open the Subscribe to a Calendar dialog box, and then visit the Windows Calendar Web site to find a volleyball calendar. With the appropriate Web page open in Internet Explorer, press the Alt+Print Screen keys to capture an image of the Internet Explorer window. Start Paint, paste the screen image in a new Paint file, and then save the file as **Volleyball Calendar** in the Tutorial.04\Case4 folder provided with your Data Files.

10. Restore your computer by clearing the History list in Internet Explorer, deleting the folder you added to the Favorites list, and deleting the e-mails you sent and received.

11. Close Internet Explorer and Windows Mail.

12. Submit the results of the preceding steps to your instructor, either in printed or electronic form, as requested.

| Assess | **SAM Assessment and Training** |

If you have a SAM user profile, you may have access to hands-on instruction, practice, and assessment of the skills covered in this tutorial. Log in to your SAM account (**http://sam2007.course.com**) to launch any assigned training activities or exams that relate to the skills covered in this tutorial.

| Review | **Quick Check Answers** |

Session 4.1

1. The Web is a service that the Internet provides. Whereas the Internet is a collection of networks connected by communication media such as fiber-optic cables and wireless connections, the Web is a collection of documents connected by links.
2. Web site
3. False
4. its home page
5. URL, or uniform resource locator
6. Type the URL in the Address bar or click a link on a Web page.
7. Using the Back button, Forward button, Recent Pages list, or History list
8. False

Ending Data Files

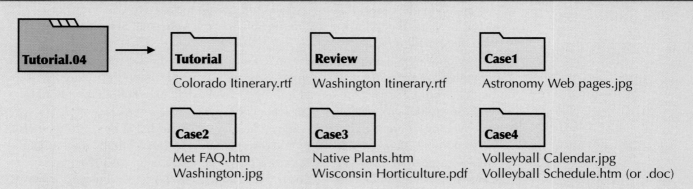

Tutorial.04 →

Tutorial
Colorado Itinerary.rtf

Review
Washington Itinerary.rtf

Case1
Astronomy Web pages.jpg

Case2
Met FAQ.htm
Washington.jpg

Case3
Native Plants.htm
Wisconsin Horticulture.pdf

Case4
Volleyball Calendar.jpg
Volleyball Schedule.htm (or .doc)

Objectives

Session 5.1
- Set up Windows Firewall and Windows Update
- Protect your computer from viruses and other malicious software
- Use Windows Defender to protect against spyware
- Manage Windows Mail security

Session 5.2
- Manage Microsoft Internet Explorer security
- Set up user accounts
- Control access to your computer
- Secure and share folders

Protecting Your Computer

Managing Computer Security

Case | Presto Global Translators

A few years ago, Curt Mickelson founded Presto Global Translators in Ithaca, New York. Presto translates written material to and from English and dozens of other languages for corporate clients around the world. Curt has hired and trained experienced translators, proofreaders, and quality assurance managers in the United States. His staff works with native speakers in other countries who specialize in technology, law, finance, and other fields so that Presto can offer top-notch translation teams of language, writing, and subject matter experts.

Presto's challenge is to keep pace with the changing terminology in these fields. Curt regularly evaluates new dictionaries and glossaries, both print and online, and maintains lists of terms that have special meaning in particular industries. A recent concern is the security of Presto's computers. Many of Curt's translators work at their client's offices, using notebook computers running Windows Vista. Although these translators can access the Internet with their computers, they can't usually connect to the Presto network, where an administrator oversees security. Instead, they must take advantage of the security tools in Windows Vista to prevent problems stemming from viruses, spyware, and other types of harmful software. Curt recently hired you to support the Presro Global translation staff. One of your first duties is to investigate the security features in Windows Vista and show Curt how to use them to address security threats.

In this tutorial, you explore the tools provided in the Windows Security Center, including Windows Firewall and Windows Update. You also learn how to set up Windows Vista to work with antivirus software. In addition, you learn how to use other security practices, including setting up user accounts, and securing and sharing folders. You also examine Microsoft Internet Explorer security settings so that you can use the Internet safely.

Starting Data Files

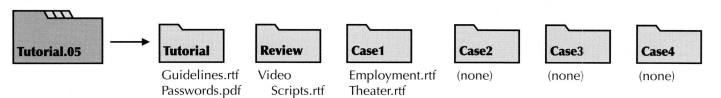

Tutorial.05 →	Tutorial	Review	Case1	Case2	Case3	Case4
	Guidelines.rtf	Video	Employment.rtf	(none)	(none)	(none)
	Passwords.pdf	Scripts.rtf	Theater.rtf			

Session 5.1

Using the Windows Vista Security Center

Many of the most improved features in Windows Vista focus on security—keeping your computer safe from threats such as harmful software, unsolicited e-mail, and invasions of your privacy. When you connect to the Internet, send and receive e-mail, or share your computer or files with others, your computer is vulnerable to harm from others who might attempt to steal your personal information, damage your files, or interrupt your work. You need to use the Windows Vista security tools and other techniques to defend against these threats and protect your computer effectively.

Harmful software (also called malicious software, or malware) includes **viruses**, which are programs that are attached to a file and run when you open the file. A virus can harm your computer by changing your desktop settings, for example, displaying an annoying image, or deleting files on your hard disk. Viruses are often spread by e-mail and run when you open an e-mail attachment or the e-mail message itself. In contrast, another type of malware called a **worm** does not have to be attached to a file—it can spread and run by itself. Worms are also usually distributed by e-mail. People who create and send malware are called **hackers**, a generic term that refers to anyone who intends to access a computer system without permission. (Hackers with criminal intent are sometimes called **crackers**.) Hackers can also invade your privacy by accessing your computer via the Internet to find information such as passwords and financial account numbers. Hackers sometimes access your computer using **spyware**, software that secretly gathers information about you and your computer actions, including sensitive information, and passes it to advertisers and others.

If you are working on a computer that is connected to a network, a network administrator probably defends the network against security threats such as viruses, worms, spyware, and hackers. Otherwise, if you are working on a home computer, for example, you should take advantage of the security features that Windows Vista provides. Windows Vista offers the following programs and options that help you keep your computer secure:

- **Security Center**: Use this Control Panel tool to manage your firewall, antivirus software, and Windows updates. All of these topics are covered in this session.
- **Windows Defender**: Use this program to prevent some types of malware from infecting your computer. You'll use Windows Defender later in this session.
- **User Account Control**: This service displays a dialog box requesting your permission to install software or open programs that could harm your computer or make it vulnerable to security breaches. You'll examine User Account Control later in this tutorial.
- **Back Up and Restore**: Use these tools to back up your files and settings regularly so that you can recover your files if they are damaged by malware or hardware problems.

The first place to go to secure your computer is the Security Center, a Control Panel tool that helps you manage security from a single window. You can manage the security settings of the features listed in Figure 5-1 when you work with the Security Center.

Security Feature	Description
Windows Firewall	Windows Firewall monitors and restricts communication with the Internet, which helps protect your computer from viruses and hackers. Before a program can send or receive information via the Internet, Windows Firewall must allow it to do so.
Windows Update	This feature checks for the latest Windows updates on the Microsoft Web site, and then downloads and installs the updates for you. Because Windows updates often include security enhancements, using this feature helps to make sure that your computer is secure against most current threats.
Malware protection	Antivirus software is your best protection against viruses, worms, and other types of harmful software. If you have antivirus software, Windows reminds you to use it regularly to scan your computer for virus infections and to monitor e-mail. If you do not have antivirus software, Windows lists vendors that provide it.
Other security settings	Security Center also checks that your Web browser is using appropriate security settings and whether the User Account Control is turned on to help prevent malware from damaging your system.

The features listed in Figure 5-1 are considered essential—you should turn on these features to keep your computer secure. If Windows detects a problem with any of these security essentials, such as when your firewall is turned off, a Security Center icon, such as 🗵 appears in the notification area of your taskbar along with a message. You can click the message or double-click the icon to open the Security Center and find out how to address the problem. Otherwise, you can open the Security Center from the Control Panel.

You'll start showing Curt how to use the security features in Windows Vista by opening the Security Center.

To open the Security Center:

▶ 1. Click the **Start** button 🪟 on the taskbar, and then click **Control Panel**. The Control Panel window opens.

▶ 2. If the Control Panel opens in Classic view, double-click **Security Center** to open the Windows Security Center window. If the Control Panel opens in Category view, click **Security**, and then click **Security Center**.

▶ 3. If necessary, maximize the Windows Security Center window and then click each heading to expand the sections. See Figure 5-2.

Figure 5-2 **Windows Security Center window**

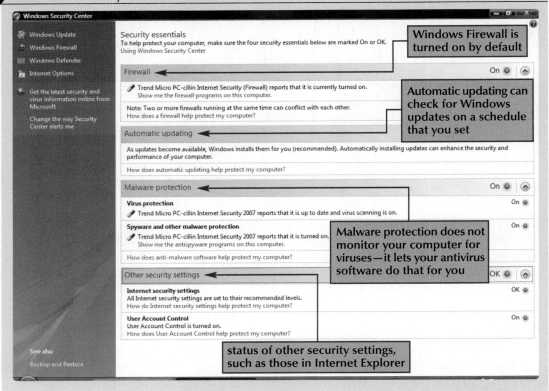

Leave the Windows Security Center window open to perform the tasks described in the following sections.

Managing Windows Firewall

Windows Firewall is software that serves as a barrier between your computer and a network or the Internet. As shown in Figure 5-3, it checks information coming from the Internet and either blocks it from your computer or allows it to pass, depending on your settings. In this way, Windows Firewall prevents unauthorized users from accessing your computer and is the first line of defense against malware.

How Windows Firewall protects your computer ◄ Figure 5-3

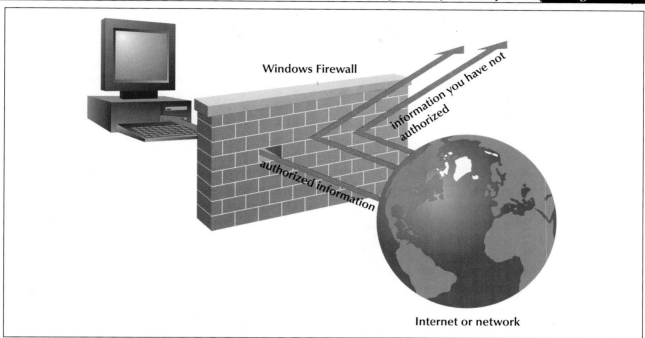

Windows Firewall

information you have not authorized

authorized information

Internet or network

Understanding What a Firewall Can Do | InSight

A firewall defends against malware trying to gain access to your computer by monitoring your network and Internet connections. However, a firewall does not scan e-mail, so it cannot detect viruses sent in e-mail messages (a common way to spread viruses). Furthermore, a firewall can't protect you from e-mail scams, called phishing, that deceive you into revealing private information, such as passwords. To protect against e-mail viruses, use antivirus software. To minimize phishing attempts, use the Internet Explorer phishing filter. (Both topics are covered later in this tutorial.)

Windows Firewall is turned on by default, so it doesn't allow communications with most programs via the Internet or a network. (One exception is Core Networking, which helps you connect to the Internet.) When someone tries to connect to your computer from the Internet, Windows Firewall blocks the connection. For example, suppose that you are running an instant-messaging program and exchanging digital photos with a friend. When your friend sends you the first photo file, Windows Firewall detects the communication and opens a dialog box asking if you want to block or allow the connection by the instant-messaging program. If you know that your friend is using the instant-messaging program to send you a file, you can allow, or unblock, the connection. Windows Firewall then adds an **exception** to its list of programs, meaning that it will allow the instant-messaging program to communicate with your computer now and in the future. Instead of turning off Windows Firewall, you can customize it by adding exceptions to its list of programs so that it maintains a level of security that's right for you. You can add a program to the Windows Firewall exception list manually, without waiting for that program to communicate with you.

- Click the Start button, click Control Panel, click Security, and then click Windows Firewall.
- In the left pane, click Allow a program through Windows Firewall, and then click the Continue button, if necessary.
- In the Program or port list, click to select a program check box. If a program does not appear in this list, click the Add program button, click a program in the Add a Program dialog box, or click the Browse button to locate and select a program.
- Click the OK button.

You select most of the Windows Firewall settings using the Windows Firewall dialog box. On the General tab of this dialog box, you can select one of three settings:

- **On (recommended)**: This setting is selected by default, meaning that most programs are blocked from communicating through the firewall.
- **Block all incoming connections**: When you connect to a public network, such as in a hotel or airport, you might want to use the Block all incoming connections settings. Windows blocks all programs, informing you when it does, and allows the programs on the exception list.
- **Off (not recommended)**: The only time you should select this setting is when another firewall is running on your computer.

The Windows Firewall dialog box also includes an Exceptions tab, where you specify which programs to allow through the firewall, and the Advanced tab, where you can specify which network connections Windows Firewall should monitor. The recommended setting is to turn on Windows Firewall for all network connections.

Curt often uses Windows Meeting Place, a Windows Vista program that lets you collaborate on documents with others on the Internet or a local network. Before remote meeting attendees can communicate with Curt's computer to let him know they are ready for the meeting, Windows Firewall must allow incoming connections from Windows Meeting Place. First, you'll make sure Windows Firewall is running on Curt's computer, and then you'll show Curt how to add Windows Meeting Place to the exception list so he can meet online without interruption.

If you are performing the following steps in a computer lab, you might not be allowed to change exceptions. Check with your instructor or technical support person to determine whether you can specify Windows Meeting Place as an exception to the Windows Firewall. If you cannot, read but do not perform the following steps.

Tip
Windows Firewall might restrict features in programs that depend on low security settings. If you are having trouble running a program, add it to the exception list to see if that solves your problem.

To verify Windows Firewall is running and add a program to the exception list:

▶ **1.** In the left pane of the Windows Security Center window, click **Windows Firewall**. The Windows Firewall window opens. See Figure 5-4. Your settings might differ.

Windows Firewall window ◀ Figure 5-4

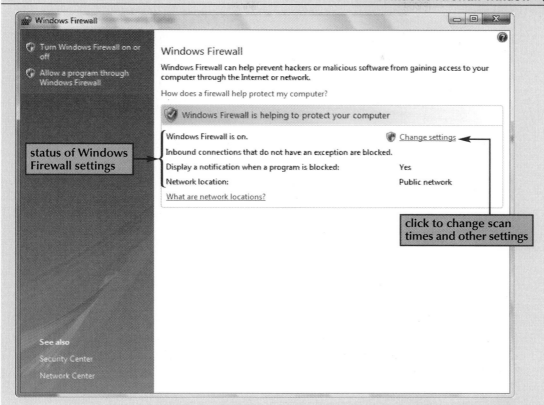

Trouble? If Windows Firewall is turned off or a firewall other than Windows Firewall is running on your computer, this window displays a warning. If the Firewall section of the Windows Security Center window (see Figure 5-2) reports that a firewall is turned on, you can ignore the warning in the Windows Firewall window. Otherwise, turn on Windows Firewall by clicking Use recommended settings, or turn on another firewall according to the manufacturer's instructions.

▶ 2. In the left pane, click **Allow a program through Windows Firewall** to open the Windows Firewall Settings dialog box to the Exceptions tab. See Figure 5-5.

Trouble? If a dialog box opens requesting an administrator password or your permission to continue, make sure you have permission to change Windows Firewall settings (check with your instructor, if necessary), and then enter the password or click the Continue button.

Figure 5-5   **Windows Firewall Settings dialog box**

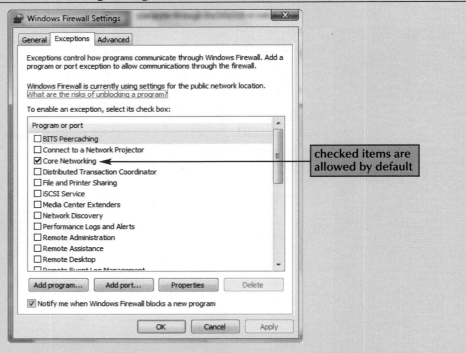

checked items are allowed by default

Tip

If the program you want to add as an exception does not appear in the Program or port list, click the Add program button and then add any program installed on your computer to the exception list.

3. Scroll to the end of the Program or port list, and then click the **Windows Meeting Space** check box, if necessary, to select it.

   Trouble? If you are not allowed to change the exceptions for Windows Firewall, click the Cancel button in the Windows Firewall Settings dialog box and then skip Step 4.

4. Click the **OK** button to add Windows Meeting Space to the exception list.

5. Close the Windows Firewall window.

Keep in mind that when you add a program to the Windows Firewall exception list, you are making your computer easier to access, and therefore more vulnerable to malware infection. If you add too many programs to the exception list, you minimize the security that Windows Firewall can provide. You should therefore allow an exception only when you really need it, and never make an exception for a program that you don't recognize—it could be a virus or a worm. Finally, be sure to remove an exception when you no longer need it.

Recall that if Windows does not detect a firewall on your computer, it displays a red Security Center icon and a periodic message in the notification area of the taskbar. If you are sure a firewall is running on your computer, click Show me my available options on the Windows Security Center window. (This option is only available if Windows does not detect that a firewall is turned on.) When the Windows Security Center dialog box opens, click I have a firewall solution that I'll monitor myself to stop receiving notifications.

Setting Up Windows Update

An **update** is a change to software that can prevent or repair problems, enhance the security of the computer, or improve the computer's performance. Microsoft Corporation occasionally releases updates to Windows Vista and provides them for download on its Web site. You can look for, download, and install these updates any time you visit the

Microsoft Web site. However, because updates often include critical security repairs and enhancements, Microsoft also makes them available to you through the Windows Update feature.

When you use the Update feature, Windows periodically checks for updates to the operating system from Microsoft, including security updates, critical updates, and service packs. If an update is available, Windows Update can download the software and install it for you. Windows downloads the updates in the background according to a schedule you set, as long as you're connected to the Internet. If you disconnect from the Internet before Windows finishes downloading, Windows continues downloading the next time you connect to the Internet.

You can specify whether Windows automatically downloads only important updates, both important and recommended updates, or does not download automatically at all. Important updates are those you should install to maintain the security and reliability of Windows. Recommended updates usually enhance your computing experience and repair problems that are not considered critical. Microsoft also provides optional updates, which don't apply to all Windows users. For example, if you use a particular piece of hardware, such as a digital music player, Windows might provide an optional update for the player's driver.

In addition to the types of updates you want Windows to download, you can also specify when Windows should install the updates. To notify you that updates are available or that Windows is ready to download or install updates, an icon appears in the notification area of the taskbar. The icon depends on the updating options you select. Figure 5-6 summarizes the download and installation options for Windows Update and the action you can take to download and install the updates.

> **Tip**
>
> To visit the Windows Update Web site and download any type of update, click the Start button, point to All Programs, and then click Windows Update.

Options for downloading and installing updates ◀ **Figure 5-6**

Option	Notification Icon	Action
Download and install updates automatically	Update icon	Windows performs all the actions. You can point to the Update icon to see a ScreenTip displaying the progress of the download and installation.
Download updates automatically, but install them yourself	Update icon	Click the Update icon to install the updates.
Check for updates, but download and install them yourself	Security Warning icon	Click the Security Warning icon to download the updates, and then click the Update icon to install them.

To view your current update status and settings for Windows Update, you open the Windows Update window from the Security category of the Control Panel. You can also use this window to review your update history by clicking the View update history link.

You recommend that Curt turn on automatic updating for important and recommended updates so he doesn't miss any for Windows Vista. He wants to check for updates every morning at 8:00 while he is typically meeting with his staff. Although he is not using his computer then, it is turned on and connected to the Internet.

As you perform the following steps, note your original settings so you can restore them later.

To set up Windows Updates:

▶ **1.** In the left pane of the Windows Security Center window, click **Windows Update**. The Windows Update window opens. See Figure 5-7. Your settings might differ.

Figure 5-7 | Windows Update window

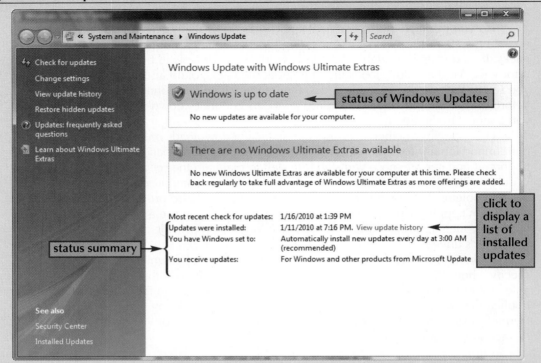

2. In the left pane, click **Change settings**. The Change settings dialog box opens. See Figure 5-8.

Figure 5-8 | Changing Windows Update settings

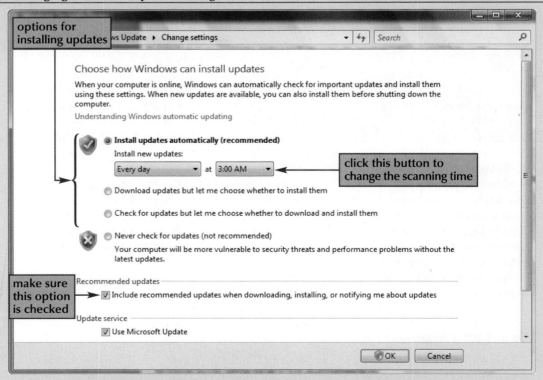

▶ 3. Click the **Install updates automatically (recommended)** option button, if necessary. Selecting this option means that Windows checks for updates according to schedule, and then downloads and installs them for you when they are available.

▶ 4. In the Install new updates section, click the time button (which appears as 3:00 AM by default), and then click **8:00 AM**.

▶ 5. If necessary, click the **Include recommended updates when downloading, installing, or notifying me about updates** check box to select it.

▶ 6. Click the **OK** button.

   Trouble? If a dialog box opens requesting an administrator password or your permission to continue, enter the password or click the Continue button.

▶ 7. Close the Windows Update window.

Now that you know Curt's copy of Windows Vista is up to date, you can turn to protecting his computer from viruses and other types of malware.

Protecting Your Computer from Malware

A virus is a program that replicates itself and attaches to files or programs, usually affects your computer's performance and stability, and sometimes damages or removes files. Viruses are often transmitted through e-mail attachments or downloaded files, but don't spread until you open the attachment or file. In contrast, a worm is harmful computer code that spreads without your interaction. A worm slips from one network connection to another, replicating itself on network computers. As it does, a worm consumes network resources, overwhelming computers until they become slow or unresponsive. Another type of malware related to viruses and worms is a Trojan horse, which is malware that hides inside other programs. These programs are usually legitimate, such as a photo viewing program you download from the Web. When you install the program, however, the Trojan horse infects the operating system, allowing a hacker to access your computer and your personal information. Trojan horses can't spread on their own; they depend on programs, including viruses and worms, to proliferate. Common symptoms of malware are when your computer runs much slower than normal, messages appear unexpectedly, programs start or close on their own, or Windows shuts down suddenly.

Your best protection against harmful software is to use current versions of antivirus software, which scans e-mail messages, attachments, and other files on your computer for viruses, worms, and other types of malware. Antivirus software locates a virus by comparing identifying characteristics of the files on your computer to a list of known viruses. When it finds a virus, or any type of malware, antivirus software notifies you about the virus and then quarantines it by moving it to an isolated place on your computer or deletes the harmful file before it damages your computer.

Most vendors of antivirus software offer a subscription service that provides regular updates for current viruses. Like Windows, antivirus programs often use an automatic update feature that downloads and installs updates to the software and adds new viruses to your virus list. Keeping the virus list current helps to protect your computer from new attacks. If your list of viruses is out of date, your computer is vulnerable to new threats.

Windows Vista does not provide antivirus software, so you should make sure that you have an antivirus program installed and running on your computer. (Your computer manufacturer probably installed antivirus software for you—look on the All Programs submenu of the Start menu and then point to the icons in the notification area of the taskbar to make sure antivirus software is installed and running on your computer.) Be sure to select the options in the antivirus software to scan incoming e-mail automatically and to scan your entire system for malware periodically (usually once a week). Windows does detect most types of antivirus software and displays their status in the Windows Security Center window.

Tip

If antivirus software is not installed and running on your computer, visit the Microsoft Web site (*www. microsoft.com*) and search for "antivirus partners" to find software publishers who provide antivirus software for Windows Vista.

Also make sure that the antivirus software uses the most current virus definitions list. If your virus list is out of date, your computer is vulnerable to new threats. Refer to the antivirus software's help system to learn how to run the software and receive regular updates. In most cases, you can also use the Security Center to determine whether your antivirus software needs to be updated.

Curt is certain that antivirus software is installed on his computer, but asks you to check to make sure it is up to date and that virus scanning is turned on.

To check for malware protection on your computer:

▶ **1.** In the Windows Security Center window, examine the settings in the **Malware protection** section, which should report that virus protection and spyware protection are both turned on.

   Trouble? If the Windows Security Center window reports that your virus protection is up to date and virus scanning is on, read but do not perform the remaining steps. If virus protection is turned on but not up to date, skip Steps 2 and 3.

   Trouble? If the Windows Security Center window reports that antivirus software is not installed on your computer, read but do not perform the remaining steps.

▶ **2.** If necessary, click the **Turn on now** button.

▶ **3.** When a dialog box opens requesting your permission to run the antivirus program, click the **Yes** button. The Windows Security Center window reports that virus scanning is on, but the antivirus program is not up to date. See Figure 5-9.

Figure 5-9	Antivirus software needs to be updated

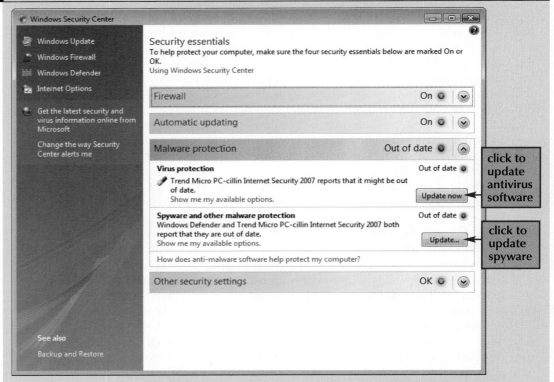

   Trouble? If your Windows Security Center window reports that virus scanning is on and up to date, read but do not perform Step 4.

▶ **4.** Click the **Update now** button. Your antivirus software starts and checks for updates on its manufacturer's Web site. When it is finished updating, close the antivirus software window.

Avoiding Viruses | InSight

You can defend against viruses in the following ways:

- Do not open unexpected e-mail attachments. If the message containing the attachment is from a trusted source, send an e-mail to that person asking about the file and what it contains.
- Regularly scan your hard drive with an antivirus program. Most antivirus software includes an option to schedule a complete system scan. You only need to make sure your computer is turned on to perform the scan.
- Set your antivirus program to scan all incoming e-mail.
- Keep your antivirus software up to date. New viruses are introduced frequently, and your antivirus software needs to use the latest virus definitions to protect your computer.
- Back up your work files periodically. Viruses can corrupt or destroy data files, which are the most valuable files on your computer.

Another security concern is spyware, which can also affect your computing experience.

Defending Against Spyware

Spyware is software that can install itself or run on your computer without your consent or control. It's called *spyware* because it monitors your computing actions, usually while you are online, to collect information about you. When spyware installs itself on your computer, it can change system settings, interrupt programs, and slow your computer's performance. Spyware often infects your computer when you visit certain Web sites or download a free program, such as a screen saver or search toolbar. Less frequently, spyware is distributed along with other programs on a CD, DVD, or other type of removable media. Sometimes, spyware passes information about your Web browsing habits to advertisers, who use it to improve their products or Web sites. Other times, a special type of spyware called **adware** changes your browser settings to open **pop-up ads**, which are windows that appear while you are viewing a Web page and advertise a product or service. Pop-up ads interrupt your online activities and can be difficult to close; they can also be vehicles for additional spyware or other types of malware. At the least, spyware is annoying; at worst, it can invade your privacy and harm your computer.

Because spyware can download, install, and run on your computer without your knowledge or consent, it's often difficult to know if spyware is infecting your computer. If you are experiencing any of the following symptoms, they are most likely due to spyware; you should scan your computer with a program that detects and removes spyware.

- New toolbars, links, or favorites appear in your Web browser unexpectedly.
- Your home page, mouse pointer, or search program changes without your consent.
- When you enter a URL for a Web site, such as a search engine, you go to a different Web site without notice.
- Pop-up ads interrupt you, even when you're not on the Internet.
- Your computer suddenly starts or runs slowly.

Scanning Your Computer with Windows Defender

To protect your computer against spyware, you can run up-to-date antispyware software. Some antivirus programs include antispyware components. Windows Vista also provides Windows Defender, which helps prevent spyware from installing itself and running on your computer and which periodically scans your computer to detect and remove spyware. Besides monitoring and scanning your computer, Windows Defender also provides access to the Microsoft SpyNet community, where you can learn how others respond to software that hasn't been classified as spyware. When you are considering whether to download a free screen saver, for example, you can check the SpyNet Web site first to see if that program includes spyware or other types of malware.

Reference Window | **Performing a Quick Scan with Windows Defender**

- Click the Start button, click Control Panel, click Security, and then click Windows Defender.
- Click the Scan button arrow on the toolbar, and then click Quick Scan.

As with antivirus software, you need to keep the spyware definitions in Windows Defender up to date. The definitions are files that list the characteristics of known spyware; Windows Defender refers to the definitions to determine if software it detects is spyware or another type of malware. When you update your computer, Windows Update installs any new spyware definitions. You can also set Windows Defender to check for updated definitions before scanning your computer.

To protect Curt's computer, you'll show him how to start Windows Defender and scan for spyware. You can run a quick scan or a full system scan. A quick scan checks the locations on your computer that spyware is most likely to infect. A full scan checks all your files and programs, but takes longer than a quick scan and can make your computer run slowly. You recommend that Curt run a quick scan every day and run a full system scan only if he suspects spyware is infecting his computer.

To start Windows Defender and perform a quick scan:

▶ 1. In the left pane of the Windows Security Center window, click **Windows Defender**. The Windows Defender window opens. See Figure 5-10. Your settings might differ.

Windows Defender ◀ Figure 5-10

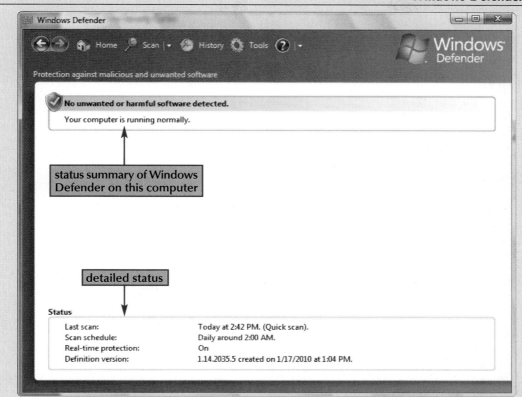

Trouble? If a dialog box opens indicating that Windows Defender is turned off, click the Turn on Windows Defender link, and then close the dialog box. When a dialog box opens requesting an administrator password or your permission to continue, enter the password or click the Continue button.

2. Click the **Scan button arrow** on the toolbar, and then click **Quick Scan**. Windows Defender scans your computer, displaying first its progress and then the results of the scan. Depending on the number of programs on your computer, your scan might take a few minutes. Wait for the scan to finish and for the results window to open before continuing. Figure 5-11 shows the results of a scan. Your results might differ.

Figure 5-11 | **Results of a quick scan**

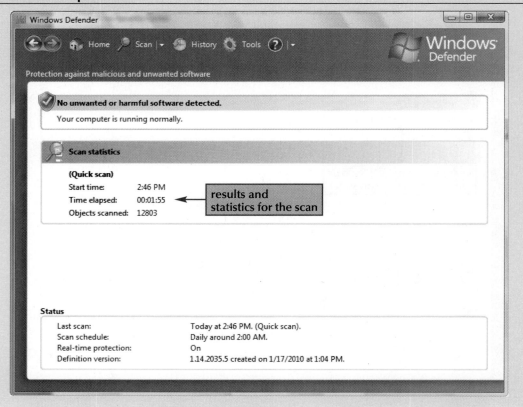

If Windows Defender finds files that might be spyware, it **quarantines** the files, which means it moves them to another location on your computer where it prevents them from running until you remove or restore the files. You can open the Quarantined items page to review the quarantined files. Windows Defender lists the quarantined files by their name, alert level, and date of quarantine. Figure 5-12 summarizes the alert levels and their recommended actions.

Figure 5-12 | **Windows Defender alert levels**

Alert Level	Description	Recommended Action
Severe	Malicious spyware that can damage your computer	Remove
High	Spyware that invades your privacy, often by collecting information or changing settings without your knowledge or consent	Remove
Medium	Software that might affect your privacy or change your settings	If you do not recognize and trust the software publisher, remove
Low	Software that might collect information about you or change settings, but is running according to its license agreement	If you do not recognize and trust the software publisher, remove
Not yet classified	Software that is usually not harmful unless it was installed without your knowledge	If you're a SpyNet community member, check the member ratings to see if other users trust the software

The Quarantined items page also provides alert details to help you determine your best course of action. For example, it might indicate that a file is an adware program that has potentially unwanted behavior. The alert details sometimes include a link to a Web page on the Microsoft Web site, separate from the SpyNet community, that provides an up-to-date description of the program and identifies whether it is a known threat.

If Windows Defender quarantined any items, you should review the quarantined files and then remove or restore them.

To remove a quarantined file:

▶ **1.** In the Windows Defender window, click the **Tools** button on the toolbar to open the Tools and Settings page, and then click **Quarantined items**. The Quarantined items page opens. See Figure 5-13.

Quarantined items in Windows Defender ◀ **Figure 5-13**

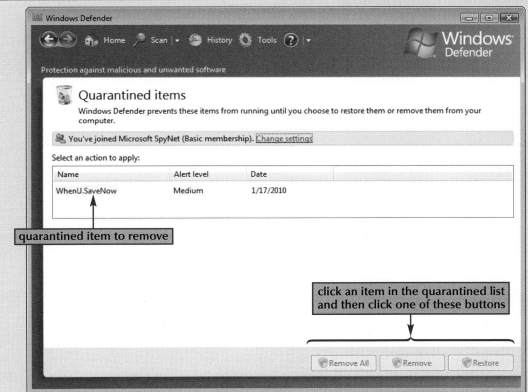

Trouble? If Windows Defender did not quarantine any items after its quick scan or you do not have permission to work with quarantined items, read but do not perform Step 2.

The item shown in Figure 5-13, WhenU.SaveNow, has a Medium alert level, and its details indicate this is adware that can behave in an unwanted manner. Curt does not recognize the publisher of this program, so you should remove it.

▶ **2.** In the Quarantined items list, click **WhenU.SaveNow** (or other item with a Severe, High, or Medium alert level and a publisher you do not recognize), and then click the **Remove** button.

Trouble? If a dialog box opens requesting an administrator password or your permission to continue, enter the password or click the Continue button.

Now that you've scanned Curt's computer and handled the items Windows Defender found, you can set options to make sure Windows Defender runs effectively.

Setting Windows Defender Options

The Options page in Windows Defender lets you set five categories of options: automatic scanning, default actions, real-time protection, advanced, and administrator options. When you select automatic scanning options, you choose whether you want Windows Defender to scan your computer according to a schedule, and then set the frequency, approximate time, and type of scan (quick scan or full system scan). You can also indicate whether Windows Defender should check for updated definitions before scanning, which is the recommended setting for keeping the spyware definitions up to date.

Default actions are those you want Windows Defender to perform when it detects potentially unsafe software installed or trying to install itself on your computer. You can specify default actions according to alert level. For example, if Windows Defender detects a program with a Low alert level, you can automatically ignore the program.

By default, Windows Defender is set to constantly monitor your computer for spyware activity. Windows Defender then alerts you when suspicious software attempts to install itself or to run on your computer, and notifies you when programs try to change important Windows settings. Real-time protection options let you turn this constant monitoring on and off, specify which Windows programs and settings it should monitor, select the type of activity Windows Defender should notify you about, and choose when a Windows Defender icon appears in the notification area: only when it detects activity or always.

The Advanced options on the Windows Defender Options page let you specify four additional options when scanning your computer for spyware. You can scan the contents of archived files and folders, which increases the scan time but might find spyware and other unwanted software concealed in these locations. Windows Defender can also use heuristics, or problem solving by trial and error, in addition to definition files to detect potentially harmful software. Scanning archived files and using heuristics is a good idea if you suspect spyware is infecting your computer but Windows Defender does not find the program during a quick or full system scan. Before applying actions to detected items, you can create a restore point, a collection of system file settings that your computer can return to if it becomes unstable. Finally, you can list any files or folders that you don't want Windows Defender to scan.

You use the two Administrator options to specify whether you want to turn Windows Defender on or off and who should use it. Windows Defender is turned on by default so it can monitor your computer for suspicious software activity, check for new definitions, scan your computer according to schedule, and automatically remove harmful software it detects during a scan. In addition, all users on your computer are set to use Windows Defender by default. If you turn off this option, only the administrator can use Windows Defender.

Curt wants to follow your recommendation of performing a quick scan every day. You'll show him how to schedule the daily spyware scan for 5:00 p.m., just before he leaves the office.

As you perform the following steps, note your settings so you can restore them later.

To schedule a spyware scan:

▶ **1.** In the Windows Defender window, click the **Tools** button on the toolbar to open the Tools and Settings page, and then click **Options**. The Options page opens. See Figure 5-14.

2. Click the **Approximate time** button, and then click **5:00 PM**.

3. Except for the Approximate time setting, make sure the other Automatic scanning options match those in Figure 5-14. If they do not, click the appropriate check box or value to change the setting.

   Trouble? If a dialog box opens requesting an administrator password or your permission to continue, enter the password or click the Continue button.

Besides scanning your computer regularly, you should keep Windows Defender turned on whenever you are using your computer. When Windows Defender is on, it alerts all users if it detects spyware or other unwanted software trying to run or install itself on your computer. In addition, you can use a feature called real-time protection to monitor certain Windows programs and settings that spyware often attempts to change, such as Internet Explorer options that prevent programs from switching your home page or installing a toolbar without your consent. As with quarantined items, when Windows Defender detects suspicious software, it assigns an alert level to the software. Then it displays a dialog box where you can choose one of the following actions:

- **Ignore**: Install or run the software on your computer. If the software is still running during the next scan, or if the software tries to change security-related settings on your computer, Windows Defender alerts you about this software again.
- **Quarantine**: Quarantine the program. Windows Defender prevents the software from running and allows you to restore it or remove it from your computer.

- **Remove**: Permanently delete the software from your computer.
- **Always Allow**: Add the software to the Windows Defender Allowed items list and run it on your computer. Windows Defender does not alert you to risks that the software might pose to your privacy or your computer unless you remove the program from the Allowed items list.

Windows Defender also alerts you if software already running on your computer attempts to change important Windows settings. In this case, you can either permit or deny the software to make the change.

If you set Windows Defender to scan your computer unattended (such as in the middle of the night) or you want Windows Defender to always take a certain action when it detects potential spyware, you can set default actions for the items it detects. By default, Windows Defender checks its definition list, and then acts accordingly by quarantining items with a High alert level, for example. You can specify whether you want Windows Defender to ignore or remove items with High, Medium, and Low alert levels. You don't need to specify an action for Severe items because Windows Defender automatically removes them or alerts you to do so. If an item is not yet classified, you must review information about the software and then choose an action.

You'll show Curt how to make sure Windows Defender is turned on and using real-time protection, and then you'll set it to remove any items it detects with a High alert level. You perform all of these tasks on the Windows Defender Options page.

To verify and set Windows Defender options:

▶ **1.** Scroll to the bottom of the Options page in the Windows Defender window to view the Administrator options. Make sure the Use Windows Defender check box is selected. This means Windows Defender is turned on.

▶ **2.** Scroll the Options page as necessary to view the Default actions and Real-time protection options sections. See Figure 5-15.

Default actions and real-time protection options ◀ **Figure 5-15**

> **3.** Click the **High alert items** button and then click **Remove**.
>
> **4.** Make sure the Use real-time protection (recommended) check box is selected, and then click the **Save** button.
>
>   **Trouble?** If a dialog box opens requesting an administrator password or your permission to continue, enter the password or click the Continue button.
>
> **5.** Close the Windows Defender, Windows Security Center, and Control Panel windows.

Windows Defender monitors the programs and settings listed in the Real-time protection options section of the Options page. (See Figure 5-15.) For example, it monitors the programs that are allowed to run automatically when you start your computer and tracks the security settings in Internet Explorer. It issues an alert if it detects changes to these programs and settings.

Defending Against E-mail Viruses with Windows Mail

An annoying and potentially dangerous type of privacy invasion is **spam**, or junk e-mail. Spam is a form of electronic direct mail, offering products and services that are sometimes fake or misleading. Some users receive thousands of spam messages a day; the volume alone makes spam a nuisance. In addition, spam can be a vehicle for malware. Although sending and reading e-mail messages is one of the most popular activities on the Internet, e-mail is the most common way for computer viruses to spread. Because viruses and other security threats are often contained in e-mail attachments, the security settings in Windows Mail block e-mail attachments that might be harmful. Files with names that end in .exe, .bat, and .js can contain malware, and are blocked by default. When Windows Mail blocks an attachment, it displays an Information bar below the toolbar that includes a message explaining that it blocked an attachment.

To help prevent spam and potentially offensive material, Windows Mail does not download graphics with messages sent in HTML format. People sending spam (called spammers) often use graphics to access your e-mail address. Viewing a picture in a junk e-mail message might notify the sender that you have read or previewed the message. This validates your e-mail address and often results in more junk e-mail. Using plain text for e-mail messages is therefore more secure than using the HTML format. Windows Mail also displays an Information bar when it blocks graphics. If you trust the sender, you can click an option on the Information bar to download and display the pictures in an open message.

Spammers can also take advantage of vulnerabilities in your computer to use it to send spam to other computers without your permission, a practice known as an **e-mail relay**. This lets spammers work without being detected and can seriously downgrade the performance of your computer. By default, Windows Mail helps prevent spammers from using your computer for e-mail relays.

Selecting Windows Mail Security Settings

You select your e-mail security settings using the Security tab of the Windows Mail Options dialog box. This dialog box provides the following categories of settings for securing your e-mail:

- **Virus Protection**: To help protect your computer from e-mail viruses, Windows Mail uses a restricted security zone by default, which prevents some types of malware from running on your computer. It also warns you when other applications try to send mail using your identity and does not allow you to save or open attachments that could be viruses.
- **Download Images**: By default, Windows Mail blocks images and other external content in HTML mail.
- **Secure Mail**: If you're concerned about the security of your outgoing mail, you can include a digital ID with your e-mail. Digital IDs are special documents that prove your identity in electronic transactions. You can also **encrypt**, or code, the contents and attachments of your outgoing mail.

InSight	**Encrypting E-Mail Messages**

When you exchange unencrypted e-mail messages, they are sent across the Internet in a plain text format. On their way to their recipients, hackers or automated programs can intercept, read, and even change the messages. In contrast, encrypted messages have a digital ID and are sent in a scrambled format that only your recipient can read. The encryption hides the e-mail contents, and the digital ID indicates whether a message has been altered in transit. You should therefore encrypt important e-mail messages. However, to send and read encrypted messages, both the sender and receiver must have copies of one another's digital ID. If you need a digital ID for your recipient, ask your recipient to send you a digitally signed message. Whenever you receive a digitally signed email message, Windows Mail automatically adds the sender's digital ID to the appropriate record in Windows Contacts.

You'll show Curt how to examine the security settings in Windows Mail. If he is using the default settings, you don't need to change them.

To examine security settings in Windows Mail:

▶ **1.** Click the **Start** button 🏵 on the taskbar, click **All Programs**, and then click **Windows Mail** to start Windows Mail.

▶ **2.** Click **Tools** on the menu bar, and then click **Options**. The Options dialog box opens.

▶ **3.** Click the **Security** tab to examine the enhanced security settings. See Figure 5-16.

Security settings for Windows Mail ◀ **Figure 5-16**

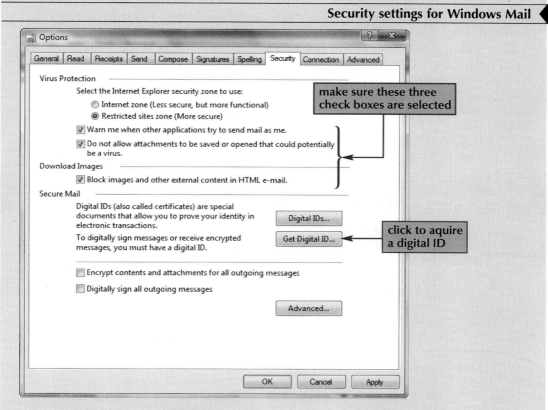

▶ **4.** Three check boxes are for enhanced security features in Windows Mail: Warn me when other applications try to send mail as me, Do not allow attachments to be saved or opened that could potentially be a virus, and Block images and other external content in HTML e-mail. Make sure that each box is checked, and then click the **OK** button.

In addition to selecting security settings in Windows Mail, some of the security settings you select for Internet Explorer apply to Windows Mail. You'll work with Internet Explorer security settings in the next session.

Blocking Spam and Other Junk Mail

Windows Mail includes a junk e-mail filter that catches obvious spam messages and moves them to a built-in Junk E-mail folder. You can then examine the messages in the Junk E-mail folder and delete them, open them, or move them back to your Inbox, if necessary. Windows Mail also maintains two lists of senders. The Safe Senders list contains addresses of messages you never want to treat as junk mail. The Blocked Senders list contains addresses of messages you always want to treat as junk mail. You can add e-mail addresses to these lists to customize the kind of security Windows Mail provides.

Usually, you add an address to the Safe Senders or Blocked Senders list when you receive a junk e-mail message. You can block further messages from that same sender by adding that sender to the Block Senders List. Alternatively, you can add the sender's domain to the Blocked Senders list. For example, if you receive spam from *JSmith@domain.net*, you can block all future e-mail from either that specific address or from any address in domain.net. Any further e-mail from that sender or domain will then be stored in the Junk E-mail folder automatically. Adding people to the Safe Senders list works the same way—you can add either an address or a domain to the Safe Senders list. If you haven't received any e-mail from someone you want to add to your Safe or Blocked Senders list, you can do so manually by using the Junk E-mail Options dialog box. If you somehow include the same person on both lists, you'll receive e-mail from that person in your Inbox because the Safe Senders list has priority over the Blocked Senders list.

By default, Windows Mail includes your Windows Contacts in the Safe Senders list. You can also automatically add people to whom you send e-mail to the Safe Senders list.

Reference Window | **Adding a Sender to the Blocked Senders or Safe Senders List**

- To block a sender in Windows Mail, right-click a message whose sender you want to add to the Blocked Senders list, point to Junk E-mail, and then click Add Sender to Blocked Senders List on the shortcut menu.
- To always allow a sender, right-click a message whose sender you want to add to the Safe Senders list, point to Junk E-mail, and then click Add Sender to Safe Senders List on the shortcut menu.
- Click the OK button.

In addition, you can set the level of junk e-mail protection you want in Windows Mail. By default, Windows Mail uses a low level of junk e-mail protection; you can change this based on how much junk e-mail you receive. You can use any of the following protection levels:

- **No Automatic Filtering**: This setting does not block any junk e-mail messages except for those from senders on your Blocked Senders list.
- **Low**: This setting blocks only the most obvious spam. Choose this level if you don't receive many junk e-mail messages.
- **High**: This setting blocks as much potential spam as possible. Choose this level if you receive a large volume of junk e-mail messages. However, be sure to review the messages in your Junk E-mail folder frequently to make sure it doesn't contain legitimate e-mail messages.
- **Safe List Only**: This setting blocks all e-mail messages except for those from senders on your Safe Senders list. Also review the messages in your Junk E-mail folder frequently for legitimate e-mail.

You'll check the level of junk e-mail protection that Curt is using, and then show him how to add people to the Safe and Blocked senders list.

To set junk e-mail options:

▶ 1. Click **Tools** on the Windows Mail menu bar, and then click **Junk E-mail Options**. The Junk E-mail Options dialog box opens. See Figure 5-17.

Junk E-mail Options dialog box ◀ **Figure 5-17**

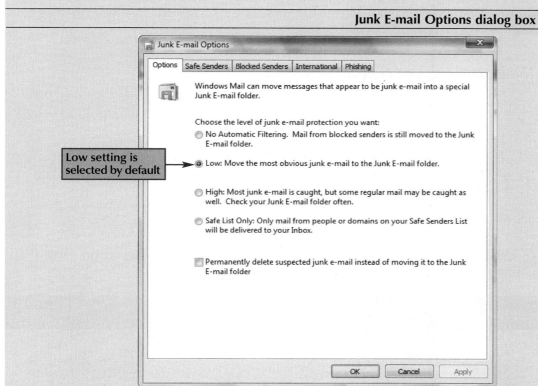

Curt doesn't receive much junk e-mail, so the Low setting is appropriate for him.

▶ 2. Click the **Safe Senders** tab to view your Safe Senders list. You can add your e-mail address to this list.

▶ 3. Click the **Add** button to open the Add address or domain dialog box.

▶ 4. Type your e-mail address, and then click the **OK** button.

▶ 5. Click the **Blocked Senders** tab to view your Blocked Senders list. Adding a sender to this list works the same way as the Safe Senders list—you click the Add button and enter an e-mail address.

Before closing the Junk E-mail Options dialog box, you want to show Curt one more way to protect his computer from harmful e-mail.

Defending Against Phishing Messages

Phishing (pronounced *fishing*) is an attempt to deceive you into revealing personal or financial information when you respond to an e-mail message or visit a Web site. A typical phishing scam starts with an e-mail message that looks like an official notice from a trusted person or business, such as a bank, credit card company, or reputable online merchant. The e-mail message asks you to reply with sensitive information, such as an account number or password, or directs you to a fraudulent Web site that requests this information. Phishers usually use the information for identity theft.

By default, if Windows Mail detects links to Web sites in the e-mail messages you receive, and the links seem fraudulent, Windows Mail blocks access to the links in that message and displays a message on the Information bar explaining its actions. If you are certain the message contains legitimate links, you can click an option on the Information bar to turn on the links in the message. You can also specify that when Windows Mail suspects a message is a phishing e-mail, it moves the message to the Junk E-mail folder. You'll show Curt how to select this setting.

To set phishing e-mail options:

▶ **1.** In the Junk E-mail Options dialog box, click the **Phishing** tab.

▶ **2.** Make sure the **Protect my Inbox from messages with potential Phishing links** check box is selected.

▶ **3.** Click the **Move phishing E-mail to the Junk Mail folder** check box, if necessary, to select that option.

▶ **4.** Click the **OK** button to close the Junk E-mail Options dialog box.

▶ **5.** Close Windows Mail.

In the next session, you'll also work with Internet Explorer settings to protect against phishing attempts.

Review | **Session 5.1 Quick Check**

1. What is malware?
2. The _____ _____ is a Control Panel tool that helps you manage security from a single window.
3. True or False. Windows Firewall checks communication coming from the Internet and either blocks it from your computer or allows it to pass.
4. Why might you add a program to the Windows Firewall exception list?
5. A(n) _____ is a change to software that can prevent or repair problems, enhance the security of the computer, or improve the computer's performance.
6. True or False. Windows Vista does not provide any type of malware protection.
7. What is the purpose of spyware?
8. _____ is a form of electronic direct mail, and can be a vehicle for malware.

Session 5.2

Managing Microsoft Internet Explorer Security

Your computer is most vulnerable to security threats when you are connected to the Internet. You should therefore take advantage of the security settings in Internet Explorer to help to protect your computer by identifying viruses and other security threats that are circulated over the Internet and to guard your privacy, making your computer and personal information more secure. Internet Explorer offers the following security and privacy features:

- **Phishing filter**: This feature helps detect online scams, such as Web sites that trick you into revealing financial account information.
- **Protected mode**: This feature guards against Web sites that try to save files or install malware on your computer.
- **Digital signatures**: Internet Explorer can detect and display digital signatures, which are electronic security marks added to files to verify their authenticity.
- **Pop-up Blocker**: Use this tool to limit or block most pop-up windows.
- **Add-on Manager**: Use this tool to disable or allow programs or controls that extend your browser's features.
- **Privacy settings and alerts**: These settings specify how to handle identifying information when you're online and alert you when a Web site you're visiting doesn't meet your criteria.
- **Secure connections**: Internet Explorer informs you when it is using a secure connection to communicate with Web sites that handle sensitive personal information.

Using the Phishing Filter

Recall that phishing is an attempt to deceive you into revealing personal or financial information when you respond to an e-mail message or visit a Web site. Internet Explorer can help protect you from phishing scams by detecting possible phishing Web sites. The Phishing Filter compares the addresses of Web sites you visit to a list of reportedly legitimate Web sites. The first time you navigate to a Web site that is not on the legitimate list, Internet Explorer asks whether you want to automatically check this Web site and others you visit for phishing history or characteristics. If you do, Internet Explorer sends the address of any potentially fraudulent Web site you visit to Microsoft, who checks it against an updated list of reported phishing sites and then alerts you. When you check Web sites automatically, the Phishing Filter also analyzes the Web pages you open to check for characteristics common to phishing sites. If they share these characteristics, Internet Explorer submits them to Microsoft for verification.

If you do not choose to check Web sites automatically, Internet Explorer displays a Phishing Filter security icon in the status bar when you visit a Web site that might be fraudulent. See Figure 5-18.

> **Tip**
> To make sure you have a secure connection with a Web site, look for a padlock icon in the Internet Explorer status bar and "https" (rather than "http") at the beginning of the Web address.

Phishing Filter security icon ◀ **Figure 5-18**

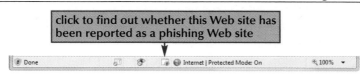

click to find out whether this Web site has been reported as a phishing Web site

You can check the Web site manually by clicking the Phishing Filter security icon, and then clicking Check This Website. If the security icon does not appear in the status bar, you can manually check a Web site by clicking the Tools button on the Internet Explorer toolbar, clicking Phishing Filter, and then clicking Check This Website. Internet Explorer then sends the Web site address to Microsoft to check it against a list of reported phishing sites.

After checking a Web site, Internet Explorer lets you know if it is a reported phishing site or is suspicious. A suspicious site shares some characteristics of typical phishing sites, but is not listed as a reported site nor as a legitimate site. You should not submit personal or financial information to a suspicious site unless you are sure it is trustworthy. If you're not sure whether to trust a Web site with your sensitive information, look for the Web site's privacy policy. Most Web sites that collect personal information provide a link to their privacy statement, which you should read carefully. Conditions that allow the Web site to share your information with others or require you to accept e-mail or advertising might indicate that the site will misuse your information.

InSight	**Protecting Yourself from Phishing Attempts**

In addition to using the Internet Explorer Phishing Filter, use the following guidelines to protect yourself from online phishing:
- Never provide personal information in an e-mail, instant message, or pop-up window.
- Do not click links in e-mail and instant messages from senders you do not know or trust. Even messages from friends and family can be faked, so check with the sender to make sure they actually sent the message.
- Only use Web sites that provide privacy statements or indicate how they use your personal information.

You'll show Curt how to check a Web site to make sure it is not a phishing site, and then turn on the Phishing Filter so Internet Explorer does this automatically.

To turn on the Phishing Filter and check a Web site:

▶ 1. Click the **Start** button 🔵 on the taskbar, and then click **Internet Explorer** to start Internet Explorer. Your home page opens.

▶ 2. Click the **Tools** button on the toolbar, point to **Phishing Filter**, and then click **Check This Website**. Internet Explorer sends the URL of your home page to Microsoft for verification.

Trouble? If a dialog box opens explaining how the Phishing Filter works, click the OK button.

Trouble? If you are not connected to the Internet, skip Steps 2 and 3.

▶ 3. When the Phishing Filter dialog box opens to indicate this is not a phishing Web site, click the **OK** button.

▶ 4. Click the **Tools** button on the toolbar, point to **Phishing Filter**, and then click **Turn On Automatic Website Checking**. The Microsoft Phishing Filter dialog box opens. See Figure 5-19. Internet Explorer selects the Turn on automatic Phishing Filter option button for you.

Tip
You can also click the Phishing Filter Security icon and then click Phishing Filter Settings to open the Microsoft Phishing Filter dialog box.

Microsoft Phishing Filter dialog box ◄ Figure 5-19

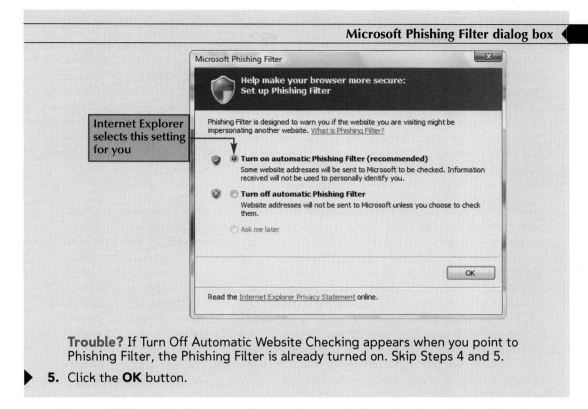

Internet Explorer selects this setting for you

Trouble? If Turn Off Automatic Website Checking appears when you point to Phishing Filter, the Phishing Filter is already turned on. Skip Steps 4 and 5.

► **5.** Click the **OK** button.

Next, you'll show Curt how to make sure Internet Explorer is using protected mode, which helps to keep your computer free of harmful software.

Blocking Malware with Protected Mode and Security Zones

To install or run programs on your computer, hackers often take advantage of Web programming tools, such as scripts and ActiveX controls that are designed to enhance your online experience. A **script** is programming code that performs a series of commands, and can be embedded in a Web page. For example, a Web site designer might use a script to verify that you've completed all the necessary fields in an online form. In contrast, hackers use scripts on a Web page to automatically download programs that can collect and transmit information about you without your knowledge or authorization. A common way for hackers to distribute adware and spyware is to download **ActiveX controls**, which are small, self-contained programs, from a Web page to your computer. Some ActiveX controls make it easier to perform tasks, such as submit information to a Web site. Other ActiveX controls can harm your computer and files, especially those controls that lack **digital signatures**, meaning they are unverified. Internet Explorer offers a few ways to protect against malicious scripts and ActiveX controls, including protected mode and security zones.

| InSight | | **Digital Signatures** |

Internet Explorer (and other programs, including Windows Vista) detects whether a file has a digital signature, which is an electronic security mark that identifies the publisher of a file and verifies that the file has not changed since it was signed. A file without a valid digital signature might not be from the stated source or might have been tampered with (possibly by a virus) since it was published. Avoid opening an unsigned file unless you know for certain who created it and whether the contents are safe to open. However, even a valid digital signature does not guarantee that the contents of the file are harmless. When you download a file, determine whether to trust its contents based on the identity of the publisher and the site providing the file.

Internet Explorer runs in protected mode by default, making it difficult for hackers to install malware on your computer. When protected mode is turned on, a notification appears in the Internet Explorer status bar. If a Web page tries to install any type of software or run a script, Internet Explorer displays a dialog box warning you about the attempt. If you trust the program, you can allow it to run once or always. If you are not familiar with the program or don't want to run it, you can deny it once or always.

In addition to protected mode, Internet Explorer uses security zones so you can tailor your security needs to the kind of online computing you do. Internet Explorer classifies all Web sites in one of four security zones: Internet, Local intranet, Trusted sites, and Restricted sites. Each zone uses a certain level of security settings ranging from Low to High. You can also select custom settings, which mix levels. For example, Web sites in the Trusted sites zone use Medium-level security settings. If a Web site you've assigned to the Trusted sites zone tries to download files onto your computer, Internet Explorer asks your permission only if the files are potentially unsafe. When you visit a Web site that has been assigned to a security zone, the appropriate icon appears in the Internet Explorer status bar. Figure 5-20 summarizes the four security zones. Note that the security zones you set in Internet Explorer also apply to Windows Mail.

Figure 5-20 ▶ **Internet Explorer security zones**

Security Zone	Description	Protected Mode Default
Internet	Internet Explorer assigns all Internet Web sites to this zone by default, and applies a Medium-high security level, which is appropriate for most sites. You can change the level to Medium or High.	On
Local intranet	Internet Explorer assigns Web sites on your intranet (a corporate or business network) to this zone and applies a Medium-low security level. You can change this to any other level.	On
Trusted sites	To this zone you assign Web sites you trust not to damage your computer or files. This zone has a Medium level of security by default, but you can change it to any other level.	Off
Restricted sites	To this zone you assign Web sites that might damage your computer or files. Adding sites to this zone does not block them, but does prevent them from using scripts or active content. This zone has a High level of security by default and cannot be changed.	On

You'll show Curt how to check the security level of his home page.

To check the security level of your home page:

▶ **1.** With Internet Explorer open to your home page, double-click the **Protected Mode** notification in the status bar. The Internet Security dialog box opens. See Figure 5-21.

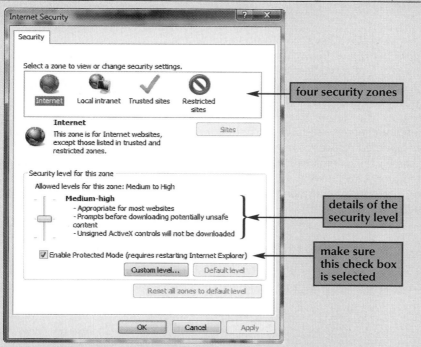

Curt's home page is assigned to the Internet zone, which uses a Medium-high security level and protected mode by default. At this level, Internet Explorer does not download unsigned ActiveX controls and requests permission before downloading content that might be unsafe.

▶ **2.** Click the **OK** button to close the dialog box.

Next, you'll show Curt how to use the pop-up blocker to limit or block most pop-up windows when he visits Web sites.

Blocking Pop-up Ads

A pop-up ad is a small Web browser window that appears when you visit a Web site and that advertises a product or service. Many legitimate advertisers use pop-up ads because they effectively get your attention while you are online and provide information or services that might interest you. However, some pop-up ads are annoying because they repeatedly interrupt your online activities, can be difficult to close, and display objectionable content. Other pop-up ads are dangerous; they can download spyware or **hijack** your browser, opening many more new windows each time you close one pop-up window until you have to close your browser or restart your computer.

To avoid the nuisance and danger of pop-up ads, Internet Explorer includes a pop-up blocker, which enables Internet Explorer to warn you about or block pop-up ads. The pop-up blocker in Internet Explorer is turned on by default, meaning that Internet Explorer blocks most pop-up ads. However, if you click a link or button to open a pop-up window, Internet Explorer does not block that window unless you change a setting. You can select settings in Internet Explorer to block all pop-up ads, allow more pop-up ads, or specify which Web sites can display pop-up ads in your browser.

Reference Window | **Blocking Pop-up Ads**

- Click Tools on the Internet Explorer toolbar, point to Pop-up Blocker, and then click Pop-up Blocker Settings.
- Click the current Filter level setting, and then click a setting ranging from High to Low.
- Click the Close button.

When you visit a Web site with pop-up ads and the pop-up blocker is turned on, an Information bar opens below the Internet Explorer toolbar and displays a message informing you that it blocked a pop-up ad. You can click the Information bar to display a menu of settings, such as to temporarily allow pop-up ads on the Web site.

Internet Explorer displays the Information bar in many situations, including when a Web site tries to install or run an ActiveX control, open a pop-up window, or download a file; when your security settings are below recommended levels; and when you need to install an updated ActiveX control or add-on program.

Curt has had problems with pop-up ads before, so he wants to block all pop-ups in Internet Explorer. You'll show him how to change the pop-up blocker settings to do so.

As you perform the following steps, note your original settings so you can restore them later.

To change the pop-up blocker settings in Internet Explorer:

▶ 1. Click the **Tools** button on the Internet Explorer toolbar, point to **Pop-up Blocker**, and then click **Pop-up Blocker Settings**. The Pop-up Blocker Settings dialog box opens. See Figure 5-22.

Figure 5-22 ▶ **Pop-up Blocker Settings dialog box**

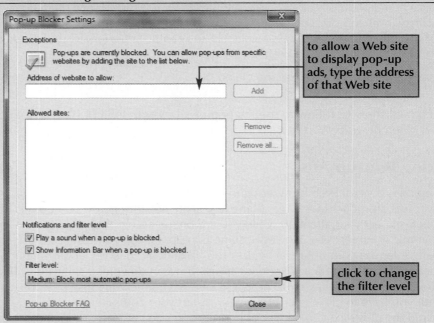

2. Click the **Filter level** button, and then click **High: Block all pop-ups (Ctrl+Alt to override)**.

Trouble? If you are working in a computer lab, you might not have permission to change the pop-up blocker settings. In that case, skip Step 2.

▶ **3.** Click the **Close** button.

Managing Add-on Programs

A browser **add-on** is a program offered by any software vendor that provides enhancements such as a toolbar or improved search feature. Some add-ons are safe and make your browser more effective; other add-ons, especially those that are installed without your permission, can affect the performance of Internet Explorer and even make it stop working. Internet Explorer provides an add-on manager so you can review, disable, update, or report add-ons to Microsoft. Other security features, such as protected mode, security levels, and the Information bar, warn you when a Web site is trying to download add-on software to your computer.

You can usually install and use browser add-ons without any problems, but some cause Internet Explorer to shut down unexpectedly. If this happens, you can update the add-on to make sure that it is compatible with your version of Internet Explorer. If the add-on continues to cause problems, you can disable it. In this case, you should also report the problem to Microsoft. Reporting is anonymous and only provides information to Microsoft about what caused the add-on problem.

Internet Explorer usually asks permission before running an add-on for the first time. If you don't recognize the program or its publisher, you can deny permission. Internet Explorer also maintains a list of preapproved add-ons that have been checked and digitally signed. It runs add-ons in this list without requesting your permission. You can view the list of preapproved add-ons in the Manage Add-ons dialog box.

Curt isn't aware of any add-ons his browser uses, so he wants to view the preapproved add-ons and any others Internet Explorer is running.

To examine and manage add-ons:

▶ **1.** Click the **Tools** button on the Internet Explorer toolbar, point to **Manage Add-ons**, and then click **Enable or Disable Add-ons**. The Manage Add-ons dialog box opens. By default, this dialog box displays the add-ons that Internet Explorer is currently using.

▶ **2.** Click the **Show** button, and then click **Add-ons that run without requiring permission**. The preapproved add-ons appear in the list. See Figure 5-23.

Figure 5-23 ▶ **Manage Add-ons dialog box**

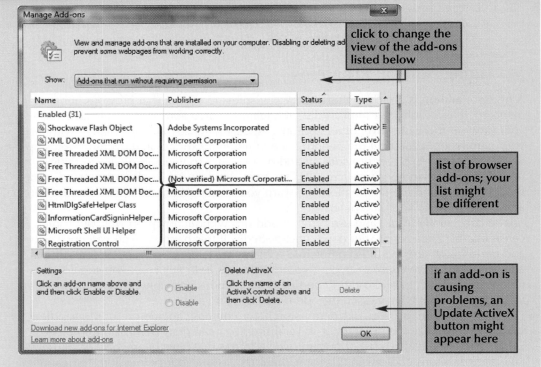

> **3.** Click the **OK** button to close the Manage Add-ons dialog box.

If you are having problems with an add-on, such as Internet Explorer closing unexpectedly when you use an add-on, you can first try to update the add-on by clicking its name in the Manage Add-ons dialog box, and then clicking the Update ActiveX button. (If the Update ActiveX button is not available, that means you cannot update the add-on.) If problems persist, you can disable the add-on by clicking it in the Manage Add-ons dialog box and then clicking the Disable option button. In some cases, you might be prompted to report a problem with an add-on to Microsoft. If you are connected to the Internet, you can follow the steps in the reporting dialog box to report the problem.

Selecting Privacy Settings

In addition to security protection, Internet Explorer also includes tools to protect your privacy. One privacy concern is cookies, which many Web sites store on your computer when you visit the site. A **cookie** is a small file that records information about you, such as the type of browser you are using, your e-mail address, and your preferences for using a Web site. Like other Web tools, cookies can enhance your online experience by helping trusted Web sites customize their service to you, but they can also pose a security risk—hackers can retrieve cookies to search for private information such as passwords or use cookies to track the Web sites you visit. In Internet Explorer, you can specify privacy settings that allow Web sites to or prevent them from saving cookies on your computer.

One way to protect your privacy with Internet Explorer is to block cookies on some or all of the Web sites you visit. You should be selective about which Web sites can store cookies on your computer. Blocking all cookies keeps your Web site visits private, but might also limit your experience or prove annoying. Allowing all cookies might compromise your privacy. Most users find that the default medium-high privacy setting provides a good balance, because it allows most **first-party cookies**, which are generated from the Web sites you visit and contain information the Web site reuses when you return. For example, to keep track of products you add to an electronic shopping cart or wish list, a Web site saves a first-party cookie on your computer. In contrast, the medium-high privacy setting blocks most **third-party cookies**, which are generated from Web site advertisers, who might use them to track your Web use for marketing purposes.

Selecting Privacy Settings | Reference Window

- Click Tools on the Internet Explorer toolbar, and then click Internet Options.
- Click the Privacy tab in the Internet Options dialog box.
- Drag the slider to select a privacy setting ranging from Block All Cookies to Accept All Cookies.
- Click the OK button.

Curt often visits his clients' Web sites for research as he prepares or performs translation projects. He wants to protect the privacy of Presto Global Translators and his clients by blocking all cookies and then allowing only those issued by sites he trusts.

As you perform the following steps, note your original settings so you can restore them later.

To change privacy settings for saving cookies:

▶ 1. Click the **Tools** button on the Internet Explorer toolbar, and then click **Internet Options**. The Internet Options dialog box opens.

▶ 2. Click the **Privacy** tab to view privacy settings. See Figure 5-24.

Privacy tab in the Internet Options dialog box ◀ Figure 5-24

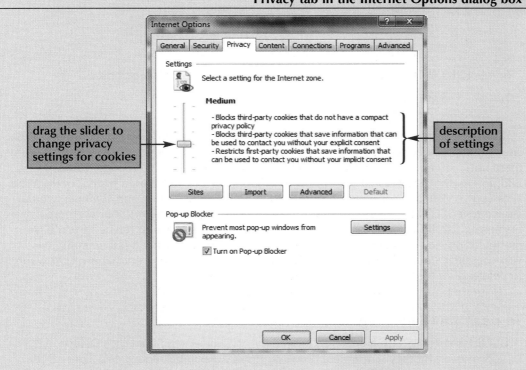

drag the slider to change privacy settings for cookies

description of settings

Trouble? If you are working in a computer lab, you might not have permission to change the privacy settings. In that case, read but do not perform Steps 3–6.

3. Drag the slider up to the **Block All Cookies** setting. Internet Explorer will not let a Web site store any cookies on your computer unless you explicitly allow it to do so.

4. Drag the slider back to **Medium**. This setting blocks cookies except for those created by Web sites you identify.

5. Click the **Sites** button to open the Per Site Privacy Actions dialog box. See Figure 5-25. You use this dialog box to specify the Web sites you want to allow to store cookies on your computer. (If you had selected a lower privacy setting, you could also use this dialog box to block certain Web sites from storing cookies.)

| Figure 5-25 | Per Site Privacy Actions dialog box |

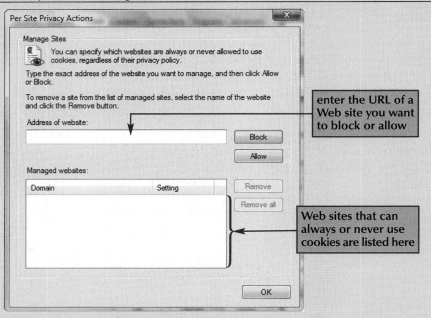

enter the URL of a Web site you want to block or allow

Web sites that can always or never use cookies are listed here

6. Click the **OK** button to close the Per Site Privacy Actions dialog box.

7. Click the **OK** button to close the Internet Options dialog box.

Tip

To view temporary files before deleting them, click the Tools button on the Internet Explorer toolbar, click Internet Options, click the General tab, click the Settings button in the Browsing history section, and then click View files.

Internet Explorer will block most cookies on Curt's computer from now on, but if Web sites stored cookies on his computer before you changed the privacy setting, they remain there until you delete them. You can delete cookies by clearing Web page history. In addition to cookies, Internet Explorer stores temporary Internet files, a history of the Web sites you've visited, information you've entered in the Address bar, and Web passwords you've saved. Usually, maintaining this history information improves your Web browsing because it can fill in information that you would otherwise have to retype. If you have particular privacy concerns, however, such as when you are using a public computer, you can clear some or all of your browsing history to delete this information. Curt wants to delete all of the cookies and the list of Web sites he has visited.

To clear your browsing history:

1. Click the **Tools** button on the Internet Explorer toolbar, and then click **Delete Browsing History**. The Delete Browsing History dialog box opens. See Figure 5-26.

Delete Browsing History dialog box ◀ **Figure 5-26**

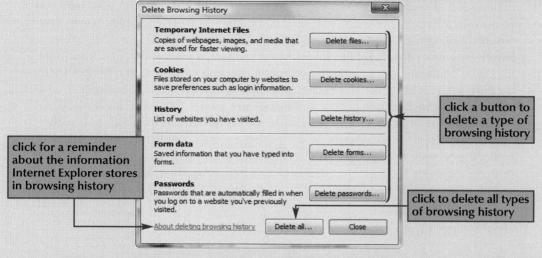

click for a reminder about the information Internet Explorer stores in browsing history

click a button to delete a type of browsing history

click to delete all types of browsing history

Trouble? If you are working in a computer lab, you might not have permission to clear your browsing history. In that case, read but do not perform Steps 2–5.

▶ **2.** Click the **Delete cookies** button to delete all the cookies stored on your computer.

▶ **3.** When asked if you are sure you want to delete cookies, click the **Yes** button.

▶ **4.** Click the **Delete history** button to delete the list of Web sites you have visited.

▶ **5.** When asked if you are sure you want to delete your browsing history, click the **Yes** button.

▶ **6.** Click the **Close** button.

Tip

When you delete all of your browsing history, you do not delete your list of favorites or subscribed feeds.

Finally, you want to examine the advanced Internet Explorer settings to make sure they are protecting Curt's computer.

Verifying Internet Explorer Advanced Settings

In addition to using the Phishing Filter, security zones, pop-up blocker, add-on programs, and privacy settings, you can manage advanced Internet Explorer settings to enhance the security of your computer. You select these settings on the Advanced tab of the Internet Options dialog box, which organizes them into categories of options you turn on or off. By default, Internet Explorer turns on settings to achieve a balance between security and performance. If you suspect your Internet activity is causing problems on your computer, you can check these settings to see if any have changed, or you can click the Restore Advanced Settings button to return the Internet Explorer settings to their original state. Some malware can gain access to your computer by changing the Advanced settings, so you should monitor the settings from time to time. If Internet Explorer becomes corrupted and unusable, you can click the Reset button on the Advanced tab to delete all of your temporary files, disable add-ons, and reset all of your changed settings.

In addition to the default settings, you can change the following Advanced settings to enhance your security when browsing:

• **Enable third-party browser extensions**: A third-party extension is a program that extends the features of Internet Explorer, such as an additional toolbars. Like add-ons, browser extensions can be benign or malicious. If you turn this setting off, browser extensions are installed only with your consent.

- **Do not save encrypted pages to disk**: A secure Web site usually sends sensitive information in an encrypted, or coded, form that prevents others from seeing the information. Browsers save Web pages, including encrypted ones, on your hard disk. To prevent a hacker from accessing your computer and these encrypted pages, you can turn this setting on.
- **Empty Temporary Internet Files folder when browser is closed**: Because a temporary file could contain information a hacker might use, you can empty the Temporary Internet Files folder (also called the **cache**) whenever you close Internet Explorer.
- **Warn if changing between secure and not secure mode**: When you are viewing a secure Web site, a padlock icon appears in the status bar and the URL starts with "https" instead of "http." When you are visiting a regular site that is not secure, the padlock icon does not appear and the URL starts with "http." You can have Internet Explorer display a Security Alert dialog box to inform you that you are switching from one kind of Web site to another.

You'll show Curt which Advanced settings to change in Internet Explorer. Note your original settings so you can restore them later.

To change Internet Explorer Advanced settings:

▶ 1. Click the **Tools** button on the Internet Explorer toolbar, and then click **Internet Options**. The Internet Options dialog box opens.

▶ 2. Click the **Advanced** tab, and then scroll the list to view most of the Browsing category. See Figure 5-27.

Figure 5-27 ▶ **Internet Explorer Advanced settings**

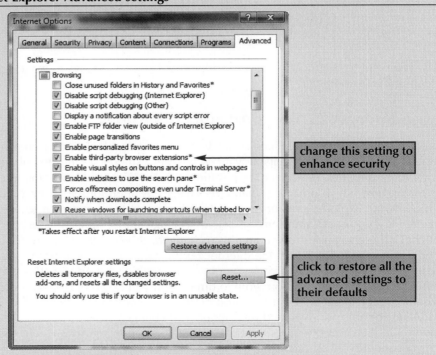

Trouble? If you are working in a computer lab, you might not have permission to change the Advanced settings. In that case, read but do not perform Steps 3–6.

▶ **3.** Click the **Enable third-party browser extensions** check box, if necessary, to remove the check mark.

▶ **4.** Scroll down to the Security category, and click the **Do not save encrypted pages to disk** check box to select it.

▶ **5.** Click the **Empty Temporary Internet Files folder when browser is closed** check box to select it.

▶ **6.** Click the **Warn if changing between secure and not secure mode** check box to select it.

▶ **7.** Click the **OK** button to close the Internet Options dialog box.

▶ **8.** Close Internet Explorer.

Now that you have thoroughly explored the security settings in Internet Explorer, you can review another way to protect your computer—by using user accounts.

Setting Up User Accounts

In Windows Vista, a **user account** is a collection of information that indicates the files and folders you can access, the types of changes you can make to the computer, and your preferred appearance settings (such as your desktop background or color scheme). If you have a user account on a computer that you share with other people, you can maintain your own files and settings separate from other users. When you start Windows Vista, the Welcome screen appears and displays the accounts that are available on the computer. To access your user account, you select your user name. For security purposes, you can also set Windows to request your password.

Windows Vista provides the following three types of user accounts, and each type gives the user a different level of control over the computer.

- **Standard**: This type of account is designed for everyday computing, and can protect your computer and data by preventing users from changing settings that affect all users. To make this type of change, such as installing software or changing security settings, Windows requests permission or a password for an Administrator account. Microsoft recommends that every regular user on a computer have a Standard account.
- **Administrator**: This type of account is created when Windows Vista is installed, and provides full access to the computer. The Administrator can access the files of any user, install software, and change any settings. The intention is that when you install Windows Vista, you first log on to the computer as the Administrator and then create a Standard user account for yourself and for each person who will use the computer.
- **Guest**: This type of account is primarily for people who need temporary access to the computer and is not used often.

To create an account, you provide a user name and select an account type. You are not required to protect every account with a password, but Microsoft strongly recommends that you do so. Using a password is one of the most effective ways you can keep your computer secure. When your computer is protected with a password, only someone who knows the password can log on to it.

Reference Window | **Creating a Password-Protected User Account**

- Open the Control Panel in Category view, click User Accounts and Family Safety, and then click User Accounts.
- Click Manage another account.
- Click Create a new account.
- Type the new account name, click the Standard user option button or the Administrator option button, and then click the Create Account button.
- Click Create a Password.
- Click in the New password text box, and then type your password.
- Click in the Confirm new password text box, and then type your password again.
- Click in the Type a password hint text box, and then type a hint to help you remember your password.
- Click the Create password button.

Curt is concerned that he and his staff at Presto Global Translators are all using the Administrator accounts that Windows created when it was installed. He wants to make sure that everyone creates a Standard user account with a password. Some part-time employees share a single computer, and Curt wants those employees to create separate Standard accounts on the same computer.

Creating a Password-Protected Standard User Account

When you create a user account, you provide a name for the account, which is usually your name, and then select the account type. You can then change the picture for the account and create a password. In Windows Vista, a password is a series of letters, numbers, spaces, and symbols that you provide to access your files, programs, and other resources on the computer. Windows passwords are case sensitive, so CuBote18 is different from cubote18. Passwords strengthen computer security because they help to make sure that no one can access the computer unless they are authorized to do so. You should therefore not give your passwords to others or write it in a place where others can see it.

When creating a password, make sure you devise a **strong password**, one that is difficult to guess but easy for you to remember. Strong passwords have the following characteristics:

- Contain at least eight characters
- Do not include your user name, real name, or company name
- Are not words you can find in the dictionary
- Are significantly different from your previous passwords
- Contain characters from each of the following categories: uppercase letters, lowercase letters, numbers, and symbols (including spaces)

Creating Strong Passwords | InSight

Microsoft provides the following guidelines for creating strong passwords:

- Create an acronym that's easy for you to remember. For example, select a phrase that is meaningful to you, such as "My birthday is February 12." From that phrase, you could create Mbdi02/12 as your password.
- Use numbers, symbols, and misspellings in place of letters or words in an easy-to-remember phrase. For example, you could change "My birthday is February 12" to MiBD I$ Two12.
- Relate your password to something that interests you, such as a hobby, sport, pet, or goal. For example, *Travel to Central America* could become Trvl 2 Cntrl@mrca.

Curt wants to start by creating a Standard user account on his computer with a strong password to protect it. If you can use an Administrator account to perform the following steps, log on to Windows using that Administrator account. If you do not have access to an Administrator account, read but do not perform the following steps.

To create a Standard user account:

▶ **1.** Click the **Start** button 🪟 on the taskbar, and then click **Control Panel** to open the Control Panel.

▶ **2.** In Category view, click **User Accounts and Family Safety**. The User Accounts and Family Safety window opens.

Trouble? If the Control Panel opens in Classic view, click Category View in the left pane, and then repeat Step 2.

▶ **3.** Click **User Accounts** to open the User Accounts window. See Figure 5-28. Your window will differ.

User Accounts window ◀ **Figure 5-28**

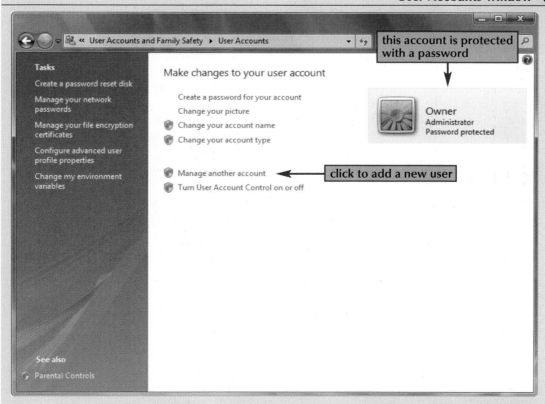

▶ **4.** Click **Manage another account** to open the Manage Accounts window.

Trouble? If a dialog box opens requesting an Administrator password or confirmation, enter the password or click the Continue button.

▶ **5.** Click **Create a new account**. The Create New Account window opens. See Figure 5-29.

Figure 5-29 **Create New Account window**

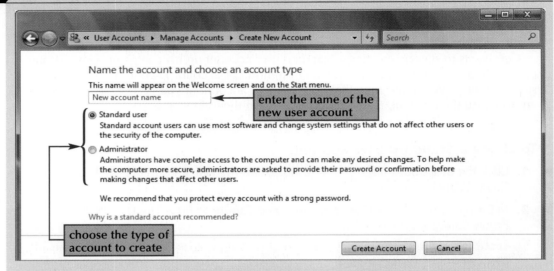

Name the account and choose an account type
This name will appear on the Welcome screen and on the Start menu.

[New account name] ← enter the name of the new user account

◉ Standard user
Standard account users can use most software and change system settings that do not affect other users or the security of the computer.

○ Administrator
Administrators have complete access to the computer and can make any desired changes. To help make the computer more secure, administrators are asked to provide their password or confirmation before making changes that affect other users.

We recommend that you protect every account with a strong password.

Why is a standard account recommended?

choose the type of account to create

[Create Account] [Cancel]

▶ **6.** Type **Curt** as the new account name, and then click the **Standard user** option button, if necessary.

▶ **7.** Click the **Create Account** button. The Manage Accounts window opens, listing the new account.

After you create a user account, you can change its properties, such as the user picture, account type, or account name, and you can create a password for the account. When you create a password, you can also create a hint to help you remember it. Using a hint is a more secure way to remember a password than writing it where others might see it. You'll create a password for Curt's account. For security, he can log on to his account later and change the password. For now, you'll use Prsto! 08 as the password, a combination of the name of Curt's company and the year it was founded.

To create a password:

▶ **1.** In the Manage Accounts window, click the **icon** for Curt's account, and then click **Create a password**. The Create Password window opens. See Figure 5-30.

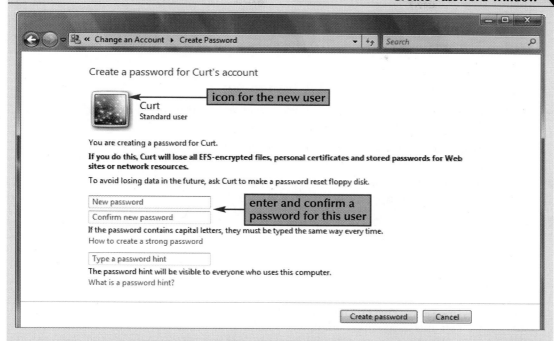

2. In the New password text box, type **Prsto! 08**. Be sure to include a space after the exclamation point. You must type the password again to confirm it.

3. Click in the Confirm new password text box, and then type **Prsto! 08**.

4. Click in the Type a password hint text box, and then type **Company and first year**.

5. Click the **Create password** button. The Change an Account window opens, displaying the new account and indicating that it is password protected.

6. Click **User Accounts** in the Address bar to return to the User Accounts window.

Now you and Curt can show all of the Presto Global employees how to create accounts and passwords on their computers.

Controlling Access to Your Computer

One way to manage access to your computer is to take advantage of User Account Control (UAC), a feature that is turned on by default and can help prevent unauthorized changes to your computer. As you performed the previous steps, you might have seen UAC at work, asking for permission or an Administrator password before performing actions that could affect your computer's settings. A UAC dialog box usually opens when a program or action is about to start. The dialog box requests an Administrator password or your permission to start the program. By notifying you, UAC can help prevent malware from installing itself on or changing your computer without permission. When a UAC dialog box opens, make sure the name of the action or program it mentions is one that you intended to start. The dialog box indicates whether the program or action is part of Windows, is not part of Windows, is unidentified, or is blocked by the Administrator. The dialog box also indicates whether the program has a digital signature. If you are working on your own computer on which you've set up an Administrator account and one or more Standard accounts, the UAC dialog box helps to protect your computer by asking for an Administrator password so that software can't be installed without your knowledge or permission.

The UAC feature is turned on by default, and should not be turned off. You'll show Curt how to make sure UAC is turned on for all the Presto Global computers.

To verify User Account Control is turned on:

▶ **1.** In the User Accounts window, click **Turn User Account Control on or off**. The Turn User Account Control On or Off window opens.

Trouble? If a User Account Control dialog box opens requesting an Administrator password or confirmation, enter the password or click the Continue button.

▶ **2.** Make sure the **Use User Account Control (UAC) to help protect your computer** check box is selected, and then click the **OK** button.

▶ **3.** Close the User Accounts window.

Locking Your Computer

Another way to protect your privacy and reduce power consumption is to let your computer go to sleep after a specified amount of idle time, which it does by default. Before going to sleep, Windows saves your files, settings, and the current state of your desktop in temporary memory, so you can return to work easily, and then plays a screen saver or blanks the screen. To wake the computer, you might move the mouse, press a key, or press the Power button, depending on your settings. Windows then displays your user account icon, and indicates the account is locked. If you use a password to log on to Windows, you must click your user icon and enter your password. Take this extra precaution of locking your account to protect the confidential information you store on your computer. To manually lock your computer, click the Start button, and then click the Lock button.

Besides controlling access to your computer with passwords and User Account Control, you can secure folders that contain files you share with other users.

Securing and Sharing Folders

If more than one person uses your computer, you can share files and folders with them in two ways: by explicitly allowing another user to share a folder or by storing files in the Public folder. The Public folder is designed for files any user can access. To share files from the Public folder, you copy or move your files to your Public folder so that other users can access them. Be aware, however, that any user on your computer can view all the files in the Public folder. You cannot restrict users from viewing only some of the files in the Public folder, though you can restrict them from changing the files or creating new ones. Use the Public folder for sharing if you prefer sharing your files from a single location on your computer, you want to monitor your shared files by opening a single folder, you want to keep your shared files separate from your other personal files, or you don't need to set sharing permissions for individual users.

When you explicitly share files, you set sharing permissions that determine who can change your files and what kinds of changes they can make. In this way, you can allow only some users on your computer to view, change, or create files in your folders. Set permissions to share any folder if you prefer to share folders directly from their original location (such as when you store many large photos in your Pictures folder), or when you want to allow only some users to access the folder.

Curt has a document named Guidelines that contains some general guidelines for translating documents. He wants to create a Translation folder in the Public folder on his computer and add other documents to it so that any user can access the documents. You'll show him how to do so.

To share a document in the Public folder:

▶ 1. If necessary, insert the USB flash drive containing your Data Files into a USB port on your computer.

   Trouble? If you do not have a USB flash drive, insert a different type of removable disk, such as a Zip disk, but not a CD, into the appropriate drive.

▶ 2. In a folder window, open the **Tutorial.05** and then the **Tutorial** folder in your Data Files.

▶ 3. Right-click the **Guidelines** document, and then click **Copy** on the shortcut menu.

▶ 4. If necessary, click the **Folders** button in the Navigation pane to display the Folders list.

▶ 5. In the Folders list, right-click the **Public** folder, point to **New**, and then click **Folder.**

   Trouble? If User Account Control dialog boxes open requesting your permission, an Administrator password or confirmation, enter the password or click the Continue button.

▶ 6. Type **Translation** as the name of the new folder, and then press the **Enter** key.

   Trouble? If User Account Control dialog boxes open requesting your permission, an Administrator password or confirmation, enter the password or click the Continue button.

▶ 7. Right-click the **Translation** folder, and then click **Paste** on the shortcut menu.

Now any user logged on to Curt's computer can access the Translation folder and its files.

Assigning Permissions to Folders

To specify which users can access a folder you want to share, you click the folder in a folder window, click Share on the toolbar, and then enter the account name of another user on the computer. Then you indicate whether that user is a Reader (can only read the files in the shared folder), Contributor (can read all files in the shared folder and can add, change, or delete their own files in the folder), or Co-owner (can read, change, add, or delete any file in the shared folder).

Curt has a sample password policy that he wants you to review before he revises it and distributes it to his employees. He wants to store it in a shared folder that only you can access and contribute to. First, you'll create a folder for the policy document. You also need to create a user account for yourself on Curt's computer, which you can do just before you assign permissions to the new folder.

To create a folder and a new account:

▶ 1. Click the **Documents** folder in the Favorite Links list in your Navigation pane.

▶ 2. Create a folder named **Policies** in the Documents folder.

3. Copy the **Password Policy** file in the Tutorial.05\Tutorial folder in your Data Files to the Policies folder.

4. Click the **Policies** folder, and then click the **Share** button on the toolbar. The File Sharing dialog box opens. See Figure 5-31.

Figure 5-31 > **File Sharing dialog box**

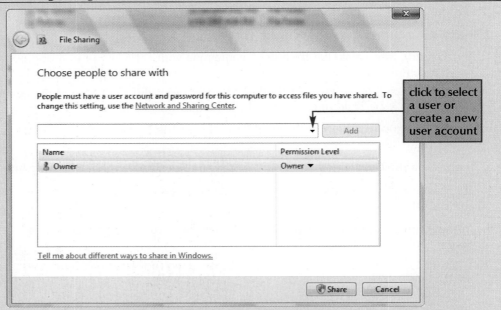

5. Click the **arrow button** to the right of the first list box (see Figure 5-31), and then click **Create a new user**. The User Accounts window opens.

6. Click **Manage another account**, and then click **Create a new account**.

   Trouble? If a dialog box opens requesting an Administrator password or confirmation, enter the password or click the Continue button.

7. Type **your first name** as the new account name, click the **Standard user** option button, if necessary, and then click the **Create Account** button.

8. Click the icon for the new account, and then click **Create a password**.

9. In the New password text box, type **T5 Pw-2010**. (Be sure to type the hyphen before 2010).

10. Click in the Confirm new password text box, and then type **T5 Pw-2010**.

11. Click the **Create password** button.

12. Close the Change an Account window.

Now you can share the folder Policies folder so that only you and Curt can access it.

To share a folder:

1. In the folder window, click the **Policies** folder, and then click the **Share** button on the toolbar. The File Sharing dialog box opens.

2. Click the **arrow** button to the right of the top (empty) list box, and then click your user name.

> **3.** Click the **Add** button to add your user name to the list.

> **4.** Click the **permission level** (such as Reader) for your user name. See Figure 5-32.

> **5.** Click **Contributor** so that you can view, add, and change your own files.

> **6.** Click the **Share** button. Windows displays the progress of the sharing process, and then confirms your folder is shared.
>
> **Trouble?** If a dialog box opens requesting an Administrator password or confirmation, enter the password or click the Continue button.

> **7.** Click the **Done** button.

> **8.** Close all open windows.

After you receive confirmation that your folder is shared, you can send a link to your shared files to the people with whom you are sharing the files. That way, the other users will know the files are shared and how to access them. You can click "e-mail these links" in the File Sharing confirmation window to open a Windows Mail e-mail message with the link to your shared files.

Restoring Your Settings

If you are working in a computer lab or a computer other than your own, complete the steps in this section to restore the original settings on your computer. If a User Account Control dialog box opens requesting an Administrator password or confirmation after you perform any of the following steps, enter the password or click the Continue button.

To restore your settings:

> **1.** Open the Control Panel in Category view, click **Security**, and then click **Security Center**.

▶ **2.** In the left pane of the Windows Security Center window, click **Windows Firewall**, and then click **Change settings** to open the Windows Firewall Settings dialog box. Click the **Exceptions** tab to view the exception list.

▶ **3.** Click the **Windows Meeting Space** check box, and the **OK** button to close the Windows Firewall dialog box, and then close the Windows Firewall window.

▶ **4.** In the Windows Security Center window, click **Windows Update**, and then click **Change settings** in the left pane. In the Install new updates section, click the update time, click the original time set for installing updates, and then click the **OK** button. Close the Windows Update window.

▶ **5.** In the Windows Security Center window, click **Windows Defender** in the left pane. Click the **Tools** button on the toolbar, and then click **Options**. Click the **Approximate time** button, click the original time set for scanning, and then click the **Save** button. Close all open windows.

▶ **6.** Start Windows Mail, click **Tools** on the menu bar, and then click **Junk E-mail Options**. Click the **Safe Senders** tab, click **your e-mail address** in the list, and then click the **Remove** button.

▶ **7.** Click the **Phishing** tab, click the **Move phishing E-mail to the Junk Mail folder** check box to remove the check mark, click the **OK** button to close the Junk E-mail Options dialog box, and then close Windows Mail.

▶ **8.** Start Internet Explorer, click the **Tools** button on the Internet Explorer toolbar, point to **Pop-up Blocker**, and then click **Pop-up Blocker Settings**. Click the **Filter level** button, and then click your original setting. Click the **Close** button to close the Pop-up Blocker Settings dialog box.

▶ **9.** Click the **Tools** button on the Internet Explorer toolbar, click **Internet Options**, click the **Privacy** tab, and then drag the slider to its original setting. Click the **OK** button to close the Internet Options dialog box.

▶ **10.** Click the **Tools** button on the Internet Explorer toolbar, click **Internet Options**, click the **Advanced** tab, and then restore your original settings for the **Enable third-party browser extensions**, **Do not save encrypted pages to disk**, **Empty Temporary Internet Files folder when browser is closed**, and **Warn if changing between secure and not secure mode** check boxes. Click the **OK** button to close the Internet Options dialog box, and then close Internet Explorer.

▶ **11.** Open the Control Panel in Category view, click **User Accounts and Family Safety**, click **User Accounts**, and then click **Manage another account**. Click the **Curt** account icon, click **Delete the account**, click the **Delete Files** button, and then click the **Delete Account** button.

▶ **12.** Click the account icon for your account, click **Delete the account**, click the **Delete Files** button, and then click the **Delete Account** button.

▶ **13.** Navigate to the **Public** folder on your hard disk, and then move the **Translation** folder to the Tutorial.05\Tutorial folder provided with your Data Files.

▶ **14.** Navigate to the **Documents** folder on your hard disk, and then move the **Policies** folder to the Tutorial.05\Tutorial folder provided with your Data Files. Delete the files in the Tutorial.05\Tutorial folder so that the folder contains only subfolders.

▶ **15.** Close all open windows.

Session 5.2 Quick Check | Review

1. How can Internet Explorer help protect you from phishing scams?
2. True or False. When you visit a Web site with pop-up ads and the pop-up blocker is turned on, you can use the Information bar to open the pop-up window.
3. A browser _____ program provides enhancements such as a toolbar or improved search feature.
4. True or False. All cookies pose some type of security risk.
5. What type of user account does Microsoft recommend for every regular user on a computer?
6. Name three characteristics of a strong password.
7. When does a User Account Control (UAC) dialog box usually open?
8. If more than one person uses your computer, you can share files and folders with them in two ways: by explicitly allowing another user to share a folder or by storing files in the _____ folder.

Tutorial Summary | Review

In this tutorial, you used the Windows Vista Security Center to manage Windows Firewall, Windows Update, and your antivirus software. You used Windows Defender to guard against spyware, and you selected options in Windows Mail to protect your computer from e-mail viruses and junk e-mail. You also used the security features in Internet Explorer to browse safely, including using the Phishing Filter, protected mode, security zones, and privacy settings. You also learned how to block pop-up ads and manage add-on programs. To enhance security, you set up a password-protected user account and learned how to share your folders.

Key Terms

ActiveX control	exception	spyware
add-on	first-party cookie	strong password
adware	hacker	third-party cookie
cache	hijack	update
cookie	phishing	user account
cracker	pop-up ad	virus
digital signature	quarantine	worm
e-mail relay	script	
encrypt	spam	

| Practice | **Review Assignments** |

Practice the skills you learned in the tutorial.

Data File needed for the Review Assignments: Video Scripts.rtf

Curt Mickelson, owner of Presto Global Translators, recently bought a new Windows Vista computer for you to share with Donna Cordoza, one of his project managers who specializes in translating videos that she plays on Windows Media Player. You'll show Donna how to keep the new computer secure and set up accounts for the two of you. Complete the following steps, noting your original settings so you can restore them later:

1. Open Windows Firewall, choose to allow a program through Windows Firewall, and then add Windows Media Player to the exception list.

2. Change the settings in Windows Update to automatically check for and install updates every day at 7:00 a.m.

3. Maximize the Windows Security Center window, expand the Firewall and Automatic updating sections, and then press the Alt+Print Screen keys to capture an image of the window. Open Paint, and then press Ctrl+V to paste the image in a Paint file. Save the file as **SecurityCenterXY**, where *XY* are your initials, in the Tutorial.05\ Review folder provided with your Data Files.

4. Use Windows Defender to perform a quick scan on your computer.

5. Change the Windows Defender settings to scan every day at 10:00 p.m.

6. With the Windows Defender home page window open on your desktop, press the Alt+Print Screen keys to capture an image of the window. Open Paint, and then press Ctrl+V to paste the image in a Paint file. Save the file as **DefenderXY**, where *XY* are your initials, in the Tutorial.05\Review folder provided with your Data Files. Close all open windows.

7. In Windows Mail, add the following e-mail address to your Safe Senders list: **DonnaCordoza@presto.net**.

8. In Internet Explorer, open a Web page in your Favorites list or go to the home page of a popular search engine, such as Google (www.google.com) or Yahoo! (www. yahoo.com). Use the Phishing Filter to verify this Web site is not a phishing Web site.

9. Make sure the pop-up blocker in Internet Explorer is turned on, and then visit a popular news Web site, such as www.cnn.com, until you find one that includes pop-up windows. With the Information bar displayed in the Internet Explorer window, press the Alt+Print Screen keys to capture an image of the window. Open Paint, and then press Ctrl+V to paste the image in a Paint file. Save the file as **PopUpXY**, where *XY* are your initials, in the Tutorial.05\Review folder provided with your Data Files. Close all open windows.

10. Create Standard user accounts for you and for Donna Cordoza. Use a name and password you prefer for your user account, making sure these are different from any other account on the computer. Use **Donna** as the name and **iLuv MVs98** as the password for Donna's account.

11. With the User Accounts window open on the desktop, press the Alt+Print Screen keys to capture an image of the window. Open Paint, and then press Ctrl+V to paste the image in a Paint file. Save the file as **UsersXY**, where *XY* are your initials, in the Tutorial.05\Review folder provided with your Data Files.

12. Move the **Video Scripts** document from the Tutorial.05\Review folder provided with your Data Files to a new folder named **Marketing** created in your Documents folder.

13. Share the **Marketing** folder with Donna as a Contributor. With the final Sharing Files window open on your desktop, press the Alt+Print Screen keys to capture an image of the window. Open Paint, and then press Ctrl+V to paste the image in a Paint file. Save the file as **SharingXY**, where *XY* are your initials, in the Tutorial.05\Review folder provided with your Data Files.

14. Restore the settings on your computer. Remove Windows Media Player from the Windows Firewall exception list. Restore the settings in Windows Update and Windows Defender to install updates and scan at their original times. Remove Donna Cordoza's e-mail address from the Windows Mail Safe Senders list. Move the **Marketing** folder to the Tutorial.05\Review folder provided with your Data Files. Delete the user accounts you created for yourself and Donna Cordoza.

15. Close all open windows.

16. Submit the results of the preceding steps to your instructor, either in printed or electronic form, as requested.

Apply	**Case Problem 1**

Use the skills you learned in the tutorial to select security settings for a theater restoration company.

Data Files needed for this Case Problem: Employment.rtf and Theater.rtf

Trang Restoration   Alice and Lou Trang run a small business in Portland, Oregon, named Trang Restoration, which restores old theaters, many from the vaudeville era. Their most successful efforts are multiuse theaters that host live productions, independent films, and training classes for actors, directors, and others in the acting and film fields. Alice conducts most of her marketing work on a laptop computer running Windows Vista, and is concerned about maintaining security as she communicates with clients and researches restoration materials on the Internet. She has experienced problems with spam and wants to know how to block senders in Windows Mail. You'll help her use the Windows Vista security settings to protect her computer. Complete the following steps, noting your original settings so you can restore them later:

1. Add Wireless Portable Devices to the Windows Firewall exception list.

2. Change the settings in Windows Update to automatically check for and install updates every day at 5:00 a.m.

3. Change the Windows Defender settings to scan every day at 11:00 p.m.

4. Arrange both windows so both status summaries are visible, and then press the Print Screen key to capture an image of the desktop. Open Paint, and then press Ctrl+V to paste the image in a Paint file. Save the file as **SecurityXY**, where *XY* are your initials, in the Tutorial.05\Case1 folder provided with your Data Files. Close all open windows.

5. In Windows Mail, add your e-mail address to the Blocked Senders list. Send an e-mail to yourself. When Windows Mail receives and blocks this message, press the Alt+Print Screen keys to capture an image of the dialog box. Open Paint, and then press Ctrl+V to paste the image in a Paint file. Save the file as **BlockedMailXY**, where *XY* are your initials, in the Tutorial.05\Case1 folder provided with your Data Files. Close Windows Mail.

6. In Internet Explorer, change the security level for the Trusted sites zone to Low. Press the Alt+Print Screen keys to capture an image of the window. Open Paint, and then press Ctrl+V to paste the image in a Paint file. Save the file as **SecurityZoneXY**, where *XY* are your initials, in the Tutorial.05\Case1 folder provided with your Data Files.

7. In the Manage Add-ons dialog box, display a list of downloaded ActiveX controls. Press the Alt+Print Screen keys to capture an image of the window. Open Paint, and then press Ctrl+V to paste the image in a Paint file. Save the file as **AddOns***XY*, where *XY* are your initials, in the Tutorial.05\Case1 folder provided with your Data Files. Close all open windows.

8. Create Standard user accounts for Alice and Lou Trang. For Alice's account, use **Alice** as the name and **MiBd I$ 05/14** as her password. For Lou's account, use **Lou** as the name and **ILuv*The8tr** as his password.

9. With the User Accounts window open on the desktop, press the Alt+Print Screen keys to capture an image of the window. Open Paint, and then press Ctrl+V to paste the image in a Paint file. Save the file as **Accounts***XY*, where *XY* are your initials, in the Tutorial.05\Case1 folder provided with your Data Files.

10. Move the **Theater** document from the Tutorial.05\Case1 folder provided with your Data Files to a new folder named **Projects** in the Public folder on your computer.

11. Move the **Employment** document from the Tutorial.05\Case1 folder provided with your Data Files to a new folder named **Jobs** in your Documents folder.

12. Share the **Jobs** folder with Alice and Lou as Co-owners. Open three windows on your desktop: the Public folder window, the Documents folder window, and the final Sharing Files window. Resize and arrange all as necessary to see their contents. Press the Print Screen key to capture an image of the desktop. Open Paint, and then press Ctrl+V to paste the image in a Paint file. Save the file as **SharedFolders***XY*, where *XY* are your initials, in the Tutorial.05\Case1 folder provided with your Data Files.

13. Restore the settings on your computer. Remove Wireless Portable Devices from the Windows Firewall exception list. Restore the settings in Windows Update and Windows Defender to install updates and scan at their original times. Remove your e-mail address from the Windows Mail Blocked Senders list. Restore the security level for the Trusted sites zone to its original setting. Move the **Projects** and **Jobs** folders to the Tutorial.05\Review folder provided with your Data Files. Delete the user accounts you created for Alice and Lou Trang.

14. Close all open windows.

15. Submit the results of the preceding steps to your instructor, either in printed or electronic form, as requested.

Apply | **Case Problem 2**

Use the skills you learned in the tutorial to select security settings for a day spa.

There are no Data Files needed for this Case Problem.

Revive Day Spa Rita Patel owns the Revive Day Spa in Charleston, West Virginia, which is part of the Charleston Golf Resort. Revive offers spa services ranging from massage therapy to facial treatments for day or weeklong packages. Guests of the Charleston Golf Resort can use a spa menu to select services such as hydrotherapy and yoga for golfers. Rita uses Windows Meeting Space to meet with managers of the Charleston Golf Resort and regularly uses Windows Mail and Internet Explorer to run her business. She has experienced problems with spyware and viruses, and wants to know when to trust e-mail she receives and Web sites she visits. You'll help her use the Windows Vista security settings to protect her computer. Complete the following steps, noting your original settings so you can restore them later:

1. Add Windows Meeting Space to the Windows Firewall exception list. Capture an image of the Exceptions tab in the Windows Firewall Settings dialog box, and save it in a Paint file named **FirewallXY**, where *XY* are your initials, in the Tutorial.05\Case2 folder provided with your Data Files.

EXPLORE

2. In Windows Update, view your update history, and then check for updates. (*Hint*: In the Windows Update window, click View update history and then click Check for updates in the left pane.) When Windows Update finishes checking for updates, capture an image of the Review your update history window, and save it as a Paint file named **UpdatesXY**, where *XY* are your initials, in the Tutorial.05\Case2 folder provided with your Data Files.

3. In Windows Mail, find out how to get a digital ID. (*Hint*: Click the Get Digital ID button on the Security tab of the Options dialog box.) Find the Web page explaining how to find services that issue or use a digital ID, and then save the page as a Web Archive, single file named **Digital IDXY**, where *XY* are your initials, in the Tutorial.05\Case2 folder provided with your Data Files. Close Windows Mail.

4. In Internet Explorer, open a Web page in your Favorites list or go to the home page of a popular search engine, such as Google (www.google.com) or Yahoo! (www.yahoo.com). Use the Phishing Filter to verify this Web site is not a phishing Web site. Capture an image of the Internet Explorer window and Phishing Filter dialog box, and save it in a Paint file named **PhishingXY**, where *XY* are your initials, in the Tutorial.05\Case2 folder provided with your Data Files.

5. In Internet Explorer, change the security level for the Internet sites zone to High. Capture an image of the dialog box, and save it in a Paint file named **HighSecurityXY**, where *XY* are your initials, in the Tutorial.05\Case2 folder provided with your Data Files.

6. Create a Standard user account for Rita Patel. Use **Rita** as the name and **Re: VeyeV10** as her password.

EXPLORE

7. Create a guest account on the computer. (*Hint*: In the Manage Accounts window, click the Guest account, and then click the Turn On button.)

8. With the User Accounts window open on the desktop, capture an image of the dialog box, and save it in a Paint file named **AccountsXY**, where *XY* are your initials, in the Tutorial.05\Case2 folder provided with your Data Files.

9. Restore the settings on your computer. Remove Windows Meeting Space from the Windows Firewall exception list. Restore the security level for the Internet sites zone to its original setting. Delete the user account you created for Rita Patel and turn off the Guest account.

10. Close all open windows.

11. Submit the results of the preceding steps to your instructor, either in printed or electronic form, as requested.

Challenge | **Case Problem 3**

Go beyond what you've learned to protect a computer at a sports center.

There are no Data Files needed for this Case Problem.

Urban Sports Urban Sports is a sports center in Bloomington, Indiana, that organizes leagues in soccer, football, basketball, softball, and other sports for children and adults. Henry Lange manages the center and provides computers with Internet connections to members who want to use them. Henry is particularly concerned about the security of these computers. You'll help him use the Windows Vista security settings to protect a public computer. Complete the following steps, noting your original settings so you can restore them later:

✦ EXPLORE   1. In Windows Firewall, block all incoming connections. (*Hint*: Select an option on the General tab of the Windows Firewall Settings dialog box.)

✦ EXPLORE   2. Set Windows Defender to perform a full scan of your computer every day at 11:00 p.m. Also set default actions for High and Medium alert items so that Windows Defender removes these items.

3. Arrange the Windows Defender Options window and the Windows Firewall window to display the settings you changed, and then capture an image of the desktop. Save the image as a Paint file named **FullScan*XY***, where *XY* are your initials, in the Tutorial.05\Case3 folder provided with your Data Files. Close all open windows.

4. In Windows Mail, set the Junk E-mail protection level to High. Also specify that you want to move phishing e-mail to the Junk Mail folder. Close Windows Mail.

5. In Internet Explorer, change the privacy level for the Internet sites zone to High. Capture an image of the dialog box, and save it in a Paint file named **HighPrivacyXY**, where *XY* are your initials, in the Tutorial.05\Case3 folder provided with your Data Files.

6. Delete all temporary files and cookies in Internet Explorer.

✦ EXPLORE   7. Set Internet Explorer so that it does not store a list of browsing history. (*Hint*: On the General tab of the Internet Options dialog box, click the Settings button in the Browsing history section, and then change the Days to keep pages in history setting.) Capture an image of the dialog box, and save it in a Paint file named **NoHistoryXY**, where *XY* are your initials, in the Tutorial.05\Case3 folder provided with your Data Files.

✦ EXPLORE   8. Create a password for your account on your computer, if necessary, and then create a guest account. (*Hint*: In the Manage Accounts window, click the Guest account, and then click the Turn On button.)

9. With the User Accounts window open on the desktop, capture an image of the window, and save it in a Paint file named **GuestAccountXY**, where *XY* are your initials, in the Tutorial.05\Case3 folder provided with your Data Files.

10. Restore the settings on your computer. Restore the original general setting in Windows Firewall. Restore the settings for a Windows Defender scan to their original settings, including the default actions. Restore the Junk E-mail options in Windows Mail to their original settings. In Internet Explorer, restore the privacy level for the Internet sites zone to its original setting, and restore the number of days Internet Explorer keeps your browsing history to its original setting. Turn off the Guest account.

11. Close all open windows.

12. Submit the results of the preceding steps to your instructor, either in printed or electronic form, as requested.

Research | **Case Problem 4**

Work with the skills you've learned and use the Internet to research computer security for a group of soil scientists.

There are no Data Files needed for this Case Problem.

Osborne & Associates   Tyler Osborne is the head scientist for Osborne & Associates, a firm providing soil science services in Columbia, Missouri. Osborne & Associates maps and classifies soils for land planners and managers and conducts research on soil degradation or erosion. Tyler wants to protect the computers his scientists use against security threats. To do so, he first wants to understand who typically attacks computers and their data. He also wants to learn more about the types of attacks people use to access computers, and how much damage attacks have caused. He asks you to research these topics and report your findings. Complete the following steps:

1. Use your favorite search engine to find information about the types of people behind attacks on desktop computers. (Attacks on networks are in a separate category.) Try searching for information about the following types of attackers:
   - Hackers
   - Crackers
   - Computer spies
   - Social engineers
2. Use your favorite search engine to find information about the types of attacks that can affect a desktop computer. Try searching for information about the following types of attacks:
   - Malicious software, or malware
   - Viruses
   - Worms
   - Logic bombs
   - Password guessing
3. Use your favorite search engine to find information about the costs to businesses and individual computer users to recover from an attack, such as a virus infestation.
4. Use a word processor to summarize your findings in one or two pages. Be sure to define any new terms and cite the Web sites where you found your information. Save your document as Attacks.docx in the Tutorial.05\Case4 folder provided with your Data Files. (The filename extension of your document might differ.)
5. Submit the results of the preceding steps to your instructor, either in printed or electronic form, as requested.

Assess | **SAM Assessment and Training**

If you have a SAM user profile, you may have access to hands-on instruction, practice, and assessment of the skills covered in this tutorial. Log in to your SAM account (**http://sam2007.course.com**) to launch any assigned training activities or exams that relate to the skills covered in this tutorial.

6. Strong passwords contain at least eight characters; do not include your user name, real name, or company name; are not words you can find in the dictionary; are significantly different from your previous passwords; and contain characters from each of the following categories: uppercase letters, lowercase letters, numbers, and symbols (including spaces)

7. when a program or action is about to start

8. Public

Ending Data Files

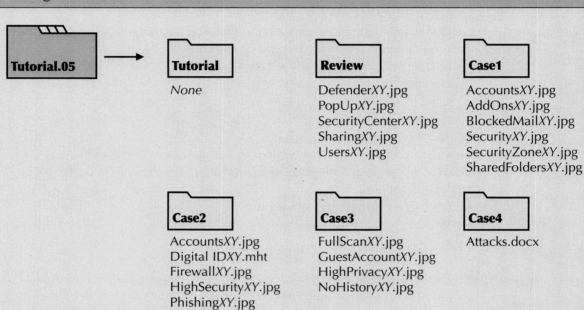

Tutorial.05 →

Tutorial

None

Review

Defender*XY*.jpg
PopUp*XY*.jpg
SecurityCenter*XY*.jpg
Sharing*XY*.jpg
Users*XY*.jpg

Case1

Accounts*XY*.jpg
AddOns*XY*.jpg
BlockedMail*XY*.jpg
Security*XY*.jpg
SecurityZone*XY*.jpg
SharedFolders*XY*.jpg

Case2

Accounts*XY*.jpg
Digital ID*XY*.mht
Firewall*XY*.jpg
HighSecurity*XY*.jpg
Phishing*XY*.jpg
Updates*XY*.jpg

Case3

FullScan*XY*.jpg
GuestAccount*XY*.jpg
HighPrivacy*XY*.jpg
NoHistory*XY*.jpg

Case4

Attacks.docx

Objectives

Session 6.1
- Develop search strategies
- Find files by name, type, and category
- Examine search results and save a search
- Add tags and other details to files
- Use Boolean filters in advanced searches

Session 6.2
- Speed searches by indexing
- Search the Internet
- Narrow searches using advanced search features
- Select search providers in Internet Explorer
- Collaborate with others using Windows Meeting Space

Searching for Information and Collaborating with Others

Finding and Sharing Information

Case | TrendSpot Magazine

TrendSpot is an online magazine for marketing professionals that features articles, profiles, and commentary about consumer trends. Kendra Cho, the founder of *TrendSpot*, works out of offices in Roswell, Georgia, though she collaborates with *TrendSpot* editors around the country. As Kendra's editorial assistant, your duties include organizing the information submitted with articles and finding supporting material, such as photos and quotations.

In this tutorial, you'll learn how to develop search strategies for finding information, and then use the Windows Vista search tools to find files. You'll refine your searches by using advanced techniques such as Boolean filters and multiple criteria, and then index your computer to speed searches. You'll also learn how to apply these search strategies when using Internet Explorer to find information on the Web. To share this information, you'll use Windows Meeting Space to collaborate and distribute the information to others.

Starting Data Files

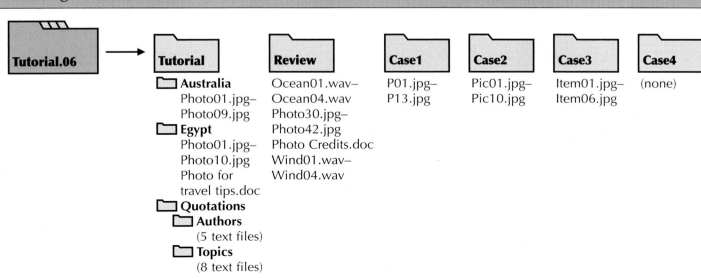

Tutorial.06 →	Tutorial	Review	Case1	Case2	Case3	Case4
	Australia Photo01.jpg– Photo09.jpg **Egypt** Photo01.jpg– Photo10.jpg Photo for travel tips.doc **Quotations** **Authors** (5 text files) **Topics** (8 text files)	Ocean01.wav– Ocean04.wav Photo30.jpg– Photo42.jpg Photo Credits.doc Wind01.wav– Wind04.wav	P01.jpg– P13.jpg	Pic01.jpg– Pic10.jpg	Item01.jpg– Item06.jpg	(none)

Session 6.1

Developing Search Strategies

As you install programs and store data on your computer, the number of files and folders you have grows, and it becomes harder to locate a particular item. Using an effective organization scheme helps you find files and folders when you need them. However, if pinpointing an item means browsing dozens or hundreds of files and folders or if you don't know where to look, you can use a Windows Vista search tool. You have already used the Search box in a folder window to find files by name and file contents. Windows Vista provides three other tools for finding files and folders: the Search pane in a folder window, the Start Search box on the Start menu, and the Search folder. Figure 6-1 recommends when to choose one search tool over another.

Figure 6-1	Choosing a search tool

Search Tool	When to Use	Notes
Search box in a folder window	When you know where to start looking for a file or folder and want to search by filename or contents	Windows searches in the current folder and all of its subfolders.
Search pane in a folder window	When you want to use criteria other than text in the filename or contents or you want to combine search criteria	Windows can search any single folder and its subfolders.
Search box on the Start menu	When you want to find a program, a Web site included in your browser's history, or a file or folder stored in your personal folder	Your personal folder includes Documents, Pictures, Music, Desktop, and other common locations.
Search folder	When you don't know where a file or folder is located or are looking for files from several folders	Windows can search one, some, or all of the folders on your computer.

When you use any of the Windows Vista search tools, you provide **search criteria**, which are conditions that the file or folder must meet to have Windows find it. These conditions help you define and narrow your search so you can quickly find the item you want. For example, if you provide a filename such as Budget as the search criterion, Windows locates and displays every file that matches that criterion—in other words, all files whose filename contains a word starting with *Budget*.

If you use text in the filename or the file contents as search criteria, you are conducting a basic search. If you use other properties such as tags or authors as search criteria, you are conducting an advanced search. A **tag** is a word or phrase you add to photos and other types of files to describe them. The other properties you can use as search criteria include any detail you can display as a column in a folder window. (Recall that you can display columns in a folder window by right-clicking a column heading, and then clicking a detail on the shortcut menu. If the detail you want to display does not appear on the shortcut menu, you can click More to open the Choose Details dialog box.) Figure 6-2 describes common criteria you can use when you conduct basic and advanced searches to find a file.

Typical search criteria ◄ Figure 6-2

File Property	Description	Example
Basic Searches		
Filename	All or part of the filename	To find a file named April sales.xlsx, enter *Apr* or *sales* as the criterion.
File type	Filename extension	To find all of your photos, enter *JPG*.
Contents	Text the file contains	To find a file that uses "Trends for June" as a heading, start typing *Trends for June*.
Advanced Searches		
Date	Date the file was modified, created, or accessed	To find a document edited on May 2, 2010, enter *5/2/10* as the criterion.
Size	Size of the file in kilobytes (KB)	To find files larger than 1 MB, enter *1000* as the criterion.
Tag	Word or phrase added to the file	To find a photo with "winter, vacation, ski" as tags, enter *winter* as the criterion.
Author	Name of the person who created the file	To find a document that Kendra created, enter *Kendra* as the criterion.

When you combine criteria, such as to find a file named Agenda that you created last Monday, you are also conducting an advanced search. You'll learn how to combine search criteria later in the tutorial.

Before you start looking for a file or folder on your computer, determine what you already know about the item; this helps you develop a search strategy. Choose the search tool that best fits your needs, and use search criteria that are most likely to find the item. For example, suppose you want to find a photo that you took last New Year's Eve and stored somewhere in the Pictures folder. Because you know the location of the photo, you can use the Search box in the Pictures folder window. You also know when you took the photo, so you can conduct an advanced search using *12/31/09* as the search criterion.

Kendra asks you to help her prepare a column on travel trends for the upcoming issue of *TrendSpot*. She has received photos and text files from contributors and asks you to help find the right content for the travel column. You'll use the Windows Vista search tools to assist Kendra and complete this task.

Searching in a Folder Window

You have already used the Search box in a folder window to find files based on their filenames and contents. To conduct these kinds of basic searches, you type text in the Search box. Windows then displays only those files in the current folder or its subfolders that match the criterion: files whose contents or filename includes a word starting with the text you typed. In addition to text in the filename or file contents, you can enter a filename extension as the search criterion to find files by type, such as JPG to find files with a .jpg extension (usually photo files). When you search for files by type, you can enter the filename extension on its own (JPG or jpg) or using an asterisk and a dot before the filename extension (*. JPG or *.jpg). In this case, the asterisk is a **wildcard**, a symbol that stands for one or more unspecified characters in the search criterion.

Using a wildcard is a good idea if you want to search for certain types of files, such as those with a DOC filename extension, but some of your filenames include words that start with the extension text, such as Doctor Visit, June Docket, or Kendra Docs. In this case, using a wildcard makes it clear that you are searching by filename extension only, and produces more accurate search results.

You can also conduct advanced searches from a folder window. To search only certain types of files, such as e-mail messages, documents, or pictures, you can display the **Search pane**. You use the Search pane to narrow a search to a specified category of files. For example, if you click the Document button on the Search pane and then type text in the Search box, Windows displays only the text files, spreadsheets, presentations, and other documents that meet your criteria.

Reference Window | **Searching for a File by Type**

- Open the folder you want to search.
- Click in the Search box, and then type the filename extension on its own, such as JPG, or using a wildcard character, as in *.jpg.

Kendra is writing her travel column about two places that are emerging as hot spots for budget travelers: Australia and Egypt. First, she wants to know how many photos her contributors submitted featuring these two locations. Because all of these photos are stored in two subfolders, you can provide the information Kendra wants by conducting a basic search in a folder window using the filename extension JPG as the search criterion.

To search for files by type:

▶ 1. If necessary, insert the USB flash drive containing your Data Files into a USB port on your computer.

   Trouble? If you do not have a USB flash drive, make sure you can access your Data Files from your computer.

▶ 2. In a folder window, open the **Tutorial.06** folder and then the **Tutorial** folder in your Data Files.

▶ 3. Click in the Search box, and then type **JPG**. Windows displays only the files with a .jpg extension in the folder window.

▶ 4. If necessary, click the **Views** button arrow, and then click **Large Icons** to see the contents of the files clearly. See Figure 6-3.

Searching for files with a JPG filename extension ◀ Figure 6-3

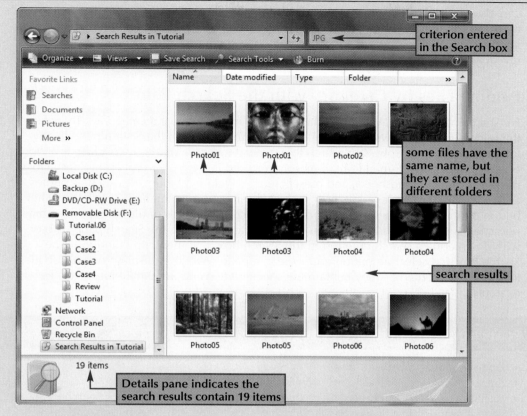

Note that the Details pane at the bottom of the folder window indicates that the subfolders in the Tutorial folder contain 19 JPG files.

Searching Versus Sorting, Filtering, Grouping, and Stacking | InSight

Recall that instead of using the Search box, you can find files by sorting, filtering, grouping, or stacking files using the column headings in a folder window. The method you choose depends on the number of files you want to search, the location of the files, and their names. For example, suppose you need to find JPG files. If you want to search the current folder *and* its subfolders, use the Search box—the other options find files only in the current folder. If you're searching a single folder, the Search box is also preferable if the folder contains similar filenames (because sorting would list together many files that start with the same text) or many different types of files (because grouping or stacking would produce many groups or stacks). If you want to find a particular file in a very large folder, it is often easier to use the Search box rather than deal with a long file list; however, if the folder doesn't contain too many files, then sorting, grouping, stacking, or filtering is usually a quicker method.

The 19 JPG files you found all have filenames starting with *Photo* followed by a number, such as Photo01 and Photo02. Kendra asked the contributors to name the files this way to streamline the layout and publication of the magazine. As Kendra prepares the column on Egypt, for example, she'll indicate where to insert photos in sequence. For the first photo, she'll include a note such as *Insert Egypt Photo01 here*, for the second photo,

Insert Egypt Photo02 here, and so on. That way, when the page designers compose the column on travel in Egypt, they don't have to find files with long or cryptic names. They can also tell from the filenames the number of files to include and the sequence in which they should appear. Although this file-naming scheme works well for editing and producing the magazine, it poses challenges for your research because the filenames do not reveal anything about the content except that they are photos.

Finding Files by Category with the Search Pane

For searching purposes, Windows classifies files into five general categories. By default, the folder window shows all categories of files. You can open the Search pane in any folder window to narrow your search to a general category of files by clicking a button on the Search pane: E-mail (e-mail messages stored in the folder or its subfolder), Document (text files, spreadsheets, and presentations), Picture (graphic files such as photos and drawings), or Music (audio files such as music and speech). If you click the Other button on the Search pane, you narrow the search to all kinds of files except for e-mail, documents, pictures, and music. You can select an option on the Search pane with or without entering a search criterion in the Search box. If you enter a criterion in the Search box and select an option on the Search pane, Windows displays only those files that meet both criteria—they contain the specified text and are e-mail messages, for example.

Reference Window | **Searching for a File by Category**

- Open the folder you want to search.
- Enter a filename or file contents search criterion in the Search box.
- Click the Organize button on the toolbar, point to Layout, and then click Search Pane. If you are working in a Search Results window, click the Search Tools button, and then click Search Pane.
- Click a button on the Search Pane to select a category.

Kendra now wants to find a text file that Sam Moriarity, a novice contributor, submitted. As Kendra requested, Sam created a short document describing the type of photograph that would best illustrate a sidebar he wrote listing travel tips for budget travelers. He does not recall where he saved the file or its filename, though it's likely the word *photo* appears in the filename or contents. If you conduct a basic search by entering *photo* in the Search box, you will find the 19 JPG files as well as any other files containing the word *photo* in their filenames or contents. To narrow the search to documents only, you'll use the Search pane.

To narrow a search using the Search pane:

1. Click the **Back** button ⊙ to return to the Tutorial folder window, click the Search box, and then type **pho** to begin entering *photo*. Windows displays all the files in the Tutorial subfolders with a filename that contains a word beginning with *pho*.

2. Click the **Search Tools** button on the toolbar, and then click **Search Pane** to open the Search pane. See Figure 6-4.

Tip

The Search Tools button appears on a folder window toolbar only after you've used the Search box to search for files or folders.

3. Click the **Document** button on the Search pane. Windows reduces the search results to files that meet both criteria—only documents whose filenames contain a word beginning with *pho*.

Examining the Search Results

After you enter search criteria using the Search box or the Search pane, Windows filters the view of the folder window to display files that meet your criteria. These are your search results. Figure 6-5 shows the results of the search performed in the preceding set of steps: documents whose filenames contain a word beginning with *photo*. When a folder window displays search results, it provides extra tools to help you work with the files you found. For example, the toolbar contains a Save Search button for saving the criteria you used to perform a search. If you often look for a certain group of files, you can save the search so you don't have to reconstruct the criteria each time you want to find the files. The toolbar still contains a Search Tools button, which provides additional search options. (You'll use the Search Tools button later in this tutorial.)

Figure 6-5 Search results

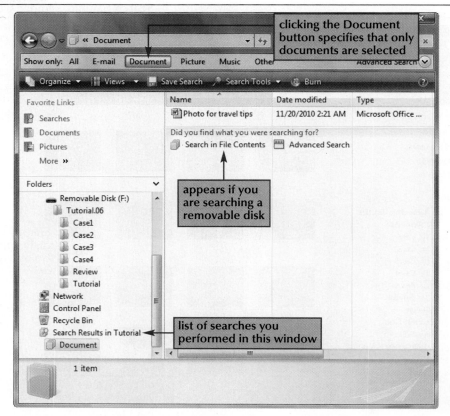

At the bottom of the Folders list in a Search Results window, Windows includes the searches you performed in that window, and stores them there until you close the window. If you want to redisplay the results of a previous search, you can click the appropriate search results in the Folders list. In the right pane of a search results window, Windows asks, "Did you find what you were searching for?" and provides links to perform an advanced search. (If you are searching files on a removable disk, you can also choose to search in the file contents.)

In addition to the extra tools provided in a search window, you can use the standard folder window tools to open, move, copy, rename, or delete a file. You can also verify that a file you found is one you want without opening the file. First, you can select the file in the folder window and then review the information in the Details pane. If you're not sure this is the right file, you can open the Preview pane, which displays the contents of the selected file. You'll verify the Photo for travel tips file you found is the document Sam sent describing the type of photograph that would best illustrate his list of travel tips.

To verify you found the right file:

▶ **1.** In the folder window, click the **Photo for travel tips** file. Information about the file appears in the Details pane, including the file type, size, and the date it was modified. (Your window might show additional information.)

▶ **2.** Click the **Organize** button on the toolbar, point to **Layout**, and then click **Preview Pane**. The Preview pane opens in the folder window, displaying the contents of the Photo for travel tips file. See Figure 6-6.

Verifying a found file ◀ **Figure 6-6**

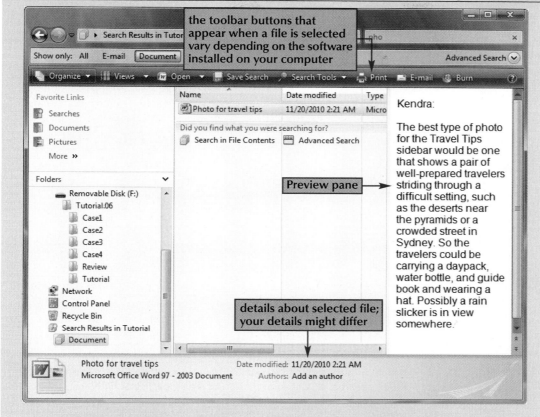

Trouble? If the Preview pane doesn't seem to open, widen the folder window to display the Preview pane.

The Photo for travel tips file appears to be the file that Kendra needs. Now she needs to find the most recent photos she has of Australia and Egypt. To do that, you can conduct an advanced search in the Search pane.

Conducting Advanced Searches with the Search Pane

The Search box and the default Search pane make it easy to use multiple criteria, as long as you want to find files by specifying text and a file category. To use other types of criteria, such as date modified, size, or tags, you conduct an advanced search using the expanded Search pane. When you expand the Search pane, you can conduct an advanced search by specifying one or more of the criteria shown in Figure 6-7.

Figure 6-7 Advanced search criteria

Expanded Search Pane Option	When to Use	How to Refine the Option
All Files		
Location	To search locations other than the current folder	Specify any drive or folder on your computer, including indexed locations.
Date	To search for files by date created, date modified, or date accessed	Specify a particular date or dates before or after a particular date.
Size	To search for files by size	Specify any size or one equal to, less than, or greater than a particular size.
Filename	To search for files by filename	Specify all of the filename or only the first few characters.
Tags	To search for files by their tags	Specify one or more tags.
Authors	To search for files by their authors	Specify one or more authors.
Additional Options for E-mail		
Date	To search for e-mail by date received, sent, modified, created, or accessed	Specify a particular date or dates before or after a particular date.
Subject	To search for e-mail by subject	Specify all or part of the text in the Subject line.
From names	To search for e-mail by sender	Specify one or more sender names.
To names	To search for e-mail by recipient	Specify one or more recipient names.
Additional Options for Pictures		
Date	To search for pictures by date taken, modified, created, or accessed	Specify a particular date or dates before or after a particular date.
Title	To search for pictures by title	Specify all or part of the picture title.
Additional Options for Music		
Title	To search for music by title	Specify all or part of the picture title.
Artists	To search for music by artist	Specify contributing artist.
Album	To search for music by album	Specify album name.

One of the locations you can search is your **indexed locations**, a group of folders including all of the folders in your personal folder (Documents, Pictures, Music, Desktop, and other common locations), e-mail, and offline files. (You'll work with these indexed locations later in the tutorial.) Windows indexes these folders so it can search them quickly. By default, Windows searches *both* filenames and contents when you are searching in an indexed location. Searching filenames and contents can take a long time in large folders that are not indexed. Because removable disks are not included in the indexed locations, Windows searches only the names of the files on a removable disk by default, and then offers to search in file contents, as shown in Figure 6-6.

You can expand the Search pane in two ways: by clicking the Advanced Search button on the Search pane or by clicking the Advanced Search link in a search results window. For example, when you entered JPG as the search criterion earlier, Windows displayed 19 .jpg files and asked, "Did you find what you were searching for?" If the JPG search criterion did not produce the results you needed, you could have clicked the Advanced Search link in the folder window to expand the Search pane.

Selecting Criteria in the Expanded Search Pane

When you set criteria in the expanded Search pane, you select or enter details about the properties of the files you want to find. For example, for the size property, you can specify that you are looking for files that are equal to, smaller than, or larger than the size you enter. You can combine the size criterion with another property, such as date created or filename, to narrow your search. The more criteria you specify, the more you narrow the search. You need to select the properties you use carefully, however, so you don't use criteria that inadvertently eliminate a file that you want. For example, if you want to find only documents you created last week, make sure you select the Date created property, not the default Date property, which finds files created, modified, or accessed on the date you specify.

Searching for a File Using Multiple Criteria | Reference Window

- Open the folder you want to search.
- Enter filename or file contents search criteria in the Search box.
- If Windows does not find the files you want, click Advanced Search in the Search Results window or click the Search Tools button, click Search Pane, and then click the Advanced Search button.
- Select additional criteria using the options in the expanded Search pane.
- Click the Search button.

In her travel trends column, Kendra wants to use recent photos of Egypt and Australia, which are those taken after September 30, 2010. To find these files, you can start with the same criterion you used to find JPG files, using a wildcard this time, and combine it with additional date criteria in the expanded Search pane.

To find JPG files taken after September 30, 2010:

▶ 1. In the folder window, click the **Tutorial** folder in the Folders list to return to the Tutorial window. Maximize the window. If the Preview pane is open click the **Organize** button on the toolbar, point to **Layout**, and then click **Preview Pane** to close the Preview pane.

▶ 2. Click the **Search** box, and then type ***.jpg**. Windows displays the 19 .jpg files in the search results. Next, you'll enter additional criteria to narrow the results to JPG files taken after September 30, 2010.

▶ 3. Click the **Advanced Search** link to open the expanded Search pane. See Figure 6-8.

Expanded Search pane ◀ Figure 6-8

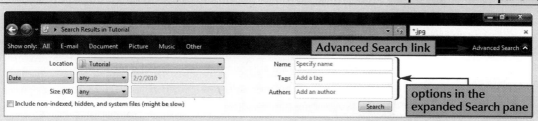

▶ 4. In the Search pane, click the **Date** button, and then click **Date modified**.

▶ 5. Click the **any** button next to Date modified, and then click **is after**.

▶ **6.** Click the button displaying today's date to open a calendar.

▶ **7.** Use the calendar controls to select **September 30, 2010**. To change the month, click the **left arrow** ◀ and **right arrow** ▶ buttons. When the calendar page for September 2010 appears, click **30**. See Figure 6-9.

Figure 6-9	**Setting date criteria**

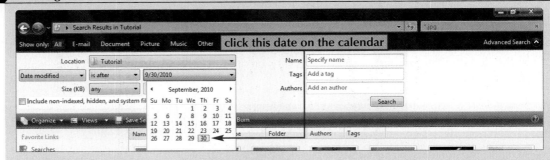

▶ **8.** Click the button displaying **9/30/2010** to close the calendar.

▶ **9.** Click the **Search** button. Windows finds the files that meet your criteria and displays them in the window.

This search worked well, and Kendra anticipates that she'll want to conduct this search again. You'll save the search so you can use it later.

Saving a Search

If you conduct a successful search, especially one that uses two or more criteria, you can save the search. Saving a search preserves your original criteria and folder location so you can perform the search again without reconstructing the criteria. By default, Windows saves the search in the Searches folder, which you can open from the Navigation pane. The Searches folder lists your searches by name so you can easily find the one you want. Because a saved search includes folder and file location information, you can conduct a saved search only on the same computer where you conducted the original search or on one that mirrors the folder and file location of the original search. For this reason, the contents of the Searches folder are called **virtual folders**, which means they don't contain actual files, only criteria to find files. To search using a virtual folder, you open the Searches folder and then double-click a virtual folder.

To save a search and perform it again:

▶ **1.** In the search results window, click the **Save Search** button on the toolbar. The Save As dialog box opens, providing .jpg modified9-30-2010 as the filename. See Figure 6-10.

Figure 6-10	**Saving a search**

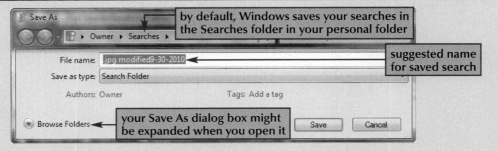

▶ 2. Change the filename to **JPG Oct**, and then click the **Save** button to save the search in the Searches folder.

▶ 3. To view the saved search, click the **Searches** folder in the Navigation pane. The JPG Oct search appears in the folder.

▶ 4. To perform the search again, double-click **JPG Oct** in the Searches folder. Windows conducts the search again, and finds the JPG files modified after September 30, 2010. See Figure 6-11.

Performing saved search ◀ Figure 6-11

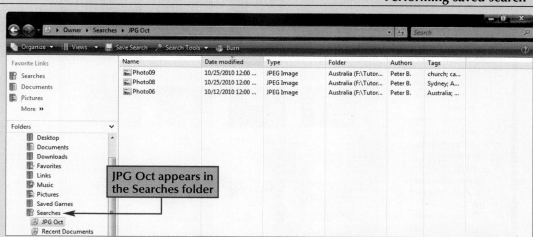

As you've been performing searches, Kendra has noticed the Tags property and wonders if using tags would help to find and identify files. In fact, one of the most useful properties you can use when searching for files is a file tag, which is one or more descriptive words you store with a file to help define its purpose or contents. You are sure that adding tags to the photo files would save you and Kendra a lot of time when searching for photos. You'll show her how to do so next.

Using Tags and Other Properties

As you know, properties are characteristics of files, such as their name and size, that provide detailed information about a file. You set some file properties when you create or modify a file, including the filename, location, and date created or modified. You can add other properties later, including tags, ratings, titles, authors, and comments. Tags are often the most useful because they make files easier to find.

To add properties to a file, you can use the Details pane or the file's Properties dialog box. To use the Details pane, you select a file, click a property text box in the Details pane, and then enter the appropriate information, such as the author's name or comments about the file. Figure 6-12 shows the Details pane when the Winter Leaves photo in the Sample Pictures folder is selected.

Figure 6-12 ▷ **File properties in the Details pane**

details, including tags, in the Details pane (yours might differ)

Most of the other properties you can add using the Details pane work the same way, and vary by file type. For photos, you can specify tags, authors, comments, title, and subject by using the appropriate text box in the Details pane. You can also rate photos by clicking a star in a series of five stars. If you click the first star, you apply a one-star rating. If you click the fourth star, you apply a four-star rating.

If you want to specify file properties other than the ones that appear in the Details pane by default, you can open the Properties dialog box for a file. To do so, you right-click a file, and then click Properties on the shortcut menu. On the Details tab, you can add or modify dozens of properties. Figure 6-13 shows the Properties dialog box for the Winter Leaves photo file. (The details for this file might differ on your computer.)

File details in the Properties dialog box ◀ **Figure 6-13**

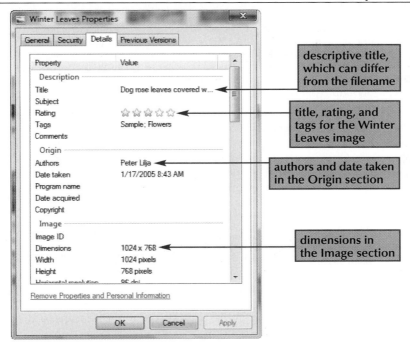

Adding Tags to Files

You can add a tag to a file by using the Save As dialog box when you save the file or by using the Details pane or the file's Properties dialog box after you save the file. To use the Details pane, you select the file, click the Tags text box in the Details pane, and then type a word or phrase that will help you find the file later. To add more than one tag, separate each word or phrase with a semicolon. For example, if you have a photo of yourself on the peak of the Blackrock Mountain in Virginia, you could use *Blackrock; mountain; Virginia* as tags.

Adding Tags to Files   │ Reference Window

- In a folder window, click the file to which you want to add a tag.
- Click the Tags text box in the Details pane, and then type a tag. To enter another tag, type a semicolon (;) followed by the next tag.
- Click the Save button on the Details pane.

   Much of the research you do for Kendra involves finding photos suitable for the columns and articles published in *TrendSpot Magazine*. Some photographers already add details to files, including tags, to help identify their photos. To facilitate your research, you'll review the files photographers recently submitted for Kendra's column on budget travel in Australia and Egypt and add tags to the files that need them.

To add tags to files:

▶ **1.** Open the **Australia** folder in the Tutorial.06\Tutorial folder, and then switch to Details view, if necessary.

▶ **2.** Display the Tags column, if necessary, by right-clicking any column heading and clicking **Tags** on the shortcut menu. Note that Photo02 and Photo04 do not have any tags.

▶ **3.** Click **Photo02** and then point to the **Title** text box in the Details pane. The photographer has provided "Middleton Beach, Western Australia" as the title.

   Trouble? If the Title text box does not appear in the Details pane, maximize the folder window and then drag the top border of the Details pane to increase its height, if necessary.

▶ **4.** Click the **Tags** text box in the Details pane, and type **Australia** as the first tag. Type **;** and then type **L** to begin to enter "Landscape." Windows might suggest typical or already used tags that start with the letter L. See Figure 6-14. The suggestions on your computer might differ.

| Figure 6-14 | Adding tags to a file |

▶ **5.** Click the **Landscape** check box or type **Landscape**, if necessary, and then click the **Save** button in the Details pane. Windows saves the tags you added.

▶ **6.** Add the following tags to the Photo04 file: **Beach; Landscape; Australia**, and then click the **Save** button. Note that after you add a tag to one file, that tag appears in the list of suggested tags for other files.

Tip

Be sure to click the Save button or press the Enter key to save the changes you make to properties in the Details pane.

▶ **7.** Resize the **Tags** column in the folder window to display all of the tag text.

| InSight | **Selecting Tags for Files** |

To create tags that will help you find files later, keep the following guidelines in mind:
- **Include the obvious**: Use words or phrases that describe the overall purpose or content of the file. For photo files, use tags that list the people in the picture, the location of the photo, and the occasion. For documents, describe the type of document, such as a proposal or report, and its subject.
- **Consider the sample tags**: You can find typical tags for files by typing a letter in the Tags text box in the Details pane. For example, type *p* to find sample tags that start with *p*, such as People, Pet Owners, Pets, and Photography.
- **Use complete words and phrases**: Avoid abbreviations and codes because you might not remember them later. Assign complete words or use phrases to be as clear as possible. Feel free to use text that appears in the filename; doing so might help you find other related files with the same tag but different filename.

Adding Other Details to Files

You can add dozens of details to files to help you identify or find the files later. The Details pane provides the most common ones, and a file's Properties dialog box includes those and many others. Kendra wants to add details to the Photo for travel tips document that Sam sent earlier. In particular, she wants to add a subject, tags, and the name of Sam's manager in California, who is Taylor Baldwin. To do so, you'll use the Properties dialog box.

To add details using a file's Properties dialog box:

▶ **1.** Open the **Egypt** folder in the Tutorial.06\Tutorial folder.

▶ **2.** Right-click **Photo for travel tips** and then click **Properties** on the shortcut menu. The Photo for travel tips Properties dialog box opens.

▶ **3.** Click the **Details** tab to work with the details for this file. See Figure 6-15. Windows scanned the first line of this file, which is *Kendra:*, and provided that text as the title.

Photo for travel tips Properties dialog box ◀ **Figure 6-15**

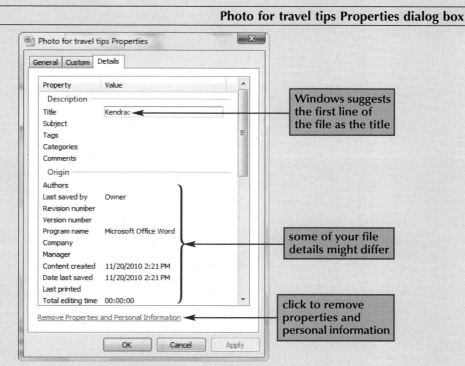

▶ **4.** In the Title text box, delete **Kendra:**, type **Travel Tips**, and then press the **Enter** key.

▶ **5.** Point to the right of Subject, and then click in the **Subject** text box. Type **General photo suggestions**, and then press the **Enter** key.

▶ **6.** Click the **Tags** text box, type **Sam; sidebar; travel tips; photo suggestions**, and then press the **Enter** key.

▶ **7.** Click the **Manager** text box, and then type **Taylor Baldwin**.

▶ **8.** Click the **OK** button to save the details with the file and close the dialog box.

Tip

Before sending a file to others, you can remove properties by opening the file's Properties dialog box, clicking the Details tab, and then clicking Remove Properties and Personal Information. The Remove Properties dialog box opens, listing the properties you can remove.

Now that you've entered tags and other properties for files, you're ready to use this information to build advanced criteria for smarter searching.

Using Advanced Criteria in the Search Box

As you know, when you enter text in a folder window's Search box, Windows looks in the name of the folders and files in the folder window. If you enter *photo*, for example, Windows finds files named Photo01, Photo for travel tips, and Understanding photons. If you are searching an indexed location, such as in the Documents folder on your hard disk, Windows also looks in the file contents. For example, using *photo* as the criterion also finds files containing words and phrases such as *art photography*, *photorealism* and *twenty-four hour photos*. You can use the Search box to find files in two other ways: searching for files by property, and searching for files that meet multiple criteria.

Searching for Files by Property

If you don't want to search for a file by name or contents, you can use the Search box to search for other properties, including date, size, and tags. To use any property as criteria in the Search box, you specify the property using the following shorthand notation: *property name:criterion*. For example, if you want to search for files modified on November 1, 2010, you could enter *Modified:11/1/2010*. (The properties are not case sensitive, so you could also enter *modified:11/1/2010*.) The properties you can use as search criteria include any detail you can display as a column in a folder window. Figure 6-16 provides examples of the shorthand notation you can use to specify file properties as search criteria in the Search box.

| Figure 6-16 | Examples of using file properties in the Search box |

Property	Example	Finds
Name	Name:City	Files and folders with names that contain a word beginning with *city*
Date modified	Modified:10/28/2010	Files and folders modified on October 28, 2010
	Modified:<10/28/2010	Files and folders modified before October 28, 2010
Date created	Created:>10/28/2010	Files and folders created after October 28, 2010
	Created:2010	Files and folders created during the year of 2010
Size	Size:200KB	Files with a size of 200 KB
	Size:>1MB	Files larger than 1 MB
Type	Filename:doc	Files with a .doc filename extension
Tags	Tag:(Egypt)	Files that include *Egypt* as a tag
Authors	Author:Peter	Files that specify Peter as the author
Artists	Artist:Elvis	Files that specify artists with *Elvis* in their names, such as Elvis Presley and Elvis Costello

Although the expanded Search pane guides you to select properties and specify criteria, you are restricted to the properties the Search pane contains: date (created or modified), size, filename, tags, and authors. When you use the shorthand notation in the Search box, however, you can use any file detail; this is especially useful when you are working with photos, music, and videos, because they have file properties that don't appear in the Search pane, such as Artists, Album, Rating, and Length.

As Kendra plans her travel trends column, she wants to include at least two photos of Sydney, Australia's largest city. Besides showing the Sydney Opera House, she'd like to show a contrasting work of architecture. You recall that some photographers provided titles for their photos. You'll use the Title property in the Search box to find photographs of Sydney.

To find files by specifying a property in the Search box:

▶ 1. Open the **Australia** folder in the Tutorial.06\Tutorial folder. Restore the folder window to its original size.

2. Click the **Search** box, and then type **title:Sydney**. As you type, Windows filters the view of the files in the folder window, and finally displays two files that contain the word *Sydney* in their Title property: Photo08 and Photo09.

3. Click **Photo08** and look for the title in the Details pane. (Resize the Details pane, if necessary.) This is a photo of the Sydney Opera House.

4. Click **Photo09**. Point to the Title text box in the Details pane to display the title in a ScreenTip. See Figure 6-17.

Tip

To learn which properties you can use in a search, click a file and check its details in the Details pane. To search by rating, enter a criterion such as rating:4 stars in the Search box.

Title property in the Details pane ◀ **Figure 6-17**

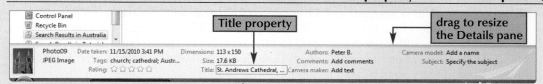

By searching for text in the Title property, you found two photos for Kendra—one showing the Sydney Opera House and the other showing St. Andrews Cathedral in Sydney.

Combining Criteria When Searching File Contents

To perform a precise search, you can combine criteria in the Search box. For example, suppose you store your financial documents on your computer and need to find a list of charitable donations you made in 2010. You don't recall where you've stored this information and scanning the filenames in your Financial folder doesn't reveal the file. If you search the content of the files using *donation* as the search criteria, you'll find lists of donations for many years as well as other documents, including e-mail messages with text such as "Thanks for your support! Every donation helps." If you search the contents of files using *2010* as the search criteria, you'll find dozens of documents that mention that year. If you search for *donations 2010*, you won't find files that include the text *donations for 2010* or *donations in 2010*. To pinpoint your search, you can combine the criteria to find files that contain the word *donations* and the date *2010*. When you search file contents, you can use **Boolean filters**, which let you search for specific information using the words AND, OR, and NOT to combine search criteria. You can use quotation marks and parentheses to refine the search conditions further. Figure 6-18 describes how to use AND, OR, and NOT along with quotation marks and parentheses when combining search criteria.

Combining search criteria ◀ **Figure 6-18**

Word or Punctuation	Example	When to Use
AND	donations AND 2010	To narrow the search to files that contain *donations* and *2010* even if the words are not next to each other
OR	donations OR 2010	To broaden the search to files that contain *donations* or *2010*
NOT	donations NOT 2010	To restrict the search to files that contain *donations* but not *2010*
" " (quotation marks)	"donations 2010"	To pinpoint the search to files that contain the exact phrase *donations 2010*
( ) (parentheses)	(donations 2010)	To open the search to files that contain both items next to each other, but in any order

Note that when you use the words AND, OR, and NOT, you must enter them using all uppercase letters.

One of your ongoing projects for *TrendSpot Magazine* is maintaining an archive of quotations on wide-ranging subjects. Kendra started the archive years ago, and now she and the *TrendSpot* editors use these quotations in columns and articles, and often request a quotation from a particular author or on a particular topic just before publishing an issue of the magazine. You have therefore created a Quotations folder with two subfolders: an Authors folder that contains documents of quotations listed alphabetically by author, and a Topics folder that contains documents of quotations listed by general topic. Because authors and editors use a variety of word-processing programs, you've stored collections of quotations in TXT documents to make sure anyone at *TrendSpot* can use the documents. However, this means that you cannot add tags or other properties to the files—you can add these details only to Microsoft Office documents. To find quotations that Kendra and others want, you can use Boolean logic to combine search criteria in a folder window's Search box.

In one part of her column, Kendra plans to highlight a few contemporary Australian writers, and wants to start that section with a quotation about Australian writers. You can combine search criteria to search the contents of the Quotations folder to find suitable quotations. Before you do, first select the text you will use in your search criteria. Then determine whether you should use AND, OR, or NOT to combine the criteria and whether you need quotation marks or parentheses to find the files you want. Using AND is the most common way to combine search criteria, followed by OR, and then NOT. Using quotation marks is more common than using parentheses. To determine the best criteria, test each method in order starting with AND.

Although you want to find quotations about Australian writers, using *Australian* and *writers* as search criteria won't find quotations that include *Australia* or *writer* or even *write*, which might be appropriate quotations. A good rule of thumb when selecting search text is to use the root of the word, such as *writ* to find documents containing *writer*, *writers*, *writes*, and *writing*. For your purposes, you should use *Australia* and *writ* as search criteria.

Next, determine the best way to combine the criteria, as shown in the following list.

- Australia AND writ finds documents that include both words.
- Australia OR writ finds documents that include at least one of the words.
- Australia NOT writ finds documents that include *Australia*, but not those that include *writ*.
- "Australia writ" finds documents that include the exact phrase *Australia writ*.
- (Australia writ) finds documents that include the exact words *Australia* and *writ* consecutively in either order.

Because *Australia* AND *writ* produces the results you want, you'll use that as your search criteria to find quotations about Australian writers.

To find files using AND criteria:

▶ 1. Open the **Quotations** folder in the Tutorial.06\Tutorial folder.

▶ 2. Click the **Search** box, and then type **Australia AND writ**. As you type, Windows searches filenames that meet your criteria.

▶ 3. If necessary, click **Search in File Contents** to search the file contents instead of filenames. Windows finds one file that meets your criteria. See Figure 6-19.

Finding files that contain *Australia* AND *writ* **Figure 6-19**

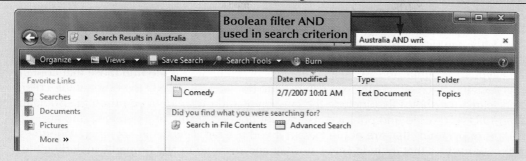

4. To verify this file contains a quotation you can use, double-click **Comedy** to open it in a text-editing program such as Notepad.

5. Page through the file until you find a quotation by Geoffrey Cottrell (*In America only the successful writer is important, in France all writers are important, in England no writer is important, and in Australia you have to explain what a writer is*), and then close the text-editing program.

Kendra mentions that she could use quotations that either mention Australia or mention writers—she can work either type into her column. You can try your search again, this time using the Boolean filter OR to find files that contain either *Australia* or *writ*.

To find files using OR criteria:

1. Display the contents of the **Quotations** folder again.

2. Click the **Search** box, and then type **Australia OR writ**.

3. If necessary, click **Search in File Contents** to search the file contents instead of filenames. Now Windows finds three files that contain the word *Australia* or the text *writ*. See Figure 6-20.

Finding files that contain *Australia* OR *writ* **Figure 6-20**

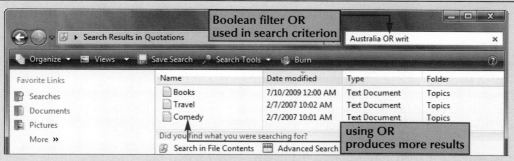

To really pinpoint what you want to find and refine your search criteria, you can combine Boolean filters and file properties.

Combining Boolean Filters and File Properties

When you search files by file property, you can use Boolean filters to combine criteria. For example, suppose you want to find files where Kendra or Sam is specified as the author. You can use *author: Kendra OR Sam* as the search criteria. This search finds files where Kendra is the author or where *Sam* is included in any file property, including author or filename. To restrict the search to files authored by Kendra or Sam, use parentheses, as in *author: (Kendra OR Sam)*. You can also use quotation marks to search literally for more than one word. For example, *author: "Sam Moriarity"* finds files only where Sam's full name is provided as the author.

Kendra is working on the Egypt section of her travel column, and requests a photo of an Egyptian pyramid. You can search the tags of the photo files to find those that contain this text. To search efficiently, you can use the Boolean filter AND to combine the criteria and search for photos that include the tags *Egypt* and *pyramid*. (If you used the Boolean filter OR, you would find photos of Egypt, but not necessarily of a pyramid, and also photos of pyramids that are not in Egypt.) If you use *tag: Egypt AND pyramid*, Windows searches for files that include *Egypt* as a tag and *pyramid* in any property, including filename and contents. To restrict the search to tags only, enclose the criteria in parentheses.

To find files by combining file property criteria:

▶ 1. Display the contents of the **Tutorial** folder.

▶ 2. Click the **Search** box, and then type **tag: (Egypt AND pyramid)**. Windows finds five files that meet your criteria. See Figure 6-21.

| Figure 6-21 | Combining Boolean filters with file properties |

When you tell Kendra that you found a number of photos of Egyptian pyramids, she mentions that Denyce, one of the photographers, said she took a terrific shot of Giza, one of the major Egyptian pyramids. Kendra asks you to find the photo of an Egyptian pyramid that Denyce took. You can search for this file by adding criteria to your search text, which could become complicated. Another way to search for files is to use a natural language search, which is especially helpful when you want to use many criteria.

Finding Files with Natural Language Criteria

Besides using Boolean filters to combine search criteria, you can turn on the Windows natural language search and perform searches in a simpler way, without using colons and Boolean filters such as AND and OR. For example, instead of using *tag: (Egypt AND pyramid)* as the search criteria, you could use either *Egypt pyramid* or *photos Egypt pyramid*. As you'll see when you search the Internet in the next section, natural language criteria let you search your files using the same kind of casual search text you use when you search the Internet.

To use natural language search, you turn it on in the Folder Options dialog box. After you turn it on, you can search files using natural language criteria or the stricter shorthand notation (specifying properties and using colons, quotation marks, and parentheses) and Boolean filters. Natural language search also examines the same file properties as default searching, including filenames, contents, tags, and dates.

To find the photo of an Egyptian pyramid taken by Denyce, you can first turn on natural language searching and then enter search text using natural language criteria.

To turn on natural language searching and use it to find files:

▶ 1. Display the contents of the **Tutorial** folder, click the **Organize** button on the toolbar, and then click **Folder and Search Options**. The Folder Options dialog box opens.

▶ 2. Click the **Search** tab, and then click the **Use natural language search** check box to turn on natural language searching. Click the **OK** button.

▶ 3. Click the **Search** box, and then type **photo Egypt pyramid**. If necessary, click **Search in file contents**. Windows finds the same five files shown earlier in Figure 6-21. These are photos that contain *Egypt* and *pyramid* as tags.

▶ 4. Type **Denyce** to add that to the search text to find photos of Egyptian pyramids taken by Denyce. See Figure 6-22. Now you can give that photo to Kendra so she can use it in her column.

Conducting a natural language search ◀ **Figure 6-22**

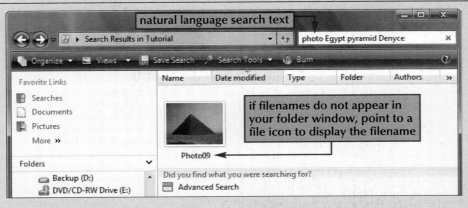

▶ 5. Close the folder window.

You've already explored many ways to search for files on your computer. Besides searching filenames and contents, you've learned how to use the Search pane to conduct advanced searches, how to use shorthand notation to specify tags and other file properties in search criteria, and how to combine criteria using Boolean filters. You've also learned how to simplify the search text by using natural language searching. In the next session, you'll apply these techniques to search for programs and for files that could be stored anywhere on your computer. You'll also examine the Windows index, develop techniques for searching the Internet, and collaborate with other people.

Review | **Session 6.1 Quick Check**

1. What are search criteria?
2. True or False. When you develop a search strategy, you choose the search tool that best fits your needs and select search criteria that are most likely to find the item.
3. You can narrow your search to a general category of files by clicking a button on the _____ _____ .
4. Name two ways you can verify that a file you found is one you want without opening the file.
5. Your _____ _____ include your personal folder (Documents, Pictures, Music, Desktop, and other common locations), e-mail, and offline files.
6. True or False. Saving a search saves the results in a folder you specify.
7. Name three types of properties you can add to photo files.
8. If you use *tag: landscape OR beach*, what files would you find?

Session 6.2

Searching for Programs from the Start Menu

As you've learned, you can use the Search box or the Search pane to find any file or folder on your computer. But if you're looking for a program, a Web page stored in your browser's History list, or a file or folder saved in your personal folder, you can use the Start Search box on the Start menu. (Recall that your personal folder contains your most frequently used folders, such as Documents, Pictures, Music, and Favorites, and other folders specific to your user account. Your personal folder is labeled with the name you use to log on to your computer and is the first folder listed on the right side of the Start menu, by default.)

When you use the Start Search box on the Start menu, you enter text just as you do when you use the Search box in a folder window. As you type, Windows displays the programs and files that meet your criteria, filtering the list with every character you type. Windows lists the search results on the left side of the Start menu. At the top of the list are programs that meet your criteria, followed by files. First are files with filenames that match your criteria and then are the files with tags that match your criteria. Windows also displays two links at the bottom of the search results—See all results and Search the Internet. You can click the See all results link to display the files in a search results window that identifies the path and other details about the file. You can click the Search the Internet link to perform the same search in your browser. You'll search the Internet later in this session.

Reference Window | **Searching for Programs on the Start Menu**

- Click the Start button, and then click the Start Search text box.
- Type your search criteria.

To search for programs from the Start menu:

▶ **1.** Click the **Start** button 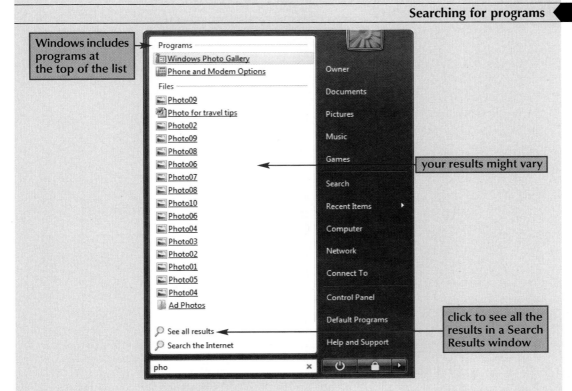, and then click in the **Start Search** text box.

▶ **2.** Type **pho** to start entering *photo* as the search text. The Start menu lists programs for working with photos at the top of the Start menu. It also lists files whose filenames contain a word starting with *photo*, and files with tags that start with *photo*. See Figure 6-23.

Searching for programs ◀ Figure 6-23

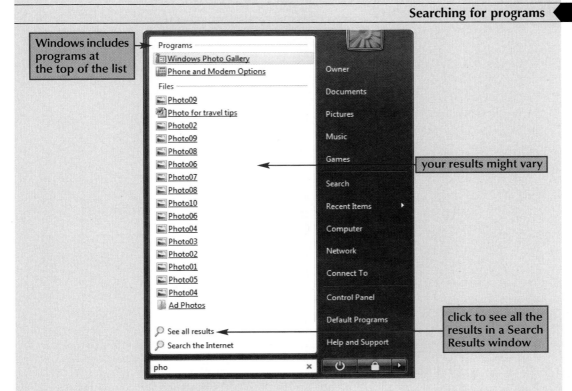

Windows includes programs at the top of the list

your results might vary

click to see all the results in a Search Results window

▶ **3.** Click **Windows Photo Gallery** to open that program. See Figure 6-24.

Figure 6-24 ▶ **Windows Photo Gallery**

4. Click the **first photo** in the window. (The images displayed with a filmstrip icon are videos, not photos.) By default, the first photo in the window is one of the sample photos provided in your Pictures folder.

5. Click the **Fix** button on the toolbar. The photo opens in a window where you can adjust the image, including its color, and crop it if necessary.

6. Close Windows Photo Gallery.

Now that you've found a program Kendra can use to edit photos, you want to explore one more way to search for files on her computer. Before you do, you can set search options, including those for indexing, to speed up your searches.

Setting Search Options

You can set search options to improve the efficiency of your searches. When Windows Vista searches for a file in a folder window, it checks every file in the folder and its sub-folders to see if the file meets your search criteria. When you are searching your personal folder or your entire computer, searching this way takes too much time. Instead of look-ing through your entire hard disk for a filename or property, Windows scans the **index**, which keeps track of the files on your computer similar to the way an index in a book keeps track of its contents. Using an index allows Windows to find most results in a frac-tion of the time that a search without the index would take.

Another way to set search options is to use the Search tab in the Folder Options dialog box to fine-tune what Windows searches and how it searches. By default, it searches filenames and contents only in indexed locations, which include any files in your personal folder and its subfolders. If necessary, you can set Windows to always search filenames and contents outside of your personal folder. Be aware, however, that setting this option can slow the search considerably. You can also set Windows to search only filenames and not contents, which can speed searches.

As you know, when you type a search criterion in the Search box, Windows searches the current folder and its subfolders by default. It also finds files that match your criterion even if you haven't finished entering the complete criterion. You can change this searching behavior on the Search tab of the Folder Options dialog box.

Verifying Search Options

You rarely need to change the Windows search options unless your searches take a long time. If you don't want to search file contents, you can set Windows to search filenames only when you enter text in the Search box. If you often start searching in a folder that is likely to contain the file you want, you can speed searches by not including subfolders when you use the Search box.

You want to make sure that the Windows Search options are set to their defaults, so you'll open the Search tab on the Folder Options dialog box.

To verify search options:

▶ **1.** Open the **Tutorial** folder provided with your Data Files.

▶ **2.** Click the **Organize** button on the toolbar, and then click **Folder and Search Options**. The Folder Options dialog box opens.

▶ **3.** Click the **Search** tab. Figure 6-25 shows the Search tab and the default indexing options and the natural language search option selected.

Search tab in the Folder Options dialog box ◀ Figure 6-25

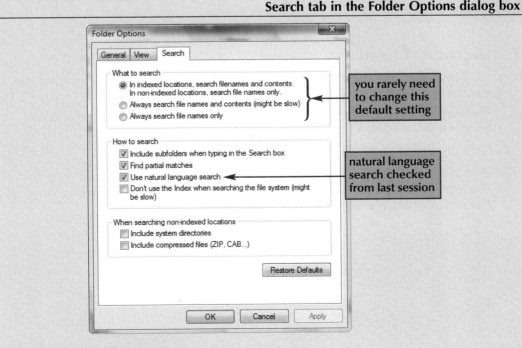

▶ **4.** Click the **OK** button to close the dialog box.

Another way to make sure Windows is performing searches efficiently is to check its indexing options.

Setting Index Options

The Windows index stores information about files, including the filename, date modified, and other properties such as tags, authors, and rating. By default, Windows indexes the files most people use often, including those in your personal folder, your e-mail, and offline files. (Offline files are those usually stored on a network resource, but saved in a location you can access when you're not connected to the network.) Windows does not index program files and system files because you rarely need to search the contents of those files.

Although you can't access the index, you can see a complete list of the locations that are indexed on your computer. To do so, you open the Indexing Options dialog box, which also reports the status of the indexing service. If you regularly search a different location, such as a Public folder, you can add that folder to the list of indexed locations. (Only users with Administrator accounts can change indexed locations.) To do so, you click the Modify button in the Indexing Options dialog box, and then select the folders on your computer you want to include. You can also exclude folders you rarely search in the same way.

InSight	**Selecting Index Locations**

Make sure you don't index too many locations for searching, or index a very large location, such as your entire computer. Doing so increases the size of the index, which hampers the efficiency of your searches. For best results, Microsoft recommends that you only add folders to the index that contain your personal files.

You want to make sure Windows is indexing your files efficiently, so you'll open the Indexing Options dialog box to view the list of indexed locations and check the status of the indexing service.

To view indexed locations:

Tip

You can also open the Indexing Options dialog box from a folder window displaying search results. Click the Search Tools button on the toolbar, and then click Modify Index Locations.

1. Click the **Start** button ⊕, and then click **Control Panel** to open the Control Panel window in Category view.

   Trouble? If your Control Panel opens in Classic view, click Category View in the left pane of the Control Panel window.

2. Click the **System and Maintenance** category.

3. Click **Indexing Options**. The Indexing Options dialog box opens. See Figure 6-26. The status of the indexing service is indicated at the top of the dialog box, and the indexed locations are listed in the Included Locations list.

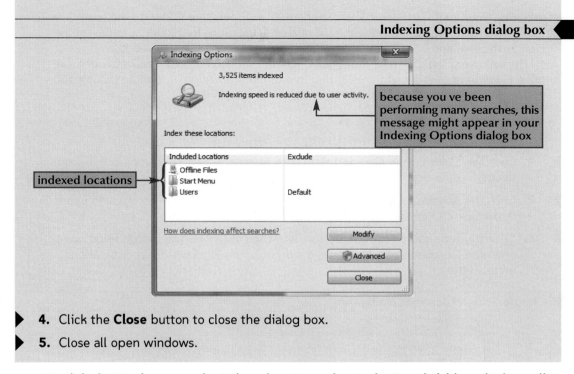

indexed locations

because you ve been performing many searches, this message might appear in your Indexing Options dialog box

▶ **4.** Click the **Close** button to close the dialog box.

▶ **5.** Close all open windows.

By default, Windows uses the index when it searches in the Search folder, which you'll do next.

Using the Search Folder

Besides using the Search box or Search pane in a folder window, or the Start Search box on the Start menu, you can find files using the Windows Search folder. Use the Search folder if the file you want to find could be located anywhere on your computer. The Search folder is also a good choice if you want to include files from more than one folder, especially if these folders are two or more of your common folders, such as Pictures and Music. Because the Search folder uses the same Search pane that you can open in a folder window, you can easily conduct searches using more than one criterion.

Selecting a Search Location

When you use the Search folder, by default Windows searches your indexed locations, which you examined in the previous set of steps. If you want to search additional locations or a different location, you can specify the locations before conducting the search. The locations you specify in this way override the defaults, so if you want to search a particular folder plus the usual indexed locations, you must specify both.

TrendSpot contributors often send articles, photos, and other material to Kendra via e-mail. Some of this material includes files that you need to work with. If Kendra receives only a few small files, she usually forwards them to you as attachments to an e-mail message. However, when she receives many files or a few large files, she saves them on a USB flash drive and gives that to you. Windows does not include the drives for removable media in its index. Because it's efficient for you to include your USB flash drive in your searches, you can include this drive in the list of search locations.

Kendra wants to use a quotation about Cleopatra for her travel column, and thinks one from Shakespeare's *Antony* and *Cleopatra* would be appropriate. She knows she gave you a file of Shakespeare quotations, but you're not sure where you stored it. It might be in a folder on your USB flash drive or somewhere in your personal folder on the hard disk. To speed your search, you'll modify the list of search locations to include a folder on the USB flash drive and your indexed locations so that Windows searches both.

The following steps assume that your Data Files are stored on a removable disk on drive F. If you are using Data Files stored in a different location, substitute that location in these steps.

To search multiple locations using the Search folder:

▶ **1.** Click the **Start** button 🪟 , and then click **Search**. A Search Results window opens displaying the Search pane and Search box.

▶ **2.** Click the **Advanced Search** button on the Search pane. The Search pane expands in the Search Results window.

▶ **3.** Click the **Indexed Locations** button, and then click **Choose search locations** to open the Choose Search Locations dialog box. See Figure 6-27. Your locations might differ.

Figure 6-27	Choose Search Locations dialog box

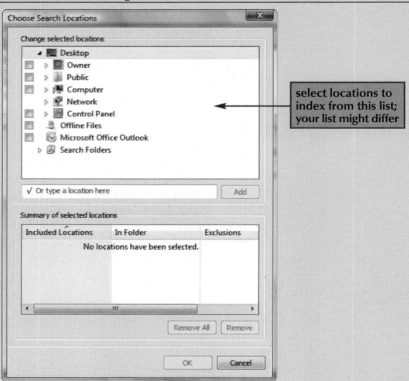

4. In the list of locations, expand the **Computer** icon, expand **Removable Disk (F:)**, and then click the **Tutorial** folder in the Tutorial.06 folder provided with your Data Files.

Tip

You can select Everywhere in the Choose Search Locations dialog box to search your entire computer.

The Tutorial folder is now the only location for this search. You need to add the indexed locations to the list.

▶ **5.** Scroll to the end of the locations list, and then expand **Search Folders**. A list of saved searches, including Indexed Locations, appears in the list.

▶ **6.** Click the **Indexed Locations** check box to select it. Two locations appear in the Summary of selected locations. See Figure 6-28.

Setting two search locations ◀ Figure 6-28

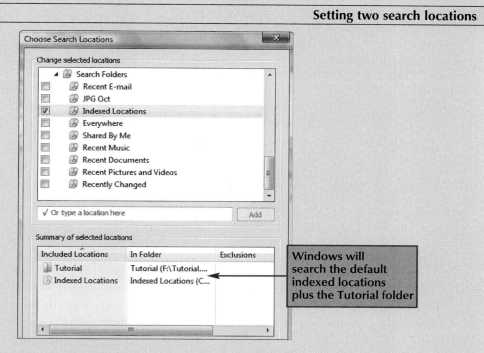

7. Click the **OK** button to accept the settings and close the dialog box. Your expanded Search pane should look similar to the one in Figure 6-29.

Expanded Search pane with two locations ◀ Figure 6-29

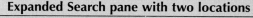
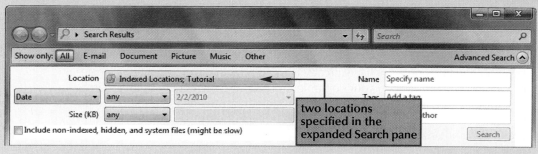

Now you can search indexed locations and the Tutorial folder on your removable disk for Shakespeare quotations to find one about Cleopatra.

To search specified locations using the Search folder:

▶ **1.** Click in the **Search** box, and then type **Shakespeare**. Windows finds one file named Shakespeare in the Tutorial folder on the removable disk. See Figure 6-30.

Figure 6-30 | **Searching specified locations**

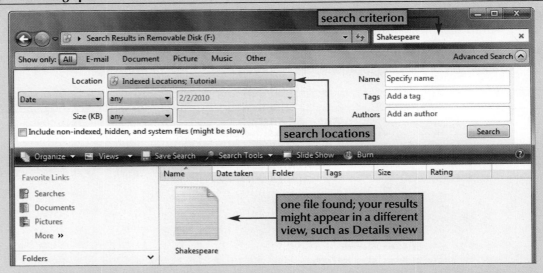

> **2.** Click **Shakespeare** in the file list, click the **Organize** button on the toolbar, point to **Layout**, and then click **Preview Pane** to open the Preview pane and view the contents of the Shakespeare file. Quotations from *Antony and Cleopatra* appear at the beginning of the document.

> **3.** Close all open windows.

Now that you found the file of Shakespeare quotations, you can send the quotations from *Antony and Cleopatra* to Kendra. She wants you to continue researching information for her column on budget travel in Australia and Egypt. However, the information she now wants you to find is not available in any of the files on your computer. Instead, you can use Internet Explorer to search the Internet for the information. Most of the searching techniques you've learned for searching files apply to searching for information in the millions of Web sites on the Internet.

Searching the Internet

The Internet provides access to a wealth of information; the challenge is to find the information you need or want. You have already learned how to develop search strategies and specific criteria to find files on your computer. You can use many of the same search strategies to find information on the Internet. Instead of using tools provided in a folder window, such as the Search box and Search pane, you use the search tools provided in Internet Explorer. Figure 6-31 summarizes the search tools you can use in Internet Explorer.

Figure 6-31 | **Internet Explorer search tools**

Search Tool	Description
Live Search box	Type a word or phrase to find Web pages associated with that topic.
Address bar	Type Find, Go, or ? followed by a word or phrase to find Web pages associated with that topic. If the word or phrase you enter is the name of a Web site, its main page opens in Internet Explorer.
Search provider	Click the Live Search button arrow, and then select a search provider to use their tools to search the Internet.

The terminology that you use when searching the Internet is slightly different from the terminology you use to search for files on your computer. The word or phrase on which you search is typically called a **search expression**. Each word in the search expression is usually called a **keyword**. After you enter a search expression using one of Internet Explorer's search tools, Internet Explorer displays the results, which are links to Web pages that meet your criteria. You can click these links, or **hits**, to access Web pages that contain the keywords in your search expression.

When you provide a search expression to Internet Explorer, it uses a search provider, which is a Web site that specializes in searching the Internet. Popular search providers include Google and Windows Live Search. Because searching all of the Web pages on the Internet to find those that contain your search expression would take a prohibitive amount of time, search providers typically search a database of indexed Web pages. These databases are updated periodically, though not often enough to keep all of the indexed Web pages up to date. This is why a page of search results might include inactive or broken links.

Web site designers and owners can make their Web pages easier for search providers to find by **optimizing** the site. In its Web page headings, an optimized site lists keywords and phrases that you and other Web users are likely to use to find the information on the Web page. Conversely, you are more likely to find the Web pages you want if you are aware of the types of keywords Web designers often use.

Searching the Internet Effectively | InSight

Keep the following guidelines in mind to search the Internet efficiently.

- **Be specific**: If you search for general categories, you'll find an overwhelming number of pages. Searching for specific terms or details is more likely to provide results you can use. For example, instead of searching for *desserts*, search for *pear cake recipe*.
- **Form a question**: Think of your search expression as a question you want answered, such as *Are there restaurants in the Denver area that serve vegetarian food?* Eliminate the articles and common words to form a workable search expression, such as *restaurants Denver vegetarian*.
- **Search the results**: Most search providers let you reduce the number of pages to search by searching your results. For example, suppose you search for *pear cake recipe* and find many thousands of results. Because you want a recipe similar to the one your Swedish grandmother made, you can search the results using *Swedish* as your search expression.

Kendra is now working on a section of her column that describes the popular restaurants in the capital cities of Australia and Egypt. So far, she has plenty of information on the restaurants in Sydney, but she wants to know more about the restaurants in Cairo. As her editorial assistant, you offer to search the Internet to find the information. You'll start by using *Cairo Egypt restaurants* as the search expression to find Web pages describing restaurants in Cairo.

Because Web pages and search indexes change frequently, the search results you find when you perform the steps in this section will differ from those shown in the figures.

To search using a search expression:

▶ **1.** Start Internet Explorer.

▶ **2.** Click in the Live Search box, type **Cairo Egypt restaurants**, and press the **Enter** key. The Live Search provider looks for Web pages containing the search expression you entered, and then displays the results. See Figure 6-32.

Figure 6-32 **Search results for the search expression *Egypt restaurants***

Using *Cairo Egypt restaurants* as the search expression produced thousands of results, which is typical. Although the first few Web pages listed might provide the information you seek, to find more useful Web pages, you need to narrow your search.

Narrowing Your Search

You can narrow your Internet search by modifying your search expression or by limiting the kinds of Web pages you want in your results. One way to modify your search expression is to use quotation marks to search for specific phrases. If you enclose a phrase in quotation marks, you restrict the results to Web pages that contain that exact phrase. For example, using a search expression such as *Radcliffe College Library* finds Web pages that include those three words anywhere on the page. If you enclose the search expression in quotation marks, as in *"Radcliffe College Library"*, you find only Web pages that include the exact text in the specified order.

Another way to modify your search expression is to use the advanced search features that search providers typically offer. Figure 6-33 shows the Advanced Search page from Google, a popular search provider.

Google Advanced Search page — **Figure 6-33**

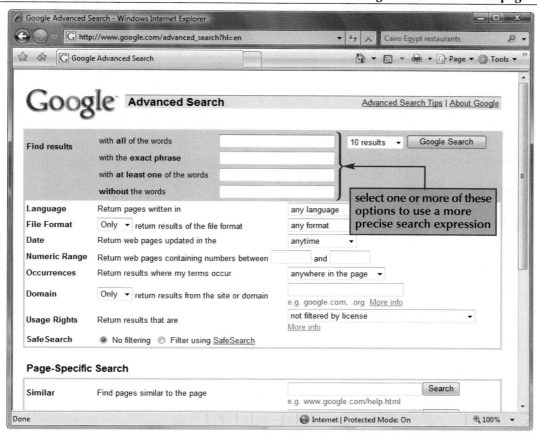

Similar to the expanded Search pane for searching files, an advanced search page lets you specify and combine search conditions. Most advanced search pages provide the following types of options:

- Find pages that include all of the words. This is the default for most search providers.
- Limit the results to pages that match the exact phrase. This is the same as using quotation marks to enclose an expression.
- Find pages that include at least one of the words in the search expression.
- Specify keywords that you do not want included in the Web page.
- Search only pages written in a particular language.
- Find pages of a certain type, such as Microsoft Word or Adobe Acrobat PDF.
- Search pages that have been updated within a specified period of time.
- Limit results to pages in a specified Web site or domain.

Besides providing an advanced search page for narrowing your search expression, most search providers include tabs or links that specify the kind of results you want. For example, the Live Search results page shown in Figure 6-32 includes six tabs: Web, Images, News, Maps, Classifieds, and More. By default, Live Search displays Web pages in the results. If you are searching for images, such as photos and drawings, you can click the Images tab before or after you enter a search expression to restrict the results to pages including images that meet your criteria.

Some of the Web pages you found when you used *Cairo Egypt restaurants* as a search expression described Cairo, Egypt, but didn't necessarily focus on restaurants. You can try narrowing your search by enclosing the expression in quotation marks to see if the results are more useful.

To narrow a search to an exact match:

▶ **1.** On the search results page, click in the search text box at the top of the page.

▶ **2.** Edit the text so it appears as **"Cairo Egypt restaurants"** and press the **Enter** key. This time, you find many fewer results because the search is restricted to only those Web pages that include the exact phrase you entered. See Figure 6-34.

Figure 6-34	Search results for an exact phrase search expression

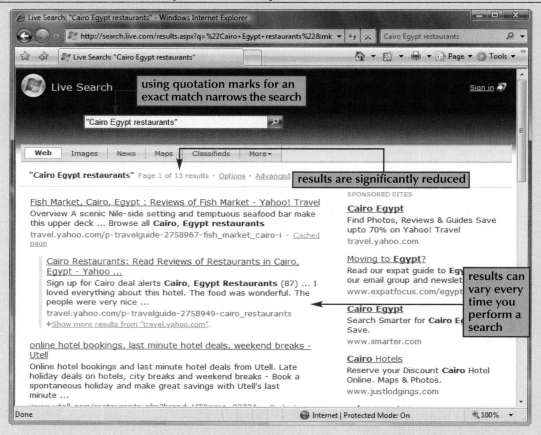

Using an exact phrase produced a list of restaurants in Cairo, Egypt, that is useful to you and Kendra. Now Kendra wants to briefly mention quality restaurants in other parts of Egypt that budget travelers might want to visit. These are any budget restaurants that are not located in Cairo. To specify this kind of search condition, you can use a search provider's advanced search page. You have used Google in the past, so you can try this search using Google instead of Live Search. You'll specify that you want to search for budget restaurants in Egypt, but not those in Cairo.

To narrow a search by excluding keywords:

▶ **1.** Click the Address bar, type **www.google.com**, and then press the **Enter** key to open the main page on the Google Web site. See Figure 6-35.

Main page on the Google Web site | **Figure 6-35**

▶ **2.** Click the **Advanced Search** link to open the Advanced Search page.

▶ **3.** In the Find results section, click the **with all of the words** text box, and then type **Egypt budget restaurants**.

▶ **4.** Click the **without the words** text box, type **Cairo**, and then press the **Enter** key. The search results list more than a million Web pages, including many for hotels. You'll exclude the keyword *hotel* from the search.

▶ **5.** Click the **Advanced Search** link, click the **without the words** text box, and then type **hotel** so that "Cairo" and "hotel" both appear in the text box.

▶ **6.** Click the **Google Search** button. The search results page includes fewer hits, with the best matches on the first page, which will help you find a few restaurants for Kendra's column.

| **Evaluating Web Pages in the Search Results** | | InSight |

Although a Web page might be listed at the top of the search results, that doesn't guarantee the page provides reliable and up-to-date information that meets your needs. Before using a Web page or citing it as a source, review the content with a critical eye. At the bottom of the Web page, look for the author and evidence of the author's credentials. Look for links to the original source of quoted information, which tends to validate the information on a Web page. Also look for signs of bias, such as unsubstantiated claims or extreme points of view.

Kendra also wonders if you can find any photos of Egyptian restaurants that she can include in her column. She'd prefer those that show restaurant interiors. To fulfill her request, you can use the Images tab in Google. Recall that Live Search and other search providers include a similar tool.

To limit the results to Web pages with images:

▶ **1.** In the Google search results page, click the **Images** link near the top of the page. Google looks for Web pages containing images that meet your search criteria—those of budget restaurants not in Cairo. See Figure 6-36.

Figure 6-36 ▶ **Searching for images**

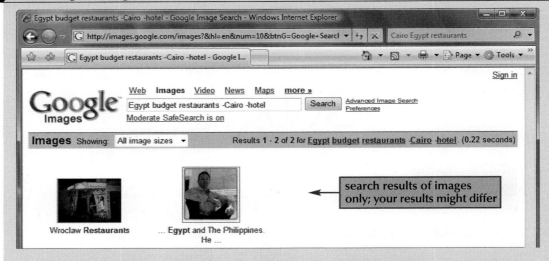

These are not promising results. However, Kendra said the photos could be of any Egyptian restaurant, so you can change the search expression.

Tip

The -*Cairo* in the search expression is a shorthand way of excluding *Cairo* from the search.

▶ **2.** Click the **search** text box near the top of the Images page, and edit the search expression to be **Egypt restaurants**.

▶ **3.** Click the **Search** button. Google displays images that meet your criteria, including many that show restaurant interiors.

Choosing Search Providers

In Internet Explorer, you can choose which provider you want to use when you search for information on the Internet. You can change the search provider for a specific search, and you can specify which search provider you prefer to use by default. When you first install Internet Explorer, only one provider might be available. You can add search providers to increase your searching options.

Reference Window | **Selecting a Search Provider**

- Click the Live Search button arrow next to the Address bar, and then click Find More Providers.
- Click a provider in the list, and then click Add Provider.

Your installation of Internet Explorer includes Windows Live Search as a search provider, but not Google, which you and Kendra use often. You'll add this search provider to the provider list, which you can access by clicking the Live Search button arrow. You can also choose to make a new search provider the default one to use when you search from the Address bar or Search box.

To add a search provider to the provider list:

▶ **1.** Click the **Live Search button arrow**, and then click **Find More Providers**. A list of possible search providers appears. See Figure 6-37.

Adding search providers

Figure 6-37

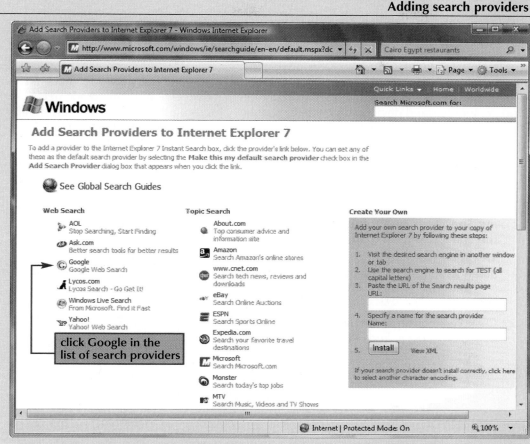

2. Click **Google** in the list to open the Add Search Provider dialog box.

3. Click the **Add Provider** button.

4. Click the **Live Search** button arrow to verify that Internet Explorer added Google to the list of search providers.

5. Close Internet Explorer.

Now Internet Explorer makes Google and Live Search available as search providers. To set the default search provider to use, you can click the Live Search button arrow, click Change Search Defaults, and then select the provider you want to use regularly.

Collaborating with Other People

Because people often work together from separate locations, they occasionally need a way to meet online to exchange information or collaborate on projects without physically traveling to convene in the same place. You can use Windows Meeting Space to meet and collaborate with others who are not in your same location. Using Windows Meeting Space, you can share documents, programs, and your desktop with other meeting participants. Similar to meeting in a physical location, you can distribute and collaborate on documents, pass notes to other participants, and connect to a network project to give a presentation. To do so, you start a meeting and invite other people to join it, or you join an existing meeting.

Setting Up Windows Meeting Space

Before you can use Windows Meeting Space for the first time, you need to set it up by turning on some services and signing onto People Near Me, a feature that identifies people using computers near you so you can use Windows Meeting Space. If you are working on a network, Windows Meeting Space uses that network to connect meeting participants. Otherwise, Windows Meeting Space sets up an **ad hoc network**, which is a temporary network used for sharing files or an Internet connection. In an ad hoc network, computers and devices are connected directly to each other instead of to a central device, such as a hub or router. By setting up an ad hoc network, Windows Meeting Space lets you meet in a conference room, outside the office, or anyplace else.

To set up Windows Meeting Space:

▶ 1. Click the **Start** button 🪟, point to **All Programs**, and then click **Windows Meeting Space**. Because this is the first time you are using Windows Meeting Space, the Windows Meeting Space Setup window opens.

   Trouble? If a message appears indicating that Windows cannot start Windows Meeting Space because of a Windows Firewall setting, click the OK button, open the Windows Firewall Settings dialog box, and then click the Block all incoming connections check box to remove the check mark. Repeat Step 1.

▶ 2. Click **Yes, continue setting up Windows Meeting Space**. The People Near Me dialog box opens. See Figure 6-38.

Figure 6-38 ▶ People Near Me dialog box

   Trouble? If this is not the first time you are using Windows Meeting Space, the Windows Meeting Space window opens. Skip Steps 2–4.

   Trouble? If a User Account Control dialog box opens, provide a password, if necessary, and then click the Continue button.

▶ 3. In the Your display name text box, type **Kendra**.

▶ 4. Click the **OK** button. The Windows Meeting Space window opens so you can start or join a meeting. A People Near Me icon 👥 also appears in the notification area of the taskbar.

Now you can start a new meeting, and invite Bev to attend.

Starting a New Meeting

After you set up Windows Meeting Space, you can use it to start new meetings or join existing ones. In either case, you need to provide a name and password for the meeting. If you are starting a meeting, Windows assigns your display name and the current time as the meeting name. You can set your own password, though the password must be at least eight characters long and should be a strong password. (Recall that strong passwords are easy for you to remember but difficult for others to guess. Furthermore, strong passwords do not contain your name in any form or a complete word, and include one or more uppercase letters, lowercase letters, numbers, and keyboard symbols.)

Starting a Meeting and Inviting Participants | Reference Window

- Start Windows Meeting Space, and then click Start a new meeting.
- Provide a meeting name, if necessary, and a password.
- Click the Create a meeting button.
- Click Invite people.
- Click the check boxes for the people you want to invite, and then click the Send Invitations button.

Kendra is nearly finished with her column, and wants to meed online with Bev Parkinson, a *TrendSpot* page designer, to discuss the layout and illustrations for the column. You'll start the meeting by entering a password and then inviting Bev to join.

If you are not connected to a network, read but do not perform the following steps.

To start a meeting and invite a participant:

▶ **1.** In the Windows Meeting Space window, click **Start a new meeting**. The window displays text boxes for providing a meeting name and password. See Figure 6-39.

Starting a new meeting ◀ **Figure 6-39**

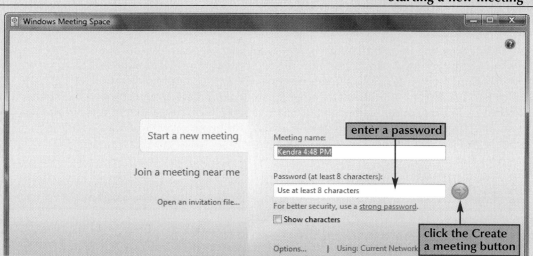

▶ **2.** In the Password text box, type **tSpot 24#**, and then click the **Create a meeting** button ⊚. Windows opens a window for the new meeting. See Figure 6-40.

| Figure 6-40 | Windows Meeting Space window |

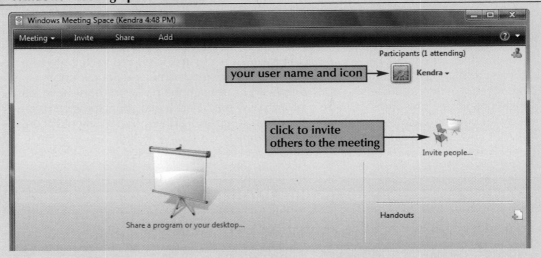

3. Click **Invite people** to open the Invite People dialog box.

   Trouble? If you are working on an ad hoc network, contact the people you want to invite, and ask them to start Windows Meeting Space and click Join a meeting near me. After they select the name of your meeting and enter a password, they appear as participants in the Windows Meeting Space window.

4. Click the **Bev** check box to invite her to the meeting, and then click the **Send invitations** button. After a few minutes, Bev receives the invitation and joins the meeting.

   Trouble? If the Invite People dialog box does not include a participant named Bev, click the check box for another person you know to invite him or her to the meeting.

   Trouble? If the Invite People dialog box does not include any participants, contact the people you want to invite, and ask them to start Windows Meeting Space and click Join a meeting near me. If they are not connected to the same network and using Windows Vista, they cannot join the meeting. Read but do not perform the remaining steps in the Windows Meeting Space section, and then close Windows Meeting Space.

Besides inviting people directly during a meeting, you can also invite people using e-mail or by creating an invitation file. To send an invitation via e-mail, click Invite people during a meeting, click Invite others in the Invite People dialog box, and then click Send an invitation in e-mail. To create an invitation file, you also open the Invite People dialog box during a meeting. Click Invite others and then click Create an invitation file. After you save the file, you can give it to others as you would any other file, such as on removable media.

Now that you've started a meeting and invited Bev to join, Kendra wants to share some of the photos for the travel trends column. You do so by distributing handouts to the meeting participants.

To distribute files to the meeting participants:

1. In the Windows Meeting Space window, click **Add a handout**. A dialog box opens, notifying you that the handouts, or files, will be copied to each participant's computer.

▶ **2.** Click the **OK** button. The Select files to add dialog box opens.

▶ **3.** Navigate to the **Tutorial** folder in the Tutorial.06 folder provided with your Data Files, and then open the **Australia** folder.

▶ **4.** Click **Photo08**, hold down the **Ctrl** key, and then click **Photo09** to select the two photos.

▶ **5.** Click the **Open** button. Windows displays the two handouts in the Windows Meeting Space window and distributes them to the meeting participants.

Bev could modify the files, if necessary, and then return them to you. Before you end the meeting, Kendra wants to show Bev the photos you found of Egyptian restaurants. To do so, you'll share your desktop with Bev.

To share your desktop:

▶ **1.** In the Windows Meeting Space window, click **Share a program or your desktop**.

▶ **2.** When asked if you want other people to see your desktop, click the **OK** button. The Start a shared session window opens.

▶ **3.** Click **Desktop**, and then click the **Share** button. The desktop colors might briefly change as Windows shows your desktop to the meeting participants. The meeting participants can now see all the activity on your desktop. See Figure 6-41.

Sharing your desktop in Windows Meeting Space **Figure 6-41**

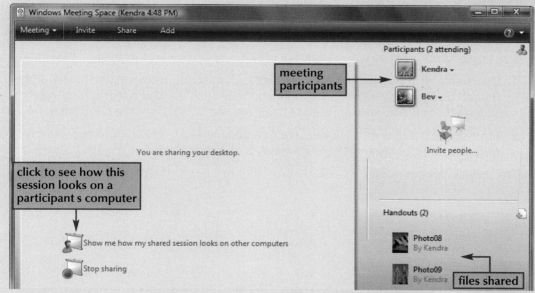

Trouble? If a message appears indicating that Windows changed your color scheme, click the OK button. You can verify your color scheme settings when you restore your computer.

▶ **4.** Start Internet Explorer.

▶ **5.** In the Address box, type **www.google.com**, and then press the **Enter** key.

▶ **6.** In the Google text box, type **Egypt restaurants**, click the **Images** link near the top of the page, and then click the **Search Images** button. Photos of Egyptian restaurants again appear in the search results. This time, however, your meeting participants can see the results. Windows Meeting Space lets you verify what participants can see.

▶ **7.** In the Windows Meeting Space window, click **Show me how my shared session looks on other computers**. Windows displays an image of your desktop as it appears on a participant's desktop; it might appear with a telescoping effect, which is normal.

Now that Kendra has provided two photo resources to Bev, you can end the meeting. Bev will examine the photos she received, return to the Web page listing photos of Egyptian restaurants, and use all the photos as she begins to work on the layout of the magazine.

To end the meeting:

▶ **1.** Close Internet Explorer.

▶ **2.** Click the **Meeting** button on the toolbar, and then click **Leave Meeting**. A dialog box opens asking if you want to save handouts.

▶ **3.** Click the **No** button. The original Windows Meeting Space window opens.

▶ **4.** Close the Windows Meeting Space window.

▶ **5.** Right-click the **People Near Me** icon 👤 in the notification area of the taskbar, and then click **Exit**.

Restoring Your Settings

If you are working in a computer lab or a computer other than your own, complete the steps in this section to restore the original settings on your computer.

To restore your settings:

▶ **1.** Open a folder window, click the **Organize** button on the toolbar, click **Folder and Search Options**, click the **Search** tab, and then click the **Use natural language search** check box to turn off natural language searching. Click the **OK** button.

▶ **2.** Start Internet Explorer, click the **Live Search** arrow button, click **Change search defaults**, click **Google**, click the **Remove** button, and then click the **OK** button.

▶ **3.** Close all open windows.

Session 6.2 Quick Check | Review

1. What is a search provider?
2. True or False. When you enter a search expression, a search provider searches all of the Web pages on the Internet to find those that match your criteria.
3. One way to modify a search expression is to use _____ _____ to search for specific phrases.
4. True or False. Search providers let you limit the search results to pages of a certain type.
5. Name three guidelines for searching the Internet efficiently.
6. You can use Windows Meeting Space on an _____ _____ network, which is a temporary network used for sharing files or an Internet connection.

Tutorial Summary | Review

In this tutorial, you developed search strategies for finding files on your computer and information on the Internet. You used the Search box in a folder window to find files by type, and used the Search pane to find files by category. You also conducted advanced searches using the expanded Search pane and saved a search so you could use it again. After adding tags and other properties to a file, you searched for these details in files. You also learned how to set search options, including those for indexing, and performed searches on the Search menu and in the Search folder. Finally, you used Internet Explorer and its search providers to find information on the Internet and collaborated with others using Windows Meeting Space.

Key Terms

ad hoc network	keyword	Search pane
Boolean filter	optimize	tag
hit	search criteria	wildcard
index	search expression	virtual folder
indexed locations		

Practice the skills you learned in the tutorial.

For a list of Data Files in the Review folder, see page 267.

You are now working with Kendra Cho on an article for *TrendSpot Magazine* on a disturbing trend: the incidents of extreme or destructive weather have increased in recent years. Kendra is editing an article on weather and needs your help to research the photos she'll use in the upcoming issue of the magazine. As an online publication, the magazine often includes multimedia files so that readers can play sound, music, and videos as they read articles. Kendra also wants you to help her search for audio and video files and find a program that can play them. Complete the following:

1. In a folder window, open the **Review** folder in the Tutorial.06 folder provided with your Data Files.
2. Use the Search box to search for WAV files. Move the WAV files to a new subfolder named **Sounds** in the Review folder.
3. Display the **Review** folder again, and then use the Search box and the Search pane to find documents whose filenames start with the text **pho**. Verify that the file you found lists credits for the photos in the Review folder. If it does, move the file you found to a new subfolder named **Documents** in the Review folder. Otherwise, do not move the file you found.
4. Add the following tags to Photo32: **Island; Ocean**.
5. Add the following tags to Photo41: **Lightning; Night; Sky; Thunderstorm**.
6. In the folder window, verify that the new tags are now assigned to Photo32 and Photo41. If necessary, maximize the folder window, switch to Details view, right-click a column heading, and then click Tags to display the Tags column.
7. In the Review folder, search for photos that have *tornado* as a tag. Move the files you found to a new subfolder named **Tornado** in the Review folder.
8. In the Review folder window, find a photo that has *snow* and *winter* as tags. Change the name of this file to **Winter**.
9. Search for a program on your computer that lets you play media files. Start the program, and then explore its toolbars. (If you need to set up the program, choose the Express Setup option.) Press Alt+Print Screen to capture an image of the program window, and then paste the image in a new Paint file. Save the file as **Media Program** in the Tutorial. 06\Review folder provided with your Data Files. Close the media program.
10. Use the Search folder to find video files in the indexed locations on your computer. (*Hint*: Use *video* in your search criteria.) Press Alt+Print Screen to capture an image of the Search Results window, and then paste the image in a new Paint file. Save the file as **Videos** in the Tutorial.06\Review folder provided with your Data Files.
11. Start Internet Explorer, and use Windows Live Search to find Web pages providing information about extreme weather in the current year. Narrow the search by finding only images of extreme weather in the current year. Press Alt+Print Screen to capture an image of the first screen of search results, and then paste the image in a new Paint file. Save the file as **Weather Images** in the Tutorial.06\Review folder provided with your Data Files.
12. Switch to Google as your search provider, and display the results of the search for Web pages providing information about extreme weather in the current year. Perform an advanced search to find Web pages that contain the exact text *extreme weather* but not for the current year. Press Alt+Print Screen to capture an image of the first screen of search results, and then paste the image in a new Paint file. Save the file as **Weather** in the Tutorial.06\Review folder provided with your Data Files. Close Internet Explorer.

13. Start Windows Meeting Space and start a meeting. If possible, invite someone you know to the meeting. Share your desktop with the meeting participants, and open Internet Explorer. Use the default search provider to find news stories about recent extreme weather. Resize the windows so that both are mostly visible. Press Print Screen to capture an image of the desktop, and then paste the image in a new Paint file. Save the file as **Weather Meeting** in the Tutorial.06\Review folder provided with your Data Files.

14. Close Paint and Internet Explorer, leave the meeting, close Windows Meeting Space, and then exit from People Near Me.

15. Submit the results of the preceding steps to your instructor, either in printed or electronic form, as requested.

Apply	**Case Problem 1**

Use the skills you learned in the tutorial to research images for a graphic arts firm.

Data Files needed for this Case Problem: P01.jpg–P13.jpg

G & K Graphic Arts   Marco Garcia and Joel Knightly own G & K Graphic Arts, a small firm in Nashville, Tennessee, that provides graphic design services to local businesses. They are currently working on a project for a recording studio to design a Web page and a CD insert for a CD featuring the work of studio musicians, tentatively called Bluegrass Studio. Marco and Joel ask you to help them find images they can use for the Web page and CD. They also want to back up their files on a DVD later, and ask you to find information about programs they can use to do so. Complete the following steps:

1. Open the **Case1** folder in the Tutorial.06 folder provided with your Data Files.

2. Review the tags and other properties already assigned to the files in the Case1 folder. Then add the tag **fiddle** or **bluegrass** to files as appropriate.

3. Using a file's Properties dialog box, add **Marco** as the author of the following photos: P01, P05, and P12.

4. Use the expanded Search pane and the Search box to find photos that include the tag *guitar* and have Marco as the author. Move the file(s) you found to a new subfolder named **Marco Guitar** in the Case1 folder.

5. In any of the indexed locations on your computer, search for WMA music files. Save the search as **WMA** in the Case1 folder.

6. Remove all the properties and personal information from the **P09** file in the Case1 folder. (*Hint*: Click the appropriate link in the P09 Properties dialog box, click the option button to Remove the following properties from this file, click the Select All button, and then click the OK button.)

7. Search for a program on your computer that lets you store files on a DVD. Start the program, and then press Alt+Print Screen to capture an image of the program window. Paste the image in a new Paint file. Save the file as **DVD Program** in the Tutorial.06\Case1 folder provided with your Data Files. Close the DVD program.

8. Search for a program on your computer that lets you back up and restore files. Start the program, and then press Alt+Print Screen to capture an image of the program window. Paste the image in a new Paint file. Save the file as **Backup Program** in the Tutorial.06\Case1 folder provided with your Data Files. Close the backup program.

9. Start Internet Explorer, and use Windows Live Search to find Web pages providing information on bluegrass music in Nashville. Narrow the search to find only images of bluegrass music in Nashville. Press Alt+Print Screen to capture an image of the first screen of search results, and then paste the image in a new Paint file. Save the file as **Nashville Images** in the Tutorial.06\Case1 folder provided with your Data Files.

10. Switch to any other search provider, and display the results of the original search for information about bluegrass music in Nashville. Modify the search to show information about bluegrass music not in Nashville. Press Alt+Print Screen to capture an image of the first screen of search results, and then paste the image in a new Paint file. Save the file as **Not Nashville** in the Tutorial.06\Case1 folder provided with your Data Files.

11. Close all open windows.

12. Submit the results of the preceding steps to your instructor, either in printed or electronic form, as requested.

Apply	**Case Problem 2**

Use the skills you learned in the tutorial to search for files and information for a pet adoption organization.

Data Files needed for this Case Problem: Pic01.jpg–Pic10.jpg

Amherst Pet Adoption   Michelle Rangely is the director of the Amherst Pet Adoption agency in Amherst, Massachusetts. She is developing a presentation to give to local groups such as parent-teacher organizations, neighborhood associations, and senior centers about the pets available at the agency and the value they provide to people and families. She asks you to help her organize the pictures she has of pets and research information about the benefits of keeping a pet. She also wants to find photographs of wildlife for part of her presentation. Because she will eventually distribute the presentation via e-mail, she wants to be aware of file size so that she can select small image files. Complete the following steps:

1. Open the **Case2** folder in the Tutorial.06 folder provided with your Data Files.

2. Add a tag to each file in the Case2 folder to identify the type of animal shown in the photo. Use **cat**, **dog**, **duck**, **rabbit**, or **parrot** as a tag. (*Hint*: Use a Large Icons or Extra Large Icons view to see the images clearly.)

3. Using a file's Properties dialog box, add **Available for adoption** as the comment in the following photos: Pic01, Pic04, Pic06, and Pic09.

✧ EXPLORE 4. Search for photos of cats that are available for adoption. (*Hint*: Start your search using **comment** as the property name in the Search box.) Move the files you found to a new subfolder named **Cats to Adopt** in the Case2 folder.

✧ EXPLORE 5. Using **Dimensions** as the property name in the search box, find files that are 120 pixels wide. Press Alt+Print Screen to capture an image of the search results window showing the files you found. Paste the image in a new Paint file, and save the file as **Dim 120** in the Tutorial.06\Case2 folder provided with your Data Files.

6. In any of the indexed locations on your computer and in the Tutorial.06\Case2 folder, search for files that are exactly 16 KB in size. Press Alt+Print Screen to capture an image of the search results window showing the files you found. Paste the image in a new Paint file, and save the file as **16 KB** in the Tutorial.06\Case2 folder provided with your Data Files.

7. In any of the indexed locations on your computer, search for picture files that have *wildlife* as a tag. Press Alt+Print Screen to capture an image of the search results window showing the files you found. Paste the image in a new Paint file, and save the file as **Wildlife** in the Tutorial.06\Case2 folder provided with your Data Files.

8. In any of the indexed locations on your computer, search for picture files that have *wildlife* as a tag and a file size less than 200 KB. Press Alt+Print Screen to capture an image of the search results window showing the files you found. Paste the image in a new Paint file, and save the file as **Small Pix** in the Tutorial.06\Case2 folder provided with your Data Files.

9. Search for a program on your computer that lets you connect to a network projector to play presentations. Start the program, and then press Alt+Print Screen to capture an image of the opening window. Paste the image in a new Paint file. Save the file as **Projector Program** in the Tutorial.06\Case2 folder provided with your Data Files. Close the projector program.

10. Start Internet Explorer, and use Windows Live Search to find Web pages providing information on the benefits of adopting pets. Narrow the search to Web pages that provide this information only about Amherst, Massachusetts. Press Alt+Print Screen to capture an image of the first screen of search results, and then paste the image in a new Paint file. Save the file as **Amherst Pets** in the Tutorial.06\Case2 folder provided with your Data Files.

11. Switch to any other search provider, and use it to conduct the original search for information about providing information on the benefits of adopting pets. Modify the search to show only news items in the search results. Press Alt+Print Screen to capture an image of the first screen of search results, and then paste the image in a new Paint file. Save the file as **Pet News** in the Tutorial.06\Case2 folder provided with your Data Files. Close Paint and Internet Explorer.

12. Submit the results of the preceding steps to your instructor, either in printed or electronic form, as requested.

| Create | **Case Problem 3** |

Using the figures as guides, find files and information for a small antiques shop.

Data Files needed for this Case Problem: Item01.jpg–Item06.jpg

Vandemain Antiques   Harold Dougal recently bought an antiques shop named Vandemain Antiques in Asheville, North Carolina. Harold wants to promote his most unusual objects in the local visitor's magazine. He asks you to help him find appropriate images and to research information about his competitors in Asheville. Complete the following steps:

1. Open the **Case3** folder in the Tutorial.06 folder provided with your Data Files.
2. Conduct a search to produce the results shown in Figure 6-42.

Figure 6-42

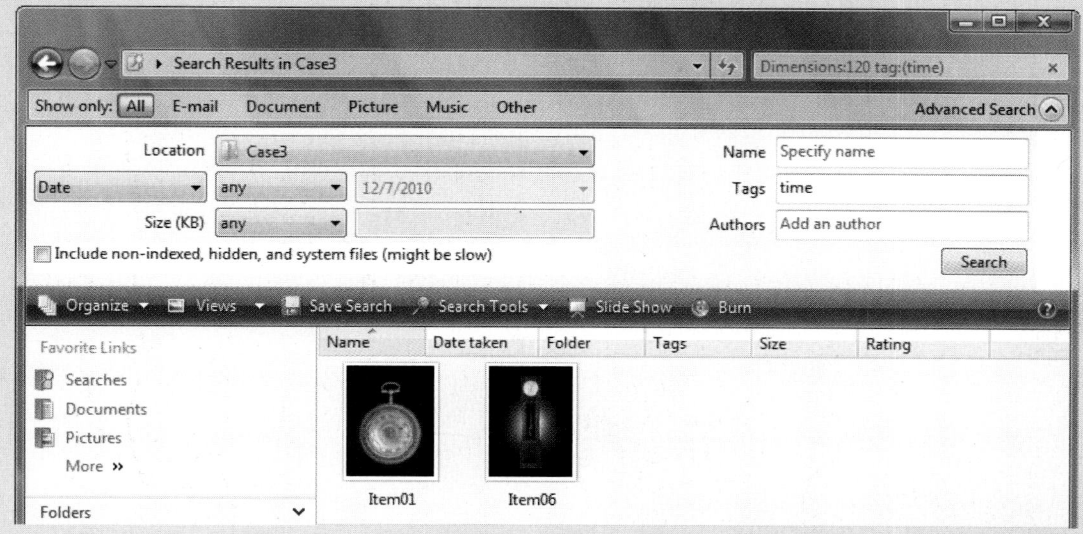

Figure 6-44

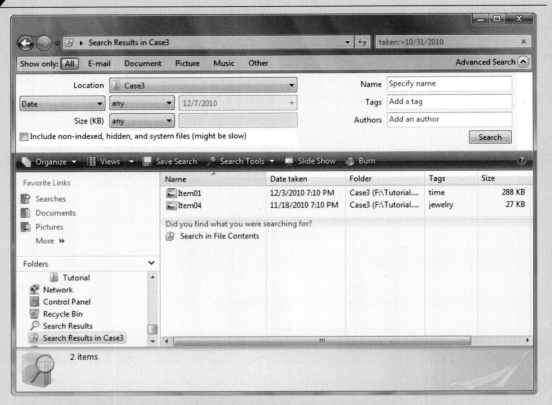

7. Press Alt+Print Screen to capture an image of the first screen of search results, and then paste the image in a new Paint file. Save the file as **Search3** in the Tutorial.06\ Case3 folder provided with your Data Files.

8. Start Internet Explorer, and conduct a search to produce the results shown in Figure 6-45.

Figure 6-45

9. Press Alt+Print Screen to capture an image of the first screen of search results, and then paste the image in a new Paint file. Save the file as **Search4** in the Tutorial. 06\Case3 folder provided with your Data Files. Close Paint and Internet Explorer.

10. Submit the results of the preceding steps to your instructor, either in printed or electronic form, as requested.

| Research | **Case Problem 4** |

Work with the skills you've learned, and use the Internet, to learn about other ways to search for information.

There are no Data Files needed for this Case Problem.

Ask Me Anything Diana and Paul Seefert are former librarians who recently started a company called Ask Me Anything in San Antonio, Texas. They provide a wide range of research services, including finding marketing and demographic information for businesses, answering questions about trivia, and uncovering local history stories. When they were trained as librarians, they learned to use mostly print documents as source materials. They hired you as an intern to help them learn how to take full advantage of the Internet. Complete the following steps:

1. Start Internet Explorer and use any search provider to research the difference between search engines, metasearch engines, and subject directories.

Research	**Case Problem 4**

Work with the skills you've learned, and use the Internet, to learn about other ways to search for information.

There are no Data Files needed for this Case Problem.

Ask Me Anything Diana and Paul Seefert are former librarians who recently started a company called Ask Me Anything in San Antonio, Texas. They provide a wide range of research services, including finding marketing and demographic information for businesses, answering questions about trivia, and uncovering local history stories. When they were trained as librarians, they learned to use mostly print documents as source materials. They hired you as an intern to help them learn how to take full advantage of the Internet. Complete the following steps:

1. Start Internet Explorer and use any search provider to research the difference between search engines, metasearch engines, and subject directories.

2. Find an example of each type of search tool and capture an image of its main page. Save the search engine image in a file named **Search Engine** in the Case4 folder. Save the metasearch engine image in a file named **Metasearch** in the Case4 folder. Save the subject directory image in a file named **Subject Directory** in the Case4 folder.

3. Use any search provider to find information about Boolean logic or Boolean operators. Narrow the results to find pages that explain how to use Boolean logic or operators to find information on the Web. Create a document using WordPad or another word-processing program with four column headings: **Operator**, **Alternate Operator**, **Description**, and **Example**. Enter information in each column to describe at least four Boolean operators you can use to search the Web. Complete the columns according to the following descriptions.

Operator	Alternate Operator	Description	Examples
List text terms for Boolean operators.	*List symbols used for Boolean operators, if any.*	*Provide a brief description of the operator or its purpose.*	*Give examples of how to use the operator, one using the text operator, and one using the symbol (if possible).*

4. Save the document as **Boolean** in the Case4 folder provided with your Data Files.

5. Submit the results of the preceding steps to your instructor, either in printed or electronic form, as requested.

Assess	**SAM Assessment and Training**

If you have a SAM user profile, you may have access to hands-on instruction, practice, and assessment of the skills covered in this tutorial. Log in to your SAM account (**http://sam2007.course.com**) to launch any assigned training activities or exams that relate to the skills covered in this tutorial.

Review	**Quick Check Answers**

Session 6.1

1. one or more conditions that a file or folder must meet to have Windows find it
2. True
3. Search pane

Ending Data Files

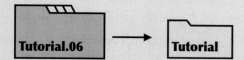

Review

Media Program.jpg
Videos.jpg
Weather.jpg
Weather Images.jpg
Weather Meeting.jpg

Case1

Backup Program.jpg
DVD Program.jpg
Nashville Images.jpg
Not Nashville.jpg
WMA.search-ms

Case2

16 KB.jpg
Amherst Pets.jpg
Dim 120.jpg
Pet News.jpg
Projector Program.jpg
Small Pix.jpg
Wildlife.jpg

Case3

Search1.jpg
Search2.jpg
Search3.jpg
Search4.jpg

Case4

Boolean.rtf
Metasearch.jpg
Search Engine.jpg
Subject Directory.jpg

Reality Check

Now that you are familiar with the Windows Vista tools that can help you personalize your computer, make it more secure, and communicate with others, set up your computer to suit your style of work. As you select settings, capture and save images of your computer so you can document what you've done. Complete the following tasks:

1. Start Windows Vista and log on, if necessary.
2. Set up shortcuts on your desktop to the folders, devices, and documents you use often.
3. Change the desktop image, screen saver, Quick Launch toolbar, and Start menu to suit your preferences.
4. Use Internet Explorer to research themes you can use on your computer. If you find a theme you like, download and install it on your computer.
5. Open the dialog box showing your screen saver, and then capture an image of the desktop.
6. In Internet Explorer, add the Web pages that you visit often to your Favorites list. Open the Favorites Center, and then capture an image of the Internet Explorer window.
7. Using Windows Contacts, create contacts for your correspondents. Capture an image of the main Windows Contacts window.
8. Using Windows Calendar, set up your appointments and tasks for the upcoming week. Capture an image of the appointment calendar.
9. Open the Windows Vista Security Center and make sure you are using all of the recommended security settings. Capture an image of the Security Center window. Do the same for Windows Mail and Internet Explorer.
10. Submit the images you captured to your instructor, either in printed or electronic form, as requested.

Objectives

Session 7.1
- Examine computer graphics
- Create graphics in Paint
- Add text to a graphic
- Apply color and draw shapes in an image

Session 7.2
- Acquire and import photos
- View and edit photos
- Organize and play music
- Burn files to a CD or DVD

Session 7.3
- Acquire and import videos
- Play and edit movies
- Create a multimedia slide show

Managing Multimedia Files

Working with Graphics, Photos, Music, and Movies

Case | Oak Park Landscaping

Bernie Quinn and Hector Torres own Oak Park Landscaping in Oak Park, Illinois, which provides landscaping and design services for businesses and homeowners. You are a part-time designer helping Bernie and Hector prepare landscaping proposals and create graphics used to market and sell their services. Your first projects are to create a logo for the company's Web site and e-mail stationary and a multimedia presentation to showcase its designs and services.

In this tutorial, you'll learn how to create, acquire, and modify multimedia files, including graphics, photos, and videos. You'll also explore how to organize and play music files. To share multimedia files with others, you'll learn how to burn the files to a CD or DVD and how to create a multimedia slide show that combines text, graphics, and other multimedia elements in a single file.

Starting Data Files

Tutorial.07 →

Tutorial
Frame.jpg
Garden01.jpg-
  Garden13.jpg
Oak.jpg

Review
Border.jpg
Buttercup.jpg
Dahlia.jpg
Fuschia.jpg
Iris.jpg
Lily.jpg

Lupin.jpg
Phlox.jpg
Plan.jpg
Rose.jpg
Violet.jpg

Case1
Austen.jpg
Bronte.jpg
Browning.jpg
Cather.jpg
Flourish.jpg

Letters AZ.jpg
McCullers.jpg
Millay.jpg
Moore.jpg

Case2
LH01.jpg-
  LH08.jpg
Lighthouse.png
Ocean.wav

Case3
Bird01.jpg-
  Bird10.jpg
BirdSong.wav
WaterFowl.wav
Window.tif
Wren.tif

Case4
Apples.jpg
Banner.jpg
Berries.jpg
Garlic.jpg
Globe.jpg
Green Tom.jpg

Market.jpg
Market02.jpg
Onions.jpg
Oranges.jpg
Peppers.jpg

Potatoes.jpg
RedPeps.jpg
Squash.jpg
Tomatoes.jpg
Variety.jpg

Session 7.1

Exploring Computer Graphics

Pictures and other images enhance your experience of working on a computer and make the documents you produce more appealing and engaging. Pictures on a computer are called **graphic images**, or **graphics**. A computer graphic is different from a drawing on a piece of paper because a drawing is an actual image, whereas a computer graphic is a file that displays an image on a computer monitor. Computer graphics come in two fundamental types: bitmapped and vector. A **bitmapped graphic** is made up of small dots that form an image. When you manipulate a bitmap graphic, you work with a grid of dots, called **pixels**, which is short for picture elements. A bitmapped graphic (or *bitmap* for short) is created from rows of colored pixels that together form an image. The simplest bitmaps have only two colors, with each pixel being black or white. Bitmaps become more complex as they include more colors. Photographs or pictures with shading can have millions of colors, which increases file size. Bitmaps are appropriate for detailed graphics, such as photographs and the images displayed on a computer monitor. See Figure 7-1. Typical types of bitmap file formats include JPG, GIF, and BMP. (You'll learn more about graphic file formats later.) You create and edit bitmaps using painting programs such as Adobe Photoshop and Windows Paint.

| Figure 7-1 | Bitmapped graphics |

Photograph

Detailed image

Pixels in bitmapped images

In contrast, a **vector graphic** is created by mathematical formulas that define the shapes used in the image. When you work with a vector graphic, you interact with a collection of lines. Rather than a grid of pixels, a vector graphic consists of shapes, curves, lines, and text that together make a picture. While a bitmapped image contains information about the color of each pixel, a vector graphic contains instructions about where to place each component. Vector images are appropriate for simple drawings, such as line art and graphs, and for fonts. See Figure 7-2. Typical types of vector file formats include WMF, SWF, and SVG, a standard for vector images on the Web. You use drawing programs such as Adobe Illustrator and CorelDRAW to create and edit vector images.

Vector graphics | **Figure 7-2**

Aa Bb Cc

Aa Bb Cc

Fonts are a kind of vector image

Edges stay smooth when a vector image is enlarged

A vector shape is a collection of points, lines, and curves

InSight | **Comparing Bitmapped and Vector Graphics**

When determining whether to use bitmapped or vector graphics, keep the following strengths and weaknesses in mind:

- In general, a bitmap file is much larger than a similar vector file, making vector files more suitable for displaying on Web pages.
- Avoid resizing bitmapped graphics because resolution (the number of pixels in an image) affects their quality. If you enlarge a bitmapped graphic, it often looks jagged because you are redistributing the pixels in the image. If you reduce the size of a bitmapped graphic, its features might be indistinct and fuzzy. On the other hand, you can resize vector graphics without affecting quality because vectors redraw their shapes when you resize them.
- To edit vector graphics, you often need to use the same drawing program used to create the graphic. Before you acquire vector graphics from various sources, make sure you have the right program if you need to edit them. In contrast, most painting programs can open multiple types of bitmapped graphic formats.
- Bitmaps are suitable for photographs and photorealistic images, while vector graphics are more practical for typesetting or graphic design.

By default, Windows Vista provides sample bitmapped graphics in its Pictures folder. You can add your own graphic files to your computer in a few ways. One way is to use a **scanner**, which converts an existing paper image into an electronic file that you can open and work with on your computer. Another popular method is to use a digital camera to take photos and then transfer the images to your computer. Software and Web sites also provide graphics you can use, including clip art, which are usually line drawings and therefore vector images. Many Web sites maintain online catalogs of drawings, images, and photographs that are available for download. Some of these sites charge a membership fee, some charge per image, and others provide copyright-free images that are also free of charge.

To edit a graphic or create one from scratch, you use a **graphics program**, which is software that includes drawing and graphics-editing tools. Windows Vista includes a basic graphics program called **Paint**, which lets you create, edit, and manipulate bitmap graphics, though not vector graphics. Many programs designed for Windows Vista, including Microsoft Office, include tools for creating and editing vector graphics such as charts, flowcharts, and other drawings in a document or worksheet, for example. Because the two images Bernie wants to combine are bitmapped graphics, you can use Paint to create the Oak Park logo.

Creating Graphics in Paint

As you already know, Paint is a Windows Vista accessory program that you can use to create and modify bitmapped graphics. Using Paint, you can draw shapes, add and change colors, include text, remove parts of a picture, and copy and paste images, including those you capture on your computer screen. Bernie is ready to learn about Paint, so you can start the program and introduce him to its graphic tools.

To start Paint:

▶ 1. Click the **Start** button 🟢 on the taskbar, point to **All Programs**, and then click **Accessories**. The Accessories folder opens in the Start menu.

▶ 2. Click **Paint**. The Paint window opens. If necessary, maximize the window. See Figure 7-3.

Paint window   **Figure 7-3**

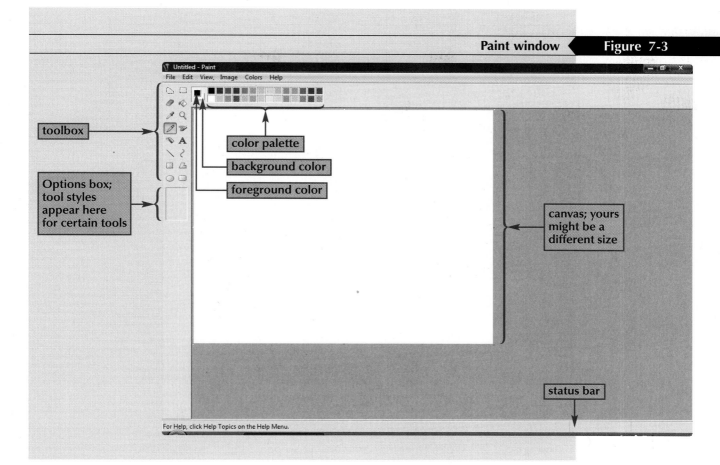

When you start Paint without opening a picture, the Paint window is mostly blank, providing a few tools for drawing and painting. The white area in the Paint window is the canvas, where you work with your graphic. Above the canvas is the color palette, which displays available colors for the **foreground color**—lines, borders of shapes, and text—and **background color**—the inside of enclosed shapes and the background of text. The left side of the palette contains two overlapping color boxes, the top for the foreground color and the bottom for the background color of any object you draw. The status bar at the bottom of the window provides information about the tools you select and about the location of the pointer when it's in the canvas.

To the left of the canvas is the **toolbox**, a collection of tools that you use to draw and edit graphics. The tools all work the same way: you click a tool, the pointer changes to a shape representing the tool, and then you either click or drag on the canvas to draw with the tool. Some tools offer different widths or shapes, which are identified in an **Options box** that appears below the toolbox.

Figure 7-4 describes the tools you can use in Paint to create and edit graphics.

Figure 7-4 ▶ **Paint tools**

Tool	Icon	Description
Free-Form Select		Select an irregularly shaped part of the graphic
Select		Select a rectangular part of a graphic
Eraser/Color Eraser		Erase a part of a graphic
Fill With Color		Fill an enclosed area with the selected color
Pick Color		Pick up a color in the graphic to set the current foreground or background color
Magnifier		Change the magnification and zoom in or out of the graphic
Pencil		Draw a free-form line or one pixel at a time
Brush		Paint free-form lines and curves using a brush in a variety of widths
Airbrush		Create an airbrush effect in a variety of widths
Text		Insert text into a graphic
Line		Draw a straight line
Curve		Draw a smooth, curved line
Rectangle		Draw a rectangle or square
Polygon		Draw a shape with any number of sides
Ellipse		Draw an ellipse or circle
Rounded Rectangle		Draw a rectangle or square with rounded corners

Opening a Graphic in Paint

You open a graphic in Paint the same way you open a file in any Windows Vista program—use the Open dialog box to navigate to where you store the image file, select the file, and then open it. Paint can keep only one graphic open at a time, similar to the way Notepad handles files. If you are working with a graphic and want to open another one, Paint closes the first graphic and gives you a chance to save your changes before opening the new graphic. If you want to work with a second image at the same time as the first image, you can start another session of Paint and open the second image.

Bernie asks you to show him how to open the two JPG files he found so you can discuss how to combine them to create a single image.

To open the Oak Park graphics:

▶ 1. Make sure you have created your copy of the Windows Vista Data Files, and that your computer can access them.

   Trouble? If you don't have the starting Data Files, you need to get them before you can proceed. Your instructor will either give you the Data Files or ask you to obtain them from a specified location (such as a network drive). In either case, make a backup copy of the Data Files before you start so that you will have the original files available in case you need to start over. If you have any questions about the Data Files, see your instructor or technical support person for assistance.

▶ 2. Click **File** on the Paint menu bar, and then click **Open**. The Open dialog box opens.

▶ 3. Navigate to the Tutorial folder in the Tutorial.07 folder provided with your Data Files.

▶ 4. Click **Oak** and then click the **Open** button. The Oak file opens in the Paint window. See Figure 7-5.

Oak picture open in Paint ◄ **Figure 7-5**

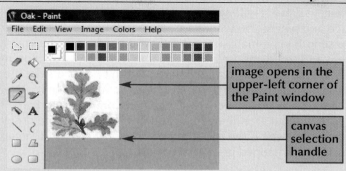

5. To examine the second picture, click **File** on the menu bar, and then click **Open**.

6. In the file list, click **Frame** and then click the **Open** button. The oak picture closes and the frame picture opens in the Paint window.

Now that you've seen the two images Bernie wants to use, you can plan the logo graphic. Clearly, the best way to combine these images is to insert the oak picture inside the frame picture. You also need to add the name of Bernie's company—Oak Park Landscaping—to the picture. After making a few sketches, you and Bernie agree on the design shown in Figure 7-6.

Design for Oak Park Landscaping logo ◄ **Figure 7-6**

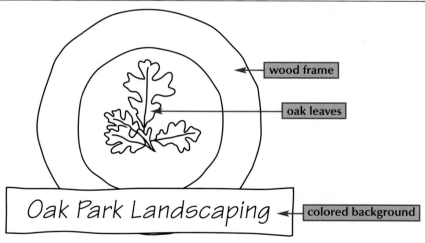

To start creating this design, you need to add the oak picture to the center of the round frame. You'll show Bernie how to do this shortly. Before you do, you should save the Frame graphic file with a new name in case you need the original again in its unchanged state.

Saving a Graphic File

When you save a graphic file with a new name, you use the Save As dialog box as you do in other Windows Vista programs. In the Save As dialog box, you select a location for the file, provide a filename, and select a file type, or format, if necessary. Paint can save and open images in many bitmap formats, and each format has its pros and cons. To work effectively with graphics, you should understand the basics of the most popular Paint file formats: JPG, GIF, BMP, and TIF.

When you create a graphics file, you choose its format based on what you intend to do with the image and where you want to produce it. If you want to display the image on a Web site or send it via e-mail, for example, you need an image with a small file size. In this case, you should choose a file format that compresses color information. For example, if a picture has an area of solid color, it doesn't need to store the same color information for each pixel. Instead, the file can store an instruction to repeat the color until it changes. This space-saving technique is called **compression**. Some compression methods save space without sacrificing image quality, and others are designed to save as much space as possible, even if the image is degraded. Figure 7-7 summarizes the pros and cons of these four bitmapped graphics formats.

Figure 7-7	Graphic file formats

File Format	Advantages	Disadvantages	When to Use
Graphics Interchange Format (GIF)	Compresses images without losing quality and allows animation	Not suitable for photographs	Graphics such as logos, line drawings, and icons
Joint Photographic Experts Group (JPG or JPEG)	Efficiently compresses photographic images	Can reduce quality	Designed for photographs and images with fine detail
Tagged Image File Format (TIF or TIFF)	Maintains image quality in print and on screen	Some Web browsers cannot display TIF images	Images used in desktop publishing, faxes, and medical imaging
Windows Bitmap (BMP)	Simplest way to store a bitmapped graphic	Can waste large amounts of storage space	Basic shapes and images with few colors

A fifth bitmap file format called Portable Network Graphics (PNG) is quickly becoming a popular alternative to GIF. It is well-suited to nonphotographic images and compresses images efficiently without losing quality. It is specifically designed for use on the Web.

The Frame and Oak files are both JPG files, which is the right file format for displaying images on a Web page or distributing via e-mail. You'll save a copy of the Frame file as a JPG file. However, if you need to provide a graphic in a different file format, you can convert it in Paint by choosing that format when you save the file.

To save the Frame image with a new name:

▶ 1. Click **File** on the menu bar, and then click **Save As**. The Save As dialog box opens.

▶ 2. If necessary, click the **Browse Folders** button to open the Navigation pane, and then navigate to the **Tutorial** folder in the Tutorial.07 folder provided with your Data Files.

▶ 3. In the File name text box, type **Logo**. The file type is already displayed in the Save As dialog box. See Figure 7-8.

Saving the Frame image with a new name ◀ Figure 7-8

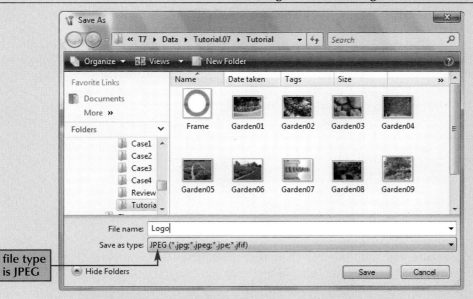

▶ **4.** Click the **Save** button. Paint saves a copy of the frame image as Logo.

| Saving a Bitmapped Graphic in a Different File Type | | InSight |

In general, you cannot improve the quality of a compressed image by saving it in a different file format. For example, suppose you convert a JPG graphic, which omits some color information to compress the file, to a format such as TIF, which doesn't sacrifice quality to reduce file size. The colors from the original JPG file remain the same, but the file size increases if the TIF file provides an expanded color palette.

Now you are ready to create the Oak Park logo by combining the picture of the oak leaves with the frame image.

Copying and Pasting to Create a Graphic

Bernie wants to insert the oak picture inside the image of the frame. One way you can do this is to open the Oak file again, select the entire image, cut or copy it, open the Logo file with the frame image, and then paste the oak picture in the frame. To reduce the number of steps you need to perform, Paint provides a shortcut method, the Paste From command on the Edit menu. You can use this command when you want to copy an entire image from another file and paste it in your current image.

To paste the oak picture in the logo image:

▶ **1.** Click **Edit** on the menu bar, and then click **Paste From**. The Paste From dialog box opens, which has the same controls as the Open dialog box.

▶ **2.** In the file list, click **Oak** and then click the **Open** button. The oak image appears in the upper-left corner of the logo picture in a selection box. See Figure 7-9.

Figure 7-9 | **Pasting the oak picture in the Logo file**

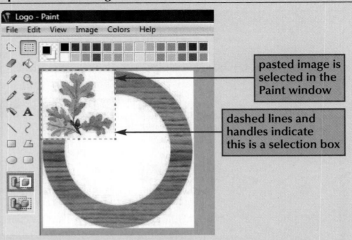

pasted image is selected in the Paint window

dashed lines and handles indicate this is a selection box

> **3.** Because you need to move the oak picture, do not click anywhere in the Paint window. If you do, you remove the selection box from the oak picture and its pixels replace the ones from the logo picture underneath it.
>
> **Trouble?** If you click in the Paint window and remove the selection box from the oak picture, click Edit on the menu bar, click Undo, and then repeat Steps 1 and 2.

If you make a mistake while working in Paint, click Edit on the menu bar, and then click Undo. You can reverse up to your last three actions.

The selection box around the oak image indicates that you can manipulate the image by moving, copying, or deleting it. You can think of the selected image as floating on top of the frame picture because any changes you make to the oak picture do not affect the Logo file until you click to remove the selection box. You want to show Bernie how to move the oak picture to the center of the frame. You can do so by dragging the selected oak picture.

To move the selected oak image:

Tip

Besides pasting elements from another graphic file, you can select an area of a graphic, and then use the Copy To command on the Edit menu to save the selected area to a new file.

> **1.** Point to the selected **oak image**. The pointer changes to ⊕.
>
> **2.** Drag the **oak image** to the center of the frame, and then release the mouse button. See Figure 7-10. The oak picture is still selected, but now appears in the middle of the frame.

Moving the oak picture to the center of the frame | Figure 7-10

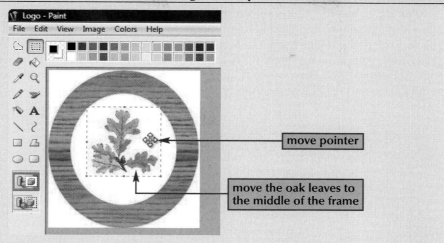

3. Click anywhere outside of the selected image to remove the selection box. The oak image is now part of the Logo file.

Now that you have created the first major part of the graphic, you should save the Logo file so you don't inadvertantly lose your changes.

To save the Logo graphic:

1. Click **File** on the menu bar, and then click **Save**. Paint saves the current image using the same name and location as you used the last time you saved the graphic.

Next, you need to add the name of Bernie's company to the graphic to make it a true logo. According to your sketch, the company name should appear in a colored rectangle that extends to the right and left of the circular frame. Right now, there's not enough room in the graphic to accommodate this band. You need to modify the graphic by resizing the canvas and then moving the image to create space for inserting the company name.

Modifying Graphics in Paint

After you create and save an image in Paint, you can modify it by adding graphic elements, such as lines, shapes, and text; changing colors; and cropping, or removing parts. According to your design for Oak Park Landscaping, you need to add a text box below the oak leaves. To provide enough work space for creating the text box, you should first resize the canvas.

Resizing the Canvas and Moving an Image

When you open a graphic, it fills the canvas—the white part of the Paint window—if the graphic is the same size or larger than the canvas. If the graphic is smaller than the canvas, you can resize the canvas to fit snugly around the image. Doing so reduces file size and eliminates a border around your picture. Reducing the width or height of the canvas is one way to **crop**, or remove, a row or column of pixels from an edge of a graphic. You can also resize the canvas if you want to make it larger than the image so you can add more graphic elements to the picture. When you enlarge the canvas, the image remains in the upper-left corner of the Paint window as you drag a selection handle on the canvas to make it longer, wider, or both.

After increasing the size of the canvas, you often need to move the image so it fits more aesthetically within the enlarged space. To move all or part of an image in Paint, you first select the image using the Select tool or the Free-Form Select tool. With the Select tool, you draw a selection box around the area you want to select. With the Free-Form Select tool, you draw a line of any shape around the area. To select the entire graphic, you can use the Select All command on the Edit menu.

To resize the canvas and then move the logo graphic:

▶ **1.** Point to the selection handle in the lower-right corner of the canvas, and then begin to drag down and to the right, watching the dimensions in the lower-right corner of the status bar. See Figure 7-11.

Figure 7-11	Resizing the canvas

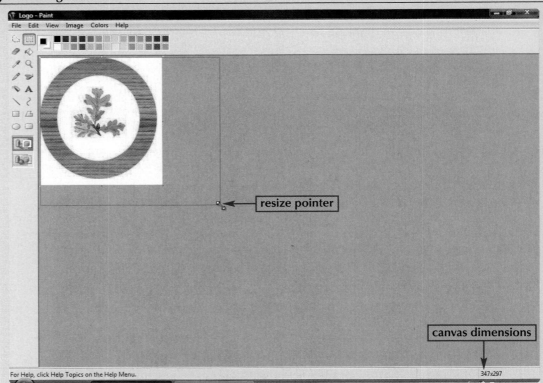

▶ **2.** When the dimensions are 400 x 500, release the mouse button.

▶ **3.** Click **Edit** on the menu bar, and then click **Select All** to select the entire graphic.

▶ **4.** Drag the graphic to the upper-middle part of the canvas. See Figure 7-12.

Moving the logo graphic | **Figure 7-12**

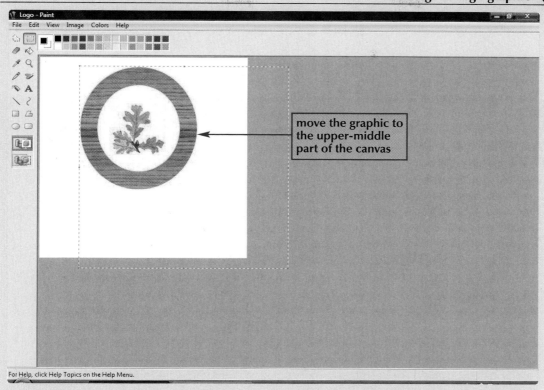

move the graphic to the upper-middle part of the canvas

▶ **5.** Click any part of the canvas outside of the selected image to remove the selection box.

When you move a graphic, part of the selection box can extend past the edges of the canvas. Because Paint saves only the part of the graphic that appears on the canvas, make sure all parts of a moved graphic appear on the canvas before you remove the selection box. You lose any part that extends past the canvas when you remove the selection.

As you've already noticed, while you are drawing shapes or dragging selections, Paint helps you identify and control your location as you draw. The **pixel coordinates** in the status bar specify the exact location of the pointer on the canvas relative to the pixels on your screen. Paint displays the pixel coordinates in an (x,y) format (x representing the horizontal location and y the vertical location). Pixel coordinates of 138 x 25, for example, indicate that the pointer is 138 pixels from the left edge of the screen and 25 pixels from the top. Using these coordinates helps you position a shape or image on the canvas and position graphic elements in relation to one another. In addition, when you draw a shape, you can use the **sizing coordinates**, immediately to the right of the pixel coordinates, to determine the size of the shape you are dragging. For example, when you draw a text box, you might start at pixel coordinates 15 x 15 and drag with sizing coordinates of 300 x 30—so your text box is long and narrow and appears in the upper-left corner of the graphic.

Resizing the canvas and moving the image provides plenty of room for your next step—adding the company name to the graphic.

Adding Text to a Graphic

To add words to a graphic in Paint, you use the Text tool. You first use the Text tool to create a text box, and then you type your text in this box. By default, the Text toolbar, also called the Fonts toolbar, appears when you select the Text tool so you can select a font, style, and size for the text. If your text exceeds the length and width of the text box, you can drag the sizing handles to enlarge the box.

Reference Window | **Adding Text to a Graphic**

- Click the Text tool and then drag a text box on the canvas.
- If the Text toolbar does not appear, click View and then click Text Toolbar.
- Use the Text toolbar to select a font, font size, or attributes (bold, italic, or underline).
- Type the text in the text box, using the sizing handles to resize the text box, if necessary.
- Adjust the font, font size, or attributes (bold, italic, or underline), and resize the text box as necessary.
- Click outside the text box.

When you add text to a graphic, by default Paint displays black text on a white rectangle. You can change these colors by changing the foreground and background colors, which are shown in the color boxes to the left of the color palette. Recall that Paint uses the foreground color for lines, borders of shapes, and text. The background color determines the background of text rectangles and the inside color of enclosed shapes. To set the foreground color, you click a color in the color palette. To set the background color, you right-click a color in the color palette. If the color palette does not contain a color you want to use, you can select one from your image using the Pick Color tool. Click the Pick Color tool in the toolbox, and then click a color in the image to change the foreground color to the color you clicked. Do the same with the right mouse button to change the background color.

According to your design, "Oak Park Landscaping" should appear in a colored rectangle that crosses the lower part of the round frame in the logo graphic. To match the font and style that Bernie and Hector use for other promotional materials, you'll use Verdana italic as the font and style of the text. You suggest picking a color from the oak leaves as the background color of the text box and using white as the foreground color for the text. When you use the Pick Color tool to change the foreground color, it is often helpful to zoom in, or increase the magnification of the image, so you can see the pixels of color more clearly. To do so, you use the Magnifier tool. When you select the Magnifier tool, a zoom slider appears in the Options area below the toolbox. You can increase the magnification by dragging the slider up or by clicking the image. You can decrease the magnification, or zoom out, by dragging the slider down or by right-clicking the image.

Tip

You can also change the magnification by clicking View on the menu bar, pointing to Zoom, pointing to Custom, and then clicking a percentage.

Reference Window | **Magnifying a Graphic**

- To zoom in, click the Magnifier tool, and then click the graphic one or more times or drag the magnification slider up to increase the magnification.
- To zoom out, click the Magnifier tool, and then right-click the graphic one or more times or drag the magnification slider down to decrease the magnification.

To zoom in and pick a color:

1. Click the **Magnifier** tool in the toolbox, and then click the center of the oak leaves image twice to increase the magnification to 400% and center the Paint window on the oak leaves. See Figure 7-13.

Changing the magnification of the image | Figure 7-13

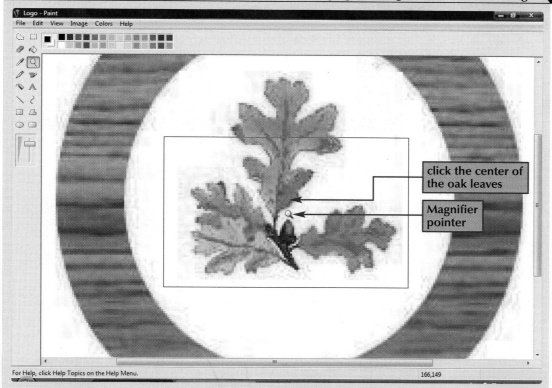

Trouble? If you magnified a different area of the graphic, use the scroll bars to display the center of the oak leaves as shown in Figure 7-13.

2. Click the **Pick Color** tool in the toolbox, and then right-click a **dark orange pixel** in the top leaf. The background color box displays the color you clicked.

Trouble? If you clicked the dark orange pixel with the left mouse button instead of the right, repeat Step 2.

3. Click the **white color square** in the color palette (bottom row, first column).

4. Click the **Magnifier** tool in the toolbox, and then drag the magnification slider to its middle position, so the graphic appears at 100% zoom.

Now you are ready to use the Text tool to add the company name to the graphic. You can only use the Text tool in 100% zoom. To avoid mistakes to the current logo graphic, you'll create the text box at the bottom of the canvas and then move it. The text box you draw will be dark orange, and the text you type will be white. In addition, the text will appear with the font style, size, attributes, and language shown in the Fonts toolbar. As you probably know, the font size of the letters is measured in points, where a single point is 1/72 inch. That means a one-inch tall character is 72 points, and a half-inch tall character is 36 points. Attributes are characteristics of the font, including bold, italic, and underline. You can change the font, size, style, and language using the Fonts toolbar before you type, after you type, or as you edit the text. When you are satisfied with the text and its appearance, you click outside the text box, and Paint anchors the text into place, making it part of the bitmapped graphic. After the text is anchored in a graphic, you can change the font or its attributes only by deleting the text and starting over with the Text tool.

To add text to the graphic:

▶ **1.** Click the **Text** tool [A] in the toolbox.

▶ **2.** Below the framed oak leaves, drag to create a text box at least 300 pixels wide by 60 pixels tall. Refer to the right side of the status bar for the size coordinates. Then release the mouse button. The Fonts toolbar opens in the Paint window. See Figure 7-14.

Figure 7-14 ▶ **Creating a text box**

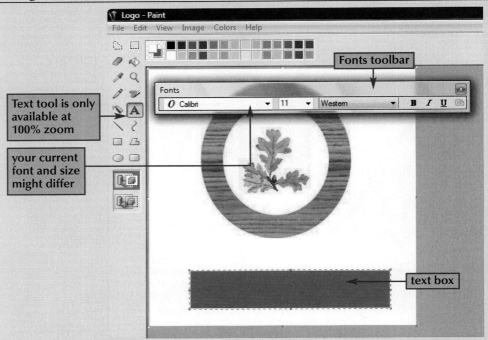

Trouble? If the Fonts toolbar does not open, click View on the menu bar, and then click Text Toolbar.

Trouble? If the text box you created is not at least 300 x 60 pixels, click outside of the selected text box, and then repeat Steps 1 and 2.

▶ **3.** Click the **Fonts** arrow button, scroll the fonts list as necessary, and then click **Verdana**.

▶ **4.** Click the **Font Size** arrow button, and then click **18**.

▶ **5.** Click the **Italic** button [I] .

▶ **6.** Click inside the text box, and then type **Oak Park Landscaping**. See Figure 7-15.

Adding text with the Text tool ◀ **Figure 7-15**

Trouble? If the text wraps within the text box, you probably selected a font or size that's too large for the text box. Repeat Steps 3 and 4, and then drag the lower-right sizing handle to make the text box match the one shown in Figure 7-15.

▶ **7.** Click a blank area of the canvas outside the text box to anchor the text.

Next, you'll show Bernie how to move the text to another part of the graphic.

Moving Part of a Graphic

To move part of a graphic, you select the area you want to move, and then drag the selection to a new location. You can also move or copy part of a graphic using the Clipboard: select an area, choose Cut or Copy on the Edit menu to store the selection on the Clipboard, and then choose Paste on the Edit menu to paste the selection into the graphic, where it floats in the upper-left corner of the canvas until you drag it to the desired location.

Before you move part of a graphic, you might need to change the background color so it's the same as the color of the surrounding area. Before moving the text box, for example, you can change the background color to white. Otherwise, the background of the selected area would appear as dark orange after you move the text box.

When you move or copy part of a graphic using the Select tool, you can paste the image with a solid background (the default) or a transparent background. Choose the Solid Background option to include the background color in your selection when you paste it somewhere else in the picture. For example, if the background of a shape you are moving is white, it stays white when you move it to a colored area of the graphic. Choose the Transparent Background option to omit the background color from the selection, so any areas using that color become transparent and allow the colors in the underlying picture to appear in its place. For example, if you use the Transparent Background option to move a shape with a white background, the background becomes transparent when you move it to a colored area of the graphic.

Tip

To delete an area of a graphic, select the area using the Select or Free-Form Select tool, and then press the Delete key.

InSight	**Using a Solid or Transparent Background**

Using the Transparent Background option in Paint can be an effective way to move an image that is not rectangular, such as the oak leaves in the logo graphic. If you select the oak leaves using the Solid Background option and move them to an orange area of the graphic, they remain in a white rectangle. If you select them using the Transparent Background option, however, they appear against an orange background when you move them into an orange area. The Transparent Background option works best in a graphic that does not use thousands or millions of colors. A white background in a JPG file, for example, often includes hundreds of shades of white, and only one of those shades is set to be transparent when you use the Transparent Background option.

First, you'll show Bernie how to move the Oak Park Landscaping text to center it within the orange rectangle. You need to select all of the text but as little of the background as possible. To work at this level of detail, you can zoom into the graphic again before selecting the text.

To zoom in and move the text:

▶ **1.** Click the **Magnifier** tool 🔍 in the toolbox, and then click the **L** in "Landscaping" in the text box. The magnification increases to 200%.

▶ **2.** Click the **Select** tool ⬚ in the toolbox. The Solid Background option is selected by default.

▶ **3.** Drag to select all of the text but only as much background as necessary. Then drag the selected text to the middle of the orange rectangle. See Figure 7-16.

Moving the text within the text box ◀ Figure 7-16

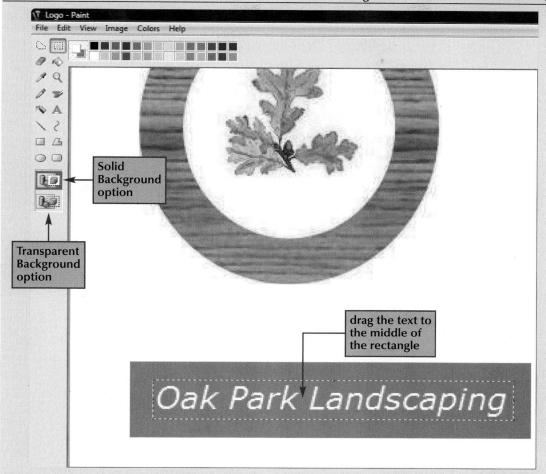

Trouble? If part of the text remains in its original location, click Edit on the menu bar, click Undo, and then repeat Steps 2 and 3.

▶ **4.** Click the **Magnifier** tool Q in the toolbox, and then right-click the graphic to return to 100% zoom and remove the selection box from the text.

Because the background color is still set to orange, moving the text does not introduce new colors into the text box. Before you move the entire text box, however, you need to change the background color to white so the area the text box now occupies doesn't remain orange after you move the text box.

To move the text box:

▶ **1.** Right-click a white color box in the palette to change the background color to white.

▶ **2.** Click the **Select** tool [□] in the toolbox.

▶ **3.** Drag a 300 x 60 pixel selection box to select the Oak Park Landscaping text box. A dashed outline appears around the text box.

Trouble? If the selection box you created is not within one or two pixels of 300 x 60 pixels, click outside of the selection, and then repeat Steps 2 and 3.

4. Use the pointer to drag the text box so that it is centered just below the oak leaves. See Figure 7-17.

Figure 7-17 **Moving the text box**

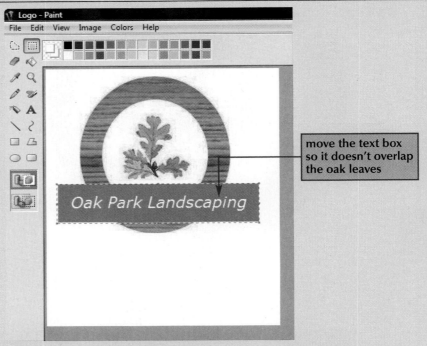

move the text box so it doesn't overlap the oak leaves

Trouble? If the text box does not move when you drag it, but the selection box changes size, you probably dragged a sizing handle instead of the entire selection. Click Edit, click Undo, and then repeat Step 4.

Trouble? If part of the orange text box remains in its original location, continue with the steps. You'll remove this part of the graphic shortly.

5. When the text box is in position similar to the one shown in Figure 7-17, click a blank area of the canvas to anchor the text box into place.

The entire image now matches your original sketch, but you and Bernie discuss adding other graphic elements to enhance the logo. In particular, you suggest adding a row of squares below the text box to balance the image and draw the eye to the company name.

Drawing Shapes

To draw closed shapes, such as squares and circles, you use the Rectangle, Polygon, Ellipse, or Rounded Rectangle tool in the Paint toolbox. After you select one of these tools to draw a shape, you can choose a foreground color to set the color of the shape's outline and a background color to set the color of the shape's fill, or interior area. You can also select the shape's style and line thickness in the Options box below the toolbox. For example, you can choose to draw a rectangle using an Outline style with no fill and a line that is two pixels thick. To draw a rectangle or rounded rectangle, you select the appropriate tool, and then drag diagonally to create the shape. To draw a square, you hold down the Shift key while dragging. Similarly, you draw an ellipse, or oval, by selecting the Ellipse tool and then dragging to create the shape. To draw a circle, hold down the Shift key while dragging.

Besides using the Rectangle, Polygon, Ellipse, or Rounded Rectangle tools to draw shapes, you can also draw using the Pencil, Brush, Line, and Curve tools, as described in

Figure 7-4. You use the Pencil tool to draw a line or image one pixel at a time, making it an effective choice when you want to edit details of an image to smooth lines or eliminate unnecessary dots, for example. Unlike the Pencil tool, the Brush tool offers a variety of widths and brush styles you can use to draw. You can use the Line tool to draw straight lines; to draw a horizontal, vertical, or diagonal line, press the Shift key while you drag in one of those directions.

You want to add three filled squares to the left and right of the circular frame, just below the text box. You'll show Bernie how to do so using the Solid rectangular style. Before you draw the shapes, however, you need to select a fill color. Bernie suggests using the same color as the background of the text box. You also want to zoom in to the graphic so you can work accurately.

To draw a square:

▶ **1.** Click the **Magnifier** tool in the toolbox, and then click the word **Oak** twice to magnify the left side of the text box and the area just below it by 400%.

▶ **2.** Click the **Pick Color** tool in the toolbox, and then click the background of the text box to change the foreground color to dark orange.

▶ **3.** Click the **Rectangle** tool in the toolbox. See Figure 7-18.

Preparing to use the Rectangle tool   **Figure 7-18**

▶ **4.** Click the **Solid** style in the Options box.

▶ **5.** Use the Drawing pointer to point to the lower-left corner of the text box, and note the position coordinates shown in the status bar.

▶ **6.** Move the Drawing pointer about 10 pixels below the text box and at the same horizontal position so the shape you draw is left-aligned with the text box.

▶ **7.** Hold down the **Shift** key, drag to draw an 11 x 11 pixel square, and then release the mouse button. Figure 7-19 shows the square before releasing the mouse button.

Figure 7-19 ▶ **Drawing a square**

square with drawing pointer

position coordinates in the status bar; the first number is the horizontal position

size coordinates in the status bar

Trouble? If the shape you drew is not similar to the one in Figure 7-19, click Edit on the menu bar, click Undo, and then repeat steps as necessary to redraw the square.

The element you added is the right size and shape and is in the right position, but repeating the color from the text box doesn't create enough of a contrast. You can change the square's color to a different one in the oak leaves image to determine if that suits the design of the logo.

Changing Colors

You can add color to a graphic in one of two ways: choosing colors as you draw or applying color to shapes after you finish drawing them. Before you use a drawing tool, you can select a color for the line or shape, as you did when you drew the text box and the square. If you want to add color to an existing image or color a large area of an image, you use the Fill With Color tool. When you use the Fill With Color tool to click a pixel in a graphic, Paint changes the color of that pixel to the current foreground color. (To change the color to the current background color, right-click a pixel.) If adjacent pixels are the same color as the one you clicked, Paint also changes those colors to the foreground color. In this way, you can use the Fill With Color tool to fill any enclosed area with color. Make sure the area you click is a fully enclosed space. If it has any openings, the new color extends past the boundaries of the area you are trying to color.

Tip

Another way to add color to an image is to use the Airbrush tool, which scatters color a few pixels at a time over an area as you drag.

Filling an Area with Color

- Click the Fill With Color tool.
- Click the desired color in the color palette.
- Click inside the border of the area you want to color.

You suggest to Bernie that a contrasting color, such as the green that appears in the lower-left oak leaf, would make the squares more appealing, and offer to show him how to quickly change the color of the square you drew.

To change the color of the square:

▶ **1.** Click the **Pick Color** tool in the toolbox, and then click a green pixel in the lower-left oak leaf to change the foreground color to medium olive green.

▶ **2.** Click the **Fill With Color** tool and move the pointer into the graphic. The pointer changes to a paint can shape , indicating that any pixel you click will change to the foreground color.

▶ **3.** Click inside the **square** to change its color from dark orange to the foreground color of medium olive green. See Figure 7-20.

Changing the color of the square ◀ **Figure 7-20**

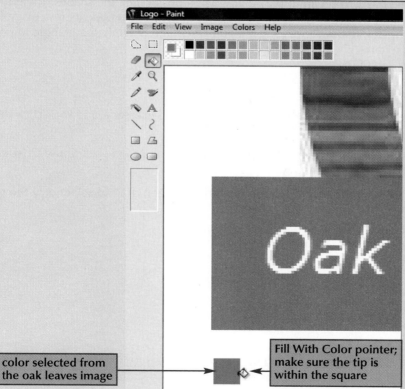

color selected from the oak leaves image

Fill With Color pointer; make sure the tip is within the square

Trouble? If your square is a different shade of green from the one shown in Figure 7-20, continue with the steps. If your square is not green at all, however, click Edit on the menu bar, click Undo, and then repeat Steps 1–3.

Trouble? If the background of the logo graphic turns green instead of the square, you clicked the background instead of the square. Click Edit on the menu bar, click Undo, and then repeat Step 3, making sure the tip of the paint can pointer is within the border of the square.

▶ **4.** To view the entire image with the new color, click the **Magnifier** tool 🔍 in the toolbox, and then right-click the graphic twice to return to 100% magnification.

Coloring the square green creates contrast, which makes that graphic element more interesting. Now you can complete the logo graphic by copying the square so three squares appear to the left of the circular frame and three appear to the right of the frame.

Copying an Image

Recall that to copy an image you use a method similar to the one used for moving an image: you select the area you want to copy, copy it to the Clipboard, and then paste the copy in your graphic. Because the copied image appears in a selection box in the upper-left corner of the graphic, you usually must drag the image to a new location after pasting it. You'll show Bernie how to copy the green square and then paste it to create a row of three squares in the lower-left area of the logo graphic. To create an appealing arrangement, you must make sure that the squares are evenly spaced and their tops and bottoms are aligned. When the bottoms of the squares are aligned, for example, the lower edge of each square is on the same row of the bitmap grid. To space and align shapes effectively, you can display a grid when positioning the shapes. The grid does not become a part of the graphic—it is only a visual guide that appears in a magnified view. You'll show Bernie how to display the grid when you magnify the graphic to copy and paste the squares.

To copy and paste the square:

▶ **1.** Click the **Magnifier** tool 🔍 in the toolbox, if necessary, and then click the **green square** twice to magnify the image 400%.

▶ **2.** Click **View** on the menu bar, point to **Zoom**, and then click **Show Grid** to display a grid in the Paint window.

▶ **3.** Click the **Select** tool ⬚ in the toolbox, and then drag to select only the **green square**. See Figure 7-21.

Selecting the square to copy it ◀ **Figure 7-21**

drawing grid appears in
magnified views over 200%

Trouble? If the selection box includes part of the background or does not include the entire green square, click outside the selection box and repeat Step 3.

▶ 4. Click **Edit** on the menu bar, and then click **Copy** to copy the square to the Clipboard.

▶ 5. Click **Edit** on the menu bar, and then click **Paste** to paste the square in the upper-left corner of the Paint window.

▶ 6. Drag the selected square next to the first square, leaving about 11 pixels of white space, or 11 dots on the grid, between the two shapes. In other words, the white space between the squares should be the same width as each square. If necessary, drag up or down to adjust the vertical position of the selected square to align it with the first square. Its lower edge should be on the same row of the grid as the lower edge of the first square.

▶ 7. Click **Edit** on the menu bar, and then click **Paste** to paste another copy of the square in the upper-left corner of the Paint window.

▶ 8. Drag the selected square next to the first two squares, again leaving about 11 pixels of white space between the second and third squares and positioning the square vertically to align its bottom with the other two squares. See Figure 7-22.

Figure 7-22   Pasting and positioning a copy of the square

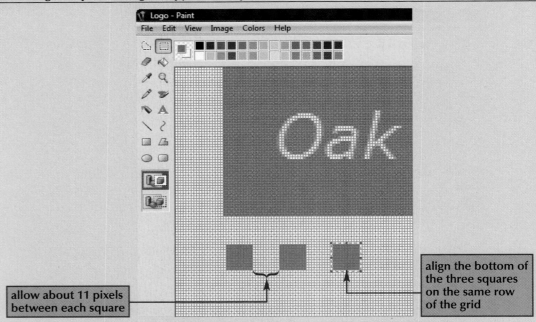

allow about 11 pixels
between each square

align the bottom of
the three squares
on the same row
of the grid

Trouble? If the three squares are not evenly spaced or bottom-aligned, use the Select tool to select a square and then drag it to change its position to match the squares in Figure 7-22.

▶ **9.** Click outside the selection, and then point to the bottom edge of a green square. Note the vertical coordinate of this pixel.

▶ **10.** To view the entire image with the three squares, click the **Magnifier** tool [Q], and then right-click the graphic twice to return to 100% magnification.

Now you can copy the three squares to the right side of the graphic to balance the image. To copy the squares precisely, it helps to work in a magnified view.

To copy and paste the three squares:

▶ **1.** Click the **Magnifier** tool [Q] in the toolbox, if necessary, and then click the **middle green square** twice to magnify the image 400%. Note that the grid still appears in the magnified view until you hide it.

▶ **2.** Click the **Select** tool [⬚] in the toolbox, and then drag to select the **three green squares**. This time, it doesn't matter if some of the background is included in the selection box. Be sure, however, that the selection box includes all parts of the three squares.

▶ **3.** Click **Edit** on the menu bar, and then click **Copy** to copy the square to the Clipboard.

▶ **4.** Drag the bottom scroll bar to the right to display the right side of the Oak Park Landscaping text box.

▶ **5.** Click **Edit** on the menu bar, and then click **Paste** to paste the squares in the upper-left corner of the Paint window.

6. Drag the selected squares below the Oak Park Landscaping text box so that the right edge of the third square aligns with the right edge of the text box, and then click outside of the selection box.

7. Point to the lower-right corner of the third square, and then look in the status bar to find its position. The vertical coordinate should match the one you noted in the previous set of steps. See Figure 7-23.

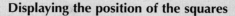

Displaying the position of the squares ◄ **Figure 7-23**

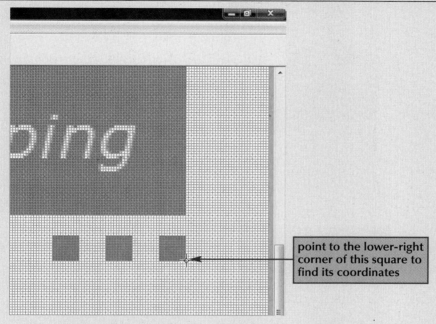

point to the lower-right corner of this square to find its coordinates

8. If necessary, select the three squares again and then drag them to align with the text box and the three squares on the left side of the graphic.

9. To hide the grid, click **View** on the menu bar, point to **Zoom**, and then click **Show Grid** to remove the check mark from that command.

10. To view the logo image with all graphic elements, click the Magnifier tool in the toolbox, and then right-click the graphic twice to return to 100% magnification. See Figure 7-24.

Figure 7-24 | **Logo with all graphic elements**

Your graphic doesn't have to look exactly like Figure 7-24, but it should look similar. Your last task is to position the image on the canvas to minimize the amount of unnecessary white space in the graphic.

Cropping a Graphic

Recall that you can crop an image to remove one or more rows or columns of pixels from the edge of a picture. When you crop a graphic to eliminate unnecessary white space by resizing the canvas, you reduce file size and prevent a border from appearing around your picture when you paste it into another file. Before you crop the white space from the logo graphic, you should move the image into the upper-left corner of the Paint window. Then you can drag the canvas to fit tightly around the image.

To move and crop the logo graphic:

1. Click **Edit** on the menu bar, and then click **Select All**.

2. Drag the image to the upper-left corner of the Paint window, making sure that the entire image appears in the window. See Figure 7-25. Then click outside the selection box to remove the selection.

Dragging the image before cropping | **Figure 7-25**

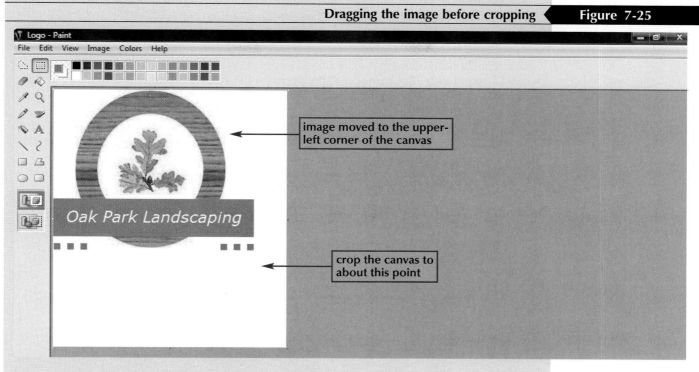

Trouble? If parts of the logo image are cut off, click Edit on the menu bar, click Undo, and then repeat Steps 1 and 2.

3. Point to the sizing handle on the lower-right corner of the canvas, and then drag to reduce its size so that it fits tightly around the graphic without hiding any part of it. See Figure 7-26.

Completed Logo graphic | **Figure 7-26**

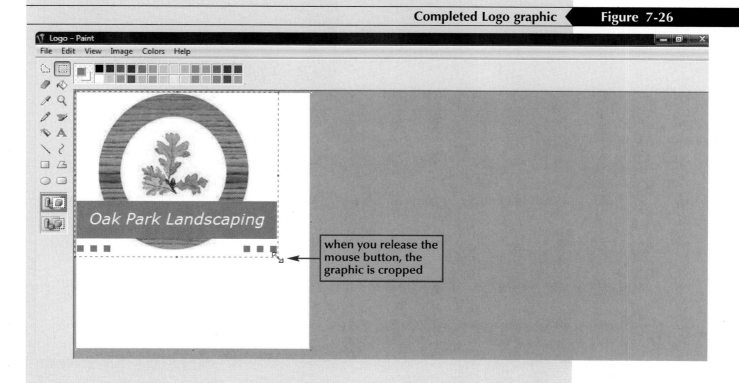

Trouble? If you made the canvas too small so that parts of the logo image are cut off, click Edit on the menu bar, click Undo, and then repeat Step 3.

Cropping is the best way to resize a bitmapped graphic. Although you can resize a graphic in Paint to make the entire image larger or smaller, recall that the results are often disappointing. Because you cannot change the size of an individual pixel, resizing the overall image tends to distort it. For example, when you try to enlarge a bitmapped graphic, Paint duplicates the pixels to approximate the original shape as best it can—often resulting in jagged edges. On the other hand, when you shrink a bitmapped graphic, Paint removes pixels, and the drawing loses detail. In either case, you distort the original graphic. Sometimes the resized bitmapped graphic looks fine, as when it contains many straight lines, but just as often the resized graphic's image quality suffers. For example, Figure 7-27 shows how the current logo image looks when it's enlarged.

Figure 7-27	Enlarging a bitmapped graphic

How do you bypass this problem? In Paint, there is no easy solution to resizing graphics, because they are all bitmapped. If your work with graphics requires resizing—for example, if you want a graphic that looks good on a small business card and a large poster—using vector graphics is a better choice. Because vector graphics are mathematically based, you can resize them as necessary without sacrificing image quality. You need to buy a graphics program that allows you to work with vector graphics, however.

You've completed the graphic for Oak Park Landscaping, so you can save the Logo file and close Paint.

To save the file and close Paint:

▶ 1. Click **File** on the menu bar, and then click **Save**.

▶ 2. Close the Paint window.

Now that you've shown Bernie how to use Paint to create and modify bitmapped graphics, you can get ready to work with Hector to develop a multimedia presentation.

Session 7.1 Quick Check | Review

1. The small dots on your screen are called _____ .
2. What command do you use to copy an entire image from another file and paste it in your current image?
3. True or False. You can open only one graphic in Paint at a time.
4. How do you resize the canvas?
5. When you draw a shape, the foreground color controls the shape's _____ , whereas the background color controls its _____ .
6. To change a shape's fill color, you use the _____ tool.

Session 7.2

Working with Photos

Recent developments in digital cameras and computers have transformed the field of photography, letting anyone edit and print photos without using a darkroom or professional photo lab. Instead, you can transfer photos from your digital camera to your Windows Vista computer, where you can fine-tune the images, display them in a slide show, use them as a screen saver or wallpaper, and e-mail them to others.

As a part-time graphic designer for Oak Park Landscaping, you are preparing to work with Hector Torres, one of two partners in the landscaping firm. Hector wants to create a multimedia presentation that Oak Park Landscaping can use to showcase its designs and services. He'd like to include a slide show of photos with a musical accompaniment in the presentation. Hector has already transferred photos of landscaping projects from his digital camera to his computer. You'll show him how to view, organize, and edit the photos so he can assemble them into a slide show to play at landscaping trade shows and expositions.

Acquiring and Importing Photos

Before you can create a slide show on your computer, you need to acquire and then import photos. The most popular way to acquire photos is to use a digital camera to take the photos yourself. Cameras store photos as JPG image files, so you can work with them using any photo editor or painting graphics program. Using a digital camera lets you control the subject matter and maintain the legal rights to the images, two notable advantages. Unless you're a trained photographer, the main disadvantage is that your images are not professional quality, though you can improve them using Windows Vista editing tools. If you are using the photos for the enjoyment of family and friends, you might not need to do more than snap the photos on your digital camera and then transfer them to your Windows Vista computer.

If you need professional photos, such as for a product brochure or company Web site, you have a few options. Hiring a photographer to create and prepare the images can be effective, though expensive. You can also purchase stock photo collections, typically provided on a CD or DVD. These collections usually contain royalty-free images that you can use for any purpose, and cost anywhere from thousands of dollars to under $20 for hundreds or thousands of images. As mentioned earlier, you can also purchase photos from Web sites, usually for a licensing fee. You can download photos free of charge and copyright only if the photos are in the public domain and are freely available for use. If you have conventional photographs printed on paper, you can use a scanner to convert the photos into digital pictures.

InSight | **Using Copyright-Protected, Royalty-Free, and Public-Domain Photos**

Although you can easily copy photos displayed on Web sites, that doesn't mean that you should. Most photos and other media on the Web are protected by copyright law. A copyright gives photographers (and other types of creators) the exclusive right to control their images. They can decide who can copy, distribute, or derive material from their photographs. Before you can use a copyrighted photo, you must receive permission from the photographer.

Some Web sites and services offer royalty-free photos, meaning that the photographers do not receive payment each time their photos are used. However, royalties are not related to copyright—the photographers still retain the rights to the photos even if they don't receive royalties.

Only photos in the public domain are not protected by copyright law. These include photos for which the copyright has expired, government images, and those explicitly identified as in the public domain.

If you want to copy photos from the Web or other digital source, the following guidelines help you respect the photographer's rights:

- Ask the owner of the copyright for permission.
- Keep a copy of your request and the permission received.
- Find out if the author provides information on how to use the material.
- If explicit guidelines are given, follow them, and credit the source of your material.

If you acquire photos from a Web site, CD, or DVD, you only have to copy them to a folder on your computer so you can edit and organize them. If you are using a digital camera, however, you need to perform an additional step of importing the photo files from your camera to your computer. One way to do this is to connect the camera directly to the computer using a cable that plugs into the computer's USB port. Another way is to import pictures using a memory card reader, a device that plugs into your computer's USB port. Most digital cameras store pictures on a flash memory card. If you have a memory card reader attached to your computer, you can remove the memory card from your camera and then slide it into the card reader to import the photos stored on the card. In either case, Windows Vista should recognize your camera or card (it recognizes most makes and models of digital cameras and cards), and guide you through the steps of importing pictures. You have the chance to add tags to the photo files so you can identify them easily later, to erase the image files on your camera or card so you can use it to store more photos, and to correct your picture's rotation, if necessary. After importing the images, Windows Vista stores them in the Pictures folder and then opens them in the Windows Photo Gallery, which you'll explore next.

Viewing and Organizing Photos

The Pictures folder and its subfolders are the best places to store your digital photos because they offer viewing tools that are not available in other folders. Figure 7-28 reviews the Pictures folder and its tools.

Pictures folder and its viewing tools   **Figure 7-28**

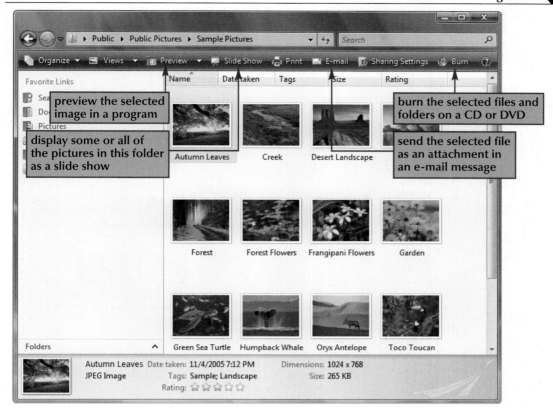

Any pictures stored in the Pictures folder, including those you've imported, also appear in the Windows Photo Gallery, a built-in Windows Vista accessory program that lets you view, organize, edit, share, and print your digital images. The Windows Photo Gallery and the Pictures folder share some features. For example, both let you view and print pictures and organize them into a slide show. In addition, Windows Photo Gallery lets you edit the photos to fix problems with lighting or color, to crop an image, and to remove red eye.

Your first task in developing a presentation with Hector is to review the photos he's taken of the Oak Park Landscaping gardening and landscaping projects. Start by copying the photos in your Tutorial folder to a subfolder of the Pictures folder.

To copy photo files to the Pictures folder:

▶ **1.** Open a folder window that displays the contents of the Tutorial.07\Tutorial folder provided with your Data Files.

▶ **2.** Copy the thirteen garden photos (**Garden01–Garden13**) to a new folder in the Pictures folder named **Gardens**.

▶ **3.** Close all open windows.

Now you can start Windows Photo Gallery and show Hector how to use it to view and organize photos.

To start Windows Photo Gallery:

▶ **1.** Click the **Start** button 🪟 on the taskbar, point to **All Programs**, and then click **Windows Photo Gallery**. Windows Photo Gallery opens and displays all of the pictures and videos in the Pictures and Videos folders, including the Public Pictures and Public Videos folders. Maximize the Windows Photo Gallery window. See Figure 7-29. The pictures included in your window might differ.

Figure 7-29	Windows Photo Gallery

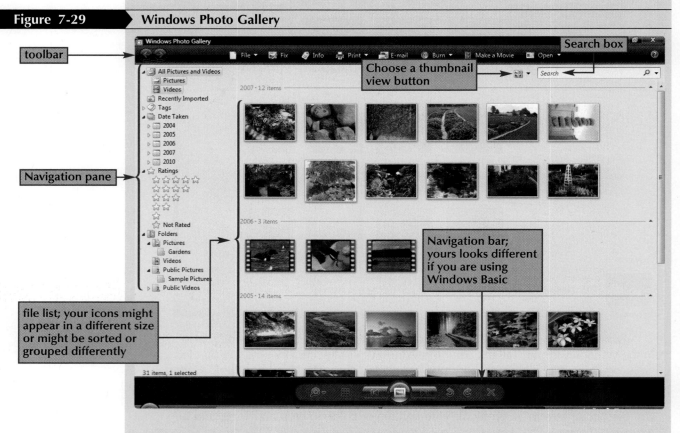

▶ **2.** To display only photos, click **Pictures** in the Navigation pane.

▶ **3.** In the Folders list at the bottom of the Navigation pane, expand the **Pictures** folder, if necessary, and then click the **Gardens** folder to display Hector's photos.

The Windows Photo Gallery window is similar to a folder window because it includes a Navigation pane, toolbar, Search box, and file list. However, each of these areas provides tools specialized for work with photos. The Windows Photo Gallery window also includes a navigation bar for navigating your collections of photos. Figure 7-30 describes the parts of the Windows Photo Gallery window.

Elements of the Windows Photo Gallery window **Figure 7-30**

Window Element	Description
Toolbar	Provides buttons that let you work with image files, adjust photos, show or hide the Info pane, print photos, e-mail image files, burn files to a CD or DVD, create a slide show or movie, and open a file for editing in another program
Navigation pane	Lists properties of pictures and videos that you can use to sort your files
Navigation bar	Includes controls for viewing photos in sequence, and for working with the thumbnails of the photos displayed in the Windows Photo Gallery window
File list	As in a folder window, this area displays thumbnails of your photos
Search box	Lets you search for files by tags, date, name, and other properties
Thumbnail view button	Provides options for working with thumbnails, such as displaying them with text or grouping them by date taken or rating

You need to get acquainted with Hector's photos, so you'll show him various ways to use Windows Photo Gallery to view the photos in the Gardens folder.

To view photos:

▶ **1.** To change the size of the thumbnails, click the **Zoom** button on the navigation bar, and then drag the slider to its highest position. The photos are displayed at the highest magnification. See Figure 7-31.

Photos displayed at the highest magnification **Figure 7-31**

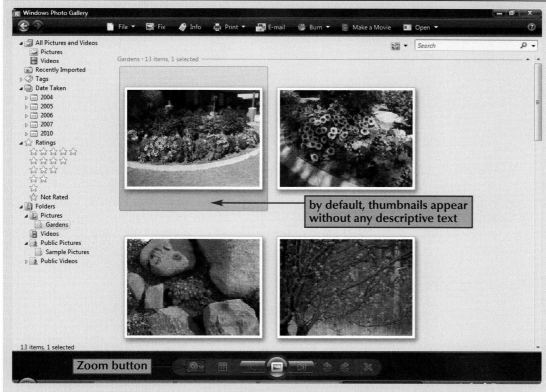

by default, thumbnails appear without any descriptive text

Zoom button

▶ **2.** To view the photos in sequence, click the **first photo**, if necessary, and then click the **Next (Right Arrow)** button on the navigation bar a few times.

3. To return to the original view of medium-sized thumbnails, click the **Reset Thumbnails to Default Size** button ▦ on the navigation bar.

4. Click the **Choose a thumbnail view** button next to the Search box, and then click **Thumbnails with Text**. By default, Windows identifies the photos by the dates they were taken. To display the filenames instead of the dates, you change the sort order—the text Windows displays in this view is determined by the sort order.

   Trouble? If your thumbnails appear with filenames, skip Step 5.

5. Click the **Thumbnail View** button , point to **Sort By**, and then click **File Name**. Filenames, including extensions, appear below each thumbnail.

6. Scroll the window and then point to the **Garden13.jpg** thumbnail to display the photo's properties such as its size, date taken, and tags that Hector assigned when he imported the photo.

7. Double-click **Garden13.jpg** to open the picture in the preview window. See Figure 7-32.

Tip

Even if Windows Vista is set to hide file extensions in folder windows, it displays the filename extension in Windows Photo Gallery.

Figure 7-32 ▶ **Photo open in the preview window**

The preview window gives you a close-up view of the photo and opens the Info pane, which lists the photo's properties and lets you change them, similarly to the way you change the properties for files in a folder window's Details pane. For example, you can click Add Tags to add keywords to the photo, click a star to assign a rating from 1–5, or click the description box at the bottom of the Info pane to add or change the photo's description.

Playing a Simple Slide Show

You can start playing a simple slide show by clicking the Slide Show button on the toolbar in the Pictures folder or by clicking the round Play Slide Show button on the navigation bar in the Windows Photo Gallery. In either case, the slide show includes all the photos in your current folder and its subfolders, and plays the photos one after another at various speeds. You can also create more sophisticated slide shows and save them on a CD or DVD, which you will do later in this session.

Playing a Slide Show		Reference Window

- In the Pictures folder window, click the Slide Show button on the toolbar.

or

- In Windows Photo Gallery, click the Play Slide Show button on the navigation bar.

If you are using Windows Aero and your computer has a Windows Experience Index base score of 3.0 or higher, you can choose a theme for your slide show. The Windows Experience Index measures the capability of your computer's hardware and software and calculates a base score. The higher the base score, the faster your computer performs advanced and resource-intensive tasks, such as slide shows. You can determine your computer's base score by opening the Performance Information and Tools window. (Open Control Panel, click System and Maintenance in Category view, and then click Performance Information and Tools.) If you don't see a base score and subscores for hardware components, click Score this computer. If you have upgraded your hardware recently, click Update my score. Otherwise, Windows Vista displays your scores so you can determine the software and features that run reliably on your computer.

To choose a theme for your slide show, start playing a slide show and then point to the bottom of the screen to display the slide show bar. Click the Themes button on the slide show bar and then click a theme. The Spin theme, for example, flips the photos to change from one to the next. Certain slide show themes are included only in Windows Vista Home Premium and Windows Vista Ultimate.

If you are not running Windows Aero or your computer has a base score lower than 3.0, you can play slide shows, but without the effects of the themes.

You want to return to the main Windows Photo Gallery window so you can examine Hector's photos again and see if any need adjustments to fix problems such as washed-out colors. You can do so by watching a simple slide show that displays one photo after another.

To play a simple slide show:

▶ 1. Click the **Back to Gallery** button ⬅ on the toolbar to return to the main Windows Photo Gallery window.

▶ 2. Click the **Garden01.jpg** thumbnail, which is the first photo file in the window.

▶ 3. Click the **Play Slide Show** button ⊡ on the navigation bar. The monitor darkens, and then Windows Vista fills the screen with the first photo, displays it for a few seconds, and then displays the next photo.

▶ 4. To slow the slide show so you can examine the photos, right-click a slide and then click **Slide Show Speed-Slow** on the shortcut menu.

   Trouble? If you are not using Windows Aero, a shortcut menu does not open. Skip Step 4.

▶ 5. After viewing one photo that needs to be rotated (Garden07) and one photo that seems to have too much contrast (Garden11), right-click a slide and then click **Exit** on the shortcut menu.

   Trouble? If you are not using Windows Aero, press the Esc key to exit the slide show.

Tip
You can play a slide show of only a few photos by selecting the photos before you click the Play Slide Show button.

You found at least two photos that could be improved by using Windows Photo Gallery editing tools. You'll show Hector how to fix these photos next.

Editing Photos

Windows Photo Gallery offers a number of useful tools to touch up your photos. When you import photos from a digital camera, Windows Vista usually detects photos that you've taken by turning the camera sideways, typically to capture an image of a tall object such as a tree or tower, and offers to rotate those photos when it imports them. If you don't accept the offer (or if Windows doesn't detect that they need to be rotated), those vertical pictures appear in the wrong orientation in Windows Photo Gallery. You can rotate photos to the correct orientation clockwise or counterclockwise.

Reference Window | **Editing a Photo**

- To rotate a photo, click the photo and then click the Rotate Counterclockwise or the Rotate Clockwise button on the navigation bar.
- To correct exposure or color problems, click the photo, click the Fix button on the toolbar, and then click Auto Adjust.
- To fine-tune exposure or color problems, click the photo, click the Fix button on the toolbar, click Adjust Exposure or Adjust Color in the Fix pane, and then adjust the settings as necessary.
- To crop a photo, click the photo, click the Fix button on the toolbar, click Crop Picture, drag the frame to select the area you want to keep, and then click the Apply button.
- To fix red eye, click the photo, click the Fix button on the toolbar, click Fix Red Eye, and then drag to draw a rectangle around the area you want to fix.

Besides rotating your pictures, the Windows Photo Gallery provides photo repair tools for correcting problems such as red eye from flash photos, dark or washed-out images, and unbalanced composition. To use the photo repair tools, select a picture, click the Fix button on the toolbar to open the Fix pane, and then select one of the following tools:

- **Auto Adjust**: Automatically select the best settings for light exposure and color. Try Auto Adjust before selecting any other repair method. If Auto Adjust doesn't fix the problem with the photo, you can change one of the other settings yourself.
- **Adjust Exposure**: Photos with inaccurate exposure are too bright or too dark. Correct this problem by changing the **brightness** (the amount of light displayed in the picture) or the **contrast** (the difference between the brightest and darkest parts of the picture).
- **Adjust Color**: Change up to three color settings. To set the overall tone of the picture, change the **color temperature** to make the image appear warmer (with more red tones) or cooler (with more blue tones). If one color dominates your picture and makes the other colors look inaccurate—an effect called **color cast**—adjust the tint by adding or removing green. If the colors in your photo look too vivid or dull, change the **saturation**, which determines the amount of color in an image.
- **Crop Picture**: Improve the composition of your picture by trimming distracting or unnecessary elements. You can crop a picture by specifying its proportions or by dragging to select the part of the picture you want to keep.
- **Fix Red Eye**: If you used a flash to snap a photo of one or more people, they might have red eyes, a common problem caused by the flash reflecting off the eyes. Reduce or eliminate this effect by replacing the red with a more natural black.

Following the Digital Workflow | InSight

Digital photographers edit their pictures in a particular order, which is called the digital workflow. Through trial and error, they've found that adjusting the exposure first, then the color, then the composition, and finally the red eye results in the highest-quality pictures. Windows Photo Gallery lists the photo touch-up tools in this order on the Fix pane, so you should change your pictures by working from the top of the list to the bottom.

The adjustments you make to photos are not permanent. If you crop part of an image you want to keep, you can click the Undo button as you can in other Windows Vista programs. Furthermore, you can revert to the original photo at any time by reversing all the changes you made to it. To do so, you click the Undo button arrow and then click Undo All.

Next, you'll show Hector how to rotate the photo of the tall topiary tree in Garden07, which should appear in a vertical rather than horizontal orientation. You can also increase the magnification of the thumbnails to see the images more clearly.

To rotate a photo:

▶ 1. In the Windows Photo Gallery window, click the **Zoom** button 🔍▾ on the navigation bar, and then drag the slider so that four thumbnails appear in each row of the window.

▶ 2. Click the **Garden07.jpg** thumbnail.

▶ 3. Click the **Rotate Counterclockwise** button ↺ on the navigation bar. See Figure 7-33.

Rotating a photo ◀ **Figure 7-33**

rotated picture

rotation buttons on the navigation bar

Now you can show Hector how to improve the quality of a couple of photos. The contrast in the Garden11 picture seems too high—the difference between the dark and light parts of that picture are too great. The colors in Garden12 are difficult to see, which could be caused by more than one problem. Finally, you think you can improve the composition of the rock garden in Garden03 by cropping that photo. You'll start by adjusting the settings in the Garden11 photo automatically.

To use Auto Adjust on a photo:

▶ 1. Scroll down, if necessary, click **Garden11.jpg**, and then click the **Fix** button on the toolbar. The photo and the Fix pane open in the preview window. See Figure 7-34.

Figure 7-34 ▶ **Preparing to fix a photo**

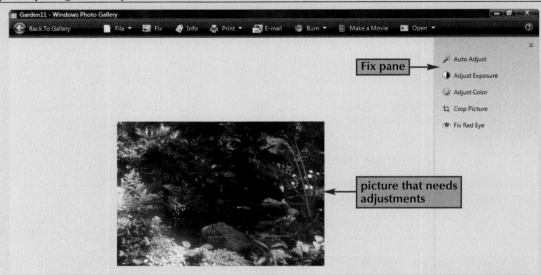

▶ 2. Click **Auto Adjust** in the Fix pane. Windows improves the exposure and adjusts the color of the picture, and then displays a check mark next to Auto Adjust and Adjust Color to indicate it has applied those tools.

Using Auto Adjust fixed the exposure problems in the photo of the garden pond, and now the image of the koi appears more clearly. You'll use Auto Adjust again to improve the image of the backyard garden in Garden12, which is too dark. If that doesn't solve the problem, you can show Hector how to manually fix the photo.

To manually adjust a photo:

▶ 1. Click the **Back to Gallery** button ⊙ on the toolbar to save the changes to the Garden11 photo and return to the main Windows Photo Gallery window.

▶ 2. Click **Garden12.jpg** and then click the **Fix** button on the toolbar. The photo and the Fix pane open in the preview window.

▶ 3. Click **Auto Adjust** in the Fix pane. Although the photo looks better, its light and color could still be improved.

▶ 4. Click **Adjust Exposure** in the Fix pane. The Brightness and Contrast sliders are both set to their middle positions. You want to increase the brightness to add more light to the picture.

▶ 5. Drag the **Brightness** slider slightly to the right. See Figure 7-35.

Increasing the brightness in a photo **Figure 7-35**

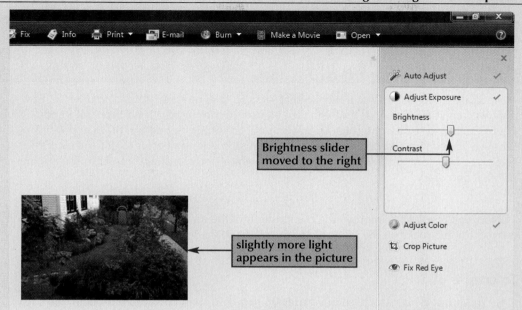

- **6.** Click **Adjust Color** in the Fix pane. You want to increase the saturation to make the colors in the picture more vivid.

- **7.** Drag the **Saturation** slider to the right. See Figure 7-36.

Adjusting the color in a photo **Figure 7-36**

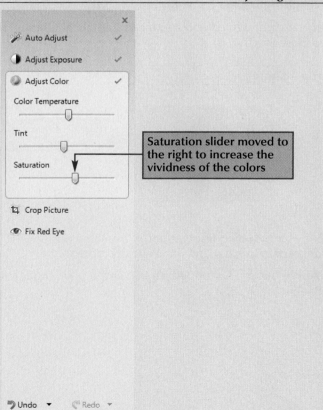

▶ **8.** Click the **Back to Gallery** button ⊙ to save the changes to the Garden12 photo and return to the main Windows Photo Gallery window.

InSight | **Creating Black-and-White Photos**

Most digital cameras provide a setting that lets you take pictures in black and white. However, Microsoft recommends that you take all your photos in color, and then use Windows Photo Gallery to reduce the color saturation until the image appears in black and white. Because you cannot add color to a black-and-white image, it's better to use the saturation setting to transform a color photo to black and white. You can always revert to the original colors if necessary.

Now you're ready to improve the composition of the rock garden photo. You want to crop out most of the rocks on the right side of the photo so the focus is on the three plants.

To crop a photo:

▶ **1.** Scroll up, if necessary, click **Garden03.jpg**, and then click the **Fix** button on the toolbar.

▶ **2.** Click **Crop Picture** in the Fix pane. A cropping frame appears in the middle of the photo. The area you want to preserve is taller than it is wide, so you need to rotate the frame.

Tip

You can also change the size and shape of the cropping frame by clicking the Proportion button and then clicking a dimension or shape.

▶ **3.** Click **Rotate Frame**. The cropping frame now appears taller than it is wide.

▶ **4.** Drag the **cropping frame** to the upper-left corner of the photo.

▶ **5.** Drag the lower-right sizing handle to include all of the plant in the center of the photo. See Figure 7-37.

Figure 7-37 ▶ **Preparing to crop a photo**

rotated and resized crop frame

Trouble? If your cropping frame is not in the same position as the one shown in Figure 7-38, repeat Steps 4 and 5 to reposition the frame.

▶ **6.** Click the **Apply** button. A cropped version of the photo appears in the preview window. See Figure 7-38.

Preview of the cropped photo ◄ Figure 7-38

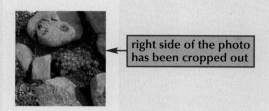

right side of the photo has been cropped out

▶ **7.** Click the **Back to Gallery** button ⬅ on the toolbar to save the changes to the Garden03 photo and return to the main Windows Photo Gallery window.

Instead of changing photos one at a time, you can select two or more photos and then click the Fix button on the toolbar. When the first picture appears in the preview window, use the Fix pane to make adjustments. Then click the Next button to adjust the next picture you selected.

Now that you've improved some of Hector's photos, you're ready to show him how to share the photos with potential clients.

Sharing Photos

When you share your photos, you make them available for other people to view on their computers. The most popular ways to share photos are to post them on a photo-sharing Web site, send them to others in e-mail, or print them. A photo-sharing Web site lets you share and store pictures, often free of charge. (Check the Web site's policies before copying your files to an online album.) You can then invite others to visit the Web site and view your photo albums. Use your Web browser to find a photo-sharing Web site, and then follow their instructions to post your photos.

Although Windows Vista does not provide tools for posting your photos on a Web site, it does help you e-mail and print your photos.

Distributing Photos via E-Mail

Although it seems natural to share your photos with others using e-mail, the problem is that the photos digital cameras take are usually large files, even if they are saved in a JPG format. E-mail prefers and sometimes requires small files. Windows Photo Gallery can solve this problem by compressing the photos before you attach them to an e-mail message. Your e-mail is then transferred more quickly and takes up less space on your recipient's computer. Compressing the photos in this way does not affect the original files.

Before you can send photos by e-mail, you need to have an e-mail profile set up in your e-mail program. The e-mail profile specifies which e-mail account settings Windows Photo Gallery should use if more than one person uses the e-mail program on your computer. You also need to make sure that an e-mail program is specified as the default. (To set an e-mail program as the default, click the Start button on the taskbar, click Default Programs, click Set your default programs, click an e-mail program in the Programs list, click Set this program as default, and then click the OK button.)

Reference Window | **Setting Up an E-Mail Profile**

- Open Control Panel in Category view.
- Click the User Accounts and Family Safety category.
- Click Mail.
- If necessary, click the Show Profiles button in the Mail Setup dialog box.
- In the Mail dialog box, click the Add button.
- Enter a name for the new profile, and then click the OK button.
- Enter your e-mail account information, and then click the Next button.
- After your e-mail program contacts your e-mail server, click the Finish button.
- Click the OK button.

Hector and Bernie often receive e-mail messages from potential clients requesting information about their designs and services. Hector is ready to respond to a message he received earlier today asking for examples of water features they've designed and installed. He wants to send a few appropriate photos along with his response. You'll show him how to find photos of water features and then send them via e-mail. You'll find the photos by searching their tags in Windows Photo Gallery, which offers a shortcut to find photos according to tags. Although you can use the Search box in Windows Photo Gallery the same way you search for any type of file in a folder window, you can use the Navigation pane to quickly find photos in the current folder by tag, date taken, or rating.

To find and e-mail photos:

▶ **1.** In the Navigation pane of the Windows Photo Gallery window, expand the list of tags, if necessary, and then click **water feature**. Three photos appear in the file list. See Figure 7-39.

Figure 7-39 ▶ **Photos with "water feature" as a tag**

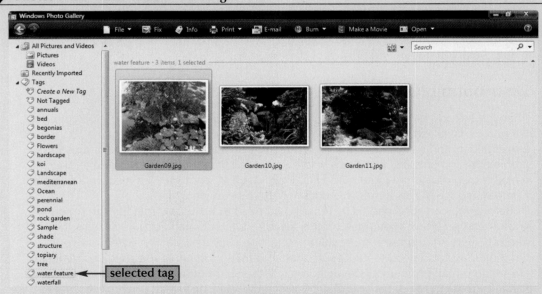

▶ **2.** Select the **three photos**, and then click the **E-mail** button on the toolbar. The Attach Files dialog box opens, estimating the size of the attachment.

▶ **3.** Click the **Picture size** button, and then click **Small: 800 x 600**. This doesn't change the size of the original photo; it only resizes the version you are sending by e-mail.

4. Click the **Attach** button. Windows Vista opens your default e-mail program, such as Windows Mail, and attaches the three photos to the new message.

5. Enter your e-mail address to send the message to yourself, type **Water feature photos** as the subject, and then click the **Send** button to send the message and attachments.

6. Click the **Back** button ⬅ on the toolbar to return to the main Windows Photo Gallery window.

Tip

You can also send photos via e-mail from the Pictures folder window by selecting the photos and then clicking the E-mail button on the toolbar.

Hector is also planning to meet with a client who wants Oak Park Landscaping to build a fence and freestanding trellis for a climbing rose. He wants to print a copy of the Garden13 photo to provide an example of a fence and trellis that Oak Park Landscaping could build. You'll show Hector how to print that photo from Windows Photo Gallery.

Printing Photos

To print your photos, you can use your own printer, order the prints online, or use a store that offers digital photo-printing services. To print sharp, appealing photos, you need a photo-quality printer and photo paper. Inkjet and dye-sublimation printers can produce high-quality photos when you print them on photo paper. Using Windows Photo Gallery, you can print a single photo, more than one photo on a page, or a contact sheet, which is a page of thumbnails arranged in a grid.

Because the paper and ink required for printing photos is expensive, especially if you print often, many people prefer to use a store or online service to print their photos. In many places, you can take your camera's memory card or a CD containing your photos to a store that provides digital photo-printing services. Some stores have self-serve photo kiosks that let you edit and print photos yourself. Look for retailers in your area that provide photo kiosks or digital photo-printing services.

To use an online photo-printing service, you copy your photo files to a Web site, and then order prints in a variety of sizes and formats. For example, you can often print your photos on a calendar, mug, or t-shirt. You can also order prints directly from Windows Photo Gallery or the Pictures folder. To do so, select the pictures you want to print, click the Print button on the Windows Photo Gallery or Pictures folder toolbar, and then click Order prints. Windows Vista connects to the Internet and displays a Web page listing photo-printing companies. Select the company you want to use, and then click Send Pictures. Follow the instructions provided by the printing company to complete your order.

Hector wants to print an 8 x 10-inch copy of the Garden13 photo so he can give it to a client. After loading photo paper in the printer and making sure this photo-quality printer is connected to your computer and turned on, you are ready to show Hector how to print this photo.

To print a photo:

1. In the Windows Photo Gallery window, click **Garden13.jpg** to select that photo.

2. Click the **Print** button on the toolbar, and then click **Print**. The Print Pictures dialog box opens. See Figure 7-40.

Figure 7-40 **Printing a photo**

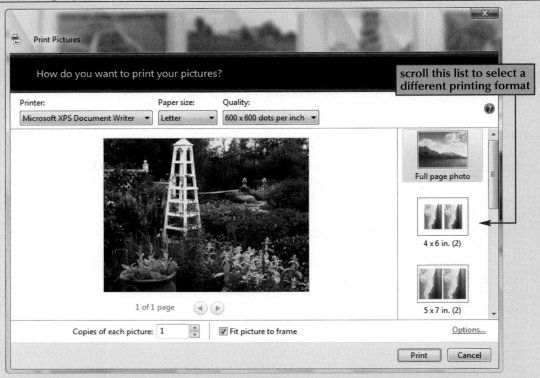

3. Scroll the list of photo layouts, and then click **8 x 10 in. (1)**.

4. Click the **Print** button. Windows Vista prints the photo on the attached printer.

5. Close all open windows.

Tip

Follow the manufacturer's instructions for inserting photo paper into your printer to make sure it prints your photo correctly.

Now that you have prepared Hector's photos for clients, you are ready to assemble them into a multimedia slide show that he can play at expositions and trade shows.

Review | Session 7.2 Quick Check

1. True or False. Only royalty-free photos are not protected by copyright law.
2. How does the Windows Photo Gallery differ from the Picture folder?
3. How do you display thumbnails with filenames in Windows Photo Gallery?
4. To have Windows Vista automatically select the best light and exposure settings for a selected photo, click _____ _____ on the Fix pane.
5. True or False. The Fix pane lists tools in a particular order that corresponds to the digital workflow that digital photographers follow when editing their pictures.
6. Why should you generally take advantage of Windows Vista's offer to compress photos before attaching them to an e-mail message?

Session 7.3

Using Windows Media Player

To play and organize digital music files on your Windows Vista computer, use the Windows Media Player. You can find and play music stored on your computer, CDs, or Web sites; download music files you've purchased from online stores; and create your own albums of songs and burn them onto CDs or sync them to a portable music player. You can use Windows Media Player to perform some or all of the following tasks:

- **Play an audio or video file**: To play a music or video file stored anywhere on your computer, right-click the file and then click Play. You can play music and videos stored in a Windows Media format, such as Windows Media Audio (WMA) and Windows Media Video (WMV). In addition, you can play video files with an AVI filename extension and music files with an MP3, MPG, or WAV filename extension—all popular media file formats. (MP3 is the industry standard for music files.)

- **Play a CD or DVD**: To play an audio CD, you only need to insert the CD in your CD drive, and then choose the Play audio CD using Windows Media Center option if an AutoPlay dialog box opens. Do the same to play a video DVD.

- **Organize your media collection in the library**: Even if you store your media files in many folders on your computer, you can organize your media collection in the Windows Media Player library. Then you can easily find and play a file, or choose content to burn to a CD or sync to a portable device. You can also create **playlists**, a list of media files, such as songs, that you want to play in specified order.

- **Burn your own CDs and DVDs**: If you have a drive that can read and write CDs or DVDs, you can copy a playlist of media files to a CD or DVD, a process called *burning* a CD or DVD.

- **Rip music from a CD**: You can copy, or *rip*, tracks from your audio CDs onto your computer, where Windows Media Player stores them as WMA or MP3 files. As with graphics, make sure you have permission to duplicate tracks on a CD or you might be in violation of copyright law.

- **Copy songs to a portable music player**: If your portable music player can play WMA or MP3 songs, you can use Windows Media Player to copy, or sync, files from your Player library to the portable device. To do so, you connect your portable player to your computer, usually by plugging a cable into a USB port, and then start Media Player. If your portable device can store more than 4 GB of songs and your entire library can fit on the device, Windows Media Player automatically syncs your entire library. Every time you connect your portable device to your computer after that, Windows Media Player updates the device to match your library. You can also choose what to sync automatically by specifying the playlists you want to sync.

  If the storage capacity of your portable music player is less than 4 GB or your entire library cannot fit on the device, Windows Media Player lets you sync manually. You select the files or playlists you want to sync each time you connect the device to your computer.

- **Shop for music and movies at online stores**: Use Windows Media Player to find and subscribe to music, video, radio services, and other media content from online stores. If you download songs or other content, it appears in your library. Before you purchase or download files, make sure you understand the rights that the store grants you to use the file. The content that stores provide is typically protected with *media usage rights*, which specify what you can do with the content. For example, these rights might specify that you cannot burn the file to an audio CD, or they might limit the number of times you can burn or sync the file.

InSight | **Using the Windows Media Center to Watch and Record TV Shows**

Besides the Windows Media Player, which is designed primarily for playing music and videos, Windows Vista also includes the Windows Media Center, which is designed primarily for watching and recording TV shows. Windows Media Center is included only with the Windows Vista Home Premium and Ultimate editions. To use it effectively, your computer needs a TV tuner, which is a built-in circuit board that lets you view TV on a monitor and change channels. So that your PC receives a TV signal, you plug a TV cable into your computer's TV tuner. If you also want to watch TV shows on a television monitor, your computer's tuner needs a jack where you can plug in your TV set.

Hector wants to find music he can use with his promotional slide show, but he's not sure what type of music would work best. You suggest playing a few sample music files provided in the Windows Vista Music folder to get a feel for the style and musical genre that would be appropriate for his slide show. First, you'll show him how to start Windows Media Player and store all of the default Windows Vista sample music files in the Windows Media Player Library.

To start Windows Media Player and add music to the Library:

▶ **1.** Click the **Start** button 🪟 on the taskbar, point to **All Programs**, and then click **Windows Media Player**. The Windows Media Player window opens.

Trouble? If this is the first time you are running Windows Media Player, a dialog box opens before the main program window does, giving you the option to choose Express or Custom settings. Unless your instructor specifies otherwise, click Express.

▶ **2.** If necessary, maximize the window. See Figure 7-41. Your window might contain different music or might not contain any music yet.

Figure 7-41	Windows Media Player window

Next, you can make sure the Windows Media Player Library includes all the sample music files in your computer.

▶ **3.** Click the **Library** button on the toolbar, and then click **Other**.

▶ **4.** Click the **Click here** link. The Add To Library dialog box opens. See Figure 7-42.

Add To Library dialog box | **Figure 7-42**

make sure the My personal folders option is selected

Trouble? If the Click here link does not appear after you click Other, your library already contains music files. Skip steps 4-6.

▶ **5.** Click the **OK** button to scan your personal folders and include media files in the Media Player Library.

▶ **6.** Click the **Close** button.

▶ **7.** Click the **Library** button on the toolbar, and then click **Music**. You return to the main Windows Media Player window, which displays albums and songs.

After Windows Media Player initially stocks your library with songs and other media files, it monitors folders containing media files, including your Music folder, and updates the library when you add or remove files. (This is a good reason to store your media files in the Music, Pictures, and Videos folders and their subfolders.) It also adds any music files you play on your computer or the Internet and music that you rip from a CD or download from an online store.

Playing Music

To play music in Windows Media Player, double-click a song, album, or playlist. While a song is playing, Windows Media Player provides information and controls at the bottom of the window. A progress bar and timer track the progress of the song, and information such as the song title, album title, musician name, and composer name flashes as the song plays. You can use the playback controls, which are similar to the controls on a CD player, to play, stop, rewind, fast-forward, mute, or change the volume for the current song. If you click the Now Playing button on the toolbar, you can view **visualizations**, which are patterns of colors and abstract shapes that move with the music you are playing. To change the appearance of the Windows Media Player window, you can switch to a different display mode: full (the default), compact (controls only), skin (a customized design, such as one that matches the Windows XP Media Player), or mini (controls appear only on the taskbar).

One of the albums in Hector's library is called Quiet Songs and is included in the Jazz genre. Hector thinks that sounds promising. He also likes Beethoven, and notices that a Best of Beethoven album is included in the library. You'll show him how to play songs on those albums, which are samples provided by Windows Vista in the Music folder.

Before performing the following steps, make sure that your computer has a sound card and speakers, and that the speakers are plugged into a power source, turned on, and connected to your computer. Also make sure that the speaker volume is not muted, but is low enough to hear without disturbing others. If you don't have speakers but do have a sound card, you might be able to plug headphones into a headphone jack to listen to music. If your computer does not have the hardware necessary to play music, you can still perform the following steps, though you won't be able to hear the song.

To play a song:

▶ 1. Locate the **Quiet Songs** album by Aisha Duo, and then double-click it. The first song on the album, titled Despertar, begins to play, and information appears next to the playback controls. See Figure 7-43.

   Trouble? If the Quiet Songs album does not appear in the album list, double-click any other album or song in the Jazz genre.

Figure 7-43	Playing a song

information about the song appears as it plays

▶ 2. Click the **Stop** button ■ in the playback controls.

▶ 3. Double-click **The Best of Beethoven** album in the album list.

   Trouble? If The Best of Beethoven does not appear in the album list, double-click any other album or song in the Classical genre.

▶ 4. Listen to the symphony for a few seconds, and then click the **Stop** button ■.

Tip

To listen to music, you can also click a song or album and then click the Play button in the playback controls.

Hector thinks both of those albums would work to accompany his slide show of landscaping projects, but wants Bernie to listen to the songs as well. Bernie often listens to CDs on a portable player as he works, so Hector wants to burn those songs onto a CD that Bernie can listen to. Then Bernie can choose one of the songs in the playlist for the slide show. You'll show Hector how to add the songs to a new playlist so they are easy to burn onto a CD.

Creating a Playlist

A playlist contains one or more digital media files and provides a way to organize files that you want to work with as a group. For example, you can create a playlist of lively songs that you play to wake up in the morning or a playlist of your favorite songs that you burn on a CD or transfer to a portable music player. By default, items in a playlist are played in the order they appear in the list. You can change the order of the items by dragging and dropping them within the list, or you can shuffle the items in the list, which means they play in a random order.

Creating a Playlist | Reference Window

- In the Navigation pane, click Create Playlist.
- Enter a name for the playlist, and then press the Enter key.
- Drag albums, songs, and other music from the file list to the List pane.
- Click the Save Playlist button.

You can create two types of playlists in Windows Media Player—regular and auto. A regular playlist does not change unless you add or delete songs or other items from the list. As its name implies, an auto playlist changes automatically according to criteria you specify. For example, you could add any song rated four stars or more to an auto playlist. As Windows Media Player monitors your folders for new songs, it adds any rated at least four stars to that auto playlist.

Now that you and Hector have listened to selections from two albums, you'll add their songs to a new regular playlist.

To create a regular playlist:

▶ 1. In the Navigation pane, click **Create Playlist**. Windows Vista displays *New Playlist* as a placeholder for the playlist you are creating.

▶ 2. Type **Slide Show Music** and then press the **Enter** key. The Slide Show Music playlist opens in the List pane. See Figure 7-44.

Creating a playlist ◀ **Figure 7-44**

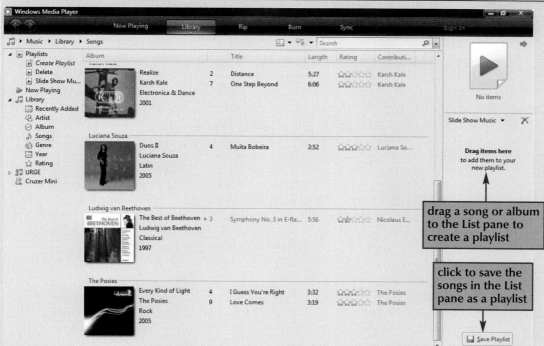

▶ 3. Drag the **Quiet Songs** album (or other Jazz album) from the album list to the List pane. The two songs on that album appear in the new playlist.

> **Trouble?** If a song you added to the playlist begins to play, click the Stop button on the playback controls.
>
> ▶ **4.** Drag **The Best of Beethoven** album (or other Classical album) to the List pane.
>
> ▶ **5.** Click the **Save Playlist** button.

If you want to change the order of the songs in the playlist, you can drag a song to a new position in the List pane. To edit a playlist by adding or removing songs, right-click the playlist in the Navigation pane and then click Edit in List Pane. To play the songs in a playlist in order, right-click the playlist in the Navigation pane and then click Play. To play the songs in random order after you click Play, click the Turn shuffle on button in the playback controls.

Next, you can burn the songs in the Slide Show Music playlist onto a CD.

Burning Files to a CD

If your computer has a CD or DVD recorder you can copy files to a writeable disc, a process called *burning* a disc. Using Windows Media Player, you can burn songs from your library to an audio CD and then play the CD in any standard CD player. However, you cannot burn music played live, such as from online radio stations, to a CD or DVD.

Reference Window | **Burning Files to a CD**

- Click the Burn button on the Windows Media Player toolbar, and then click Audio or Data, depending on the type of CD you want to burn.
- Insert the blank CD into the appropriate drive.
- Drag files from the file list to the List pane.
- Click Start Burn.

To burn music on a CD, your computer needs a CD burner, a drive that can read and write files to a CD. Depending on the type of burner you have, you can copy files to a blank compact disc-recordable (CD-R) or a blank compact disc-rewriteable (CD-RW). However, not all CD players can play CD-RW discs, so make sure your computer hardware is compatible with your CD player before burning discs.

You can use Windows Media Player to burn two types of CDs: audio and data CDs. You can play the music files on an audio CD in most computers and in CD players that play CD-R or CD-RW disks. You must copy WMA, MP3, or WAV files to create an audio CD. A data CD, also called a media CD, can store music, video, or other types of files, including documents and photos. However, not all CD players and computers can play music on a data CD, so check your destination device before you burn a CD.

After finding a blank CD-R, you are ready to burn the music files in the Slide Show Music playlist to an audio disc.

To perform the following steps, make sure your computer has a CD burner and that you have the appropriate type of CD, either a CD-R or CD-RW. If you are not equipped with the proper hardware, read but do not perform the following steps.

To burn files to a CD:

Tip

To change burn settings, click Burn on the toolbar, and then click Options.

▶ **1.** Click the **Burn** button arrow on the Windows Media Player toolbar, and then click **Audio CD**. The List pane opens, indicating that you need to insert a blank CD into the appropriate drive.

▶ **2.** Insert the blank CD into the appropriate drive.

> **Trouble?** If you are using a rewriteable disk such as a CD-RW that includes files, make sure that you don't need the files, right-click the drive in the Navigation pane, and then click Erase disc. You must erase the files before you can burn the disc again.
>
> **3.** Drag the **Slide Show Music** playlist from the Navigation pane to the List pane. The three songs in the Slide Show Music playlist appear in the Burn list, and Windows Vista displays how many minutes and seconds of empty space remain on the disc after it adds each song.
>
> **4.** Click **Start Burn**. A progress bar appears in the Burn list. Burning the disc takes a few minutes.
>
> **5.** When Windows Vista is finished burning the disc, close all open windows.

Now Hector can give the CD to Bernie so he can listen to the three songs on the disc. The promotional slide show you create will probably be long enough to play only one song, so you'll ask Bernie to listen to the CD at his convenience, and then select one of the three songs for the slide show.

Creating and Viewing Digital Movies and Slide Shows

If you have a digital video (DV) camera, you can use Windows Movie Maker to import audio and video to your computer from your DV camera, and then assemble the imported content into a movie. You can also import existing audio, video, and still pictures into Windows Movie Maker to use in movies. Windows Vista also considers photo slide shows to be movies. To create a professional-quality slide show, you import photos, arrange them in order, create **transitions** between each photo, add a musical soundtrack, and burn them to a DVD. A transition controls how your movie or slide show plays from one video clip or picture to the next. For example, a video clip can start by fading in from a black screen or one picture can play by sliding across the screen to reveal another picture.

Creating a movie typically involves completing three major steps:

1. Importing video, pictures, and music
2. Editing the movie to arrange and fine-tune video clips and pictures, add transitions, and coordinate music
3. Publishing the edited movie or slide show

Keep in mind that creating movies can consume a lot of hard disk space. A 10-minute movie consisting of video clips and transitions can easily take up 2 or more gigabytes, so make sure you have enough hard disk space before you start creating a movie. Windows Vista also recommends that you set your screen resolution to 1024 x 768 or higher before working in Windows Movie Maker. (Right-click the desktop, click Personalize, click Display Settings, and then drag the Resolution slider.)

The movie that Hector wants to create is a slide show of the photos stored in the Gardens folder. To make the slide show professional and appealing, he'd like to add transitions, slide titles, and music. To get acquainted with Windows Movie Maker, you suggest starting the program and playing a sample video provided with Windows Vista.

To start Windows Movie Maker:

▶ 1. Click the **Start** button 🔵 on the taskbar, point to **All Programs**, and then click **Windows Movie Maker**. The Windows Movie Maker window opens. Maximize the window, if necessary. See Figure 7-45.

| Figure 7-45 | Windows Movie Maker window |

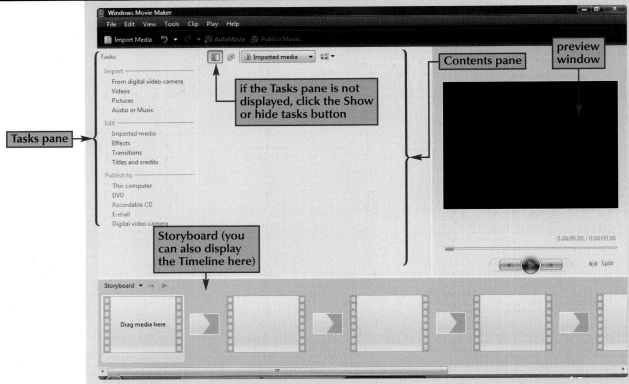

Trouble? If the Timeline opens at the bottom of the window instead of the Storyboard, click the Timeline button, and then click Storyboard.

▶ 2. In the Tasks pane, click **Videos** in the Import category. The Import Media Items dialog box opens, displaying the Sample Videos folder by default.

Trouble? If the Import Media Items dialog box does not open to the Sample Videos folder, open the Folders list, expand the Public folder if necessary, expand the Public Videos folder if necessary, and then click Sample Videos.

Trouble? If the Sample Videos folder appears unopened in the Import Media Items dialog box, double-click the Sample Videos folder to open it.

▶ 3. Double-click the **Butterfly** video to import it to Windows Movie Maker. See Figure 7-46.

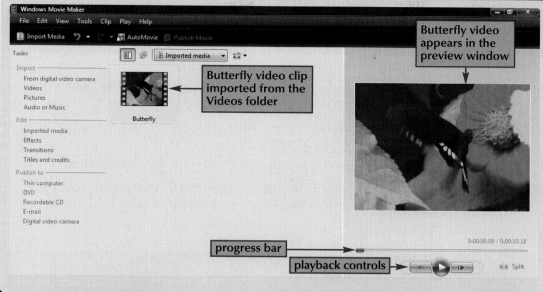

Importing a video to Windows Movie Maker Figure 7-46

4. If your computer has a sound card and speakers, make sure the speaker volume is set to be audible but not too loud. Then click the **Play** button ⊙ to play the movie. The Butterfly movie plays with a soundtrack, including background music.

Next, you'll show Hector how to import his garden photos to Windows Movie Maker so he can assemble them into a slide show.

Importing Movie Content

To create a movie in Windows Movie Maker, you need to import content such as footage from a digital video camera, video clips, pictures, and audio or music. To copy footage from a digital video camera to your computer, start Windows Movie Maker and then use a cable to connect the camera to your computer's FireWire or USB 2.0 port. (FireWire, or IEEE 1394 ports, are designed for this sort of transfer, and copy the files faster than a USB 2.0 port.) Click Import Video in the Tasks pane, and then enter details about the video such as a name, format, and whether to import the entire videotape or only parts of it. You can choose one of three formats when importing video. The Audio Video Interleaved (single file) format copies the entire video as a single file without any loss in quality. This format requires 13 GB for each hour of footage, so make sure you have enough room on your hard disk before choosing this format. The Windows Media Video (single file) format also copies the entire video as a single file, but compresses the content so it consumes only 2 GB per hour. The Windows Media Video (one file per scene) format requires the least amount of hard disk space because it breaks each shot into a separate file.

If you want to use files from a different source in your movie, such as photos, music, or existing video clips, make sure your computer can access them. Then select the appropriate option in the Import category on the Tasks pane: Videos (for video already stored on your computer), Pictures (for digital photos), or Audio or Music (sounds or music).

After listening to the three songs in the Slide Show Music playlist that you burned on a CD, Bernie thinks the Beethoven piece would work best for the landscaping slide show. You'll show Hector how to gather the Beethoven music file and the photos he needs for his slide show. First, you'll remove the Butterfly video from the Contents pane so you don't inadvertently include that video in the slide show. Then you'll save the project—the term Windows Vista uses to refer to a Windows Movie Maker file—with a descriptive name.

To import photos and music:

1. Right-click the **Butterfly** video in the Contents pane, and then click **Remove**. Windows Vista removes the video from the Contents pane, which does not affect the original Butterfly file.

2. Click **File** on the menu bar, and then click **Save Project** to open the Save Project As dialog box, which is identical to the Save As dialog box.

3. Navigate to the **Gardens** folder in your Pictures folder, type **Garden Show** in the File name text box, and then click the **Save** button.

4. In the Tasks pane, click **Pictures** to open the Import Media Items dialog box, which is similar to the Open dialog box.

5. Open the **Gardens** folder, and then select all the picture files in the folder.

6. Click the **Import** button. The 13 pictures appear in the Contents pane, with the last selected picture displayed in the preview window. See Figure 7-47.

Tip

To import any type of media, click the Import Media button on the toolbar.

Figure 7-47	Importing pictures

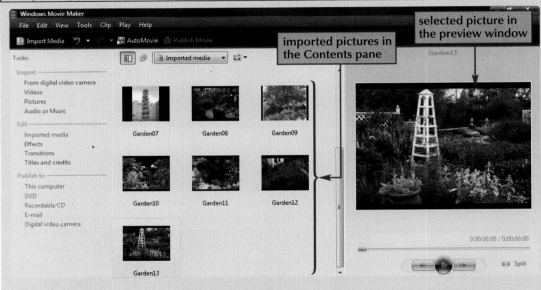

7. In the Tasks pane, click **Audio or Music** in the Import category. The Import Media Items dialog box opens.

8. In the Sample Music folder, double-click **Symphony No. 3 in E-flat major...** to import the music to Windows Movie Maker.

9. Click **File** on the menu bar, and then click **Save Project** to save your work on the Garden Show project so far.

The Contents pane now includes all the raw content you need to create Hector's slide show. You're ready to assemble them into a movie.

Editing a Movie

To edit a movie, you start by examining your imported media, including video clips and photos, and remove any content that's not appropriate for the movie. You can reduce the file size of your movie by selecting only high-quality shots, photos, and music that are essential and eliminating all the unnecessary ones, particularly if you are working with video clips.

Next, you arrange your media in the order you want them to play in the movie. You do this by dragging video clips or pictures from the Contents pane to the Storyboard. The Storyboard is your workspace for linking media files in logical order. You can fine-tune the arrangement by dragging media from one slot on the Storyboard to another. When you're satisfied with the order, you can add effects and transitions. Recall that a transition plays between clips or pictures, such as a fade or dissolve. An effect changes the appearance of a clip or picture. For example, you can apply a Blur effect to make a photo look blurred. You can also add a title, your name, the date, credits, and other text to your movie.

To edit video clips and add a soundtrack, you open the Timeline, which provides a detailed view of your movie project. Using the Timeline, you can shorten video clips, adjust the length of transitions, and add music or other audio. You can also use the Timeline to review and modify the timing of the clips and pictures.

As you edit a movie project, preview the movie by playing it from time to time, and then save it so you don't lose your creative work.

With the garden photos and music files in the Contents pane of the Garden Show movie project, you're ready to assemble this raw content into a polished slide show. Hector wants to start by showing the flower borders and beds (Garden01, Garden02, Garden03, Garden05, Garden06, Garden12, and Garden13), followed by trees (Garden04, Garden07, and Garden08), and ending with water features (Garden09, Garden10, and Garden11). You can switch to Details view in the Contents pane to work with the media files more easily.

To arrange photos in the Storyboard:

▶ **1.** Click the **Views** button 🔳 ▾ on the Contents pane toolbar, and then click **Details**. The media files appear in Details view.

▶ **2.** Drag **Garden12** from the Contents pane to the **first frame** in the Storyboard. See Figure 7-48.

Adding media to the Storyboard ◀ **Figure 7-48**

▶ 3. Select the remaining picture files in the Contents pane, click **Clip** on the menu bar, and then click **Add to Storyboard**. The photos appear in the Storyboard in the order you selected them, which is alphabetical order by filename.

▶ 4. Save your work.

▶ 5. In the Storyboard, drag **Garden13** to the **Garden07** frame. At first, the pointer might change to a No sign pointer ⃠. Continue dragging in the Storyboard until the pointer changes to a ⬚ pointer. When a blue line appears to the left of the Garden07 frame, release the mouse button. The Garden13 picture now appears before Garden07 in the Storyboard.

▶ 6. Finish arranging the photos of flower borders and beds by moving **Garden04** so it appears before Garden07. The order of the pictures should be Garden12, Garden01, Garden02, Garden05, Garden06, Garden03, Garden13, Garden04, Garden07, Garden08, Garden09, Garden10, and Garden 11.

▶ 7. Save the project.

Next, you can add effects to the first and last photos in the slide show. This is often a good way to let viewers know when the slide show begins and ends, especially if you plan to play the show on an endless loop. Before you apply an effect, you can preview one or two effects to see how they look.

To preview movie effects:

▶ 1. In the Tasks pane, click **Effects** in the Edit category. Dozens of movie effects appear in the Contents pane.

▶ 2. To see thumbnails of the effects, click the **Views** button ⊞▾ and then click **Thumbnails**, if necessary. See Figure 7-49.

Selecting effects ◀ Figure 7-49

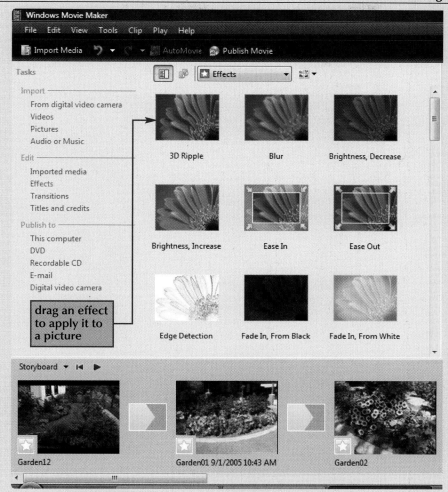

3. Click the **3D Ripple** effect to display it in the preview window.

4. Click the **Play** button ▶ to preview this effect.

5. Preview the **Fade In, From Black** effect.

Selecting Effects and Transitions | InSight

Effects and transitions are more appropriate for slide shows than movies assembled from video clips. In a slide show, transitions help to hold the viewer's interest as the show switches from one image to the next. Effects are often helpful to signal the beginning and end of the show. They can also be effective to create a stylized look for an entire video. For example, you can apply a Film Age effect to make a movie look like historic footage or a black-and-white classic. However, you should use transitions only sparingly in a movie, if at all, because they distract from the other moving images.

Hector likes both of those effects, and you agree that they would both work well in the slide show. You suggest applying the Fade In, From Black effect to the first image because that type of effect is often associated with the start of a show. The 3D Ripple effect would work well with the last photo, which displays a pond.

To apply movie effects:

▶ 1. Scroll the Storyboard to the far left to display the Garden12 picture in the first frame.

▶ 2. Drag the **Fade In, From Black** effect from the Contents pane to the **Garden12** picture in the Storyboard. The star icon in the lower-left corner of the frame is highlighted, indicating that frame includes an effect. See Figure 7-50.

| Figure 7-50 | Applying an effect to a frame |

highlighted star means an effect is applied →

Trouble? If you dragged the effect to a picture other than the Garden12 picture, click the Undo button on the toolbar and repeat Step 1.

▶ 3. Preview the effect by clicking **Garden12** in the Storyboard, and then clicking the **Play** button ⏵ in the preview window. When the next image appears in the preview window, click the **Pause** button ⏸.

▶ 4. Scroll the Storyboard to the right to display the Garden11 picture.

▶ 5. Drag the **3D Ripple** effect from the Contents pane to the **Garden11** picture.

▶ 6. Preview the effect on the Garden11 picture, and then pause the slide show.

▶ 7. Save the project.

Next, you can apply transitions to play between each slide. To avoid having the transitions distract from your content, play the same transition between each slide or group of slides. As with effects, you can preview the transitions before adding them to your movie.

To preview transitions:

▶ 1. In the Tasks pane, click **Transitions** in the Edit category. Dozens of transitions appear in the Contents pane. See Figure 7-51.

Selecting transitions ◀ Figure 7-51

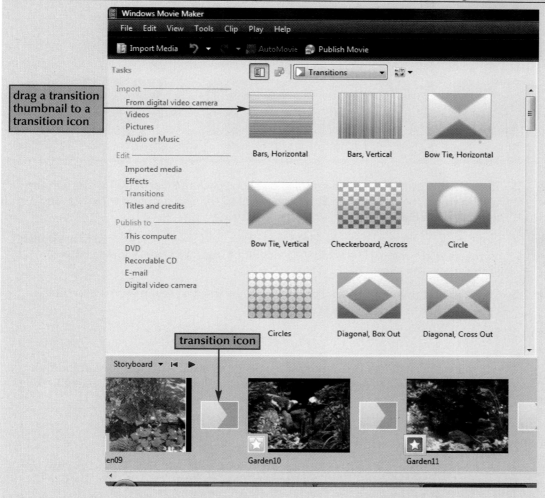

2. Click the **Bars, Horizontal** transition, and then click the **Play** button ▶ to preview this transition.

3. Scroll the Contents pane to find and then click the **Wipe, Normal Right** transition.

4. Click the **Play** button ▶ to preview the Wipe, Normal Right transition.

The Wipe, Normal Right transition would work well in Hector's slide show, so you show him how to apply that transition to each slide.

To apply a transition:

1. Scroll the Storyboard pane to display the Garden12 picture in the first frame.

2. Drag the **Wipe, Normal Right** transition from the Contents pane to the **transition icon** between the first two pictures in the Storyboard. The transition icon now displays an image of the Wipe, Normal Right transition. See Figure 7-52.

Figure 7-52 | **Applying a transition between frames**

3. To apply this transition to the entire slide show, click the **Garden01** picture in the second frame, hold down the **Shift** key, scroll to the end of the Storyboard, and then click the **Garden11** picture in the last frame.

4. Right-click the **Wipe, Normal Right** transition, and then click **Add to Storyboard** on the shortcut menu. The Wipe, Normal Right transition icon appears between each slide in the show.

5. Click the first frame in the Storyboard, preview the first few pictures and transitions, and then stop the slide show.

6. Save the project.

Next, you want to add a title to the Garden Show project. You'd like to start the show with a slide that introduces the movie and provides information about contacting Oak Park Landscaping.

To add titles to the slide show:

Tip

To display a title on a slide, select the slide, click Titles and credits in the Tasks pane, and then click Title overlay on the selected clip.

1. In the Tasks pane, click **Titles and credits** in the Edit category. Windows Vista asks where you want to add a title.

2. Click **Title at the beginning**.

3. In the first Enter text for title text box, type **Garden Designs by Oak Park Landscaping**. In the second text box, type **Oak Park, IL**, press the **Enter** key, and then type **(312) 555-4156** so the phone number appears together on one line. A preview plays in the preview window. You and Hector like the animation and font used for this title, but you'd like to change the background color to green, which coordinates with the green in many of the pictures.

4. Click **Change the text font and color**. Controls appear so you can change the font, text color, background color, and other options.

5. Click the **Change the background color** icon ▣ to open the Color dialog box.

6. Click the **dark green** square (fourth row, third column), and then click the **OK** button. Windows Vista previews the title with the new background color. See Figure 7-53.

Creating a title slide ◄ **Figure 7-53**

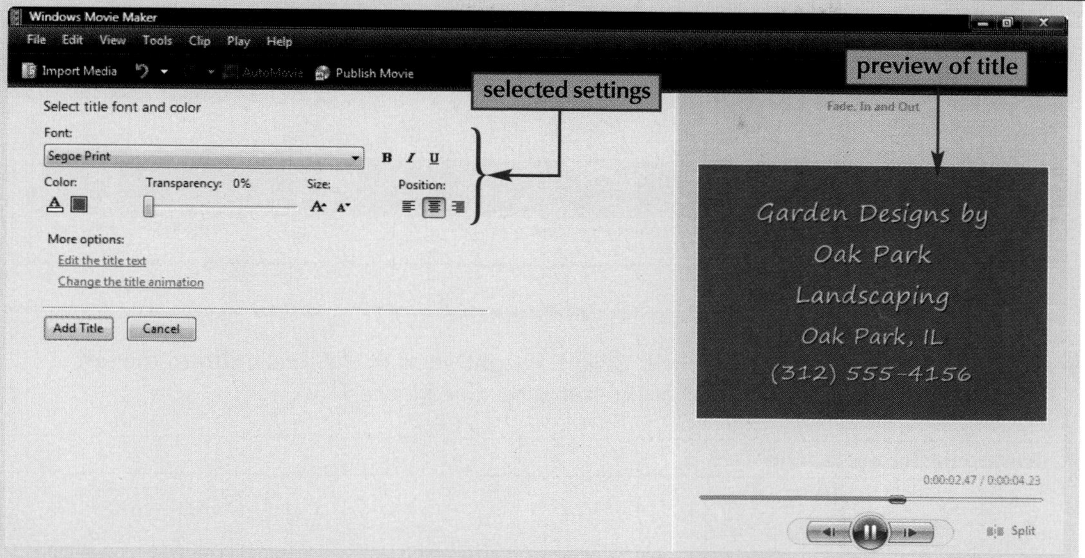

7. Click the **Add Title** button. The title appears as the first frame in the Storyboard.

8. Save the project.

Note that no transition plays between the title and the first picture. Recall that the first picture includes the Fade In, From Black effect. Including a transition before the first slide could seem confusing or distracting, so you won't add a transition between the first and second frames.

The last element you want to add to the movie is a soundtrack. You can do so by dragging a music file from the Contents pane to the audio track on the Timeline. The piece that Bernie and Hector agreed on is the Beethoven symphony.

To add an audio track to the movie:

1. Click **View** on the menu bar, and then click **Timeline**. The Timeline replaces the Storyboard at the bottom of the Windows Movie Maker window.

2. Click the **Transitions** button on the Contents pane toolbar, and then click **Imported media**.

3. Drag **Symphony No. 3 in E-flat major** from the Contents pane to the beginning of the **Audio/Music** track in the Timeline. See Figure 7-54.

Figure 7-54 **Adding a music track to the Timeline**

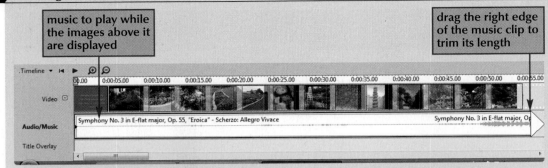

4. To set the length of the music, drag the right edge of the music clip to the left until it aligns with the end of the last slide. See Figure 7-55.

Figure 7-55 **Trimming the music clip**

5. Click the **Title** frame, and then click the **Play** button ⊙ in the preview window to play the movie with the soundtrack.

6. Stop the playback, and then save the project.

Now that you've created and edited the Garden Show movie, you are ready to publish it.

Publishing a Movie

To save an edited movie or slide show in a format that can play in Windows Media Player or other video device, you publish the project. You can publish the movie to a Windows Media file with a WMV filename extension or to an Audio Video Interleaved file with an AVI filename extension. Then you can share the movie with others by playing it on your computer, burning it to a CD or DVD so you can play it on a portable device, sending it as a compressed attachment in an e-mail, or copying it to a blank videotape in your digital video camera.

Publishing a Movie | Reference Window

- Click an option in the Publish to category in the Windows Movie Maker Tasks pane.
- If you are publishing to a folder on your computer, the Publish Movie Wizard starts. Enter a name and location for the movie, click Next, choose the settings for your movie, and then click the Publish button.
- If you are publishing to a DVD, Windows DVD Maker opens. Customize the opening menu, and then click Burn.
- If you are publishing to a recordable CD, the Publish Movie Wizard starts. Insert a recordable CD in the appropriate drive, click Next, enter a name and location for the movie, click Next, choose the settings for your movie, and then click the Publish button.
- If you are publishing the movie as an e-mail attachment, Windows Vista publishes the movie to a compressed file. When it's finished, click Save a copy of my movie on my computer, enter a name and location for the file, click Save, and then click Attach Movie.
- If you are publishing to a videotape in a digital video camera, connect your camera to your computer, click Next, rewind or fast-forward the tape in your camera to where you want to record your movie, click Next, click Yes, and then click Finish.

When you select a Publish to option in the Tasks pane and appropriate settings, Windows Vista creates your movie, choosing the appropriate file size and quality for the destination you selected. Publishing involves arranging all of your clips and pictures, creating effects and transitions, adding soundtracks, and compressing everything into a single file. All of that processing can take a long time. Also keep in mind that the higher the quality of the movie, the larger the file size. Movies you save on a videotape in a digital video camera have the highest quality and the largest file size. Movies saved for e-mail have the lowest quality and smallest file size. Those you save on your computer can take a few gigabytes of storage space, even if you sacrifice quality and compress the files. Make sure you have plenty of time and storage space before you publish a movie.

Before publishing Hector's movie, he wants Bernie to review it. If he wants to make any changes, you can do so in Windows Movie Maker, and then publish the final movie file. For now, you are finished with Windows Movie Maker so you can close the program.

To close Windows Movie Maker:

▶ **1.** Click the **Close** button [X] on the Windows Movie Maker title bar.

Restoring Your Computer

If you are working in a computer lab or a computer other than your own, complete the steps in this section to restore the original settings on your computer.

To restore your computer:

▶ **1.** Navigate to the **Pictures** folder on your computer.

▶ **2.** Move the **Gardens** folder to the **Tutorial.07\Tutorial** folder provided with your Data Files.

▶ **3.** Delete the **Slide Show Music** playlist from Windows Media Player.

▶ **4.** Close all open windows.

| Review | **| Session 7.3 Quick Check** |

1. A(n) _____ is a list of media files, such as songs, that you want to play in specified order.
2. True or False. As you play music in Windows Media Player, you can view patterns of colors and abstract shapes that move with the music you are playing.
3. What are the two types of CDs you can burn using Windows Media Player?
4. What is typically the first step you perform when creating movies in Windows Movie Maker?
5. True or False. An effect in a movie is an animation that plays only at the beginning of a movie.
6. What must you do to save an edited movie or slide show in a format that can play in Windows Media Player or other video device?

| Review | **| Tutorial Summary** |

In this tutorial, you explored computer graphics, learning how to create and modify bitmapped graphics in Paint by combining images, adding text, drawing shapes, changing colors, and cropping a graphic. You also used the Windows Photo Gallery to work with photos. You imported photos into the gallery, viewed and organized them, improved their appearance, and then shared them with others by e-mailing and printing them. To explore Windows Vista's music tools, you used Windows Media Player to play music files, create a playlist, and burn files to a CD. Finally, you used Windows Movie Maker to create a movie, a professional-quality slide show featuring effects, transitions, and a title.

Key Terms

background color	foreground color	playlist
bitmapped graphic	graphic images	saturation
brightness	graphics	scanner
color cast	graphics program	sizing coordinates
color temperature	Options box	toolbox
compression	Paint	transition
contrast	pixel	vector graphic
crop	pixel coordinates	visualization

Practice	Review Assignments

Practice the skills you learned in the tutorial.

For a list of Data Files in the Review folder, see page 321.

Oak Park Landscaping is conducting a series of seminars on garden design to help promote its business. Hector Torres wants to create a postcard he can mail to current and prospective clients to invite them to attend a seminar. He's found two graphics that he wants to use on the postcard, and asks you to show him how to combine these into an effective design. Bernie Quinn has taken photos of some of the most popular flowers they feature in gardens, and wants to showcase these in a slide show he can play at the seminar on selecting bedding plants. He asks you to help him prepare the photos and assemble them into a professional slide show. Complete the following steps:

1. Start Paint, open the **Border** picture, and then save it as **Seminar** in the Tutorial.07\Review folder provided with your Data Files.
2. Paste the Plan picture into the Seminar picture, and center it within the border.
3. Increase the size of the canvas to at least 600 x 400 pixels to create a larger work area.
4. Increase the magnification as necessary to select a dark red color from the Border graphic as the forecolor and a light yellow-green color from the Plan graphic as the background color.
5. Return to 100% zoom. Near the bottom of the canvas, use the Solid style and then *right*-drag to draw a rectangle 255 x 30 pixels.
6. Above the rectangle, create a text box slightly larger than the rectangle. Choose Verdana as the font, 16 as the point size, and Italic as the style. Type **Oak Park Landscaping** in the text box.
7. Move the text, including as little background as possible, from the text box to the light green rectangle, centering the text in the rectangle. Save your work.
8. Near the bottom of the canvas, use the Solid style to draw a dark-red rectangle 275 x 30 pixels.
9. Switch the foreground and background colors—make the light green the foreground color and the dark red the background color.
10. Create a text box slightly larger than the red rectangle. Choose Verdana as the font, 16 as the point size, and Italic as the style. Type **Garden Design Seminars** in the text box.
11. Move the text, including as little background as possible, from the text box to the dark-red rectangle, centering the text in the rectangle. Save your work.
12. Change the background color to white, and then delete the original text boxes that no longer contain any text.
13. Arrange the rectangles so that they are right next to each other with no white space between them, the "Oak Park Landscaping" rectangle on the left, aligned with the left edge of the canvas, and the "Garden Design Seminars" rectangle on the right. Save your work.
14. Copy both rectangles, which now form a two-color bar, and then resize the canvas to 530 x 250 pixels. If any remnants of the rectangles remain, delete them.
15. Paste the rectangles into the picture, and then move them to the bottom of the canvas, taking care not to extend any part of the rectangles past the borders of the canvas. Save your work.

16. Working in a magnified view, draw a 12 x 12 pixel square in the upper-right corner of the picture, using the same shade of light-green you used in the rectangles or a slightly darker shade selected from the Plan image. Display the grid and move the square so it is 12 pixels to the right of the Border image and 12 pixels from the top of the canvas.

17. Copy and paste the square to create a row of four squares with 12 pixels of white space between each square. The final picture should look similar to Figure 7-56.

Figure 7-56

18. Make any final modifications as necessary, save your work, and then close Paint.

19. Copy the nine flower garden photos from the Tutorial.07\Review folder provided with your Data Files to a new folder in the **Pictures** folder named **Flowers**.

20. Start Windows Photo Gallery, and then play a simple slide show of the pictures in the **Flowers** folder.

21. Fix three photos as follows:
    a. Automatically adjust the exposure and color in the Buttercup photo.
    b. Slightly increase the brightness in the Fuschia photo.
    c. Crop the Dahlia photo by rotating and resizing the frame to remove about 20% of the photo on the right.

22. Close Windows Photo Gallery.

23. Start Windows Media Player, and then create a playlist named **Flower Slide Show** consisting of **OAM's Blues** and **Muita Bobeira**. (*Hint:* Add these files to the Library from the Sample Music folder first, if necessary.)

24. Close Windows Media Player.

25. Start Windows Movie Maker, remove any clips in the Contents pane, and then create a project named **Seminar Show** in the **Flowers** folder. Import the nine pictures from the **Flowers** folder and OAM's Blues from the **Sample Music** folder into the Seminar Show project.

26. Edit the movie as follows, saving your work after each step:
    a. Add each photo to the Storyboard in alphabetical order.
    b. Apply the Brightness, Increase effect to the first photo and the Brightness, Decrease effect to the last photo.
    c. Include the Fade transition between each photo.

    d. Add a title slide at the beginning of the show with the text **Oak Park Landscaping** on the first line and **Flower Identification Guide** to the second line. Choose a dark red background for the title.

    e. Add OAM's Blues to the Audio/Music track, and then trim it so it doesn't play past the last slide.

27. Save your work, play the show from the beginning, and then close Windows Movie Maker.

28. Move the **Flowers** folder from the Pictures folder to the Tutorial.07\Review folder provided with your Data Files.

29. Submit the results of the preceding steps to your instructor, either in printed or electronic form, as requested.

| Apply | **Case Problem 1** |

Use the skills you learned in the tutorial to manage multimedia files for a stationery shop.

For a list of Data Files in the Case1 folder, see page 321.

Alpha-Zeta   Marianne Zeta owns Alpha-Zeta, a stationery store in Greenwich, Connecticut, that offers paper making, calligraphy, and other hand-printing services. You are working as Marianne's assistant and help her serve customers, fill orders, and create promotional materials. Marianne asks you to work with two calligraphy images she has to develop a logo for the store and to create a slide show of female authors. She plans to play the slide show in the store during Women's History Month. Complete the following steps:

1. Start Paint, open the **Flourish** picture, and then save it as **AZLogo** in the Tutorial.07\Case1 folder provided with your Data Files.

2. Increase the size of the canvas to at least 400 x 400 pixels to create a larger work area.

3. Paste the Letters AZ picture into the AZ Logo picture, and move them to a blank spot on the canvas.

4. Working in a magnified view as necessary, select the letters *A* and *Z* again without selecting any white space around them. Move the letters next to the flourish image, so that they appear to the right of the vertical bar in the flourish image. Do not allow any white space between the flourish image and the letters. Save your work.

5. Near the bottom of the canvas, create a text box and choose 16-point Monotype Corsiva for the text. Type **Alpha-Zeta** in the text box. Make sure all the text appears on one line.

6. Select the text, including as little background as possible, and then move it under the calligraphic letter *Z*, so that it is roughly right-aligned with the black box containing the letter *Z*.

7. Change the foreground color to a dark red selected from elsewhere in the picture.

8. Near the bottom of the canvas, create another text box and choose 12-point Monotype Corsiva italic for the text. Type **Stationery &** and then press the Enter key. Type **Calligraphy**. Make sure the text appears on two lines.

9. Move the new text so that it is right-aligned under "Alpha-Zeta." Save your work.

10. Resize the canvas so its dimensions are about 195 x 220. The final logo should look similar to Figure 7-57.

Figure 7-57

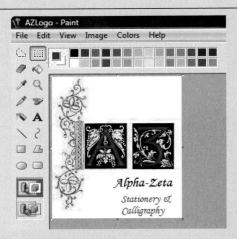

11. Make any final modifications as necessary, save your work, and then close Paint.

12. Copy the seven portraits of female authors from the Tutorial.07\Case1 folder provided with your Data Files to a new folder in the **Pictures** folder named **Authors**.

13. Start Windows Photo Gallery, and then play a simple slide show of the pictures in the **Authors** folder.

14. Automatically adjust the exposure in all seven photos.

15. Rotate the Browning photo so it appears in the correct orientation.

16. Close Windows Photo Gallery.

17. Start Windows Movie Maker, remove any clips in the Contents pane, and then create a project named **Author Slide Show** in the **Authors** folder.

18. Import the seven portraits from the **Authors** folder into the Author Slide Show project.

19. Edit the movie as follows, saving your work after each step:
    a. Add each photo to the Storyboard in alphabetical order.
    b. Apply the Fade In, From White effect to the first photo and the Fade Out, To White effect to the last photo.
    c. Include the Reveal, Right transition between each photo.
    d. Add a title to the beginning of the show with the text **Alpha-Zeta Stationery & Calligraphy** to the first line, and **Notable Women Authors** to the second line. Change the font to Monotype Corsiva.

20. Play the show, save your work, and then close Windows Movie Maker.

21. Move the **Authors** folder from the Pictures folder to the Tutorial.07\Case1 folder provided with your Data Files.

22. Submit the results of the preceding steps to your instructor, either in printed or electronic form, as requested.

| Apply | | **Case Problem 2** |

Use the skills you learned in the tutorial to work with multi-media files for a lighthouse preservation society.

For a list of Data Files in the Case2 folder, see page 321.

Landmark Lighthouses   Since the United States Coast Guard automated the nation's coastal lights, the federal government has been transferring ownership of lighthouses to state and local governments and to nonprofit organizations. With this in mind, Stanley and Debra Keene started Landmark Lighthouses in Superior, Wisconsin, a nonprofit company dedicated to preserving historic lighthouses. You volunteer regularly for the organization, and offer to help Stan and Debra create fundraising materials. Stan asks you to show him how to use Paint to create an image for their Web site and to create a slide show they can make available for download. Complete the following steps:

1. Start Paint, open the **Lighthouse** file, and then save it as **Landmark** in the Tutorial. 07\Case2 folder provided with your Data Files.
2. Increase the size of the canvas to at least 600 x 600 pixels to create a larger work area.
3. Change the foreground color to a shade of pale yellow that appears in the lighthouse lantern.
4. Near the top of the canvas and to the right of the lighthouse, use the Solid style to draw an ellipse about 140 x 140 pixels round.
5. If necessary, move the yellow circle so that its top edge touches the top of the canvas. Save your work.
6. Select the lighthouse, choose the Transparent Background option, and then move the lighthouse to the circle so that the lantern and the first red segment of the lighthouse appear to be surrounded by a halo of yellow light. See Figure 7-58.

Figure 7-58

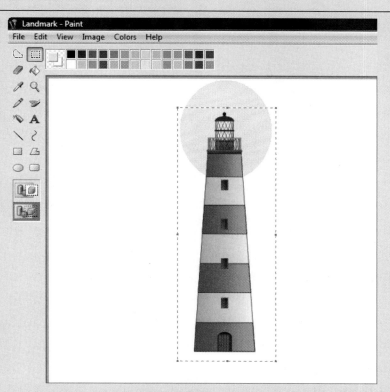

7. Change the foreground color to a shade of gray selected from the lighthouse, change the background color to a shade of red selected from the lighthouse.

8. Using the Outline with fill style, draw a rectangle 300 x 42 pixels near the bottom of the canvas.

9. Change the foreground color to a shade of light gray selected from the lighthouse.

10. Near the bottom of the canvas, but away from the rectangle, create a text box at least 290 pixels wide and choose 20-point Book Antiqua for the text. Select the Solid Background option in the Options box, if necessary, and then type **Landmark Lighthouses** in the text box. Make sure the text appears on one line.

11. Move the text, including as little background as possible, from the text box to the red rectangle, centering the text in the rectangle. Save your work.

12. Change the background color to white, and then delete the box that no longer contains any text.

13. Select the entire remaining rectangle, choose the Transparent Background option, and then move the rectangle so it is centered under the lighthouse and no white space appears between the lighthouse and the rectangle.

14. Move the entire image so that the left edge of the rectangle touches the left edge of the canvas. (The top edge of the halo should still touch the top edge of the canvas.)

⊕ **EXPLORE** 15. Point to the lower-right corner of the rectangle and note its pixel coordinates. Click Image on the menu bar and then click Attributes to open the Attributes dialog box. Enter the pixel coordinates in the appropriate text boxes, which should be close to 300 for the Width and 460 for the Height. Click the OK button. Your image should look similar to Figure 7-59.

Figure 7-59

16. Make any final modifications as necessary, save your work, and then close Paint.

17. Copy the eight lighthouse photos and the Ocean sound file from the Tutorial.07\Case2 folder provided with your Data Files to a new folder in the **Pictures** folder named **Lighthouses**.

18. Start Windows Photo Gallery, and then play a simple slide show of the pictures in the **Lighthouses** folder.

19. Fix three photos as follows:
    a. Automatically adjust the exposure and color in the LH04 photo.
    b. Slightly increase the brightness in the LH06 photo.
    c. Crop the LH03 photo to focus more tightly on the lighthouse.

20. Close Windows Photo Gallery.

21. Start Windows Movie Maker, remove any clips in the Contents pane, and then create a project named **Lighthouse Show** in the **Lighthouses** folder. Import the eight photos and the Ocean sound file from the **Lighthouses** folder into the Lighthouse Show project.

22. Edit the movie as follows, saving your work after each step:
    a. Add the photos to the Storyboard so that LH04 is the first picture, LH08 is the seventh picture, and LH06 is the last picture.
    b. Apply the Fade In, From Black effect to the first photo and the Fade Out, To Black effect to the last photo.
    c. Include the Diagonal, Down Right transition between each photo.
    d. Add a title slide with the text **Landmark Lighthouses** on the first line. Change the font to Book Antiqua.
    e. Add the Ocean sound file to the Audio/Music track four times, and then trim the last clip so it doesn't play past the last slide.

23. Play the show from the beginning, save your work, and then close Windows Movie Maker.

24. Move the **Lighthouses** folder from the Pictures folder to the Tutorial.07\Case2 folder provided with your Data Files.

25. Submit the results of the preceding steps to your instructor, either in printed or electronic form, as requested.

| Challenge | **Case Problem 3** |

Extend what you've learned to discover other ways to customize Windows for a bird supply store.

For a list of Data Files in the Case3 folder, see page 321.

Backyard Birds Backyard Birds is a store with two locations in Silver Spring, Maryland, that specializes in wild bird supplies, quality bird seed, field guides, and other distinctive equipment and gifts for birding enthusiasts. Tricia Knowles recently opened her second store in the area and hired you to manage it. When she learned that you have some graphic design training, she asked you to help her design a graphic she can use on her newsletter and business correspondence. She also wants you to develop a slide show highlighting backyard birds. Complete the following steps:

1. Start Paint, open the **Window** picture, and then save it as **Backyard Birds** in the Tutorial.07\Case3 folder provided with your Data Files.

2. Increase the size of the canvas to at least 700 x 600 pixels to create a larger work area.

3. Paste the **Wren** picture into the backyard birds picture, and move the bird to a blank spot on the canvas.

EXPLORE 4. With the image of the bird still selected, rotate the image 90 degrees to the left by clicking Image on the menu bar, clicking Flip/Rotate, clicking Rotate by angle, making sure that the 90 option button is selected, and then clicking the OK button.

EXPLORE 5. Select the image of the window frame without selecting any white space around it. Choose the Transparent Background option, and then move the window frame over the bird so that the bird appears mostly in the top two panes. The lower-right frame should contain almost all white space. Save your work.

6. Change the foreground color to a shade of dark olive green that appears in the bird image.

7. In a blank spot on the canvas, create a text box at least 170 pixels wide. Choose the Solid Background option, and select 20-point Goudy Old Style for the text. Type **Backyard Birds** in the text box so that the text appears on two lines. Save your work.

8. Move the "Backyard Birds" text into the lower-right pane of the window frame. See Figure 7-60.

Figure 7-60

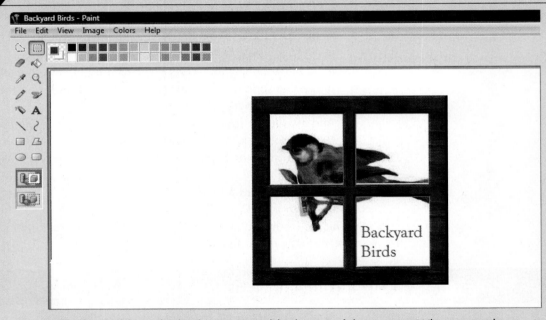

9. Copy the leaf from the bird image to a blank area of the canvas. When you select the leaf, you will probably include some pixels from the frame or bird.

EXPLORE 10. Erase the unnecessary pixels from the leaf by clicking the Eraser tool, clicking the smallest size in the Options box, and then clicking the pixels you want to erase from the leaf. Save your work.

11. Move the leaf to the lower-right window pane next to "Birds."

12. Move the entire image to the upper-left corner of the canvas. No white space should appear above and to the left of the graphic.

EXPLORE 13. Resize the canvas to precisely 386 x 344 by clicking Image on the menu bar, clicking Attributes, entering 386 in the Width text box and 344 in the Height text box, and then clicking the OK button.

14. Change the foreground color to a shade of light brown that appears in the bird image.

15. Fill the white part of the canvas outside of the window frame with the foreground color. Your image should look similar to Figure 7-61.

Figure 7-61

16. Make any final modifications as necessary, save your work, and then close Paint.

17. Copy the 10 bird photos and the two sound files from the Tutorial.07\Case3 folder provided with your Data Files to a new folder in the **Pictures** folder named **Birds**.

18. Start Windows Photo Gallery, and then play a simple slide show of the pictures in the **Birds** folder.

⊕ **EXPLORE** 19. Fix the photos as follows:

   a. Automatically adjust the exposure and color in each photo.

   b. Slightly reduce the color temperature of the Bird10 photo.

   c. Crop the Bird10 photo to focus more tightly on the group of ducks.

20. Close Windows Photo Gallery.

21. Start Windows Movie Maker, remove any clips in the Contents pane, and then create a project named **Bird Show** in the **Birds** folder. Import the 10 photos and the two sound files from the **Birds** folder into the Bird Show project.

⊕ **EXPLORE** 22. Edit the movie as follows, saving your work after each step:

   a. Add the photos to the Storyboard in numeric order.

   b. Remove the Bird10 picture from the Storyboard.

   c. Apply the Ease In effect to the first photo and the Ease Out effect to the last photo.

   d. Include the Wipe, Narrow Right transition between each photo.

   e. Switch to Timeline view, click the first picture, and then add a title on that picture with the text **Backyard Birds** on the first line. Change the font to Goudy Old Style.

   f. Add four copies of the BirdSong audio file so it plays with Bird01, Bird07, Bird08, and Bird09.

   g. Add the **WaterFowl** audio file to the audio track so it starts playing with the Bird02 picture.

23. Save your work, and then close Windows Movie Maker.

24. Move the **Birds** folder from the Pictures folder to the Tutorial.07\Case3 folder provided with your Data Files.

25. Submit the results of the preceding steps to your instructor, either in printed or electronic form, as requested.

Create | **Case Problem 4**

Using Figures 7-62 and 7-63 as guides, create a graphic for a farmer's market.

For a list of Data Files in the Case4 folder, see page 321.

Farmer's Market West Franklin Bieder is the manager of Farmer's Market West in Spokane, Washington. Farmer's Market West offers fresh fruits, vegetables, and other farm products during the growing months in Spokane. Franklin hired you as his assistant to provide marketing and graphic design services to the organization. He asks you to design a logo he can use in print and online. He'd also like you to create a slide show that promotes the market's products. Complete the following steps:

1. Create a logo for Farmer's Market West using Figure 7-62 as a guide. Save the graphic as **FMWest** in the Tutorial.07\Case4 folder provided with your Data Files.

Figure 7-62

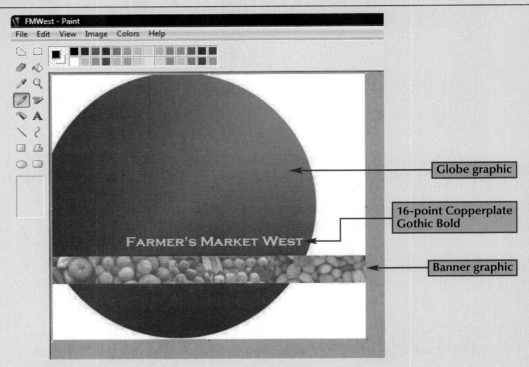

Keep the following information in mind as you create the logo:

- The Globe and Banner graphics files are in the Tutorial.07\Case4 folder provided with your Data Files.
- Be sure to save your work after making a significant change to the graphic.

2. Create a slide show for Farmer's Market West using Figure 7-63 as a guide. Save the project as **Market Show** in the Tutorial.07\Case4 folder provided with your Data Files.

Keep the following information in mind as you create the slide show:

- The 14 photos you need are in the Tutorial.07\Case4 folder provided with your Data Files.
- Be sure to save your work after making a significant change to the project.

Figure 7-63

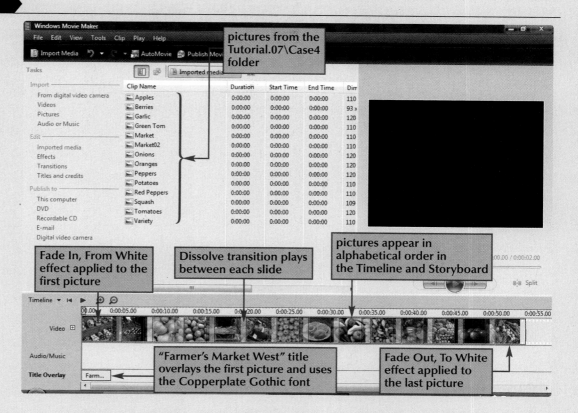

3. Submit the results of the preceding steps to your instructor, either in printed or electronic form, as requested.

Assess | **SAM Assessment and Training**

If you have a SAM user profile, you may have access to hands-on instruction, practice, and assessment of the skills covered in this tutorial. Log in to your SAM account (**http://sam2007.course.com**) to launch any assigned training activities or exams that relate to the skills covered in this tutorial.

Review | **Quick Check Answers**

Session 7.1

1. pixels
2. Paste From
3. false
4. Click the canvas, and then drag a selection handle.
5. outline or border, fill or inside color
6. Fill With Color

Session 7.2

1. False
2. Only Windows Photo Gallery lets you edit the photos to fix problems with lighting or color, to crop an image, and to remove red eye.
3. Click the Thumbnail View button to sort the thumbnails by filename, and then click the Thumbnail View button and select Thumbnails with Text.
4. Auto Adjust
5. True
6. Photos from a digital camera are usually large, and e-mail works best with small file attachments.

Session 7.3

1. playlist
2. True
3. audio and data CDs
4. importing media such as video, pictures, and music
5. False
6. Publish the movie project.

Ending Data Files

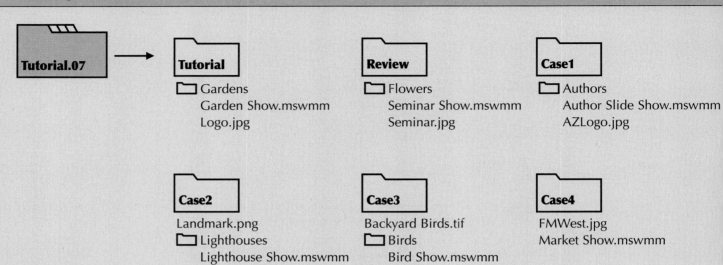

Tutorial.07 →

Tutorial
- Gardens
  - Garden Show.mswmm
  - Logo.jpg

Review
- Flowers
  - Seminar Show.mswmm
  - Seminar.jpg

Case1
- Authors
  - Author Slide Show.mswmm
  - AZLogo.jpg

Case2
- Landmark.png
- Lighthouses
  - Lighthouse Show.mswmm

Case3
- Backyard Birds.tif
- Birds
  - Bird Show.mswmm

Case4
- FMWest.jpg
- Market Show.mswmm

Objectives

Session 8.1
- Manage mobile computing devices
- Present information to an audience
- Explore network concepts
- Manage network connections

Session 8.2
- Connect to another computer
- Access shared network folders
- Synchronize folders
- Allow remote access to your computer

Connecting to Networks with Mobile Computing

Accessing Network Resources

Case | KATE Consultants

Kevin Adelson and Tay Endres are partners in KATE Consultants, a firm in Portland, Oregon, that provides financial and management consulting to businesses throughout western Oregon. Founded in the last two years, KATE is one of the fastest growing consulting firms in the state. Kevin and Tay attribute most of their success to their "roving professional" service, which involves working at a client's site to gather management, financial, and other business information and then provide analysis and advice. In addition, KATE consultants help clients set up business systems ranging from databases and custom programs to small networks.

You have been working for KATE as an associate for a few months, specializing in helping clients upgrade to Microsoft Windows Vista. Kevin and Tay are preparing to visit their client Rowley & Klein, a small law firm in Klamath Falls that wants to automate more of its operations. After an initial consultation, Kevin and Tay are returning to the law firm and ask you to accompany them. They plan to create a custom database for the firm and configure its wireless network. Kevin has developed a presentation to describe the details of the proposed database and show what it can do. He wants you to help him prepare his computer for the presentation, and then set it up when you arrive. Tay asks you to work with him to manage the wireless network so Rowley & Klein can use it effectively. He knows how to perform networking tasks in earlier versions of Windows, but not in Windows Vista. Because Kevin plans to work on his laptop computer during the five-hour drive to Klamath Falls, he also asks you to change mobility settings on his computer so he can use it during the trip without worrying about losing power or disturbing you and Tay.

In this tutorial, you will explore mobile computing, including maintaining power and accessing other computing resources. You will also examine network concepts and learn how to connect two or more computers in a network, and then use the network to share files, folders, and resources.

Starting Data Files

There are no starting Data Files needed for this tutorial.

Session 8.1

Managing Mobile Computing Devices

A **mobile computing device**, or a **mobile personal computer (PC)**, is a computer you can easily carry, such as a laptop, notebook, or Tablet PC. Currently, more people are buying mobile PCs than desktop PCs, preferring their portability and flexibility. Although a desktop PC must be plugged into a power source and use cables to connect most of its components and devices, a mobile PC contains all of its necessary parts in a single package, including a display screen, processor, keyboard, and pointing device. See Figure 8-1.

| Figure 8-1 | Comparing desktop and mobile computers |

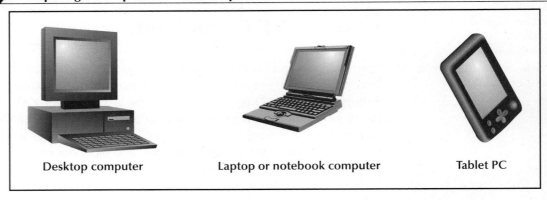

Desktop computer   Laptop or notebook computer   Tablet PC

The terms **laptop computer** and **notebook computer** are interchangeable, although *laptop* is the older term and *notebook* is sometimes associated with a smaller, lighter computer. Both refer to portable computers smaller than the average briefcase and light enough to carry comfortably. A laptop or notebook has a flat screen and keyboard that fold together and a battery pack that provides power for a few hours so that you don't have to plug the computer into a wall outlet. A **Tablet PC** is smaller than a laptop or notebook, and works like an electronic slate. You use a stylus and a touch screen to make selections and enter information instead of using a keyboard and a pointing device.

Contemporary mobile computers are just as powerful as desktops and let you use your computer almost anywhere, especially while traveling and meeting with others. However, the portability of mobile computers introduces two problems that desktop computers typically do not have: managing power and keeping your files synchronized. When you're using a notebook computer while traveling, for example, you need a way to conserve battery power so you don't lose data or have to shut down unexpectedly. If you do some of your work on a mobile computer, such as at a client meeting, and other work at a desktop computer, especially one connected to a network, you need a way to update the files stored on your desktop computer or network with the work you did at your client's site and vice versa.

Windows Vista solves these problems with the Mobility Center, power plans, and the Sync Center. The **Mobility Center** organizes mobile computer controls into a single location. These controls let you view and adjust the settings you use most often on a mobile computer, including the screen brightness, speaker volume, and battery status. While working in the Mobility Center, you can also select a **power plan**, a collection of hardware and system settings that define how a computer consumes power. For example, you can choose a plan designed to minimize power consumption, maximize system performance, or strike a balance between the two. The Mobility Center also provides access to the **Sync Center**, a place where you can move files from one PC, such as a notebook computer, to another device, such as a desktop PC, network computer, portable music player, digital camera, or mobile phone. While moving the files, the Sync Center helps you maintain consistency among two or more versions of the same file stored in different locations, so you don't use an out-of-date file on a portable device, for example, when you have a more current version on your desktop PC.

Using the Mobility Center

The Mobility Center provides a small control panel for managing a mobile computer. Although hardware vendors can add and change features in the Mobility Center, by default Windows Vista lets you adjust power settings such as the brightness of the computer screen, the speaker volume, and the current power-saving scheme. If your mobile computer is equipped to access a wireless network, the Mobility Center displays your network status (connected or not connected) and lets you quickly open the Network and Sharing Center, which you'll explore later in this tutorial. The Mobility Center also lets you manage settings you often need when you are working away from your desk, such as those for synchronizing files, using an external display, and controlling what appears on a projector when you give a presentation. See Figure 8-2.

Windows Mobility Center ◀ **Figure 8-2**

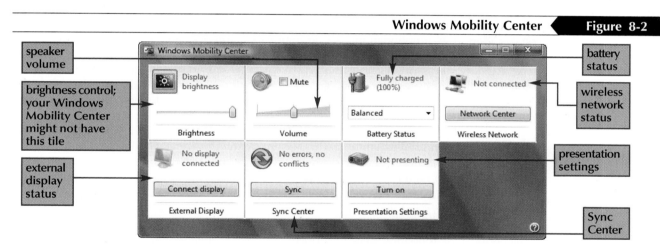

Each control in the Mobility Center is called a tile. Although not shown in Figure 8-2, if you use a Tablet PC, the Mobility Center includes a Screen Orientation tile for setting the screen orientation of your Tablet PC. Also, your Mobility Center might not include a Brightness tile for dimming or increasing the brightness of your screen. Computer manufacturers sometimes remove this tile if their hardware provides a brightness control. Figure 8-3 describes the purpose of each tile.

Figure 8-3 ▶ **Settings in the Windows Mobility Center**

Tile	Description
Brightness	Dim or increase the brightness of your screen.
Volume	Use the slider to control the volume of the computer's speakers or mute the speakers to turn off the sound completely.
Battery Status	Select a power scheme that suits how you are working with your computer.
Wireless Network	View whether your computer is connected to a wireless network, and access the Windows Vista Network and Sharing Center.
Orientation	Set the screen orientation on your Tablet PC to portrait or landscape.
External Display	Connect your computer to another monitor or projector.
Sync Center	Open the Sync Center to identify devices containing files to synchronize and then exchange information.
Presentation Settings	Control what appears on a projector when your computer is connected to one.

Setting Speaker Volume

You can set the speaker volume using the Volume tile in the Mobility Center or the speaker icon in your notification area. In both cases, you drag a slider to increase or decrease the volume. As you drag, a ScreenTip displays the current volume setting, which ranges from a low of 0 to a high of 100. When you stop dragging, Windows plays a sound at the current volume so you can hear how loud or soft it is. You can also use the Volume tile or the speaker icon to mute sound, which effectively turns off the speakers. You use the same controls to turn the sound back on.

As you help Kevin prepare for your trip to Klamath Falls, you ask him what type of work he wants to do on his laptop computer during the drive. He says he is planning to view the presentation he will give to Rowley & Klein. Because the presentation includes audio, you suggest he turn off the speakers on his laptop during the trip so that the presentation does not distract Tay while he is driving. You'll show Kevin how to test the volume of the speakers and then mute them using the Windows Mobility Center. Note the original volume setting so you can restore it later.

To perform the following steps or most of the steps in this tutorial, you need to be working on a mobile PC such as a laptop computer. If you are not working on a mobile PC, read but do not perform the steps.

To open Windows Mobility Center and adjust the speaker volume:

▶ **1.** Click the **Start** button 🟦 on the taskbar, point to **All Programs**, click **Accessories**, and then click **Windows Mobility Center**. The Windows Mobility Center opens as shown in Figure 8-2.

▶ **2.** To test the speaker volume, drag the **Volume** slider to **30**. Windows plays a sound at that volume.

  Trouble? If your speakers are already set to 30, drag the Volume slider to 40.

▶ **3.** Click the **Mute** check box to insert a check mark. Windows turns the speakers off.

Tip

You can also open the Mobility Center by opening Control Panel, clicking Mobile PC, and then clicking Windows Mobility Center.

Now that you've shown Kevin how to control the volume of his notebook speakers, you'll demonstrate how to manage battery power with power plans.

Selecting a Power Plan

One advantage of mobile PCs over desktop computers is that you can use mobile PCs without plugging them into a power outlet. Instead, mobile PCs get the power they need from a battery, which is usually installed within the computer case. However, even with recent improvements in battery cell technology, you can use a mobile computer powered by a battery for only a limited time before you need to recharge the battery. You can track the status of the battery charge in the Windows Mobility Center and in the notification area of the taskbar. Both places display a battery meter icon that shows how much charge remains in the battery. See Figure 8-4.

Battery status   **Figure 8-4**

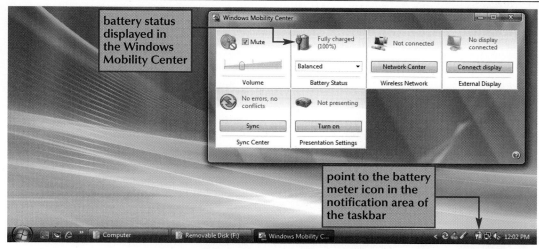

Although a battery meter icon always appears on the taskbar of a mobile computer, it can also appear on a desktop computer that is plugged into an uninterruptible power supply (UPS) or other short-term battery device. If your computer has more than one battery, you can click the battery meter icon in the notification area of the taskbar to display the charge remaining on one battery, click it again to see the charge remaining on the second battery, and so on. Point to the battery meter icon to see the combined charge.

You can also point to the battery meter icon to display the amount of time and percentage of battery power remaining. The battery meter icon changes appearance to display the current state of the battery so that you can see how much charge remains even when you are not pointing to the icon. When the battery charge is above 25 percent, the battery icon is green. When the battery charge reaches 25 percent, a yellow warning sign appears on the icon. When the charge is 10 percent or lower, a critical sign appears and Windows displays a notification so you can recharge the battery. See Figure 8-5.

Changes in the battery meter icon   **Figure 8-5**

Your mobile PC is plugged in and the battery is charging	**Battery is fully charged**	**Your mobile PC is running on battery power**	**Battery charge is low**	**Battery charge is critical**

Besides displaying the percentage of charge remaining in the battery, the battery meter icon and the Battery Status tile in the Mobility Center display your current power plan. Recall that a power plan is a collection of hardware and system settings that manages how your computer uses and conserves power. To match how you are using your mobile computer with how it consumes energy, you select a power plan. Windows Vista provides three default plans that let you save energy, maximize system performance, or balance energy conservation with system performance. The three default plans are called Power saver, High performance, and Balanced, and are described in Figure 8-6.

Figure 8-6 ▶ **Default power plans**

Power Plan	Description
Power saver	Saves power on your mobile computer by reducing system performance and extending battery life
High performance	Provides the highest level of performance on your mobile computer but consumes the most energy
Balanced	Balances energy consumption and system performance by adjusting your computer's processor speed to match your activity

You can select a power plan by clicking the Change power settings button in the Mobility Center or by clicking the battery icon in the notification area of the taskbar and then clicking a power plan option button. Most mobile computers include the kind of hardware Windows Vista expects to support power management settings. However, if your computer does not have the proper kind of hardware or if Windows cannot identify it, the Battery Status button or battery icon menu displays only the plans your computer supports.

Reference Window | **Selecting a Power Plan**

- Click the Start button, point to All Programs, click Accessories, and then click Windows Mobility Center.
- Click the Change power settings button, and then click a power plan.

or

- Click the battery icon in the notification area of the taskbar.
- Click a power plan option button.

Because Kevin plans to run his laptop computer on battery power during the trip to Klamath Falls, you show him how to monitor his power consumption by pointing to the battery meter icon in the notification area of the taskbar. Next, you'll show him how to change his power plan to Power saver, which is designed for mobile computer users who are working away from power outlets for several hours. Note your original settings so you can restore them later.

To perform the following steps, you need to be working on a mobile PC such as a laptop computer. If you are not working on a mobile PC, read but do not perform the steps.

To change the power plan:

▶ **1.** In the Windows Mobility Center, click the **Change power settings** button, and then click **Power saver**.

Trouble? If your Battery Status is already set to Power saver, skip Step 1.

Trouble? If the Power saver setting is not available when you click the Battery Status button, skip Step 1.

▶ **2.** Minimize the Windows Mobility Center window.

If you are using the Aero experience, Windows sometimes turns off transparency when you are using the Power saver plan. If you don't want Windows to turn off transparency, switch to the Balanced plan.

Choosing a Power Plan | InSight

When working with mobile computers or desktop computers that are connected to a battery, choose a battery plan that best fits your current activities to conserve battery power and to save energy in general. If you are engaging in activities that don't require a lot of power, such as reading e-mail messages or listening to music, switch to the Power saver plan. If you need a lot of computing power, such as when you are working with complex spreadsheets or creating movies, use the High performance plan. If you are performing a variety of tasks, select the Balanced power plan so that the processor can run at full speed when you are playing a game or watching a video, but slow down to save power when you are checking your e-mail.

Kevin thinks the Power saver plan is perfect for conserving the battery charge while he's traveling. He can then change to the Balanced plan when he arrives in Klamath Falls, but wants to fine-tune that plan to suit his needs. During his presentation, he wants to use power settings that are not offered in any of the default plans. You'll show him how to modify a default plan and then create one of his own.

Customizing Power Options

If the default power plans provided by Windows Vista or your computer manufacturer do not address your power needs, you can change one of the default plans or create a new one. All of the plans specify how long the computer can be idle before Windows turns off the display and how long to wait before Windows puts the computer to sleep when you are using battery power or a wall outlet. When putting your computer to **sleep**, Windows saves your data and system settings in temporary memory and then suspends operations as it goes into a power-saving state. During sleep, the screen is blank and the computer does not perform any activities, which conserves power. In fact, while a mobile computer is asleep, it typically uses one to two percent of battery power per hour, which is a fraction of what it uses when running on full power. (You can put a computer to sleep yourself by clicking the Power button on the Start menu, pressing a sleep button if your mobile device has one, or closing the lid on your notebook computer.) To wake a mobile computer from sleep, you usually press the hardware power button. To wake a desktop computer, you usually move the mouse or press a key. In a few seconds, Windows displays the desktop in its presleep state, including open windows and running programs.

Besides changing sleep and displaying turn-off times for each default power plan, you can specify advanced settings such as whether to allow hybrid sleep and how long to wait before hibernating. **Hybrid sleep** is an alternative to sleep in which Windows saves your open documents and programs to temporary memory and to your hard disk and then goes into a low-power state. You resume from hybrid sleep the same way and almost as quickly as from sleep. The advantage is that if a power failure occurs while your computer is asleep, Windows can restore your documents because it saved them to your hard disk. If you turn on hybrid sleep and then click the Power button on the Start menu, Windows puts your computer into hybrid sleep instead of standard sleep. Note that not all computers support hybrid sleep.

Like hybrid sleep, **hibernation** saves your work to your hard disk and puts your computer into a power-saving state. However, it then turns off your computer. Of the three power-saving states in Windows Vista, hibernation uses the least amount of power. Because both sleep states require some power, Windows automatically puts a mobile computer into hibernation after a specified period of time. Windows also puts a mobile PC into hibernation when the battery charge is critically low. If you know that you won't use your mobile computer for a while and you can't charge the battery during that time, you should put your computer into hibernation yourself. To do so, click the Lock arrow button on the Start menu, and then click Hibernate.

In short, power plans include settings that determine how long Windows should wait before putting your computer into a power-saving state: sleep, hybrid sleep, or hibernation. You can also put your computer to sleep or hibernation yourself by using a button on the Start menu.

| InSight | **Choosing a Power-Saving State** |

Sleep, hybrid sleep, and hibernation are three power-saving states Windows uses to conserve battery power on mobile computers. Keep the following guidelines in mind when choosing a power-saving state:

- **Sleep**. If you are not planning to use your computer for several hours, Microsoft recommends putting it to sleep rather than turning it off. Sleep is preferable to turning off your computer because when you're ready to use your computer again, it wakes quickly so you can resume your work where you left it. If you put a computer to sleep yourself, be sure to save your data first so you don't lose it in case of a power failure. Even if you let Windows put your computer to sleep after a specified amount of idle time, standard sleep is the best power-saving state for average computing because it resumes operations faster than hybrid sleep or hibernation.
- **Hybrid sleep**. If you are concerned that you might lose power while the computer is asleep, such as when your battery charge is low and you cannot recharge it, turn on hybrid sleep so that Windows saves your data on the hard disk before it puts your computer to sleep.
- **Hibernation**. When you are finished working and know you won't use your mobile computer for a day or longer and that you won't have a chance to recharge the battery during that time, put the computer into hibernation yourself. Otherwise, you can generally let Windows determine when to use hibernation.

Modifying a Power Plan

When you modify a power plan, you can adjust up to two basic settings and dozens of advanced settings that apply when your computer is running on battery power and when your computer is plugged into a power outlet. For example, in the Balanced plan, Windows is set to turn off the display after five minutes of idle time if the computer is using battery power and after 20 minutes of inactivity if the computer is plugged into an outlet. You can increase or decrease these times in the Edit Plan Settings window, which you open from the Power Options category (in Hardware and Sound) in Control Panel. To change advanced settings, such as whether to use hybrid sleep instead of standard sleep, click the Change plan settings link in the Power Options window, and then click Change advanced power settings to open the Power Options dialog box.

Modifying a Power Plan | Reference Window

- Click the Start button on the taskbar, and then click Control Panel.
- In Category view, click Hardware and Sound, and then click Power Options. In Classic view, double-click Power Options.
- Click Change plan settings for the power plan you want to modify.
- Click a button for a power setting, and then click the amount of time to wait before applying the setting.
- Click Change advanced power settings.
- Expand an advanced setting, change the setting, and then click the OK button.
- Click the Save changes button.

Kevin wants to make two changes to the Balanced power plan on his mobile computer. First, he wants Windows to wait for more than 20 minutes of idle time before it turns off the display when his computer is plugged in. During his presentation, members of the audience might raise questions that lead him to step away from his computer for more than 20 minutes of discussion. Also, because he has only one copy of the presentation on his laptop, he wants to take an extra precaution to prevent losing that document if a power outage occurs while his computer is asleep. You'll show Kevin how to change basic and advanced settings for the Balanced power plan.

To change basic power plan settings:

1. If the Power Options window is not open, click **Control Panel Home** in the left pane of the Control Panel window, click **Hardware and Sound**, and then click **Power Options**. The Power Options window opens. See Figure 8-7.

> **Tip**
>
> You can also open the Power Options window by clicking the battery icon in the notification area and then clicking More power options.

Power Options window ◄ **Figure 8-7**

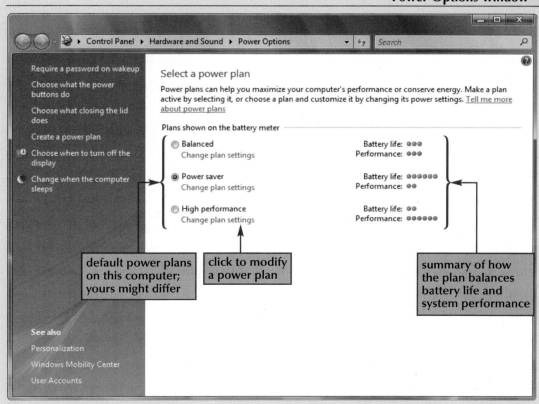

This window lists power plans on the left; on the right, it summarizes how each plan balances battery life with system performance.

2. Click **Change plan settings** for the Balanced power plan. The Edit Plan Settings window opens for the Balanced plan. See Figure 8-8. Your settings might differ. If you are using a desktop computer, your options also differ.

Figure 8-8 ▶ **Edit Plan Settings window**

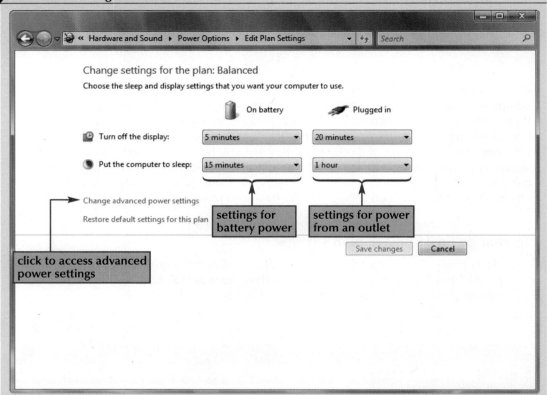

3. For the Turn off the display setting, click the **arrow button** in the Plugged in column, and then click **30 minutes**.

   Trouble? If you are working on a desktop computer, click the arrow button for the Turn off the display setting, and then click 30 minutes.

4. Click the **Save changes** button. Windows saves the new setting and closes the Edit Plan Settings window.

You can change the other basic power plan settings the same way—click a button for the Turn off the display or Put the computer to sleep setting, and then select an amount of idle time Windows should wait before activating that setting. You can turn off the setting by selecting Never. For example, if you do not want Windows to put the computer to sleep when it's plugged in, click the arrow button in the Plugged in column for the Put the computer to sleep setting, and then click Never. However, you might lose data if you prevent a mobile computer from sleeping or hibernating and the battery runs out of power.

Next, you'll show Kevin how to use hybrid sleep instead of sleep as an extra precaution to prevent losing updates he makes to his presentation. To do so, you need to change an advanced power plan setting.

To change advanced power plan settings:

▶ **1.** In the Power Options window, click **Change plan settings** for the Balanced power plan to open the Edit Plan Settings window again.

▶ **2.** Click **Change advanced power settings** to open the Power Options dialog box. See Figure 8-9.

Power Options dialog box ◀ Figure 8-9

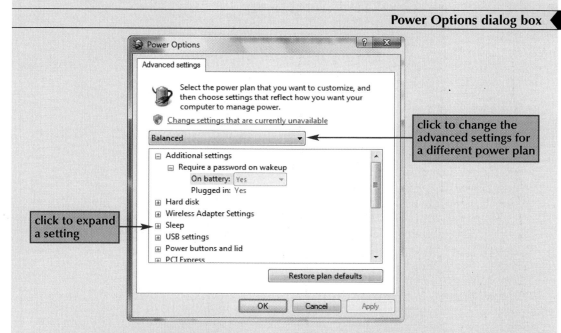

▶ **3.** Click the **expand** button ⊞ for the Sleep setting, and then click the **expand** button ⊞ for the Allow hybrid sleep setting. See Figure 8-10. If you are using a desktop computer, your options differ.

Preparing to allow hybrid sleep ◀ Figure 8-10

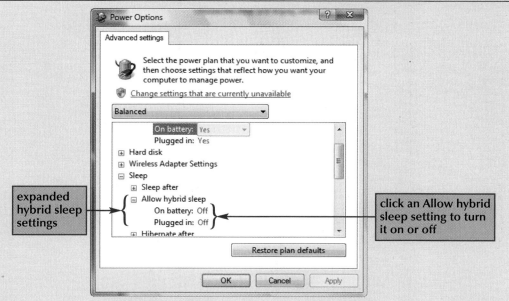

> **Trouble?** If the Allow hybrid sleep setting is not included in your Power Options dialog box, skip Step 3 and read but do not perform the remaining steps.
>
> ▶ **4.** Click **On battery**, click the **Off** button, and then click **On**.
>
> **Trouble?** If you are working on a desktop computer, click Setting below Allow hybrid sleep, click the Off button, and then click On. Skip Step 5.
>
> ▶ **5.** Click **Plugged in**, click the **Off** button, and then click **On**.
>
> ▶ **6.** Click the **OK** button to close the Power Options dialog box.
>
> ▶ **7.** Click the **Back** button ⊙ to return to the Power Options window.

You've changed basic and advanced settings in Kevin's Balanced power plan. Next, you'll show him how to create a power plan based on one of the default plans.

Creating a Power Plan

Creating a power plan is similar to modifying one—you customize the basic settings in one of the default plans and then save it with a new name. If you want to adjust advanced settings, you modify the new plan. To start, you select a default plan on which to base the new plan. Because the battery meter icon in the notification area and the Battery Status button in the Mobility Center display only three power plans, the new power plan you create replaces the base default plan in those lists.

After Kevin makes his presentation to the law firm, he'll meet with the partners in a conference room. He's not sure he can plug his notebook into a power outlet there, so he wants to be prepared to use battery power instead. During the meeting, he'll probably make some notes and might need to edit the presentation, which will serve as his proposal to the firm. He needs a little more battery power than the Power saver plan offers, but not as much as the Balanced plan requires. In addition, he does not want to change the settings in those two default plans—they both suit his needs in other circumstances. Instead, you'll create a power plan for him that uses settings that fall between the two default plans. Because Kevin will use the Balanced, Power saver, and your new plan, you'll base the new plan on the High performance plan, which Windows will hide when it displays the battery meter and Battery Status button lists.

To create a power plan:

▶ **1.** In the Power Options window, click **Create a power plan** in the left pane. The Create a Power Plan window opens. See Figure 8-11.

Create a power plan window ◀ Figure 8-11

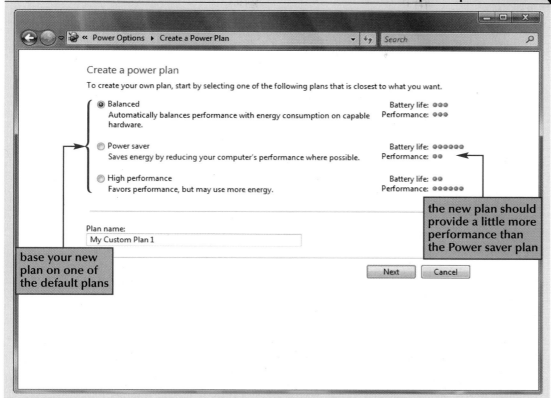

▶ **2.** Click the **High performance** option button to base the new plan on the High performance default plan.

▶ **3.** Type **Conference** in the Plan name text box, and then click the **Next** button. The Edit Plan Settings window opens, the same window you used earlier.

▶ **4.** For the Turn off the display setting, click the **arrow button** in the On battery column, and then click **5 minutes**.

   Trouble? If you are using a desktop computer, click the arrow button for the Turn off the display setting, and then click 5 minutes.

▶ **5.** For the Put the computer to sleep setting, click the **arrow button** in the On battery column, and then click **30 minutes**.

   Trouble? If you are using a desktop computer, click the arrow button for the Put the computer to sleep setting, and then click 30 minutes.

▶ **6.** Click the **Create** button to close the Edit Plan Settings dialog box. The new Conference plan is now selected in the Power Options window.

The High performance plan now appears in a category titled Hide additional plans, meaning Windows does not display it when you click the battery meter icon in the notification area or the Battery Status button in the Mobility Center. If you're using a *mobile PC*, the Conference plan appears in the category titled Plans that is shown on the battery.

Selecting Other Power Options

Besides using power plans, you can control other power settings, such as what Windows should do when you press the hardware power button or close the lid on your mobile PC. You can apply the following settings to all of your power plans or only to a specific plan.

- **Define power button and lid settings**. Recall that by default, Windows puts a mobile computer to sleep when you press the hardware power button or close the lid. It also puts the computer to sleep when you press the hardware sleep button (if your computer has one). You can change the power button, sleep button, and lid settings to hibernate, shut down, or do nothing when your computer is running on battery power or is plugged in.
- **Password protection on wakeup**. If you log on to your computer by providing a password, Windows locks your computer for security when it sleeps and requires that password to unlock the computer when it wakes from sleep. This is especially helpful if you need to protect confidential information on your computer. However, if you're the only one who uses your computer and you use it at home or another private place, you can change this setting if you don't want to enter a password every time your computer wakes.

Kevin is in the habit of using the Power button on the Start menu to put his notebook computer to sleep and likes having the computer go to sleep when he closes the lid, which he does when he moves the computer. However, if his computer is running on battery power, he wants to save the battery charge by having the computer hibernate and eventually turn off when he presses the hardware power button on the computer case. In addition, although he wants to maintain password protection during the trip to Klamath Falls, he wants to know how to turn off the password protection on wake-up setting so he doesn't need to provide the password when he works from home. You'll show Kevin how to change the power button and password protection on wake-up settings.

To change power options:

1. In the Power Options window, click **Choose what the power buttons do** in the left pane. The System Settings window opens. See Figure 8-12. If you are using a desktop computer, your options differ.

System Settings window   Figure 8-12

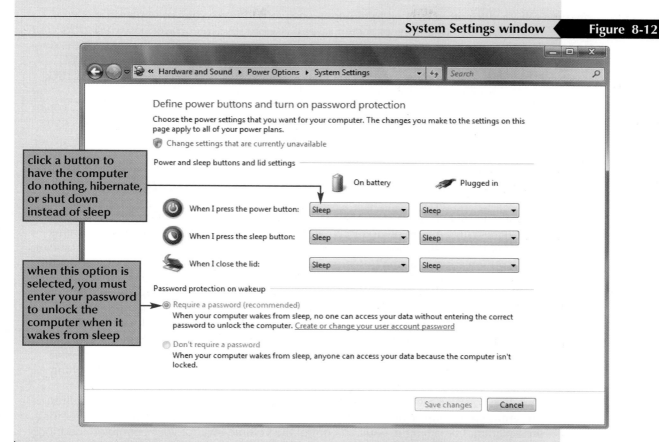

click a button to have the computer do nothing, hibernate, or shut down instead of sleep

when this option is selected, you must enter your password to unlock the computer when it wakes from sleep

▶ **2.** For the When I press the power button setting, click the **arrow button** in the On battery column, and then click **Hibernate**.

Trouble? If you are using a desktop computer, click the arrow button for the When I press the power button setting, and then click Hibernate.

▶ **3.** Click the **Don't require a password** option button. This means that when your computer wakes from sleep, it is unlocked and anyone can access your data and settings.

Trouble? If this option is unavailable, click the "change settings that are currently unavailable" link, and then click the Continue button.

▶ **4.** Click the **Require a password (recommended)** option button. This means that when your computer wakes from sleep, it is locked and you or another user must enter your Windows password to unlock it.

▶ **5.** Click the **Save changes** button.

▶ **6.** Close the Power Options window.

The change you made to the power button now applies to all of the power plans on Kevin's computer. To make these changes to only a particular power plan, you open the Edit Plan Settings window, and then open the Advanced settings tab in the Power Options dialog box as you did earlier, and then change the Require a password on wakeup and Power buttons and lid settings.

If you turn off the setting to require a password to wake your computer from sleep, you should also turn off your screen saver password. (A screen saver password locks your computer when the screen saver is on. The screen saver password is the same as the one you use to log on to Windows.) To turn off the screen saver password, open Control Panel, click Appearance and Personalization, click Change screen saver, and then click the On resume, display logon screen check box to remove the check mark.

Now that you've shown Kevin how to control the power state of his mobile PC, you're ready for the trip to Klamath Falls. When you arrive, you can help him prepare his computer for the presentation to Rowley & Klein.

Presenting Information to an Audience

Giving a presentation is a common practice in business and education. When you use a computer to give a presentation to an audience, you can combine images, text, animation, sound and visual effects, and audio to educate, inform, or entertain others. You can give a presentation to a small or large group of people while you are in the same room, or you can present the information remotely to people with whom you share a network connection. To create a presentation, you can use Microsoft Office PowerPoint, Windows Movie Maker, the slide show feature in the Pictures folder, or any other presentation program. You can then connect your computer to a projector to broadcast the presentation or use Windows Meeting Space to share the presentation with others. To start and control the presentation, you use the keyboard and pointing device on your computer and the tools provided in the presentation program to perform tasks such as switching from one image or slide to another and ending the presentation.

Before you give a presentation, you can use the Windows Mobility Center to adjust **presentation settings**, which are a collection of options that prepare your computer for a presentation. For example, you can control the volume level of your computer and block distractions such as notifications and reminders. You can also use the Mobility Center to connect your computer to an external display, such as a larger monitor or projector. To connect to a network projector, which is a projecting device connected to your network, you can use the Connect to a Network Projector wizard, an accessory program available on the Start menu.

Preparing a Computer for a Presentation

Using the Windows Mobility Center, you can specify the settings that Windows Vista uses when you are giving a presentation. By default, your computer stays awake and Windows blocks notifications during a presentation. You can also choose to turn off the screen saver, adjust the speaker volume, and change your desktop background image. Windows saves these settings and applies them when you turn on presentation settings in the Windows Mobility Center. To turn on presentation settings, you can click the Turn on button in the Presentation Settings tile of the Windows Mobility Center. Windows also turns on presentation settings when you connect your mobile PC to a network projector or additional monitor. To turn off presentation settings, you can click the Turn off button in the Mobility Center. Windows also turns off presentation settings when you disconnect your computer from a projector or when you shut down or log off from your PC.

Now that you, Kevin, and Tay have arrived in Klamath Falls, you have some time to prepare for Kevin's presentation, which he'll give in the Rowley & Klein conference room. First, you'll customize the presentation settings to turn off the screen saver, turn up the volume, and change the desktop background to black. Then you'll show Kevin how to turn the presentation settings on and off. Note your original settings so you can restore them later.

To perform the following steps, you need to be working on a mobile PC such as a laptop computer. If you are not working on a mobile PC, read but do not perform the steps.

To customize presentation settings:

▶ **1.** Restore the Windows Mobility Center window.

▶ **2.** In the Presentation Settings tile, click the **Change presentation settings** icon . The Presentation Settings dialog box opens. See Figure 8-13.

Presentation Settings dialog box ◀ **Figure 8-13**

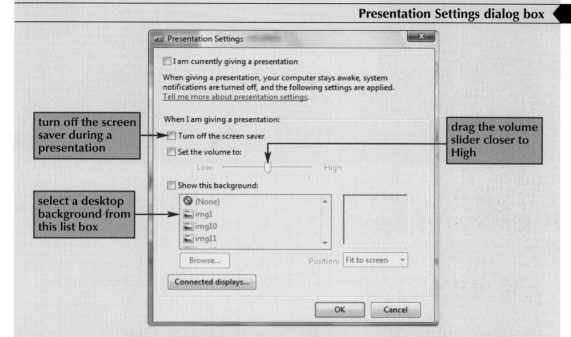

turn off the screen saver during a presentation

select a desktop background from this list box

drag the volume slider closer to High

▶ **3.** Click the **Turn off the screen saver** check box.

▶ **4.** Click the **Set the volume to:** check box, and then drag the slider to **85**.

▶ **5.** Click the **Show this background:** check box, and then click **(None)**.

▶ **6.** Click the **OK** button.

Now Windows will turn off the screen saver, turn up the speaker volume, and display a black desktop background when Kevin turns on the presentation settings, which you'll show him how to do next.

Tip

To change the screen saver delay time, right-click the desktop, click Personalize, click Screen Saver, and then change the minutes value in the Wait box.

To turn presentation settings on and off:

▶ **1.** In the Presentation Settings tile, click the **Turn on** button. The presentation icon appears in the notification area of the taskbar. See Figure 8-14.

Figure 8-14 ▶ **Turning on presentation settings**

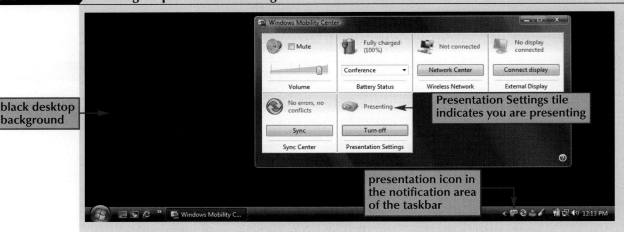

black desktop background

Presentation Settings tile indicates you are presenting

presentation icon in the notification area of the taskbar

It's not yet time for Kevin's presentation, so you can turn off the settings for now.

▶ **2.** In the Presentation Settings tile, click the **Turn off** button.

▶ **3.** Minimize the Windows Mobility Center window.

Next, you'll help Kevin select display settings when he connects his notebook computer to a projector.

Displaying Information on an External Display Device

When you connect a mobile PC to a projector or any other type of additional display device such as a flat-screen monitor, Windows Vista detects the extra display and applies the video settings that correspond to that device. It then opens the New Display Detected dialog box so you can customize display settings such as resolution and color depth and choose how you want your desktop to appear on the additional display device. When you connect an external display device to a mobile PC, the computer's screen is called the primary monitor or display and the external device is called the secondary monitor or display. Use the New Display Detected dialog box to select one of the display options described in Figure 8-15.

Display options in the New Display Detected dialog box   Figure 8-15

Display Option	Description	When to Use
Mirrored	Duplicates your desktop on each display device	When you are giving a presentation on a projector or a fixed display, such as a TV-type monitor
Extended	Extends your desktop across all of your display devices	When you want to increase your work space, such as by displaying one program window on your primary monitor and another window on a secondary monitor
External display only	Shows your desktop on the external display devices, but not on your mobile PC screen	When you want to conserve battery power

When you disconnect the external display device, Windows restores the original display settings to your primary monitor. It also moves all open files and program windows to the primary display. The next time that you connect the same monitor, Windows automatically applies the display settings that you used the last time that you connected this monitor.

Connecting to an External Display Device | Reference Window

- Connect your mobile computer to an external display device, such as a projector or secondary monitor.
- If Windows does not automatically detect the external display and open the New Display Detected dialog box, open the Windows Mobility Center and then click the Connect display button in the External Display tile.
- Click the appropriate option button to mirror (the default), extend, or show your desktop on the external display only.
- If you are extending your desktop, click the Left or Right option button to extend your desktop in one of these directions.
- Click the OK button.

Before adding a second display device to your computer, make sure that you have a video card that supports multiple monitors or that your computer has more than one video card. A video card that supports multiple monitors has two video ports—check the back of your computer to find these ports. Turn off your computer before connecting the second display device. When you turn on your computer, Windows should recognize the secondary monitor and open the New Display Detected dialog box.

Kevin connects his notebook computer to the projector in the conference room. When the New Display Detected dialog box opens, you click the OK button to accept the mirrored setting. Kevin's desktop is now displayed on his notebook and is projected on a large white screen in the conference room.

Connecting to a Network Projector

As you'll learn shortly, you can share resources such as Internet access and a printer if you connect your computer to one or more other computers to form a network. (**Network resources** are files, folders, software, and hardware devices that computers on a network can access.) If you are connected to a network that includes a projector as one of its shared resources, you can use that network projector to give a presentation from a desktop or mobile computer. To do so, you use the Connect to a Network Projector Wizard, which guides you through the steps of connecting to any available projector on your network. You can use the wizard to connect to a network projector in one of two ways: select from a list of available projectors or enter the network address of the projector. See Figure 8-16.

Figure 8-16 | **Starting the Connect to a Network Projector Wizard**

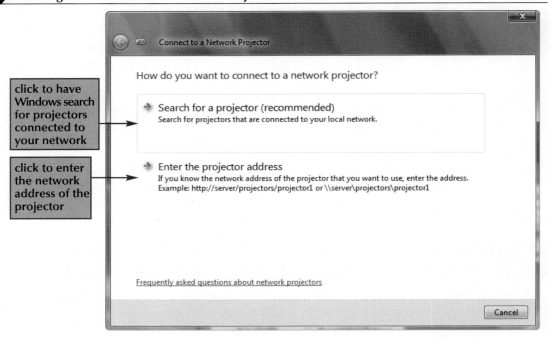

click to have Windows search for projectors connected to your network

click to enter the network address of the projector

When you choose to search for a projector with the Connect to a Network Projector Wizard, Windows searches for projectors on your network, and then displays up to five projectors that you have used recently. To use one of these projectors, you select it from the list. If you want to use a different projector, you can enter the projector's network address, which you can enter as a URL such as http://server/projectors/projector01 or as a path such as \\server\projectors\projector01. (The wizard can only find a network projector if the projector is connected to the same network segment to which your computer is connected.) However, when you enter a projector's network address, the wizard can find the projector regardless of where it's located on the network.

Reference Window | **Connecting to a Network Projector**

- Click the Start button on the taskbar, point to All Programs, click Accessories, and then click Connect to a Network Projector. If you are asked for permission to connect, click Yes. If you are then asked for permission to continue, click the Continue button.
- Select Search for a projector (recommended) or Enter the projector address.
- Click an available projector in the list or enter the network address, enter the projector password, if necessary, and then click the Connect button.

After you finish using the wizard to connect to a network projector, a Network Presentation icon appears in the notification area of the taskbar. You can click the icon to open the Network Presentation dialog box to pause, resume, or end your presentation by disconnecting your computer from the network projector.

Because Kevin can use the projector in Rowley & Klein's conference room, he doesn't need to use a network projector. However, after you help Tay configure the law firm's network, Kevin can use the Connect to a Network Projector Wizard to remotely connect to the law firm's projector if necessary.

Exploring Network Concepts

As you know, a **network** is a collection of computers and other hardware devices linked together so they can exchange data and share hardware and software. If more than one person uses a computer at work or home, networks offer many advantages. Groups of computers on a network can use the same printer, so you don't have to purchase a printer for each computer. Network computers can also share an Internet connection, so you don't need to purchase and install a broadband modem for each computer. Networks also facilitate group projects because one person can save a document in a folder that other users on other computers can access. A network also improves communication in a company because coworkers can easily share news and information.

Large companies that want to connect their computers on a network usually hire a team of network specialists to determine what type of hardware the company should purchase and how to connect the devices to form a **local area network (LAN)**, a network of computers and other hardware devices that reside in the same physical space, such as an office building. Small office and home users can set up a simplified LAN to enjoy the advantages of networking. Like large companies, you also need to decide what type of network technology and hardware you will use if you want to set up a small network. (**Network technology** is the way computers connect to one another.) The most common types of network technology for a small office or home network are wireless, Ethernet, and home phone line (HPNA). These are compared in Figure 8-17.

Comparing network technologies | Figure 8-17

Network Technology	How It Sends Information Between Computers	Pros	Cons
Wireless	Uses radio waves, microwaves, or infrared light	Setting up the network and moving computers are easy because there are no cables.	Wireless technology is more expensive and often slower than Ethernet or HPNA. Wireless connections can be interrupted by interference.
Ethernet	Uses Ethernet cables	Ethernet is a proven and reliable technology, and Ethernet networks are inexpensive and fast.	Ethernet cables must connect each computer to a hub, switch, or router, which can be time consuming and difficult when the computers are in different rooms.
HPNA	Uses existing home telephone wires	You can connect computers without using hubs or switches.	You need a phone jack in each room where you want to have a computer, and all jacks must be on the same phone line.

Small office and home networks use a variety of special hardware, including the following devices:

- **Network adapters**. Also called network interface cards (NICs), these adapters connect computers to a network. Network adapters are often installed inside your computer, though you can also plug one into a USB port. See Figure 8-18.

| Figure 8-18 | Network interface card |

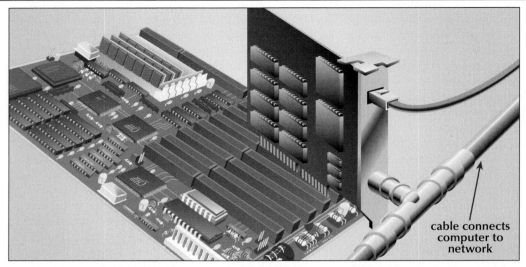

cable connects computer to network

- **Network hubs and switches**. Used on an Ethernet network, these devices connect two or more computers to the network.
- **Routers and access points**. Routers connect computers and networks to each other and let you share a single Internet connection among several computers. Wireless devices can connect to access points, which are cabled to wired networks. If you want to share an Internet connection over a wireless network, you need a wireless router or an access point.
- **Modems**. To connect your computer to the Internet, you need a modem, which sends and receives information over telephone or cable lines.
- **Cables**. On an Ethernet or HPNA network, cables connect computers to each other and to other devices, such as hubs and routers.

Figure 8-19 describes the hardware you need for each type of network technology.

Hardware needed for each type of network technology ◀ **Figure 8-19**

Network Technology	Hardware You Need
Wireless	• Wireless network adapter installed on each computer in the network • Wireless access point or router
Ethernet	• Ethernet network adapter on each computer in the network • Ethernet hub or switch if you want to connect more than two computers • Ethernet router if you want to connect more than two computers and share an Internet connection • Ethernet cables • Crossover cable if you want to connect two computers directly to each other and not use a hub, switch, or router
HPNA	• Home phone line network adapter on each computer in the network • Telephone cables

Setting Up a Small Office or Home Network

After you determine what type of network you want and acquire the hardware you need, you can set up a small office or home network by performing the following tasks:

• **Install the hardware**. Install the network adapters in the computers that need them, if necessary.

• **Set up an Internet connection**. If you want the network computers to access the Internet, set up a connection to the Internet. (See Appendix A for complete instructions.)

• **Connect the computers**. On an Ethernet network, you can use crossover cables to connect two computers in the same room. If you want to connect more than two computers or link computers in different rooms on an Ethernet network, you need a hub, switch, or router to connect the computers. Use a router to share an Internet connection. Connect the router to the computer that is connected to the modem.

If you only want to share an Internet connection on a wireless network, you can set up a wireless router and then use Windows Vista to connect to that network. If you want to also share files and printers, run the Set up a wireless router or access point wizard to guide you through the steps of adding computers and other devices to the network.

On an HPNA network, use cables to connect two or more computers.

• **Test the connections**. Turn on all the computers and devices, and then open the Network window by clicking the Start button and then clicking Network. In the Network window, an icon should appear for your computer and all the other computers and devices connected to the network.

If you only want to share an Internet connection on a wireless network, you need to complete two steps:

• Configure the wireless router to broadcast signals.
• Set up Windows Vista on each computer to receive the signals.

In the first step, you install a wireless router or wireless access point and configure it to start broadcasting and receiving information to and from your computer. Often, a wireless access point is built into your router or can be plugged into one of your router's ports. To have the router start broadcasting radio signals, you need to run the setup software provided with your router. The steps to run this software vary depending on your router, but usually, you need to provide a network name, or service set identifier (SSID), which is a name you use to identify your wireless network. You'll see this name later when you use Windows Vista to connect to your wireless network. The setup software also lets you turn on security settings to encrypt your data when you transmit it, which helps to prevent unauthorized people from accessing your data or your network. To do so, you need to provide a password so that you can access the network. See Figure 8-20.

| Figure 8-20 | Wireless network sharing an Internet connection |

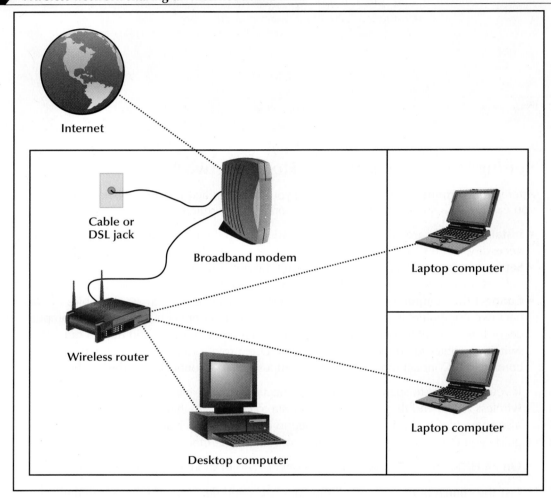

Internet

Cable or DSL jack

Broadband modem

Laptop computer

Wireless router

Desktop computer

Laptop computer

The following "Managing Network Connections" section shows you how to set up Windows Vista to receive the wireless signals.

If you want to share files and printers as well as an Internet connection on a wireless network, you first install a wireless router as described earlier in this section. Next, you run the Set up a wireless router or access point wizard on the computer that is connected to the wireless router. To start the wizard, open Control Panel in Category view, in the Network and Internet category click Set up file sharing, click Set up a connection or network, and then click Set up a wireless router or access point. The wizard guides you through the necessary steps, which vary depending on which operating system is running on each computer, the type of wireless technology your router uses, and the types of printers you want to connect. To save time, you can save your selections on a USB flash drive and then plug the USB flash drive into each computer you add to the network so it uses the same settings.

Managing Network Connections

After you connect two or more computers through cables or wireless connections, you can use Windows Vista to monitor and manage your network connections. If your network is set up to share a printer or Internet connection, Windows works behind the scenes to organize requests to use these resources. For example, if two people want to print documents at the same time on the network printer, Windows lines up the printer requests in a queue and prints the documents one after the other. It also lets all the network users share a single Internet connection so they can visit Web sites and exchange e-mail without interrupting each other. For other networking tasks, such as verifying you are connected to a network, finding and connecting to a wireless network, and determining which other computers are connected, you use the Network and Sharing Center window. See Figure 8-21.

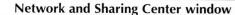 **Network and Sharing Center window** Figure 8-21

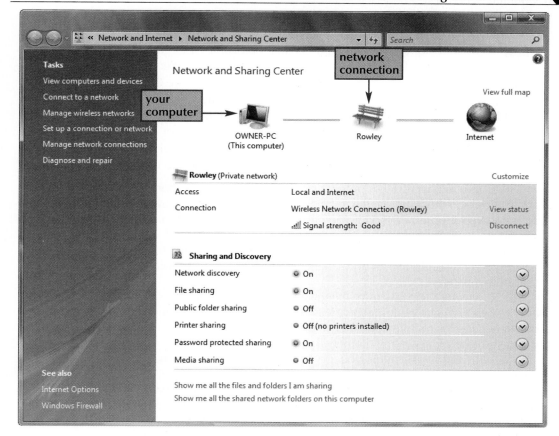

You can now show Tay how to connect his mobile PC to the Rowley & Klein wireless network. He has prepared some sample network policy documents and wants to copy them to a folder on the network that the Rowley & Klein partners can access. Tay might also need to retrieve a document stored on their network. Before he can perform those tasks, he needs to connect to the wireless network.

Connecting to a Wireless Network

If you have a mobile PC with a wireless network adapter, you can display a list of available wireless networks and then connect to one of those networks, whether it's your own private wireless network or a public one. You'll show Tay how to use the Mobility Center to open the Connect to a network window, which you can use to connect to available wireless networks. Windows displays the following information about each available wireless network:

- **Network name**. This is the SSID you or someone else provided when the network was set up. Because wireless signals extend past the boundaries of your home or office, the wireless adapter in your computer often detects more than one network within its range.
- **Security**. Unsecured networks don't require a password, whereas security-enabled networks do. Security-enabled networks also encrypt data before transmitting it, meaning that unauthorized people cannot intercept sensitive information such as a credit card number when you send it across the network. When you set up a wireless network, you can create a strong password or passphrase (more than one word). A **strong passphrase** includes at least 20 characters and is not a common phrase that other people are likely to know. If you don't create a passphrase, the network is protected with a network security key, which is usually a series of hexadecimal numbers.
- **Signal strength**. Windows displays a series of bars that indicate the strength of the signal. The more bars highlighted, the stronger the connection. The strongest signal (five bars highlighted) means that the wireless network is nearby or there is no interference. To improve the signal strength, you can move your computer closer to the wireless router or access point, or move the router or access point so it's not close to sources of interference such as brick walls or walls that contain metal support beams.

Unless you are accessing a public network, such as in an airport or hotel, be sure to connect only to the wireless network you are authorized to use, even if you can access an unsecured private network. If you are authorized to connect to more than one wireless network, you should generally use the one with the strongest signal. However, if an unsecured network has a stronger signal than a security-enabled one, it's safer for your data if you connect to the security-enabled network as long as you are an authorized user of that network.

The Rowley & Klein law firm already has a wireless network set up in their offices. Tay asks you to help him perform some basic tasks to manage the Rowley & Klein network by connecting his mobile computer to their wireless network. Frank Rowley gives you the passphrase for accessing the network, which is R&Kuser10 klamath Law01.

The following steps assume you are not connected to a network and are equipped to connect to a wireless network named Rowley. Substitute the name of your network and your network password when you perform the following steps. If you are already connected to a network or are not equipped to connect to a wireless network, read but do not perform the following steps.

To connect to a wireless network:

▶ **1.** In the Windows Mobility Center, click the **Change wireless network settings** icon 🖥️ . The Connect to a network window opens. See Figure 8-22.

Connect to a network window ◀ Figure 8-22

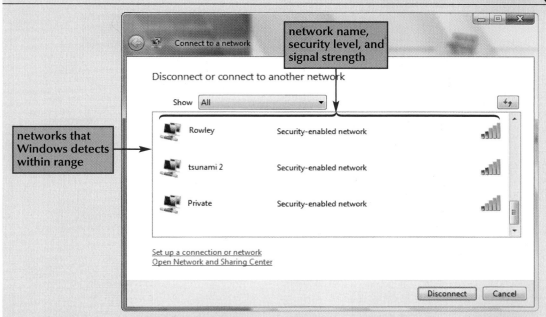

networks that Windows detects within range

network name, security level, and signal strength

2. Click your network, such as **Rowley**, in the list of available networks, and then click the **Connect** button. A dialog box opens requesting your security key or passphrase.

Trouble? If your network is not listed in the Connect to a network window, the signal strength might be low. Move your computer closer to the wireless router or access point, if possible, and then click the Refresh button.

Trouble? If your network is not listed in the Connect to a network window, but one or more networks are listed as *Unnamed Network*, click an unnamed network, click Connect, and then enter the network's name.

3. Enter your passphrase, such as **R&Kuser10 klamath Law01**, and then click the **Connect** button. Windows connects to the network.

4. Click the **Close** button.

5. In the Connect to a network window, click the **Open Network and Sharing Center** link. The Network and Sharing Center window now shows your computer connected to the network. See Figure 8-23.

Tip

You can also open the Network and Sharing Center window by clicking the Network Center button in the Windows Mobility Center window.

Figure 8-23	Computer connected to the network

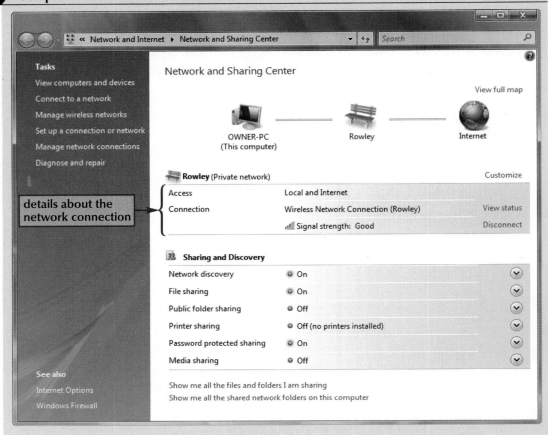

Tay's mobile computer is now connected to the Rowley & Klein wireless network. Because cordless phones and other devices can interfere with a wireless connection, you should periodically check the status of the connection. You can do so by opening the Network and Sharing Center or the Windows Mobility Center or by using the network icon in the notification area of the status bar. You'll show Tay how to check the status using the Mobility Center and the network icon. The Mobility Center indicates whether your computer is connected to or disconnected from the network. The network icon provides more information, including the name of the network and the type of access you have, which can be Local (network resources only), Local and Internet (network resources and the Internet), or Not connected.

To check the status of a wireless connection:

▶ **1.** Minimize the Network and Sharing Center window so you can see the entire Windows Mobility Center window. The Wireless Network tile indicates whether your computer is connected or disconnected from the network.

▶ **2.** Click the **network** icon 🖥 in the notification area of the taskbar. A small notification window shows the status of your network connection. See Figure 8-24. Your network status might differ.

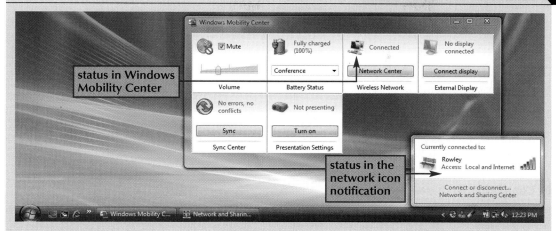

Status of wireless connection | Figure 8-24

3. Click the desktop to close the notification window, and then close the Windows Mobility Center window.

Now that Tay is connected to the Rowley & Klein wireless network, he can get ready to copy the files to and from a folder on their network. Before he does, he wonders if he can connect to wired networks at other client sites when necessary. You'll briefly explain how to connect remotely to a wired network.

Connecting Remotely to a Wired Network

If you use a wired LAN at your workplace or school, you can connect to that network even when you are not using one of the network computers. To do so, you use a **virtual private network (VPN)** connection, which is a secure connection to a large network, such as a business network, using the Internet. To set up a VPN connection, you use the Connect to a workplace wizard, which you start from the Network and Sharing Center window. One of the dialog boxes in the wizard asks for the Internet address and name of the VPN server, so make sure you have this information before you start the wizard. The network administrator of the larger network usually supplies the address, name of the VPN server, your user name, and any password you might need.

| **Connecting Remotely to a Wired Network** | Reference Window |

- Click the Start button on the taskbar, click Control Panel, click Network and Internet, and then click Network and Sharing Center.
- In the left pane of the Network and Sharing Center window, click Set up a connection or network.
- Click Connect to a workplace, and then click the Next button.
- To connect to the VPN using the Internet, click Use my Internet connection (VPN).
- Enter the Internet address of the VPN server.
- Enter the name of the VPN server, and then click the Next button.
- Enter your user name and password, and then click the Connect button.
- After the wizard creates the connection, click Connect now, if necessary, to connect to the network.

Next, you'll show Tay how to find out another detail about the Rowley & Klein network—whether the network his computer is connected to is a workgroup or a domain.

Identifying Workgroups and Domains

Most networks at a medium-size or large company organize the computers as a **domain**, which is a collection of computers on a network that are administered as a whole with common rules and procedures. In contrast, a small office or home network organizes computers as a **workgroup**, which is a group of computers on a network that share resources, such as printers and files. The differences between domains and workgroups are summarized in Figure 8-25.

Figure 8-25 ⟩ **Comparing workgroups and domains**

Characteristic	Workgroup	Domain
Role of each computer	All computers are peers, meaning that no computer has control over another computer.	At least one computer on the network is a server. A network administrator uses the server to control the security and permissions for all the computers on the domain.
User accounts	To use a computer in the workgroup, you need an account on that computer.	If you have a user account on the domain, you can use any computer on the domain without having an account.
Permissions	If you have an account on a computer, you can change settings for that account.	Unless you are the network administrator, you can make only limited changes to settings.
Number of computers	Workgroups usually have no more than 20 computers.	Domains can have thousands of computers.
Location of computers	All computers must be on the same local network.	Computers can be on different local networks.

You suspect that the Rowley & Klein network is set up as a workgroup, but you want to make sure before you configure Tay's computer to perform any tasks on the network. You'll use the System window to check to see if the Rowley & Klein network organizes computers as a workgroup or domain. The System window also provides valuable information that you often need when working with networks, including the name of your computer and the name of your workgroup or domain. You'll need both of these names later in this tutorial, so record them when you open the System window.

To check if a computer is connected to a workgroup or domain:

▶ 1. Click the **Start** button 🌐 on the taskbar, click **Control Panel**, click **System and Maintenance**, and then click **System**. The System window opens. See Figure 8-26.

System window showing domain and workgroup settings ◄ Figure 8-26

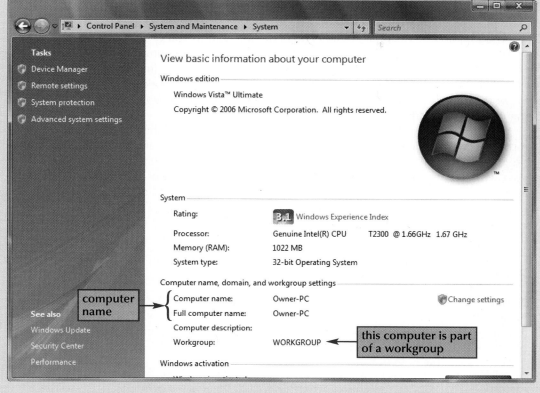

▶ **2.** Close the System window.

Now that you've helped Tay connect to the Rowley & Klein wireless network, you are ready to perform some typical network tasks, which involve connecting to and sharing files with other computers on the network. You'll do that in the next session.

Session 8.1 Quick Check | Review

1. What is a mobile PC?
2. Which of the following settings is *not* included in the Windows Mobility Center?
   a. Battery status
   b. Speaker volume
   c. Workgroup or domain status
   d. Presentation settings
3. A(n) _____ _____ is a collection of hardware and system settings that manages how your computer uses and conserves power.
4. True or False. Hybrid sleep is an alternative to sleep in which Windows saves your work and then immediately turns off the computer.
5. Name two settings you can set before you give a presentation.
6. The most common types of network technology for a small office or home network are wireless, _____ , and home phone line (HPNA).
7. When you use the Connect to a network window to connect to an available wireless network, what three details does the window provide about each wireless network?

Session 8.2

Connecting to Another Computer

After setting up a network and connecting computers to it, you can browse the network by opening the Network window to display all the connected computers, and then double-clicking a computer to see the drives and folders it contains. You can also share files and resources with other computers connected to the network. You share files on the network similarly to the way you share files with other users on your computer: by storing the files you want to share in the Public folder.

You can also connect to another computer remotely and use the programs, files, and resources available on that computer. For example, suppose you are in the middle of a project at work that involves Microsoft Office. You can set up a remote connection to your work computer from your home computer so that you can use all the tools that are available from your desktop on your work computer, including Microsoft Office and your project files.

Before you connect to another computer, you need to find that computer on the network. You can do so using the Network window.

Browsing a Network

If your computer is connected to a network, you can see all of the computers and devices that are part of the network in the Network window. Then you can use a network resource, such as a printer; open files on another computer; or confirm that a computer or device was added to your network.

You'll show Tay how to browse the Rowley network.

To browse the network:

1. Click the **Start** button 🔘 on the taskbar, and then click **Network**. The Network window opens, displaying all the computers and devices on your network. See Figure 8-27.

Network window showing computers on the network ◀ Figure 8-27

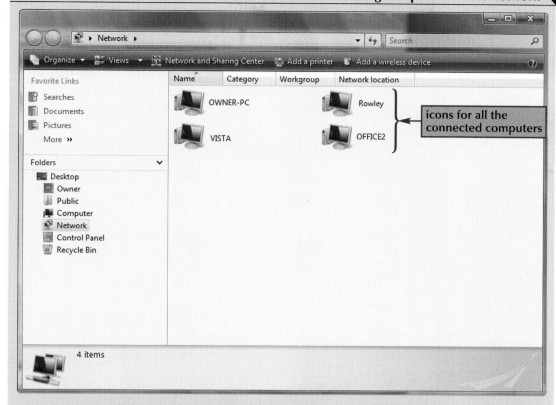

Trouble? If you don't see computers that you expect to see, the network discovery setting on your computer or another computer might be blocking access. Run Network Diagnostics by right-clicking the network icon in the notification area of the taskbar and then clicking Diagnose and repair.

Trouble? If other computers on your network are running Windows XP and you don't see them in the Network window, you might need to change the workgroup name on those computers. Find the name of the Windows Vista computer connected to the router by opening the System window from Control Panel. On the Windows XP computers, change their name to match the Windows Vista name.

▶ **2.** Double-click the **VISTA** computer icon to see its drives and folders.

Trouble? If a computer named VISTA is not part of your network, double-click a different computer icon.

Now that Tay has examined the computers on the Rowley & Klein network, you're ready to turn on file sharing so he can share files with the Rowley & Klein partners.

Sharing Files on the Network

To share files, you use the Network and Sharing Center window to turn on file sharing. You'll do so on Tay's mobile computer so that he can share sample network policy documents from his Public folder with the Rowley & Klein partners. Note your original settings so you can restore them later.

To turn on file sharing:

▶ 1. Click the **Back** button ⬅ to return to the Network window.

▶ 2. Click the Network and Sharing Center button on the toolbar. The Network and Sharing Center window opens.

▶ 3. In the Sharing and Discovery section, click the **expand** button ⌄ to the right of Public folder sharing, and then click the **Turn on sharing so anyone with network access can open, change, and create files** option button. See Figure 8-28.

| Figure 8-28 | Turning on file sharing |

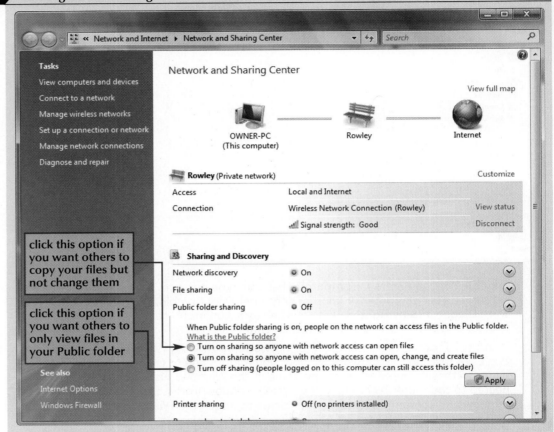

▶ 4. Click the **Apply** button, and then close the Network and Sharing Center window.

Trouble? If you are asked for an administrator password or confirmation, type the password or provide confirmation.

▶ 5. Close the Network window.

When you turn on sharing, the Public folder on your computer is available to anyone else on the network who wants to open, change, or leave files in that folder. If you want to let other people copy the files in your Public folder but not change your copies, you click Off in the Public folder sharing section, and then click Turn on sharing so anyone with network access can open files.

If you want to access files stored on a different computer on the network, you open the Network window and then double-click the computer you want to access. If the user of that computer has turned on file sharing, you can navigate to the Public folder on the networked computer and access those files.

Now Tay can place in his Public folder the files he wants to share with the Rowley & Klein partners.

Although files you delete from your computer's hard drive are stored in the Recycle Bin until you empty it, this is not true for computers you access on your network. If you delete a file from the Public folder of a computer on your network, Windows Vista does not store that file in the Recycle Bin on your computer or on the networked computer. You should therefore avoid deleting files from the Public folder of a computer to which you are connected.

Next, you'll show Tay how to use Remote Desktop Connection to connect to another computer.

Using Remote Desktop Connection

Another way to share information among computers is to use **Remote Desktop Connection**, a technology that allows you to use one computer to connect to a remote computer in a different location. For example, you can connect to your school or work computer from your home computer so you can access all of the programs, files, and network resources that you normally use at school or work. If you leave programs running at work, you can see your work computer's desktop displayed on your home computer, with the same programs running.

Suppose you are planning to use a mobile computer at home and want to connect to your computer at work. To use Remote Desktop Connection, the home computer and work computer must both be running Windows and must be connected to the same network or to the Internet. The work computer must be turned on, have a network connection, and Remote Desktop must be turned on. The home computer must have network access to the work computer, which could be through the Internet, and you must have permission to connect to your work computer. However, you cannot use Remote Desktop Connection to connect computers running Windows XP Home Edition. Furthermore, you cannot connect to your work computer if it is running Windows Vista Starter, Windows Vista Home Basic, or Windows Vista Home Premium, though you can establish an outgoing connection on a computer running those versions of Windows Vista.

Setting up Remote Desktop Connection is a two-part process. First, you allow remote connections on the computer to which you want to connect, such as your work computer. Next, you start Remote Desktop on the computer you want to connect from, such as your home computer. When you allow remote connections on your computer, you can allow connections from computers running any version of Remote Desktop, including those in earlier versions of Windows. If you know that the computers connecting to your computer are also running Windows Vista, you should allow connections only from computers running Remote Desktop with Network Level Authentication (NLA). This option provides more security and can protect remote computers from hackers and malware.

After viewing the presentation and discussing the proposal, the Rowley & Klein partners decide that they want Kevin and Tay to create the custom database described in their proposal. Tay will be managing this part of the project, and will spend some time in Klamath Falls meeting with Rowley & Klein, and will then send an associate to the law firm to continue working on the database. Rowley & Klein are providing a computer in the conference room where Tay and his employee can develop the database when they are in Klamath Falls. Tay anticipates that he will also need to access this computer when he is not in Klamath Falls. You'll show him how to allow remote connections on that conference room computer.

First, you need to determine whether the conference room computer is running a version of Remote Desktop with NLA.

To see if your computer is running a version of Remote Desktop with NLA:

▶ 1. Click the **Start** button ⊕ on the taskbar, point to **All Programs**, click **Accessories**, and then click **Remote Desktop Connection**. The Remote Desktop Connection dialog box opens. See Figure 8-29.

| Figure 8-29 | Remote Desktop Connection dialog box |

click this icon and then click About

▶ 2. Click the **Remote Desktop Connection** icon in the upper-left corner of the dialog box, and then click **About**. A window opens describing Remote Desktop Connection. See Figure 8-30. Look for the phrase "Network Level Authentication supported."

| Figure 8-30 | About Remote Desktop Connection window |

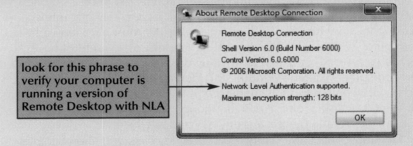

look for this phrase to verify your computer is running a version of Remote Desktop with NLA

▶ 3. Click the **OK** button.

▶ 4. Click the **Cancel** button to close the Remote Desktop Connection window.

Now you are ready to set up your computer to allow a remote desktop connection from another computer. Before performing the following steps, log on to your computer as an Administrator. If you are not allowed to use an Administrator account on your computer, read but do not perform the following steps.

To set up Remote Desktop Connection:

▶ 1. Click the **Start** button ⊕ on the taskbar, click **Control Panel**, click **System and Maintenance**, and then click **System**. The System window opens.

▶ 2. In the left pane, click **Remote settings**. If necessary, click the **Continue** button. The System Properties dialog box opens to the Remote tab. See Figure 8-31.

Trouble? If you are asked for an administrator password or confirmation, type the password or provide confirmation.

Remote tab in the System Properties dialog box ◀ Figure 8-31

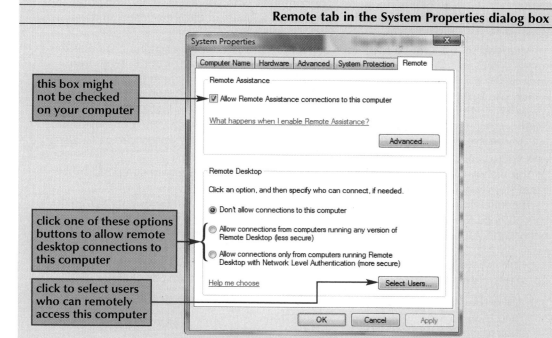

this box might not be checked on your computer

click one of these options buttons to allow remote desktop connections to this computer

click to select users who can remotely access this computer

3. Click the **Allow connections only from computers running Remote Desktop with Network Level Authentication (more secure)** option button.

Trouble? If a dialog box opens regarding your power settings, click the OK button.

4. Click the **Select Users** button. The Remote Desktop Users dialog box opens. See Figure 8-32.

Remote Desktop Users dialog box ◀ Figure 8-32

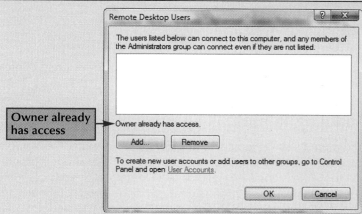

Owner already has access

On this computer, the Owner account already has access because that is the Administrator account used to set up the remote connection.

5. Click the **OK** button to close the Remote Desktop Users dialog box.

6. Click the **OK** button to close the System Properties dialog box. Close the System window.

If you want to allow users other than the Administrator to use a remote desktop connection to your computer, you could click the Add button in the Remote Desktop Users dialog box, enter the name of the user or computer who can access your computer, and then click the OK button. The name you entered appears in the list of users in the Remote Desktop Users dialog box.

After you set up Remote Desktop Connection on your remote computer, such as the one at work, you can start Remote Desktop on the computer you want to work from, such as the one at home. Before you do, you need to know the name of the computer to which you want to connect. You can also enter the IP address instead of the computer name. To find the name of a computer, you open the System window by opening Control Panel, clicking System and Maintenance, and then clicking System. The computer name is listed in the *Computer name, domain, and workgroup settings* section. You can also find your computer name in the Welcome Center window.

You'll show Tay how to start Remote Desktop on a computer so he can perform the same steps when he returns to the KATE offices in Portland.

The following steps assume that you are set up to connect to a remote computer. To do so, you need to know the name of the computer to which you want to connect. If you are not set up to connect to a remote computer, read but do not perform the following steps.

To start Remote Desktop to connect to a remote computer:

▶ **1.** Click the **Start** button 🪟 on the taskbar, point to **All Programs**, click **Accessories**, and then click **Remote Desktop Connection**. The Remote Desktop Connection dialog box opens.

▶ **2.** In the Computer text box, type **Conference**. This is the name of the computer in the Rowley & Klein conference room.

  Trouble? If the name of the remote computer to which you want to connect is not named Conference, enter its name instead of *Conference* in the Computer text box.

▶ **3.** Click the **Connect** button to connect to that computer on your network.

▶ **4.** Enter your user name and password, and then click the **OK** button to establish the connection.

▶ **5.** Click the **Close** button.

Now Tay and his associate can access the computer in the Rowley & Klein conference room when they are working in the KATE offices in Portland.

Enabling and Disabling Remote Assistance

Although you can use Remote Desktop to access one computer from another remotely, such as your work computer from your home computer, you can use another program with a similar name—Remote Assistance—to give or receive help with your computer. For example, a friend or technical support professional can access your computer from a remote location to help solve a computer problem or show you how to perform a task. When the person giving remote assistance is connected to your computer, you both see the same desktop and you can both control the pointer. In this way, you can learn how to complete a computer task or solve a problem.

| Reference Window

Enabling and Disabling Remote Assistance

- Click the Start button on the taskbar, click Control Panel, click System and Maintenance, and then click System.
- In the left pane of the System window, click Remote settings. (If you are asked for permission to continue, click the Continue button.)
- To enable Remote Assistance, make sure the Allow Remote Assistance connections to this computer check box is selected.
- To disable Remote Assistance, click the Allow Remote Assistance connections to this computer check box to remove the check mark.
- Click the OK button.

To enable Remote Assistance, you use the same Remote settings tab in the System Properties dialog box that you used to set Remote Desktop settings. Make sure the Allow Remote Assistance connections to this computer check box is selected to enable Remote Assistance.

However, when someone uses Remote Assistance to connect to your computer, that person can see your desktop, any open documents, and any visible private information. In addition, if you allow the person giving you remote assistance to control your computer, that person can delete files or change settings. Only allow people you trust to access or share control of your computer. You can also disable Remote Assistance if you are concerned about security.

Connecting by Mapping a Drive

A third way to connect to another computer is to create a shortcut on your computer to a shared folder or computer on a network, which is also called **mapping a network drive**. Then you can find and use the network drive the same way you use a folder on your hard drive—you open a folder window and navigate to the file or folder you want.

| InSight

Choosing a Connection Method

So far, you've learned about three ways to access files on a network computer other than your own: sharing files by using the Public folder, using Remote Desktop Connection, and mapping a network drive. The easiest method is to share files using the Public folder because if you are already connected to the network, you only need to navigate to the Public folder, which is listed in the Navigation pane of any folder window by default. However, someone must store the files you need in that Public folder. If you need to access more than files, such as programs and other tools, or when you need to access files not stored in the Public folder, use Remote Desktop Connection. If you want to open a shared file using older software, such as older database programs, and the software does not recognize shared network folders, you can map the network drive to your computer so that you can use the database program or other software to open and save the files.

When you map a drive, you assign a drive letter to a network drive or folder, such as Z or Y. Windows recognizes the drive letter and gives you direct access to the files it contains. You map a drive to connect your computer to a folder or drive on another computer. (You can map a drive only after the user of the computer or the network administrator has given you access to the drive).

You'll show Tay how to map the Public Documents folder on the Rowley & Klein network to a drive named Z:. Later, when he works on the database project, he might need to map a different folder to a drive.

To map a drive:

1. Click the **Start** button 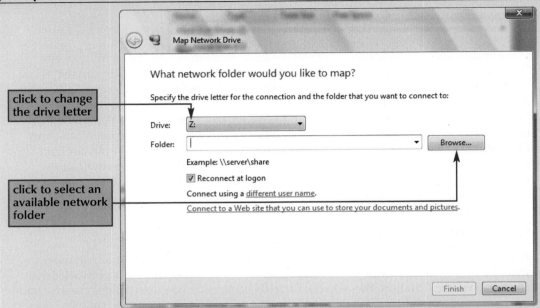 on the taskbar, and then click **Computer**. The Computer window opens.

2. Press the **Alt** key to open the menu bar.

3. Click **Tools** on the menu bar, and then click **Map Network Drive**. The Map Network Drive window opens. See Figure 8-33.

Figure 8-33 | Map Network Drive window

click to change the drive letter

click to select an available network folder

4. Click the **Browse** button to open the Browse For Folder dialog box, which displays a list of computers on the network.

   Trouble? If a dialog box opens regarding network discovery, click the OK button, click Cancel, click the Start button, click Network, and then click the Information bar in the Network window to turn on network discovery.

5. Navigate to and then click the **Public Documents** folder on the Rowley computer.

   Trouble? If your network does not include a computer named Rowley, select a different computer.

6. Click the **OK** button to close the Browse For Folder dialog box.

7. Click the **Finish** button.

8. Click **Computer** in the Navigation pane to display the contents of your computer. The mapped drive now appears in the Computer window. See Figure 8-34. Your Computer window might open in a different view.

Computer window with mapped drive ◀ Figure 8-34

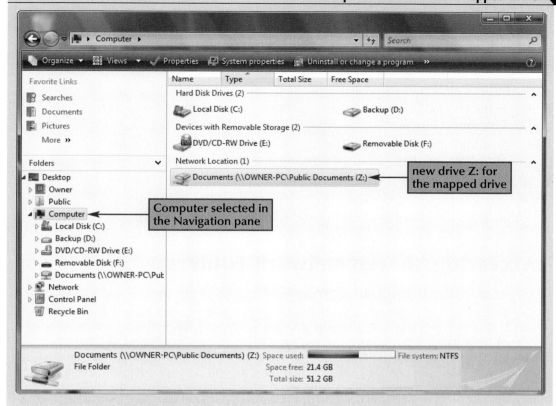

To access the files on a mapped drive, you work with the mapped drive as you would any other drive or folder—double-click its icon in the Computer window to open it, for example.

When you map a drive, the Map Network Drive window shows the location of the drive you are going to map, which is displayed as a pathname. Windows Vista pathnames follow the **Universal Naming Convention** (**UNC**), an accepted set of rules for expressing pathnames, including those for mapped drives and network folders. The general form is \\server\sharename, where sharename is the name or drive letter you used when sharing the folder. Thus the pathname to the Public Documents network folder is \\Rowley\Public Documents, indicating a shared resource named Public Documents located on the server named Rowley.

Removing Drive Mapping

When you no longer plan to use a mapped drive, you should remove the drive mapping to maintain security—an unauthorized user might gain access to your files through the mapped drive. When you remove drive mapping, you disconnect the drive from your computer. You can also assign a computer or shared folder to a different drive letter by disconnecting from the drive and then reassigning it to a new drive letter. When you are ready to remove drive mapping, you can do so from the Computer window.

Reference Window | **Removing Drive Mapping**

- Open the Computer window.
- Right-click the mapped drive and click Disconnect on the shortcut menu.

To remove drive mapping:

▶ **1.** In the Computer window, right-click **Public Documents (Z:)**, and then click **Disconnect** on the shortcut menu.

    Trouble? If your mapped drive has a name other than Public Documents (Z:), right-click the drive you mapped in the preceding set of steps.

▶ **2.** Close the Computer window.

The drive letter associated with the network folder is removed from your system.

Accessing Shared Network Folders

After setting up and sharing files and folders on a network, you might need to work with files that are stored on the network, but can't access them because your network connection is not available. To avoid this problem, you can create **offline files**, which are copies of your network files that you can access even when you are not connected to the network. To create offline files, you choose the network files you want to make available offline, and Windows creates copies of these files for you on your computer. Every time you connect to the network folder, Windows updates, or synchronizes, the offline files so they remain exact duplicates. When you are not connected to the network, you can open the offline files on your computer knowing that they have the same content as the network files. When you're finished working with the offline files, you can synchronize (*sync* for short) the offline files and network files yourself, or you can wait for Windows to do it the next time you access the network files.

You can synchronize files whenever you copy and save network files to your computer. When you first create offline files, Windows Vista transfers the files from the network to a specified folder on your hard disk. After that, when you connect to the network folder that contains the files you've also stored offline, Windows makes sure that both the folder containing the offline files and the network folder contain the most recent versions of the files.

Besides providing convenience when you are away from your network, offline files protect you from network problems caused by power outages, maintenance, or system trouble. If you are linked to your network with a slow connection, you can also continue to work efficiently by switching to the offline copies and avoiding the wait times for accessing a shared network folder.

You explain to Tay that offline files are especially popular with mobile computer users. For example, if he is working with files stored on the Rowley & Klein network using his notebook computer and wireless connection, he loses that connection when he leaves the law office. He can continue working on those files at the KATE offices in Portland if he creates offline versions of those files. You'll show Tay how to set up his notebook to use offline files, and then you'll make a Public folder on the Rowley & Klein network available to him offline.

Setting Up a Computer to Use Offline Files

Before you specify that a network file or folder should be available offline, make sure that offline files are enabled on your computer, which it is by default. When this feature is turned on, Windows synchronizes the offline files on your computer with the network files as soon as you reconnect to the network.

To make sure offline files are enabled on your computer:

▶ **1.** Click the **Start** button 💿 on the taskbar, click **Control Panel**, click **Network and Internet**, and then click **Offline Files**. The Offline Files dialog box opens. See Figure 8-35.

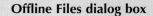 Offline Files dialog box ◀ Figure 8-35

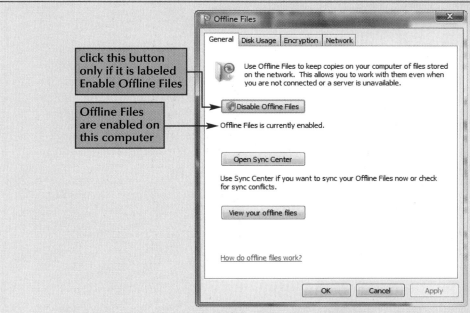

click this button only if it is labeled Enable Offline Files

Offline Files are enabled on this computer

Trouble? If offline files are disabled on your computer, click the Enable Offline Files button.

▶ **2.** Click the **OK** button to close the dialog box.

Next, you'll access a network folder and make it available to Tay offline.

Making a File or Folder Available Offline

To use a file or folder offline, you specify that it is always available offline. (When you make a folder available offline, all the files in the folder are also available offline.) Afterwards, you will be able to open the file or folder even if the network version is unavailable. You'll show Tay how to use offline files and folders by making the Public Documents folder on the Rowley computer available offline.

The following steps assume that a computer named Rowley is connected to your network. If your network does not include a computer named Rowley, substitute the name of a different network computer that you can access in the following steps. The steps also assume that you have permission to access the Public Documents folder on the network computer. If you do not have permission to access this folder, ask your instructor which folder you can make available offline.

To make network files available offline:

▶ **1.** In the Network and Internet window, click **View network computers and devices** to open the Network window.

▶ **2.** Double-click the **Rowley** computer to display the users and resources on the computer.

▶ **3.** Double-click the **Users** folder, and then double-click the **Public** folder.

▶ **4.** Right-click the **Public Documents** folder, and then click **Always Available Offline** on the shortcut menu if this command is not checked.

Trouble? If the Always Available Offline command does not appear on the short-cut menu, navigate to and right-click a folder you have permission to access offline. If you do not have permission to access any folders offline, read but do not perform the remaining steps.

▶ **5.** Close the folder window.

▶ **6.** Close the Network and Internet window.

Tip

To view all your offline files, open the Offline Files dialog box, and then click the View your offline files button.

Now you can show Tay how to work with the files in the Public Documents folder offline.

If you made a different folder available offline, substitute that folder for the Public Documents folder in the following steps. If you did not make any folders available offline, read but do not perform the following steps.

To work with offline files:

▶ **1.** Navigate to the Public folder on the network again, and then open the **Public Documents** folder.

▶ **2.** Click the **Work offline** button on the toolbar. This button appears only if you have already made this folder available offline.

▶ **3.** Close the folder window.

Tip

When you are finished working offline, click the Work online button on the toolbar to sync the changes you made with the files on the network.

Windows turns on offline files when you lose your network connection. Windows copies to your computer the files you designate as offline files so you can work on them. When you are reconnected to network, Windows syncs the two copies. You can find out if you're working offline by opening the network folder that contains the file you are working on, and then looking in the Details pane of the folder window. If the status is offline, you are working with a copy of the file on your computer. If the status is online, you are working with the file on the network.

Synchronizing Folders

Recall that keeping files in sync is one of the problems mobile computer users often have that desktop computer users do not. If you use more than one computer, such as a desktop computer and a mobile PC, it can be difficult to keep track of all your files. To make sure that you have the most recent versions of your files on your mobile PC before you travel, for example, you can synchronize information on your mobile PC, desktop computer, and other devices by using Sync Center. To do so, you create a set of rules that tells Sync Center what files you want to sync, where to sync them, and when. You can schedule Sync Center to run as frequently as you want, such as daily or weekly, or you can sync files manually before you travel. In this way, Sync Center makes it easy to move files from one computer to another device, such as another computer, network server, portable music player, digital camera, or mobile phone. Besides copying files from one device to another, Sync Center can maintain consistency among two or more versions of the same file stored in different locations. If you add, change, or delete a file in one location, Sync Center can add, overwrite, or delete an earlier version of the file in other locations.

Synchronizing Folders Between Computers with Sync Center | Reference Window

- Set up a folder on another computer for synchronizing. (Right-click the folder on another computer, and then click Always Available Offline.)
- Click the Start button, point to All Programs, click Accessories, and then click Sync Center.
- To synchronize manually, click the Offline Files folder, and then Sync All. To synchronize automatically, click Next, click At a scheduled time or On an event or action, and then click Finish to accept the default time or event.

You can also use Sync Center to manage offline files in Windows Vista Business, Enterprise, and Ultimate editions. In this case, Sync Center compares the size and time stamp of an offline file with a network file to see if they are different. For example, suppose you have changed an offline file, but have not made the same changes in the network copy. Sync Center copies the offline file to the network so they are identical. If Sync Center finds a new file in an offline folder, for example, it copies the file to the network folder. The same is true for deleted files—if Sync Center finds that a file has been deleted from the network folder, for example, it deletes the same file in the offline folder.

Sometimes, Sync Center discovers a conflict, which means that you have changed both a network file and its offline copy. A sync conflict occurs whenever differences can't be reconciled between a file stored in one location and a version of the same file in another location, which stops the sync from being completed. This usually happens when a file has changed in both locations since its last sync, making it difficult to determine which version should be left unchanged (or kept as the master copy) and which should be updated. In this case, Sync Center asks you to select the version you want to keep.

When you are synchronizing between a mobile device, such as a portable music player, and your computer, Sync Center gives you the option of setting up a one-way or two-way sync. In one-way sync, every time you add, change, or delete a file or other information in one location, such as the Music folder on your hard disk, the same information is added, changed, or deleted in the other location, such as your portable music player. Windows does not change the files in the original location, such as the Music folder on your hard disk, because the sync is only one way.

In two-way sync, Windows copies files in both directions, keeping files in sync in two locations. Every time you add, change, or delete a file in either location, the same change is made in the other sync location. You often use two-way sync in work environments, where files are often updated in more than one location and then synchronized with other locations.

Using the Sync Center

At one time, the synchronizing process was so complex, especially in work environments, that companies relied on a system administrator to set up sync for them. Now you can use Sync Center to set up the sync yourself by specifying which files and folders you want to sync, where to sync them, and when. This set of rules—which represents a partnership between two or more sync locations—is called a **sync partnership**.

You'll show Tay how to open Sync Center and set up a sync partnership.

To perform the following steps, you must be working on a mobile computer. If you are not working on a mobile computer, read but do not perform the following steps.

To open Sync Center:

▶ 1. Click the **Start** button 🪟 on the taskbar, point to **All Programs**, click **Accessories**, and then click **Windows Mobility Center** to open the Windows Mobility Center window.

▶ 2. Click the **Sync settings** button in the Sync Center tile. The Sync Center window opens. See Figure 8-36.

| Figure 8-36 | Sync Center window |

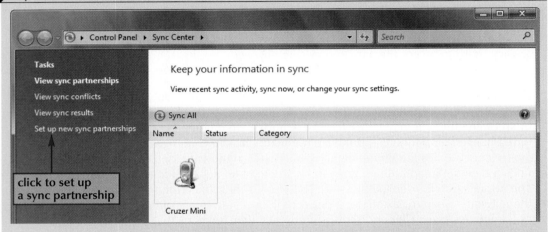

▶ 3. In the left pane, click **Set up new sync partnerships**. The Sync Setup window opens. See Figure 8-37.

| Figure 8-37 | Sync Setup window |

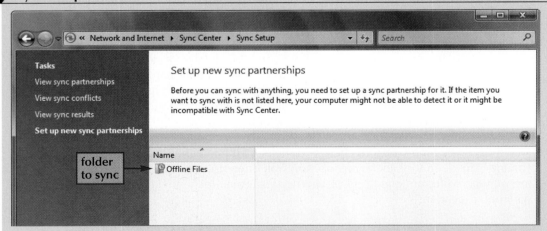

▶ 4. Click **Offline Files**, and then click **Set up**. The Offline Files Sync Schedule window opens. You can schedule the sync for a particular time or choose an event or action, such as every time you log on to your computer.

▶ 5. Click **At a scheduled time**, and then click the **Finish** button to accept the default sync time of 2 a.m.

Next, you'll show Tay how to manually sync his files. You recommend that he does so when he is getting ready to disconnect his mobile computer from the Rowley & Klein network and wants to make sure he has the latest copies of his files.

To synchronize files:

▶ **1.** Click the **Back** button ⊖ to return to the Sync Center window.

▶ **2.** Click the **Offline Files** sync partnership, click **Sync** on the toolbar. Windows Vista begins synchronizing your files. See Figure 8-38.

> **Tip**
>
> To sync only the contents of a particular file or folder, right-click the file or folder, and then click Sync.

Synchronizing files ◀ Figure 8-38

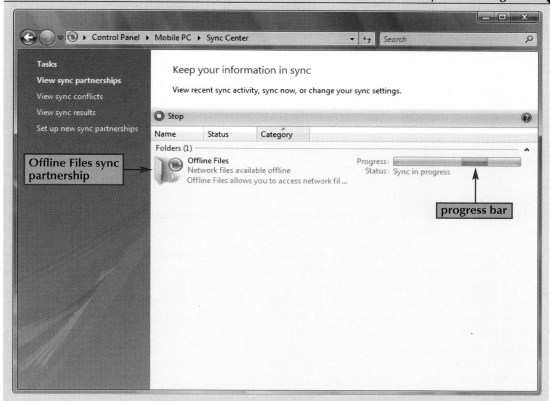

▶ **3.** When the sync is finished, click **View sync results** in the left pane of the Sync Center window to display the results. See Figure 8-39.

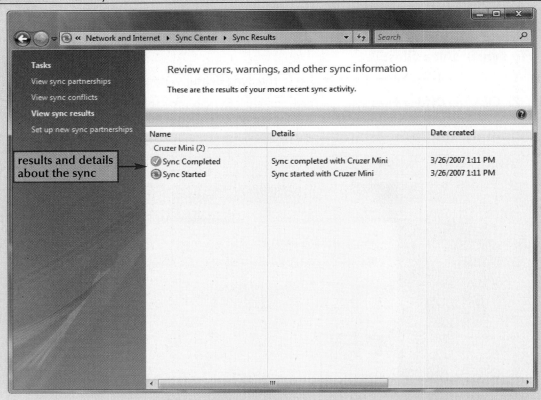

Figure 8-39 **Results of the sync**

results and details about the sync

Windows reports that the sync was successful, which streamlines your sync tasks. During the sync, if Sync Center finds that the offline file is identical to the network file, Sync Center does nothing because the files are already in sync. If Sync Center finds that an offline file differs from its network version, Sync Center determines which version of each file to keep and copies that version to the other location. It selects the most recent version to keep, unless you have set up the sync partnership to sync differently. If you have added a new file in one location but not the other, Sync Center copies the file to the other location. If you have deleted a file from one location but not the other, Sync Center deletes the file from the other location. If Sync Center finds a conflict, however, you should know how to resolve it.

Resolving Synchronization Conflicts

If you or Windows performs a sync and Sync Center finds that a file has changed in both locations since the last sync, Sync Center flags this as a sync conflict and asks you to choose which version to keep. You must resolve this conflict so that Sync Center can keep the files in sync. When Sync Center detects a conflict, it displays a message similar to the one displayed in Figure 8-40.

Conflict window | Figure 8-40

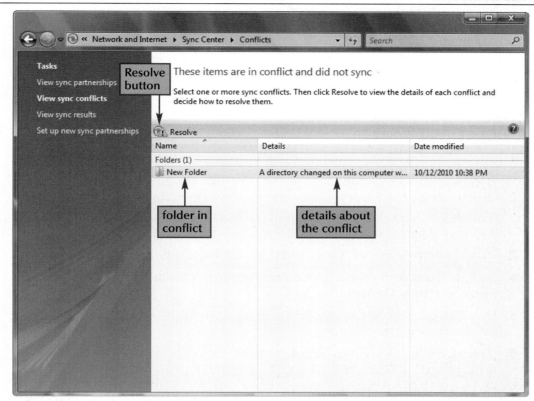

To resolve this conflict, you click the Resolve button. When you do, the Resolve dialog box opens and asks if you want to keep this version and copy it to the other location, or if you want to delete both copies. Click the appropriate option, and then click the OK button.

Distinguishing Between Sync Conflicts and Sync Errors | InSight

A sync conflict occurs when differences can't be reconciled between a file stored in one location and a version of the same file in another location. This stops sync from being completed for this file until you decide how to reconcile the differences. You don't need to resolve all sync conflicts, but it improves the integrity of your files if you do so.

In contrast, a sync error is a problem that usually prevents sync from being completed, such as a mobile device that is not plugged in or turned on, or a network server that is unavailable. Unlike sync conflicts, sync errors are not caused by problems reconciling two versions of a file. Rather, sync errors usually occur when there is a problem with the device, computer, or folder you are trying to sync with. To complete a sync successfully, you must resolve all sync errors.

You've given Tay a good grounding in basic network information, so he should be able to continue working on the Rowley & Klein network productively.

Restoring Your Settings

If you are working in a computer lab or on a computer other than your own, complete the steps in this section to restore the original settings on your computer. If a User Account Control dialog box opens requesting an Administrator password or confirmation after you perform any of the following steps, enter the password or click the Continue button.

To restore your settings:

▶ 1. Open the Windows Mobility Center, and then drag the **Volume** slider to its original setting.

▶ 2. Click the **Mute** check box to remove the check mark and turn the speakers on.

Trouble? If your speakers were turned off when you originally opened Windows Mobility Center in Session 8.1, skip Step 2.

▶ 3. Click the **Battery Status** button, and then click **Balanced**.

▶ 4. Click the **Start** button , click **Control Panel**, click **Hardware and Sound**, and then click **Power Options**.

▶ 5. Click **Change plan settings** for the Balanced power plan, and then click **Restore default settings for this plan**.

▶ 6. Click the **Yes** button, and then click the **Back** button to return to the Power Options window.

▶ 7. Click **Change plan settings** for the Conference power plan.

▶ 8. Click **Delete this plan**, and then click the **OK** button.

▶ 9. Repeat Steps 5 and 6 to restore the defaults for the Power saver and High performance plans.

▶ 10. In the Windows Mobility Center window, click the **Change presentation settings** icon , and then restore the screen saver, volume, and background controls to their original settings. Then click the **OK** button.

▶ 11. Open the Network and Sharing Center window. In the Public folder sharing section, restore your original settings, and then click the **Apply** button.

▶ 12. Click the **Start** button on the taskbar, point to **All Programs**, click **Accessories**, and then click **Remote Desktop Connection**. In the Computer text box, select the name of the computer to which you have a remote desktop connection, such as **Conference**, and then click the **Disconnect** button.

▶ 13. Open the Network window, and then navigate to the Public Documents folder on the network. Right-click the **Public Documents** folder, and then click **Always Available Offline** on the shortcut menu to remove the check mark. Close the folder window.

▶ 14. In the Windows Mobility Center window, click the **Sync settings** button, and then click **View sync partnerships**, if necessary. Right-click **Offline Files**, and then click **Delete**.

▶ **15.** Click the **Start** button 🔵 on the taskbar, click **Control Panel**, click **System and Maintenance**, and then click **System**. Click **Remote settings**, click the **Don't allow connections to this computer** option button, and then click the **OK** button to close the System Properties dialog box.

▶ **16.** Close all open windows.

Session 8.2 Quick Check | Review

1. Which window do you use to browse a network to which you are connected?
2. True or False. When you delete a file from a shared folder on a network computer, the file is stored in your Recycle Bin.
3. The first major step in setting up Remote Desktop Connection is to allow remote connections on the computer to which you want to connect. What is the second step?
4. Which of the following programs can you use to give or receive help with your computer?
   a. Sync Center
   b. Remote Desktop
   c. Network Sharing
   d. Remote Assistance
5. One way to connect to another computer is to create a shortcut on your computer to a shared folder or computer on a network, which is called _____ a network drive.
6. _____ _____ are copies of your network files that you can access even when you are not connected to the network.
7. Identify an advantage Sync Center offers if you work on more than one computer, such as a mobile computer and a network computer.

Tutorial Summary | Review

In this tutorial, you managed mobile computing devices by configuring power plans and selecting presentation settings. You also explored network concepts and learned how to manage network connections on a wireless network. You also learned how to manage remote access to your computer, and explored three ways to connect to another computer. Finally, you shared network folders and then synchronized the folders using Sync Center.

Key Terms

domain

hibernate

hybrid sleep

laptop computer

local area network (LAN)

map a network drive

mobile computing device

mobile PC

Mobility Center

network

network resource

network technology

notebook computer

offline file

power plan

presentation settings

Remote Desktop Connection

sleep

strong passphrase

Sync Center

sync partnership

Tablet PC

Universal Naming Convention (UNC)

virtual private network (VPN)

workgroup

| Practice | | Review Assignments |

Practice the skills you learned in the tutorial.

There are no Data Files needed for the Review Assignments.

You are now working with Tay Endres to help him prepare for a meeting with a client in Eugene, Oregon—a small video production studio named Eugene Video. Tay asks you to help him prepare his mobile computer for the trip and for a presentation he plans to make to Eugene Video when he arrives. Kevin Adelson also requests your help in connecting his Windows Vista notebook computer to the Eugene Video wireless network and sharing some of its resources. Complete the following steps, noting your original settings so you can restore them later:

1. Open the Windows Mobility Center, change the speaker volume to 25, and then mute the speakers.

2. Open Control Panel, click Hardware and Sound, and then click Power Options. Change the plan settings for the Power saver plan so that the display turns off after five minutes of idle time when running on battery power and after 15 minutes when plugged in. (If you are not using a mobile computer, set the Power saver plan to turn off the display after 15 minutes of idle time.) Save your changes.

3. Create a power plan based on the High performance plan and name it **Eugene**. Set the Eugene plan to turn off the display setting after 10 minutes of idle time when running on battery power and after 30 minutes when plugged in. Also set the plan to put the computer to sleep after 45 minutes of idle time when running on battery power. (If you are not using a mobile computer, set the Eugene plan to turn off the display after 30 minutes of idle time and put the computer to sleep after 45 minutes of idle time.) Save your changes.

4. Select the Power saver plan, and then press Alt+Print Screen to capture an image of the window. Paste the image in a new Paint file, and save the file as **Power Options** in the Tutorial.08\Review folder provided with your Data Files.

5. Change what the power button does so that when you press the power button when running on battery power, your computer shuts down. (If you are not using a mobile computer, do the same for the default type of power.) Press Alt+Print Screen to capture an image of the window. Paste the image in a new Paint file, and save the file as **Power Button** in the Tutorial.08\Review folder provided with your Data Files. Save your changes, and then close the Power Options window.

6. Use Windows Mobility Center or Control Panel to change presentation settings so that when you give a presentation, you turn off the screen saver, set the volume to 75, and show img11 as the desktop background. Press Alt+Print Screen to capture an image of the window. Paste the image in a new Paint file, and save the file as **Presentation** in the Tutorial.08\Review folder provided with your Data Files.

7. Connect to an available wireless network, entering a security key or passphrase as necessary. (If you are not equipped to connect to a wireless network, connect to a wired network.) Capture an image of the Network and Sharing window. Paste the image in a new Paint file, and save the file as **Wireless** in the Tutorial.08\Review folder provided with your Data Files.

8. Browse the network you connected to in the previous step. Display the drives and folders of any network computer (other than your own) in the Network window. Press Alt+Print Screen to capture an image of the window. Paste the image in a new Paint file, and save the file as **Network** in the Tutorial.08\Review folder provided with your Data Files.

9. Return to the Network and Sharing Center window, and then turn on sharing for the Public Downloads folder, if necessary, so that anyone with network access can open, change, and create files. Press Alt+Print Screen to capture an image of the window. Paste the image in a new Paint file, and save the file as **Sharing** in the Tutorial.08\Review folder provided with your Data Files. Close the Network and Sharing Center window.

10. From Control Panel, open the System window. In the left pane, click Remote settings, and then allow connections only from computers running Remote Desktop with NLA. Press Alt+Print Screen to capture an image of the window. Paste the image in a new Paint file, and save the file as **Remote Desktop** in the Tutorial. 08\Review folder provided with your Data Files. Close all open dialog boxes.

11. From Control Panel, click Network and Internet, and then click Offline Files. Make sure offline files are enabled on your computer. If possible, make the Public Downloads folder on a network computer always available offline.

12. Open the Sync Center and set up a sync partnership with offline files. Accept the default scheduled time for synchronizing.

13. Synchronize the offline files now. When the sync is finished, view the sync results and then press Alt+Print Screen to capture an image of the window. Paste the image in a new Paint file, and save the file as **Sync** in the Tutorial.08\Review folder provided with your Data Files. Close all open dialog boxes.

14. Restore your original settings. Change the speaker volume to its original setting, and then turn on the speakers. Change the power plans to their default settings, delete the Eugene power plan, and then select your original plan. Restore the original action to the power button. Restore the presentation settings to their original form. Turn off sharing for the Public Downloads folder on the network computer. Delete the sync partnership with offline files. Disconnect from the network, if necessary, and then close all open windows.

15. Submit the results of the preceding steps to your instructor, either in printed or electronic form, as requested.

Apply | **Case Problem 1**

Use the skills you learned in the tutorial to enhance mobile computing for a visiting nurse service.

There are no Data Files needed for this Case Problem.

Tempe Visiting Nurse Service Sarah Shepard is the director of the Tempe Visiting Nurse Service (TVNS) in Tempe, Arizona. During flu season in the fall, TVNS sets up mobile clinics in offices thoughout the city to provide flu shots and give presentations on avoiding the flu, pneumonia, and other viruses. Sarah recently hired you to train her and her staff in using Windows Vista to perform mobile computing tasks, including managing power options and connecting to wireless networks when working at offices in Tempe. Complete the following steps, noting your original settings so you can restore them later:

1. Open the Windows Mobility Center and then mute the speakers.

2. Change the plan settings for the Balanced plan so that the display turns off after 10 minutes of idle time when running on battery power and after 1 hour when plugged in.

3. Create a power plan based on the High performance plan and name it **Visits**. Set the Visits plan to do the following when running on battery power: turn off the display setting after 5 minutes of idle time and put the computer to sleep after 45 minutes of idle time. (If you are not using a mobile computer, use these settings for the default type of power.)

4. Set the Visits plan to use hybrid sleep instead of sleep when running on battery power (or any time if you are not using a mobile computer). Arrange the Power Options dialog box and the Edit Plan Settings window so you can see the settings in both windows, and then press Print Screen to capture an image of the desktop. Paste the image in a new Paint file, and save the file as **Power Plans** in the Tutorial. 08\Case1 folder provided with your Data Files. Save your changes.

5. Set the mobile computer to hibernate when you close its lid and are running on battery power. Press Alt+Print Screen to capture an image of the window. Paste the image in a new Paint file, and save the file as **Lid** in the Tutorial.08\Case1 folder provided with your Data Files. Save your changes, and then close the Power Options window.

6. Use the Windows Mobility Center window to change presentation settings so that when you give a presentation, the volume is set to High and the screen saver is turned off. Press Alt+Print Screen to capture an image of the Presentation Settings dialog box. Paste the image in a new Paint file, and save the file as **Present** in the Tutorial.08\Case1 folder provided with your Data Files. Save your changes.

7. Display a list of wireless networks within range of your computer. Capture an image of the Connect to a network window. Paste the image in a new Paint file, and save the file as **Connect** in the Tutorial.08\Case1 folder provided with your Data Files.

8. If a public wireless network is within range of your computer, attempt to connect to the network. Display the Network and Sharing Center window after this attempt. Press Alt+Print Screen to capture an image of the window. Paste the image in a new Paint file, and save the file as **Public** in the Tutorial.08\Case1 folder provided with your Data Files.

9. Open the Remote Desktop Connection dialog box, and then determine whether your computer supports Network Level Authentication. Press Alt+Print Screen to capture an image of the window that provides this information. Paste the image in a new Paint file, and save the file as **NLA** in the Tutorial.08\Case1 folder provided with your Data Files. Close all Control Panel windows.

10. Disconnect from the public wireless network, if necessary, and then restore your original settings. Turn on the speakers. Change the power plans to their default settings, delete the Visits power plan, and then select your original plan. Restore the presentation settings to their original form. Close all open windows.

11. Submit the results of the preceding steps to your instructor, either in printed or electronic form, as requested.

Challenge | **Case Problem 2**

Use the skills you learned in the tutorial to set mobile computing options for an event planner.

There are no Data Files needed for this Case Problem.

Celebration Event Planners   Alissa Hanley started Celebration Event Planners in Omaha, Nebraska, for families and businesses who sponsor events such as anniversaries, retirement parties, and product introductions. Alissa often travels around Omaha to meet with potential clients and vendors, so she wants to know more about the Windows Vista mobile computing features. Many of the events she organizes involve slide shows that run on a notebook computer. As Alissa's assistant, you help her with a wide range of tasks, including planning events and managing the company's computers. She asks you to help her use Windows Vista to perform mobile computing tasks, including managing power options, giving presentations, and selecting other options for setting up a network. Complete the following steps, noting your original settings so you can restore them later:

1. Change the speaker volume to 30, and then mute the speakers.

2. Change the plan settings for the Power saver plan so that the display turns off after five minutes of idle time when running on battery power and after 30 minutes when plugged in. (If you are not using a mobile computer, set the display to turn off after 30 minutes of idle time.)

3. Create a power plan based on the High performance plan and name it **Events**. Set the Events plan to the following settings when running on battery power: turn off the display setting after 5 minutes of idle time and put the computer to sleep after 30 minutes of idle time. (If you are not using a mobile computer, set the display to turn off after 5 minutes of idle time.)

⊕ EXPLORE   4. Set the Events plan to use hybrid sleep instead of sleep for all types of power. Arrange the Power Options dialog box and the Edit Plan Settings window so you can see the settings in both windows, and then press Print Screen to capture an image of the desktop. Paste the image in a new Paint file, and save the file as **Events** in the Tutorial.08\Case2 folder provided with your Data Files.

5. Set the mobile computer to shut down when you close its lid and are running on battery power. Make sure a password is required to access your computer when it wakes up. (*Hint*: Click the Change settings that are currently unavailable link to activate this setting.) Press Alt+Print Screen to capture an image of the window. Paste the image in a new Paint file, and save the file as **Password** in the Tutorial.08\Case2 folder provided with your Data Files. Save your changes, and then close the Power Options window.

6. Change presentation settings so that when you give a presentation, the volume is set to high, the screen saver is turned off, and a black background is displayed. Press Alt+Print Screen to capture an image of the Presentation Settings dialog box. Paste the image in a new Paint file, and save the file as **Present** in the Tutorial.08\Case2 folder provided with your Data Files. Save your changes.

⊕ EXPLORE   7. Begin to set up a wireless ad hoc network named **Celebration**. Use **CelebR08** as the passphrase. Capture an image of the Set up a wireless ad hoc (computer-to-computer) network window that shows the network is ready to use. Paste the image in a new Paint file, and save the file as **Ad Hoc** in the Tutorial.08\Case2 folder provided with your Data Files.

⊕ EXPLORE   8. Begin to set up a new connection to a workplace. Choose to use your Internet connection (VPN). Use **VPN** as the Destination name, and choose not to connect now. Press Alt+Print Screen to capture an image of the window. Paste the image in a new Paint file, and save the file as **VPN** in the Tutorial.08\Case2 folder provided with your Data Files.

9. Open the System window to determine what your computer's name is and whether it is part of a workgroup or domain. Press Alt+Print Screen to capture an image of the window. Paste the image in a new Paint file, and save the file as **System** in the Tutorial.08\Case2 folder provided with your Data Files.

10. Restore your original settings. Change the speaker volume to its original setting, and then turn on the speakers. Change the power plans to their default settings, delete the Events power plan, and then select your original plan. Restore the original action to the closing the lid setting. Restore the presentation settings to their original form. Close all open windows.

11. Submit the results of the preceding steps to your instructor, either in printed or electronic form, as requested.

Challenge | **Case Problem 3**

Go beyond what you've learned to work with mobile computing and network settings for a market researcher.

There are no Data Files needed for this Case Problem.

Amity Market Research   Ron Amity is a marketing analyst who consults with companies who need market research to improve sales or develop new products. His company, Amity Market Research in Hartford, Connecticut, employs researchers who often work on mobile computers at their clients' offices. As a project assistant, part of your job is to make sure the researchers are using their computers effectively. Ron asks you to show him how to use Windows Vista to perform mobile computing tasks, including conserving battery power, connecting to networks, and sharing files. Complete the following steps, noting your original settings so you can restore them later:

⊕ EXPLORE

1. Click the battery meter icon in the notification area of the taskbar, and then click Learn how to conserve power. Read the Help topic about conserving power. Leave the Help window open.

2. In the Windows Mobility Center, change settings to conserve as much power as you can on your computer. Press Print Screen to capture an image of the desktop. Paste the image in a new Paint file, and save the file as **Conserve** in the Tutorial.08\Case3 folder provided with your Data Files.

3. Create a power plan based on the High performance plan and name it **Amity**. Set the Amity plan to turn off the display after five minutes of idle time when running on battery power and after 15 minutes when plugged in. (If you are not using a mobile computer, set the display to turn off after 15 minutes of idle time.) Also set the plan to put the computer to sleep after 30 minutes of idle time when using any type of power. Press Alt+Print Screen to capture an image of the window. Paste the image in a new Paint file, and save the file as **Amity** in the Tutorial.08\Case3 folder provided with your Data Files.

4. Change presentation settings so that when you give a presentation, the volume is set to 75, the screen saver is turned off, and img10 is shown as the desktop background. Press Alt+Print Screen to capture an image of the window. Paste the image in a new Paint file, and save the file as **Show** in the Tutorial.08\Case3 folder provided with your Data Files.

5. Connect to an available wireless network, entering a security key or passphrase as necessary. (If you are not equipped to connect to a wireless network, connect to a wired network.)

⊕ EXPLORE

6. Check the status of the network connection. Diagnose and repair the connection, and then capture an image of the results window. Paste the image in a new Paint file, and save the file as **Diagnose** in the Tutorial.08\Case3 folder provided with your Data Files.

⊕ EXPLORE

7. Turn on sharing for the Public Documents folder so that anyone with network access can open files. Press Alt+Print Screen to capture an image of the window that shows Public folder sharing turned on. Paste the image in a new Paint file, and save the file as **Open** in the Tutorial.08\Case3 folder provided with your Data Files. Close the Network and Sharing Center window.

8. Make sure offline files are enabled on your computer. If possible, make the Public Documents folder on a network computer always available offline.

9. Open the Sync Center and set up a sync partnership with offline files. Accept the default scheduled time for synchronizing.

10. Synchronize the offline files now. When the sync is finished, view the sync results and then press Alt+Print Screen to capture an image of the window. Paste the image in a new Paint file, and save the file as **Sync Center** in the Tutorial.08\Case3 folder provided with your Data Files.

⊕ EXPLORE 11. In the Network and Sharing Center window, click Show me all the shared network folders on this computer. Capture an image of the window. Paste the image in a new Paint file, and save the file as **Shared** in the Tutorial.08\Case3 folder provided with your Data Files.

12. Restore your original settings. Restore the power plans to their default settings, delete the Amity power plan, and then select your original plan. Restore the presentation settings to their original form. Turn off sharing for the Public Documents folder on the network computer. Delete the sync partnership with offline files. Disconnect from the network, if necessary, and then close all open windows.

13. Submit the results of the preceding steps to your instructor, either in printed or electronic form, as requested.

Research	**Case Problem 4**

Work with the skills you've learned and use the Internet to research networks for a group of city planners.

There are no Data Files needed for this Case Problem.

Columbia City Planning The city planning office for Columbia, Missouri, is considering connecting their computers on a network. Nelson Ochoa is the lead project manager, and asks you, an administrative assistant, to help him research small office networks using the Internet and Windows Help and Support. Complete the following steps:

1. The Columbia City planning office has the following characteristics and requirements:
   - There are nine users, seven on mobile computers and two on desktop computers.
   - All computers are running Windows Vista.
   - Most of the city planners use their computers outside of the office.
   - All users often distribute large files to other users.

2. Use the Internet to research appropriate networks for the Columbia City planning office. Choose two types of networks to recommend. Create a document with four column headings: **Network Technology**, **Hardware Requirements**, **Speed**, and **Cost**. Complete the columns according to the following descriptions:

Network Technology	Hardware Requirements	Speed	Cost
List two types of networks.	*List devices and other hardware required.*	*List speed considerations or rates*	*List Cost considerations.*

3. Save the document as **Networks** in the Tutorial.08\Case4 folder provided with your Data Files.

4. Submit the results of the preceding steps to your instructor, either in printed or electronic form, as requested.

| Assess | **SAM Assessment and Training** |

If you have a SAM user profile, you may have access to hands-on instruction, practice, and assessment of the skills covered in this tutorial. Log in to your SAM account (**http://sam2007.course.com**) to launch any assigned training activities or exams that relate to the skills covered in this tutorial.

| Review | **Quick Check Answers** |

Session 8.1

1. a computer you can easily carry, such as a laptop, notebook, or Tablet PC
2. c
3. power plan
4. False
5. screen saver on or off, volume, and desktop background image
6. Ethernet
7. Network name, security status, and signal strength

Session 8.2

1. Network window
2. False
3. Start Remote Desktop on the computer you want to connect from.
4. d
5. mapping
6. offline files
7. If you add, change, or delete a file in one location, Sync Center can add, overwrite, or delete an earlier version of the file in other locations.

Ending Data Files

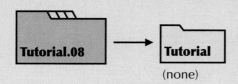

Tutorial

(none)

Review

Power Options.jpg
Power Button.jpg
Presentation.jpg
Network.jpg
Wireless.jpg
Sharing.jpg
Remote Desktop.jpg
Sync.jpg

Case1

Connect.jpg
Lid.jpg
NLA.jpg
Power Plans.jpg
Present.jpg
Public.jpg

Case2

Ad Hoc.jpg
Events.jpg
Password.jpg
System.jpg
VPN.jpg

Case3

Amity.jpg
Conserve.jpg
Diagnose.jpg
Open.jpg
Shared.jpg
Show.jpg
Sync Center.jpg

Case4

Networks.doc

Objectives

Session 9.1
- Back up and restore files
- Create a system restore point
- Install and uninstall software

Session 9.2
- Maintain hard disks
- Enable and disable hardware devices
- Install and update device drivers

Session 9.3
- Adjust monitor settings
- Set up multiple monitors
- Install and set up printers

Maintaining Hardware and Software

Managing Software, Disks, and Devices

Case | Northbrook Farmers Market

The Northbrook Farmers Market is a grocery store in Manchester, New Hampshire, that specializes in fresh food grown and raised on nearby New England farms. Shelly McCormick, the general manager of the store, spends most of her time meeting with farmers and other vendors, analyzing customer requests and sales trends, and training her store employees. When she needs to complete office work, she conducts much of her business on her Windows Vista PC. As her assistant back office manager, one of your responsibilities is to maintain the hardware and software at the store.

Shelly has heard that software and hardware problems can affect files, and she wants to make sure she can protect her files from corruption and accidental loss. You suggest she back up her files now, and set up a schedule to back them up on a regular basis. You also want to set up systems for maintaining Windows Vista and her hardware, including her hard disk and monitor. Finally, Shelly bought a new printer and wants to install it in the back office.

In this tutorial, you will back up and restore files and folders and create a schedule to do so automatically. You will also prepare for installing new programs, and then install software and view your updates. You will manage a hard disk by checking for problems and learn to improve performance. You will also learn how to maintain the devices attached to a computer, including your monitor and printer.

Starting Data Files

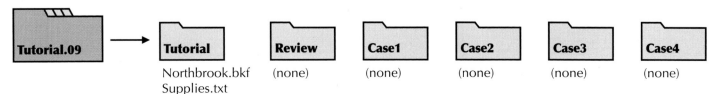

Tutorial.09 →	Tutorial	Review	Case1	Case2	Case3	Case4
	Northbrook.bkf Supplies.txt	(none)	(none)	(none)	(none)	(none)

Session 9.1

Backing Up and Restoring Files

No one is safe from computer problems that result in data loss. Problems such as a power surge, a power loss, a failed section of a hard disk, or a computer virus can strike at any time. Rather than risk disaster, you should make copies of your important files regularly. You have already learned how to copy data to and from your hard disk and a removable disk. Making a copy of a file or folder on a removable disk is one way to protect data.

To protect data on a hard disk, however, you should use a backup program instead of a copy procedure. A **backup program** copies and then automatically compresses files and folders from a hard disk into a single file, called a **backup file**. A backup file is a copy of one or more files that you store in a separate location from the original. The backup program stores a backup file on a **backup medium** such as an external or internal hard disk, or writeable CD or DVD. To back up files in Windows Vista, you use the Back Up Files Wizard, which guides you through the following steps of backing up your files:

- Specify where you want to save your backup file.
- Select the folders and files you want to back up.
- Indicate how often you want to create a backup.

| Reference Window | **Backing Up Files** |

- Click the Start button, click Control Panel, click System and Maintenance, and then click Backup and Restore Center.
- Click Back up files.
- Follow the steps in the wizard. If you are prompted for an administrator password or confirmation, type the password or provide confirmation.

Suppose you store all of your important files on drive C in three folders named Projects, Accounts, and Clients. Figure 9-1 shows how the Back Up Files Wizard backs up the files in these folders.

Backing up data   **Figure 9-1**

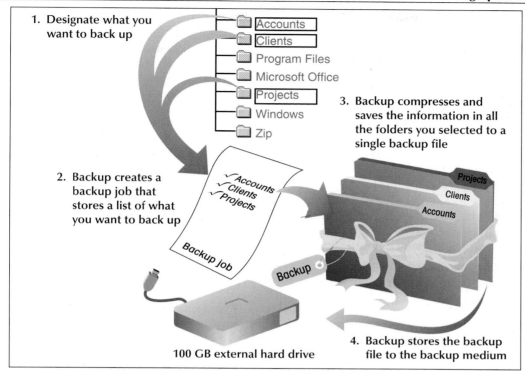

1. Designate what you want to back up

   - Accounts
   - Clients
   - Program Files
   - Microsoft Office
   - Projects
   - Windows
   - Zip

2. Backup creates a backup job that stores a list of what you want to back up

   Backup job
   - ✓ Accounts
   - ✓ Clients
   - ✓ Projects

3. Backup compresses and saves the information in all the folders you selected to a single backup file

   Projects
   Clients
   Accounts

   Backup

4. Backup stores the backup file to the backup medium

100 GB external hard drive

Backing up is different from copying files, because the Back Up Files Wizard copies files into a single, compressed file, whereas a copy simply duplicates the files. Figure 9-2 points out the differences between copying and backing up, showing why backing up files is a better data-protection method than copying files.

Comparing copying and backing up files   **Figure 9-2**

Copy	Backup
Copying your files can be time consuming and tedious because you must navigate to and select each file and folder that you want to copy.	Using the Back Up Files Wizard is faster because you select the files and folders in one step, and the wizard navigates to the folders and selects the files during the backup.
Because a copy of a file occupies the same amount of space as the original file, making a copy of all the files on a hard disk is impractical.	The Back Up Files Wizard can back up your entire computer and store the contents in a compressed file, which is much smaller than the original files combined.
You need to manually note which files and folders have changed since your last backup.	The Back Up Files Wizard keeps track of which files and folders are new or modified. When you create a backup, you can back up only the files that have changed since your last backup.
You need to set reminders on your own to create backups periodically.	If you set up automatic backups, Windows regularly backs up your files and folders so that you don't have to remember to do it.
If you do lose data because of a computer failure, it is not easy to locate a file you need in your backups.	The Back Up Files Wizard keeps track of the files you have backed up, and makes it easy to find and recover a file.

| **Determining Which Files to Back Up**

The most valuable files on your computer are your data files—the documents, pictures, videos, projects, and financial records that you create and edit. You should back up any data files that would be difficult or impossible to replace, and regularly back up files that you change frequently. You don't need to back up programs because you can use the original product disks to reinstall them, and programs typically take up a lot of space on backup media.

After you back up files, you should store the backups in a safe place where unauthorized people cannot access them. For example, if you create a backup of your personal folder by burning those files on a CD, you should store the CD away from the computer where the CD is unlikely to be tampered with or damaged. For your most valuable files, create two backups and store one off site, such as in a safe deposit box. If you accidentally delete or replace files on your hard disk or lose them due to a virus or worm, software or hardware trouble, or a complete hard disk failure, you can **restore** your files from the backup. When you restore files, Windows Vista extracts the files you want from the backup and then copies them to a location you specify.

Specifying Where to Save Your Backup File

With Windows Vista, you can create backups on a hard disk, writeable CD or DVD, or a network folder. To select the location that is best for you, consider the hardware installed on your computer and the number and size of files that you want to back up. You can back up files to any of the following locations:

- **Internal hard drive**. If you have an additional internal hard drive in your computer, you can use it to back up files. However, you cannot back up files to a folder on the same hard drive on which Windows Vista is installed because if your computer suffers a virus or software failure, you might have to reformat the drive and reinstall Windows to recover from the problem.
- **External hard drive**. If your computer has a USB port, you can attach an external hard drive to it and then back up files to the external drive. If you plan to backup your entire computer, the external hard drive must have plenty of space for your backups; at least 200 GB is often recommended. You need less storage space if you plan to back up only selected files. For extra security, keep your external hard drive in a fireproof location separate from the computer. Because of its portability, capacity, and ease of use, backing up to an external hard drive is the option experienced computer users prefer.
- **Writeable disc**. If your computer has a CD or DVD burner, you can back up your files to writeable CDs or DVDs. (A writeable CD means that you can add, delete, or change its contents.) The Back Up Files Wizard estimates how much space you need each time you perform a backup. If you are backing up to writeable discs, make sure you have enough to store the complete backup.
- **Network folder**. If your computer is on a network, you can create a backup on a network folder. You need to have permission to save files in the folder and set sharing options so that unauthorized users cannot access the backup.

If your computer is not equipped with an extra internal hard disk, USB port, or disc burner, or if you are not connected to a network, you can purchase this hardware or use an Internet-based file storage service. These services let you store personal, password-protected backups, usually on a server you can access via the Internet.

If you are backing up only certain types of files, such as documents, you might be able to use a USB flash drive as your backup medium. The USB flash drive should have plenty of free space—at least twice the amount you plan to back up. If you use a USB flash drive with 1 GB of storage space or more, for example, Windows Vista treats the flash drive like an external hard drive plugged into the USB port.

Selecting the Folders and Files to Back Up

When you use the Back Up Files Wizard, you can select personal data files to back up, such as documents, financial records, pictures, and projects. Besides backing up these personal files, you can back up your entire computer, including programs and system settings, using an option called Windows Complete PC Backup. (This option is not available with Windows Vista Home Basic or Home Premium.) Backing up your entire computer creates a complete image of the computer, which includes a copy of your programs, system settings, and files and a record of their original locations. You can then use the complete backup if your computer stops working. Microsoft recommends that you update the complete backup image every six months. Figure 9-3 describes backing up files and backing up your entire computer.

Backing Up Files or Your Computer ◀ Figure 9-3

Back Up Option	What It Backs Up	When to Use
Back up files	Personal files such as pictures, music, and documents	On a regular schedule and before you make system changes
Back up computer	All the files, folders, and settings on your computer	When you first set up your computer and every six months afterwards

When you back up personal files, the Back Up Files Wizard lets you back up the most common file types, including documents, pictures, music, and compressed folders. It does not let you back up system files, program files, Web e-mail not stored on your hard disk, files in the Recycle Bin, temporary files, or user profile settings. In addition, you cannot back up files that have been encrypted using the Encrypting File System (EFS), which is a feature of Windows that allows you to store information on your *hard disk* in an *encrypted* format. (EFS is not fully supported in Windows Vista Starter, Home Basic, or Home Premium.) Furthermore, you can back up only files stored on hard disks formatted with the NT File System (NTFS), not the earlier versions of the file allocation table (FAT) file system.

When you backup an entire computer, the Windows Complete PC Backup image contains copies of your programs, system settings, and files. This is usually a very large backup file that you can use to restore the contents of your computer if your hard disk or entire computer stops working.

> **Tip**
>
> To determine what type of file system a disk uses, open the Computer window, right-click the disk, and then click Properties.

Indicating How Often to Back Up

The Back Up Files Wizard lets you create automatic backups on a daily, weekly, or monthly basis. You can also create backups manually at any time. You should back up your personal files regularly, preferably at least once a week. If you're working on an important project and can't afford to lose even a few hours worth of work, back up your files once or twice a day. You should also back up your files before making any system changes, such as adding new hardware or making significant changes to Windows by installing a service pack, for example. If you create many files at a time, such as dozens or hundreds of digital photos you took at a special occasion, back up those files as soon as you can.

You should create a complete PC image when you first set up your computer, when it contains only programs and files provided by the computer manufacturer. Microsoft recommends that you update the complete backup image every six months.

The first time you back up your personal files and your complete computer, you need media with enough space to store the files. The Back Up Files Wizard can create a backup file that spans more than one optical disc, so you can back up your complete computer using a few DVDs, for example. Note that you need to be available to insert additional discs as necessary during the backup. If you run out of discs, however, you can suspend the backup and finish it later. After you create the first backup file, Windows keeps track of the files that have been added or modified since your last backup so you only have to update the existing backup, which saves time and space on your backup media.

Before you create a back up file, you want to copy files to Shelly's computer so that Windows includes them in the backup. You'll store the files in a folder named Shelly so that you can find them easily later.

To copy files to the Shelly folder:

▶ 1. Navigate to the **Documents** folder in your personal folder on the hard disk of your computer.

   Trouble? If you are not allowed to access the Documents folder, navigate to another folder in your personal folder.

▶ 2. Click **Organize** on the toolbar, and then click **New Folder**.

▶ 3. Type **Shelly** as the name of the folder.

▶ 4. Copy the files from the Tutorial.09\Tutorial folder provided with your Data Files to the Shelly folder.

▶ 5. Close the folder window.

Now you're ready to back up Shelly's documents.

Backing Up Files

Before you back up your personal files, make sure you know where you want to store the backup file, which files you want to back up, and when you want to schedule automatic backups. The first dialog box in the Back Up Files Wizard lets you choose where to save your backup. The wizard searches your computer and displays a list of all locations you can use for the backup. Windows Vista cannot create backups in the following types of locations:

• Tape drives
• The hard disk on which Windows Vista is installed
• CD-ROM drive

Most of the work Shelly does on her computer involves documents, such as text documents and spreadsheets, and she has not backed up her documents on her Windows Vista computer yet. You'll show her how to back up these files onto an external hard drive named EXTERNAL on drive F. Substitute the name of your backup location for EXTERNAL (F:) in the following steps.

To perform the steps, your computer needs access to an additional internal hard drive, an external hard drive, a network folder, or a writeable CD or DVD drive. You also need to log on to the computer using an Administrator account. If your computer cannot access these locations, or you cannot log on as an Administrator, read but do not perform the following steps. If you do perform the steps, note the original settings so you can restore them later.

To back up personal files:

▶ **1.** If necessary, insert a writeable CD or DVD into the appropriate drive or attach an external hard drive to your computer by plugging it into a USB port. Close any dialog boxes that open.

▶ **2.** Click the **Start** button 🔘 on the taskbar, click **Control Panel**, click **System and Maintenance**, and then click **Backup and Restore Center**. The Backup and Restore Center window opens as shown in Figure 9-4.

Backup and Restore Center ◀ **Figure 9-4**

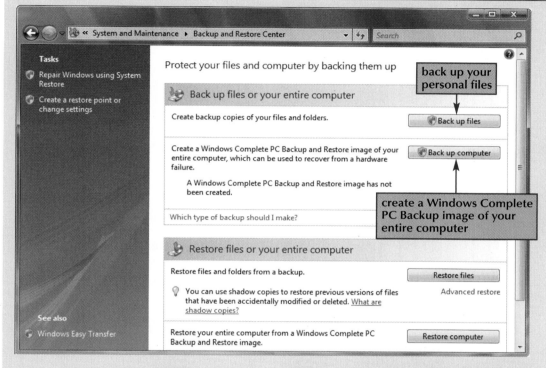

▶ **3.** Click the **Back up files** button. The Back Up Files Wizard starts and asks where you want to save your backup. See Figure 9-5.

Trouble? If a User Account Control dialog box opens requesting your permission or a password to continue, enter the password or click the Continue button.

Trouble? If your computer is already set up to make backups, the wizard starts backing up files. Click the notification message, click the Stop backup button, click Change settings, and then click Change backup settings.

Figure 9-5 | **Back Up Files Wizard**

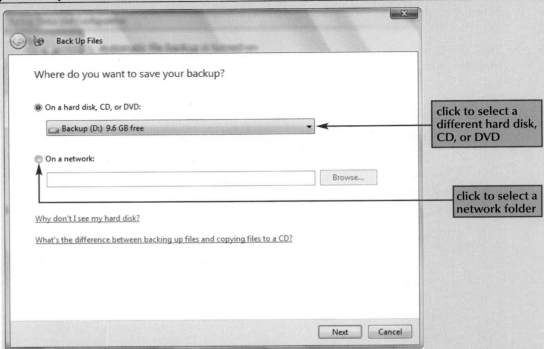

4. If necessary, click the **On a hard disk, CD, or DVD** option button, click the **arrow button**, and then click **EXTERNAL (F:)**.

   Trouble? If you are creating a backup on a different drive, click the arrow button, and then click the appropriate location.

   Trouble? If you need to create a backup on a network, click the On a network option button, and then click the Browse button to navigate to the network drive.

5. Click the **Next** button. The next wizard dialog box asks which file types you want to back up.

   Trouble? If a dialog box opens asking which disks you want to include in the backup, your computer has more than one hard drive. Click Local Disk (C:) (System) and then click the Next button unless your instructor prefers otherwise.

6. Click to remove check marks from the check boxes so that only the **Documents** check box is selected. See Figure 9-6.

Selecting file types to back up ◄ Figure 9-6

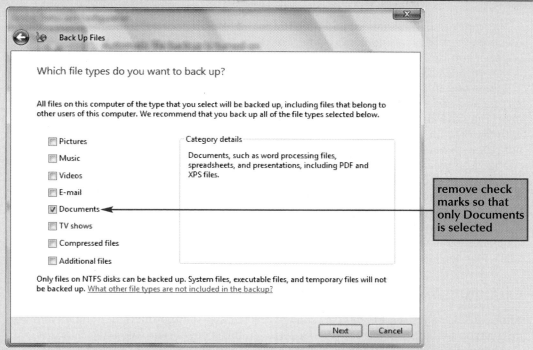

7. Click the **Next** button. The next wizard dialog box asks how often you want to create a backup. Shelly wants to create an automatic weekly backup on Sundays at 9:00 p.m.

8. Click the **What time** button, and then click **9:00 PM**. The other settings should match those shown in Figure 9-7.

Scheduling the backups ◄ Figure 9-7

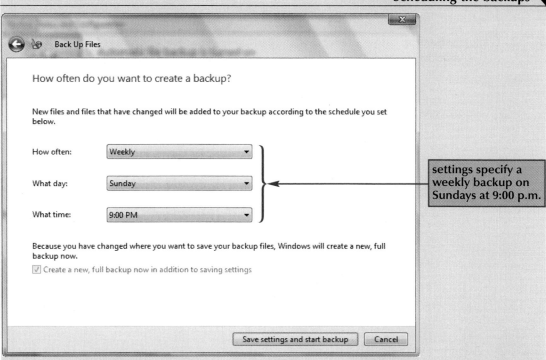

▶ **9.** Click the **Save settings and start backup** button. The backup starts, storing the specified files in a backup file, which might take a few minutes.

Backups are named and saved in the following format: *backup location\computer name\Backup Set year-month-day time*. For example, if your computer name is Desktop, your backup location is F, and you backed up on April 2, 2010, at 10:16:00, that backup is named Backup Set 2010-04-02 101600 and is stored in F:\Desktop.

When you make a full backup, a backup folder is created and labeled with that date. As you add updates, the date in the label stays the same, though your backup is up to date. The next time you make a full backup, a new backup folder is created and labeled with the date for that day, and any updates are then added to that new folder. You should not delete the current backup folder, because Windows uses it to track the files that have changed on your computer.

Keep in mind that after Windows Vista makes the first full backup, it backs up only files that have changed since your last backup. That means it doesn't need as much storage space to create the subsequent backups. Eventually, after many files have changed, Windows Vista will need to create another full backup, which it stores in a different folder. As you add personal files to the folders on your computer, each full backup might require more storage space than the last full backup, so keep additional storage media handy.

Changing Your Backup Settings

After you create a backup, you can change any backup settings, including the location of the backup file, the types of files to backup, and the schedule for automatic backups. You do so by selecting Change settings in the Backup and Restore Center window, which starts the Back Up Files Wizard.

Shelly decides that she wants to schedule automatic backups on Fridays at 9 p.m. instead of Sundays. She has scheduled her antivirus software to run on Sunday evenings, and doesn't want the two programs to conflict. You'll show Shelly how to change the backup settings.

To change backup settings:

▶ **1.** Make sure your computer can still access your backup media.

▶ **2.** Click the **Backup and Restore Center** button on the taskbar to make that the active window. It now displays the results of your last backup. See Figure 9-8.

Details about your last backup | **Figure 9-8**

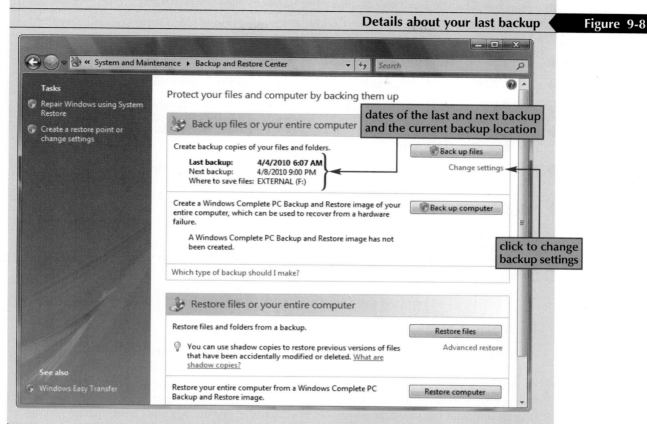

3. Click **Change settings**. The Back Up Status and Configuration window opens. See Figure 9-9.

Back Up Status and Configuration window | **Figure 9-9**

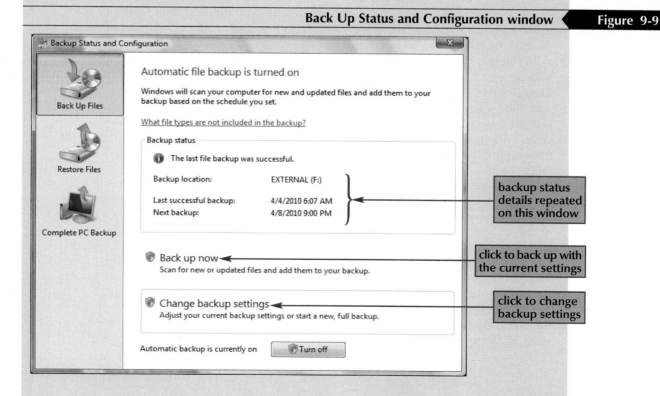

▶ **4.** Click **Change backup settings**. The Back Up Files Wizard starts.

> **Trouble?** If a User Account Control dialog box opens requesting your permission or a password to continue, enter the password or click the Continue button.

▶ **5.** Click the **Next** button to accept your current drive as the backup drive.

▶ **6.** If necessary, click **Local Disk (C:) (System)**, and then click the **Next** button.

▶ **7.** Click the **Next** button to accept Documents as the only type of file to back up.

▶ **8.** Click the **What day** button, and then click **Friday**. The backup schedule is now set to a weekly backup on Fridays at 9 p.m.

▶ **9.** Click the **Save settings and exit** button. Windows Vista saves your settings and will apply them for the next backup.

▶ **10.** Close the Backup Status and Configuration window.

> **Tip**
>
> Click the Create a new, full backup now in addition to saving settings check box to change settings and create a backup at the same time.

If you want Windows to back up files on your computer automatically late at night, remember to leave your computer turned on during the scheduled time. It can't make backups if your computer is turned off.

Next, you'll show Shelly how to restore the files that she backed up.

Restoring Files and Folders

All hard disks eventually fail, even if you maintain them conscientiously. When a hard disk fails, you can no longer access the files it contains. For that reason alone, you should back up your personal files regularly. If your hard disk does fail, and a computer maintenance expert believes data recovery is hopeless, you'll need to install a new hard disk or reformat the one that you have. Practically everyone who has been using computers for very long has a data loss story to tell. Many computer owners who now make regular backups learned the hard way how important it is to protect data. Backing up your files is one of the most effective ways to save time and maintain data integrity when you are working on a computer. Create the first backup file, and then set up an automatic schedule to update it regularly. If you do lose data, your backup file allows you to easily restore the files you lost.

When you restore personal files, Windows Vista extracts the files you want from the backup media and then copies them to a location you specify. You can restore individual files, groups of files, or all files that you have backed up. In addition to selecting the files and folders you want to restore and specifying where you want to restore them, you can also set other restore options. For example, you can specify that you do not want Windows Vista to replace any current files on your computer, or to replace files only if the ones on the hard disk are older. Either option prevents you from overwriting files you might need.

You restore files using the Restore Files Wizard, which you also start from the Backup and Restore Center window. If you want to restore files from your latest backup or an older one, you click the Restore files option. If you want to restore files from a backup made on another computer, you click the Advanced restore option. In either case, you specify the files to restore by adding files and folders from the backup file to a list. You can also search for files to restore. Windows Vista restores all the files you add to the list. You can restore the files to their original location (that is, the location from which you backed them up) or a different location you specify.

When you restore files from a Windows Complete PC Backup image, you are restoring the entire computer, so you don't need to choose files or folders to restore. Windows Vista replaces all of your current programs, system settings, and files.

If you have a backup file with a BKF filename extension, that backup file was created using a previous version of Windows. You can restore a BKF file by using Windows NT Backup - Restore Utility, a program you can download from the Microsoft Web site, which you will do later in this tutorial.

You'll show Shelly how to restore the documents she backed up using her latest backup.

To restore files from a backup:

▶ **1.** In the Backup and Restore Center window, click the **Restore files** button. The Restore Files Wizard starts and asks what you want to restore.

▶ **2.** Click the **Files from the latest backup** option button, if necessary, and then click the **Next** button. The next dialog box in the wizard opens where you can select the files and folders you want to restore. See Figure 9-10.

Selecting files and folders to restore   Figure 9-10

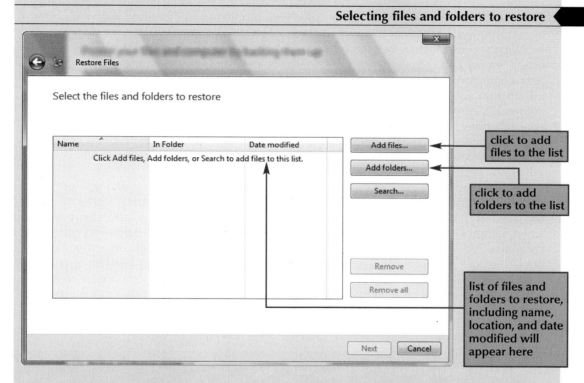

▶ **3.** Click the **Add folders** button, and then navigate to and click the **Shelly** folder in your Documents folder. Click the **Add** button. The Shelly folder is added to the list of files and folders to restore.

▶ **4.** Click the **Next** button. The next wizard dialog box asks where you want to save the restored files.

▶ **5.** Click the **In the original location** option button, if necessary, and then click the **Start restore** button. The Copy File dialog box opens and indicates the Shelly folder already includes a file with the same name.

▶ **6.** Click **Copy and Replace**. Windows restores the files from the backup. Restoring might take a few minutes, depending on the size of the files you backed up.

▶ **7.** When a dialog box opens indicating the files were successfully restored, click the **Finish** button.

▶ **8.** Close all open windows.

Besides restoring files that you have backed up manually or through an automatic backup, you can restore files that Windows Vista creates when you create a restore point, which you'll explore next.

Managing Software

Although your personal files are the most valuable files you have on a computer, they are useful to you only if you have the right programs to create, edit, and otherwise enhance those files. To safeguard your data and your programs, recall that you can create a Windows Complete PC Backup image using the Backup and Restore Center window. To save system files without affecting your personal files, you can use **System Restore**, a Windows tool that helps you restore your computer's system files to an earlier point when your system was working reliably. If your system becomes unstable or starts to act unpredictably after installing software, you can try uninstalling the software to see if that solves your problem. If uninstalling does not solve your problem, you can undo system changes by restoring your computer to an earlier date when the system worked correctly.

When you use System Restore, it tracks changes to your computer's system files and uses a feature called System Protection to create a **restore point**, which is a snapshot of your computer's system files. A restore point contains information about Windows system information and settings in the **registry**, which is a database of information about your computer's configuration. If your system becomes unstable, use System Restore to return your computer settings to a particular restore point. System Restore creates restore points at regular intervals (typically once a day) and when it detects the beginning of a change to your computer, such as a Windows Update. You can also create a restore point yourself at any time.

Because System Restore reverts to previous system settings without affecting your personal files, it usually cannot help you recover a personal file that has been lost or damaged. To protect your data, you still need to back up your files regularly. However, when System Protection is turned on (which it is by default for all the hard disks on your computer), Windows does save copies of data files that you've modified since it made the last restore point. These files are called **shadow copies**, or previous versions of your files. You can use shadow copies to restore files that you accidentally modified, deleted, or damaged. For your own data files, you can open the shadow copy, save it to a different location, or restore a previous version. (Only Windows Vista Business, Ultimate, and Enterprise editions create shadow copies.)

InSight	**Selecting a Tool to Restore Your Files**

Windows Vista offers a few tools for restoring files. If you accidentally delete a file, the easiest way to recover it is to retrieve it from the Recycle Bin. If you've already emptied the Recycle Bin, the most reliable way to recover the file is to restore it from a backup. If you don't have a backup that contains the file you need, your next step is to restore a shadow copy, which provides a previous version of the file.

Whereas System Restore helps you manage system software, you can also use Windows Vista tools to manage your applications. To make sure the programs provided with Windows are running smoothly and include the latest features, you can use Windows Update to install a software update. You can also install other programs, such as office productivity suites, games, and security programs. Typically, you install programs from a CD, DVD, Web site, or network. If you no longer use a program or need to free up space on your hard disk, you can uninstall a program. You'll learn how to do both later in this section.

Creating a System Restore Point

Although Windows Vista automatically creates system restore points periodically and before a significant system event such as installing new software, you can create a restore point yourself at any time. When a restore point is created, Windows saves images of its system files, programs, and registry settings. It might also save images of files that help to run programs, such as scripts and batch files. As with backup files, Windows can only create restore points on NTFS disks, not FAT disks. To create restore points, you need at least 300 MB of free space on a hard disk that has at least 1 GB of storage space. As this space fills up with restore points, System Restore deletes older restore points to make room for new ones. Also note that Windows Vista does not recognize restore points created in earlier versions of Windows because it uses a different method to create them.

Creating a System Restore Point	Reference Window

- Click the Start button, point to All Programs, click Accessories, click System Tools, and then click System Restore. (If you are prompted for an administrator password or confirmation, enter the password or provide confirmation.)
- Click the open System Protection link in the System Restore dialog box.
- Click the System Protection tab, if necessary, and then click the Create button.
- Enter a description to help you identify the restore point, and then click the Create button.
- Click the OK button.

Shelly's computer is working well right now, so you'll show her how to create a restore point to protect her system. Before you do, you want to make sure that System Protection is turned on for her computer.

To make sure System Protection is turned on:

1. Click the **Start** button 🪟 on the taskbar, click **Control Panel**, click **System and Maintenance**, and then click **System**. The System window opens.

2. In the left pane, click **System protection**. The System Properties dialog box opens. See Figure 9-11. The Available Disks list shows for which disks System Protection is turned on. Make sure the Local Disk (C:) check box is selected, indicating that System Protection is turned on for the drive where Windows Vista is installed on Shelly's computer.

Figure 9-11 System Properties dialog box

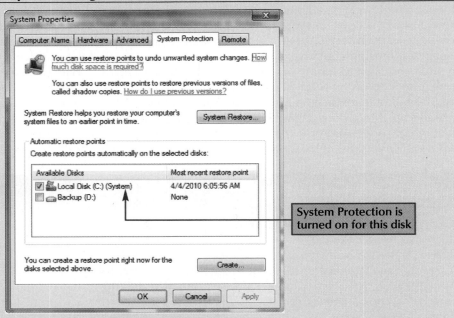

Trouble? If a User Account Control dialog box opens requesting your permission or a password to continue, enter the password or click the Continue button.

You can use this same dialog box to create a restore point yourself.

To create a restore point:

1. In the System Properties dialog box, click the **Create** button. The System Protection dialog box opens.

2. Type **Shelly** as the description for this restore point. Windows will add the current date and time automatically.

3. Click the **Create** button. Windows creates a restore point, which might take a few minutes, and then displays a message indicating it was created successfully.

4. Click the **OK** button.

At any point after you or Windows Vista create a restore point, you can select one to undo changes made to your system up to that restore point. Every time you use System Restore, Windows creates a restore point before proceeding, so you can undo the changes if reverting to a restore point doesn't fix your problem. If you need to restore your computer, Windows recommends using the most recent restore point created before a significant change, such as installing a program. You can also choose from a list of restore points. It's a good idea to select restore points in descending order, starting with the most recent. If that doesn't solve your problem, try the next most recent, and so on. Although System Restore doesn't delete any of your personal files, it removes programs installed after the restore point you select, requiring you to reinstall those programs.

You'll show Shelly how to restore her computer in case she has system problems and wants to revert to a previous point. You won't actually restore her computer in the following steps because it doesn't need it right now. You'll work as far as you can through the System Restore dialog boxes, and then click the Cancel button instead of the Finish button. You also inform Shelly that she should save any open files and close any running programs before using System Restore.

To begin restoring a computer:

▶ 1. In the System Properties dialog box, click the **System Restore** button. The System Restore Wizard starts.

▶ 2. If necessary, click the **Choose a different restore point** option button. Then click the **Next** button. The next System Restore dialog box opens where you can choose a restore point. See Figure 9-12.

> **Tip**
>
> You can also open the System Restore dialog box by clicking the Start button, pointing to All Programs, clicking Accessories, clicking System Tools, and then clicking System Restore.

Choosing a restore point ◀ Figure 9-12

▶ 3. Click the **second restore point** in the list, which is probably named Manual:Shelly, the one Windows created when you backed up Shelly's documents, and then click the **Next** button. The last System Restore dialog box opens so you can confirm your restore point.

▶ 4. Click the **Cancel** button to close the dialog box without creating a restore point.

Trouble? If you clicked the Finish button instead of the Cancel button, wait until System Restore finishes and restarts your computer. Open the System Properties dialog box, click the System Restore button, click Undo System Restore, click Next, and then click Finish.

▶ 5. Close all open windows.

Recall that Windows Vista saves restore points until they fill up the hard disk space reserved by System Restore. As you and Windows create new restore points, System Restore deletes old ones. If you turn off System Protection on a disk, Windows deletes all the restore points from that disk. When you turn System Protection back on, Windows starts creating new restore points.

Restoring a Shadow Copy of a File

Besides saving an image of your system when it creates a restore point, Windows Vista also saves shadow copies of files that have been modified since the last restore point. As with restore points, Windows creates shadow copies of files on a hard disk only if System Protection is turned on for that disk. You can restore a single file or an entire folder. Note that Windows saves only one version of a file as a shadow copy. For example, if you modify a file several times in one day, Windows saves only the version that was current when the restore point was created.

When you created a restore point earlier, Windows created a shadow copy of the Supplies text file at the same time. You can change this file now, save it, and then restore its shadow copy.

To change the Supplies file and then restore a previous version:

▶ **1.** Open the Shelly folder window.

▶ **2.** In the Shelly folder window, double-click **Supplies**. The Supplies file opens in the default text editor, such as Notepad.

▶ **3.** Enter your name at the end of the document, save the file, and then close it.

▶ **4.** Right-click the **Supplies** file, and then click **Restore previous versions**. The Supplies Properties dialog box opens to the Previous Versions tab. See Figure 9-13.

Figure 9-13 ▶ **Previous Versions tab in the Supplies Properties dialog box**

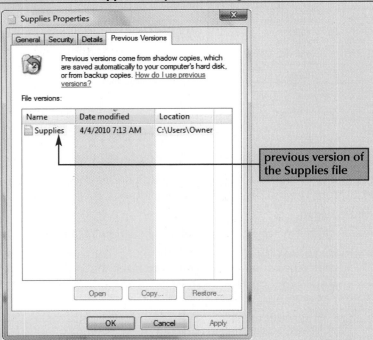

▶ **5.** Click **Supplies** in the File versions list, and then click the **Restore** button. The Previous Versions dialog box opens, asking you to confirm that you want to restore the Supplies.txt file.

▶ **6.** Click the **Restore** button. After restoring the file, Windows displays a message indicating that the file was successfully restored.

▶ **7.** Click the **OK** button.

▶ **8.** Click the **OK** button to close the Supplies Properties dialog box.

▶ **9.** Close all open windows.

Windows restores the previous version of the Supplies file to the Shelly folder. Next, Shelly mentions that she has a backup file that she created on her old Windows XP computer. She'd like to restore a file from that backup. To do so, she needs to install a program from the Microsoft Web site.

Installing Software

You can install software from at least three locations: from a CD or DVD, Web site, or network folder. Installing typically involves starting a setup program, copying the files you need from the installation medium to a folder on your computer, and then changing Windows Vista settings so that the program runs properly. Most programs come with a setup wizard that asks you for some information, such as where you want to store the program, and then takes care of the rest of the tasks.

If the software you want to install is provided on a CD or DVD, you insert the disc into the appropriate drive on your computer. In most cases, as soon as Windows detects the disc in the drive—a feature called AutoPlay—a dialog box opens and asks if you want to run the setup wizard. If you choose to run the wizard, the Setup program starts and guides you through the installation steps. If a dialog box does not open to ask about the setup wizard, you can browse the disk and open the program's setup file yourself by double-clicking a file named Setup.exe or Install.exe.

You install a program from a Web site by using your browser to visit the Web site and then clicking a link to download the program. When you click the link, a dialog box usually opens and gives you the choice of running the setup program now or saving it to install the program later. If you choose Run (or Open), you can install the program immediately by following the instructions in a dialog box or wizard. However, if your transmission is interrupted, you'll have to start downloading the program again. More importantly, downloading and running a program in the same step introduces the risk of a virus. That's why choosing to save the program file when you download it is a safer option—your antivirus software can then scan the file for known viruses or you can do so yourself. In either case, be sure you trust the publisher of any program you download from a Web site. You have already learned some ways to gauge the legitimacy of a Web site, such as by using the phishing filter. In addition, use the following guidelines to determine whether a Web site is trustworthy:

- **The Web site is certified by an Internet trust organization**. Look for a privacy certification seal from a trust organization such as TRUSTe, BBB Online, or Web Trust. These seals usually appear on the home page of the Web site. However, some unscrupulous Web sites display fake trust logos. You can find out if a Web site is registered with an Internet trust organization by visiting that organization's Web site.
- **The Web site is owned by an organization you know well**. If you are using a Web site for a brick-and-mortar store where you have shopped or if you or others have visited the Web site in the past with no problems, you can probably trust the files provided by the Web site.

In contrast, be wary of downloading files from Web sites you are invited to visit in an e-mail message sent by someone you don't know, Web sites that offer objectionable content, and those that make offers that seem too generous, indicating a possible sale of illegal or pirated software.

If your computer is on a network, such as an internal network at your school or office, the network administrator might make programs available that you can install. To do so, you use the Programs category in Control Panel, and then open the Get Programs Online window. You select a program from the list, click Install, and follow the instructions that usually appear in a wizard.

You'll show Shelly how to download a program from the Microsoft Web site and then install it so that she can restore files from her BKP backup file. A BKP file is one made with the Backup program provided in earlier versions of Windows. The Windows Vista Back Up Files Wizard cannot restore files in a BKP backup, so you need a special program designed for that purpose.

To perform the following steps, make sure you have permission to download software from a Web site. If your school does not allow you to download files, read but do not perform the following steps. If you do have permission, you need to know whether you are running a 32-bit or 64-bit version of Windows Vista. To find out, open the System window from Control Panel. The operating system is listed under *System type* and indicates whether it is 32-bit or 64-bit.

To download a program from the Microsoft Web site:

▶ **1.** Start Internet Explorer.

▶ **2.** Type **www.microsoft.com/downloads** in the Address bar, and then press the **Enter** key. The Microsoft Download Center Web page opens.

▶ **3.** In the Search box next to the All Downloads text box, type **backup restore**, and then click the **Go** button. The Search Results Web page lists programs you can download to backup or restore files.

▶ **4.** Click the **Windows NT Backup – Restore Utility** link. The Windows NT Backup - Restore Utility page opens. See Figure 9-14.

Figure 9-14	Windows NT Backup – Restore Utility Web page

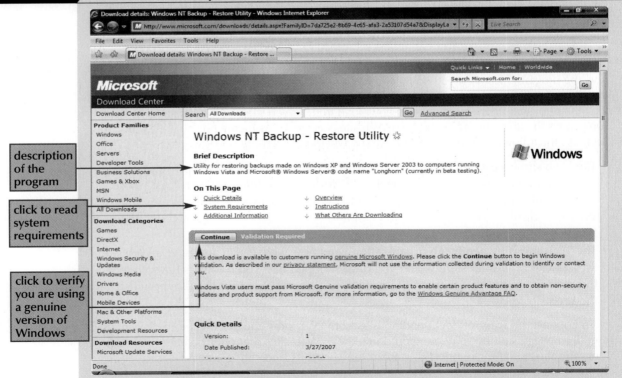

Trouble? If the Windows NT Backup – Restore Utility link or a similar link does not appear on the Search Results Web page, click the Next link to view another page of search results. If you do not find a link to the Windows NT Backup – Restore Utility page, close Internet Explorer and then read but do not perform the remaining steps.

5. Click the **Continue** button, if necessary, to validate your copy of Windows, and then follow the instructions on the Web page. After validating Windows (which might take a few minutes), a Download files below link appears on the page.

Trouble? If Windows Vista asks if you want to install an ActiveX control, click the Yes button.

6. Click the **Download files below** link. Shelly needs the program designed for the 32-bit version of Windows Vista.

7. Click the **Download** button for the file named NtBackupRestore_x86.msi. The File Download – Security Warning dialog box opens. See Figure 9-15.

Trouble? If you are using a 64-bit version of Windows Vista, click the Download button for the file named NtBackupRestore_Win64.msi.

File Download – Security Warning dialog box ◀ Figure 9-15

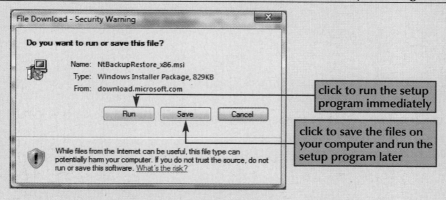

8. Click the **Save** button. The Save As dialog box opens.

9. Navigate to the **Shelly** folder in the Documents folder, and then click the **Save** button. The Microsoft Web site downloads the file, which might take a few minutes, and then closes the dialog box.

Trouble? If the Download complete dialog box does not close, click the Close button.

10. Close Internet Explorer.

Before you install the software you just downloaded, you need to turn on the Removable Storage Management setting for Windows. This also gives you an opportunity to open the Programs and Features window, which you'll use later to uninstall a program.

To turn on a Windows setting:

1. Click the **Start** button 🪟 on the taskbar, click **Control Panel**, click **Programs**, and then click **Programs and Features**. The Programs and Features window opens.

2. In the left pane, click **Turn Windows features on or off**. The Windows Features dialog box opens, scans the features in Windows Vista, and then displays them in the dialog box. See Figure 9-16.

Figure 9-16 ▶ **Windows Features dialog box**

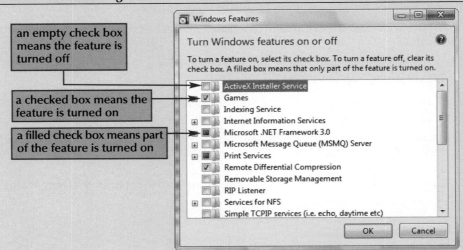

an empty check box means the feature is turned off

a checked box means the feature is turned on

a filled check box means part of the feature is turned on

Trouble? If a User Account Control dialog box opens requesting your permission or a password to continue, enter the password or click the Continue button.

▶ **3.** Click the **Removable Storage Management** check box to select it.

▶ **4.** Click the **OK** button to close the Windows Features dialog box. It might take a few minutes for Windows to configure the new features.

▶ **5.** Minimize the Programs and Features window.

When you use the Save option in the File Download – Security Warning dialog box to download files, Windows saves in the folder you specify all the files it needs to install the program. To install the program, you double-click the file you downloaded.

To install the downloaded program:

▶ **1.** Navigate to the **Shelly** folder.

▶ **2.** Double-click the **NtBackupRestore_x86** file.

Trouble? If you downloaded NtBackupRestore_Win64.msi, double-click the NtBackupRestore_Win64 file.

▶ **3.** If the Open File – Security Warning dialog box opens, click the **Run** button to start the Setup Wizard.

▶ **4.** Click the **Next** button to start the Setup Wizard.

▶ **5.** Read the License Agreement, click the **I Agree** option button, and then click the **Next** button.

▶ **6.** Click the **Next** button to start the installation. Windows Vista installs the program in its default location.

Trouble? If a User Account Control dialog box opens requesting your permission or a password to continue, click the Continue button.

▶ **7.** Click the **Close** button.

▶ **8.** Close the Shelly folder window.

Now you can show Shelly how to start the Windows NT Backup – Restore Utility program to restore files to Windows Vista from a BKP backup file. Like any other Windows Vista program, it is available on the Start menu. After starting this program, you can use it to restore a file from the BKP backup in the Shelly folder.

To restore a file from a BKP backup:

▶ 1. Click the **Start** button 🕐 on the taskbar, point to **All Programs**, and then click **Windows NT Backup – Restore Utility**. (It should appear at the bottom of the All Programs list.)

▶ 2. Click **NTBackup-RestoreUtility**. The program starts and opens its main window. See Figure 9-17.

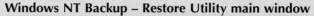
Windows NT Backup – Restore Utility main window   Figure 9-17

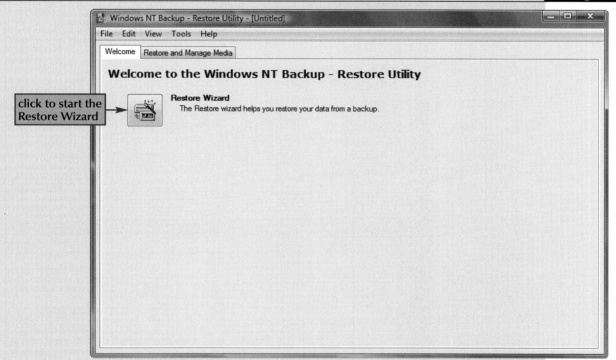

Trouble? If a User Account Control dialog box opens asking whether you want to allow or deny a request to run a program from an unknown source, click Allow.

▶ 3. Click the **Restore Wizard** button, and then click the **Next** button. The What to Restore dialog box opens.

▶ 4. Click the **Browse** button. In the Open Backup File dialog box, click the **Browse** button, and then navigate to the **Shelly** folder in your Documents folder. Double-click the **Northbrook** file, and then click the **OK** button. Windows displays the files in the Northbrook backup.

▶ 5. Double-click **File** in the left pane, and then double-click **Test Backup created**.

▶ 6. Click the three **C:** check boxes to select them, and then click the **Next** button. The Restore wizard confirms your selection.

▶ 7. Click the **Finish** button.

▶ 8. Click the **OK** button. Windows restores the files.

> **9.** Click the **Close** button, and then close all open windows.

Now that you've restored the file from a BKP backup, you can uninstall the Windows NT Backup – Restore Utility program because you no longer need it.

Uninstalling a Software Program

Tip

For some programs, you can click the Start button, point to All Programs, point to the program name, and then click an uninstall command to uninstall the program.

You can uninstall a program from your computer if you no longer use it. Doing so frees up space on your hard disk, sometimes a significant amount of space, depending on the program. You can use the Programs and Features window to uninstall programs, which removes them from your computer. Uninstalling removes the program's files and any changes made to Windows system settings, such as in the registry.

You can also use the Programs and Features window to change a program's configuration by adding or removing certain options. Usually this means that you turn optional features of the program on or off. Not all programs let you change their features. To determine whether you can, click the program name in the Programs and Features window, and then look for the Change or Repair button on the toolbar.

You'll show Shelly how to uninstall the Windows NT Backup – Restore Utility program from the Programs and Features window.

To uninstall a program:

> **1.** Click the **Start** button 🕐 on the taskbar, click **Control Panel**, click **Programs**, and then click **Programs and Features**. The Programs and Features window opens and now includes the Windows NT Backup – Restore Utility program in the list of installed programs. See Figure 9-18.

Figure 9-18 ▶ **List of installed programs**

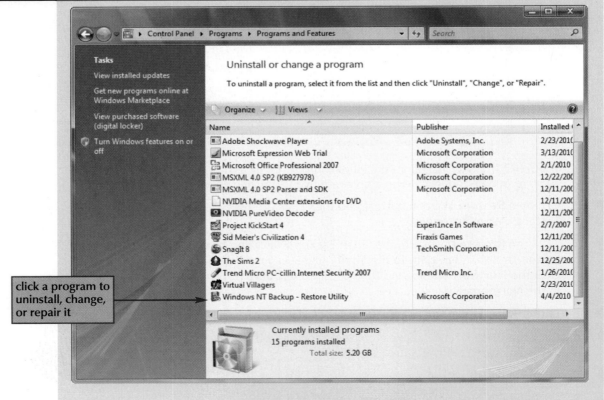

click a program to uninstall, change, or repair it

▶ **2.** Click **Windows NT Backup – Restore Utility**, and then click the **Uninstall** button. Windows asks if you are sure you want to uninstall the program.

▶ **3.** Click the **Yes** button. Windows removes the program from the computer, which could take a few minutes.

Trouble? If a User Account Control dialog box opens requesting your permission or a password to continue, click Allow.

Next, to make sure that Windows Vista on Shelly's computer is up to date, you'll check for updates and remind her how to install Windows Updates.

Installing a Software Update

Recall from an earlier tutorial that you should install updates to Windows Vista as they become available. Important updates provide significant benefits, such as improved security and reliability. To have Windows install important updates as they become available, you turn on automatic updating. You can also set Windows to automatically install recommended updates, which can address noncritical problems and help enhance your computing experience. You can also check for optional updates using the Windows Security Center on your own. Windows Update does not download or install optional updates automatically.

Installing a Software Update | Reference Window

- Click the Start button, point to All Programs, and then click Windows Update.
- In the left pane, click Check for updates, and then wait while Windows looks for the latest updates for your computer.
- If Windows finds updates, click View available updates.
- Select the updates you want to install, and then click Install. (If you are prompted for an administrator password or confirmation, type the password or provide confirmation.)
- Restart your computer, if necessary.

You can also use the Programs and Features window to verify which updates have been installed on your computer. You'll view the software updates installed on Shelly's computer to make sure her software is current.

To view installed updates:

▶ **1.** In the left pane of the Programs and Features window, click **View installed updates**. Windows scans your computer for updates, and then displays them sorted by program. See Figure 9-19.

Figure 9-19 | **Viewing installed updates**

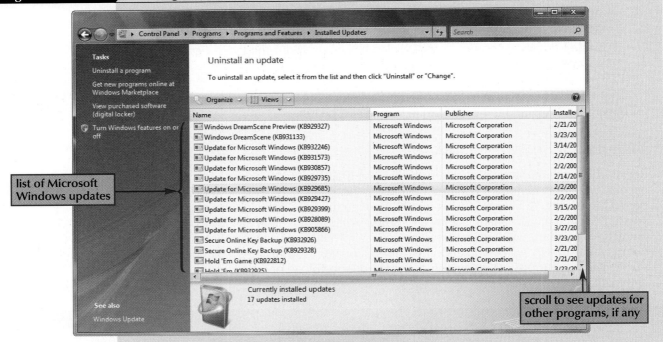

2. Click the **Installed On** column heading to sort the updates by date. An Update for Microsoft Windows should appear near the beginning of the list.

Trouble? If the Installed On column heading does not appear in your window, right-click any column heading, and then click Installed On.

3. Minimize the Installed Updates window.

Shelly's copy of Windows Vista seems to be up to date, and she verifies that she has automatic updating turned on, so you are confident she has the latest software updates.

Setting a Program to Start Automatically

If you often open the same program after starting your computer, such as Internet Explorer or Windows Mail, you can save yourself a few steps by setting the program to start automatically when you start Windows. To do so, you include a shortcut to the program in the Startup folder. Shortcuts in the Startup folder run whenever Windows starts.

If having the program start automatically becomes inconvenient, you can delete the shortcut from the Startup folder. In some cases, a software program might set itself to start automatically when Windows starts. If the Startup folder does not include a shortcut icon for that program, you can use Windows Defender to prevent the program from running automatically when Windows starts by completing the following steps:

- Start Windows Defender.
- Click the Tools button, and then click Software Explorer.
- Select Startup Programs from the Category list, if necessary.
- Select the program you want to disable, and then click Disable.

Shelly always checks her e-mail with Windows Mail as soon as she starts Windows Vista. You'll show her how to set Windows Mail to start automatically when she starts Windows.

To set Windows Mail to start automatically when Windows starts:

▶ 1. Click the **Start** button 🕮 on the taskbar, point to **All Programs**, right-click the **Startup** folder, and then click **Open** on the shortcut menu. The Startup folder window opens.

▶ 2. Click the **Start** button 🕮 on the taskbar, and then drag the **Windows Mail** icon from the pinned items list to the Startup folder window. See Figure 9-20.

Adding a shortcut to the Startup folder   **Figure 9-20**

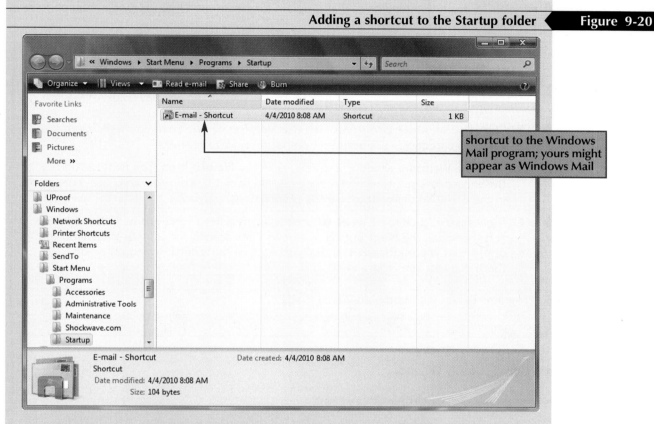

Trouble? If the Windows Mail icon does not appear in the pinned items list, click All Programs, and then drag Windows Mail to the Startup folder window.

▶ 3. Close the Startup folder window.

The next time you start Windows, Windows Mail will run automatically.

Setting Up a Program for Compatibility

If you install programs written for earlier versions of Windows, such as Windows XP, chances are that they run properly. However, some older programs might run poorly or not run at all. If an older program doesn't run correctly, you can use the Program Compatibility Wizard to select and test compatibility settings that might fix the problems in the older program. You can choose an operating system recommended for the program or one that previously supported the program correctly, including Windows XP (Service Pack 2), Windows 2000, Windows 98 or Me, Windows NT (Service Pack 5), or Windows 95. You can also select a display setting recommended for the program, which often solves compatibility problems with games. Microsoft advises that you should not use the Program Compatibility Wizard on older antivirus programs, disk utilities, or other system programs because it might remove data or create a security risk.

Shelly installed a Windows XP program called Electronic Organizer on her Windows Vista computer, and it has not displayed menus or title bars correctly since she installed it. You'll run the Program Compatibility Wizard and select the Electronic Organizer program to run it with compatibility settings, and see if that solves the problem.

The following steps select compatibility settings for Electronic Organizer. Ask your instructor to identify a program on your computer that you can use instead of Electronic Organizer. The program should not be an antivirus program, disk utility, or other system program. Substitute the name of that program for Electronic Organizer when you perform the following steps.

To use the Program Compatibility Wizard:

▶ **1.** Restore the Installed Updates window, and then click the **Back** button 🔙 twice to return to the Programs window.

▶ **2.** Click **Use an older program with this version of Windows** in the Programs and Features category. The Program Compatibility Wizard starts.

▶ **3.** Read the Welcome window, and then click the **Next** button. The next dialog box in the wizard lets you select an older program from a list of programs, use a program in the CD-ROM drive, or locate the program manually.

▶ **4.** If necessary, click the **I want to choose from a list of programs** option button, and then click the **Next** button. Windows Vista scans your computer for older programs that you might want to run with compatibility settings, and then displays them in a list. See Figure 9-21.

| Figure 9-21 | Programs to run with compatibility settings |

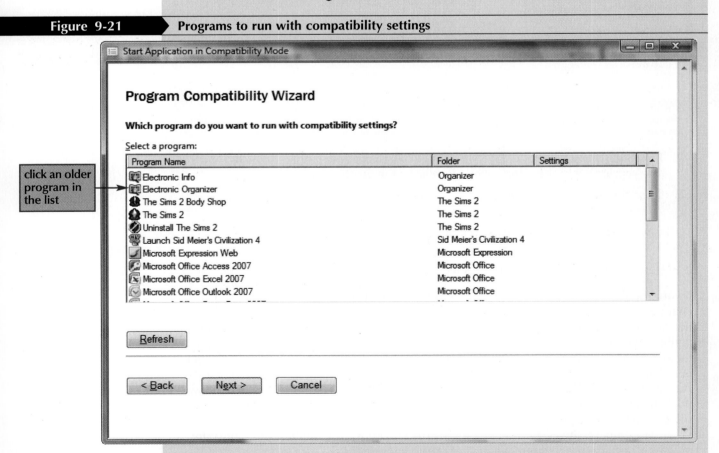

▶ 5. Click **Electronic Organizer** in the list of programs, and then click the **Next** button. The next wizard dialog box asks you to select a compatibility mode for the program.

   Trouble? If your list of programs does not include Electronic Organizer, click the program your instructor recommended.

▶ 6. Click the **Microsoft Windows XP (Service Pack 2)** option button, and then click the **Next** button. The next wizard dialog box asks you to select display settings for the program.

▶ 7. Click the **Disable visual themes** check box, and then click the **Next** button. The next wizard dialog box asks if the program requires administrator privileges.

▶ 8. Click the **Next** button. Windows verifies your settings.

▶ 9. Click the **Next** button to test the program with the new compatibility settings. After the program starts, close its window.

▶ 10. Click the **No, I am finished trying compatibility settings** option button, and then click the **Next** button. The next wizard dialog box asks if you want to send information about the compatibilty problems to Microsoft.

▶ 11. Click the **No** option button, and then click the **Next** button.

▶ 12. Click the **Finish** button, and then close all open windows.

You're finished showing Shelly how to backup and restore files and manage her software. Next, you'll examine how to maintain hard disks and monitors and work with device drivers.

Session 9.1 Quick Check | Review

1. Which of the following reasons describe why you should use a backup program instead of a copy procedure to protect data on a hard disk?
   a. You need to manually note which files and folders have changed since your last backup.
   b. You save time because you can back up only the files that have changed since your last backup.
   c. You can password-protect backups.
2. Explain the difference between using the Back Up Files Wizard and Windows Complete PC Backup.
3. If your computer becomes unstable, you can undo system changes using _____ _____ to return your system to an earlier date when it worked correctly.
4. True or False. A shadow copy is a temporary file that Windows deletes when you're finished using a program.
5. When you insert in a CD drive a CD containing a program, what happens if Windows is set to use AutoPlay?
6. True or False. To set a program to start manually, you add a shortcut to the program on the pinned items list in the Start menu.
7. If an older program doesn't run correctly in Windows Vista, you can use the _____ _____ Wizard to try to fix the problems in the older program.

Session 9.2

Maintaining Hard Disks

As a computer owner, one of your most important responsibilities is to maintain your hard disk by keeping it free of problems that could prevent you from accessing your data. Recall that the failure of a hard disk can be a headache if you have backups of your data and a disaster if you don't. Windows Vista helps you prevent disk failure from occurring in the first place by providing some valuable disk maintenance accessories. Disk maintenance accessories are available on the Tools tab of the disk's properties sheet (which you open by right-clicking the disk icon in the System Maintenance category of Control Panel).

As part of a regular maintenance program, you should become familiar with the properties of your hard disk, including how much free space it has and whether it is partitioned. Next, you should check each disk on your computer to locate and repair errors, such as parts of corrupted files and damaged sections on the disk. Then you should defragment each disk. **Defragmenting** a drive organizes clusters so that files are stored most efficiently. If you are responsible for maintaining a computer that is used all day, you should probably run these maintenance procedures on a weekly or even daily basis. On the other hand, if you use your computer less frequently—for example, if you use a home computer only for correspondence, games, and maintaining your finances—you might only need to run disk maintenance procedures once every month or so.

Shelly has not performed any maintenance tasks on her computer, so you'll guide her through the cleanup tasks and show her how to make sure they are completed on a regular basis.

Viewing Hard Disk Properties

As you know, all of the programs and files on your computer are stored on your hard disk. You should periodically check the amount of free space on your hard disk to make sure the computer does not run out of storage space.

Reference Window	Viewing Hard Disk Properties

- Click the Start button, and then click Computer.
- Right-click a hard disk in the Computer window, and then click Properties on the shortcut menu.

View the properties of your hard disk to learn the following information:

- **File system**. Recall that Windows Vista must be installed on a disk using the NTFS file system. NTFS supports file system recovery (in the case of a hard disk failure) and can access disk drives up to 2 terabytes in size. NTFS is the preferred file system if your disk drive is larger than 32 gigabytes. Your computer might also be able to access a disk that uses the FAT32 file system, which uses an older, less efficient method of organizing data on the disk.
- **Used space, free space, and capacity**. The Properties dialog box for your hard disk shows the amount of space that files and other data use, the amount of free space remaining, and the total capacity of the disk.
- **All disk drives**. The Hardware tab of a disk's Properties dialog box lists all the disks installed in or attached to your computer. If you are having trouble with a disk, you can view more details about it, such as its status, which indicates whether it is working properly.

You'll start your maintenance session with Shelly by viewing the properties of her hard disk.

To view the properties of a hard disk:

▶ 1. Click the **Start** button ⊕ on the taskbar, and then click **Computer**. The Computer window opens.

▶ 2. Right-click **Local Disk (C:)**, and then click **Properties** on the shortcut menu. See Figure 9-22. The space details on your computer will differ.

Tip

You can also click a hard disk icon to view its total size and available free space in the Details pane of the folder window.

Local Disk (C:) Properties dialog box ◀ **Figure 9-22**

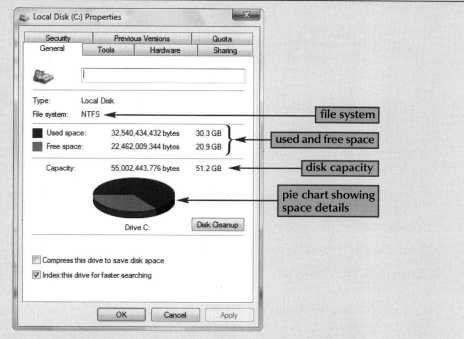

Trouble? If the hard disk where Windows Vista is installed has a different name, right-click that disk icon, and then click Properties.

▶ 3. Click the **Hardware** tab to display the disks attached to your computer. See Figure 9-23.

Figure 9-23 | **Hardware tab of the Local Disk (C:) Properties dialog box**

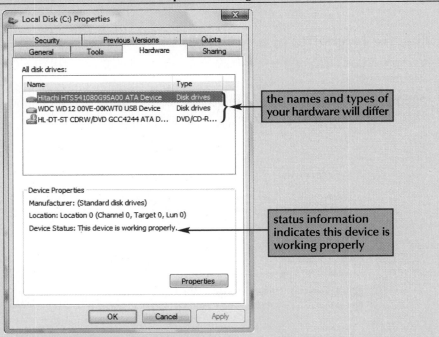

4. Click the first disk in the list, if necessary, and then click the **Properties** button. The Device Properties dialog box for that disk opens, where the Device status box indicates whether the device is working properly.

5. Click the **OK** button to close the Device Properties dialog box.

6. Close the Computer window, but leave the Local Disk (C:) Properties dialog box open.

You want to show Shelly one other way to learn more about her hard disk.

Checking for Partitions

A **partition** (sometimes called a **volume**) is part of a hard disk that works like a separate disk—it can be formatted with a file system and identified with a letter of the alphabet. A hard disk needs to be partitioned and formatted before you can store data on it. Computer manufacturers usually perform this task for you, and set up the hard disk as a single partition that equals the size of the hard disk. Partitioning a hard disk into several smaller partitions is not required, but it can be useful for organizing data on your hard disk. Some users prefer to have separate partitions each for the Windows operating system files, programs, and personal data. You can also create partitions if you want to install more than one operating system on your computer.

You can use the Disk Management window to view the partitions on your system. One partition is the system partition, and contains the hardware-related files that tell a computer where to look to start Windows. Another partition is the boot partition, and contains the Windows operating system files, which are located in the Windows file folder. Usually, these are the same partition, especially if you have only one operating system installed on your computer. If you have more than one operating system on your computer, such as Windows Vista and Windows XP (called a dual-boot or multiboot computer), you have more than one boot partition. The other partitions are for your programs and data.

You'll show Shelly how to view the partitions on her hard disk and identify the system partition in the Disk Management window. Usually, only experienced computer administrators work in this window, but you can open it to view basic information about your hard disk.

You need to log on using an Administrator account to perform the following steps. If you are not allowed to log on as an Administrator, read but do not perform the following steps.

To view the partitions on a hard disk:

▶ **1.** Click the **Start** button 🟢 on the taskbar, click **Control Panel**, and then click **System and Maintenance**.

▶ **2.** Scroll to the Administrative Tools category, and then click **Create and format hard disk partitions**. The Disk Management window opens. See Figure 9-24. The information in your Disk Management window will differ.

Disk Management window ◀ **Figure 9-24**

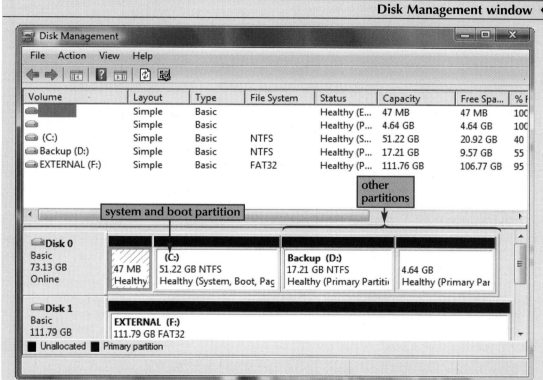

Trouble? If a User Account Control dialog box opens requesting your permission or a password to continue, enter the password or click the Continue button.

▶ **3.** Close the Disk Management window.

▶ **4.** Close Control Panel.

Now that you and Shelly are acquainted with her hard disk, you can start performing maintenance tasks. The first one is to remove unnecessary files using Disk Cleanup.

Deleting Unnecessary Files with Disk Cleanup

When you work with programs and files in Windows Vista, unnecessary files, such as temporary Internet and setup files, accumulate on your hard disk and impair system performance. The Disk Cleanup tool helps you free disk space by permanently deleting these files. When you start Disk Cleanup, it searches your disk for unnecessary files, and then lists the types of files it found in the Disk Cleanup dialog box. Figure 9-25 describes the typical types of files Disk Cleanup can remove when you choose to clean your files to free space on your hard disk. Your Disk Cleanup dialog box might include a different set of files depending on your computer activity.

Figure 9-25 ▶ **Typical types of files to remove when using Disk Cleanup**

Category	Description
Downloaded program files	Program files downloaded automatically from the Internet when you view certain Web pages
Temporary Internet files	Web pages stored on your hard disk for quick viewing, stored in the Temporary Internet Files folder
Offline Web pages	Web pages stored on your computer so you can view them without being connected to the Internet
Hibernation File Cleaner	Information about your computer stored in the Hibernation file; removing this file disables hibernation
Recycle Bin	Files you deleted from your computer, which are stored in the Recycle Bin until you delete them
Setup log files	Files Windows created during setup
Temporary files	Files generated by programs to be used temporarily; usually these are deleted when you close the program, but if the program isn't shut down properly, the temporary files remain on your disk
Thumbnails	Copies of your picture, video, and document thumbnails if you are using Windows Aero

You can also choose to clean files for all users on a computer if you are using an Administrator account. In that case, the Disk Cleanup dialog box includes an additional tab named More Options. Using the More Options tab, you can uninstall programs that you no longer use and delete all but the most recent restore point on the disk.

You'll clean Shelly's hard disk by starting the Disk Cleanup tool from the Local Disk (C:) Properties dialog box.

To use Disk Cleanup:

▶ 1. In the Local Disk (C:) Properties dialog box, click the **General** tab.

▶ 2. Click the **Disk Cleanup** button. A dialog box opens asking which files to clean up.

▶ 3. Click **My files only**. Disk Cleanup calculates how much space you can free and then opens the Disk Cleanup for (C:) dialog box. See Figure 9-26. The information in your Disk Cleanup dialog box will differ.

Tip

You can also start Disk Cleanup by clicking the Start button, pointing to All Programs, clicking Accessories, clicking System Tools, and then clicking Disk Cleanup.

Disk Cleanup dialog box | **Figure** 9-26

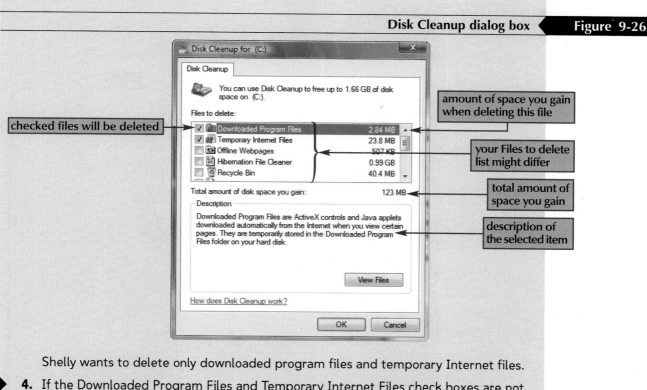

checked files will be deleted

amount of space you gain
when deleting this file

your Files to delete
list might differ

total amount of
space you gain

description of
the selected item

Shelly wants to delete only downloaded program files and temporary Internet files.

▶ **4.** If the Downloaded Program Files and Temporary Internet Files check boxes are not selected, click to select them.

▶ **5.** Scroll the list and then click to remove check marks from any other boxes.

▶ **6.** Click the **OK** button. A dialog box opens asking if you're sure you want to permanently delete these files.

▶ **7.** Click the **Delete Files** button. It might take a few minutes to clean the files from your hard disk.

Next, you'll check Shelly's hard disk for errors and other problems.

Checking a Hard Disk for Errors

A computer hard disk is a magnetic storage device that contains several metal platters that are usually sealed in your computer. Sections of the magnetic surface of a disk sometimes get damaged. Regularly scanning your disks for errors can be an effective way to head off potential problems that would make data inaccessible. The Windows Vista error-checking tool not only locates errors on a disk, but it also attempts to repair them, or at least to mark the defective portions of the disk so that Windows doesn't try to store data there. In earlier versions of Windows, the error-checking tool was called Check Disk or ScanDisk.

To understand what problems the error-checking tool looks for and how it repairs them, you need to understand the structure of a disk. A hard disk is organized as a concentric stack of disks or platters. Each platter has two surfaces, and each has its own read/write head, which reads and writes data magnetically on the surface. The data is stored on concentric circles on the surfaces called **tracks**. An individual block of data is one **sector** of a track, as shown in Figure 9-27.

Figure 9-27 | **Single platter on a hard disk**

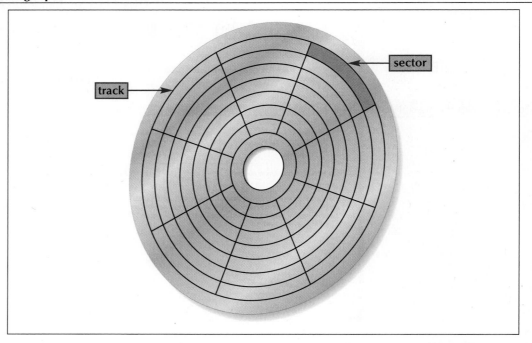

Corresponding tracks on all surfaces on a drive, when taken together, make up a cylinder. The number of sectors and tracks depends on the size of the disk. A 40 GB hard disk, for example, has 16,384 cylinders. Each cylinder has 80 heads, with one head per track. Each track has 63 sectors, with 512 bytes per sector. That makes 42,278,584,320 bytes, which is considered 40 GB.

Although the physical surface of a disk is made up of tracks and sectors, a file is stored in clusters. A **cluster** is one or more sectors of storage space—it represents the minimum amount of space that an operating system reserves when saving the contents of a file to a disk. Most files are larger than 512 bytes (the size of one sector). That means a file is often stored in more than one cluster. If Windows loses track of which clusters contain the data that belongs to a single file, that causes a file system error known as a **lost cluster**. The error-checking tool identifies file system errors and can repair them if necessary.

InSight	**Checking for Errors After Power Failures**

If your computer suffers a power surge, a power failure, or any problem that locks it up, Windows might lose one or more clusters from a file that was open when the problem occurred, and you might lose the data stored in those clusters. The presence of lost clusters on a disk is not damaging, but lost clusters do take up valuable space, and too many of them can lead to other types of file system errors. To prevent an accumulation of file system errors, you should check your hard disk for errors immediately after a power failure.

When you use the Windows Vista error-checking tool to scan your disk for errors, you can specify whether you want it to automatically repair problems with files that the scan detects, such as lost clusters, or only report problems and not fix them. You can also perform a thorough disk check by scanning for and repairing physical errors on the hard disk itself, including **bad sectors**, which are areas of the disk that do not record data reliably. Performing a thorough disk check can take much longer to complete.

You'll show Shelly how to check her hard disk for file system errors. Because her computer is still relatively new, it's unlikely the hard disk has any bad sectors. But after she's used her computer awhile, she should check the hard disk for bad sectors as well as file system errors.

To check the hard disk for errors:

▶ **1.** In the Local Disk (C:) Properties dialog box, click the **Tools** tab. See Figure 9-28.

Tools tab of the Local Disk (C:) Properties dialog box ◀ Figure 9-28

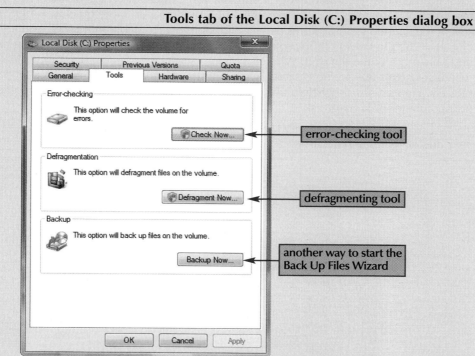

▶ **2.** Click the **Check Now** button. The Check Disk Local Disk (C:) dialog box opens. See Figure 9-29.

Check Disk Local Disk (C:) dialog box ◀ Figure 9-29

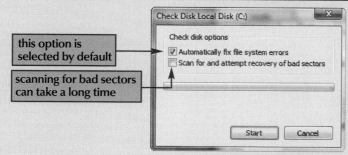

Trouble? If a User Account Control dialog box opens requesting your permission or a password to continue, enter the password or click the Continue button.

▶ **3.** Make sure only the Automatically fix file system errors box is checked, and then click the **Start** button. A dialog box opens indicating that Windows can't check the disk for errors while the disk is in use and asks if you want to check for hard disk errors the next time you start your computer.

▶ **4.** Click the **Cancel** button.

Shelly doesn't need to check her disk now, but when she does, she can click the Schedule disk check button. Windows will then check the disk the next time she starts her computer.

Defragmenting a Disk

After correcting any errors on your hard disk, you can use Disk Defragmenter to improve the disk's performance so that programs start and files open more quickly. When you save a file, Windows Vista stores as much of the file as possible in the first available cluster. If the file doesn't fit into one cluster, Windows locates the next available cluster and puts more of the file in it. Windows attempts to place files in contiguous clusters whenever possible. The file is saved when Windows has placed all the file data into clusters. Figure 9-30 shows two files named Address and Recipes saved on an otherwise unused platter on a hard disk.

Figure 9-30 ▶ **Two files saved on a hard disk**

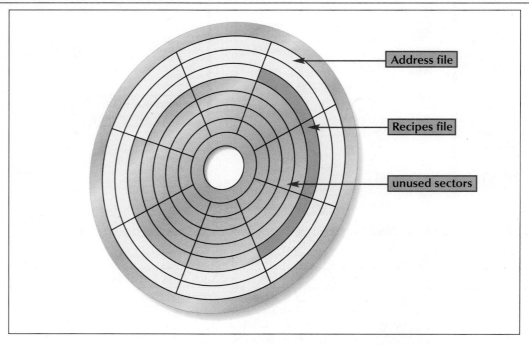

As you create and save new files, more clusters are used. If you delete a file or two, those clusters are freed. Figure 9-31 shows the disk after you save a new file, Memo, and then delete Recipes.

Adding one file and deleting another file ◀ **Figure 9-31**

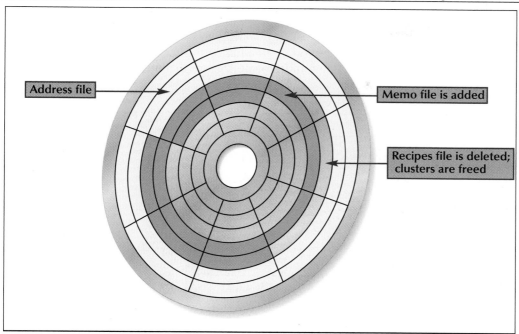

The next time you save a file, Windows Vista searches for the first available cluster, which is now between two files. Figure 9-32 shows what happens when you save a fourth file, Schedule—it is saved to clusters that are not adjacent.

Adding a new file in fragmented clusters ◀ **Figure 9-32**

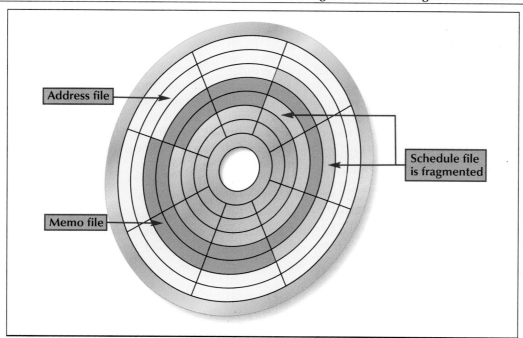

The more files you save and delete, the more scattered the clusters for a file become. A disk that contains files whose clusters are not next to each other is said to be **fragmented**. The more fragmented the disk, the longer Windows Vista takes to retrieve the file, and the more likely you are to have problems with the file. Figure 9-33 shows a fragmented disk. When a program tries to access a file on this disk, file retrieval takes longer than necessary because the program must locate clusters that aren't adjacent.

Figure 9-33 ▶ **Fragmented files**

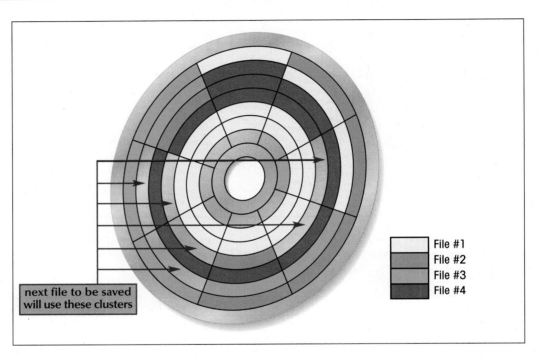

File #1
File #2
File #3
File #4

next file to be saved will use these clusters

Whenever a disk has been used for a long time, it's a good idea to defragment it. Defragmenting rearranges the clusters on the disk so each file's clusters are adjacent to one another. To do so, you use Disk Defragmenter, which rearranges the data on your hard disk and reunites fragmented files so your computer can run more efficiently. In Windows Vista, Disk Defragmenter runs on a schedule so you don't have to remember to run it, although you can still run it manually or change the schedule it uses.

You'll show Shelly how to start Disk Defragmenter and examine its schedule. Because defragmenting a hard disk can take a long time, you won't defragment now.

To start Disk Defragmenter:

▶ **1.** On the Tools tab of the Local Disk (C:) Properties dialog box, click the **Defragment Now** button. The Disk Defragmenter dialog box opens. See Figure 9-34.

Disk Defragmenter dialog box ◄ **Figure 9-34**

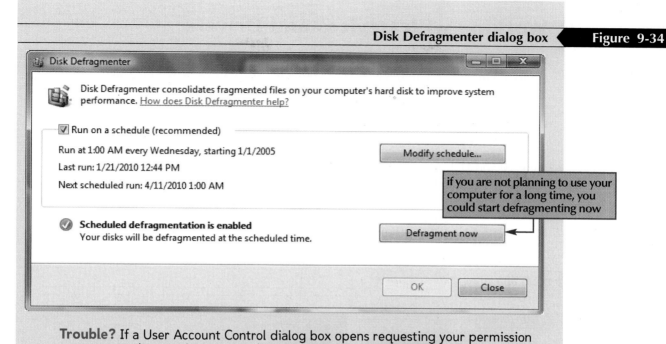

Trouble? If a User Account Control dialog box opens requesting your permission or a password to continue, enter the password or click the Continue button.

2. Click the **Modify schedule** button to examine the defragmenting schedule. The Disk Defragmenter: Modify Schedule dialog box opens. See Figure 9-35.

Disk Defragmenter: Modify Schedule dialog box ◄ **Figure 9-35**

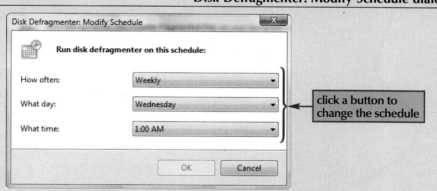

This schedule doesn't conflict with any other scheduled events, such as an antivirus scan, so Shelly doesn't need to change it.

3. Click the **Cancel** button to close the Disk Defragmenter: Modify Schedule dialog box.

4. Click the **Close** button to close the Disk Defragmenter dialog box.

5. Close the Local Disk (C:) Properties dialog box.

By default, Disk Defragmenter is set to run every week to make sure your disk is defragmented.

Working with Devices and Drivers

Hardware is any physical piece of equipment, called a **device**, that is both connected to your computer and controlled by your computer. These devices include external equipment such as keyboards, printers, and scanners, which remain outside the case of the computer, and internal equipment, such as disk drives, modems, and network adapter cards, which are placed inside the case of the computer.

External devices are connected to your computer through a **port**, which is a physical connection that is visible on the outside of the computer. Windows Vista supports serial, parallel, and USB ports for external devices, though USB ports are the most common. USB, short for Universal Serial Bus, is a thin, rectangular slot that accommodates a high-speed connection to a variety of external devices, such as removable disks, scanners, keyboards, video conferencing cameras, and printers. To use USB technology, your computer must have a USB port, and the device you install must have a USB connector, which is a small, rectangular plug. See Figure 9-36.

| Figure 9-36 | USB and other external ports |

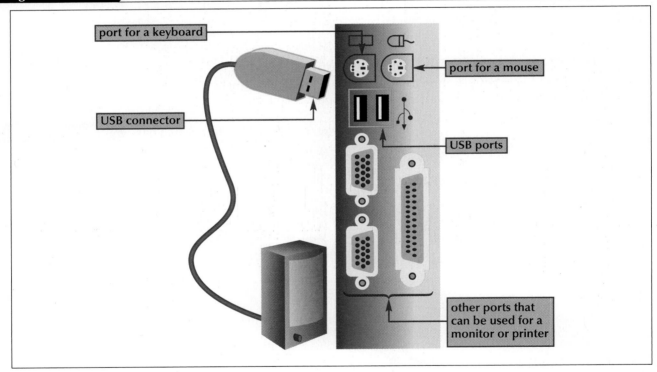

When you plug the USB connector into the USB port, Windows Vista recognizes the device and allows you to use it immediately. You can also daisy-chain up to 127 devices together, meaning that you plug one device, such as a scanner, into the USB port, and then plug a second device, such as a speaker, into the scanner, so you are no longer limited by the number of ports on your computer. Instead of daisy-chaining devices, you can also connect multiple devices to a single inexpensive **USB hub**. A hub is a box that contains many USB ports—you plug the hub into your computer, and then plug your USB devices into the hub. USB devices communicate with your computer more efficiently—a USB port transfers data many times faster than other types of ports. You can also connect and disconnect USB devices without shutting down or restarting your computer.

Internal devices are connected to the **motherboard**, a circuit board inside your computer that contains the **microprocessor** (the "brains" of your computer), the computer memory, and other internal hardware devices. Internal devices are connected either directly to the motherboard (such as the microprocessor and your memory chips) or via a socket in the motherboard called an **expansion slot**. You can insert devices such as network adapter cards or sound cards into expansion slots. Devices that you insert into expansion slots are often called **expansion cards** or **adapter cards** because they "expand" or "adapt" your computer and they look like large cards. See Figure 9-37.

Internal devices ◄ Figure 9-37

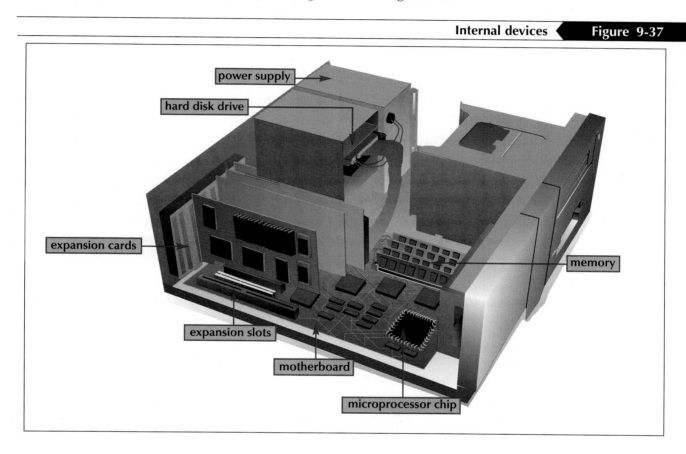

Understanding Device Resources

Windows Vista assigns each device a set of system resources to help it work with the computer. Windows can assign four resources to a device: an IRQ, a DMA channel, an I/O address, and a memory range. When two devices share a particular resource, a **device conflict** can occur, rendering one or both of the devices unusable.

A hardware device often needs to use the microprocessor in the computer to send or receive information. When you are trying to complete several computer tasks at once (for example, when you search for a Web page while you are printing a document and playing an audio CD), Windows needs a way to handle these simultaneous requests. It does so by assigning each device an **interrupt request line (IRQ)** number that signals the microprocessor that the device is requesting an action. Windows Vista makes 16 IRQ numbers, numbered from 0 to 15, available to hardware devices. Lower numbers have higher priority and receive attention first. One common hardware headache is to have more devices than available IRQs, resulting in an IRQ conflict. If you use USB devices, however, Windows Vista only uses one set of resources for all USB devices, meaning you don't have to resolve these types of IRQ conflicts.

If the device does not need to use the microprocessor, information can be transferred directly between the device and the system's memory. This channel for transferring data is called the **direct memory access (DMA) channel**. Most computers have four DMA channels, numbered from 0 to 3, available for your devices.

When the computer receives information from one of its devices, it needs a place to store that data in the computer's memory. It does this by reserving a specific section of the computer's memory for each device. The section of the computer's memory devoted to the different devices on a computer is called the **I/O address**. Each device requires a different I/O (input/output) address.

Finally, some devices, such as video cards, require additional computer memory for their own use (not related to communicating with the microprocessor). For example, a video card needs additional memory to manage video and graphics that are not essential to the operating system. This resource is called the **memory address** or **memory range**.

Your computer uses all four types of system resources—IRQs, DMA channels, I/O addresses, and memory addresses—to communicate between hardware and software.

Understanding Device Drivers

Each hardware device requires a **driver**, a software file that enables Windows Vista to communicate with and control the operation of the device. In most cases, drivers come with Windows or can be found by going to Windows Update in Control Panel and checking for updates. If Windows doesn't have the driver you need, you can find it on the disc that came with the hardware or device you want to use, or on the manufacturer's Web site. Hardware manufacturers update drivers on a regular basis to improve device performance and speed, so you should use Windows Update or periodically check the manufacturer's Web site to confirm that you're using the most current driver version.

A **signed driver** is a device driver that includes a digital signature. Recall that a digital signature is an electronic security mark that can indicate the publisher of the software, as well as whether someone has changed the original contents of the driver package. If a publisher signed a driver by verifying its identity with a certification authority, you can be confident that the driver actually comes from that publisher and hasn't been altered. Windows Vista alerts you if a driver is not signed, was signed by a publisher that has not verified its identity with a certification authority, or has been altered since it was released.

Installing a USB Device

Before installing new hardware, check the instructions included with the device to determine whether a driver should be installed before you connect the device. Typically, Windows detects a new device after you connect it, and then installs the driver automatically. However, some devices require you to install the driver before plugging the device in. Although most devices that have power switches should be turned on before you connect them, others require that you turn them on during the installation process. Differences like this one make it a good idea to read the instructions included with a new device before you connect it.

To install new devices of any type, you typically can plug the device to a port or install a new add-on card in your computer, and Windows Vista detects the hardware, automatically installs the correct driver, and notifies you when installation begins and when it's complete. The first time you plug a USB device into a USB port, Windows installs a driver for that device. After that, you can disconnect and reconnect the device without performing additional steps.

Shelly has a new USB flash drive that she wants to use with her computer. You'll show her how to install this new device. Her computer has a USB port on the front of its case, making it convenient for her new USB flash drive because she plans to connect and disconnect the device frequently.

To perform the following step, you need a USB device that you have not yet used with your computer.

To install a USB device:

▶ **1.** Plug the device into the USB port. Windows detects the device, installs a device driver automatically, and indicates that the device is ready to use. See Figure 9-38.

Installing a USB device ◀ **Figure 9-38**

notification that the device has been installed successfully → Your devices are ready to use
Device driver software installed successfully.

Next, you can show Shelly how to use the Device Manager to manage her new USB flash drive.

Enabling and Disabling Devices

Device Manager is a Windows tool that lets you manage the external and internal devices your computer uses. Using Device Manager, you can determine which *devices* are installed on your computer, update *driver* software for your devices, check to see if hardware is working properly, and modify hardware settings.

Enabling and Disabling Devices | Reference Window

- Click the Start button, click Control Panel, click System and Maintenance, and then click Device Manager. If you are prompted for an administrator password or confirmation, type the password or provide confirmation.
- Expand the list of devices as necessary, and then click a device.
- If the device is disabled, click the Enable button on the toolbar to enable it. If the device is enabled, click the Disable button on the toolbar to disable it.

You can use Device Manager to change how your hardware is configured and interacts with your programs. Advanced users can use the diagnostic features in Device Manager to resolve device conflicts and change resource settings. Typically, however, you use Device Manager to update device drivers and troubleshoot problems by checking the status of your devices. Suppose you occasionally have trouble burning files to a disc in your CD-RW drive. You can check the status of that drive in Device Manager and try to repair it by disabling it and then enabling it. When troubleshooting, you might also disable a device instead of uninstalling it to see if that device is causing a larger system problem. If the problem persists, you can enable the device and disable a different device. When you disable a device, you turn it off. When you enable a device, you turn it on.

You'll start Device Manager and show Shelly how to disable and then enable her new USB flash drive.

To perform the following steps, you need to log on using an Administrator account. The USB device you installed in the preceding set of steps should also be available and plugged into a USB port. If you cannot log on using an Administrator account or if you do not have a USB device, read but do not perform the following steps.

To disable a USB device:

▶ **1.** Click the **Start** button 🕢 on the taskbar, click **Control Panel**, click **System and Maintenance**, scroll the window, and then click **Device Manager**. See Figure 9-39.

Figure 9-39 Device Manager

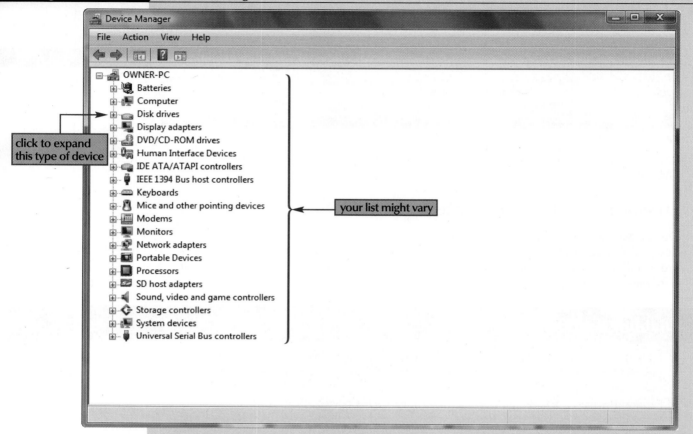

Trouble? If a User Account Control dialog box opens requesting your permission or a password to continue, enter the password or click the Continue button.

▶ **2.** Click the **expand** icon ⊞ for Disk drives, and then click the name of your USB device.

▶ **3.** Click the **Disable** button 🔯 on the toolbar to disable the device. Windows asks you to confirm that you want to disable the device.

▶ **4.** Click the **Yes** button. Windows disables the device, and then displays it in the list of devices with a disabled icon. See Figure 9-40.

Trouble? If a System dialog box opens asking if you want to restart your computer now, click the No button.

Disabling a device in Device Manager ◀ Figure 9-40

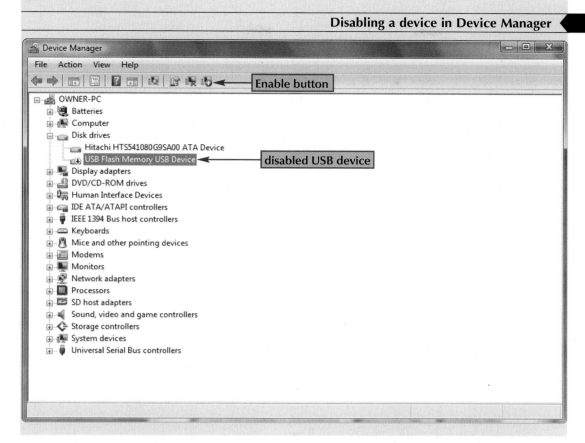

To determine whether this USB device is causing problems with your system, you could troubleshoot to see if your system now works properly with this device disabled. Shelly is not really having any problems with this USB device, so you can enable it again.

To enable a disabled device:

▶ 1. In the Device Manager window, click the disabled **USB device**, if necessary.

▶ 2. Click the **Enable** button 🔳 on the toolbar to enable the device. Windows turns on the device, scans your computer to gather information about the hardware change, and then informs you that it updated some hardware.

Another way to troubleshoot a hardware problem is to install or update device drivers.

Installing and Updating Device Drivers

If a hardware device isn't working properly, or if a program that you're installing indicates that it requires newer drivers than you currently have installed, first check Windows Update for updated drivers. Windows Update automatically installs the device drivers you need as it updates your computer. In some cases, such as when technical support personnel ask you to install drivers from a disc or from the device manufacturer's Web site, you can also manually update drivers for your device using Device Manager.

To install or update a device driver, you can use the Properties dialog box for the hardware device. The Driver tab in this dialog box lets you update the driver, roll it back, disable it, or uninstall it. You can also find out if a driver is signed. If you want to update a driver, you can have Windows search your computer and the Internet for the appropriate files. If you have a CD or DVD that contains the updated driver, you can navigate to and install the driver files yourself.

InSight | **Installing Device Drivers on Your Own**

Sometimes, you install a device in Windows Vista and find that it is working well. Then, when you visit the manufacturer's Web site, you notice that they've provided a newer driver that you can download and install. However, if you're not having any problems with the device, you don't need to download and install that updated driver. Newer drivers are not necessarily better. They might not have any improvements to help your hardware run better. Typically, device drivers not available when you use Windows Update add support for new products or technologies you don't have. For example, a manufacturer might provide new drivers when it releases new high-speed DVD devices. One of the drivers might also support the older DVD driver that you purchased from the manufacturer. Unless you have one of the new DVD drives, you probably won't benefit from the new driver. If the driver hasn't been fully tested with your older DVD driver, it might cause problems with the hardware.

In case Shelly needs to update a device driver on her own, you'll show her how to check for and manually install an updated driver.

To perform the following steps, you need to log on using an Administrator account. The USB device you installed in the preceding step should also be available and plugged into a USB port. If you cannot log on using an Administrator account or if you do not have a USB device, read but do not perform the following steps.

To update and install a device driver:

▶ 1. In the Device Manager window, double-click the USB device. Its Properties dialog box opens. See Figure 9-41.

Figure 9-41 ▶ **Properties dialog box for a USB device**

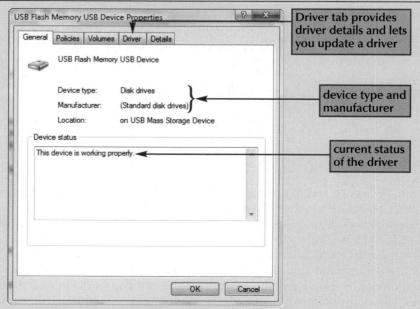

Trouble? If a User Account Control dialog box opens requesting your permission or a password to continue, enter the password or click the Continue button.

▶ **2.** Click the **Driver** tab. You can use this tab to find out if a driver is signed, update the driver, roll it back, disable it, or uninstall it. See Figure 9-42.

Driver tab in the Properties dialog box for a USB device ◀ **Figure 9-42**

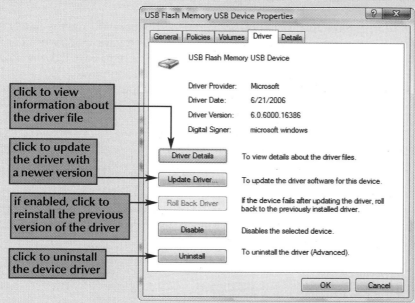

▶ **3.** Click the **Driver Details** button. The Driver File Details dialog box opens, displaying the name, location, and other details about the driver file.

▶ **4.** Click the **OK** button to close the Driver File Details dialog box.

▶ **5.** Click the **Update Driver** button. A dialog box opens asking how you want to search for driver software.

▶ **6.** Click **Search automatically for updated driver software**. Windows searches your computer and the Internet for the latest version of the driver software. For Shelly's USB device, it determined that the best driver software for the device is already installed.

Trouble? If Windows determines that you need to update the driver software for your device, it asks if you want to install the software now. Click the Yes button, and then wait until Windows finishes installing the driver.

▶ **7.** Click the **Close** button to close the Update Driver Software dialog box.

▶ **8.** Close all open windows.

Sometimes, installing an updated driver can cause more problems than it solves. In that case, you can restore the driver to a previous version.

Rolling Back a Driver to a Previous Version

If your computer or device has problems after you upgrade a driver, try restoring, or rolling back, the driver to a previous version. In many cases, that solves the problem. To roll back a driver, you use the Roll Back Driver button on the Driver tab of the device's Properties dialog box. (If this button is not available, that means no previous version of the driver is installed for the selected device.) Windows restores the previous version of the driver.

Safely Removing USB Devices

You can remove and unplug most USB devices whenever you like. The same is true for PC cards, which some mobile computers use to connect to a network or the Internet. When unplugging storage devices, such as USB flash drives, make sure that the computer has finished saving any information to the device before removing it. If the device has an activity light, wait for a few seconds after the light turns off flashing before unplugging the device.

You know you can remove a USB device or PC card when you see the Safely Remove Hardware icon in the notification area of the taskbar. This means that all devices have finished all operations in progress and are ready for you to remove. Click the icon to display a list of devices, and then click the device you want to remove.

Shelly is finished using the USB flash drive on her computer, so you'll show her how to safely remove it.

To remove a USB device from a computer:

▶ 1. Click the **Safely Remove Hardware** icon 🔌 in the notification area of the taskbar to display a list of devices you can remove.

▶ 2. Click **Safely remove USB Device**. (The wording of your notification might differ.) The Safe To Remove Hardware dialog box opens, indicating that you can now safely remove the device from the computer.

▶ 3. Click the **OK** button.

▶ 4. Unplug the USB device from the USB port.

Now that you've examined how to maintain hard disks and other hardware devices, in the next session, you'll learn how to maintain another important component in your system: your monitor.

Review | **Session 9.2 Quick Check**

1. _____ a disk organizes its files so that they are stored most efficiently.
2. Which of the following can you learn when you view the properties of your hard disk?
   a. date modified
   b. Windows version
   c. file system
   d. display settings
3. True or False. The Windows Vista error-checking tool helps you free disk space by permanently deleting unnecessary files.
4. How are external devices connected to your computer?
5. True or False. Windows Vista most often detects a new device after you connect one, and then installs the driver automatically.
6. Name two ways to update a device driver.

Session 9.3

Maintaining Your Monitor

When your monitor is installed, Windows chooses the best display settings for that monitor, including screen resolution, refresh rate, and color. If you start having display problems with your monitor or want to improve its display, you can change the following settings or restore them to their defaults.

- **Brightness and contrast**. For the best results, you can use a calibration program to adjust brightness, contrast, and color settings. (Windows Vista does not include a calibration program, but many are available from other software vendors.) Calibration programs usually work with a device that you attach to the front of your monitor to read light and color levels and to optimize your monitor's display. You can also adjust brightness and contrast manually (though not as precisely) by using the hardware controls, which are usually placed on the front of the monitor.
- **Display resolution**. As you learned in an earlier tutorial, you can adjust the screen resolution to improve the clarity of the text and images on your screen. Recall that at higher resolutions, computer images appear sharper. They also appear smaller, so more items fit on the screen. At lower resolutions, fewer items fit on the screen, but they are larger and easier to see. At very low resolutions, however, images might have jagged edges. For an LCD monitor, use its **native resolution**—the resolution a monitor is designed to display best, based on its size. The monitor manufacturer usually ships the computer with the monitor set to the native resolution, which is usually the highest available resolution. Although LCD monitors can technically support lower resolutions than their native resolution, the image might look stretched, or it might be small, centered on the screen, and edged with black.
- **Color settings**. You also learned how to adjust the number of colors your monitor displays in an earlier tutorial. Recall that the number of colors determines how realistic the images look. However, the higher the resolution and color setting, the more resources your monitor needs; the best settings for your computer balance sharpness and color quality with computer resources. Windows colors and themes work best when you have your monitor set to 32-bit color.
- **Screen refresh rate**. To reduce or eliminate flicker, you can adjust the screen refresh rate. If the refresh rate is too low, the monitor can flicker, which can cause eye strain and headaches. Most monitor manufacturers recommend a refresh rate of at least 75 Hertz.
- **Screen text and icons**. To make text and icons easier to see on your screen, you can enlarge them by increasing the dots per inch (DPI) scale. Conversely, you can decrease the DPI scale to make text and other items on your screen smaller, so that more information fits on the screen. In general, however, the higher the DPI, the better screen text looks.

Shelly already knows how to adjust the brightness, contrast, and screen resolution. You'll show her how to maintain her monitor by adjusting the display refresh rate, selecting color settings, and changing the size of the screen text and icons.

Adjusting the Display Refresh Rate

A flickering monitor can contribute to eyestrain and headaches. You can reduce or eliminate flickering by increasing the **screen refresh rate**, which determines how frequently the monitor redraws the images on the screen. The refresh rate is measured in hertz. A refresh rate of at least 75 Hertz generally produces less flicker.

Reference Window | **Adjusting the Display Refresh Rate**

- Click the Start button, click Control Panel, click Appearance and Personalization, click Personalization, and then click Display Settings.
- Click the Advanced Settings button.
- Click the Monitor tab.
- Click the Screen refresh rate button, and then click a refresh rate.

You might need to change your screen resolution before changing the refresh rate because not every screen resolution is compatible with every refresh rate. The higher the resolution, the higher your refresh rate should be. Recall that to change your screen resolution, you can right-click the desktop, click Personalize on the shortcut menu, click Display Settings, and then drag the Resolution slider.

Shelly recently increased the screen resolution on her monitor from 1024 × 768 to 1280 × 720 to improve the clarity of her icons. However, the screen flickers slightly since she changed that setting. You'll show her how to increase the screen refresh rate to reduce monitor flicker.

Tip

You can also open the Display Settings dialog box by opening Control Panel, clicking Appearance and Personalization, clicking Personalization, and then clicking Display Settings.

To change the screen refresh rate:

▶ 1. Right-click the desktop, click **Personalize** on the shortcut menu, and then click **Display Settings**. The Display Settings dialog box opens.

▶ 2. Click the **Advanced Settings** button. The Properties dialog box for your monitor opens.

▶ 3. Click the **Monitor** tab to display the monitor properties. See Figure 9-43.

Figure 9-43 ▶ | Monitor tab in the Properties dialog box for a monitor

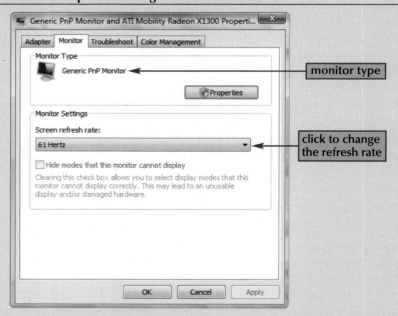

▶ 4. Click the **Screen refresh rate** button, and then click **75 Hertz**.

Trouble? If your list of refresh rates does not include 75, click any other refresh rate the same or higher than your current refresh rate.

▶ **5.** Click the **Apply** button to apply the new setting. Windows asks if you want to keep these display settings.

▶ **6.** Click the **Yes** button and leave the Display Settings dialog box open.

Next, you'll show Shelly how to manage the color settings on her computer. She is planning to update and print a four-color ad for the Northbrook Farmers Market and wants to make sure the colors she sees on her monitor are the same colors that print in the ad.

Selecting Color Settings

Recall from an earlier tutorial that you also use the Display Settings dialog box to change the color depth, which is typically medium (16 bit) or high (32 bit). To make sure that the colors displayed on your monitor match the colors produced on a color printer, for example, you use the Windows Vista color management settings.

Hardware devices that produce color, such as monitors and printers, often have different color characteristics and capabilities. Monitors can't show the same set of colors that a printer can print because they use different techniques to produce color on a screen or on paper. Scanners and cameras also have different color characteristics. Even the same type of device can display color differently. For example, the LCD monitor built into a laptop computer might display different shades of color from the LCD monitor attached to a desktop computer.

To overcome these differences, Windows Vista uses color management settings and color profiles to maintain consistent colors no matter which device produces the color content. Hardware manufacturers can create a color profile, which is a file that describes the color characteristics of a device. Profiles can also define viewing conditions, such as low-light or natural lighting. When you add a new device to your computer, the color profile for that device is included with the other installation files, so you don't need to add or remove a color profile. In addition, the default color management settings almost always produce the best results; therefore, only color professionals, such as compositors and typographers, should change them. However, you can use the Display Settings dialog box to verify that your computer is using the default color management settings.

Before Shelly updates and prints her four-color ad for the Northbrook Farmers Market, you'll show her how to make sure her computer is using the default settings for color management.

To verify the color management settings:

▶ **1.** In the Properties dialog box for your monitor, click the **Color Management** tab, and then click the **Color Management** button. The Color Management dialog box opens to the Devices tab, which identifies your hardware display and lists its color profiles, if any.

▶ **2.** Click the **Advanced** tab to display the color management settings. See Figure 9-44. All of these settings are set to the system default.

Figure 9-44 **Advanced tab in the Color Management dialog box**

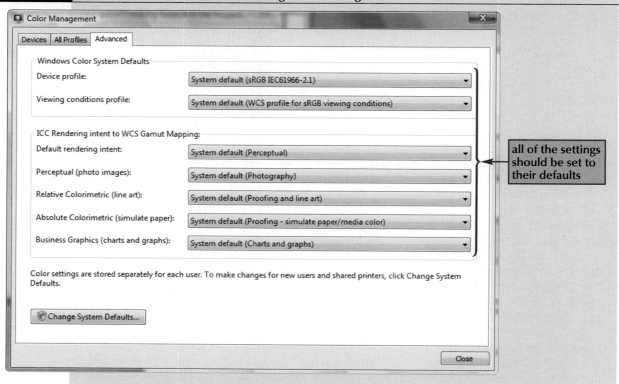

all of the settings should be set to their defaults

3. Click the **Close** button to close the Color Management dialog box.

4. Click the **OK** button to close the Properties dialog box for your monitor.

5. Click the **OK** button to close the Display Settings dialog box.

After Shelly increased her screen resolution, she noticed that the text and icons were smaller, though sharper. She'd like to enlarge the text and the icons without decreasing the screen resolution. You'll show her how to do this by increasing the DPI scale.

Changing the Size of Icons and Text

To increase the size of text, icons, and other items on your screen, you can adjust the DPI scale. The default DPI scale is 96 DPI. You can increase this scale to 120 DPI to make the text and icons easier to see. On the other hand, if you want more information to fit on your screen, you can decrease the DPI scale to make text, icons, and other items smaller. If you change the font for screen text (as you did in an earlier tutorial), you might want to set a custom DPI that seems best for that font.

You'll show Shelly how to change the DPI scale to increase the size of text and icons.

To change the DPI scale:

1. In the left pane of the Personalization window, click **Adjust font size (DPI)**. The DPI Scaling dialog box opens. See Figure 9-45.

Tip

To magnify items on the screen, open Control Panel, click Ease of Access, click Ease of Access Center, and then click Start Magnifier.

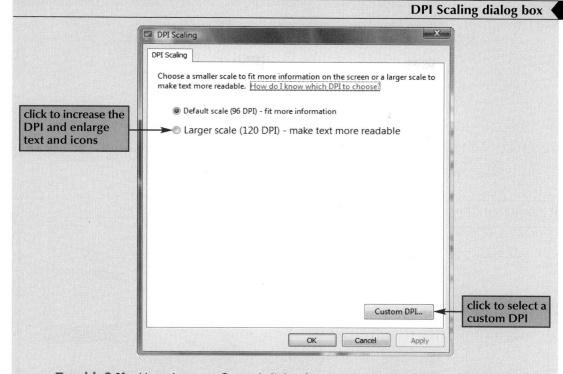

Trouble? If a User Account Control dialog box opens requesting your permission or a password to continue, enter the password or click the Continue button.

2. Click the **Larger scale (120 DPI) – make text more readable** option button.

3. Click the **OK** button.

4. Click the **Restart Later** button. Because the changes you made don't take effect until you restart the computer, the text on your screen remains the same size.

5. Close the Personalization window.

You can also set a custom DPI if you are running Windows Aero with a DPI higher than 96. In some programs that are not designed for high-DPI display, the text and other items on the screen might appear blurry. If they do, click the Custom DPI button in the DPI Scaling dialog box, and then click the Use Windows Vista style DPI scaling check box.

Setting Up Multiple Monitors

If you have an extra monitor, you can double your desktop workspace by connecting the extra monitor to your computer. Windows Vista can stretch the desktop across both monitors so you can display a presentation or report on the primary monitor, for example, and browse the Internet on the secondary monitor. To use multiple monitors, your computer should have a video card with at least two ports. When you plug in a second monitor, Windows detects and identifies it, and then applies the video settings that are best suited to the new display. When you disconnect the additional monitor, Windows restores the original display settings, including screen size, resolution, and color depth, and then moves all open files and program windows to your primary monitor. If you connect that monitor again, Windows applies the same display settings you used when you last connected the monitor.

Reference Window | **Setting Up and Extending the Desktop on Multiple Monitors**

- Physically connect the additional monitor to your computer.
- In the New Display Detected dialog box, click the Show different parts of my desktop on each display (extended) option button.
- Click the Left or Right option button.
- Click the OK button.

The first time you connect an additional monitor, you can choose how you want your desktop to appear on the displays: mirrored, extended, or external only. Figure 9-46 illustrates these options. In the figure, the laptop computer display is the primary monitor, and the flat-screen display is the secondary monitor.

Figure 9-46 ▶ **Options for displaying the desktop with multiple monitors**

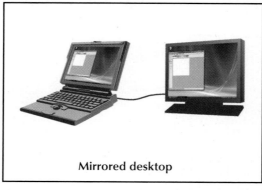

Mirrored desktop

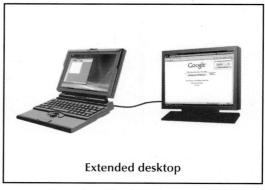

Extended desktop

Desktop on external monitor only

A mirrored desktop—the default display option—is useful if you plan to use one computer, such as your mobile PC, to give a presentation on a projector or TV-type monitor. (You learned how to do this in a previous tutorial.) When you want to increase your desktop area, you can extend your desktop across both displays, so you can move program windows between the different displays. You can also show your desktop only on the external display, such as when you play a video on a mobile PC. You can save battery power by turning off the mobile PC display and using only the external display.

When Shelly works on her ad for the Northbrook Farmers Market, she needs to follow detailed instructions that her printing company provided about how to lay out the ad. To avoid switching frequently from the program window containing the ad image to the program window containing the instructions, she wants to use two monitors. She can then display the current version of the ad on her primary monitor and the instructions on her secondary monitor. You'll show her how to set up an additional monitor on her laptop computer.

To perform the following steps, you need an extra monitor. Your computer also needs to have a video card with at least two ports. (Check the back of your computer for an additional video port.) If you do not have the required hardware, read but do not perform the following steps.

To extend the desktop to an additional monitor:

▶ **1.** Physically connect the extra monitor to your computer by plugging the monitor into an available video port. Windows Vista detects the extra monitor and opens the New Display Detected dialog box. See Figure 9-47.

New Display Detected dialog box ◀ **Figure 9-47**

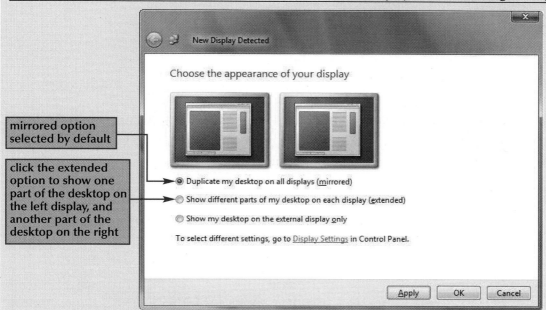

mirrored option selected by default

click the extended option to show one part of the desktop on the left display, and another part of the desktop on the right

Trouble? If the New Display Detected dialog box does not open and you are using a mobile computer, press the Fn+F5 keys or click the Start button, click Control Panel, click Mobile PC, click Windows Mobility Center, and then click the Connect display in the External Display tile.

▶ **2.** Click the **Show different parts of my desktop on each display (extended)** option button, and then click the **Left** option button, if necessary, to extend the desktop to the left.

▶ **3.** Click the **OK** button. Windows extends your desktop across the two monitors.

If Windows can't identify the monitor that you connect, it applies the last display settings that you used (if any) for that type of monitor and asks whether you want to keep the settings. Click OK to keep the settings. If you click Cancel or do nothing, the Display Settings dialog box opens so that you can choose the display settings yourself. You'll examine how to adjust the resolution of the secondary monitor next.

Setting the Resolution of a Secondary Monitor

When you connect an additional monitor to your computer, you don't have to use the same display settings you use for the primary monitor. You can use the Display Settings dialog box to adjust the resolution, color depth, and other options. For example, if you're using two monitors to give a presentation from a mobile PC, you can decrease the brightness and refresh rate on your mobile PC display to conserve battery power. Then you can increase the screen resolution and DPI settings on the secondary monitor so that others can easily read the information you're presenting.

You can also use the Display Settings dialog box to set up three or more monitors connected to your computer. Windows can detect only one additional display. If you connect two or more monitors, you designate the primary display, arrange your desktop, and apply display settings, such as screen resolution and color depth using the Display Settings dialog box. The next time that you connect these monitors, Windows identifies the primary display and applies the settings that you specified.

You'll show Shelly how to examine the display settings to specify which monitor is the primary monitor and to set the resolution of the secondary monitor.

If you did not connect a second monitor to your computer, read but do not perform the following steps.

To set display settings for multiple monitors:

1. Right-click the desktop, click **Personalize** on the shortcut menu, and then click **Display Settings** to open the Display Settings dialog box.

2. Click the monitor identified as 1, and then click the **This is my main monitor** check box.

3. Click the monitor identified as 2. See Figure 9-48.

| Figure 9-48 | Identifying monitors |

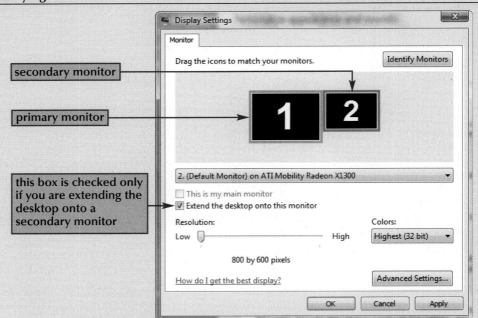

4. Drag the **Resolution** slider to 1024 by 768 to match the resolution of your primary monitor. The preview window displays the effect of your changes.

5. Click the **Yes** button to accept your changes and close the dialog box.

6. Close the Personalization window.

Shelly doesn't need to use the additional monitor right now, so you can disconnect it. The next time she connects the extra monitor to her computer, Windows will apply the same settings so she can start using the monitor immediately.

If you did not connect a second monitor to your computer, read but do not perform the following step.

To disconnect the extra monitor:

▶ **1.** Unplug the monitor from the video port in the back of the computer.

Now you can turn to a final hardware task: installing and setting up a printer.

Installing and Setting Up a Printer

Before you can print anything from your computer, you either need to connect a printer directly to your computer, making it a **local printer**, or else create a connection to a network or shared printer. Before using Windows Vista to install a printer, check the manual that came with your printer. For some printers, you plug the printer into your computer, usually using a USB port, turn on the printer, and then Windows Vista detects the new printer and installs its driver. For other printers, you need to install their software first, and then plug in and turn on the printer.

Most contemporary printers are USB printers, meaning you connect them by plugging the printer's cable into a USB port on your computer. Other printers use a parallel cable that connects to your computer's printer port (also called the LPT1 port). If you are installing a second or third printer, you might also need to use a parallel cable to attach the printer to the printer port if you need to use the computer's USB ports for other devices.

After you physically connect a local printer, you open the Printers window and start the Add Printer Wizard, which guides you through the steps of installing the printer and its drivers. You use the same wizard to set up a network printer for which you've turned on printer sharing.

Shelly bought a new color printer that she wants to use to print drafts of her ad for the Northbrook Farmer's Market. You'll show her how to install that printer and set it as the default.

Installing a Local Printer

Using the printer manufacturer's directions, attach or connect the printer to your computer. Windows usually installs the printer without further action from you. If Windows does not recognize the printer, you can open the Printers window from Control Panel to install it yourself.

Reference Window | **Installing a Local Printer**

- Follow the printer manufacturer's instructions to connect the printer to your computer.
- If Windows does not automatically detect the printer and install its drivers, click the Start button, click Control Panel, click Hardware and Sound, and then click Printers.
- Click the Add a printer button on the toolbar.
- In the Add Printer Wizard, click Add a local printer.
- Click the Next button to accept the existing printer port.
- Select the printer manufacturer and the printer name, and then click the Next button.
- Enter a printer name, and then click the Next button.
- Click the Finish button.

Shelly wants to install a color printer that she recently purchased to print full-color ads and other documents. She already has one laser printer that is connected to a USB port on her computer, and she needs to connect the color printer to her computer using a parallel cable plugged into the printer port. You'll show her how to install a Hewlett-Packard color laser printer.

If you are working on a school or institutional network, you probably cannot install a printer on your computer. In that case, read but do not perform the following steps.

To install a local printer:

▶ **1.** Physically connect your printer to your computer. The Printers window opens. See Figure 9-49.

Figure 9-49 ▶ **Printers window**

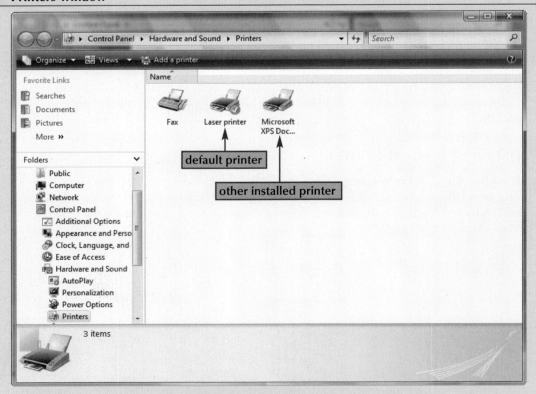

Trouble? If you plugged the printer into a USB port, Windows detects the printer and installs the drivers automatically. The printer is ready to use. Read but do not perform the following steps.

Trouble? If the Printers window does not open, click the Start button, click Control Panel, click Hardware and Sound, and then click Printers.

▶ 2. Click the **Add a printer button** on the toolbar. The Add Printer Wizard starts and lets you choose whether to add a local or network printer.

▶ 3. Click **Add a local printer**. The next wizard dialog box opens where you can choose a printer port.

▶ 4. Make sure the Use an existing port option button is selected, and then click the **Next** button. The next wizard dialog box opens where you can select the manufacturer and model of your printer. See Figure 9-50.

Installing the printer driver ◀ **Figure 9-50**

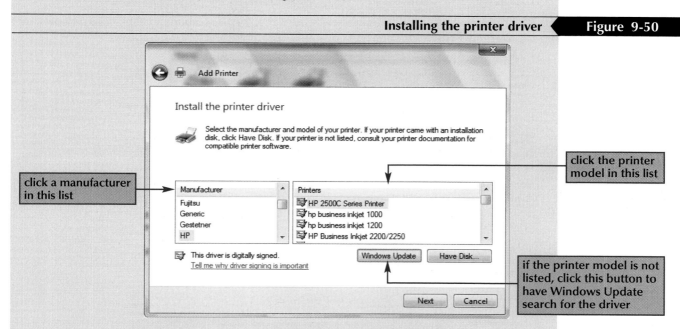

click a manufacturer in this list

click the printer model in this list

if the printer model is not listed, click this button to have Windows Update search for the driver

▶ 5. Scroll the Manufacturer list, click **HP**, scroll the Printers list, and then click **HP Color LaserJet 2500 PS**.

Trouble? If you have a different printer, select the appropriate manufacturer and printer from the lists.

▶ 6. Click the **Next** button. The next wizard dialog box asks you to confirm the printer's name or enter a different one.

▶ 7. Click the **Next** button. The final wizard dialog box confirms that the printer is installed, and lets you print a test page, if necessary.

▶ 8. Click the **Finish** button.

Tip

To verify the printer works correctly, click the Print a test page button before clicking the Finish button.

After you successfully install the color laser printer for Shelly, she notices that it is now the default printer, meaning that all the documents she prints will be directed to that printer unless she changes that setting using the Print dialog box. She prints far more often on the black-and-white laser printer. You'll show her how to specify that printer as the default.

Changing the Default Printer

If you have more than one printer connected to your computer, you can select the one you want to use by default. When you use Windows or your programs to print, a Print dialog box opens and lets you select settings, including a printer. The Print dialog box selects the default printer automatically, though you can change it if you like. In some programs, when you click a Print button, the content prints on the default printer without opening a Print dialog box. You should therefore select the printer you use most often as your default printer. You can do so in the Printers window.

Shelly wants to make her black-and-white laser printer the default instead of her color printer. You'll show her how to change her default printer using the Printers window.

To change the default printer:

1. In the Printers window, right-click the **Laser printer** icon, and then click **Set as Default Printer** on the shortcut menu. Windows displays a default icon on the Laser printer. See Figure 9-51.

Figure 9-51	Select a default printer

Tip

To delete a printer you no longer use, right-click it and then click Delete on the shortcut menu.

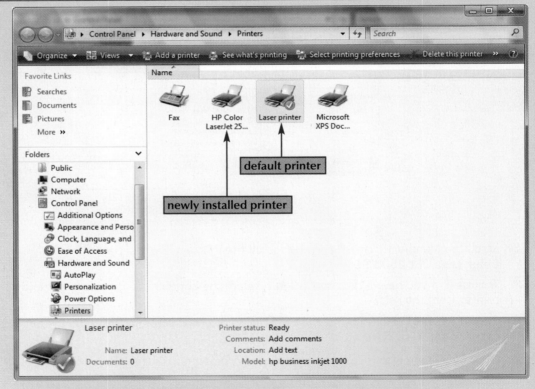

Trouble? If the printer you want to set as the default is named something other than Laser printer, right-click that printer icon in Step 1.

Trouble? If the printer you want to set as the default printer is already designated as the default printer, skip Step 1.

Shelly occasionally connects to a wireless network, which includes a wireless printer as a resource. You'll show her how to use this printer when she needs it.

Finding and Installing a Network Printer

On most small office and home networks, a printer is installed as a device on the network, and a connection to the printer is added to each computer on the network. The printer then becomes a network printer, meaning it is available to one or more computers on the network. A network printer can be a wireless printer, which plugs into a power source and uses a built-in wireless card so that a network router can detect it. Other network printers are connected directly to the network using a USB or Ethernet cable plugged into the network hub or router. Some hubs and routers can support more than one printer, meaning you can use more than one printer on your network.

If you connect a printer to a computer on the network, you can share that printer with others on the network by turning on printer sharing in the Network and sharing Center window. You learned how to work with this window in an earlier tutorial. You turn on printer sharing the same way you turned on file sharing: click the Printer sharing Off button to display a menu, and then click Turn on printer sharing. This means that anyone on the network can use the printer after you install it.

You'll show Shelly how to share the printers attached to her computer.

To perform the following steps, you need to be connected to a network and have permission to share a printer. If you don't, read but do not perform the following steps.

To share a printer on the network:

▶ **1.** Click the **Start** button 🪟 on the taskbar, and then click **Network**. The Network window opens, displaying all the computers on your network.

▶ **2.** Click the **Network and Sharing Center** button on the toolbar. The Network and Sharing Center window opens, which you worked with in Tutorial 8.

▶ **3.** In the Sharing and Discovery section, click the **expand** button ⊙ to the right of Printer Sharing, and then click **Turn on printer sharing**.

▶ **4.** Click the **Apply** button. Printer sharing is now turned on for your network.

   Trouble? If a User Account Control dialog box opens requesting your permission or password to continue, enter the password or click the Continue button.

▶ **5.** Close the Network and Sharing Center window, and then close the Network window.

After you connect the printer and turn on printer sharing, you can install the printer on the network using the Printers window. This step lets other networked computers use the printer you just shared. When you start the Add Printer Wizard, it scans the network for printing devices and then displays the available printers. Available printers can include all printers on a network, including wireless printers or those that are plugged into another computer and shared on the network. To use one of these printers, you must have permission to do so before you can add them to the computer. If you have permission, you can select the printer that you want Windows to install. If the wizard doesn't find the printer you want to install, you can examine the printers attached to other computers on your network, and then select one of those. You'll show Shelly how to use the Add Printer Wizard to make her laser printer a network printer.

To perform the following steps, you need to be connected to a network that has one or more printers available for sharing. If you don't, read but do not perform the following steps.

To find and install a network printer:

▶ 1. In the Printers window, click the **Add a printer** button on the toolbar.

▶ 2. Click **Add a network, wireless, or Bluetooth printer**. The wizard scans your network and displays available printers.

▶ 3. Click **Laser printer** in the list of printers, click the **Next** button, and then click the **Finish** button. The wizard installs the network printer and displays it in the Printers window. See Figure 9-52.

Figure 9-52 ▶ Installing a network printer

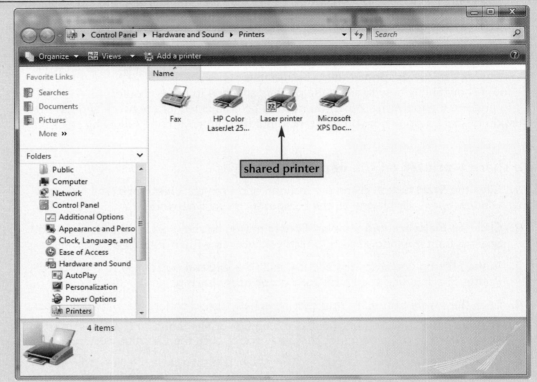

Trouble? If your network provides a different printer, click that printer in Step 3.

Trouble? If your printer is not available, click The printer that I want isn't listed, click the Browse button to navigate to and double-click the printer on the network, and then click the Next button.

▶ 4. Close the Printers window.

To print using a shared printer not directly attached to your computer, you can use the Start Search box on the Start menu to find and use the printer. To do so, you need to know the network name of the computer to which the shared printer is attached. In the Start Search box, you type \\ followed by the name of the computer connected to the shared printer you want to use, such as \\NetworkMobile, and then press the Enter key. If Windows finds the computer on the network, it displays a folder for the computer, which includes a Printers folder. Open the Printers folder, and then double-click the shared printer you want to use. Windows installs the printer driver and then displays the printer in your Printers window. You can now use that printer as you would any other printer in the Printers window.

If you have computers on your network that run different versions of Windows, you can make the appropriate drivers available so other users can connect to a shared printer. For example, if you want to share the printer connected to a computer running Windows XP, you should install the driver so users on the Windows Vista computers don't have to search for it when they access the printer.

To make printer drivers available for other versions of Windows, right-click the shared printer in the Printers window, and then click Properties on the shortcut menu toopen the Properties dialog box for the printer. Click the Sharing tab, and then click the Additional Drivers button. Click the check boxes corresponding to the Windows version for which you want to install drivers. Navigate to where the driver files are stored, and then click the OK button. Users running different versions of Windows can now connect to your printer and download the drivers.

Restoring Your Settings

If you are working in a computer lab or a computer other than your own, complete the steps in this section to restore the original settings on your computer. If a User Account Control dialog box opens requesting an Administrator password or confirmation after you perform any of the following steps, enter the password or click the Continue button.

To restore your settings:

▶ 1. Click the **Start** button 🌐 on the taskbar, click **Control Panel**, click **System and Maintenance**, and then click **Backup and Restore Center**.

▶ 2. Click **Change settings**.

▶ 3. If Automatic backup was originally turned off for your computer, click the **Turn off** button, and then close the Backup Status and Configuration window.

▶ 4. Transfer the **Backup Set** folder containing your backup file to the Tutorial. 09\Tutorial folder provided with your Data Files.

▶ 5. Move the **Shelly** folder in your Documents folder to the Tutorial.09\Tutorial folder provided with your Data Files.

▶ 6. Click the **Start** button 🌐 on the taskbar, click **All Programs**, right-click the **Startup** folder, and then click **Open** on the shortcut menu. The Startup folder window opens.

▶ 7. Right-click the **Windows Mail** icon, and then click **Delete** on the shortcut menu. Click the **Yes** button to confirm.

▶ 8. Close the Startup folder window.

▶ 9. Right-click the desktop, click **Personalize** on the shortcut menu, and then click **Display Settings**.

▶ 10. Click the **Advanced Settings** button, and then click the **Monitor** tab. Click the **Screen refresh rate** button, and then click your original refresh rate, such as **61 Hertz**. (Your refresh rates might differ.) Click the **OK** button to close the Properties dialog box for your monitor. Click the **OK** button to close the Display Settings dialog box.

▶ 11. In the left pane of the Personalization window, click **Adjust font size (DPI)**. Click the **Default scale (96 DPI) – fit more information** option button, and then click the **OK** button. Choose to restart the computer later. Close the Personalization window.

▶ 12. Click the **Start** button 🌐 on the taskbar, click **Control Panel**, click **Hardware and Sound**, and then click **Printers**.

▶ **13.** Right-click one of the extra printers you installed in this tutorial, and then click **Delete** on the shortcut menu. Right-click any other extra printer you installed in this tutorial, and then click **Delete** on the shortcut menu. Click the **Yes** button to confirm.

▶ **14.** Close all open windows.

Review | **Session 9.3 Quick Check**

1. You can reduce or eliminate flickering on your monitor by increasing the screen _____ rate.
2. True or False. If you increase the DPI scale to 120 DPI, you reduce the size of the desktop.
3. When you are using multiple monitors, which display option is best if you are giving a presentation?
4. The printer directly connected to your computer is called the _____ printer.
5. Which printer should you select as your default printer?
6. True or False. A network printer can be the one connected to your computer.

Review | **Tutorial Summary**

In this tutorial, you protected your data by backing up and restoring selected files. You protected your system by creating a system restore point. You also installed software downloaded from the Internet, and then uninstalled it. To keep your computer in good working order, you learned how to maintain your hard disk by using Windows Vista tools such as Disk Cleanup and Disk Defragmenter. You also installed, disabled, and enabled hardware devices, and then learned how to install and update device drivers. In addition to maintaining your hard disk, you learned how to maintain your monitor by adjusting its settings. You also set up multiple monitors and installed printers.

Key Terms

adapter card
backup file
backup medium
backup program
bad sector
cluster
defragment
device
device conflict
direct memory access
   (DMA) channel
driver
expansion card

expansion slot
fragmented
hardware
I/O address
interrupt request line (IRQ)
local printer
lost cluster
memory address (or
   memory range)
microprocessor
motherboard
native resolution
partition

port
registry
restore
restore point
screen refresh rate
sector
shadow copy
signed driver
System Restore
track
USB hub
volume

Practice	Review Assignments

There are no Data Files needed for the Review Assignments.

You are now working with Stuart Hansen, the front-end manager of the Northbrook Farmers Market. He has recently acquired a new Windows Vista computer and asks you to show him how to maintain its hardware and software. He is particularly concerned about protecting the photos he uses to promote the market and its products. Complete the following steps, noting your original settings so you can restore them later:

1. Insert a writeable CD or DVD into the appropriate drive or attach an external hard drive to your computer by plugging it into a USB port.

2. Open the Backup and Restore Center window, and then change the backup settings to save your backup to the CD, DVD, or external hard drive that you prepared in Step 1. Choose to back up only the Picture files on your computer. With the Back Up Files window open showing the types of files you are backing up, press Alt+Print Screen to capture an image of the window. Paste the image in a new Paint file, and save the file as **Picture Backup** in the Tutorial.09\Review folder provided with your Data Files. To save time and disk space, click the Cancel button to close the window without creating a backup.

3. Accept the default backup schedule, and then back up the Picture files. Save the Backup Set folder containing the Picture files in the Tutorial.09\Review folder provided with your Data Files.

4. Create a restore point named **Stuart**. With the System Restore window open and displaying the restore points on your computer, press Alt+Print Screen to capture an image of the window. Paste the image in a new Paint file, and save the file as **System Restore** in the Tutorial.09\Review folder provided with your Data Files.

5. Display the installed updates on your computer. Sort the updates by the date they were installed, and then press Alt+Print Screen to capture an image of the window. Paste the image in a new Paint file, and save the file as **Updates** in the Tutorial.09\Review folder provided with your Data Files.

6. Set Windows Photo Gallery to start automatically when Windows starts. With the Startup folder window open, press Alt+Print Screen to capture an image of the window. Paste the image in a new Paint file, and save the file as **Startup** in the Tutorial.09\Review folder provided with your Data Files.

7. Display the amount of free space and used space on your hard disk. With the dialog box open showing this information, press Alt+Print Screen to capture an image of the window. Paste the image in a new Paint file, and save the file as **Disk Space** in the Tutorial.09\Review folder provided with your Data Files.

8. Open the Disk Cleanup dialog box for your hard disk, and then choose to clean up only your thumbnails. Press Alt+Print Screen to capture an image of the window. Paste the image in a new Paint file, and save the file as **Disk Cleanup** in the Tutorial.09\Review folder provided with your Data Files.

9. Display the schedule for defragmenting your hard disk. Press Alt+Print Screen to capture an image of the window. Paste the image in a new Paint file, and save the file as **Defragment** in the Tutorial.09\Review folder provided with your Data Files.

10. Install a USB device you have not used with your computer or plug it into a USB port you have not yet used with the device. After installing it successfully, disable the device. With the Device Manager window open, press Alt+Print Screen to capture an image of the window. Paste the image in a new Paint file, and save the file as **Disabled** in the Tutorial.09\Review folder provided with your Data Files. Enable, and then disconnect the USB device.

11. Increase the size of the DPI scale on your computer, and then press Alt+Print Screen to capture an image of the DPI Scaling window. Paste the image in a new Paint file, and save the file as **DPI** in the Tutorial.09\Review folder provided with your Data Files. Restore the original DPI scale.

12. Install a local printer named **Front End** in the Printers window. (*Hint*: You can install a local printer even if it is not connected to your computer.) With the Printers window open, press Alt+Print Screen to capture an image of the window. Paste the image in a new Paint file, and save the file as **Printer** in the Tutorial.09\Review folder provided with your Data Files.

13. Restore your settings by deleting the Front End printer from the Printers window. Remove the Windows Photo Center program from the Startup folder. Close all open windows.

14. Submit the results of the preceding steps to your instructor, either in printed or electronic form, as requested.

| Apply | | **Case Problem 1** |

Use the skills you learned in the tutorial to maintain the hardware and software for a symphony orchestra.

There are no Data Files needed for this Case Problem.

Sarasota Symphony Orchestra   Martin Prago is the business director of the Sarasota symphony orchestra, and he has recently hired you to help him automate the orchestra's business and marketing efforts. Martin has been using a Windows Vista laptop for a few months, and asks you to help him properly maintain its hardware and software. Complete the following steps, noting your original settings so you can restore them later:

1. Insert a writeable CD or DVD into the appropriate drive or attach an external hard drive to your computer by plugging it into a USB port.

2. Open the Backup and Restore Center window, and then change the backup settings to save your backup to the CD, DVD, or external hard drive that you prepared in Step 1. Choose to back up only the Music files on your computer. With the Back Up Files window open showing the types of files you are backing up, press Alt+Print Screen to capture an image of the window. Paste the image in a new Paint file, and save the file as **Music Backup** in the Tutorial.09\Case1 folder provided with your Data Files. To save time and disk space, click the Cancel button to close the window without creating a backup.

3. Create a restore point named **Martin**. With the System Restore window open and displaying the restore points on your computer, press Alt+Print Screen to capture an image of the window. Paste the image in a new Paint file, and save the file as **Restore Point** in the Tutorial.09\Case1 folder provided with your Data Files.

4. Use the Programs and Features window to display the programs installed on your computer. Select a program that lets you change or repair its settings, and then press Alt+Print Screen to capture an image of the Programs and Features window. Paste the image in a new Paint file, and save the file as **Programs** in the Tutorial.09\Case1 folder provided with your Data Files.

5. Start the Program Compatibilty Wizard and display the programs you can run with compatibility settings. Press Alt+Print Screen to capture an image of the window. Paste the image in a new Paint file, and save the file as **Compatible** in the Tutorial.09\Case1 folder provided with your Data Files.

6. Open the Properties dialog box for Local Disk (C:). (If your local hard disk uses a different drive letter, substitute that letter for C.) Display all the disk drives attached to your computer. With the dialog box open showing this information, press Alt+Print Screen to capture an image of the window. Paste the image in a new Paint file, and save the file as **Disk Drives** in the Tutorial.09\Case1 folder provided with your Data Files.

7. Use Device Manager to check for an updated driver for any device on your computer. After checking, press Alt+Print Screen to capture an image of the dialog box showing the results. Paste the image in a new Paint file, and save the file as **Driver** in the Tutorial.09\Case1 folder provided with your Data Files. If Windows found an updated driver, do not install it.

8. Increase the resolution of your monitor, and then increase the screen refresh rate, if possible. With the Display Settings dialog box open, press Alt+Print Screen to capture an image of the window. Paste the image in a new Paint file, and save the file as **Resolution** in the Tutorial.09\Case1 folder provided with your Data Files.

9. Install a local printer named **Sarasota** in the Printers window. (*Hint*: You can install a local printer even if it is not connected to your computer.) With the Printers window open, press Alt+Print Screen to capture an image of the window. Paste the image in a new Paint file, and save the file as **Sarasota** in the Tutorial.09\Case1 folder provided with your Data Files.

10. Restore your settings by deleting the Sarasota printer from the Printers window and restoring your original screen resolution. Close all open windows.

11. Submit the results of the preceding steps to your instructor, either in printed or electronic form, as requested.

Apply		**Case Problem 2**

Use the skills you learned in the tutorial to manage the hardware and software for a semiprofessional hockey team.

There are no Data Files needed for this Case Problem.

Salem Hockey Ducks Guy Larousse is the owner of the Hockey Ducks, a semiprofessional hockey team in Salem, Oregon. You are a part-time assistant for the Hockey Ducks and primarily help Guy perform computer tasks using his Windows Vista computer. Guy recently lost some data during a power failure and asks you to help him back up his e-mail messages. He is also concerned about maintaining the software on his computer. You'll also show him how to complete these maintenance tasks. Complete the following steps, noting your original settings so you can restore them later:

1. Insert a writeable CD or DVD into the appropriate drive or attach an external hard drive to your computer by plugging it into a USB port.
2. Open the Backup and Restore Center window, and then change the backup settings to save your backup to the CD, DVD, or external hard drive that you prepared in Step 1. Choose to back up only the e-mail files on your computer. With the Back Up Files window open showing the types of files you are backing up, press Alt+Print Screen to capture an image of the window. Paste the image in a new Paint file, and save the file as **E-mail Backup** in the Tutorial.09\Case2 folder provided with your Data Files. To save time and disk space, click the Cancel button to close the window without creating a backup.
3. Make sure System Protection is turned on for your computer. With the window open displaying this information, press Alt+Print Screen to capture an image of the window. Paste the image in a new Paint file, and save the file as **Protection** in the Tutorial.09\Case2 folder provided with your Data Files.
4. Begin restoring Guy's computer by selecting the first restore point in the list. With the System Restore window open and displaying the restore points on your computer, press Alt+Print Screen to capture an image of the window. Paste the image in a new Paint file, and save the file as **First Restore** in the Tutorial.09\Case2 folder provided with your Data Files. Click the Cancel button to close the System Restore window.

⊕ EXPLORE

5. Use Windows Update to check for optional updates to your computer, including device drivers. (*Hint*: Open the Windows Update window, click Check for updates, and then wait while Windows looks for the latest updates for your computer.) Display only optional updates, and then press Alt+Print Screen to capture an image of the window. Paste the image in a new Paint file, and save the file as **Updates** in the Tutorial.09\Case2 folder provided with your Data Files. Close the Windows Update window without installing any updates.
6. In the Programs and Features window, display the Windows features that are turned on and off on your computer. Press Alt+Print Screen to capture an image of the window. Paste the image in a new Paint file, and save the file as **Features** in the Tutorial.09\Case2 folder provided with your Data Files.

⊕ EXPLORE

7. Use Windows Defender to display the software installed on your computer. (*Hint*: Open Control Panel, open the Programs window, and then click View currently running programs in the Windows Defender category.) With the Windows Defender window open showing the software installed on your computer, press Alt+Print Screen to capture an image of the window. Paste the image in a new Paint file, and save the file as **Defender** in the Tutorial.09\Case2 folder provided with your Data Files.

8. If your Programs window includes a category named Get Programs Online, click Get Programs Online. When the Web page opens, press Alt+Print Screen to capture an image of the page. Paste the image in a new Paint file, and save the file as **Online** in the Tutorial.09\Case2 folder provided with your Data Files.

9. Install a local printer named **Salem** in the Printers window. With the Printers window open, press Alt+Print Screen to capture an image of the window. Paste the image in a new Paint file, and save the file as **Salem** in the Tutorial.09\Case2 folder provided with your Data Files.

10. Restore your settings by deleting the Salem printer from the Printers window. Close all open windows.

11. Submit the results of the preceding steps to your instructor, either in printed or electronic form, as requested.

Challenge | **Case Problem 3**

Go beyond what you've learned to maintain the hardware for a group of designers.

There are no Data Files needed for this Case Problem.

Pacific Design Group Ali Johanssen is the founder of the Pacific Design Group in West Hollywood, California. The Pacific Design Group is a cooperative venture that shares design and office space for interior and industrial designers. Ali has hired you to help her maintain the computer hardware for the Pacific Design Group members. Complete the following steps, noting your original settings so you can restore them later:

1. Install a USB flash drive or external hard disk on your computer.

2. Display the amount of free space and used space on the removable disk. With the dialog box open showing this information, press Alt+Print Screen to capture an image of the window. Paste the image in a new Paint file, and save the file as **General** in the Tutorial.09\Case3 folder provided with your Data Files.

3. Open the Disk Cleanup dialog box for the removable disk, and then display the files you can delete. Press Alt+Print Screen to capture an image of the dialog box. Paste the image in a new Paint file, and save the file as **Removable** in the Tutorial.09\Case3 folder provided with your Data Files.

4. Display the schedule for defragmenting your removable disk. Press Alt+Print Screen to capture an image of the window. Paste the image in a new Paint file, and save the file as **Schedule** in the Tutorial.09\Case3 folder provided with your Data Files.

⊕ EXPLORE

5. Click the ReadyBoost tab in the Properties dialog box for the removable disk. Test the device, and then press Alt+Print Screen to capture an image of the window. Paste the image in a new Paint file, and save the file as **ReadyBoost** in the Tutorial.09\Case3 folder provided with your Data Files.

♦ EXPLORE 6. Click the Hardware tab in the Properties dialog box for the removable disk. Click the removable disk device in the list of all disk drives, and then click the Properties button. Press Alt+Print Screen to capture an image of the window. Paste the image in a new Paint file, and save the file as **Properties** in the Tutorial.09\Case3 folder provided with your Data Files.

♦ EXPLORE 7. Open the Device Manager window, and then display all the devices by connection. (*Hint*: Click View on the menu bar, and then click Devices by connection if it is not selected.) Press Alt+Print Screen to capture an image of the window. Paste the image in a new Paint file, and save the file as **Devices** in the Tutorial.09\Case3 folder provided with your Data Files. Return the view to Devices by type.

♦ EXPLORE 8. In the Hardware and Sound window, select an option to learn about Windows SideShow. Open a window displaying information about using a device with Windows SideShow, and then press Alt+Print Screen to capture an image of the window. Paste the image in a new Paint file, and save the file as **SideShow** in the Tutorial.09\ Case3 folder provided with your Data Files.

9. Install a local printer named **Ali** in the Printers window. With the Printers window open, press Alt+Print Screen to capture an image of the window. Paste the image in a new Paint file, and save the file as **Ali** in the Tutorial.09\Case3 folder provided with your Data Files.

10. Restore your settings by deleting the Ali printer from the Printers window and removing the USB device from your computer. Close all open windows.

11. Submit the results of the preceding steps to your instructor, either in printed or electronic form, as requested.

| Research | **Case Problem 4** |

Work with the skills you've learned and use the Internet to research accessibility features in Windows Vista.

There are no Data Files needed for this Case Problem.

Council for the Hearing and Visually Impaired   Rose Mellenhoff is the director of the Council for the Hearing and Visually Impaired in Columbia, Missouri. You volunteer for the council, and usually offer your services to provide data entry, computer hardware maintenance, and other computer tasks. Rose is interested in learning more about making computers accessible to her clients and asks you to conduct research into the Windows Vista hardware and software accessibility features. Complete the following steps:

1. Use your favorite search engine to find information about how to make a computer easier to use for the hearing and visually impaired. Try searching for information about the following types of information:
   • Accessible computing
   • Assistive technology
   • Accessibility features

2. Use Windows Help and Support and your favorite search engine to find information about the features Windows Vista provides for the hearing and visually impaired.

3. Select two or three features that interest you, and then write a paragraph about each feature. Be sure to explain how to use the feature and how to change the setting, if any, in Windows Vista. Also describe the benefits the feature provides to the hearing or visually impaired.

4. Save the paragraphs in a document named **Accessible** in the Tutorial.09\Case4 folder provided with your Data Files.

5. Submit the results of the preceding steps to your instructor, either in printed or electronic form, as requested.

| Assess | **SAM Assessment and Training** |

If you have a SAM user profile, you may have access to hands-on instruction, practice, and assessment of the skills covered in this tutorial. Log in to your SAM account (**http://sam2007.course.com**) to launch any assigned training activities or exams that relate to the skills covered in this tutorial.

| Review | **Quick Check Answers** |

Session 9.1

1. b
2. The wizard lets you specify which personal files to back up, whereas Windows Complete PC Backup backs up the entire computer.
3. System Restore
4. False
5. A dialog box opens and asks if you want to run the setup wizard as soon as Windows detects the CD in the drive.
6. False
7. Program Compatibility

Session 9.2

1. Defragmenting
2. c
3. False
4. through a port
5. True
6. Use Windows Update or use the Driver tab in the Properties dialog box for the hardware device.

Session 9.3

1. refresh
2. False
3. mirrored
4. local
5. the printer you use most often
6. True

Ending Data Files

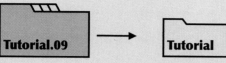

Tutorial

Backup Files
date number
Shelly

Review

Defragment.jpg
Disabled.jpg
Disk Cleanup.jpg
Disk Space.jpg
DPI.jpg
Picture Backup.jpg
Printer.jpg
Startup.jpg
System Restore.jpg
Updates.jpg

Case1

Compatible.jpg
Disk Drives.jpg
Driver.jpg
Music Backup.jpg
Programs.jpg
Resolution.jpg
Restore Point.jpg
Sarasota.jpg

Case2

Defender.jpg
E-mail Backup.jpg
Features.jpg
First Restore.jpg
Online.jpg
Protection.jpg
Salem.jpg
Updates.jpg

Case3

Ali.jpg
Devices.jpg
General.jpg
Properties.jpg
ReadyBoost.jpg
Removable.jpg
Schedule.jpg
SideShow.jpg

Case4

Accessible.doc

Objectives

Session 10.1
- Optimize computer performance
- Monitor system tasks
- Examine system information
- Increase memory capacity with ReadyBoost

Session 10.2
- Find trouble-shooting steps
- Troubleshoot printer and network problems
- Respond to software and operating system errors
- Manage remote assistance

Improving Your Computer's Performance

Enhancing Your System and Troubleshooting Computer Problems

Case | SafeRecords

SafeRecords in Indianapolis, Indiana, provides secure storage facilities for local businesses. In addition to a climate-controlled warehouse for storing documents and other records, SafeRecords shreds, recycles, and tracks paper documents and electronic media. You work for SafeRecords as a computer specialist, and your supervisor is Amar Gupta, the company's systems administrator. Your job is to help Amar keep the SafeRecords computers running at peak performance. Amar is familiar with system maintenance and troubleshooting tools in earlier versions of Windows, but he is new to Windows Vista. Besides managing company computers, Amar often trains employees on how to improve the performance of their computers and troubleshoot problems they have with hardware and software. You plan to spend some time with Amar showing him how to perform these same tasks on his Windows Vista computer.

In this tutorial, you will improve your computer's performance by disabling startup programs, optimizing system settings, and increasing processing speed. You'll monitor system performance, examine important information that reflects your computer's health, and find troubleshooting information. You'll also diagnose and repair errors with printers and network connections and learn how to respond to software errors, including recovering the operating system and repairing the Windows Vista installation. Finally, you'll request and manage remote assistance.

Starting Data Files

There are no starting Data Files needed for this tutorial.

Session 10.1

Improving System Performance

After you use your computer for awhile, and especially after installing software and saving and deleting files, you might notice changes in your **system performance**: how well your computer does what it is supposed to do. These changes usually mean that your computer is not as quick to respond to your actions or to perform system tasks as it was when Windows Vista was first installed. In that case, you can improve system performance by completing maintenance tasks. Start by opening the Performance Information and Tools window from Control Panel, shown in Figure 10-1.

| Figure 10-1 | Performance Information and Tools window |

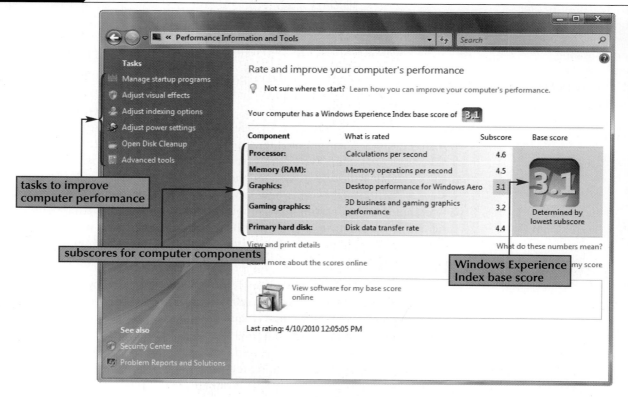

The Performance Information and Tools window lets you view and complete the information and performance tasks described in Figure 10-2.

Tasks and information provided in the Performance Information and Tools window ◀ **Figure 10-2**

Task or Information	Description	How to
Windows Experience Index base score	Indicates the capability of your computer's hardware and software to run Windows Vista and perform computing tasks	Click the Update my score link to calculate your base score.
Manage startup programs	If too many programs start automatically when you start Windows, they can slow down your computer. Preventing some programs from starting when Windows starts can improve performance.	Use Windows Defender to disable startup programs.
Adjust visual effects	How Windows displays menus and windows can affect performance.	Use the Performance Options dialog box to optimize how Windows displays menus and windows.
Adjust indexing options	Indexing helps you find files on your computer quickly.	Use the Indexing Options dialog box to specify what locations to index.
Adjust power settings	How Windows consumes or conserves power directly affects performance, especially for mobile computers.	Use the Power Options window to change power plans and their settings.
Open Disk Cleanup	Temporary or unnecessary files can take up too much storage space.	Use the Disk Cleanup tool to delete unnecessary files.
Advanced tools	Examining advanced performance information helps avoid related problems.	Use the Advanced Tools window to view notifications about performance problems and how to solve them.

You have already explored some of these tools in earlier tutorials. This tutorial discusses each item in the Performance Information and Tools window to help improve the performance of your computer.

Rating Your Computer's Performance

Recall that your computer's Windows Experience Index **base score** provides a general indication of your computer's performance. It reflects the speed and performance of your computer's components, including the processor, random access memory (RAM), graphics card, and hard disk. A higher base score generally means that your computer performs better and faster than a computer with a lower base score, especially when working on more advanced and resource-intensive tasks. Windows Vista calculates the base score by rating each hardware component that can affect performance and giving it a subscore. The base score is the lowest subscore, not an average, so if the subscore for general graphics is 2.7 but all the other subscores are 4.5 or higher, the base score for your computer is 2.7.

Viewing and Calculating Your Base Score | Reference Window

- Click the Start button, click Control Panel, click System and Maintenance, and then click Performance Information and Tools.
- View the Windows Experience Index base score and subscores for your computer. If these scores are not displayed, click Score this computer.
- To find out if your score has changed, click Update my score.

When you open the Performance Information and Tools window, it displays the base score calculated the last time Windows Vista rated the hardware components on your computer. If it has never rated the components, you can click a link to score the computer. After you install new hardware, you can recalculate the rating by clicking a link to update the score.

Software publishers other than Microsoft might identify the minimum base score your computer needs to run their software. You can therefore use the base score to make decisions when purchasing software. For example, if your computer has a base score of 3.1, you can confidently purchase software designed for Windows Vista that requires a computer with a base score of 3 or lower. If you want to use a particular program or feature of Windows Vista that requires a higher score than your base score, note the lowest subscore in the Performance and Tools window. You might need to upgrade the component with that subscore to meet the necessary base score.

You can generally interpret your computer's base score according to the descriptions in Figure 10-3.

Figure 10-3 | **Interpreting base scores**

Base Score	What the Computer Can Do
1–1.9	Complete general computing tasks, such as running office productivity programs and searching the Internet, but not use Windows Aero or the advanced multimedia features of Windows Vista
2–2.9	Respond more quickly than computers in the 1.0 range while running the same types of programs; some computers in this range can run Windows Aero, though performance might decline
3–3.9	Run Windows Aero and other new Windows Vista features at a level adequate for most computer users; for example, the computer can display a desktop theme at a high resolution, but not on multiple monitors
4 or higher	Use all the new features of Windows Vista, including advanced, graphics-intensive experiences, such as multiplayer and 3-D gaming

In addition, consider how you use your computer when interpreting the subscores. If you use your computer primarily to perform office productivity tasks by working with word processing, spreadsheet, e-mail, and Web browsing software, then your CPU and memory components should have high subscores. If you use your computer to play games or run high-end graphics programs, such as a video editor, then your RAM, graphics, and gaming graphics components should have high subscores. If you use your computer as a media center, such as to play multimedia slide shows or record digital TV programs, then your CPU, hard disk, and graphics components need high subscores.

SafeRecords mostly uses office productivity programs and custom databases to track the documents and other files it stores and tracks. Amar wants to make sure that his base score is high enough to run Windows Aero and that his subscores are appropriate for his typical tasks, which involve producing spreadsheets and reports that analyze the SafeRecords storage capacity. You'll show Amar how to view and calculate the Windows Experience Index base score for the first time on his Windows Vista computer.

To view and calculate a computer's base score:

▶ 1. Click the **Start** button 🔵 on the taskbar, and then click **Control Panel**. The Control Panel window opens.

▶ 2. Click the **System and Maintenance** category, and then click **Performance Information and Tools**. The Performance Information and Tools window opens.

3. Click the **Score this computer** link to assess the hardware and calculate a base score, which might take a few minutes. Windows displays the subscores and base score in the Performance Information and Tools window. See Figure 10-4.

Results of calculating the base score ◄ **Figure 10-4**

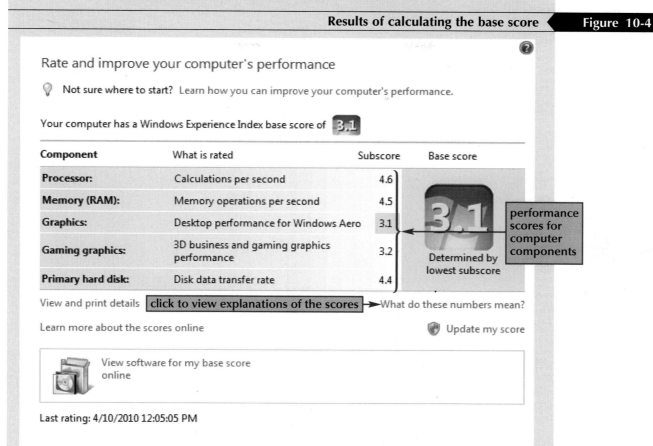

Rate and improve your computer's performance

💡 Not sure where to start? Learn how you can improve your computer's performance.

Your computer has a Windows Experience Index base score of **3.1**

Component	What is rated	Subscore	Base score
Processor:	Calculations per second	4.6	
Memory (RAM):	Memory operations per second	4.5	
Graphics:	Desktop performance for Windows Aero	3.1	**3.1**
Gaming graphics:	3D business and gaming graphics performance	3.2	Determined by lowest subscore
Primary hard disk:	Disk data transfer rate	4.4	

performance scores for computer components

View and print details | click to view explanations of the scores ► What do these numbers mean?

Learn more about the scores online 🛡 Update my score

View software for my base score online

Last rating: 4/10/2010 12:05:05 PM

Trouble? If a User Account Control dialog box opens requesting your permission or a password to continue, enter the password or click the Continue button.

Trouble? If Windows Vista has already calculated a base score, the Score this computer link does not appear. Instead, you can click Update my score to have Windows recalculate the base score.

Tip

To further interpret the scores, click Learn more about the scores online.

The subscores for Amar's computer are high for the processor, memory, and hard disk, which is appropriate for the type of tasks he performs. His graphics score of 3.1 is the lowest subscore, and is therefore his base score. This is very good for his current computing needs. However, because he is considering using two monitors to improve his productivity, he will need to increase this score by upgrading his graphics components. You suggest that Amar view the details about the components so he knows what to upgrade.

To view system details:

1. In the Performance Information and Tools window, click **View and print details**. The More details about my computer window opens displaying detailed information about Amar's system. See Figure 10-5.

Figure 10-5 ▶ **Displaying system details**

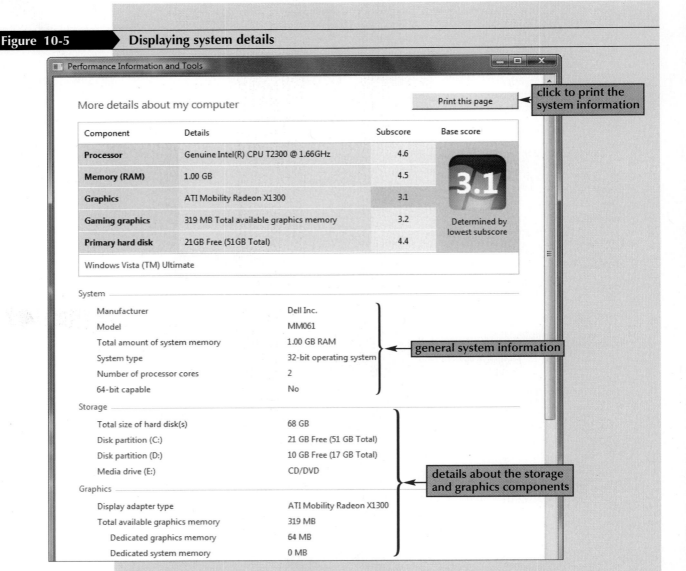

2. Close the More details about my computer window.

Amar has noticed that his computer is performing more slowly than it was when he first started using it. It is particularly slow to restart and wake up from sleep. You'll help him identify ways to improve his computer performance.

Disabling Startup Programs

In a previous tutorial, you learned how to add a program to the Windows Startup folder so that the program starts automatically when Windows starts. However, specifying that too many or unnecessary programs start when Windows does can increase the amount of time it takes to restart your computer after turning it off. To disable a startup program and improve performance, you can remove the program from the Startup folder or use Windows Defender.

Choosing the Startup Folder or Windows Defender | InSight

When you want to prevent a program from running automatically when Windows starts, open the Startup folder to remove any of its programs. You can add a program to the Startup folder by dragging it from the Start menu or by selecting the appropriate startup option when you install the program. Windows Defender, on the other hand, manages programs that start when Windows does with or without your knowledge. These programs include those that start by default, such as Windows Sidebar; software that can affect your privacy or the security of your computer, such as your antivirus software; and software related to networking, which lets you connect to the Internet or a network. Use Windows Defender when you want to manage the startup settings for these types of programs.

Windows Defender includes a tool called Software Explorer that provides detailed information about the types of programs described in Figure 10-6. These programs include those that start automatically when Windows does, programs currently running on your computer that can affect your privacy or the security of your computer, and programs that interact with networking and operating system services.

Types of programs monitored by Software Explorer ◄ **Figure 10-6**

Type of Program	Description	Example
Startup	Programs that run automatically with or without your knowledge when you start Windows	Windows Sidebar
Currently running	Programs that are currently running on the desktop or in the background	Antivirus software
Network	Programs or processes that can connect to the Internet or to your home or office network	People Near Me
Winsock service providers	Programs that perform low-level networking and communication services for Windows and programs that run on Windows	Any program governing network protocols

To help Amar determine how to improve the performance of his computer when starting and waking from sleep, you'll start by opening Software Explorer in Windows Defender and examining the programs it manages.

To open Software Explorer:

▶ **1.** In the Performance Information and Tools window, click **Manage startup programs** in the left pane. Windows Defender starts and opens Software Explorer. See Figure 10-7.

Figure 10-7 **Software Explorer in Windows Defender**

2. In the list of programs, click **Microsoft Windows Sidebar**. Its details appear in the right pane.

Trouble? If Microsoft Windows Sidebar does not appear in the list of programs, click the Category arrow button, click Currently Running Programs, then click Microsoft Windows Sidebar. If Sidebar is not listed as a running program, ask your instructor which program to select in the Startup Programs list.

When you display startup programs in the left pane, the right pane displays general information about the selected program, including its name, location, publisher, version, and startup details. The Startup Value line shows the path to the program. If the path ends with */autoRun*, that means the program is set to start automatically when Windows starts and run as it normally does. The Startup Value line for other programs, such as Windows Defender itself, might end with *–hide*, meaning that Windows Defender starts and then runs in the background.

You can prevent a program from starting when Windows does by disabling or removing the program. Disabling the program leaves it in the list of startup programs, but doesn't allow it to start automatically. Removing the program removes it from the list of startup programs.

Amar rarely uses Windows Sidebar, so you'll show him how to disable it so it doesn't start when Windows does.

To disable a startup program:

▶ **1.** In the Software Explorer window, make sure **Microsoft Windows Sidebar** is selected in the left pane, and then click the **Disable** button. A dialog box opens asking if you're sure you want to disable the program.

▶ **2.** Click the **Yes** button.

▶ **3.** Close the Software Explorer window.

Recall that the base score for Amar's computer is 3.1, reflecting the lowest subscore for his graphics component. Until Amar can upgrade his graphics hardware, he can improve his computer's performance by adjusting its visual effects.

Optimizing Visual Effects and Other Options

Windows Vista uses visual effects to enhance your computing experience, especially if you are using Windows Aero. For example, it shows thumbnails instead of icons to help you identify files in a folder window. It also fades menu items after you click them to reinforce your selection. However, these visual effects consume system resources related to the general graphics and gaming graphics components. If a subscore for one of these components is less than four, your computer might be working especially hard to display visual effects. In that case, you can improve performance by displaying some effects and not others using the Visual Effects tab in the Performance Options dialog box. This tab lists settings for visual effects such as animating windows when minimizing and maximizing and provides the following four option buttons:

• Let Windows choose what's best for my computer: Windows selects the visual effects that achieve the best balance of appearance and performance for your computer hardware.
• Adjust for best appearance: Use all the visual effects listed.
• Adjust for best performance: Use none of the visual effects listed.
• Custom: Select only the visual effects you want to use.

You'll show Amar how to turn off window animation to improve performance.

To adjust visual effect settings:

▶ **1.** In the Performance Information and Tools window, click **Adjust visual effects** in the left pane. The Performance Options dialog box opens to the Visual Effects tab. See Figure 10-8.

| Figure 10-8 | Performance Options dialog box |

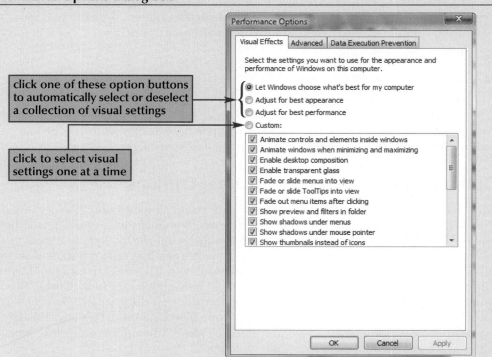

click one of these option buttons to automatically select or deselect a collection of visual settings

click to select visual settings one at a time

Trouble? If a User Account Control dialog box opens requesting your permission or a password to continue, enter the password or click the Continue button.

2. Click the **Animate controls and elements inside windows** box to remove the check mark. This automatically selects the Custom option button.

3. Click the **Animate windows when minimizing and maximizing** box to remove the check mark.

4. Click the **OK** button to change the visual effects Windows uses.

The Performance Information and Tools window also includes three tools you have already used: indexing options, power settings, and Disk Cleanup. Recall that you can set indexing options to help you find files on your computer. Click *Adjust indexing options* in the left pane of the Performance Information and Tools window to open the Indexing Options dialog box, where you can specify which folders to include in your indexed locations. You can search more efficiently and improve performance by excluding folders from your indexed locations and including only those that you commonly use. To remove a folder from the indexed locations, click the folder name in the Indexing Options dialog box, click the Modify button, clear the check box for the folder in the Change selected locations list, and then click OK.

As you learned in a previous tutorial, changing your power settings also affects performance. Click *Adjust power settings* in the left pane of the Performance Information and Tools window to open the Power Options window, where you can select a default power plan or create a new one. The High performance plan chooses settings that optimize performance and minimize battery life.

You also learned how to use Disk Cleanup to delete temporary and other unnecessary files. Click *Open Disk Cleanup* in the left pane of the Performance Information and Tools window to open the Disk Cleanup Options dialog box, where you can choose to clean up your files only or files from all users on the computer. After selecting your files only, for example, you select the drive you want to clean up, such as drive C. Windows Vista calculates how much space you can free by permanently deleting files such as temporary Internet files and downloaded program files. You can also select other types of files, such as those in the Recycle Bin. After you select the files to remove, click the OK button to delete the files.

Using Advanced Performance Tools

System administrators and information technology (IT) professionals often use advanced system tools, such as Event Viewer and System Information, to solve problems. These performance tools are collected in a central location, the Advanced Tools window, which also notifies you about performance issues and suggests how to address them. For example, if Windows detects that a driver is reducing performance, the Advanced Tools window displays a notification you can click to learn which driver is causing the problem and to view help on how to update the driver. Performance issues are listed at the top of the Advanced Tools window in order of importance. In other words, issues at the beginning of the list affect the system more than issues at the end of the list. The Advanced Tools window also provides access to the advanced performance tools described in Figure 10-9.

Advanced performance tools ◀ Figure 10-9

Advanced Tool	Description
Event Viewer	Event Viewer tracks details of system events that might affect your computer's performance.
Reliability and Performance Monitor	This monitor displays graphs of system performance and collects data about resource usage.
Task Manager	Task Manager provides details about programs, processes, and how your computer is using system resources, such as RAM.
System Information	This tool displays details about the hardware and software components on your computer.
Performance Options	This dialog box is the same one you used to adjust visual effects. You can also use it to manage memory and Data Execution Prevention (DEP), a Windows Vista tool that protects against damage from viruses and other security threats.
Disk Defragmenter	Use the Disk Defragmenter window to schedule disk defragmentation or start defragmenting now.
System Diagnostics	This tool generates a report about the status of hardware resources, system response times, and other system information, and provides suggestions for maximizing performance.

You'll explore these advanced performance tools with Amar shortly. Right now, you want to open the Advanced Tools window to see if it detects any performance issues that Amar should resolve.

To view performance issues:

▶ **1.** In the Performance Information and Tools window, click **Advanced tools** in the left pane. The Advanced Tools window opens. See Figure 10-10. Windows identifies two issues that might affect the performance of Amar's computer.

Figure 10-10 | **Advanced Tools window**

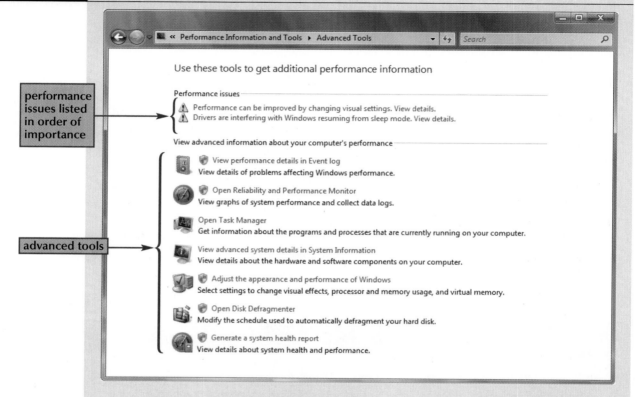

performance issues listed in order of importance

advanced tools

Trouble? If the Advanced Tools window does not list any Performance issues for your computer, read but do not perform Steps 2–5.

▶ **2.** Click the first issue in the list, **Performance can be improved by changing visual settings. View details.** A Performance Information and Tools dialog box opens to suggest how to address the issue. See Figure 10-11.

Figure 10-11 | **Suggested resolutions for performance issue**

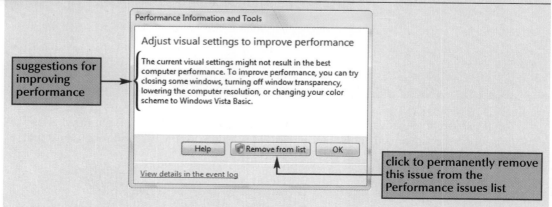

suggestions for improving performance

click to permanently remove this issue from the Performance issues list

> **Trouble?** If a different performance issue is listed first in your Advanced Tools window, click that issue. If no issues are listed in your Advanced Tools window, read but do not perform the remaining steps.
>
> ▶ **3.** Click the **Help** button to open a Windows Help and Support window that describes how to change visual settings.
>
> ▶ **4.** Read the suggestions, and then close the Windows Help and Support window.
>
> ▶ **5.** Click the **OK** button to close the Performance and Information and Tools dialog box.

Amar can perform these same steps to learn more about remaining performance issues and how to resolve them. Next, you want to explore some of the advanced performance tools that Amar has not encountered before.

Viewing Details About System Events

When you are troubleshooting problems with Windows and other programs, it is often helpful to view details about system events, such as a user logging on to Windows or a program closing unexpectedly. Windows records these system events in an **event log**, a special text file that contains details about the event. You can read event logs by using Event Viewer, an advanced performance tool that tracks system events, including the following types:

- **Program events**. Windows classifies each program event as an error, warning, or information, depending on its severity. An error is a significant problem, such as loss of data. A warning is an event that might indicate a potential problem. An information event indicates that a program, driver, or service performed successfully.
- **Security events**. These events are called audits and are either successful or failed. For example, when you log on to Windows, Event Viewer records that as a successful audit.
- **System events**. Similar to program events, Windows classifies each system event as an error, warning, or information.

To view details about an event, double-click it in the Event Viewer window to open the Event Properties window, which describes the event and provides details helpful to a PC professional. You can copy the event properties to the Windows Clipboard, and then paste it in a text file or e-mail message to send to a technician, for example.

You'll show Amar how to open the Event Viewer window and find information about critical events.

To perform the following steps, you must be logged on using an Administrator account. If you are not logged on as an Administrator, you can only change settings that apply to your *user account*, and some event logs may not be accessible. However, you can still complete the following steps.

To use Event Viewer:

▶ **1.** In the Advanced Tools window, click **View performance details in Event log**. The Event Viewer window opens. See Figure 10-12. If this is the first time you are opening the Event Viewer window, a message appears briefly indicating that Windows is setting up the program.

Figure 10-12 | **Event Viewer window**

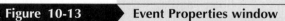

description bar identifies the types of events displayed in the window

console tree lists folders where Windows stores event logs

list of events

Preview pane shows details about the selected event

Trouble? If a User Account Control dialog box opens requesting your permission or a password to continue, enter the password or click the Continue button.

2. Scroll the list of events, and then double-click a **Critical** event. The Event Properties window opens. See Figure 10-13. Note that this event has an Event ID of 100. If necessary, you could provide this Event ID to a PC technician who is trying to troubleshoot your computer.

Figure 10-13 | **Event Properties window**

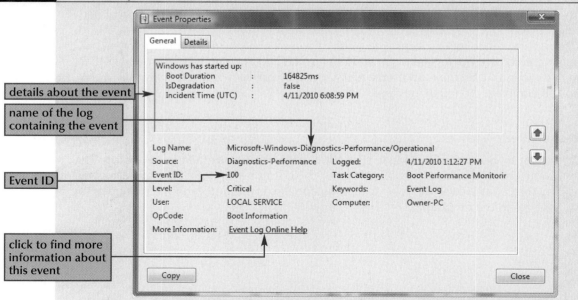

details about the event

name of the log containing the event

Event ID

click to find more information about this event

Trouble? If no Critical events are listed in your Event Viewer, click any type of event.

▶ **3.** Click the **Close** button to close the Event Properties window.

▶ **4.** Close the Event Viewer window.

Next, you want to show Amar how to use the Reliability and Performance Monitor to view graphs of system performance.

Monitoring System Performance

A common complaint from computer users is that their computer seems to be running more slowly than usual. If you are experiencing this same symptom, too many programs might be running at the same time, causing a loss of performance. Or the computer might be low on memory or need to have its processor upgraded to a faster one. To determine the cause, you need to measure the performance of the system in numerical terms.

Tip

You can also open Event Viewer by clicking the Start button, clicking Control Panel, clicking System and Maintenance, clicking Administrative Tools, and then double-clicking Event Viewer.

| **Monitoring System Performance** | Reference Window |

- Click the Start button, click Control Panel, click the System and Maintenance category, and then click Performance Information and Tools.
- Click Advanced tools in the left pane.
- Click Open Reliability and Performance Monitor.
- In the left pane, click Reliability and Performance, if necessary, to display an overview of system resources.
- Click Performance Monitor to graph system performance.
- Click Reliability Monitor to display a chart of system stability information.

One way of accomplishing this task is to use the Windows Reliability and Performance Monitor, which provides tools for analyzing system performance. These tools let you monitor the performance of programs and hardware, customize the data you want to collect in logs, and generate reports. Windows Reliability and Performance Monitor consists of three monitoring tools, which are described in Figure 10-14.

Reliability and Performance Monitor tools ◀ Figure 10-14

Tool	Description
Resource View	Lets you monitor the usage and performance of the CPU, disk, network, and memory resources as your computer is using them
Performance Monitor	Displays graphs or generates reports of current or historic performance data
Reliability Monitor	Provides an overview of system stability and analyzes trends about events that can affect system stability, such as software installations, operating system updates, and hardware failures, starting from the time of system installation

When you open the Reliability and Performance Monitor window, it opens to the Resource View page by default. With this page, you can view four graphs and detailed information to monitor the usage of CPU, disk, network, and memory as your computer is using these resources. Each bar below the graphs summarizes resource usage. You can click a bar or an expand button to display details about each resource.

The CPU graph shows how much of the central processing unit (CPU) is being used at the moment. The CPU is the main circuit chip in a computer, and performs most of the calculations necessary to run the computer. A high percentage of CPU usage means that the currently running programs or processes require a lot of CPU resources, which can slow your computer. If the percentage appears frozen at or near 100%, then some programs might not be responding. You can use Task Manager to stop running the program, which you'll do shortly. Click the CPU bar to view the processes, or images, using CPU resources. (A **process** is a task performed by a program and usually contains information about starting the program.)

The Disk graph and bar indicates how active your hard disk is, measured by the number of times a program reads (retrieves) data from the hard disk or writes (stores) data on the hard disk. Click the Disk bar to see which files are reading or writing data to your hard disk.

The Network graph and bar indicates the amount of network activity your computer is experiencing, measured in kilobytes per second (kbps). Click the Network bar to see the network address of the programs exchanging information with your computer.

The Memory graph and bar displays the percentage of RAM currently being used and the number of hard faults occurring per second. A hard fault, or page fault, occurs when a program retrieves data from RAM and stores it on the hard disk. If a program is responding slowly to your commands, look here for a high number of hard faults, which indicate that the program is continually reading data from disk rather than RAM.

SafeRecords employees occasionally report to you or Amar that their computers are suddenly running more slowly than normal. You'll show Amar how to open the Reliability and Performance Monitor window and view the resources Windows is currently using to diagnose the problem with the employee's computer.

To perform the following steps, you must be logged on using an Administrator account. If you are not logged on as an Administrator, read but do not perform the following steps.

To examine an overview of resource usage:

▶ **1.** In the Advanced Tools window, click **Open Reliability and Performance Monitor**. The Reliability and Performance Monitor window opens to the Resource Overview. See Figure 10-15.

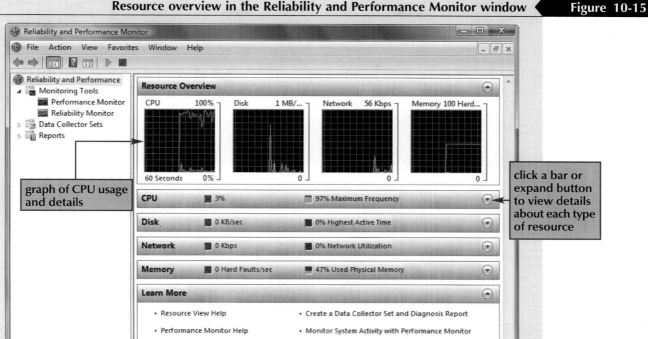

Trouble? If a User Account Control dialog box opens requesting your permission or a password to continue, enter the password or click the Continue button.

2. Click the **expand** button ⊙ on the CPU bar to display details about CPU activity.

Next, you can use Performance Monitor to produce a graph that reflects system performance. See Figure 10-16.

Tip

To determine the type of CPU installed on your computer, open Control Panel, click System and Maintenance, click System, and then look for the CPU speed and type in the System section under Processor.

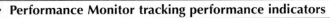

Performance Monitor tracking performance indicators

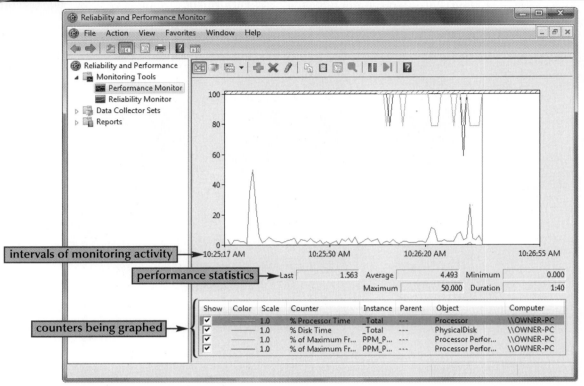

The Performance Monitor tracks the percentage of time your processor is working by default, which is one measure of how busy your system is. You can also track other performance indicators, such as how fast your computer retrieves data from the hard disk. Tracking performance information can locate the source of trouble in a slow system, and can help you determine what needs to be done to speed up the system.

To track performance indicators other than processor time, you add an item, called a **counter**, to track a particular part of the system performance and track the values of the counter in the graph. The counter is updated at intervals you specify—usually every few seconds. To add a counter to the graph, you click the Add button on the Performance Monitor toolbar to open the Add Counters window. This window lists performance counters that are included with Windows Vista.

You'll show Amar how to use the Performance Monitor to track processor time. In this case, the graph in the Performance Monitor window measures the percentage of time that the processor is not idle. A value near 100% suggests that the processor is almost never idle. If so, that indicates the processor might be so busy that it can't perform tasks efficiently. When a SafeRecords employee reports that a computer is working slowly, you and Amar can track the processor time to see if the employee is running too many programs or processes at the same time.

Another common problem that affects performance is low memory. Your computer has two types of memory: RAM and virtual memory. All programs use RAM, so if you have many programs running or are using a program that requires a lot of RAM, Windows might not have enough RAM to run a program. In that case, Windows temporarily moves information that it would normally store in RAM to a file on your hard disk called a **paging file**. The paging file is a hidden file on the hard disk that Windows uses to hold parts of programs and data files that do not fit in RAM. Windows moves data from the paging file to RAM as needed and moves data from RAM to the paging file to make room for new data. Because Windows swaps data in and out of the paging file, it is also known as a swap file. The amount of information temporarily stored in a paging file is called

virtual memory. Using virtual memory—in other words, moving information to and from the paging file—frees up enough RAM for programs to run correctly.

Preventing and Solving Low Memory Problems | InSight

If you try to open a menu or dialog box in a program and the program responds slowly or seems to stop working, your computer is probably low on memory. You can prevent or solve low memory problems by observing the following guidelines:

- Run fewer programs at the same time, especially those that show signs of requiring lots of memory.
- Increase the size of the paging file. Windows increases virtual memory the first time your computer becomes low on memory, but you can increase it up to the amount of RAM installed. However, this might cause your programs to run more slowly overall.
- Install more RAM. Open the System window to view the amount of RAM your computer has installed, and then contact the computer manufacturer to find out if you can install more.
- Determine if a program uses too much memory. Track the paging file usage in Performance Monitor or Task Manager when you are running a particular program. If these tools show frequent activity, check for updates to the program and install them.

Besides tracking processor time on Amar's computer, you'll also track the paging file usage to diagnose memory problems. If a SafeRecords employee indicates that a program is responding slowly or that Windows reports a low memory problem, you can track the paging file usage and increase its size, if necessary. (You'll learn how to increase the size of the paging file shortly.)

To perform the following steps, you must be logged on using an Administrator account. If you are not logged on as an Administrator, read but do not perform the following steps.

To track processor time:

▶ 1. In the Reliability and Performance Monitor window, click **Performance Monitor** in the left pane. The Performance Monitor graph appears in the right pane, tracking the percentage of time that the processor is in use each second. See Figure 10-17. The graph on your computer will show different activity.

Figure 10-17 **Tracking processor time**

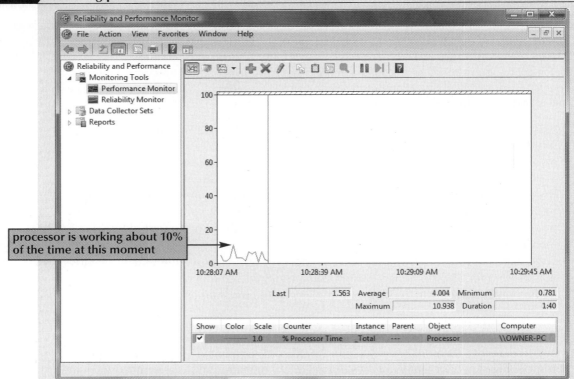

processor is working about 10% of the time at this moment

Trouble? If your Performance Monitor is not tracking any counters, click the Add button in the toolbar, click Processor in the Available counters list, click the Add button, and then click the OK button to track processor time.

2. Click the **Add** button on the Performance Monitor toolbar. The Add Counters dialog box opens. See Figure 10-18.

Adding a counter to the Performance Monitor ◀ Figure 10-18

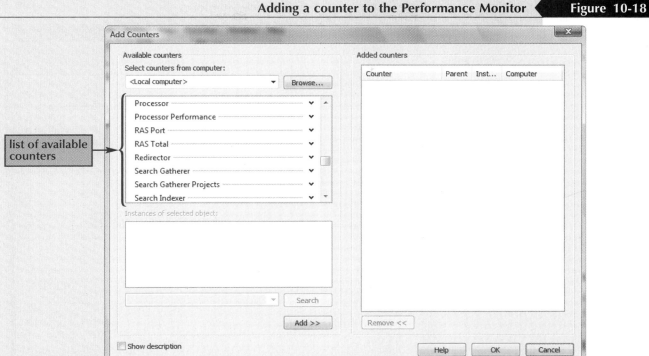

list of available counters

3. Scroll the Available counters list, and then double-click **Paging File**. Details you can track appear below the Paging File entry.

4. Click **% Usage**, and then click the **Add** button to include that counter in the Added counters list.

5. Click the **OK** button. The Performance Monitor begins tracking paging file usage. See Figure 10-19.

Figure 10-19 **Adding a paging file counter to the Performance Monitor**

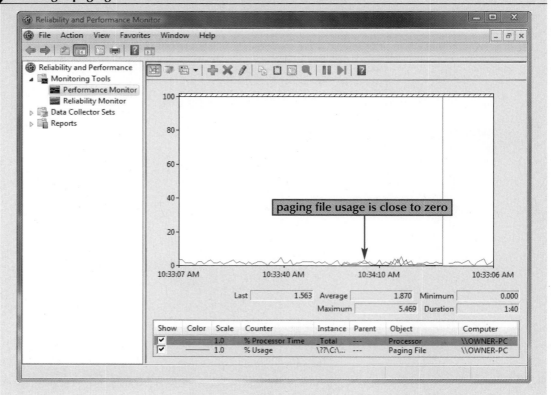

The processor time and paging file usage on Amar's computer do not indicate any performance problems. However, you and Amar can track these counters to diagnose problems for the SafeRecords employees.

Finally, you'll open the Reliability Monitor window to view a chart of the system stability of Amar's computer. The Reliability Monitor maintains up to a year of history for system stability and reliability events. For example, the Reliability Monitor tracks program failures, such as a program shutting down unexpectedly, and problems with the hard disk and memory. It then displays these events on a chart and calculates a stability index, which is a number from 1 (least stable) to 10 (most stable) and reflects the number of failures of various types during the last year.

To view the System Stability chart and index:

1. In the Reliability and Performance Monitor window, click **Reliability Monitor** in the left pane. The Reliability Monitor chart appears in the right pane. See Figure 10-20. The chart and other system information on your computer will differ.

System Stability chart in the Reliability Monitor window ◄ Figure 10-20

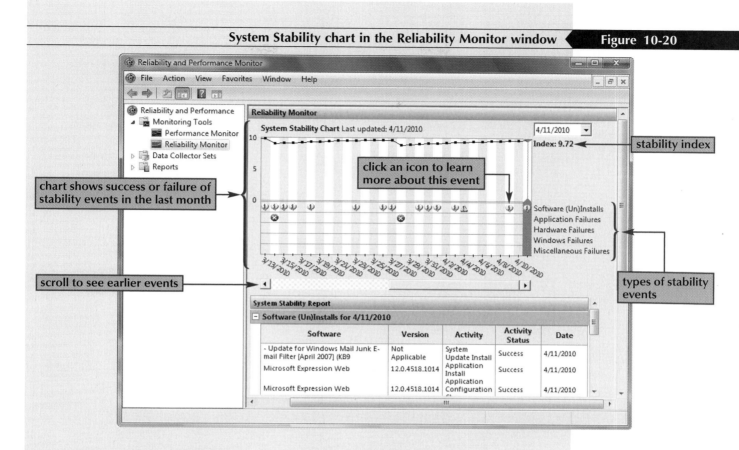

2. Click an **Information** icon on the chart. Details about that event appear in the System Stability Report pane. See Figure 10-21.

Figure 10-21 Viewing information about a system stability event

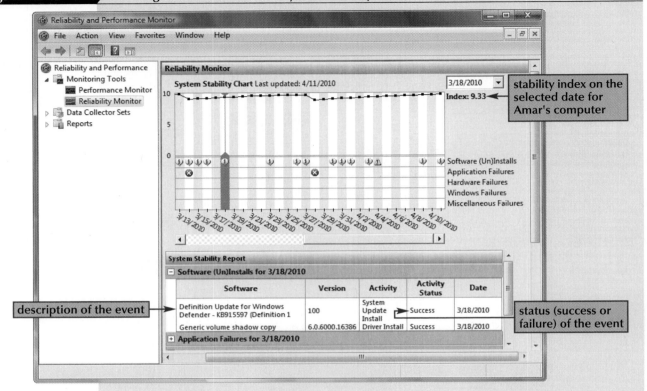

3. Close the Reliability and Performance Monitor window.

The stability index on Amar's computer is over 9, which means his system has been stable and reliable over the past year.

Using Task Manager to Examine System Information

Besides using the Reliability and Performance Monitor to track system information, you can also use Task Manager to view information about the programs and processes running on your computer. Task Manager does not provide as much information as the Reliability and Performance Monitor, but any user can open Task Manager, whereas only Administrators can use the Reliability and Performance Monitor.

You can use Task Manager to monitor your computer's performance or to close a program that is not responding. If you are connected to a network, you can also use Task Manager to view network status and see how your network is functioning. If more than one user is connected to your computer, you can see who is connected and what they are working on, and you can send them a message.

Task Manager is a dialog box that contains the tabs described in Figure 10-22.

Tabs in the Task Manager dialog box ◄ **Figure 10-22**

Task Manager Tab	Description
Applications	Lists the programs running on your computer, including those that are not responding
Processes	Lists the processes running on your computer
Services	Lists current services, which are the background programs or processes that support other programs
Performance	Provides details about how your computer is using system resources, such as RAM and the CPU
Networking	Provides details about network connections
Users	Identifies the current users of the computer and their status

You typically use the first four tabs in the Task Manager dialog box to troubleshoot system problems and improve performance. The Applications tab displays each currently active program and its status, which is either Running or Not Responding. If a program has a Not Responding status, you can close the program by clicking it and then clicking the End Task button. Note that closing a program this way discards any unsaved changes you made with that program.

Although viruses and other malware rarely appear as programs listed on the Applications tab, they sometimes appear on the Processes tab. To learn more about a process, right-click it on the Processes tab, and then click Properties on the shortcut menu. Click the Details tab in the Properties dialog box to view a description of the file, the program it's associated with, and its copyright information. Typically, the Details tab for malware files does not provide any information. You can also search the Windows Vista help or the Internet for more information about the files listed on the Processes tab. If you are sure a process is associated with malware, click the file, and then click the End Process button. Make sure you know the purpose of a process before ending it. If you end a process associated with an open program, such as a word-processing program, the program closes without saving your data. If you end a process associated with a system service, some part of the system might not function properly.

Recall that a **service** is a program or process running in the background that supports other programs; currently running services appear on the Services tab in the Task Manager dialog box. You can see which process is associated with a service (if any) by right-clicking a service on the Services tab, and then clicking Go to Process on the shortcut menu. The Processes tab opens and selects the process associated with that service.

Similar to the Reliability and Performance Monitor window, the Performance tab displays graphs to illustrate how your computer is using system resources, including CPU and RAM. The status bar in the Task Manager dialog box also displays the percentage of CPU and physical memory (RAM) currently being used. Recall that if the CPU Usage percentage appears frozen at or near 100%, a program might not be responding. In that case, you should open the Applications tab and end that program as previously described.

You'll explore the first four tabs in the Task Manager dialog box with Amar to show him the kinds of information they provide.

To explore Task Manager:

▶ **1.** In the Advanced Tools window, click **Open Task Manager** to open the Windows Task Manager dialog box.

▶ **2.** Click the **Applications** tab, if necessary, to see a list of programs running on your computer. See Figure 10-23. Your list of applications might differ.

Figure 10-23 ▶ **Applications tab in the Task Manager dialog box**

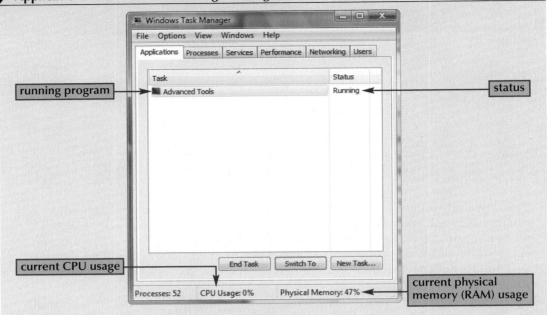

3. Click the **Processes** tab to display the processes running for your user account. See Figure 10-24. Your list of processes might differ.

Figure 10-24 ▶ **Processes tab in the Task Manager dialog box**

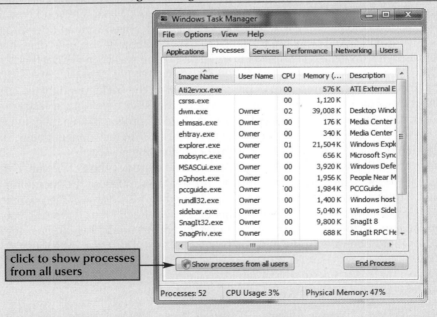

▶ **4.** Right-click **explorer.exe** and then click **Properties** on the shortcut menu. The explorer Properties dialog box opens. Drag it to an open area of the desktop, if necessary.

▶ **5.** Click the **Details** tab to view details about the explorer.exe process file. This file is associated with the Windows Explorer program.

▶ **6.** Click the **OK** button to close the explorer Properties dialog box.

▶ **7.** Click the **Services** tab in the Task Manager dialog box to display the services associated with the programs and processes running on your computer.

▶ **8.** Click the **Performance** tab to display graphs of CPU and RAM usage. See Figure 10-25.

Performance tab in the Task Manager dialog box ◀ **Figure 10-25**

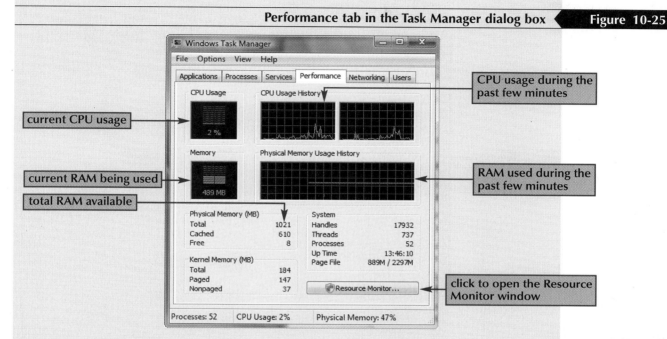

▶ **9.** Close the Windows Task Manager dialog box.

Although Task Manager provides information about software running on your computer and displays some resource information also included in the Reliability and Performance Monitor, you can use another window to examine a summary of hardware on your computer.

Tip

You can also open Task Manager by right-clicking the taskbar and then clicking Task Manager.

Examining System Information

The System Information window collects detailed information about your computer system, some of which is also provided in other windows, including the Device Manager and the System window. Advanced users often find it more convenient to use the System Information window to learn details such as the computer name, operating system version, processor type, and total amount of RAM.

Although Amar is comfortable using Device Manager to view hardware information, including device conflicts, drivers, and component names, you'll show him how to use the System Information window to learn this same hardware information and other system details that computer administrators often need to know.

To examine system information:

▶ **1.** In the Advanced Tools window, click **View advanced system details in System Information** to open the System Information window. By default, this window opens to show a system summary. See Figure 10-26.

Figure 10-26 System Information window

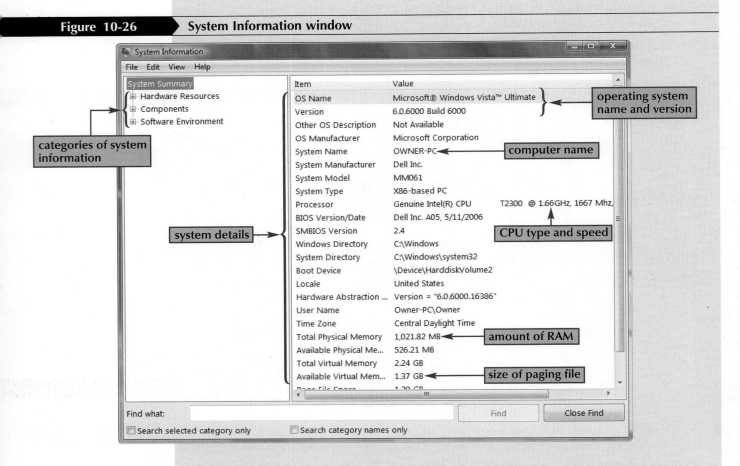

Trouble? If your System Information window does not open showing a system summary, click System Summary in the left pane.

▶ **2.** Click the **expand** icon ⊞ next to Hardware Resources, and then click **IRQs** to display a list of hardware resources, including the IRQ number, device, and status. (Recall that Windows assigns each hardware device an IRQ number and ranks them, giving lower numbers higher priority so they receive attention first.)

▶ **3.** Click the **expand** icon ⊞ next to Components to display a list of the types of devices installed on your computer.

▶ **4.** Click **CD-ROM** in the Components list to display details about this device, including its drive letter and location of its driver file.

Trouble? If CD-ROM does not appear in your Components list, click any other device type.

▶ **5.** Click the **expand** icon ⊞ next to Software Environment to display a list of software details.

▶ **6.** Click **Running Tasks** in the Software Environment list to display a list of running processes, similar to the one displayed in the Task Manager dialog box.

▶ **7.** Click **Startup Programs** to display details about programs that start when Windows does, similar to the list displayed in the Software Explorer window in Windows Defender.

▶ **8.** Close the System Information window.

Now that you've shown Amar a few ways to track the paging file usage, you explore how to increase the size of this file when necessary.

Increasing Memory Capacity

If you receive warnings that your virtual memory is low, you can increase the minimum size of your paging file. Windows sets the initial minimum size of the paging file at the amount of RAM installed on your computer plus 300 MB. It sets the maximum size at three times the amount of RAM installed on your computer. If you see warnings at these recommended levels, then increase the minimum and maximum sizes.

Although Amar's computer has enough virtual memory to perform efficiently, you'll show him how to increase the minimum and maximum size of the paging file for future reference. To do so, you use the Performance Options dialog box, which is the same dialog box you used to select visual effects.

To increase the size of the paging file:

▶ **1.** In the Advanced Tools window, click **Adjust the appearance and performance of Windows** to open the Performance Options dialog box.

Trouble? If a User Account Control dialog box opens requesting your permission or a password to continue, enter the password or click the Continue button.

▶ **2.** Click the **Advanced** tab to display paging file information. See Figure 10-27.

Advanced tab in the Performance Options dialog box ◀ Figure 10-27

▶ **3.** Click the **Change** button to open the Virtual Memory dialog box. See Figure 10-28.

Figure 10-28 — **Virtual Memory dialog box**

when this box is checked, Windows
manages your paging file

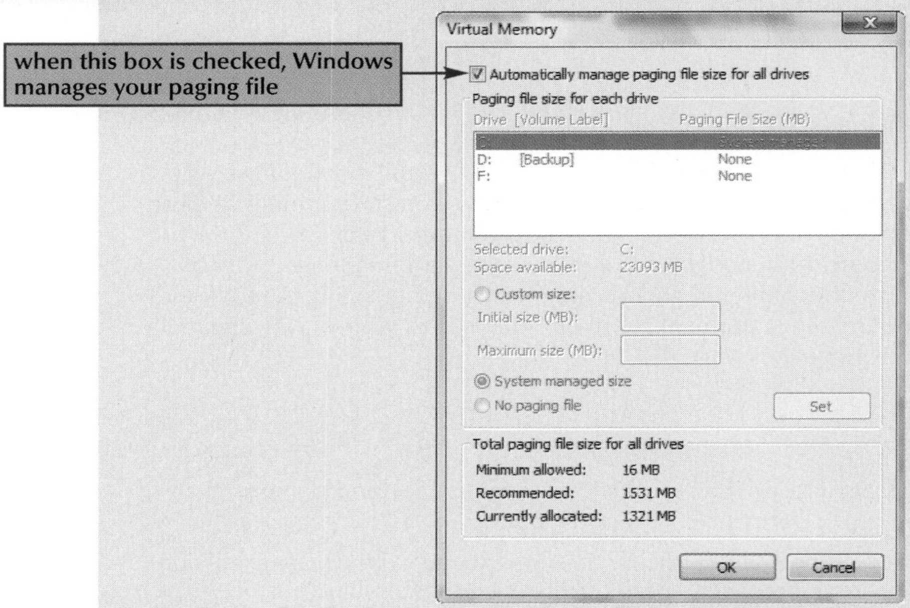

4. If Amar wanted to manage the paging file size himself, he could click the
   Automatically manage paging file size for all drives box to remove the check mark,
   click the drive he wants to manage, click the Custom size option button, enter the
   initial (minimum) and maximum size for the paging file, and then click the
   Set button.

5. Click the **Cancel** button to close the Virtual Memory dialog box without making any
   changes.

6. Click the **OK** button to close the Performance Options dialog box.

Two tools remain in the Performance Information and Tools window: Disk
Defragmenter and a system health report. You and Amar already know how to defragment a disk—you open the Disk Defragmenter dialog box and then click the Defragment
now button or set a schedule to have Windows defragment a disk automatically. You'll
show Amar how to generate a system health report next.

Generating a System Health Report

To have Windows collect data about your system and diagnose any problems, you can generate a Systems Diagnostics report. This report includes nine sections. The first section identifies the computer, the date of the report, and the length of time Windows needed to collect
the data for the report. The second section, Diagnostic Results, is especially helpful to system
administrators. This section lists problems found on the computer, if any, and assigns them a
severity, such as Critical or Warning. This section also shows the results of basic system
checks, such as a survey of the attributes of the operating system, and a resource overview,
such as CPU and network usage. Other sections, such as the Software Configuration and
Hardware Configuration sections, provide details about these checks. The last section, Report
Statistics, lists details about the computer, files, and events.

Because Amar's system is performing well right now, you'll generate and save a system health report to use as a baseline, which is a snapshot of the computer's performance when it's running at a normal level. When the system has problems, Amar can generate another system health report to compare to the baseline report. Using baseline reports, he can anticipate and then prevent problems.

To generate a system health report:

1. In the Advanced Tools window, click **Generate a system health report**. The Reliability and Performance Monitor window opens and displays a progress bar as Windows collects data about your system for 60 seconds. When it's finished collecting data, Windows generates and displays the System Diagnostics Report. See Figure 10-29.

System Diagnostics report | Figure 10-29

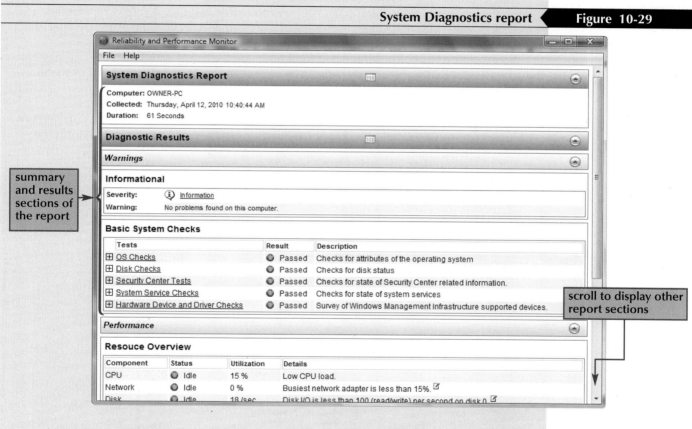

summary and results sections of the report

scroll to display other report sections

Trouble? If a User Account Control dialog box opens requesting your permission or a password to continue, enter the password or click the Continue button.

2. Click **File** on the menu bar, and then click **Save As** to open the Save As dialog box.

3. Navigate to the Tutorial.10\Tutorial folder provided with your Data Files, type **Diagnostics** as the name of the report, and then click the **Save** button.

4. Close the report window.

5. Close the Advanced Tools window.

You want to show Amar another useful way to increase memory capacity using a USB flash drive and a feature called ReadyBoost.

Using ReadyBoost to Increase Memory Capacity

Windows ReadyBoost can use storage space on some removable media devices, including USB flash drives, to speed up your computer. When you insert a device with this capability, the AutoPlay dialog will offer you the option to speed up your system using Windows ReadyBoost. If you select this option, you can then choose how much memory to use for this purpose. However, there are some situations where you may not be able to use all of the memory on your storage device to speed up your computer.

Some USB storage devices contain both slow and fast flash memory, and Windows can only use fast flash memory to speed up your computer. So if your device contains both slow and fast memory, keep in mind that you can only use the fast memory portion for this purpose.

The recommended amount of memory to use for ReadyBoost acceleration is one to three times the amount of RAM installed in your computer. For instance, if your computer has 512 megabytes (MB) of RAM and you plug in a 4 gigabyte (GB) USB flash drive, setting aside from 512 MB to 1.5 GB of that drive will offer the best performance boost.

You can turn ReadyBoost on or off for a flash drive or other removable storage device, as long as the removable media device contains at least 256 megabytes (MB) of space to work with Windows ReadyBoost.

You'll show Amar how to increase his memory capacity using ReadyBoost.

To perform the following steps, you need a USB flash drive that has at least 50 percent of its storage space free. If you do not have such a device, read but do not perform the following steps.

To use ReadyBoost:

▶ **1.** Plug a USB flash drive into an available USB port on your computer. The AutoPlay dialog box opens. See Figure 10-30.

Figure 10-30 ▶ **AutoPlay dialog box**

click to use this device to increase the memory capacity of your computer

Trouble? If the AutoPlay dialog box does not open, open Computer, right-click the USB flash drive, and then click Open Autoplay.

▶ **2.** Click **Speed up my system** to open the Properties dialog box for the USB flash drive. If necessary, click the **ReadyBoost** tab. See Figure 10-31.

USB flash drive's Properties dialog box open to the ReadyBoost tab ◀ Figure 10-31

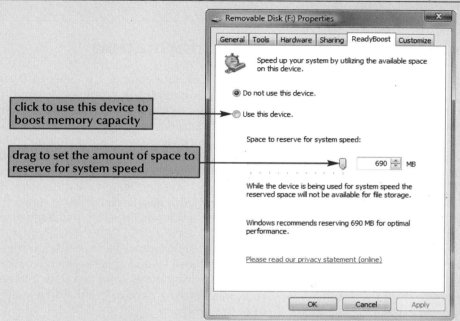

click to use this device to boost memory capacity

drag to set the amount of space to reserve for system speed

Trouble? If the Speed up my system option does not appear on the AutoPlay dialog box, the USB flash drive might not have the required performance characterisitics for boosting memory. Find a different USB flash drive and repeat Steps 1 and 2.

▶ **3.** Click the **Use this device** option button to turn on ReadyBoost.

▶ **4.** Drag the slider to the far right, if possible, to select the maximum amount of available space on your USB flash drive to reserve for boosting your system speed.

▶ **5.** Click the **OK** button.

Now Amar has an extra 690 MB of memory that Windows can use to improve system performance.

In the next session, you'll show him how to continue to optimize his computer by troubleshooting hardware and software problems.

Session 10.1 Quick Check | Review

1. What is system performance?
2. True or False. The Windows Experience Index base score is the lowest subscore, not an average.
3. To disable a startup program and improve performance, you can remove the program from the Startup folder or use _____ _____ in Windows Defender.
4. Name two ways to find the CPU usage of your computer.
5. True or False. One way to solve memory problems is to disable the paging file.

6. Name two ways to increase memory capacity.
7. If you open Task Manager and find that the CPU Usage percentage appears frozen at or near 100%, what can you do to solve the problem?

Session 10.2

Finding Troubleshooting Information

When you have problems with Windows, its programs, your computer, or other hardware, you can find troubleshooting information in at least two resources: Windows Help and Support and the Microsoft Knowledge Base (KB). You can find Help topics designed to help you troubleshoot and solve problems by clicking Troubleshooting on the Windows Help and Support home page. The Troubleshooting in Windows page provides access to troubleshooting problems with networking, using the Web, exchanging e-mail, using hardware and drivers, and using your computer. On the Windows Help and Support home page, you can also click the Ask button to open a page listing ways to get customer support or other kinds of help, including access to the online **Microsoft Knowledge Base**, a repository of support information for Microsoft product users. The KB includes articles that provide troubleshooting steps to help you solve or identify a problem.

Amar wants to train SafeRecords employees to use Windows Help and Support to troubleshoot typical computer problems, such as those involving network connections and hardware. One problem that Amar often helps employees solve is a slow Internet connection. You'll show him how to find troubleshooting steps in Windows Help and Support that employees can follow to solve this problem.

To troubleshoot Internet problems:

▶ 1. Click the **Start** button 🔵 on the taskbar, and then click **Help and Support**. The Windows Help and Support window opens.

▶ 2. Click **Troubleshooting** to open the Troubleshooting in Windows page. See Figure 10-32.

Troubleshooting in Windows Help page | **Figure 10-32**

categories of troubleshooting information

> **3.** In the Using the web category, click **Why is my Internet connection so slow?** to open an article that identifies three reasons an Internet connection might be slow.

> **4.** Scan the article and then click the **Back** button ⊙ to return to the Troubleshooting in Windows page.

> **5.** In the Using the web category, click **Repair Internet Explorer** to display trouble-shooting information for Internet Explorer. See Figure 10-33.

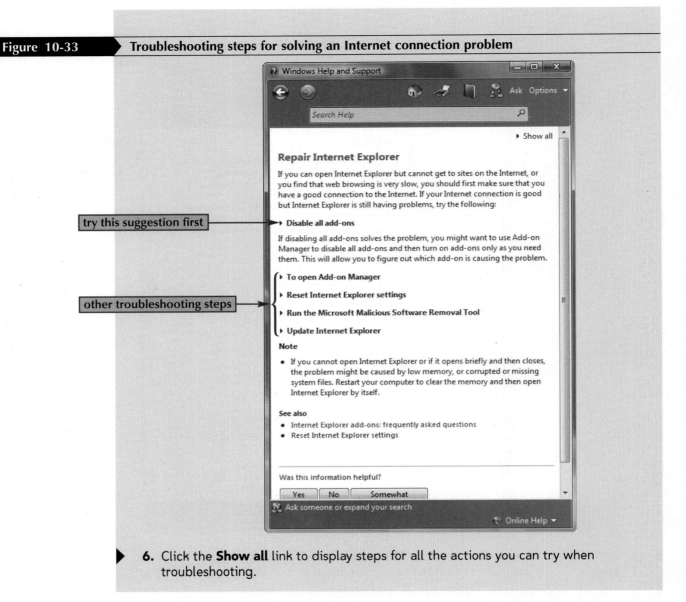

try this suggestion first

other troubleshooting steps

▶ **6.** Click the **Show all** link to display steps for all the actions you can try when troubleshooting.

Amar can now train SafeRecords employees to use the Troubleshooting page in Windows Help and Support to solve common computer problems. You'll show him the next step to take if employees can't find answers to their questions in Windows Help and Support.

Searching the Microsoft Knowledge Base

Because the Microsoft Knowledge Base contains support information about all of the Microsoft software products, it is a valuable resource when you are troubleshooting computer problems. However, it can be difficult to pinpoint the answer to your question. Just as you search for information on the Internet, you search for answers in the Knowledge Base by entering one or more keywords. The Knowledge Base then displays the support articles associated with those keywords.

A SafeRecords employee recently asked Amar why Windows no longer displays the Internet Explorer icon on the desktop by default. You'll show Amar how to search the Microsoft Knowledge Base from Windows Help and Support to find the answer.

To find information in the Microsoft Knowledge Base:

▶ **1.** Click the **Ask** button on the Windows Help and Support toolbar. The Get customer support or other types of help window opens.

▶ **2.** Click the **Knowledge Base** link. Internet Explorer starts and opens to the Search the Support Knowledge Base (KB) Web page. See Figure 10-34.

Search the Support Knowledge Base (KB) Web page ◀ Figure 10-34

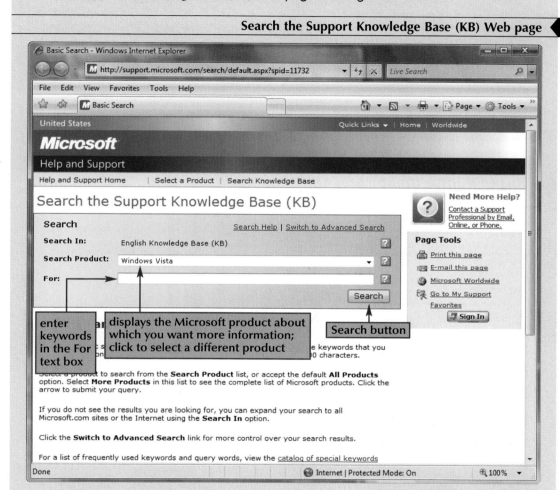

Trouble? If your Internet Explorer window is maximized and elements on the Search the Support Knowledge Base (KB) Web page do not appear as they do in Figure 10-34, click the Restore Down button to resize the window.

▶ **3.** In the For text box, type **Internet Explorer icon**, and then click the **Search** button. A list of search results appears below the Search box.

▶ **4.** Click **Internet Explorer 7 Desktop icon missing** to display the KB article with that title. See Figure 10-35.

Figure 10-35   **Internet Explorer 7 Desktop icon missing KB article**

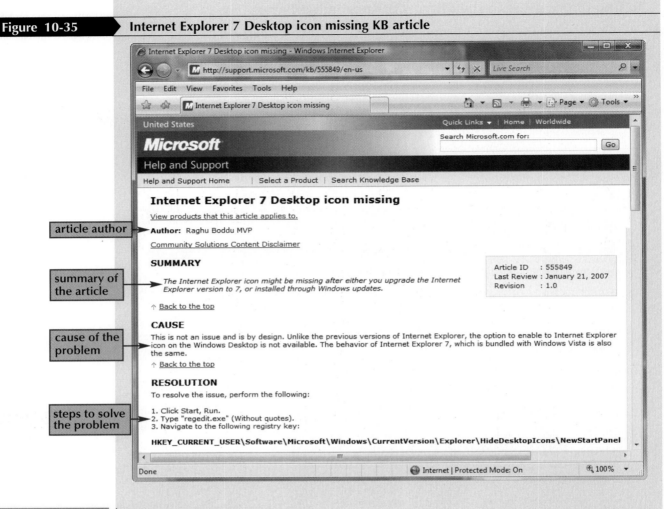

5. Close all open windows.

Tip

If you search for Windows Vista help on the Microsoft Web site (*windowshelp. microsoft.com/ windows*), you can also click a link in the search results to perform the same search in the Microsoft Knowledge Base.

When SafeRecords employees have trouble with hardware, it usually involves printers. You'll show Amar how to troubleshoot printing errors so he can help his employees solve those problems.

Troubleshooting Printing Errors

You have already learned how to use the Printers window to install a printer and select the default printer to use with Windows programs. You can also use this window to troubleshoot some typical printing errors, such as problems with print quality. You need to address other printing problems, such as running out of paper or clearing a print jam, directly at the printer. For example, when the printer runs out of paper, you need to restock the paper tray with printer paper. To clear a jam, you need to follow the printer manufacturer's recommendations, which might involve pressing a button to clear the jam or opening the printer to remove paper. However, these printing errors can cause problems with the **print queue**, which is the list of documents waiting to be printed. While you clear a printer jam, for example, you might need to pause and then restart the print jobs in the print queue. The print queue also displays information about documents that are waiting to print, such as the printing status, document owner, and number of pages to print. You can use the print queue to view, pause, resume, restart, and cancel print jobs.

Amar often tries to help SafeRecords employees respond to printing errors. In fact, he has not been able to print with a laser printer installed on his system. You'll try printing to the laser printer, and then show Amar how to discover the status of this printer in the Printers window and then use the print queue to troubleshoot that printing problem.

To simulate a printing problem and perform the following steps, turn off the printer to which your computer is connected, if possible. The following steps use *Laser printer* as the name of the printer causing problems. Substitute the name of the printer you turned off for *Laser printer*. If you cannot turn off a printer connected to your computer, read but do not perform the following steps.

To troubleshoot printing errors:

▶ 1. Start Notepad, type your name in the Notepad document, click **File** on the menu bar, and then click **Print**. The Print dialog box opens.

▶ 2. Click **Laser printer** in the Select Printer list, and then click the **Print** button.

▶ 3. In the Notepad window, press the **Enter** key and type today's date.

▶ 4. Repeat Steps 1 and 2 to print the document, and then minimize the Notepad window.

▶ 5. Click the **Start** button 🔵 on the taskbar, click **Control Panel**, click **Hardware and Sound**, and then click **Printers** to open the Printers window.

▶ 6. If necessary, click the **Views arrow button**, and then click **Details** to display the window in Details view. See Figure 10-36.

Printers window in Details view　　　**Figure 10-36**

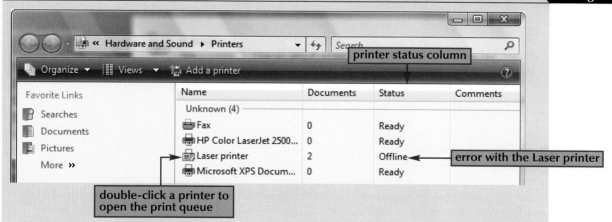

▶ 7. Double-click the **Laser printer** to open the print queue. See Figure 10-37.

Figure 10-37 | Laser printer print queue

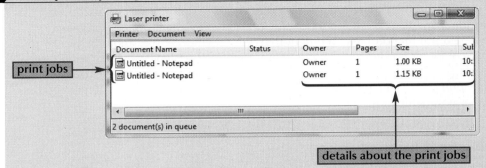

> **8.** Right-click the second **Untitled – Notepad** print job in the queue, and then click **Pause** on the shortcut menu. This pauses the print job so you can solve the printer problem.

> **9.** Right-click the first **Untitled – Notepad** print job in the queue, and then click **Cancel** to prevent this print job from printing and delete it from the print queue. Click the **Yes** button when asked if you are sure you want to cancel the document.

> **10.** Reconnect the printer to your computer and turn it on, if necessary.

> **11.** In the Laser printer print queue, right-click the paused **Untitled – Notepad** print job, and then click **Resume** on the shortcut menu. The Notepad document prints on the Laser printer.

> **12.** Close all open windows without saving any changes.

Network connections are another common problem area for SafeRecords employees. Recently, an employee mentioned that he received an error message stating "There is an IP address conflict" when he tried to connect to the SafeRecords network. You'll show Amar how to troubleshoot and repair network connection problems.

Troubleshooting Network Connections

You have already learned how to use the Windows Network Diagnostics tool to identify and resolve small office and home network problems, such as trouble connecting to the Internet or a wireless network. Troubleshooting network and Internet connection problems can be difficult because many factors might be causing the problem. Your first step is to use Network Diagnostics to have Windows solve the problem for you. If this doesn't solve your connection problem, you can use advanced network troubleshooting tools, which involve entering commands in the Command Prompt window.

Reference Window | **Repairing a Network Connection**

- Right-click the network icon in the notification area of the taskbar, and then click Diagnose and repair on the shortcut menu.
- Follow the suggestions that appear in the Windows Network Diagnostics window, if any.
- Click the Close button.

One problem users occasionally have is an IP address conflict. Recall that an IP address, short for Internet Protocol address, is a number that identifies a computer connected to the Internet or a network. An IP address usually consists of four groups of numbers separated by periods, such as 192.202.54.62. You sometimes need your computer's IP address if you want to set up an Internet connection, allow other people to connect to your computer, or troubleshoot network problems. You can find your computer's IP address by opening the Network and Sharing Center window or by opening a Command Prompt window and then using the **ipconfig** command. To solve an IP address conflict, you can run the Network Diagnostics tool to have Windows assign a unique IP address to your computer.

If you are not sure whether your computer is successfully connected to a network, you can open the Properties dialog box for the network connection and view the status. You can also open a Command Prompt window and use the **ping** command, which verifies whether your computer is connected to the network and can access another IP address.

You'll help Amar troubleshoot the "There is an IP address conflict" error a SafeRecords employee received when he tried to connect to the SafeRecords network. To do so, you'll use the Network Diagnostics tool and the Command Prompt window. You'll show him how to run Windows Network Diagnostics, how to examine the IP address and other properties for the connection, and how to use the ping command to make sure his computer is connected to a network.

To perform the following steps, you must be connected to the Internet or a network. If you are not, read but do not perform the following steps.

To troubleshoot network connection problems:

▶ 1. Right-click the **network** icon 🔲 in the notification area of the taskbar, and then click **Diagnose and repair** on the shortcut menu. The Windows Network Diagnostics tool starts, scans your network configuration, and then displays the results. See Figure 10-38.

Results of Windows Network Diagnostics ◀ **Figure 10-38**

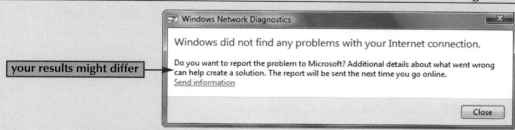

| your results might differ |

▶ 2. Click the **Close** button.

▶ 3. Click the **network** icon 🔲 in the notification area, and then click **Network and Sharing Center** to open the Network and Sharing Center window.

▶ 4. In the column next to the connection name, click **View status**. The Status dialog box for that connection opens. See Figure 10-39.

Figure 10-39 | **Status dialog box for the network connection**

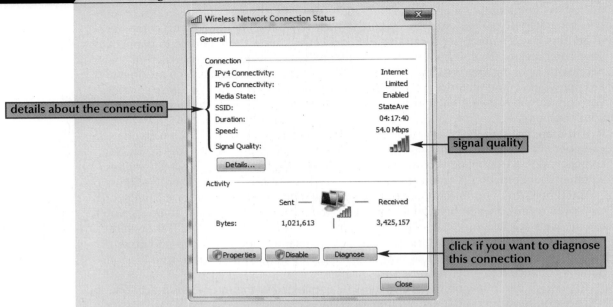

details about the connection

signal quality

click if you want to diagnose this connection

5. Click the **Details** button. The Network Connection Details dialog box opens, displaying properties about the connection, including IP address, which is shown in the IPv4 IP Address line. Record this address.

6. Click the **Close** button to close the Network Connection Details dialog box.

7. Click the **Close** button to close the Status dialog box for that connection.

8. Close the Network and Sharing Center window.

Tip

You can also open the Network and Sharing Center window by clicking the Start button, clicking Control Panel, clicking Network and Internet, and then clicking Network and Sharing Center.

Next, you'll show Amar how to use the Command Prompt window to find the IP address of his computer more quickly.

To perform the following steps, you must be connected to the Internet. If you are not, read but do not perform the following steps.

To find the IP address of your computer:

1. Click the **Start** button 🕮 on the taskbar, point to **All Programs**, click **Accessories**, and then click **Command Prompt**. The Command Prompt window opens. See Figure 10-40.

Command Prompt window ◀ **Figure 10-40**

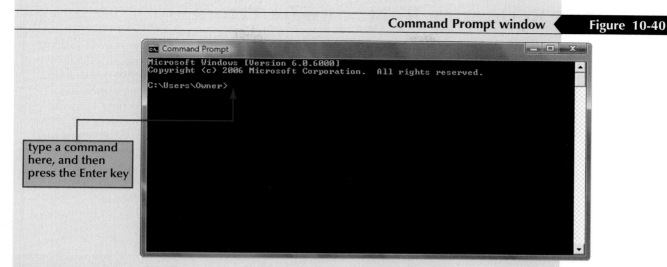

type a command here, and then press the Enter key

▶ **2.** Type **ipconfig** and then press the **Enter** key. The Command Prompt window displays the IP address of your computer along with other IP configuration details. See Figure 10-41. The IPv4 Address should be the same number you recorded when you opened the Network Connection Details dialog box.

Command Prompt window displaying IP address ◀ **Figure 10-41**

IPv4 address

▶ **3.** Close the Command Prompt window.

You can ping another computer on a network to verify that your computer is connected. You can ping using an IP address (four groups of numbers separated by periods, such as 192.202.54.62) or using a host name, which is similar to a Web address, such as www.usps.gov. For example, you could type *ping www.usps.gov* or *ping 56.0. 134.23* (the IP address for the usps.gov Web site). If your computer is connected and the site is working correctly, you would receive a few responses from the site. If your computer is not properly connected to the network, you might receive a *Request timed out* message instead. Some computers also block ping requests; in that case, you would receive an error message after using the ping command.

Recovering from Software Errors

To keep your computer running at peak performance, you need to know how to recover from two types of software errors: those produced by programs and those produced by Windows Vista itself. You have already learned to use Task Manager to respond to a program that stops working or responding to your actions. Recall that you can open the Applications tab in Task Manager to identify unresponsive programs and then click the End Task button to close the program. Another way to recover from software errors is to use the Programs and Features window to change the installed features of a program or to try to repair the installation. (To do so, you open Control Panel, click Programs, click Programs and Features, click the troublesome program, and then click the Repair button.) A third way to respond to software problems is to report the problem to Microsoft and have Windows check for a solution. Windows then notifies you if you should take steps to prevent or solve the problem or if Microsoft needs more information to find or create a solution.

Reference Window |	**Checking for Solutions to Software Problems**

- Click the Start button, click Control Panel, click System and Maintenance, and then click Problem Reports and Solutions to open the Problem Reports and Solutions window.
- Click Check for new solutions in the left pane.
- Follow any steps Windows provides, and then close the Problem Reports and Solutions window.

In addition to reporting problems when they occur and checking for solutions, you can use the Problem Reports and Solutions window to check for new solutions to past problems, to view your problem history, and to change settings so that Windows no longer checks for solutions automatically.

Reporting and Solving Software Errors

You can report software problems and check for solutions in three ways: set Windows to report and check for you automatically, check for solutions only when a problem occurs, or report problems and check solutions at any time. When you report a software problem, Windows assembles and sends a description of the problem to Microsoft to try to match the description to a known solution. If Windows finds a solution, it indicates what steps you can take to solve the problem or to find more information. If a solution is not available yet, Microsoft stores the problem report and uses it to find or create a new solution. If you have Windows set to check for solutions automatically, it notifies you about steps you can take immediately after a problem occurs. If Windows is not set to check for solutions automatically, you can manually check for a solution after a problem occurs.

Although Amar has sent reports to Microsoft about software problems, he hasn't used the Problem Reports and Solutions window yet to repair a software installation. You'll show him how to do so next. First, however, you want to make sure that Windows is set to report software problems and check for solutions automatically on Amar's computer.

To set Windows to check for software solutions automatically:

▶ **1.** Click the **Start** button 🕐 on the taskbar, click **Control Panel**, click **System and Maintenance**, and then click **Problem Reports and Solutions**. The Problem Reports and Solutions window opens. See Figure 10-42.

Problem Reports and Solutions window ◀ **Figure 10-42**

▶ **2.** Click **Change settings** in the left pane. The Choose how to check for solutions to computer problems window opens.

▶ **3.** Make sure the Check for solutions automatically (recommended) option button is selected.

Trouble? If you cannot change settings in the Choose how to check for solutions to computer problems window, skip Step 3, and then read but do not perform the following set of steps.

Now you are sure that Windows will notify Amar about any steps he can take to prevent or solve software problems. You can view any problems that Windows has identified with Amar's software, and then check for new solutions.

To view problems Windows has identified:

▶ **1.** Click the **Back** button 🔙 to return to the Problem Reports and Solutions window.

▶ **2.** Click **View problem history** in the left pane. The Problems Windows has identified window opens. See Figure 10-43.

Figure 10-43 ▶ **Problems Windows has identified window**

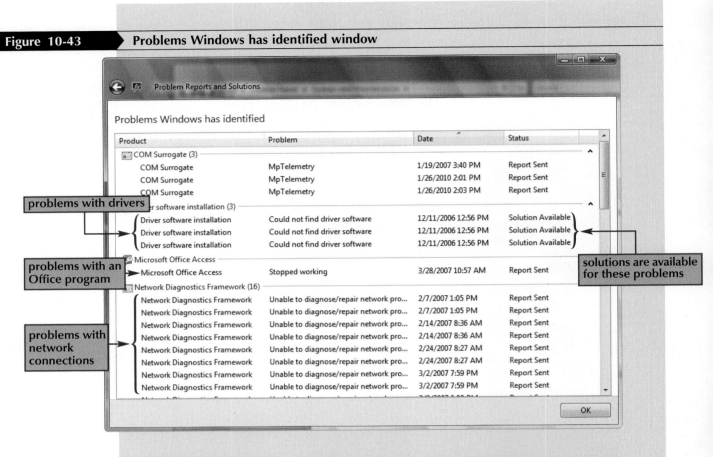

Problems Windows has identified

Product	Problem	Date	Status
COM Surrogate (3)			
COM Surrogate	MpTelemetry	1/19/2007 3:40 PM	Report Sent
COM Surrogate	MpTelemetry	1/26/2010 2:01 PM	Report Sent
COM Surrogate	MpTelemetry	1/26/2010 2:03 PM	Report Sent
...r software installation (3)			
Driver software installation	Could not find driver software	12/11/2006 12:56 PM	Solution Available
Driver software installation	Could not find driver software	12/11/2006 12:56 PM	Solution Available
Driver software installation	Could not find driver software	12/11/2006 12:56 PM	Solution Available
Microsoft Office Access			
Microsoft Office Access	Stopped working	3/28/2007 10:57 AM	Report Sent
Network Diagnostics Framework (16)			
Network Diagnostics Framework	Unable to diagnose/repair network pro...	2/7/2007 1:05 PM	Report Sent
Network Diagnostics Framework	Unable to diagnose/repair network pro...	2/7/2007 1:05 PM	Report Sent
Network Diagnostics Framework	Unable to diagnose/repair network pro...	2/14/2007 8:36 AM	Report Sent
Network Diagnostics Framework	Unable to diagnose/repair network pro...	2/14/2007 8:36 AM	Report Sent
Network Diagnostics Framework	Unable to diagnose/repair network pro...	2/24/2007 8:27 AM	Report Sent
Network Diagnostics Framework	Unable to diagnose/repair network pro...	2/24/2007 8:27 AM	Report Sent
Network Diagnostics Framework	Unable to diagnose/repair network pro...	3/2/2007 7:59 PM	Report Sent
Network Diagnostics Framework	Unable to diagnose/repair network pro...	3/2/2007 7:59 PM	Report Sent

problems with drivers

problems with an Office program

problems with network connections

solutions are available for these problems

OK

▶ **3.** Click the **OK** button to return to the Problem Reports and Solutions window.

If Windows identifies software problems, as it has for Amar's computer, Windows might have solutions for the problems, which you can check by using the Problem Reports and Solutions window. You'll show Amar how to check for new solutions and then use them to install updated drivers.

To check for new solutions and install them:

▶ **1.** Click **Check for new solutions** in the left pane. Windows contacts Microsoft online, and searches for solutions. This might take a few minutes if Windows has identified many problems on your computer. Windows then lists the solutions in the Problem Reports and Solutions window.

Trouble? If Windows Vista displays "No new solutions found" instead of listing new solutions, click the Close button.

▶ **2.** Click a solution to display details about it. See Figure 10-44, which shows a solution to a driver problem.

Solution details **Figure 10-44**

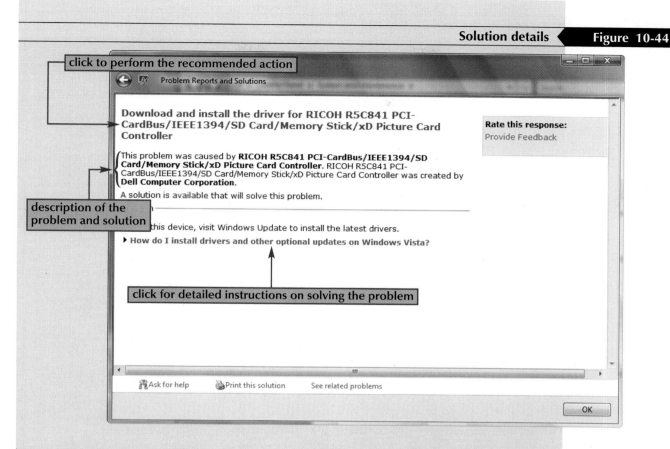

click to perform the recommended action

Download and install the driver for RICOH R5C841 PCI-CardBus/IEEE1394/SD Card/Memory Stick/xD Picture Card Controller

This problem was caused by **RICOH R5C841 PCI-CardBus/IEEE1394/SD Card/Memory Stick/xD Picture Card Controller**. RICOH R5C841 PCI-CardBus/IEEE1394/SD Card/Memory Stick/xD Picture Card Controller was created by **Dell Computer Corporation**.

A solution is available that will solve this problem.

description of the problem and solution

this device, visit Windows Update to install the latest drivers.

▶ How do I install drivers and other optional updates on Windows Vista?

click for detailed instructions on solving the problem

Rate this response:
Provide Feedback

🔍 Ask for help   🖨 Print this solution   See related problems

OK

3. If possible, click the solution title to see detailed instructions for repairing the installation.

4. Click the **OK** button to close the window.

5. Close the Problem Reports and Solutions window.

The solution to Amar's problem is to use Windows Update to check for optional updates available for his hardware devices.

Recovering the Operating System

If Windows Vista doesn't start correctly or runs erratically, you can try the troubleshooting steps shown in Figure 10-45 to solve the problem. These solutions are listed in order of complexity, with the simplest solutions listed first.

Tip

After solving the problems, click Clear solution and problem history and then click Clear All to clear the list of problems.

Figure 10-45 ▶ **Recovering the operating system**

Tool	Description	How to Access
System Restore	You can use System Restore to restore your computer's system files to an earlier point in time.	1.Click the Start button, point to All Programs, click Accessories, click System Tools, and then click System Restore. 2.Click the Next button to accept the most recent restore point. 3.Click the Finish button.
Last Known Good Configuration	This advanced startup option starts Windows using the registry settings and drives that were in use the last time the computer started successfully.	1.Restart your computer. 2.Press and hold the F8 key before the Windows logo appears. 3.On the Advanced Boot Options screen, select Last Known Good Configuration, and then press the Enter key.
Safe mode	If the Last Known Good Configuration option doesn't work, use safe mode to try to identify and fix the problem. If your computer starts only in safe mode, try disabling recently installed hardware or programs.	1.Restart your computer. 2.Press and hold the F8 key before the Windows logo appears. 3.On the Advanced Boot Options screen, select Safe Mode, and then press the Enter key.
Startup Repair	In extreme cases, you can use Startup Repair to fix missing or damaged system files that might prevent Windows from starting.	1.Insert the Windows installation disc. 2.Restart your computer. 3.Select your language settings, and then click the Next button. 4.Click Repair your computer. 5.Select the operating system to repair, and then click the Next button. 6.On the System Recovery Options menu, click Startup Repair.
Reinstall Windows	If your system has been severely damaged, you might need to reinstall Windows. A *custom (clean)* installation of Windows permanently deletes all of the files on your computer and reinstalls Windows, so only use this option if all other recovery options have been unsuccessful. After the installation, you must reinstall your programs and restore your files from backup copies.	1.Insert the Windows installation disc. 2.Restart your computer. 3.On the Install Windows page, follow any instructions, and then click Install now. 4.Follow the instructions that appear on your screen.

Last Known Good Configuration, Safe mode, and Startup Repair are advanced startup options that let you select settings before Windows Vista starts. **Last Known Good Configuration** uses the most recent system settings that worked correctly. Every time you turn your computer off and Windows shuts down successfully, it saves important system settings in the registry. If those new settings are faulty, such as a device driver causing problems, you can bypass the settings when you restart the computer by selecting the Last Known Good Configuration option on the advanced startup menu. When you do, Windows loads the settings it saved the second-to-last time you shut down the computer (the time before you shut down the computer after making the faulty new system settings). You can then disable a device or uninstall a program that it causing problems. Be sure you select the Last Known Good Configuration option before you log on to Windows—you must press the F8 key right after the computer starts and before Windows does. If you log on to Windows or start and wait for the desktop to appear, the Last Known Good Configuration includes the faulty new settings.

Safe mode is a troubleshooting option for Windows that starts your computer with only basic services and functionality. If a problem you experienced earlier does not reappear when you start Windows in safe mode, you can eliminate the default settings and basic device drivers as possible causes. While in safe mode, you can use Device Manager to disable a problematic device or restore a driver to its previous version. You can also restore your computer to an earlier point using System Restore.

Startup Repair is a Windows recovery tool that can fix problems such as missing or damaged system files, which might prevent Windows from starting. This tool is provided on the Windows installation disc and, depending on your computer, might also be stored on your hard disk.

| **Selecting a Restore Point or the Last Known Good Configuration** | InSight |

If your operating system is running erratically, the two least disruptive solutions to try are reverting to a restore point or using the Last Known Good Configuration. These two options are often confused. Use System Restore when you notice your system behaving strangely and Windows is still running. Then you can select a restore point to return the system to an earlier point in time when things worked correctly. Unlike Last Known Good Configuration, you can undo the changes made with System Restore, so troubleshoot operating system problems by selecting a restore point first. Use Last Known Good Configuration if you can't start Windows, but it started correctly the last time you turned on the computer.

Requesting and Managing Remote Assistance

If you are experiencing a computer problem and can't find a solution yourself, you can use Windows Remote Assistance to have someone show you how to fix a problem. Windows Remote Assistance is a convenient way for someone you trust, such as a friend or technical support person, to connect to your computer and step you through a solution—even if that person isn't nearby. To help ensure that only people you invite can connect to your computer using Windows Remote Assistance, all sessions are encrypted and password protected.

To request remote assistance, send an instant message or e-mail to invite someone to connect to your computer. After connecting, that person can view your computer screen and chat with you about what you both see on your computer screen. With your permission, your helper can even use a mouse and keyboard to control your computer and show you how to fix a problem. You can also help someone else the same way.

Before you can use Windows Remote Assistance to connect two computers, you must enable the feature. You'll show Amar how to enable Remote Assistance connections so that he can request help from you and vice versa.

To enable Remote Assistance connections:

▶ **1.** In the System and Maintenance window, click **System**. The System window opens.

▶ **2.** Click **Remote settings** in the left pane. The System Properties dialog box opens to the Remote tab.

   Trouble? If a User Account Control dialog box opens requesting your permission or a password to continue, enter the password or click the Continue button.

▶ **3.** If necessary, click the **Allow Remote Assistance connections to this computer** box to insert a check mark.

When you allow Remote Assistance connections to your computer, you can send and receive Remove Assistance invitations using e-mail or a file. You can also use instant messaging to correspond with your Remote Assistance partner. Windows also automatically allows the Remote Assistance program through Windows Firewall. To disable Remote Assistance invitations, you remove the check mark from the Allow Remote Assistance connections to this computer box on the Remote tab of the System Properties dialog box.

You can also use the Remote tab in the System Properties dialog box to access advanced Remote Assistance settings. For security reasons, you might want to limit the amount of time that a Remote Assistance invitation is available so that an unauthorized person cannot control your computer without your knowledge.

To select advanced Remote Assistance settings:

▶ **1.** On the Remote tab of the System Properties dialog box, click the **Advanced** button. The Remote Assistance Settings dialog box opens. See Figure 10-46.

Figure 10-46 ▶ **Remote Assistance Settings dialog box**

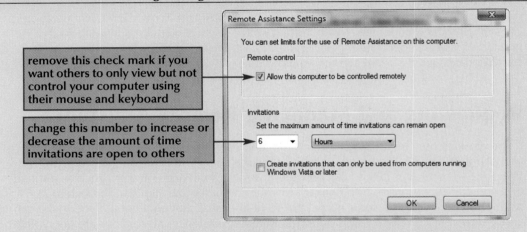

remove this check mark if you want others to only view but not control your computer using their mouse and keyboard

change this number to increase or decrease the amount of time invitations are open to others

▶ **2.** Click **6** in the Set the maximum amount of time invitations can remain open box, and then type **4** to reduce the amount of time a Remote Assistance invitation is available.

▶ **3.** Click the **OK** button to close the Remote Assistance Settings dialog box.

▶ **4.** Click the **OK** button to close the System Properties dialog box.

Although Amar doesn't need to establish a Remote Assistance session now, you'll show him how to request assistance using the Windows Remote Assistance Wizard.

Requesting Remote Assistance

When you need help from someone else, you can request Remote Assistance using the Windows Remote Assistance Wizard. The easiest way to start this wizard is from the Windows Help and Support window, though you can also start it by clicking the Start button, pointing to All Programs, clicking Maintenance, and then clicking Windows Remote Assistance.

You'll show Amar how to use the Windows Remote Assistance Wizard to send you an e-mail message inviting you to help him troubleshoot a problem on his computer. When you perform the following steps, substitute the e-mail address of a friend or classmate for Amar's e-mail address.

To request Remote Assistance:

▶ 1. Click the **Start** button 🕐 on the taskbar, and then click **Help and Support**. The Windows Help and Support window opens.

▶ 2. In the Ask someone section of the Windows Help and Support window, click **Windows Remote Assistance**. The Windows Remote Assistance Wizard starts. See Figure 10-47.

Starting the Windows Remote Assistance Wizard ◀ **Figure 10-47**

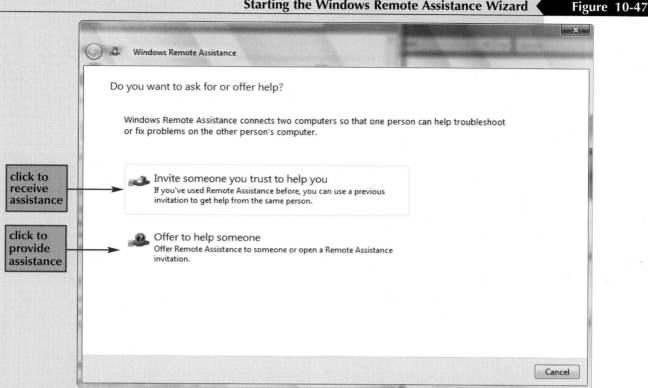

click to receive assistance

click to provide assistance

▶ 3. Click **Invite someone you trust to help you**. The next wizard dialog box opens, asking how you want to invite someone to help you.

▶ 4. Click **Use e-mail to send an invitation**. The next wizard dialog box opens, requesting a password.

▶ 5. Type **Safe0101 Records** as the password, and then retype it in the Retype the password box. Click the **Next** button. Remote Assistance opens an invitation e-mail in your default e-mail program. See Figure 10-48.

Figure 10-48 ▶ **E-mail with Remote Assistance invitation**

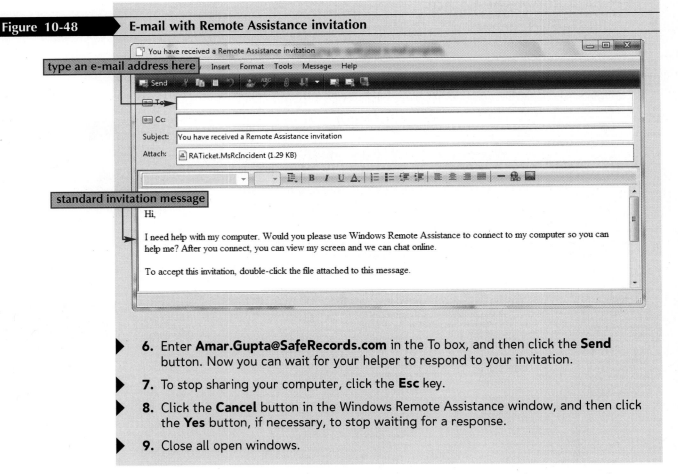

6. Enter **Amar.Gupta@SafeRecords.com** in the To box, and then click the **Send** button. Now you can wait for your helper to respond to your invitation.

7. To stop sharing your computer, click the **Esc** key.

8. Click the **Cancel** button in the Windows Remote Assistance window, and then click the **Yes** button, if necessary, to stop waiting for a response.

9. Close all open windows.

   Now that you're finished helping Amar improve his computer's performance and troubleshoot system problems, you should restore your system settings.

Restoring Your Settings

If you are working in a computer lab or on a computer other than your own, complete the steps in this section to restore the original settings on your computer. If a User Account Control dialog box opens requesting an Administrator password or confirmation after you perform any of the following steps, enter the password or click the Continue button.

To restore your settings:

1. Click the **Start** button 🔘 on the taskbar, click **Control Panel**, click **System and Maintenance**, and then click **Performance Information and Tools**.

2. Click **Manage startup programs** in the left pane.

3. Click **Microsoft Windows Sidebar**, click the **Enable** button, and then click the **Yes** button.

   Trouble? If you disabled a startup program other than Microsoft Windows Sidebar, click that program, click the Enable button, and then click the Yes button.

4. Close the Software Explorer window.

▶ **5.** In the Performance Information and Tools window, click **Adjust visual effects** in the left pane.

▶ **6.** Click the **Let Windows choose what's best for my computer** option button, and then click the **OK** button to close the Performance Options dialog box.

▶ **7.** Click **Advanced tools** in the left pane of the Performance Information and Tools window, and then click **Open Reliability and Performance Monitor**.

▶ **8.** Open the Computer window, right-click the **USB flash drive**, and then click **Properties** on the shortcut menu.

▶ **9.** Click the **ReadyBoost** tab, and then click **Do not use this device**. Click the **OK** button to close the Properties dialog box.

▶ **10.** Restore your original setting, which is **6** by default, for the maximum amount of time Remote Assistance invitations can stay open. Also disable Remote Assistance invitations if they were not enabled on your computer.

▶ **11.** Close all open windows.

Session 10.2 Quick Check | Review

1. When you have problems with Windows, its programs, or your computer, you can find troubleshooting information in Windows Help and Support and the Microsoft _____ _____ .

2. True or False. A print queue is a list of printers waiting to provide printing services.

3. Why might you use Windows Network Diagnostics?

4. Which of the following commands can you use in the Command Prompt window to help solve network connection problems?
   a. ping
   b. repair
   c. internet config
   d. index

5. Besides using Task Manager to end a task or the Programs and Features window to repair a software installation, what else can you do to troubleshoot a software problem?

6. Which is a more complex or extreme solution to a Windows Vista startup problem: Last Known Good Configuration or Startup Repair?

7. True or False. Windows Vista is always ready to let you receive Remote Assistance from a friend or expert.

Tutorial Summary | Review

In this tutorial, you learned how to improve your computer's performance by rating the performance, disabling startup programs, optimizing visual effects, and setting advanced options. You also learned how to used advanced tools to monitor system performance and view detailed system information. You used two ways to increase memory capacity, and learned various ways to find troubleshooting information. Besides recovering from software errors, you explored recovering from Windows Vista errors. Finally, you learned how to request and manage Windows Remote Assistance.

Key Terms

base score	Microsoft Knowledge Base	service
counter	paging file	Startup Repair
event log	ping	system performance
ipconfig	print queue	virtual memory
Last Known Good	process	
Configuration	safe mode	

Practice | **Review Assignments**

Practice the skills you learned in the tutorial.

There are no Data Files needed for the Review Assignments.

Now that you've helped Amar Gupta improve system performance and troubleshoot hardware and software problems on his computer, he asks you to show another SafeRecords manager, Lani Eggers, how to optimize her computer. Complete the following steps, noting your original settings so you can restore them later:

1. Open Control Panel, open the Performance and Information Tools window, and then calculate your computer's Windows Experience Index base score. Press Alt+Print Screen to capture an image of the window. Paste the image in a new Paint file, and save the file as **Base Score** in the Tutorial.10\Review folder provided with your Data Files.

2. Use the Software Explorer tool in Windows Defender to disable Microsoft Windows Sidebar as a startup program. Select Microsoft Windows Sidebar in the list of startup programs, and then press Alt+Print Screen to capture an image of the window. Paste the image in a new Paint file, and save the file as **Sidebar** in the Tutorial.10\Review folder provided with your Data Files.

3. To improve performance, adjust the visual effects on your computer so that controls and elements inside windows and minimized and maximized windows are not animated. With the Performance Options dialog box open to the appropriate tab, press Alt+Print Screen to capture an image of the window. Paste the image in a new Paint file, and save the file as **Visual** in the Tutorial.10\Review folder provided with your Data Files.

4. Open the Advanced Tools window to display any issues that Windows identifies as detracting from the performance of your computer. Press Alt+Print Screen to capture an image of the window. Paste the image in a new Paint file, and save the file as **Advanced** in the Tutorial.10\Review folder provided with your Data Files.

5. Open the Event Viewer window and display details about a critical event. If your Event Viewer window does not list any critical events, display details about an error. Press Alt+Print Screen to capture an image of the window. Paste the image in a new Paint file, and save the file as **Event** in the Tutorial.10\Review folder provided with your Data Files.

6. Open the Task Manager dialog box and display the processes running for your user account. Open the Properties dialog box for a process and display the Details tab. Arrange the dialog boxes to completely display both of them, and then press Print Screen to capture an image of the desktop. Paste the image in a new Paint file, and save the file as **Process** in the Tutorial.10\Review folder provided with your Data Files. Close the Properties dialog box for the process.

7. Display graphs of CPU and RAM usage in the Task Manager dialog box. Press Alt+Print Screen to capture an image of the dialog box. Paste the image in a new Paint file, and save the file as **Graphs** in the Tutorial.10\Review folder provided with your Data Files.

8. Display a system summary that shows details about the processor and how much RAM is installed on your computer. Press Alt+Print Screen to capture an image of the window. Paste the image in a new Paint file, and save the file as **Summary** in the Tutorial.10\Review folder provided with your Data Files.

9. Display the size of the paging file on your computer. Press Alt+Print Screen to capture an image of the dialog box. Paste the image in a new Paint file, and save the file as **Paging** in the Tutorial.10\Review folder provided with your Data Files.

10. Generate a System Diagnostics report for your computer. Save the report as **System** in the Tutorial.10\Review folder provided with your Data Files.

11. Increase the memory capacity of your system by turning on ReadyBoost. Select the maximum amount of available space on your USB flash drive to reserve for boosting your system speed. Press Alt+Print Screen to capture an image of the dialog box. Paste the image in a new Paint file, and save the file as **ReadyBoost** in the Tutorial. 10\Review folder provided with your Data Files.

12. Search the Microsoft Knowledge Base for articles about ReadyBoost. Display one article that discusses ReadyBoost, and then press Alt+Print Screen to capture an image of the window. Paste the image in a new Paint file, and save the file as **KB** in the Tutorial.10\Review folder provided with your Data Files.

13. Diagnose and repair your network or Internet connection. With the results of this task displayed on your desktop, press Alt+Print Screen to capture an image of the dialog box. Paste the image in a new Paint file, and save the file as **Repair** in the Tutorial.10\Review folder provided with your Data Files.

14. Use the Problem Reports and Solutions window to view the problem history on your computer. Press Alt+Print Screen to capture an image of the window. Paste the image in a new Paint file, and save the file as **Problems** in the Tutorial.10\Review folder provided with your Data Files.

15. Set the maximum amount of time Remote Assistance invitations can stay open to five hours. Press Alt+Print Screen to capture an image of the dialog box. Paste the image in a new Paint file, and save the file as **Remote** in the Tutorial.10\Review folder provided with your Data Files.

16. Restore your computer by completing the following tasks:
    a. Enable Microsoft Windows Sidebar as a startup program in Software Explorer.
    b. Adjust the visual effects on your computer by letting Windows choose what's best for your computer.
    c. Turn off ReadyBoost.
    d. Return the maximum amount of time Remote Assistance invitations can stay open to its original setting, which is six hours by default.

17. Close all open windows.

18. Submit the results of the preceding steps to your instructor, either in printed or electronic form, as requested.

| Apply | | **Case Problem 1** |

Use the skills you learned in the tutorial to optimize computers for a marketing research company.

There are no Data Files needed for this Case Problem.

Bodette Partners Kathleen Bodette owns a marketing research company named Bodette Partners in Salinas, California. Kathleen hired you as a computer specialist and is particularly interested in how to improve the performance of her company's computers. She also wants to know how to find troubleshooting information for e-mail problems. Complete the following steps, noting your original settings so you can restore them later:

1. Display details about your computer, including its base score, subscores, processor, memory, and storage details. Press Alt+Print Screen to capture an image of the window. Paste the image in a new Paint file, and save the file as **Details** in the Tutorial.10\Case1 folder provided with your Data Files.

2. Use the Software Explorer tool in Windows Defender to select a startup program other than one published by Microsoft Corporation. Press Alt+Print Screen to capture an image of the window. Paste the image in a new Paint file, and save the file as **Software** in the Tutorial.10\Case1 folder provided with your Data Files.

3. To improve performance, adjust the visual effects on your computer to deselect settings that involve fade or slide effects. With the Performance Options dialog box open to the appropriate tab, press Alt+Print Screen to capture an image of the window. Paste the image in a new Paint file, and save the file as **Fade** in the Tutorial. 10\Case1 folder provided with your Data Files.

4. Open the Advanced Tools window to display any issues that Windows identifies as detracting from the performance of your computer. View the details for one of the performance issues. Press Alt+Print Screen to capture an image of the window. Paste the image in a new Paint file, and save the file as **Issue** in the Tutorial.10\Case1 folder provided with your Data Files.

5. Open the Event Viewer window and display general information about a warning. Press Alt+Print Screen to capture an image of the window. Paste the image in a new Paint file, and save the file as **Warning** in the Tutorial.10\Case1 folder provided with your Data Files.

6. Open the Task Manager dialog box and display the programs running on your computer. Press Alt+Print Screen to capture an image of the desktop. Paste the image in a new Paint file, and save the file as **TaskMan** in the Tutorial.10\Case1 folder provided with your Data Files.

7. Display a resource overview, including graphs of CPU, Disk, Network, and Memory usage. Press Alt+Print Screen to capture an image of the window. Paste the image in a new Paint file, and save the file as **Overview** in the Tutorial.10\Case1 folder provided with your Data Files.

8. In the System Information window, display a list of hardware resource conflicts. Press Alt+Print Screen to capture an image of the window. Paste the image in a new Paint file, and save the file as **Conflicts** in the Tutorial.10\Case1 folder provided with your Data Files.

9. Increase the memory capacity of your system by turning on ReadyBoost. Select the minimum amount of available space on your USB flash drive to reserve for boosting your system speed. Press Alt+Print Screen to capture an image of the dialog box. Paste the image in a new Paint file, and save the file as **Minimum** in the Tutorial. 10\Case1 folder provided with your Data Files.

10. Use Windows Help and Support to find troubleshooting information about common problems with Windows Mail. Press Alt+Print Screen to capture an image of the Windows Help and Support window listing solutions to common problems with Windows Mail. Paste the image in a new Paint file, and save the file as **Mail** in the Tutorial.10\Case1 folder provided with your Data Files.

11. Search the Microsoft Knowledge Base for articles about Windows Mail. Display one article that discusses Windows Mail, and then press Alt+Print Screen to capture an image of the window. Paste the image in a new Paint file, and save the file as **MailKB** in the Tutorial.10\Case1 folder provided with your Data Files.

12. Use the Network and Sharing Center window to display the IP address of your computer. Press Alt+Print Screen to capture an image of the window. Paste the image in a new Paint file, and save the file as **IP** in the Tutorial.10\Case1 folder provided with your Data Files.

13. Start the Windows Remote Assistance Wizard and invite someone you trust to help you. Send an invitation to your instructor, and then cancel the Remote Assistance session.

14. Restore your computer by adjusting the visual effects so that Windows chooses what's best for your computer. Turn off ReadyBoost.

15. Close all open windows.

16. Submit the results of the preceding steps to your instructor, either in printed or electronic form, as requested.

| Apply | **Case Problem 2** |

Use the skills you learned in the tutorial to improve the performance of a real estate group's computers.

There are no Data Files needed for this Case Problem.

CG Real Estate Group Luis Cortes and Alex Gavin are partners in the CG Real Estate Group in Santa Fe, New Mexico. Luis and Alex upgraded their computers to Windows Vista a few months ago, and have noticed that they are not running as efficiently as they were when they were set up. As the general manager of CG Real Estate, you share responsibility for optimizing the computers. Luis asks you to help him improve the performance of his computer and to troubleshoot problems he's having playing audio files. Complete the following steps, noting your original settings so you can restore them later:

1. Find the hardware component with the lowest subscore on your computer, and then display details about it. Press Alt+Print Screen to capture an image of the window. Paste the image in a new Paint file, and save the file as **Lowest** in the Tutorial. 10\Case2 folder provided with your Data Files.

⊕ EXPLORE

2. Learn more about the Windows Experience Index online. Press Alt+Print Screen to capture an image of the Web page displaying this information. Paste the image in a new Paint file, and save the file as **Index** in the Tutorial.10\Case2 folder provided with your Data Files.

⊕ EXPLORE

3. Use the Software Explorer tool in Windows Defender to display a list of running programs. Open Task Manager to display the same information. Arrange the windows on the desktop so you can see Software Explorer and Task Manager clearly. Press Print Screen to capture an image of the desktop. Paste the image in a new Paint file, and save the file as **Running** in the Tutorial.10\Case2 folder provided with your Data Files.

4. Open the Advanced Tools window to display any issues that Windows identifies as detracting from the performance of your computer. View the details for one of the performance issues, and then click the Help button to display information about the issue in Windows Help and Support. Arrange the windows on the desktop so you can see the performance issue description and Windows Help and Support clearly. Press Print Screen to capture an image of the desktop. Paste the image in a new Paint file, and save the file as **Help** in the Tutorial.10\Case2 folder provided with your Data Files.

5. Open the Event Viewer window and display general information about an error. Press Alt+Print Screen to capture an image of the window. Paste the image in a new Paint file, and save the file as **Error** in the Tutorial.10\Case2 folder provided with your Data Files.

6. Open the Performance Monitor window and graph the percentage of processor time. Add a counter to graph the percentage of paging file usage. After the Performance Monitor graphs the two counters for a few seconds, press Alt+Print Screen to capture an image of the window. Paste the image in a new Paint file, and save the file as **Graph** in the Tutorial.10\Case2 folder provided with your Data Files.

7. In the System Information window, display details about the sound devices on your computer. Press Alt+Print Screen to capture an image of the window. Paste the image in a new Paint file, and save the file as **Sound Card** in the Tutorial.10\Case2 folder provided with your Data Files.

Reality Check

Now that you are experienced with the Windows Vista tools that can help you manage multimedia files and programs, connect to networks with a mobile computer, maintain hardware and software, and improve your computer's performance, you are ready to make the most of your Windows Vista computer. As you select settings, capture and save images of your computer so you can document what you've done. Complete the following project:

1. Select one or more of the following Windows Vista programs to use in creating a presentation:
   - Windows Photo Gallery
   - Windows Media Player
   - Windows Movie Maker
   - Paint
   - Other software, such as a word-processing program
2. Using the software you selected, prepare a presentation on how you are using or plan to use your Windows Vista computer in a project outside of class. For example, you might be writing an illustrated novel, participating in or creating a blog, providing PC repair services to other users, or producing a movie about a recent or upcoming travel experience.
3. Include at least one topic for each of the following types of information in the presentation:
   - Title and introduction, including your name
   - Graphic, such as a photo or drawing, of you participating in your activity or project. For example, if you are producing a movie about a trip, include a photo of you the day you leave or arrive.
   - Sample of your production. For example, if you are writing an illustrated novel, include a page with an illustration or a drawing of the cover.
   - Detailed description of the programs, tools, and other features of Windows Vista you are taking advantage of to complete your project. For example, if you are participating in a blog, explain how you are using Windows Vista networking features to communicate with others on a network or Internet. If you are training to become a PC repair expert, outline the administrative tools you will use to become proficient in this area.
   - Consider the skills you developed in Tutorials 7–10 of this book. Describe how these skills enhance your project.
   - Conclusion or summary.
4. Prepare the presentation as a file your instructor can view.
5. Submit the presentation to your instructor, either in printed or electronic form, as requested.

Objectives

- Prepare to connect to the Internet
- Set up a broadband connection
- Set up a wireless connection
- Set up a dial-up connection
- Troubleshoot your Internet connection

Connecting Computers to the Internet

Setting Up an Internet Connection

Appendix A

Windows Vista makes it easy to connect to the Internet, whether your computer uses a DSL modem, cable modem, or dial-up connection. This appendix is designed for you if you are working with your own computer and want to connect to the Internet. It discusses the most popular types of technologies for connecting to the Internet, and explains what you need to prepare for connecting. It also discusses the pros and cons of the various connection methods. This appendix provides step-by-step instructions for setting up a broadband Internet connection in Windows Vista, a wireless Internet connection, and a dial-up Internet connection. Finally, the appendix lists suggestions for troubleshooting these types of connections if you have trouble accessing the Internet.

Starting Data Files

There are no starting Data Files needed for this appendix.

Preparing to Connect to the Internet

Windows Vista makes communicating with computers easier than ever because it provides tools that allow you to connect your computer to other computers and to the Internet. If you are using a computer on a university or institutional network or any other type of local area network (LAN), you are probably already connected to the Internet, and you can skip this appendix. This appendix is useful for people who are not connected to the Internet but who have their own computer and devices designed for accessing the Internet, including a modem and phone line or cable connections. Figure A-1 describes what you need to set up an Internet connection.

Figure A-1 ▶ **What you need to set up an Internet connection**

Device or Service	Type	Description
Internet service provider (ISP)	National or local	An ISP provides access to the Internet. You sign up for an account with an ISP as you do for telephone service or utilities. Some ISPs, such as America Online (AOL), serve a broad area, while others are more limited.
Hardware	Broadband	A high-capacity, high-speed device that is usually included as part of the start-up hardware from your ISP when you sign up for a broadband account
	Dial-up	A device that usually comes installed in your computer and lets you connect to an ISP via telephone lines
	Cables	Cables that connect your modem to your computer or phone jack

To access the Internet, you need to connect your computer to an Internet service provider (ISP), which is a company that provides Internet access. ISPs maintain servers that are directly connected to the Internet 24 hours a day. You use hardware attached to your computer—either broadband or dial-up devices—to contact your ISP's server and use its Internet connection. You pay a fee for this service, most often a flat monthly rate.

After you set up a computer with the appropriate hardware and establish an account with an ISP, you can use Windows Vista to manage the connection to the Internet. This appendix explains how to use the tools in Windows Vista to set up a broadband or a dial-up connection to the Internet.

Using a Broadband Connection

As the popularity of the Internet has increased, the technologies for connecting to the Internet have improved, providing faster and more reliable connections. If you want to use the Internet to listen to Web radio stations, download music and videos to your computer, send digital photographs to family and friends, play online games, or browse animated Web sites, you need an Internet connection that lets you transfer data quickly. The most popular technology that provides a fast Internet connection is called a **broadband connection**, which is a high-capacity, high-speed medium for transmitting voice, video, and data at the same time. The two most common and practical broadband connections for home and small office users are digital subscriber lines (DSL) and digital cable connections. DSL and digital cable connections are fast because they have a lot of **bandwidth**, which is the amount of data that can be transmitted per second through a connection. The bandwidth for digital cable allows speeds from 64 kilobits per second (Kbps) to 20 megabits per second (Mbps), and DSL allows between 128 Kbps and 7.5 Mbps.

A DSL connection uses telephone lines to connect your computer to your ISP. See Figure A-2. Your ISP usually provides and installs a DSL modem with your computer and a DSL splitter at your home or office. The modem is plugged into your computer on one end and a telephone jack on the other. When you connect to the Internet, the DSL splitter separates the computer data signals from your voice telephone signals, so a DSL connection does not interrupt your phone service. The DSL splitter connects to the public phone lines and uses them to exchange computer data with your ISP, which provides Internet access to you.

DSL connection | Figure A-2

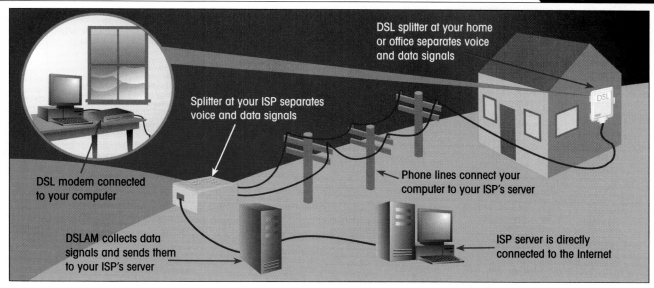

One advantage of a DSL connection is that it is always on, maintaining a constant high-speed, high-bandwidth connection to the Internet. The speed and bandwidth varies, however, depending on the distance between your DSL modem and the DSL access multiplexer (DSLAM). The greater the distance, the lower the bandwidth and speed of your connection. The maximum distance is about three miles.

A digital cable connection is also a fast and popular way to connect to the Internet. This broadband technology uses a cable modem attached to cable television lines to connect your computer to your ISP. See Figure A-3. As with DSL connections, digital cable connections are always on. One consideration for digital cable is that users within a geographic location, such as an apartment or neighborhood, share bandwidth. When only a few people in that location are online, the digital cable connection can be very fast. When many people in that location are online, the connection often slows. Because the performance of digital cable can vary, people who are seeking broadband connections and live within range of a DSLAM often opt for DSL over digital cable.

Figure A-3 ▶ **Digital cable connection**

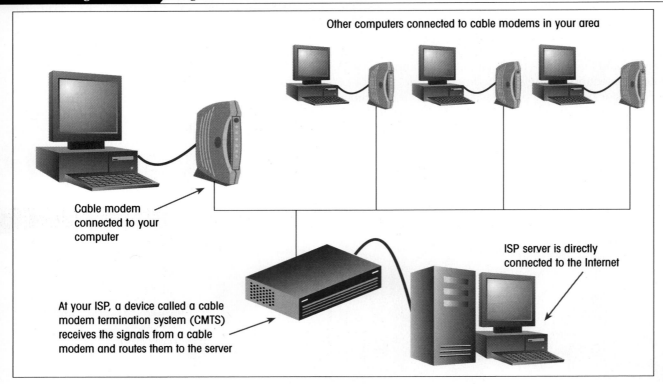

Other computers connected to cable modems in your area

Cable modem connected to your computer

At your ISP, a device called a cable modem termination system (CMTS) receives the signals from a cable modem and routes them to the server

ISP server is directly connected to the Internet

As mentioned earlier, before you can use a broadband service to connect to the Internet, you need to find an ISP that works with DSL or digital cable. The ISP often provides the special equipment you need, such as a cable modem, and establishes an account you use to connect to their server. The ISP also provides account information, including a user name and password, to identify you to the ISP's server. You need this information to set up an Internet connection in Windows Vista.

Using a Wireless Connection

Many personal computers, especially laptops and other mobile computers, use a wireless connection to access the Internet. A **wireless connection** uses infrared light or radio-frequency signals, rather than cables, to transmit data from your computer to a broadband device that connects you to the Internet. To establish a wireless Internet connection in your home, for example, you typically need the following equipment:

- **Broadband Internet connection**: Establish at least one physical connection to the Internet through a broadband connection, such as a DSL or cable modem.
- **Wireless router**: A **router** is a computer device that converts the signals from your Internet connection into a wireless broadcast.

• **Computer with wireless capabilities**: Your computer needs a wireless network adapter or a built-in wireless network card to communicate with the router. This wireless device detects and interprets the wireless broadcast signals transmitted by your wireless router. Most recent computers provide built-in wireless capabilities, especially portable computers. If your computer does not have built-in wireless capabilities, you can use a wireless network adapter, which typically plugs into a USB port on a desktop computer or a card slot on a laptop.

After you acquire the equipment you need for a wireless connection, you need to set up a **wireless network**, which is a way to share Internet access, files, and printers among a group of computers. If you are setting up a wireless network at the same time that you establish a broadband connection to the Internet, your ISP often configures the network for you. Even if your ISP does not provide this service, you can establish a wireless network by connecting your wireless router to your DSL or cable modem, as shown in Figure A-4.

Setting up a wireless Internet connection ◄ **Figure A-4**

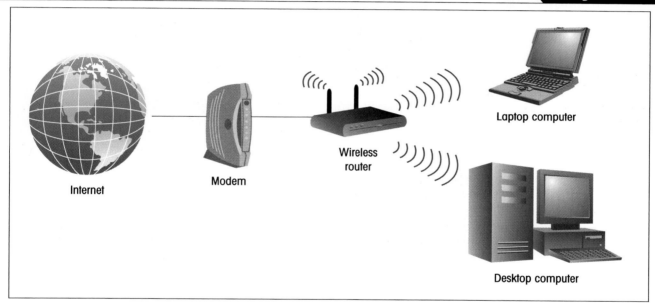

After you set up a wireless network at home, the wireless card or adapter on your computer detects the network so you can use it to connect to the Internet.

If you are away from your wireless home nework, you can connect to the Internet without cables by using a **hotspot**, a public space equipped with wireless Internet access, such as a hotel, airport, convention center, or restaurant. To connect to a hotspot, you need a computer, typically a laptop, with wireless capabilities. As mentioned earlier, most new laptops come equipped with wireless technology. Older laptops require a wireless access card. When you are in range of a hotspot, you can turn on your computer and check to see if you're receiving a network signal. You might need to sign in with information such as user name, password, and method of payment. After you do so, you are connected to the Internet.

Using a Dial-Up Connection

If affordable broadband service is not available in your area, you can connect to the Internet using a **dial-up connection**, which uses a modem in your computer connected to public telephone lines to transmit your signal to a server at your ISP. See Figure A-5.

Figure A-5 ▶ **Phone line connection to the Internet**

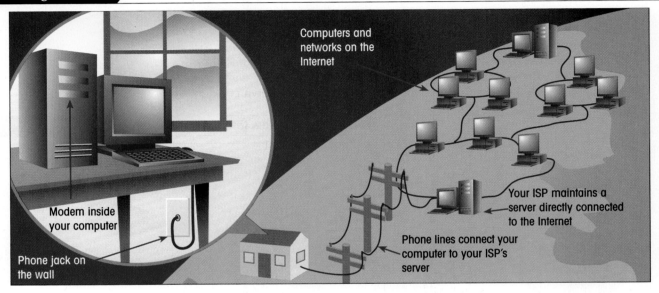

To establish a dial-up connection, you attach the modem in your computer to a phone jack and set the modem to dial the ISP's server, which is directly connected to the Internet. Although regular phone lines are often the only practical choice for some home and small business users, using a dial-up connection has a few drawbacks. Unlike a broadband connection, which is always on, you maintain a dial-up connection only as long as you need to access the Internet because it uses the same telephone lines that you use to make phone calls—if you want to talk on the phone while you are online, you need a second phone line. Phone connections are also less reliable than broadband connections. If there are any problems with the phone connection, you can lose data. Furthermore, the bandwidth of a dial-up connection is much lower than broadband connections. Although it is adequate for reading textual information and transferring small files, a dial-up connection can be inefficient when you want to work with multimedia files online. In some areas, **Integrated Services Digital Network (ISDN) lines**, which are telephone wires that provide a completely digital path from one computer to another, are dropping in price so that small businesses and homeowners can afford them. ISDN lines offer much more bandwidth and speed than regular phone lines, though you must still establish dial-up connections to use them to access the Internet.

Setting Up a Broadband Connection

After you set up an account with an ISP and configure the hardware you need to make a broadband connection to the Internet, you're ready to use Windows Vista to access the Internet. If your ISP sends a service person to your home or office to set up a broadband Internet connection, you do not need to set it up yourself. Your broadband connection is configured by the service person and ready to use.

If you need to set up a broadband connection yourself, you can do so by using the Connect to the Internet wizard. This wizard guides you through the steps of connecting to the Internet using a broadband, wireless, or dial-up connection. You choose the broadband method if your computer is connected directly to a broadband modem (a DSL or cable modem), and you have a Point-to-Point Protocol or Ethernet (PPPoE) Internet account. With this type of account, you must provide a user name and password to connect. (Your ISP indicates what type of account it is providing when you sign up for the account.)

To set up a broadband connection:

1. Click the **Start** button 🪟, and then click **Control Panel**. Control Panel opens in Category view.

   Trouble? If Control Panel opens in Classic view, click the Control Panel Home link in the left pane to open Control Panel in Category view.

2. In the Network and Internet category, click **Connect to the Internet**. The Connect to the Internet wizard starts and asks how you want to connect to the Internet. See Figure A-6.

   Trouble? If the Connect to the Internet link does not appear in the Network and Internet category, your computer might already be connected to the Internet. If you still want to set up a broadband connection, disconnect from the Internet first by clicking the network icon in the notification area of the taskbar, clicking Connect or disconnect, and then clicking the Disconnect button. Repeat Step 2.

   Trouble? If the Connect to the Internet link does not appear in the Network and Internet category and you are not connected to the Internet, click Network and Internet in Control Panel, click Network and Sharing Center, click Set up a connection or network, and then click Connect to the Internet.

Connect to the Internet wizard   **Figure A-6**

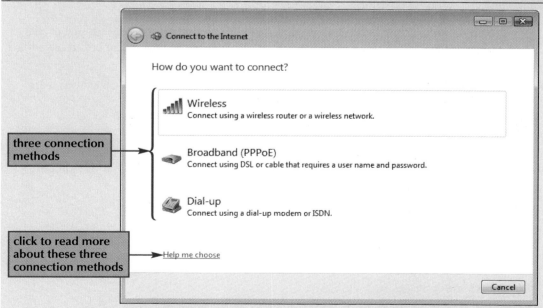

▶ **3.** Click **Broadband (PPPoE)**. The next dialog box in the wizard opens, requesting your user name and password. See Figure A-7.

▶ **Providing your user name and password**

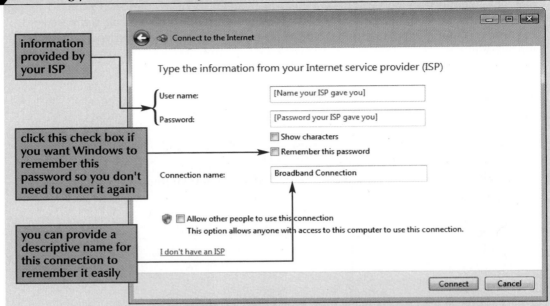

▶ **4.** In the User name text box, type the user name your ISP gave you. This is often your first and last name combined without any spaces.

▶ **5.** In the Password text box, type the password your ISP gave you.

▶ **6.** Click the **Connect** button. Windows Vista sets up a broadband connection to the Internet, and then displays a dialog box indicating the connection was successful.

Trouble? If the connection is not successful, Windows might identify the reason it cannot connect to the Internet. Follow the instructions or suggestions in the dialog box to solve the problem.

▶ **7.** Click the **Next** button. Windows tests your Internet connection and lets you know you are connected to the Internet. Click the **Close** button.

To verify the connection, start a program that uses the Internet, such as Internet Explorer. A network icon also appears in the notification area of the taskbar to indicate your computer is connected to the Internet.

Troubleshooting a Broadband Connection

After you set up a broadband Internet connection, you can access the Internet with programs such as Internet Explorer and Windows Mail. Even if you shut down and restart your computer, you can access the Internet simply by starting Internet Explorer, for example—you don't need to contact your ISP to make a connection to their server first.

If your broadband connection is interrupted, make sure all the cables and wires are connected properly. If that doesn't solve the problem, you can perform the following steps to repair the connection.

To troubleshoot a broadband connection:

▶ **1.** Right-click the **network** icon 🖳 in the notification area of the taskbar, and then click **Diagnose and repair**. Windows communicates with your network device and repairs the connection if possible. If Windows requires you to take action or it cannot solve the problem, the Windows Network Diagnostics window opens, listing possible problems. See Figure A-8. Your problems might differ.

Diagnosing broadband connection problems ◀ **Figure A-8**

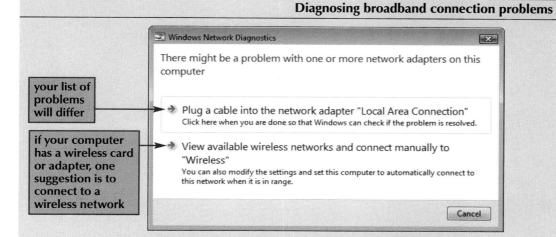

your list of problems will differ

if your computer has a wireless card or adapter, one suggestion is to connect to a wireless network

▶ **2.** Read the possible problems to find the one that seems the most likely for your computer. Take the suggested action, and then click the option, if necessary.

▶ **3.** If you still cannot connect to the Internet after attempting to repair the connection, perform the following troubleshooting tasks:

- Check the status indicator lights on the DSL or cable modem to make sure that it is connected to your ISP.
- Put the DSL or cable modem on standby (most modems have a Standby button or one with a similar name), and then make the modem active again. Wait a few minutes, and then test your Internet connection.
- Note the actions you have already performed, and then contact your ISP.

Setting Up a Wireless Connection

You set up a wireless Internet connection using the Connect to the Internet wizard. When you do, you choose the wireless method if you are using a wireless router or network or if you're connecting to a hotspot (even if you also have a broadband connection).

To set up a wireless connection:

▶ 1. Open **Control Panel** in Category view, and then click **Connect to the Internet** in the Network and Internet category. The Connect to the Internet wizard starts and asks how you want to connect to the Internet.

   Trouble? If the Connect to the Internet link does not appear in the Network and Internet category, your computer might already be connected to the Internet. If you still want to set up a wireless connection, disconnect from the Internet first by clicking the network icon in the notification area of the taskbar, clicking Connect or disconnect, and then clicking the Disconnect button. Repeat Step 1.

   Trouble? If the Connect to the Internet link does not appear in the Network and Internet category and you are not connected to the Internet, click Network and Internet in Control Panel, click Network and Sharing Center, click Set up a connection or network, and then click Connect to the Internet.

▶ 2. Click **Wireless**. The next dialog box in the wizard opens, listing the wireless networks nearby. See Figure A-9. Your list of wireless networks will differ.

Figure A-9 ▶ **Selecting a wireless network**

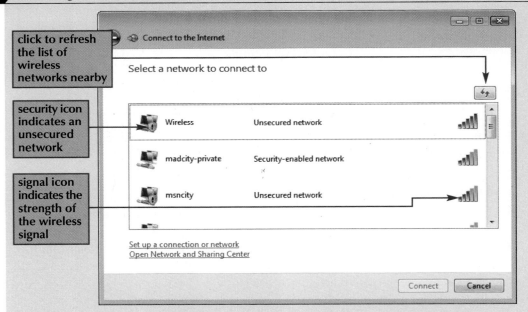

▶ 3. Click the wireless network to which you want to connect, and then click the **Connect** button.

▶ **4.** If you are connecting to a secured network, type the network security key or passphrase you need to connect to this network. (Usually, the person who set up the network gives you this security information.) Then click the **Connect** button.

If you are connecting to an unsecured network, a dialog box opens indicating this network is unsecured. Click **Connect Anyway** to connect to the unsecured network.

Trouble? If you do not want to connect to the unsecured network, click **Connect to a different network** to return to the dialog box shown in Figure A-9, and then repeat Step 3.

Windows attempts to connect to the network, and then displays a dialog box indicating the connection was successful.

▶ **5.** Click the **Next** button. Windows tests your Internet connection and lets you know you are connected to the Internet. Click the **Close** button.

To troubleshoot a wireless connection, follow the steps in the "Troubleshooting a Broadband Connection" section.

Setting Up a Dial-Up Connection

You set up a dial-up Internet connection using the Connect to the Internet wizard. When you do, you choose the dial-up method if you are using a dial-up modem (not a DSL or cable modem) or an ISDN line to connect your computer to the Internet.

To set up a dial-up connection:

1. Open **Control Panel** in Category view, and then click **Connect to the Internet** in the Network and Internet category. The Connect to the Internet wizard starts and asks how you want to connect to the Internet.

   Trouble? If the Connect to the Internet link does not appear in the Network and Internet category, your computer might already be connected to the Internet. If you still want to set up a dial-up connection, disconnect from the Internet first by clicking the network icon in the notification area of the taskbar, clicking Connect or disconnect, and then clicking the Disconnect button. Repeat Step 1.

   Trouble? If the Connect to the Internet link does not appear in the Network and Internet category and you are not connected to the Internet, click Network and Internet in Control Panel, click Network and Sharing Center, click Set up a connection or network, and then click Connect to the Internet.

2. Click **Dial-up**. The next dialog box in the wizard opens, requesting information about your ISP account. See Figure A-10.

Figure A-10	Setting up a dial-up connection

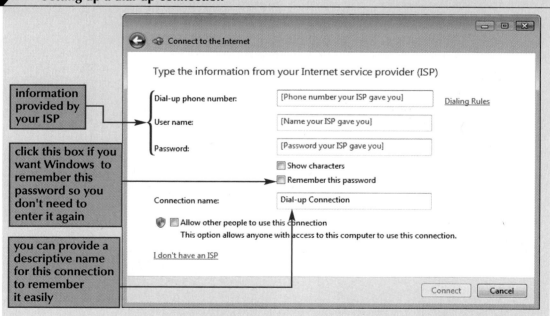

Trouble? If Dial-up does not appear as an option, click Show connection options that this computer is not set up to use.

▶ 3. In the Dial-up phone number text box, type the phone number your ISP gave you. This is the number your modem dials to contact your ISP.

▶ 4. In the User name text box, type the user name or account name your ISP gave you.

▶ 5. In the Password text box, type the password your ISP gave you.

▶ 6. Click the **Connect** button. Windows Vista sets up a dial-up connection to the Internet, and then displays a dialog box indicating the connection was successful.

Trouble? If a Create button appears instead of a Connect button, click the Create button.

▶ 7. Click the **Next** button. Windows tests your Internet connection and lets you know you are connected to the Internet. Click the **Close** button.

Your dial-up account remains connected until you disconnect from your account. In some cases, your ISP might disconnect you automatically if your computer is idle for several minutes.

To disconnect a dial-up connection:

▶ 1. Right-click the **network** icon 🖳 in the notification area of the taskbar, and then click **Disconnect**.

Troubleshooting a Dial-Up Connection

If your dial-up connection is interrupted, refer first to the "Troubleshooting a Broadband Connection" section for steps to solve the problem. If you are still having trouble making and maintaining a dial-up connection to the Internet, try performing the following steps:

- Make sure that you are dialing the correct number, including any required access numbers (such as 9), and that the number is not busy.
- Make sure that the phone jack is working by plugging in a working phone and checking for a dial tone. Similarly, make sure that the phone cable is working properly by plugging a working phone into the telephone jack of your modem and verifying you receive a dial tone.
- Make sure that the phone cable is plugged into the line jack on your modem, not the telephone jack.
- If you have call waiting, try disabling it, and then try the connection again.
- If someone picked up the phone while you were online, you might have been automatically disconnected. Try connecting again.
- Make sure that your modem is working properly. For more information, check the information that came with your modem or go to the manufacturer's Web site.
- Contact your telephone company to verify the quality of your line.

Tutorial Summary | Review

In this tutorial, you learned how to prepare to connect to the Internet if you need to set up an Internet connection on your own. You explored the hardware and technologies you need to use a broadband, wireless, or dial-up connection, and then you learned how to set up each type of connection. You also examined ways to troubleshoot your Internet connection if it is interrupted or experiences other problems.

Key Terms

bandwidth	hotspot	router
broadband connection	Integrated Services Digital	wireless connection
dial-up connection	Network (ISDN) line	wireless network

Ending Data Files

There are no ending Data Files for this appendix.

Objectives

Session B.1
- Customize mouse settings
- Change sound and other hardware settings
- Set accessibility options
- Work with user accounts and parental controls

Session B.2
- Install and remove fonts
- Explore the Welcome Center
- Play media with the Windows Media Center
- Use a tablet PC

Exploring Additional Windows Vista Tools

Using Control Panel Tools and Built-in Programs

Appendix B

Windows Vista provides a wealth of tools and programs for maintaining and enjoying your computer and for making it more productive. You have already used many Control Panel tools, including those in the Personalization, Security, Network and Internet, Programs, and System and Maintenance categories. In this appendix, you will work with tools in the Hardware and Sound category to customize your mouse and sound devices, set AutoPlay options, and learn about Windows SideShow. You will also examine other ways to protect your computer with user accounts and parental control settings. To optimize your Windows experience, you will use ease of access tools, including a narrator and speech recognition, and learn how to install fonts.

Besides Control Panel tools, Windows Vista includes a few built-in programs so you can enjoy and be productive with your computer without installing additional software. In this appendix, you will tour the Welcome Center and examine the tools and features it provides. You will also explore Windows Media Center, which you can use to play recorded television programs, DVDs, videos, and other media. If you are using or planning to use a tablet PC, this appendix also introduces features designed for this type of computer, including Sticky Notes and handwriting recognition.

Starting Data Files

There are no starting Data Files needed for this appendix.

Session B.1

Customizing the Mouse

The Mouse Properties dialog box, available through Control Panel, lets you customize the mouse settings. You can configure the mouse for the right or left hand, adjust the double-click and pointer speed, choose different pointer shapes, and turn on pointer **trails**, which are visual effects that make the pointer easier to see when you are moving it. If you have a mouse with a wheel, the Mouse Properties dialog box includes a Wheel tab where you can set the number of lines the wheel scrolls with each turn. If you have a pointing device other than a mouse, this dialog box might include additional features for customizing that type of pointing device.

Configuring the Mouse for the Right or Left Hand

You can configure the mouse for either right-handed or left-handed users. To do so, you switch the primary and secondary buttons. By default, Windows Vista considers the left button to be the primary button, and the right button to be the secondary button. If you are left-handed, you can configure the mouse settings so the right button (the one your forefinger rests on if you are left-handed) is the primary button and the left button is secondary.

You switch the primary and secondary buttons using the Buttons tab in the Mouse Properties dialog box. On this tab, you can also change the double-click speed, which is how fast you need to press the mouse button when double-clicking. You can also turn on a feature called ClickLock, which lets you drag without holding down the mouse button. When you turn on ClickLock, you can briefly press the mouse button to activate ClickLock and drag by moving the mouse. To release, you briefly press the mouse button again.

To configure the mouse for left-handed users:

▶ 1. Click the **Start** button 🏵 on the taskbar, click **Control Panel**, and then click **Mouse** in the Hardware and Sound category. The Mouse Properties dialog box opens to the Buttons tab. See Figure B-1.

Figure B-1   Mouse Properties dialog box

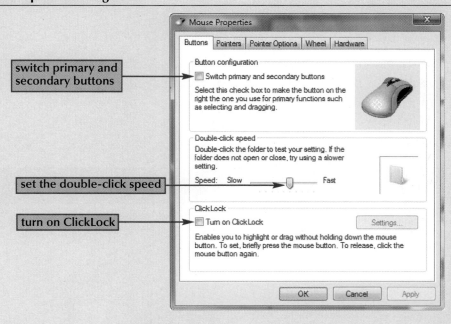

switch primary and secondary buttons

set the double-click speed

turn on ClickLock

Trouble? If the Mouse Properties dialog box does not open to the Buttons tab, click the Buttons tab.

▶ **2.** If you are left-handed, click to select the **Switch primary and secondary buttons** check box. As you change this setting, the description and picture of mouse operations change. If you are right-handed, do not select this check box.

▶ **3.** If you are working on your own computer and switched the mouse buttons in the previous step, click the **Apply** button to apply your changes, and then test the new mouse setting by dragging the Mouse Properties dialog box with the appropriate mouse button.

In addition to configuring the mouse buttons, you can also customize the double-click speed of your mouse.

Adjusting Double-Click Speed

Most Windows programs use double-clicking to select or open objects. Because some new users double-click more slowly or more quickly than others, Windows Vista lets you set your preference so you can work comfortably with the mouse. First you can test your double-click speed to see if you need to adjust it.

To test the current double-click speed:

▶ **1.** Point to the **folder icon** in the Mouse Properties dialog box.

▶ **2.** Double-click the **folder icon**. If you double-click successfully, the folder icon opens.

▶ **3.** Double-click the **folder icon** again to close it.

Trouble? If you couldn't open the folder, you probably need to adjust the double-click speed of the mouse. You'll do so in the next set of steps.

If you have trouble double-clicking, you can slow the double-click speed by using the Double-click speed slider. Before performing the following steps, note the original settings in case you need to restore them.

To slow down the double-click speed:

▶ **1.** Drag the **Double-click speed** slider to the left, toward Slow.

▶ **2.** Double-click the **folder icon** to open it.

Trouble? If you still cannot successfully double-click to open the folder, drag the Double-click speed slider even farther to the left toward Slow, and then repeat Step 2.

▶ **3.** When you can successfully double-click, try increasing or decreasing the double-click speed to find the most comfortable speed for you.

▶ **4.** If you are using your own computer, click the **Apply** button to change the double-click speed to the new setting. If you are in a lab, drag the **Double-click speed** slider to its original position to restore its original setting.

Besides setting the double-click speed, you can also set the speed of the pointer, which you'll do in the next set of steps.

Adjusting Pointer Speed

You use the Pointer Options tab in the Mouse Properties dialog box to adjust the pointer speed or the relative distance the pointer moves on the screen when you move the mouse. It can be easier to use a slower speed when you need more control. Likewise, you might need faster speed if you have limited desktop space.

Before performing the following steps, note the original settings in case you need to restore them.

To adjust the pointer speed:

▶ **1.** Click the **Pointer Options** tab in the Mouse Properties dialog box to display the Pointer Options tab. See Figure B-2.

| Figure B-2 | Pointer Options tab in the Mouse Properties dialog box |

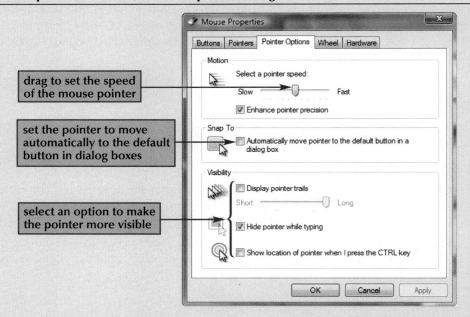

drag to set the speed of the mouse pointer

set the pointer to move automatically to the default button in dialog boxes

select an option to make the pointer more visible

▶ **2.** Drag the **Select a pointer speed** slider to the left, toward Slow, to decrease the pointer speed, and then move the pointer around the desktop.

▶ **3.** Drag the **Select a pointer speed** slider to the right, toward Fast, to increase the pointer speed, and then move the pointer around the desktop.

▶ **4.** If you are using your own computer, select the pointer speed setting that is most comfortable for you, and then click the **Apply** button. If you are using a lab computer, return the slider to its original position.

▶ **5.** Click the **OK** button to close the Mouse Properties dialog box.

You can select other mouse settings to enhance the accessibility of your computer by changing the Ease of Access options, which you'll do later in the appendix. Next, you'll adjust the sound settings to suit your preferences.

Changing Sound Settings

As you learned in a previous tutorial, you can set the volume of the computer sound using the Volume icon in the notification area of the taskbar. If you have a mobile PC, you can also set the volume using the Windows Mobility Center. Using Control Panel, you can change other sound settings, including the sounds Windows plays to signal program events, such as new e-mail arriving in your inbox, a program pausing because of an error, or the Recycle Bin emptying. You can also set the default volume for audio playback on your speakers or head-phones and for audio recording if a microphone is attached to your computer.

Changing the Sound Scheme

By default, Windows Vista plays certain sounds to signal program events, such as when you log on or connect a device to your computer. Windows stores these sounds in a **sound scheme**, a collection of sounds Windows plays when system events occur. You can create a sound scheme by selecting different sounds and saving them as a new scheme. If you have a desktop theme installed on your computer other than the default Windows Vista desktop theme, it might also have its own sound scheme that you can select in the Sound dialog box.

One way to test whether your sound devices are working is to open the Sound dialog box and play a program sound. You'll do that in the next set of steps. Then you'll change a sound for a program event and save the sounds as a new scheme.

Before performing the following steps, note the original settings in case you need to restore them.

To change a sound scheme:

▶ 1. In Control Panel, click **Hardware and Sound**, and then click **Sound** to open the Sound dialog box.

▶ 2. Click the **Sounds** tab to display the sound schemes. See Figure B-3.

Sounds tab in the Sound dialog box ◀ **Figure B-3**

after changing sounds or selecting new events, click to save the collection of sounds as a new scheme

sounds with speaker icons play in the current scheme

click a sound and then click the Test button to play the sound

click to find other sounds to play with program events

▶ 3. Click **Asterisk** in the list of program events, and then click the **Test** button. The sound stored in the Windows Error.wav file plays.

Trouble? If a sound does not play on your computer speakers, click the Volume icon in the notification area, and then click the Mute button, if necessary, to turn on the speakers. Repeat Step 3. If a sound still does not play and you are using external speakers, make sure the speakers are properly connected to your computer and are plugged into a power source, if necessary.

▶ 4. Scroll the list of program events, and then click **Open program** to assign a sound that plays when you start a program.

▶ 5. Click the **Sounds arrow button**, and then click **tada.wav**.

▶ 6. Click the **Test** button to play the tada.wav sound.

▶ 7. Click the **Save As** button to open the Save Scheme As dialog box.

▶ 8. Type **Program Open** as the name of the new sound scheme, and then click the **OK** button. Program Open is now the current sound scheme on your computer.

Next, you can work with the Playback and Recording options to make sure your speakers and microphone are working properly and change settings if necessary.

Setting Playback and Recording Options

You can use the Playback tab in the Sound dialog box to work with the properties of your speakers, whether internal or external. You can change the icon that appears in the Sound dialog box to display headphones, for example, or another image of a playback device. You can also set the default volume of your playback device and select enhancements such as virtual surround, if your playback device supports these enhancements.

If a microphone or other audio recording device is connected to your computer, you can set similar options, such as the microphone icon and default volume.

You'll change the icon for the speakers and examine the volume levels for the speakers and microphone. Before performing the following steps, note the original settings in case you need to restore them.

To change playback and recording settings:

▶ 1. In the Sound dialog box, click the **Playback** tab to display a list of playback devices attached to your computer.

▶ 2. Click **Speakers** in the list of playback devices, and then click the **Properties** button. The Speakers Properties dialog box opens to the General tab. See Figure B-4.

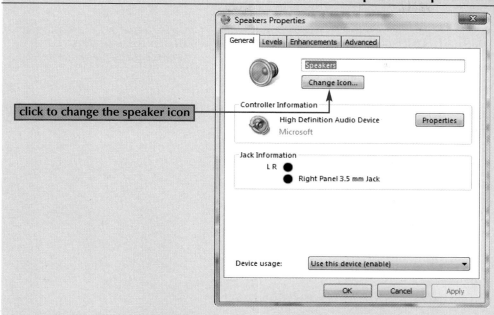

click to change the speaker icon

Trouble? If Speakers does not appear in your list of playback devices, click a different device.

Trouble? If the Speakers Properties dialog box does not open to the General tab, click the General tab.

▶ **3.** Click the **Change Icon** button. The Change Icon dialog box opens, displaying a collection of icons for playback devices.

▶ **4.** Click the **headphones** icon (bottom row, second column), and then click the **OK** button. The playback device icon now appears as a set of headphones in the Speakers Properties dialog box.

▶ **5.** Click the **Levels** tab to display the default volume for the playback device. You use the controls on this tab to increase or decrease the volume, mute the speakers, or change the volume played in the left and right speaker or headphone.

▶ **6.** Click the **OK** button to close the Speakers Properties dialog box.

▶ **7.** In the Sound dialog box, click the **Recording** tab to display a list of microphones and other recording devices attached to your computer.

▶ **8.** Click **Microphone** in the list of playback devices, and then click the **Properties** button. The Microphone Properties dialog box opens to the General tab. See Figure B-5.

Figure B-5 > **Microphone Properties dialog box**

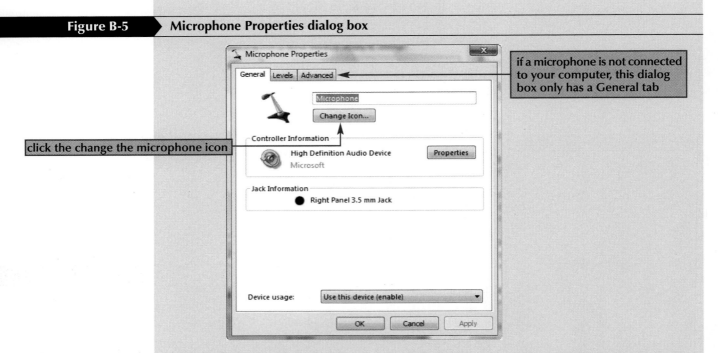

click the change the microphone icon

if a microphone is not connected to your computer, this dialog box only has a General tab

Trouble? If Microphone does not appear in your list of recording devices, click a different device. If no recording devices appear in the list, read but do not perform the remaining steps.

Trouble? If the Microphone Properties dialog box does not open to the General tab, continue to Step 9.

▶ **9.** Click the **Levels** tab to display the default volume for the recording device. You use the controls on this tab to increase or decrease the volume, mute the microphone, or boost the sound.

Trouble? If your Microphone Properties dialog box contains only the General tab, make sure a microphone is connected to your computer, and then repeat Step 9. If you cannot connect a microphone to your computer, skip Step 9.

▶ **10.** Click the **OK** button to close the Microphone Properties dialog box.

If you are working on your own computer, you can retain the new settings in the Sound dialog box. Otherwise, you should restore the original sound settings.

To restore the sound settings:

▶ **1.** In the Sound dialog box, click the **Sounds** tab to display the sound schemes.

▶ **2.** Click the **Sound Scheme arrow button**, and then click **Windows Default**.

Trouble? If your computer was originally set to use a different sound scheme, click that scheme in the list.

▶ **3.** Click the **Playback** tab, click **Speakers** (or other playback device) in the list of playback devices, and then click the **Properties** button.

▶ **4.** Click the **Change Icon** button, click the original **speakers** icon (first row, first column), and then click the **OK** button.

Trouble? If your computer was originally set to display a different speaker icon, click that icon in the Change Icon dialog box.

▶ **5.** Click the **OK** button to close the Speakers Properties dialog box.

▶ **6.** Click the **OK** button to close the Sound dialog box.

You can also change settings for other hardware devices in the Hardware and Sound category in Control Panel, which you'll explore next.

Changing Other Hardware Settings

Other hardware settings you might find useful include the AutoPlay defaults and Windows SideShow. When you attach a digital media device such as a camera or portable music player to your computer or insert a CD or DVD into the appropriate drive, the AutoPlay dialog box shown in Figure B-6 opens by default. The content of the AutoPlay dialog box depends on the files on the disk you inserted or device you attached.

AutoPlay dialog box ◀ **Figure B-6**

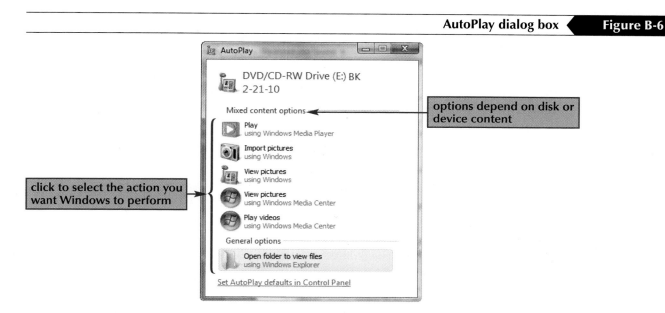

Using this dialog box, you can choose to install or run a program, play media files in Windows Media Player or Windows Media Center, or open a folder to view files, depending on the type of device you attach or insert in your computer. Instead of using this dialog box every time you insert a media device, you can choose an action you want Windows to perform by default. When you insert an audio CD, for example, you can set an AutoPlay default so that Windows always plays the CD using Windows Media Player. To set AutoPlay defaults, you use the AutoPlay tool in Control Panel.

Another Control Panel tool you might find useful is **Windows SideShow**, a technology that lets you use a mobile PC with a secondary screen, which is usually located on the lid of a notebook computer. This additional display lets you view important information even when your mobile computer is turned off, sleeping, or closed. To do so, Windows uses gadgets, or add-on programs, that extend information from your computer to the secondary display. Gadgets can also run on other devices that are compatible with Windows SideShow, such as mobile phones and media remote controls. You can then use the mobile phone, for example, to view your contacts and calendar. (To determine whether you can use a device with Windows SideShow, look for the Windows SideShow logo on the device or go to the manufacturer's Web site.)

Selecting AutoPlay Defaults

When you turn AutoPlay on in Control Panel, you can choose what should happen when you insert different types of digital media into your computer. For example, you can choose which digital media player to use to play CDs. When AutoPlay is turned off, Windows displays the AutoPlay dialog box when you insert digital media and asks you to choose what you want to do.

You'll turn AutoPlay on, and then select a default action to play audio CDs using Windows Media Player.

To turn AutoPlay on and select a default action:

▶ **1.** In the Hardware and Sound window, click **AutoPlay** to open the AutoPlay window. See Figure B-7.

Figure B-7	AutoPlay window

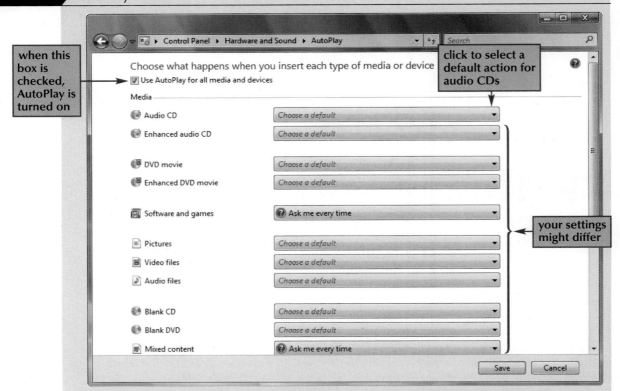

when this box is checked, AutoPlay is turned on

click to select a default action for audio CDs

your settings might differ

▶ **2.** If the Use AutoPlay for all media and devices check box does not contain a check mark, click the **Use AutoPlay for all media and devices** check box to turn AutoPlay on.

▶ **3.** Click the **Audio CD arrow button** to display a list of default actions Windows can take with this type of device. See Figure B-8.

Actions for audio CDs ◄ **Figure B-8**

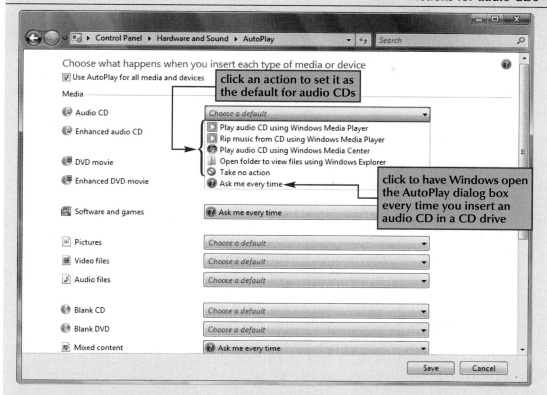

4. Click **Play audio CD using Windows Media Player**.

5. If you are using your own computer, click the **Save** button to save your settings. If you are working in a computer lab, click the **Cancel** button to restore the original settings and close the AutoPlay window.

If you have a mobile computer with a secondary display or other device compatible with Windows SideShow, you can use the Windows SideShow tool in Control Panel to use gadgets with the SideShow device.

Using Windows SideShow

Recall that Windows SideShow is a technology that uses add-on programs, or gadgets, to extend information from your computer onto devices such as a secondary display or a mobile phone. (For security reasons, information from your computer is always downloaded to your device, and never from your device to your computer.) While you're traveling, for example, you can use Windows SideShow to keep track of e-mail messages without needing to open the lid of your mobile computer. Or you can access the e-mail addresses and phone numbers of your contacts in Windows Contacts while you are using your mobile phone. See Figure B-9.

Figure B-9 ▶ Notebook computer with SideShow-compatible secondary display

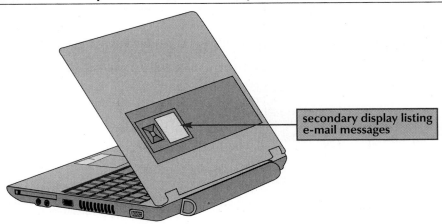

secondary display listing
e-mail messages

You use the Windows SideShow tool in Control Panel to find and download gadgets, such as a stock ticker or weather tracker, and to change gadget settings. You'll use this tool to select a gadget to use with a secondary display on a notebook computer and to view a list of gadgets you can use with Windows SideShow devices.

To find gadgets and change SideShow device settings:

▶ 1. In the Hardware and Sound window, scroll down to and click **Windows SideShow** to open the Windows SideShow window. See Figure B-10. If you don't have any SideShow devices installed on your computer, your window will differ.

Figure B-10 ▶ Windows SideShow window

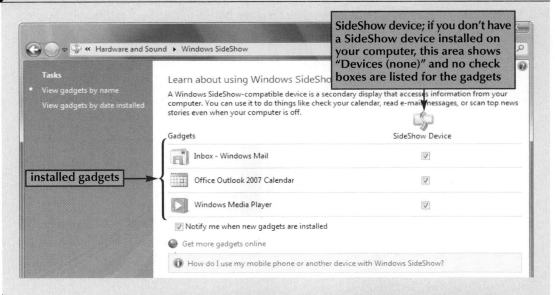

SideShow device; if you don't have a SideShow device installed on your computer, this area shows "Devices (none)" and no check boxes are listed for the gadgets

installed gadgets

▶ 2. To find more gadgets to use with the SideShow device, click **Get more gadgets online**. Your Web browser starts and opens a Web page listing gadgets you can download to use with your Windows SideShow device.

Trouble? If you are not connected to the Internet, skip Steps 2 and 3.

▶ 3. Close your Web browser.

You can also use the Windows SideShow window to change the settings for a SideShow device. To do so, click the device in the Windows SideShow window; a window opens displaying the settings you can change for the device. For example, for a secondary screen, you can change settings such as the language, screen brightness, and turn off time.

Another way to make the hardware and other settings work for you is to use ease of access settings to enhance the accessibility of your computer.

Using Accessibility Options

Accessibility options are Windows Vista settings that you can change to make it easier to interact with your computer. Although designed primarily for users with special vision, hearing, and mobility needs, all users might find it helpful to adjust accessibility settings when working with software such as graphics programs that require more control over mouse and keyboard settings or when working in a poorly lit or noisy room.

To use accessibility options, you can open the Ease of Access Center from Control Panel or from the Welcome screen when you log on. In the Ease of Access Center, you can adjust settings that make it easier to see your computer, use the mouse and keyboard, or use other input devices. You can change accessibility settings in two ways. You can open windows in the Ease of Access Center to change individual accessibility settings, or you can complete an online questionnaire to have Windows suggest the settings that work best for you. You'll examine some individual accessibility settings, and then open the online questionnaire.

To open the Ease of Access Center:

▶ 1. Click the **Back** button ⬅ twice to return to Control Panel.

▶ 2. In Control Panel, click **Ease of Access**, and then click **Ease of Access Center**. The Ease of Access Center window opens. A narrator might explain what you can do with this window as Windows moves a selection box in the Ease of Access Center window so you can easily make a selection. See Figure B-11.

Figure B-11 **Ease of Access Center window**

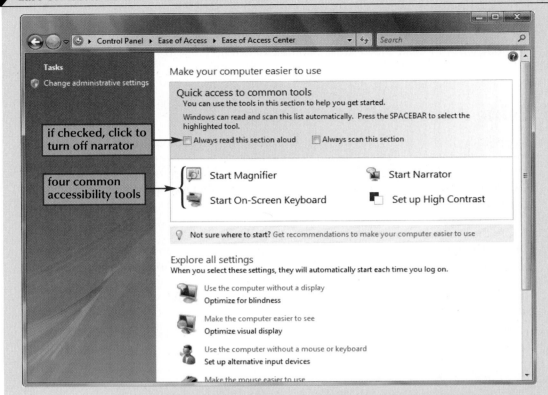

Figure B-11 **Ease of Access Center window**

▶ **3.** To turn off the narrator for now, click the **Always read this section aloud** check box to remove the check mark, if necessary.

▶ **4.** Maximize the Ease of Access Center window.

Figure B-12 describes the four common accessibility tools listed in the first section of the Ease of Access Center window. To start one of these tools, click the appropriate option. You can also press the Spacebar when the selection box highlights a tool to select that tool.

Figure B-12 **Four common Ease of Access features**

Ease of Access Tool	Description	How to Use
Magnifier	Enlarges part of the screen as you move the Magnifier pointer	Click Start Magnifier, and then move the pointer to the part of the screen that you want to magnify.
On-screen keyboard	Displays the image of a keyboard that you can use instead of a physical keyboard to type and enter data	Click Start On-Screen Keyboard, and then click keys in the On-Screen Keyboard window to enter data.
Narrator	Reads text on the screen aloud and describes some events (such as an error message appearing) that happen while you're using the computer	Click Start Narrator.
High contrast	Uses a high contrast color scheme to make the computer screen easier to see	Click Set up High Contrast.

You can start a couple of Ease of Access tools to determine whether they improve your computing experience.

To use Ease of Access tools

▶ **1.** In the Ease of Access Center window, click **Start Magnifier**. The Magnifier dialog box opens briefly, and then is minimized on the taskbar. The Magnifier pane opens at the top of the desktop and displays a magnified image of the screen near your pointer. See Figure B-13.

Using Magnifier to make the screen easier to see ◀ **Figure B-13**

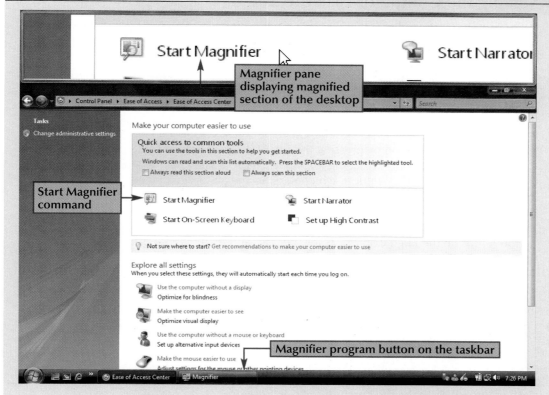

Trouble? If the Magnifier dialog box opens but does not become minimized, click to select the Minimize on Startup check box, and then click the Hide button.

▶ **2.** Move the pointer around the desktop.

▶ **3.** Right-click the **Magnifier** button on the taskbar and then click **Close** to close the Magnifier window.

▶ **4.** Click **Start On-Screen Keyboard** to open the On-Screen Keyboard window. See Figure B-14.

Using the On-Screen Keyboard to enter data ◀ **Figure B-14**

▶ **5.** Open Notepad, and then click keys on the On-Screen Keyboard to enter your name in a new Notepad document.

▶ **6.** Close Notepad without saving any changes, and then close the On-Screen Keyboard window.

The Ease of Access Center window also lists accessibility settings you can change. Each of the links listed below the four common tools opens a window where you can select settings to optimize the visual display, adjust settings for the mouse or other pointing device, and set up alternatives to sound, for example. You'll explore a few of these windows to change accessibility settings.

Making the Computer Easier to See

If you want to optimize the visual display on your computer, you can open a window where you can select settings to turn on High Contrast, read screen text or video descriptions, or turn on the Magnifier tool when you log on to Windows. By default, High Contrast uses large white letters on a black background and increases the size of the title bar and window control buttons, making objects and text stand out. If you have limited vision or if you're in a dark office, using a High Contrast color scheme can make it easier to see what's on your screen. You can also select a different High Contrast color scheme to use instead of the default white-on-black scheme. After selecting a High Contrast color scheme, you can turn it on by pressing the Alt+Shift+Print Screen keys.

If are having problems seeing text on a screen or viewing a video, you can turn on the Narrator or Audio Description, which narrates the action in a video. (This feature is available only for videos that provide audio descriptions.) You can also select a setting to turn on the Magnifier tool when you log on to Windows, set the thickness of the blinking insertion point, and remove background images when they appear in windows.

You'll turn on the High Contrast color scheme, and then explore other settings that make your computer easier to see.

To make your computer easier to see:

1. In the Ease of Access Center window, click **Make the computer easier to see** in the Explore all Settings list. A window opens providing options for optimizing the visual display. See Figure B-15.

Figure B-15   **Setting options to make the computer easier to see**

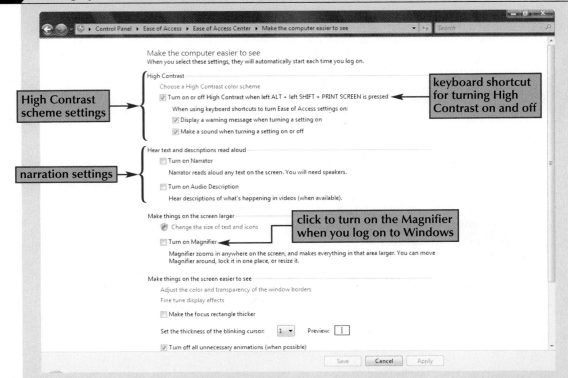

2. To test the current High Contrast color scheme, turn it on by pressing the **Alt+Shift+Print Screen** keys. A dialog box opens asking if you want to turn on High Contrast.

3. Click the **Yes** button. The desktop color scheme changes to the default High Contrast scheme. See Figure B-16.

Default High Contrast color scheme ◀ **Figure B-16**

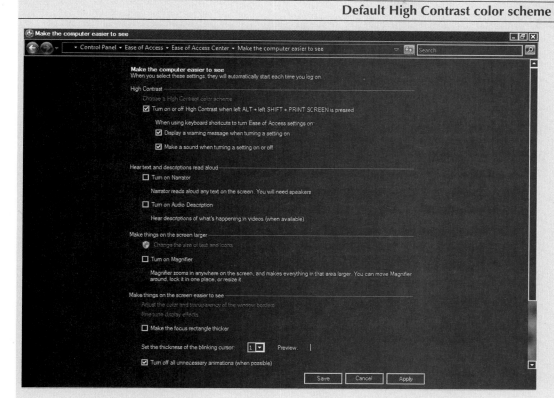

4. Press the **Alt+Shift+Print Screen** keys to turn off High Contrast.

5. Scroll the window if necessary to display the *Make things on the screen easier to see* options.

6. Click the **Set the thickness of the blinking cursor arrow button**, and then click **3**. The sample insertion point in the Preview box is thicker.

7. Click the **Set the thickness of the blinking cursor arrow button**, and then click **1** to restore this setting.

8. Click the **Back** button ⬅ to return to the Ease of Access Center window.

Note that when you use a High Contrast color scheme, that scheme affects all programs and windows you open.

Using Mouse Keys to Control the Pointer

All users occasionally have trouble using the mouse to control the pointer, especially when using drawing or graphics programs. You can turn on **Mouse Keys**, a feature that lets you control the pointer with the numeric keypad as well as with the mouse. This is also a useful feature if you have a hand injury. You turn on Mouse Keys in the Make the mouse easier to use window, which you open from the Ease of Access Center. You can also use this window to change the color and size of mouse pointers and make it easier to switch between windows by pointing to a window to activate it instead of clicking the window.

To see how Mouse Keys works, you can start Paint, turn on Mouse Keys, and then use the keys on the numeric keypad to draw on the Paint canvas.

To turn on and use Mouse Keys:

1. Start Paint the way you normally do. (Click the **Start** button, point to **All Programs**, click **Accessories**, and then click **Paint**.) Minimize the Paint window.

2. In the Ease of Access Center window, click **Make the mouse easier to use**. A window opens where you can adjust settings for the mouse or other pointing device.

3. In the Control the mouse with the keyboard section, click **Set up Mouse Keys**. The Set up Mouse Keys window opens.

4. Click the **Turn on Mouse Keys** check box to insert a check mark.

5. Click the **Apply** button to activate Mouse Keys. The Mouse Keys icon appears in the taskbar notification area. See Figure B-17.

Figure B-17	Turning on Mouse Keys

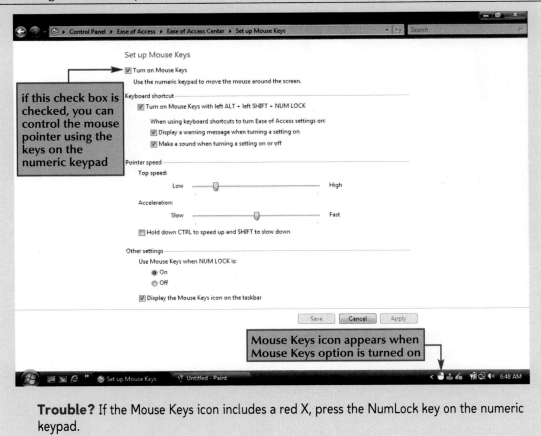

Trouble? If the Mouse Keys icon includes a red X, press the NumLock key on the numeric keypad.

Figure B-18 describes how to use the numeric keypad to perform mouse actions.

Mouse action and corresponding key ◀ **Figure B-18**

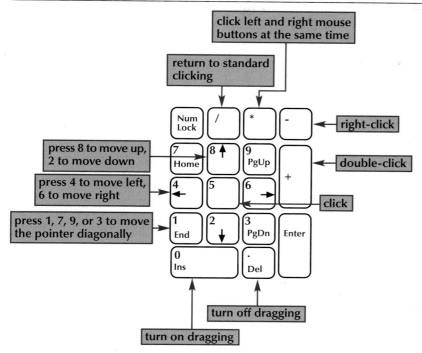

In general, you can use the numeric keypad when Mouse Keys is turned on to move the pointer, drag objects, or click objects as follows:

- To move the mouse pointer, press a directional key (an arrow, Home, End, PgUp, or PgDn key).
- To drag an object, point to the object using the directional keys, press the Ins key, press a directional key to drag the object, then press the Del key to release the object.
- To click, press the 5 key; to double-click, press the plus (+) key; to right-click, press the minus key (–) to activate right-clicking, and then press the 5 key to click or the plus key to double-click. After right-clicking, press the slash (/) key to return to standard clicking.
- To click as if you were using the left and right buttons at the same time, press the asterisk (*) key to activate simultaneous clicking, and then press the 5 key to click or the plus key to double-click. After simultaneous clicking, press the slash (/) key to return to standard clicking.

To practice using Mouse Keys:

▶ **1.** Click the **Paint** program button on the taskbar, and then use the numeric keypad to move the pointer over the Paint window.

▶ **2.** Press the **Ins** key on the numeric keypad to start drawing. Press the number keys to move the pointer and draw precise vertical, horizontal, and diagonal lines. Then press the **Del** key to stop drawing.

You've already used Paint with a pointer, so you'll notice that this is a much slower method of drawing, but it is more precise. Now you can close Paint and deactivate Mouse Keys.

To use Mouse Keys to close the Paint window:

▶ **1.** Use the keys on the numeric keypad to move the pointer over the **Close** button [X] in the Paint window.

▶ **2.** Press the **5** key to click the **Close** button [X].

▶ **3.** Use the keys on the numeric keypad to move the pointer to the **Don't Save** button on the Paint dialog box, and then press the **5** key to close Paint.

▶ **4.** Click the **Turn on Mouse Keys** check box to turn this feature off, and then click the **Apply** button.

▶ **5.** Click the **Back** button ◀ twice to return to the Ease of Access Center window.

While you can use Mouse Keys to move the pointer more precisely, you can use another feature called Sticky Keys to make the keyboard easier to use.

Simplifying Keyboard Shortcuts with Sticky Keys

You can perform many actions with either the mouse or by holding down one key while pressing another key. For example, instead of clicking the Start button to open the Start menu, you can use Ctrl+Esc (hold down the Ctrl key and then press the Esc key). Key combinations like this one are often called **keyboard shortcuts**. Some users have trouble pressing two keys at once; Sticky Keys is a feature that makes it easier. You typically use one of three keys—the Shift key, the Ctrl key, or the Alt key—with another key to perform an action, such as selecting a menu command. These three keys are also known as **modifier keys**—you hold them down while pressing another key to modify the action of the second key, which is called the **action key**.

In a window with a menu bar, you can press and hold the Alt key and then press an action key to open a menu. For example, you can press Alt+F to open the File menu. If you don't want to hold down the modifier key, such as Alt, you can turn on Sticky Keys. With Sticky Keys, you can press and release the modifier key and then press the action key, so you'd press Alt and then F to open the File menu.

To turn on Sticky Keys:

▶ **1.** In the Ease of Access Center window, click **Make the keyboard easier to use**. A window opens where you can adjust settings for the keyboard.

▶ **2.** In the Make it easier to type section, click **Set up Sticky Keys**. The Set up Sticky Keys window opens. See Figure B-19.

Set up Sticky Keys window   **Figure B-19**

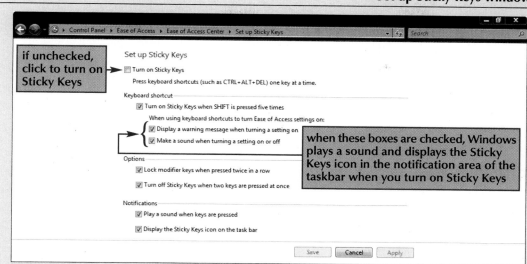

▶ **3.** Click the **Turn on Sticky Keys** check box to turn on this feature.

▶ **4.** Click the **Apply** button to activate Sticky Keys. After a few moments the Sticky Keys icon 🔲 appears in the taskbar notification area.

Now you can test the effect of Sticky Keys by using a keyboard shortcut to open the File menu.

To test the effect of Sticky Keys:

▶ **1.** Open Notepad as you usually do.

▶ **2.** Press and release the **Alt** key. A sound indicates that you pressed a Sticky Key. The sound and the icon indicate that the next key you press will be combined with the Alt key.

    Trouble? If you didn't hear a sound, sounds might not be enabled on your Sticky Keys settings or on your computer. To enable sounds, click the Play a sound when keys are pressed box in the Set up Sticky Keys window.

▶ **3.** Press the **F** key. The File menu opens. Because Sticky Keys is activated, you do not have to hold down the Alt key while you press the F key.

▶ **4.** Press the **Esc** key twice to close the File menu.

▶ **5.** Close the Notepad window without saving any changes.

▶ **6.** In the Set up Sticky Keys window, click the **Turn on Sticky Keys** check box to remove the check mark, and then click the **Apply** button to deactivate Sticky Keys. The Sticky Keys icon is removed from the taskbar.

▶ **7.** Click the **Back** button ◀ twice to return to the Ease of Access Center window.

Note that you can also start Sticky Keys by pressing the Shift key on your keyboard five times in succession.

Next, you'll explore the Ease of Access questionnaire to have Windows recommend how to make your computer easier to use.

Using the Ease of Access Questionnaire

The Ease of Access Center provides dozens of settings that can make your computer easier to use. If you prefer not to explore those settings, you can take the Ease of Access Questionnaire. Based on the answers you provide to the questions, Windows recommends accessibility settings and assistive technologies and settings that can make the computer easier to use.

You'll complete the questionnaire as if you are a user who has trouble seeing images on the screen in low light and hearing computer sounds when you are in a place with background noise.

To use the Ease of Access questionnaire:

▶ **1.** In the Ease of Access Center window, click **Get recommendations to make your computer easier to use**. The first window in the questionnaire opens, listing statements about your eyesight. See Figure B-20.

Figure B-20 ▶ **Starting the Ease of Access Center questionnaire**

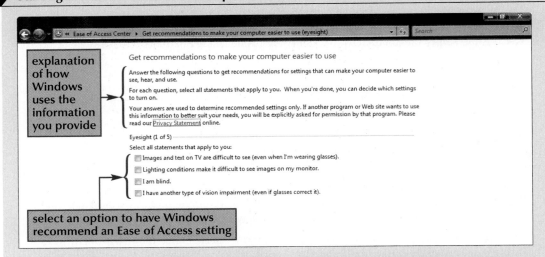

▶ **2.** Click the **Lighting conditions make it difficult to see images on my monitor** check box, and then click the **Next** button. The next window lists statements about your dexterity.

▶ **3.** Click the **Next** button. The next window lists statements about your hearing.

▶ **4.** Click the **Background noise makes the computer difficult to hear** check box, and then click the **Next** button. The next window lists statements about your speech.

▶ **5.** Click the **Next** button. The next window lists statements about your reasoning.

▶ **6.** Click the **Done** button. The Recommended settings window opens, listing the Ease of Access settings Windows suggests based on your responses. See Figure B-21.

Recommended settings after completing the Ease of Access questionnaire — **Figure B-21**

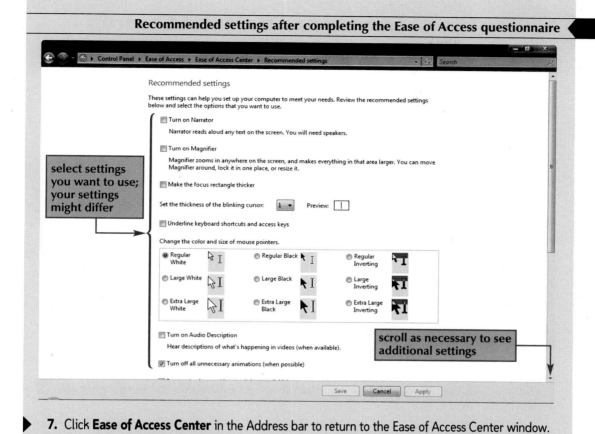

7. Click **Ease of Access Center** in the Address bar to return to the Ease of Access Center window.
8. Click **Control Panel** in the Address bar to return to Control Panel.

Next, you'll use advanced user account settings to protect your computer and set parental controls.

Adding User Accounts and Parental Controls

You've already used the User Accounts window to add a new user to a computer and to select settings such as the user picture, account name, account type, and password. You can also perform advanced tasks to manage user accounts and enhance security. You can set three important settings using the **Microsoft Management Console (MMC)**, a tool that computer administrators use to manage the hardware, software, and network components of Windows. Both Microsoft and other software vendors offer programs, called **snap-ins**, that run in the MMC to manage advanced settings in Windows. To improve the security of user accounts, you can use a snap-in called Local Users and Groups to open a user's Properties dialog box, where you can change advanced user account settings to make a user's password more secure.

Besides using the MMC and the Local Users and Groups snap-in, you can change other advanced settings using the User Accounts window in Control Panel. To prevent you or another user from permanently losing or forgetting a password, you can create a password reset disk, which is a removable disk such as a USB flash drive or CD that you can use to log on to Windows if you forget your password. You can also store passwords in Windows that you frequently use to access Web sites or networks. If you save these network passwords, you don't have to retype them each time you return to the Web site or network.

Parental Controls are related to user accounts. If children use your computer, set up an account for each child. Then use the Windows Parental Controls feature to set limits on the hours that the children can use the computer, the types of games they can play, the Web sites they can visit, and the programs they can run. Using Parental Controls prevents children from accessing inappropriate content with your computer. (Note that Parental Controls are not included with Windows Vista Business and Windows Vista Enterprise editions.)

In the following sections, you'll create a user account and set advanced options for it. You'll also set network passwords and parental controls for the new account. If you don't want to save these settings, you'll delete the account at the end of the section.

Setting Advanced Options for User Accounts

To improve the security of user accounts, you can use the Local Users and Groups snap-in in the MMC to open a user's Properties dialog box, where you can change the following settings:

- **User must change password at next logon.** Select this option so that the next time the selected user logs on to Windows, a dialog box opens indicating that the user must change the password for his or her account. The user can then change the password using the Change Password dialog box. Changing a password regularly is one way to keep your computer more secure.
- **User cannot change password.** Select this option to prevent the user from changing the password. If you manage a computer that more than one person uses, you might want to prevent a user from changing the password without your authorization.
- **Password never expires.** Select this option so that the user's password never expires, or disable this setting so that the password does expire after a specified amount of time.
- **Account is disabled.** Select this option to disable the user account so that no one can use it to access Windows Vista or the user's files. If the user is away from the computer for an extended period, such as for a long vacation, this option is preferable to removing and then recreating an account.

Before you set the advanced password options, you'll create an account for a new user. You'll provide a generic password for the new user, and then apply the advanced password settings to the new account so that the new user must change the password the next time they log on. The new user should use a strong password instead of the generic one. (Recall that a strong password cannot be guessed easily—it is at least six characters long, does not contain all or part of the user's account name, and contains a mixed collection of characters, such as uppercase and lowercase characters, numbers, and symbols.) You must be logged on using an Administrator account to complete the following steps. If you cannot use an Administrator account, read but do not perform the steps.

To create a user account:

▶ 1. In Control Panel, click the **User Accounts and Family Safety** category, and then click **User Accounts**. The User Accounts window opens.

   Trouble? If you are using Windows Vista Business or Windows Vista Enterprise, click the User Accounts category.

▶ 2. Click **Manage another account** to open the Manage Accounts window.

   Trouble? If a User Account Control dialog box opens requesting your permission or a password to continue, enter the password or click the Continue button.

▶ 3. Click **Create a new account**. The Create New Account window opens.

▶ 4. Type **New User** as the name of the new account, make sure the **Standard user** option button is selected, and then click the **Create Account** button. The new account is displayed in the Manage Accounts window.

▶ 5. Click **New User** to open the Change an Account window, and then click **Create a password**. The Create Password window opens.

▶ 6. Type **password** as the new password, press the **Tab** key, type **password** to confirm the password, and then click the **Create password** button.

▶ 7. Return to the User Accounts window, and then minimize the window.

Now you are ready to use the Microsoft Management Console to set advanced password options for the New User account. You must be logged on as an Administrator to complete the steps. If you cannot do so, read but do not perform the steps.

To set advanced password options:

▶ **1.** Click the **Start** button 🌀 on the taskbar, and then type **MMC** in the Start Search box. Windows displays programs and files that match the search criteria.

▶ **2.** Click **MMC** in the list of programs. The Microsoft Management Console opens. See Figure B-22.

Figure B-22 ▶ **Microsoft Management Console**

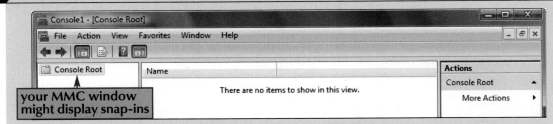

Trouble? If a User Account Control dialog box opens requesting your permission or a password to continue, enter the password or click the Continue button.

▶ **3.** If the Local Users and Groups snap-in is not installed, click **File** on the menu bar, and then click **Add/Remove Snap-in**. The Add or Remove Snap-ins dialog box opens. Scroll the list of available snap-ins, click **Local Users and Groups**, click the **Add** button, make sure the **Local computer** option button is selected, click the **Finish** button, and then click the **OK** button to add the snap-in to the Microsoft Management Console.

▶ **4.** In the left pane of the Microsoft Management Console, click the **expand** icon ▷ next to Local Users and Groups, and then double-click the **Users** folder. A list of the users on the computer appears in the right pane.

▶ **5.** Double-click **New User** in the center pane. The New User Properties dialog box opens. See Figure B-23.

New User Properties dialog box   **Figure B-23**

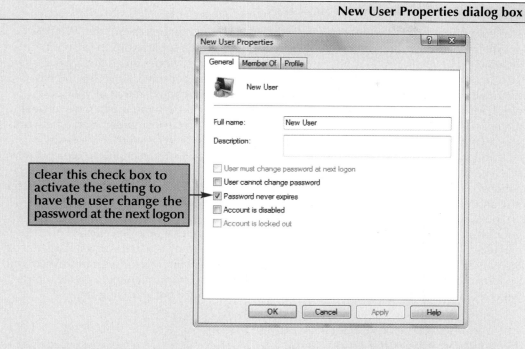

clear this check box to
activate the setting to
have the user change the
password at the next logon

Trouble? If you are using Windows Vista Business or Windows Vista Enterprise, right-click
a blank area of the window, and then click New User.

▶ **6.** Click the **Password never expires** box to remove the check mark, if necessary.

▶ **7.** Click the **User must change password at next logon** box to insert a check mark and
select this option, if necessary.

▶ **8.** Click the **OK** button to close the New User Properties dialog box.

▶ **9.** Close the Microsoft Management Console. A dialog box opens asking if you want to save
console settings.

▶ **10.** Click the **No** button.

The next time anyone logs on to Windows using the New User account, that person
will be required to change the password.

The Properties dialog box shown in Figure B-23 includes another useful option for
improving the security of user accounts. If you want to temporarily disable an account
rather than deleting it, click to select the Account is disabled check box. To reactivate the
account, you can open this Properties dialog box again, and then click to remove the
check mark from the Account is disabled box. Doing so restores all the settings and other
properties associated with the account.

Creating a Password Reset Disk

Two common problems with account passwords are entering a password that Windows doesn't recognize and forgetting your password. If you enter a password to log on to Windows, but Windows does not recognize it, check the obvious causes first. Make sure the Caps Lock key is not on; Windows passwords are case sensitive, so typing the password with the Caps Lock key on could change the correct capitalization of your password. Also make sure you are trying to log on to your account—you might have clicked the user name or picture for a different account. Finally, if your computer is on a network, check with your network administrator, who can change your password if necessary.

If you forget your account password, you can use a password reset disk to create a new one. The best time to create a password reset disk is when you create your password, although you can create a reset disk later. If you forget your password, you can insert the reset disk and Windows will guide you through the steps of using it to log on to your account.

You'll create a password reset disk for your account now so you don't lose access to your files and other information. You need a USB flash drive or an external hard drive you can use to store the password information. The following steps use Removeable Disk (F:) as the name of the drive. Substitute the name of the drive containing your reset disk when you perform the steps. You must be logged on using an Administrator account to create a password reset disk. If you cannot do so, read but do not perform the following steps.

To create a password reset disk:

▶ 1. Insert a USB flash drive or external hard drive in the appropriate drive, restore the User Accounts window, and then click **Create a password reset disk** in the left pane. The Forgotten Password Wizard starts.

▶ 2. Click the **Next** button. The next wizard dialog box opens, where you can select the drive for storing the password reset disk.

▶ 3. Make sure **Removable Disk (F:)** is selected in the text box, and then click the **Next** button. The Current User Account Password dialog box opens.

▶ 4. In the Current user account password box, type your password, and then click the **Next** button. The Creating Password Reset Disk dialog box opens, displaying the progress of creating the disk.

▶ 5. When Windows is finished creating the password reset disk, click the **Next** button. The final dialog box in the wizard opens.

▶ 6. Click the **Finish** button.

Be sure to store the password reset disk in a safe place where unauthorized users cannot access it and it cannot be damaged.

Managing Network Passwords

Besides storing the password for your user account on a reset disk, you can also store passwords you use to log on to Web sites or networks. Maintaining strong passwords for each Web site or network that requires one is prone to error, so using this feature in the User Accounts window can save you time.

In the following steps, you can store the password for logging on to a fictitious financial Web site named Bank.com. Substitute the name of the Web site or network location for which you want to store a password.

To manage network passwords:

▶ **1.** In the left pane of the User Accounts window, click **Manage your network passwords**. The Stored User Names and Passwords dialog box opens. See Figure B-24.

Stored User Names and Passwords dialog box | Figure B-24

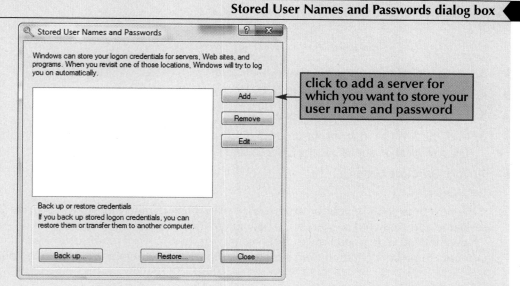

click to add a server for which you want to store your user name and password

▶ **2.** Click the **Add** button. The Stored Credential Properties dialog box opens. See Figure B-25.

Figure B-25 | **Stored Credential Properties dialog box**

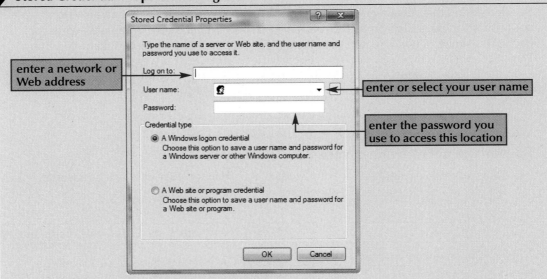

3. In the Log on to text box, type **www.bank.com**.

4. In the User name text box, type **New User**.

5. In the Password text box, type **password**.

6. Click the **A Web site or program credential** option button, and then click the **OK** button. The new location appears in the Stored User Names and Passwords dialog box.

7. Click the **Close** button.

The next time you use your browser to visit www.bank.com, Windows will provide your user name and password so you can log on automatically, if the site allows you to do so.

Now that you've learned how to make your own user account more secure, you'll learn how to prevent children from accessing inappropriate content using your computer.

Setting Parental Controls

You can use Parental Controls to set limits on the hours that children can use the computer, the types of games that they can play, the Web sites that they can visit, and the programs that they can run. Time limits prevent children from logging on during specified hours, such as very late at night. If children are allowed to use the computer on weekend nights but not week nights, for example, you can set different hours for every day of the week. You can also use Parental Controls to prevent children from playing certain games, such as those not suited for their age, or from running programs, such as utilities that could damage data on your computer. To limit content that children can view on the Web, you can restrict the Web sites children can visit. After you set up Parental Controls, you can generate activity reports that track your child's computer activity.

When Windows blocks access to a Web page or game because of Parental Control settings, it displays a notification that it is blocking a Web page or program. The child can click a link in the notification to request permission for access to that Web page or program, and you can allow access by entering your account information.

Before you set Parental Control, make sure that each child using the computer has a standard user account—you can apply Parental Controls only to standard accounts. Then you can select the following settings to limit a child's access to the computer:

- **Windows Vista Web Filter.** Use this setting to restrict the Web sites that children can visit, make sure children visit only age-appropriate Web sites, indicate whether you want to allow file downloads, and set up which content you want the content filters to block and allow. You can also block or allow specific Web sites.
- **Time limits.** Use this setting to set time limits to prevent children from logging on during the specified hours. If they are already logged on during a restricted time, Windows logs them off. You can set different logon hours for every day of the week.
- **Games.** Use this setting to control access to games, choose an age rating level, choose the types of content you want to block, and allow or block unrated or specific games.
- **Allow and block specific programs.** Use this setting to prevent children from running programs that you don't want them to run.

Recall that you set up a user with a standard account named New User. You'll set Parental Controls on the New User account so that this user can use the computer only until 8 p.m. on week nights and 9 p.m. on weekends. To do so, you need to log on using an Administrator Account. If you cannot do so, read but do not perform the following steps.

To turn on Parental Controls for a standard user account:

▶ 1. In the User Accounts window, click **User Accounts and Family Safety** in the Address bar to open the User Accounts and Family Safety window.

▶ 2. Click **Parental Controls**. The Parental Controls window opens. See Figure B-26.

Parental Controls window **Figure B-26**

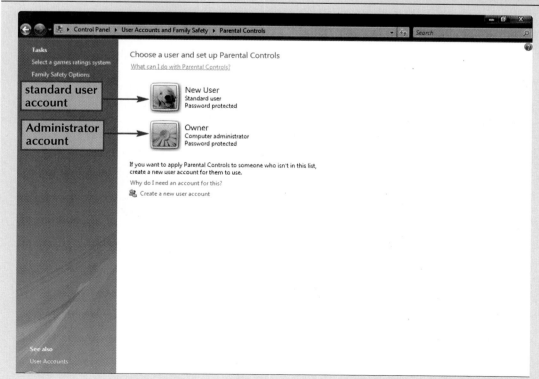

Trouble? If a User Account Control dialog box opens requesting your permission or a password to continue, enter the password or click the Continue button.

▶ 3. Click **New User** to open the User Controls window.

▶ 4. Click the **On, enforce current settings** option button. See Figure B-27.

Figure B-27	User Controls window

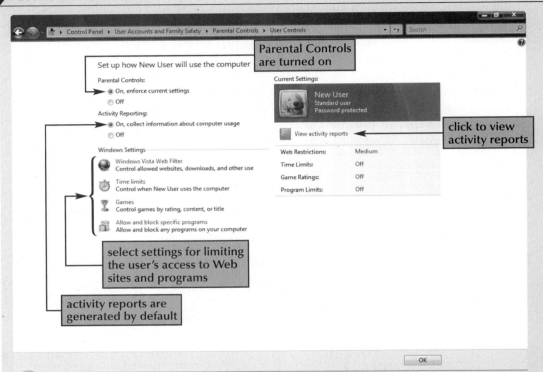

▶ 5. Click **Time limits** in the Windows Settings section. The Time Restrictions window opens.

   Trouble? If a Windows Parental Controls dialog box opens indicating that Windows detects a FAT drive, click the OK button.

▶ 6. For Sunday, drag from the first **12** to the second **6** and from the second **9** to the last **12**. Do the same for Saturday.

▶ 7. For Monday, drag from the first **12** to the second **7** and from the second **8** to the last **12**. Do the same for the remaining weekdays.

▶ 8. Click the **OK** button to close the Time Restrictions window.

▶ 9. Click the **OK** button to close the User Controls window.

▶ 10. In the User Accounts window, click **User Accounts and Family Safety** in the Address bar to open the User Accounts and Family Safety window.

If you are not working on your own computer, you should restore the original user accounts settings.

To restore the original settings:

▶ **1.** In the User Accounts and Family Safety window, click **Add or remove user accounts**. The Manage Accounts window opens.

   Trouble? If a User Account Control dialog box opens requesting your permission or a password to continue, enter the password or click the Continue button.

▶ **2.** Click **New User** to open the Change an Account window.

▶ **3.** Click **Delete the account**. A window opens asking if you want to keep New User's files.

▶ **4.** Click the **Delete Files** button. A window opens asking you to verify that you want to delete New User's account.

▶ **5.** Click the **Delete Account** button. Windows deletes the account and returns to the Manage Accounts window.

▶ **6.** Return to the User Accounts and Family Safety window, click **Parental Controls**, click **Family Safety Options** in the left pane, and then click the **Never** option button to turn off reminders about generating an activity report.

   Trouble? If a User Account Control dialog box opens requesting your permission or a password to continue, enter the password or click the Continue button.

▶ **7.** Close all open windows.

In the next session, you'll work with another feature users often want to customize—the fonts on their computer. You'll learn how to view and install fonts next.

Session B.2

Working with Fonts

From Control Panel you can open the Fonts window, which you use to manage the fonts on your computer. As you probably know, a **font** is the design of a collection of numbers, symbols, and characters. All the fonts in the Fonts window are available for use in all your Windows programs. You can use the Fonts window to open fonts to look at their style and print a test page. You can also install or delete fonts.

To view the fonts installed on your computer:

▶ **1.** Open Control Panel, click the **Appearance and Personalization** category, and then click **Fonts**. The Fonts window opens.

▶ **2.** Switch to **Details** view, if necessary. See Figure B-28.

Fonts window in Details view ◄ **Figure B-28**

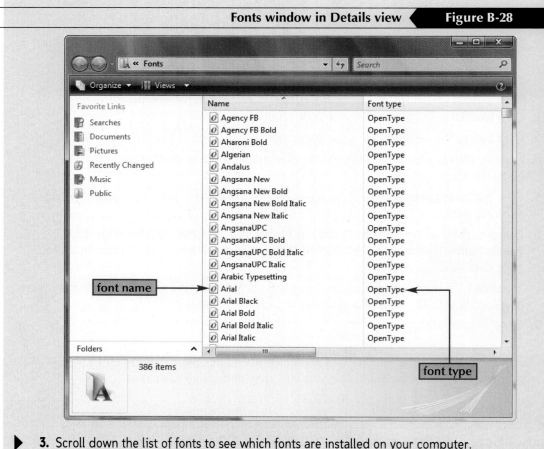

3. Scroll down the list of fonts to see which fonts are installed on your computer.

In Details view, the Fonts window shows you the name of the font and its type. You can also display the font filename. The next section explains how those font characteristics are related.

Understanding Font Types

When you view the Fonts window in Details view, you see detailed information about the font files on your computer. A font file contains the information Windows Vista needs to display the font on the computer screen or to print the font. In Windows Vista, the font name and filename are not the same. To verify this, right-click a column heading in the Fonts window, click Font file names, and then scroll to the right to display a column of filenames. The Arial Bold font, for example, is stored in a file named arialbd.ttf.

Almost all font filenames have a TTF extension, which indicates a TrueType font (or OpenType, an updated extension of TrueType). Windows Vista uses OpenType font files to both display text on your computer screen and to print text on a printer. A few font files have an FON extension, such as the Small Fonts (VGA res) font, which is a screen font. Windows uses screen fonts only to display text on your screen.

As you scroll through the Fonts window, notice that some fonts have one base font and a number of variations. For example, Times New Roman is a base font and has three variations: Times New Roman Bold, Times New Roman Bold Italic, and Times New Roman Italic. Times New Roman uses the times.ttf file, while each variation uses a separate file: timesbd.ttf, timesbi.ttf, and timesi.ttf, respectively. When you choose an attribute such as bold or italic in a program, you are actually choosing an alternate font file.

Opening a Font

You can open a font in the Fonts window to see its characteristics and how it will look in a variety of sizes. One of the fonts that comes with Windows Vista is Calibri.

To open the Calibri font:

▶ **1.** Scroll down in the Fonts window, right-click the **Calibri** font, and then click **Open** on the short-cut menu. The Calibri (OpenType) window opens, displaying the font in different sizes, along with information about the font and its creator at the top of the window. See Figure B-29.

Opening a font ◀ **Figure B-29**

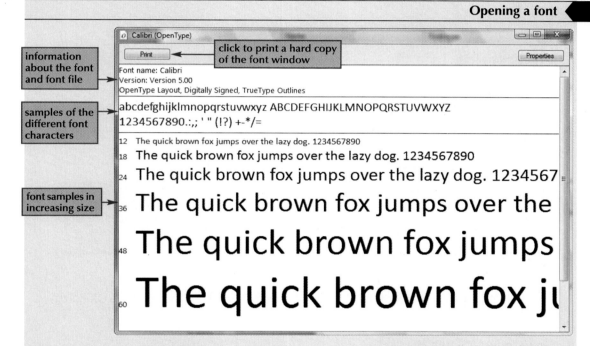

▶ **2.** Close the Calibri (OpenType) window.

In addition to using the fonts that Windows Vista or your printer provides, you can also find fonts on the Web or in font collections on disk or CD-ROM. Before you can use such a font, you must install it.

Installing a Font

When you install a font, you place it in the Fonts folder on your hard disk, and Windows Vista makes it available to other programs. You can install a font by right-clicking a blank spot in the Fonts window and then clicking Install New Font on the shortcut menu.

To install a new font:

▶ **1.** Right-click a blank spot in the Fonts window, and then click **Install New Font** on the shortcut menu. The Add Fonts dialog box opens. See Figure B-30.

Figure B-30
Installing a font

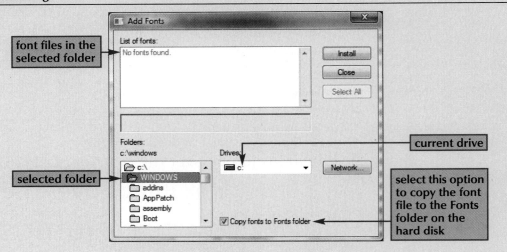

If you needed to install a font, you would select the drive and folder containing the font. It would then appear in the List of fonts box. You would click it and then click the OK button.

▶ **2.** Click the **Close** button to close the Add Fonts dialog box without installing a font.

▶ **3.** Close all open windows.

In the remaining sections, you'll explore two valuable Windows accessories—the Welcome Center and the Media Cener—and learn how to use a tablet PC.

Exploring the Welcome Center

Recall that the Welcome Center is a window that displays information you are likely to need when you start Windows Vista, including basic information such as the edition of Windows Vista running on your computer. In addition, the Welcome Center helps you perform other typical startup tasks, such as connecting to the Internet, transferring files and settings from another computer, and adding new users. If you are new to Windows Vista, you can also find out about the new features in this version of the Windows operating system.

After you connect your computer to the Internet, you can go online to get the latest information and files from Microsoft and its partners. For example, you can go online to Windows Marketplace, a Web site that provides programs you can download to enhance your Windows Vista experience. You can also go online to learn more information about protecting your computer from threats such as malware and spyware.

The Welcome Center is set to run at startup by default. If you change this setting, you can open the Welcome Center from Control Panel, where it is always available, even after you start your computer.

To open the Welcome Center:

▶ 1. Click the **Start** button 🔵 on the taskbar, click **Control Panel**, click **System and Maintenance**, and then click **Welcome Center**. The Welcome Center window opens. See Figure B-31.

Welcome Center window   **Figure B-31**

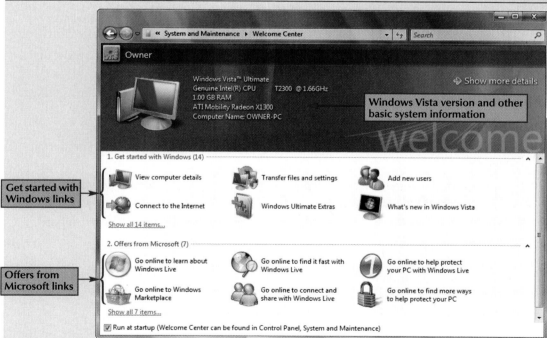

▶ 2. Click **Show more details**. The System window opens, displaying detailed information about your computer.

▶ 3. Click the **Back** button ◀ to return to the Welcome Center window.

▶ 4. If necessary, maximize the Welcome Center window.

Next, you'll explore a few links in the Get started with Windows category.

Getting Started with Windows

The Get started with Windows section of the Welcome Center window includes links to resources that you might find valuable when you first start working with Windows. For example, the Transfer files and settings link lets you transfer user accounts, files and folders, program settings, Internet settings and favorites, e-mail settings, contacts, and messages from one computer, such as a computer running a previous version of Windows, to your current computer or vice versa. If you haven't registered your copy of Windows Vista yet, you can click the Register Windows online link to open a Web page where you can register your copy.

The Get started with Windows section usually contains more links than it can display in the Welcome Center window. You'll show all the items in this category, and then explore two links that are often useful for new users.

To use the links in the Get started with Windows section:

▶ 1. Click **Show all 14 items** in the Get started with Windows section. The section expands to show 14 icons and links.

   Trouble? If your Welcome Center window can show a different number of items, click the link that shows all the items.

▶ 2. Click **What's new in Windows Vista**. The top panel of the window displays information about the features in your edition of Windows Vista.

▶ 3. Click **See more new features** in the top panel. The Windows Help and Support window opens, displaying information about the new features in your edition of Windows Vista.

▶ 4. In the Get started with Windows section, click **Windows Vista Demos**. The top panel of the window displays a list of Windows Vista demos.

▶ 5. Click **Open Windows Vista Demos**. The Windows Help and Support window opens, listing demos for using Windows Vista.

▶ 6. Scroll down as necessary, and then click **Demo: Understanding user accounts** in the Security and maintenance section. A Windows Help and Support page opens, introducing that demo.

▶ 7. Click **Watch the demo**. Windows Media Player starts and plays a demo explaining the benefits and features of user accounts.

▶ 8. Close the Windows Media Player window, and then close the Windows Help and Support window.

You can also use the Welcome Center to learn about offers from Microsoft and its partners, which you'll do next.

Learning About Offers from Microsoft

The Offers from Microsoft section of the Welcome Center window is updated to provide links to resources you can use to enhance your Windows Vista experience. When you first install Windows Vista, the Welcome Center window includes the offers shown in Figure B-31. You'll use these links to learn ways to help protect your computer and to find programs available for downloading at the Windows Marketplace Web site.

To use the links in the Get started with Windows section:

▶ 1. Click **Go online to find more ways to help protect your PC**. The top panel of the window changes to reflect information about this link.

▶ 2. Click **Learn more online**. The Windows Vista Security Software Providers Web page opens, listing software publishers that provide antivirus and other security software compatible with Windows Vista.

▶ 3. Close the Windows Vista Security Software Providers Web page.

▶ 4. Close the Windows Help and Support window.

▶ 5. Click **Go online to Windows Marketplace**. The top panel of the window displays information about Windows Marketplace.

▶ 6. Click **Go online to Windows Marketplace** in the top panel. The Windows Marketplace Web page opens, displaying software you can purchase and download in various categories, including games and security.

▶ 7. In the Search box, type **gadgets** and then click the **Go** button. The Web page lists gadgets you can download from the Internet and add to Windows Sidebar.

▶ 8. Close the Windows Marketplace Web page, and then close the Welcome Center window.

Another way to download and add gadgets to Windows Sidebar is to open Windows Sidebar, click the Add Gadgets button ➕, and then click Get more gadgets online to open the Windows Vista Sidebar Web page. Find the gadget you want, click the Download button, and then follow the instructions to download and install the gadget.

Next, you'll open a built-in program provided with Windows Vista, the Windows Media Center.

Playing Media with Windows Media Center

Although Windows Media Center includes many of the same controls available in Windows Media Player, it is designed to let you watch and record TV programs. You can also use the Windows Media Center to play other types of media, including videos, DVDs, and music, but its large menus and full screen display are best suited for TV programs.

To watch and record TV shows using the Windows Media Center, your computer needs the following hardware and software:

- **Vista Home Premium or Ultimate.** The Media Center is not available with Vista Home Basic or Vista Business versions.
- **TV tuner.** You need a hardware or software TV tuner to view TV on a monitor and change channels.
- **TV signal.** You can connect the cable that plugs into your TV set into your computer's TV tuner so you can capture TV signals.
- **Video with TV-Out port.** Your computer's tuner also needs to plug into your TV set, usually through an S-Video port, the same port used by specialty game computers, such as an Xbox.

If your computer is equipped with these four prerequisites, Windows Media Center will detect these devices and let you play and record TV programs. You can also choose to pause live TV or a movie and temporarily record it as a video file. You can then rewind or fast forward through the recorded program or movie until you return to the current part of the show.

Windows Media Center also includes a Guide that displays the programs on TV and lets you search for TV shows. The Guide displays the date and time of each TV show, the channel number, channel name, and program title.

Windows Media Center comes with a few sample programs you can play to get a feel for how it works. You'll start the Media Center, explore its main menu, and then play a sample program. If your computer has the required hardware and software to play and record TV programs, you can use the remote control that came with your TV tuner to move the pointer. Otherwise, you can use the mouse as you usually do.

To start Windows Media Center:

▶ **1.** Click the **Start** button ⊕ on the taskbar, point to **All Programs**, and then click **Windows Media Center**. The Windows Media Center starts. See Figure B-32.

Windows Media Center ◀ **Figure B-32**

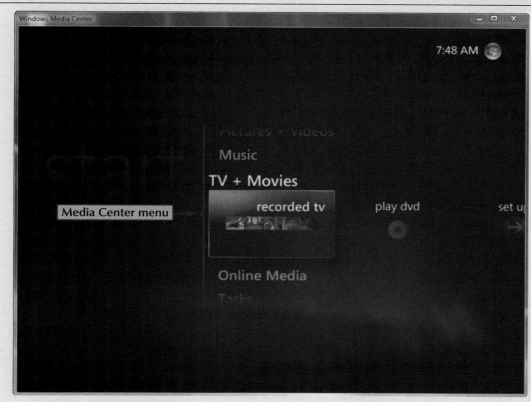

Trouble? If a setup window opens before the Windows Media Center window does, click the Express setup option button, and then click the OK button.

▶ **2.** Point to the last option in the menu (which is Online Media in Figure B-32), scroll down as necessary, and then point to the **arrow icon** that appears below that option to scroll the menu.

▶ **3.** Click **TV + Movies**, and then click **recorded TV**. The sample clips from movies and TV programs appear on the screen. See Figure B-33.

Sample movie and TV clips 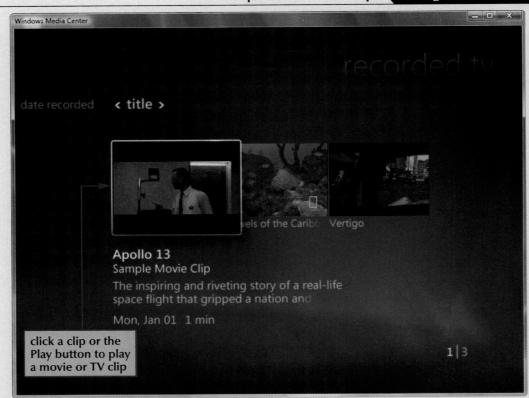 Figure B-33

click a clip or the Play button to play a movie or TV clip

4. Click **Jewels of the Caribbean**, and then click **Play**. The TV begins to play.

5. To control the sound and playback, move your pointer on the screen to display the playback controls and the window sizing buttons.

6. Click the **Stop** button to stop playing the program. The program info window opens, describing the program and listing commands you can use to resume, restart, delete or burn the program on a CD or DVD.

7. Close the Windows Media Player.

Windows Media Center lets you use your PC as a sophisticated video recording device if you have the proper hardware. You can learn more about Windows Media Center in Windows Help and Support.

Using a Tablet PC

If you use a Tablet PC, a handheld computer that includes a special screen you can use like a slate and write on with a stylus, you can use Windows Vista tools designed for use with a tablet PC. For example, you can use the Tablet PC Input Panel to enter text without using a standard keyboard, which can increase your productivity on a tablet PC. Instead of pressing keys on a physical keyboard, you enter text by tapping keys with your tablet pen. You can also create and store Sticky Notes on your desktop. A **Sticky Note** is a Tablet PC accessory you use to write or record short notes. Whether you create them by handwriting them or recording your voice, Windows stacks them on the desktop, similar to paper sticky notes. The Tablet PC tool also includes the Windows Journal, an accessory you can use to create notes, including those with drawings you create with your stylus or pictures you insert in the note.

Using the Input Panel

The Input Panel is a Tablet PC accessory that you can use to enter text by using a tablet pen instead of a standard keyboard. It includes a writing pad and a character pad to convert handwriting into typed text, and an on-screen keyboard to enter individual characters.

The Input Panel is designed for use with a Tablet PC, but you can open and move the Input Panel on any type of computer to get a feel for how it works.

To open and use the Input Panel:

▶ 1. Click the **Start** button 🚭 on the taskbar, point to **All Programs**, click **Accessories**, click **Tablet PC**, and then click **Tablet PC Input Panel**. The Input Panel opens on the desktop, including a writing pad and navigation buttons. See Figure B-34.

Input Panel accessory for a Tablet PC ◀ **Figure B-34**

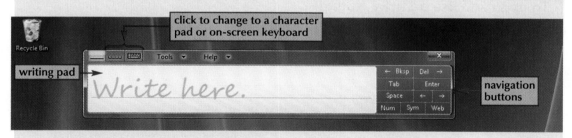

Trouble? If you are using a Tablet PC, right-click the taskbar, tap Toolbars, and then tap Tablet PC Input Panel.

▶ 2. Click or tap **Tools** on the menu bar, and then click or tap **Dock at Top of Screen**. See Figure B-35.

Figure B-35 ▶ **Inserting handwritten text**

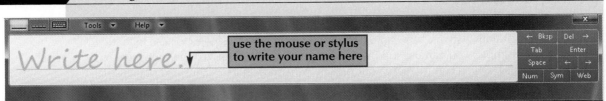

3. Use your mouse or stylus to write your name in the Input Panel. When you release the mouse button or stylus, one or more buttons appear showing the text you can insert.

4. Click the first button that appears below the text you wrote. The Input Panel displays the characters it recognizes and other words that are a close match. If you were using a program on a Tablet PC, Windows would insert the selected text when you click the Insert button.

5. Click the **OK** button to close the list of suggested entries, and then click the **Insert** button.

6. Close the Input Panel.

Next, you can explore another Tablet PC accessory, Sticky Notes.

Using Sticky Notes

When you use a Tablet PC, you can use Sticky Notes to quickly create a handwritten note or add text to a voice note. Sticky Notes looks similar to their paper counterparts, and are displayed in a stack along with other notes until you delete them.

To open and use a Sticky Note:

1. Click the **Start** button 🏁 on the taskbar, point to **All Programs**, click **Accessories**, click **Tablet PC**, and then click **Sticky Notes**. The Sticky Notes window opens. See Figure B-36.

Figure B-36 ▶ **Sticky Notes window**

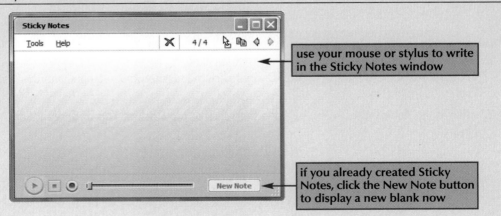

▶ **4.** To navigate from one note to another, click the **Previous Note** button ◁ on the toolbar. The first note you wrote in this session appears in the Sticky Notes window.

▶ **5.** Close the Sticky Notes window.

Notes are automatically saved when you close Sticky Notes, so you don't need to select a Save option.

Using the Windows Journal

Another Tablet PC accessory for recording notes in your own handwriting is the Windows Journal. When you open Windows Journal, you can handwrite by using your stylus or mouse. You can save your handwriting in a note, convert the writing to typed text, and then enter typed text into your notes. You can also create drawings and insert pictures in your notes. Although Sticky Notes are suitable for very short reminders, Windows Journal is designed to store longer notes.

To open and use Windows Journal:

▶ **1.** Click the **Start** button 🪟 on the taskbar, point to **All Programs**, click **Accessories**, click **Tablet PC**, and then click **Windows Journal**. The Windows Journal window opens. See Figure B-37.

Figure B-37	Windows Journal window

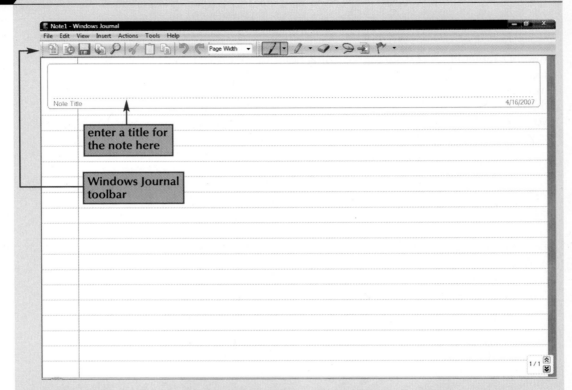

Trouble? If a Windows Journal dialog box opens asking if you want to install a Journal Note Writer print driver, click the Yes button.

▶ **2.** On the Note Title line, use your mouse or stylus to write **First note**.

▶ **3.** Below the Note Title line, use your mouse or stylus to write **1. Write text**.

▶ **4.** Click **File** on the menu bar, and then click **Save**. The Save As dialog box opens to the Notes folder. You could click the **Save** button to save the note using the Note Title as the filename, but you can discard this test note for now.

▶ **5.** Click the **Cancel** button to close the Save As dialog box.

▶ **6.** Close the Windows Journal window without saving your changes.

You're finished exploring some of the tools and accessories available in Windows Vista.

In this tutorial, you customized the mouse and changed sound settings. You also changed other hardware settings, including AutoPlay defaults and Windows SideShow setup. You also explored the accessibility settings, including those that make the computer easier to see and the mouse and keyboard easier to use. To protect your computer, you set advanced options for user accounts, created a password reset disk, and managed network passwords. You also set parental controls. To make your computer more productive and enjoyable to use, you learned how to install fonts, explored the Welcome Center, played a video in the Windows Media Center, and explored Tablet PC features.

Key Terms

action key	modifier key	Sticky Note
font	Mouse Keys	trail
keyboard shortcut	snap-in	Windows SideShow
Microsoft Management Console (MMC)	sound scheme	

Ending Data Files

There are no ending Data Files for this appendix.

Glossary/Index

Note: Boldface entries include definitions.

Special Characters

() (parentheses), WIN 284

"" (quotation marks), WIN 283

A

About Remote Desktop Connection window, WIN 436

access points, networks, WIN 422

accessibility. *See* Ease of Access Center

action key The key that is pressed along with a modifier key in a key combination. WIN B20

active program The program you are currently using. WIN 13

ActiveX control One of a set of technologies from Microsoft that enables interactive content on a Web page. WIN 237

ad hoc network A temporary network created for sharing files or an Internet connection. WIN 206

adapter card. *See* expansion card

Additional Options category, WIN 118

add-on A product designed to complement another product; specifically, a program offered by any software vendor that provides enhancement features. WIN 240–241

Address bar

Internet Explorer, WIN 298

Windows Explorer, WIN 54, WIN 59–60

Address toolbar, WIN 134

Adjust Color tool, WIN 358

Adjust Exposure tool, WIN 358

Administrator user account, WIN 247

Advanced Appearance dialog box, WIN 124

advanced performance tools, WIN 547–567

examining system information, WIN 560–564

increasing memory capacity, WIN 565–566

monitoring system performance, WIN 551–560

System Diagnostic reports, WIN 566–567

viewing details about system events, WIN 549–551

viewing issues, WIN 548–549

Advanced tab, Performance Options dialog box, WIN 565–566

adware A type of spyware that collects information about a computer user's browsing patterns in order to display advertisements in the user's Web browser. WIN 221

Aero The user interface in Windows Vista. WIN 4, WIN 13

Airbrush tool, WIN 326, WIN 342

AND, combining search criteria, WIN 283–285

antivirus software, updating, WIN 220–221

Appearance and Personalization category, WIN 118

application Software that a computer uses to complete tasks; also called program. WIN 2. *See also* program

Applications tab, Task Manager dialog box, WIN 561–562

appointment, scheduling in Windows Calendar, WIN 195–198

Appointment calendar, Windows Calendar window, WIN 195

audio file. *See also* sound entries

playing with Windows Media Player, WIN 367

audio track, adding to movies, WIN 383–384

Auto Adjust tool, WIN 358

AutoPlay dialog box, WIN 568–569, WIN B9, WIN B10–B11

B

Back button, Windows Explorer, WIN 54

Back Up and Restore, WIN 210

Back Up Files Wizard, WIN 467–468

Back Up Status and Configuration window, WIN 471

background

desktop, WIN 120–122

images, solid and transparent, WIN 338

background color The color used for the inside of enclosed shapes and the background of text in Paint. WIN 325

backing up files and folders, WIN 462–474

changing backup settings, WIN 470–472

copying compared, WIN 463

frequency, WIN 465–466

locations to save files, WIN 464–465

performing backup, WIN 466–470

restoring files and folders, WIN 472–474

selecting files and folders to back up, WIN 464, WIN 465

backup A duplicate copy of important files that you need. WIN 51

Backup and Restore Center, WIN 467

backup file A copy of one or more files that you store in a separate location from the original. WIN 462

backup medium A separate location, such as an external or internal hard disk or writeable CD or DVD, where backup files are saved. WIN 462

backup program A program that copies and then automatically compresses files and folders from a hard disk into a single file, called a backup file. WIN 462

bad sector An area of a hard disk that does not record data reliably. WIN 496

balanced power plan, WIN 406

bandwidth The amount of data that can be transmitted per second. WIN A2

base score A measure of the speed and performance of your computer's components, including the processor, random access memory (RAM), graphics card, and hard disk. WIN 539–542

battery meter icon, WIN 405–406

Bcc line, e-mail messages, WIN 182

bitmapped graphic A graphic made up of small dots called pixels that form an image. Also called a bitmap graphic. WIN 322, WIN 324

saving in different file type, WIN 328–329

black-and-white photo, WIN 362

Block Senders list, WIN 231, WIN 233

adding senders, WIN 232

BMP (Windows Bitmap) format, WIN 328

Boolean filter Any of the Boolean operators AND, OR, and NOT, which can be used to combine multiple search criteria into a single search expression. WIN 283–286

combining with file properties, WIN 285–286

brightness The amount of light displayed in a picture. WIN 358

adjusting, WIN 361

monitors, WIN 511

broadband connection A connection that uses a high-capacity, high-speed medium capable of transmitting voice, video, and data simultaneously. The two most common and practical broadband connections for home and small office users are digital subscriber lines (DSL) and digital cable connections. WIN 160, WIN A2–A4

setting up, WIN A6–A8

troubleshooting, WIN A8–A9

browser A program that locates, retrieves, and displays Web pages. Internet Explorer is the Microsoft browser. WIN 159–160

Microsoft Windows Vista Task Reference

TASK	PAGE #	RECOMMENDED METHOD
AutoPlay, turn on	WIN B10	Click ⊞, click Control Panel, click Hardware and Sound, click AutoPlay, click the Use AutoPlay for all media and devices check box
Backup and Restore Center, open	WIN 467	Click ⊞, click Control Panel, click System and Maintenance, click Backup and Restore Center
Backup settings, change	WIN 470	Open the Backup and Restore Center, click Back up files, follow the instructions in the Back Up Files Wizard
Base score, view and calculate	WIN 539	*See* Reference Window: Viewing and Calculating Your Base Score
Colors setting, change	WIN 131	Right-click the desktop, click Personalize, click Display Settings, click Colors button arrow, click a color setting, click OK
Compressed folder, create	WIN 85	In a folder window, select the files and folders to be compressed, right-click the selection, point to Send To on the shortcut menu, click Compressed (zipped) Folder, type a folder name, press Enter
Compressed folder, extract all files and folders from	WIN 86	Right-click the compressed folder, click Extract All on the shortcut menu
Connect a mobile PC remotely to a wired network	WIN 429	*See* Reference Window: Connecting Remotely to a Wired Network
Connect a mobile PC to a network projector	WIN 420	*See* Reference Window: Connecting to a Network Projector
Connect a mobile PC to a wireless network	WIN 426	Open the Windows Mobility Center, click 🖥 (or other wireless network icon), click Connect to a network, click a wireless network network, type the passphrase, click Connect, click Close
Connect a mobile PC to an external display device	WIN 419	*See* Reference Window: Connecting to an External Display Device
Connection, set up broadband	WIN A7	Click ⊞, click Control Panel, click Connect to the Internet, click Broadband (PPPoE), type user name and password, click Connect, click Next, click Close
Connection, set up dial-up	WIN A12	Click ⊞, click Control Panel, click Connect to the Internet, click Dial-up, type telephone number, user name and password, click Connect, click Next, click Close
Connection, set up wireless	WIN A10	Click ⊞, click Control Panel, click Connect to the Internet, click Wireless, select network, click Connect, type network pass phrase, click Connect, click Next, click Close
Control Panel, open	WIN 118	Click ⊞, click Control Panel
Desktop background, change	WIN 121	*See* Reference Window: Changing the Desktop Background
Desktop colors, change	WIN 124	Right-click the desktop, click Personalize, click Window Color and Appearance, click a color scheme, click OK
Desktop icon, change image for	WIN 103	Right-click the desktop, click Personalize, click Change desktop icons, click an icon, click Change Icon, select an image, click OK, click OK
Desktop icons, change location of	WIN 101	Right-click the desktop, point to View, click Auto Arrange to deselect that option, right-click the desktop, point to View, click Align to Grid to deselect that option, drag desktop icons to new location
Desktop icons, change size of	WIN 101	Right-click the desktop, point to View, click a size

TASK	PAGE #	RECOMMENDED METHOD
Desktop icons, display standard	WIN 100	*See* Reference Window: Displaying Standard Desktop Icons
Desktop icons, hide	WIN 102	Right-click the desktop, point to View, click Show Desktop Icons to deselect that option
Desktop icons, sort	WIN 115	Right-click the desktop, click Sort By, select sort criterion
Desktop image, position	WIN 123	Right-click the desktop, click Personalize, click Desktop Background, click position option button, click OK
Desktop shortcut, create to drive	WIN 109	Drag the drive icon from a folder window to desktop
Desktop shortcut, create to file, folder, or program	WIN 111	Right-drag the file, folder, or program icon to desktop, click Create Shortcuts Here
Desktop shortcut, create to printer	WIN 114	Right-click the printer, click Create Shortcut
Desktop shortcut, delete	WIN 116	Click the shortcut, press Delete key, click Yes
Desktop theme, change	WIN 126	Right-click the desktop, click Personalize, click Theme, click Theme button, click a theme, click OK
Desktop theme, save new	WIN 126	Right-click the desktop, click Personalize, click Theme, click Theme button, click My Current Theme, click Save As, type a name, click Save, click OK
Device driver, update and install	WIN 508	Open the Device Manager, double-click the device, click the Driver tab, click Update Driver, click Search automatically for updated driver software, click Yes
Device Manager, open	WIN 506	Click 🟦, click Control Panel, click System and Maintenance, click Device Manager
Device, enable and disable	WIN 505	*See* Reference Window: Enabling and Disabling Devices
Display font size, change	WIN 514	Click 🟦, click Control Panel, click Appearance and Personalization, click Personalization, click Adjust font size (DPI), select a font size, click OK
Display refresh rate, adjust	WIN 512	*See* Reference Window: Adjusting the Display Refresh Rate
Double-click, adjust speed for	WIN B3	Click 🟦, click Control Panel, click Mouse, click Buttons tab, drag the Double-click speed slider, click OK
Drive map, create	WIN 440	Click 🟦, click Computer, click Tools, click Map Network Drive, click Browse, navigate to and click a drive or folder, click OK, click Finish
Drive map, remove	WIN 442	*See* Reference Window: Removing Drive Mapping
Ease of Access Center, open	WIN B13	Click 🟦, click Control Panel, click Ease of Access, click Ease of Access Center
E-mail message, attach file to	WIN 190	Click 📎, double-click file
E-mail message, create	WIN 185	*See* Reference Window: Creating and Sending an E-mail Message
E-mail message, delete	WIN 189	Click message, click ❌
E-mail message, reply to	WIN 189	Click message, click Reply
E-Mail profile, set up	WIN 364	*See* Reference Window: Setting Up an E-Mail Profile
Event log, view	WIN 549	Open the Performance Information and Tools window, click Advanced tools, click View performance details in Event log
Favorites Links list, add file or folder to	WIN 84	Drag a file or folder to the list
Favorites list, add Web page to	WIN 174	*See* Reference Window: Adding a Web Page to the Favorites List
Favorites list, open	WIN 174	Click ⭐

TASK	PAGE #	RECOMMENDED METHOD
Favorites, list, organize	WIN 175	*See* Reference Window: Organizing the Favorites List
File sharing, turn on	WIN 434	Click ⊕, click Network, click the Network and Sharing Center button, ⊗ to the right of Public folder sharing, click Turn on sharing so anyone with network access can open, change, and create files, click Apply
File, copy	WIN 67	*See* Reference Window: Copying a File or Folder in Windows Explorer or Computer
File, create	WIN 71	Start program and enter data
File, delete	WIN 70	Right-click the file, click Delete on shortcut menu, click Yes
File, move	WIN 65	*See* Reference Window: Moving a File or Folder in a Folder Window
File, open from folder window	WIN 73	Navigate to the file, double-click the file
File, rename	WIN 69	Right-click the file, click Rename on shortcut menu, type new filename, press Enter
File, restore shadow copy	WIN 478	Right-click the file, click Restore previous versions, click Restore, click Restore, click OK, click OK
File, save	WIN 72	Click File, click Save As, navigate to a location, type filename, and then click Save
File, search for within folder	WIN 61	Click in the Search box, type word or phrase to be found in file or filename
Filename extension, show	WIN 82	Click Organize in folder window, click Folder and Search Options, click View, click Hide extensions for known file types to clear the check box
Files, back up	WIN 462	*See* Reference Window: Backing Up Files
Files, restore from backup	WIN 473	Open the Backup and Restore Center, click Restore files, follow the instructions in the Restore Files Wizard
Files, select multiple	WIN 67	Hold down the Ctrl key and click files
Flip-3D, use	WIN 16	Click ▣, press the Tab key to cycle through programs, click a program window
Folder list, expand	WIN 55	Click ▷
Folder window, return to a previously visited location	WIN 60	Click ▽, click a location in the list
Folder window, return to previous location	WIN 60	Click ⬅
Folder, copy	WIN 67	*See* Reference Window: Copying a File or Folder in Windows Explorer or Computer
Folder, create in Windows Explorer	WIN 63	*See* Reference Window: Creating a Folder Using Windows Explorer
Folder, delete	WIN 70	Right-click the folder, click Delete on shortcut menu, click Yes
Folder, filter files in	WIN 77	In a folder window, click a column heading arrow button, click a filter option
Folder, group files in	WIN 78–79	In a folder window, click a column heading arrow button, click Group
Folder, move	WIN 65	*See* Reference Window: Moving a File or Folder in a Folder Window
Folder, sort files in	WIN 75	In a folder window, click a column heading
Folder, stack files in	WIN 78	In a folder window, click a column heading arrow button, click a stacking option
Folders list, open or close	WIN 84	Click the Folders button
Font, install	WIN B35	Click ⊕, click Control Panel, click Appearance and Personalization, click Fonts, right-click a blank spot in the window, click Install New Font, navigate to and click the new font, click Insert

TASK	PAGE #	RECOMMENDED METHOD
Fonts, view installed	WIN B32	Click [icon], click Control Panel, click Appearance and Personalization, click Fonts
Gadget, customize	WIN 106	Click [icon] on gadget
Graphic file, use as desktop background	WIN 122	Right-click the desktop, click Personalize, click Desktop Background, click Browse, double-click graphic file, click OK
Hard disk, check for errors	WIN 497	Right-click the disk in a folder window, click Properties, click the Tools tab, click Check Now, click Start
Hard disk, clean up	WIN 494	Right-click the disk in a folder window, click Properties, click the General tab, click Disk Cleanup
Hard disk, defragment	WIN 500	Right-click the disk in a folder window, click Properties, click the Tools tab, click Defragment Now
Hard disk, view partitions	WIN 493	Click [icon], click Control Panel, click System and Maintenance, click Create and format hard disk partitions
Hard disk, view properties	WIN 490	*See* Reference Window: Viewing Hard Disk Properties
Help, find topic	WIN 38	In Help, click in the Search Help box, type word or phrase, click [icon]
Help, start	WIN 35	Click [icon], click Help and Support
Input Panel, open	WIN B41	Click [icon], point to All Programs, click Accessories, click Tablet PC, click Tablet PC Input Panel
Internet Explorer, block pop-up ads in	WIN 242	*See* Reference Window: Blocking Pop-up Ads
Internet Explorer, delete browsing history in	WIN 246	Start Internet Explorer, click Tools, click Delete Browsing History, click Delete cookies, click Yes, click Delete history, click Yes, click Close
Internet Explorer, manage add-ons	WIN 243	Start Internet Explorer, click Tools, point to Manage Add-ons, click Enable or Disable Add-ons
Internet Explorer, select security settings in	WIN 245	*See* Reference Window: Selecting Privacy Settings
Internet Explorer, set Phishing Filter	WIN 238	Click [icon], click Internet Explorer, click Tools, point to Phishing Filter, click Turn On Automatic Website Checking, click OK
Internet Explorer, start	WIN 162	Click [icon], click Internet Explorer
IP address, determine	WIN 578	Click, [icon], point to All Programs, click Accessories, click Command Prompt, type ipconfig, press Enter
Link, open in new tab	WIN 171	Right-click the link, click Open in New Tab
List box, scroll	WIN 24	Click the scroll down or up arrow button, or drag the scroll box
Local printer, install	WIN 520	*See* Reference Window: Installing a Local Printer
Meeting, start	WIN 307	*See* Reference Window: Starting a Meeting and Inviting Participants
Menu option, select	WIN 22	Click the option on the menu
Microsoft Knowledge Base, use	WIN 573	Click [icon], click Help and Support, click Ask, click Knowledge Base
Mobility Center, open for a mobile PC	WIN 404	Click [icon], point to All Programs, click Accessories, click Windows Mobility Center
Mouse keys, turn on	WIN B18	Open the Ease of Access Center, click Make the mouse easier to use, click Set up Mouse Keys, click the Turn on Mouse Keys check box, click Apply
Mouse, configure for a left-handed user	WIN B2	Click [icon], click Control Panel, click Mouse, click Buttons tab, click the Switch primary and secondary buttons check box, click OK

TASK	PAGE #	RECOMMENDED METHOD
Multiple monitors, set up	WIN 516	*See* Reference Window: Setting Up and Extending the Desktop on Multiple Monitors
Network connection, repair	WIN 576	*See* Reference Window: Repairing a Network Connection
Network files, make available offline	WIN 443	Click ⊞, click Control Panel, click Network and Internet, click View network computers and devices, navigate to and right-click a folder, click Always Available Offline
Network passwords, manage	WIN B28	Click ⊞, click Control Panel, click User Accounts and Family Safety, click User Accounts, click Manage your network passwords, click Add, type a URL, user name, and password, click A Web site or program credential option button, click OK, click Close
New tab, open	WIN 171	Click 🗋
Offline files, enable	WIN 444	Click ⊞, click Control Panel, click Network and Internet, click Offline Files, click Enable Offline Files, click OK
Paging file, change size	WIN 565	Open the Performance Information and Tools window, click Advanced tools, click Adjust the appearance and performance of Windows, click the Advanced tab, click Change
Paint, add text to a graphic in	WIN 334	*See* Reference Window: Adding Text to a Graphic
Paint, copy and paste a portion of the graphic in	WIN 344	Select the portion of the graphic, click Edit, click Copy, click Edit, click Paste, drag the image to the desired location
Paint, draw a square in	WIN 341	Click ▢, click a style in the Options box, click the canvas, hold down the Shift key and drag, release the mouse button
Paint, fill an area with color in	WIN 343	*See* Reference Window: Filling an Area with Color
Paint, insert an image into the current graphic in	WIN 329	Click Edit, click Paste From, navigate to the image, click the image, click the Open button, drag the image to the desired location
Paint, magnify a graphic in	WIN 334	*See* Reference Window: Magnifying a Graphic
Paint, open a graphic file in	WIN 326	Click File, click Open, navigate to the file, click the file, click the Open button
Paint, resize the canvas in	WIN 332	Drag the lower-right corner of the canvas
Paint, select a background color from a graphic in	WIN 335	Click 🖉, right-click a color in the graphic
Paint, select a foreground color from a graphic in	WIN 341	Click 🖉, click a color in the graphic
Paint, select a portion of a graphic in	WIN 338	Click ⬚, drag to select
Paint, start	WIN 324	Click ⊞, point to All Programs, click Accessories, click Paint
Parental controls, turn on	WIN B29	Click ⊞, click Control Panel, click User Accounts and Family Safety, click User Accounts, click Parental Controls, click a user, Click On, enforce current settings, set options, click OK
Password, create for user account	WIN 252	Click ⊞, click user icon, click Create a password
Password reset disk, create	WIN B27	Click ⊞, click Control Panel, click User Accounts and Family Safety, click User Accounts, click Create a password reset disk, follow the instructions in the Forgotten Passwords Wizard

TASK	PAGE #	RECOMMENDED METHOD
Permission, assign to folder	WIN 255	Click the folder, click Share, click arrow to right of first text box, click a user name, click Add, click Permission Level, click a permission level, click Share, click Done
Performance Information and Tools window, open	WIN 540	Click 🪟, click Control Panel, click the System and Maintenance category, click Performance Information and Tools
Performance issues, view	WIN 548	Open the Performance Information and Tools window, click Advanced tools
Playback settings, change	WIN B6	Click 🪟, click Control Panel, click Hardware and Sound, click Sound, click Playback tab, change settings, click OK
Pointer speed, adjust speed for	WIN B4	Click 🪟, click Control Panel, click Mouse, click Pointer Options tab, Drag the Select a pointer speed slider, click OK
Power options, change	WIN 414	Click 🪟, click Control Panel, click Hardware and Sound, click Power Options, click Choose what the power button does, change settings, click Save changes
Power plan, create	WIN 412	Click 🪟, click Control Panel, click Hardware and Sound, click Power Options, click Create a power plan, click a plan option button, type a name for the power plan, click Next, change settings, click Create
Power plan, modify	WIN 409	*See* Reference Window: Modifying a Power Plan
Power plan, select	WIN 406	*See* Reference Window: Selecting a Power Plan
Presentation settings, customize for a mobile PC	WIN 417	Open the Mobility Center, click Change presentation settings, change settings, click OK
Printer, set default	WIN 522	Click 🪟, click Control Panel, click Hardware and Sound, click Printers, right-click a printer, click Set as Default Printer
Program, check for compatibility	WIN 488	Click 🪟, click Control Panel, click Programs, click Use an older program with this version of Windows, follow the instructions in the Program Compatibility Wizard
Program, close	WIN 12	Click X
Program, close inactive	WIN 16	Right-click the program button on the taskbar, click Close
Program, set to start automatically	WIN 487	Click 🪟, point to All Programs, right-click the Startup folder, click Open, click 🪟, locate the program on the Start menu and drag it to the Startup folder window
Program, start	WIN 10	*See* Reference Window: Starting a Program
Program, switch to another open	WIN 14	Click the program button on the taskbar
Program, uninstall	WIN 484	Click 🪟, click Control Panel, click Programs, click Programs and Features, click the program, click Uninstall, click Yes
Property, add to file	WIN 281	Right-click the file, click Properties, click Details, type property, click OK
Quick Launch toolbar, add program icon to	WIN 136	Drag the program icon to the Quick Launch toolbar
ReadyBoost, use	WIN 568	Click 🪟, click Computer, right-click a USB flash drive, click Open Autoplay, click Speed up my system, click Use this device, click OK
Recycle Bin, open	WIN 7	Double-click 🗑
Recording settings, change	WIN B7	Click 🪟, click Control Panel, click Hardware and Sound, click Sound, click Recording tab, change settings, click OK

TASK	PAGE #	RECOMMENDED METHOD
Reliability and Performance window, open	WIN 552	Open the Performance Information and Tools window, click Advanced tools, click Open Reliability and Performance Monitor
Remote Assistance, enable	WIN 585	Click 🪟, click Control Panel, click System and Maintenance, click System, click Remote settings, click the Allow Remote Assistance connections to this computer
Remote Assistance, enable or disable	WIN 439	*See* Reference Window: Enabling and Disabling Remote Assistance
Remote Assistance, request	WIN 587	Click 🪟, click Help and Support, click Windows Remote Assistance, follow the instructions in the Windows Remote Assistance Wizard
Remote desktop connection, set up	WIN 436	Click 🪟, click Control Panel, click System and Maintenance, click System, click Remote settings, click Allow connections only from computers running Remote Desktop with Network Level Authentication (more secure), click OK
Screen resolution, change	WIN 130	Right-click the desktop, click Personalize, click Display Settings, drag the Resolution slider, click OK
Screen Saver delay time, change	WIN 128	Right-click the desktop, click Personalize, click Screen Saver, click Wait arrow buttons, click OK
Screen Saver, change	WIN 128	Right-click the desktop, click Personalize, click Screen Saver, click Screen saver button, click a screen saver, click OK
ScreenTip, view	WIN 5	Position pointer over an item
Search, locate file by category	WIN 272	*See* Reference Window: Searching for a File by Category
Search, locate file by type	WIN 270	*See* Reference Window: Searching for a File by Type
Search, locate file using multiple criteria	WIN 277	*See* Reference Window: Searching for a File Using Multiple Criteria
Search, locate program	WIN 290	*See* Reference Window: Searching for Programs on the Start Menu
Search, save	WIN 278	Click Save Search, click Save
Search, select Internet search provider	WIN 304	*See* Reference Window: Selecting a Search Provider
Security Center, open	WIN 213	Click 🪟, click Control Panel, click Security, click Security Center
Sidebar, add gadget to	WIN 104	Click ➕, double-click a gadget
Sidebar, keep on top of other windows	WIN 107	Right-click the sidebar, click Properties, click Sidebar is always on top of other windows, click OK
Sidebar, remove gadget from	WIN 108	Point to the gadget, click ❌
Software problems, check for solutions	WIN 580	*See* Reference Window: Checking for Solutions to Software Problems
Software update, install	WIN 485	*See* Reference Window: Installing a Software Update
Sound scheme, create new	WIN B5	Click 🪟, click Control Panel, click Hardware and Sound, click Sound, click Sounds tab, click a program event, click the Sounds arrow button, click a sound, click Save As, type a sound scheme name, click OK
Speaker volume, set in Mobility Center	WIN 404	Open the Windows Mobility Center, drag the Volume slider
Start menu icons, change size	WIN 141	Right-click 🪟, click Properties, click Customize, click Use large icons, click OK
Start menu, add command to	WIN 145	Right-click 🪟, click Properties, click Customize, select command, click OK
Start Menu, open	WIN 6	Click 🪟

TASK	PAGE #	RECOMMENDED METHOD
Start menu, pin a program to	WIN 143	Right-click the program name in the Start menu, click Pin to Start Menu
Startup program, disable	WIN 545	Open the Performance Information and Tools window, click Manage startup programs, click the program, click Disable, click Yes
Sticky Keys, turn on	WIN B20	Open the Ease of Access Center, click Make the keyboard easier to use, click Set up Sticky Keys, click the Turn on Sticky Keys check box, click Apply
Sticky Notes, open	WIN B42	Click 🙂, point to All Programs, click Accessories, click Tablet PC, click Sticky Notes
Sync Center, open	WIN 445	Open the Windows Mobility Center, click Sync settings
Sync partnership, set up on a mobile computer	WIN 446	Open the Sync Center, click Set up new sync partnerships, click Offline Files, click Set up
Synchronize files	WIN 446	Open the Sync Center, click Offline Files, click Sync
System details, view	WIN 541	Open the Performance Information and Tools window, click View and print details
System Health Report, create	WIN 567	Open the Performance Information and Tools window, click Advanced tools, click Generate a system health report
System information, view	WIN 563	Open the Performance Information and Tools window, click Advanced tools, click View advanced system details in System Information
System performance, monitor	WIN 551	*See* Reference Window: Monitoring System Performance
System restore point, create	WIN 475	*See* Reference Window: Creating a System Restore Point
System Stability chart and index, view	WIN 558	Open the Reliability and Performance window, click Reliability Monitor
System, restore	WIN 477	Click 🙂, click Control Panel, click System and Maintenance, click System, click System protection, click System Restore, follow the instructions in the System Restore Wizard
Tag, add to file	WIN 281	*See* Reference Window: Adding Tags to Files
Task Manager, open	WIN 561	Open the Performance Information and Tools window, click Advanced tools, click Open Task Manager
Taskbar, add Desktop toolbar to	WIN 138	Right-click the taskbar, point to Toolbars, click Desktop
Taskbar, create Custom toolbar for	WIN 139	*See* Reference Window: Creating a Custom Taskbar Toolbar
Taskbar, hide	WIN 135	Right-click the taskbar, click Properties, click Auto-hide the taskbar, click OK
Taskbar, move	WIN 133	*See* Reference Window: Moving and Resizing the Taskbar
Taskbar, resize	WIN 133	*See* Reference Window: Moving and Resizing the Taskbar
Troubleshooter, use	WIN 570	Click 🙂, click Help and Support, click Troubleshooting
USB device, install	WIN 505	Plug the device into a USB port
USB device, safely remove	WIN 510	Click 🔌 in the notification area of the taskbar, click Safely remove USB Device, click the device, click the OK button, unplug the USB device from the USB port
User Account, create	WIN B24	Click 🙂, click Control Panel, click User Accounts and Family Safety, click User Accounts, click Manage another account, click Create a new account, type a name, click Create Account
User account, create new	WIN 250	*See* Reference Window: Creating a Password-Protected User Account

TASK	PAGE #	RECOMMENDED METHOD
User picture, change	WIN 140	Click ⊞, click user icon, click Change the picture, click picture, click Change Picture
View, change in a folder window	WIN 32	*See* Reference Window: Changing the Icon View
Visual effects, adjust	WIN 545	Open the Performance Information and Tools window, click Adjust visual effects, change option settings, click OK
Web calendar, publish	WIN 201	*See* Reference Window: Publishing a Web Calendar
Web calendar, subscribe to	WIN 200	*See* Reference Window: Subscribing to a Web Calendar
Web page, open using URL	WIN 165	*See* Reference Window: Opening a Web Page Using a URL
Web page, print	WIN 176	Click 🖶 ▾, click Print
Web page, return to next	WIN 168	Click ➡
Web page, return to previous	WIN 168	Click ⬅
Web page, return to recent	WIN 169	Click ▾, click a page
Web page, return to using History List	WIN 169	Click ☆, click History, click a date, click a Web page
Welcome Center, open	WIN B36	Click ⊞, click Control Panel, click System and Maintenance, click Welcome Center
Window colors, change	WIN 124	Right-click the desktop, click Personalize, click Window Color and Appearance, click color, click OK (Aero only)
Window, maximize	WIN 20	Click 🗖
Window, minimize	WIN 19	Click 🗕
Window, move	WIN 20	Drag the title bar
Window, resize	WIN 21	Drag an edge or corner
Window, restore	WIN 20	Click 🗗
Windows Calendar, schedule an appointment	WIN 197	*See* Reference Window: Scheduling an Appointment in Windows Calendar
Windows Defender, perform a quick scan with	WIN 222	*See* Reference Window: Performing a Quick Scan with Windows Defender
Windows Defender, schedule scan	WIN 226	Start Windows Defender, click Tools, click Options, click Approximate time
Windows Defender, start	WIN 222	Click ⊞, click Control Panel, click Security, click Windows Defender
Windows Explorer, start	WIN 33	Click ⊞, point to All Programs, click Accessories, click Windows Explorer
Windows Firewall, add an exception	WIN 214	*See* Reference Window: Adding a Program to the Windows Firewall Exception List
Windows Journal, open	WIN B43	Click ⊞, point to All Programs, click Accessories, click Tablet PC, click Windows Journal
Windows Mail, add a contact	WIN 191	*See* Reference Window: Adding a Contact in Windows Mail
Windows Media Center, open	WIN B38	Click ⊞, point to All Programs, click Windows Media Center
Windows Media Player, burn files to a CD in	WIN 372	*See* Reference Window: Burning Files to a CD
Windows Media Player, create a playlist in	WIN 371	*See* Reference Window: Creating a Playlist
Windows Media Player, play a song in	WIN 370	Double-click a song
Windows Media Player, start	WIN 368	Click ⊞, point to All Programs, click Accessories, click Windows Media Player

TASK	PAGE #	RECOMMENDED METHOD
Windows Mail, add a sender to the Blocked Senders or Safe Senders list	WIN 232	*See* Reference Window: Adding a Sender to the Blocked Senders or Safe Senders List
Windows Mail, set junk e-mail options	WIN 232	Start Windows Mail, click Tools, click Junk E-mail Options
Windows Mail, start	WIN 181	Click 🔵, point to All Programs, click Windows Mail
Windows Movie Make, publish a movie in	WIN 385	*See* Reference Window: Publishing a Movie
Windows Movie Maker, add a file to the storyboard in	WIN 377	Drag a file to a storyboard frame
Windows Movie Maker, add a transition to the storyboard in	WIN 381	Click Transitions, drag a transition to a transition icon between two storyboard frames
Windows Movie Maker, add an effect to a storyboard in	WIN 380	Click Effects, drag an effect to a storyboard frame
Windows Movie Maker, play a video in	WIN 374	Double-click a video
Windows Movie Maker, start	WIN 374	Click 🔵, point to All Programs, click Windows Movie Maker
Windows Photo Gallery, edit a photo in	WIN 358	*See* Reference Window: Editing a Photo
Windows Photo Gallery, e-mail photos from	WIN 364	Select the photos, click the E-mail button, click the Attach button, enter an e-mail address and subject, click the Send button
Windows Photo Gallery, play a slide show in	WIN 357	*See* Reference Window: Playing a Slide Show
Windows Photo Gallery, print a photo in	WIN 365	Select a photo, click Print, click Print, click Print
Windows Photo Gallery, start	WIN 354	Click 🔵, point to All Programs, click Windows Photo Gallery
Windows Update, set up	WIN 217	Click 🔵, click Control Panel, click Security, click Security Center, click Windows Update, click Change settings
Windows Vista, log off	WIN 39	Click 🔵, point to ▶, click Log Off
Windows Vista, start	WIN 2	Turn on the computer
Windows Vista, turn off	WIN 39	Click 🔵, point to ▶, click Shut Down
Windows, arrange on desktop	WIN 132	Right-click the taskbar, click Cascade Windows, Show Windows Stacked, or Show Windows Side by Side